Tasting Cryptography

Yi Mao
Editor

Tasting Cryptography

FIPS ‘n’ Chips

Springer

Editor
Yi Mao
atsec information security corporation
Austin, TX, USA

ISBN 978-3-032-30242-7 ISBN 978-3-032-30243-4 (eBook)
https://doi.org/10.1007/978-3-032-30243-4

This Springer imprint is published by the registered company Springer Nature Switzerland AG
The registered company address is: Gewerbestrasse 11, 6330 Cham, Switzerland

To all atsec colleagues, to the cryptographic module validation community, and to the cybersecurity industry at large.

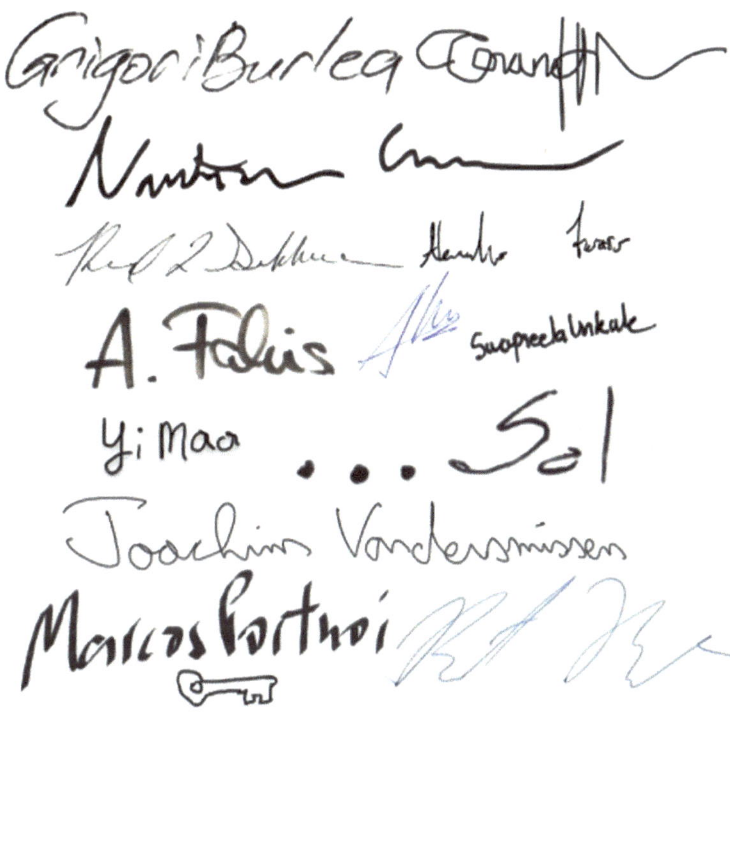

Foreword

The field of cryptographic algorithm design has advanced dramatically over the past half-century. The security assurance for an algorithm has evolved from merely resisting exhaustive search attacks to immunizing against much more sophisticated cryptanalysis methods. The concept of provable security was introduced to support security statements on a theoretical level.

However, for a complete security assurance, algorithm security is only a starting point. There is still a long way to go before achieving the final goal of a secure system, because these algorithms must be implemented on diverse platforms for a variety of application purposes. History has proved that the security measurement for a cryptographic implementation is far more difficult to tackle than the security of the algorithm.

This book tells the compelling story of how cryptographic module validation has evolved over several decades. By vividly replaying critical turning points, these accounts set the stage for the key contributors who shaped the field. Ultimately, the book assembles these historical pieces to show how validation became an essential security measurement for real-world cryptographic implementations.

Today's success in cryptographic module validation could not have been achieved without the close collaboration of a dedicated community formed by cryptographers, standard developers, implementers, and validators. Openness and transparency are critical not only for developing robust cryptographic algorithm standards—such as AES, SHA-3, and those for Post-Quantum Cryptography (PQC)—but also for pursuing effective validation techniques. The contributions from this community have been invaluable.

While technological advancement enables automated cryptographic module validation to take flight, the ubiquity of these algorithms across nearly every digital device challenges the program's agility. In this new era of booming AI and powerful quantum computing, cryptographic module validation must continue to evolve as a critical pillar of security assurance.

This book concentrates the essence of experience from decades of cryptographic module validation. It is by no means intended to draw a conclusion. Rather, it prepares readers to embrace new challenges in the journey ahead and to continue the advancement of cryptographic module validation.

Gaithersburg, Maryland, USA Dr. Lily Chen

Preface

The year 2025 is a special one. It marks the twenty-fifth anniversary of atsec information security and the twentieth year of operation for our Cryptographic Security Testing (CST) laboratory. It is also the year ISO/IEC 19790:2025 was published, representing a major revision of a standard that had remained largely unchanged for more than a decade. Several distinguished NIST cryptographic experts retired this year, closing an important chapter in the history of modern cryptography. At the same time, automation for cryptographic module validation is finally within reach. Rapid advances in artificial intelligence are increasing security threats, while also providing new tools for Information Assurance. AI is accelerating scientific discovery and may shorten the path toward practical quantum computing.

Together, these forces make 2025 an inspiring moment to write a book devoted to cryptographic modules, the standards that guide their design, implementation, testing, validation, usage, and disposal, and the people behind them from academia, industry, and government, including researchers, developers, testers, certifiers, and users.

Cryptography plays a critical role in protecting our data, yet it can feel dense, abstract, and difficult to approach. Testing cryptography is essential to ensure correct and trustworthy implementations, but the subject can easily become intimidating when presented only through formulas and formal proofs. To make this material accessible without sacrificing rigor, we adopt a storytelling approach. Readers are invited to imagine themselves at the FIPS 'n' Chips restaurant, tasting carefully prepared drinks and dishes of cryptography. Each section is served in bite-sized portions, offering a range of flavors so that every reader can find something to enjoy.

This book exists as an act of gratitude and collective identity. Over the years at atsec information security, we have achieved not only hundreds of FIPS validation certificates for cryptographic modules implemented in chips, software libraries, and applications, but also something far more enduring. We have built a team of extraordinary individuals who care deeply about our customers, our programs, and our company. Together, their work underpins today's digital world, from IoT devices and mobile platforms to supercomputers and cloud services. By contributing collectively to this book, we have created something greater than any single chapter. As

CEO, I am deeply indebted to my colleagues for their loyalty and craftsmanship. I hope each of them sees this volume as a mark of belonging and excellence. This book is our shared signature.

I believe that the highest quality work arises from free will, passion, and love for what we do. Compelled labor may produce output, but it rarely produces art. History offers compelling parallels. The pyramids of Egypt, once thought to have been built by slaves, are now understood to be the work of skilled laborers, craftsmen, artisans, and organized workers who took pride in their achievements. The precision and alignment of those monuments would have been nearly impossible under threat and desperation. Similarly, legend holds that a master Swiss watchmaker, when taken captive and housed in luxury, lost the ability to craft a precise timepiece because he had lost the freedom of mind that guided his skill.

Our colleagues at atsec are not bound by obligation. They are driven by passion. They do not work for pay alone, but for love of precision, logic, and trust. That commitment turns long nights in the lab, countless reviews, and meticulous quality control into acts of creation.

Aster, a character in this book, is intended as a stand-in for an atsec colleague. Aster represents the collective identity of the atsec global team. She steps into whatever role an atsec contributor chooses to explore. In some sections, she appears as a learner, while in others she speaks as an expert. In two sections, Aster serves as the pen name of an atsec colleague who preferred not to reveal his real name for the material he authored.

Aster's shifting and sometimes unpredictable personality is intentional. It introduces a playful element into the narrative, much like randomness in cryptography. Just as high-quality random numbers are essential for generating strong cryptographic keys, this element of unpredictability adds vitality and depth to the story.

Through this book, we share both the technical foundations and the human spirit behind them, including FIPS, ISO standards, laboratory procedures, cryptographic assurance, and collaborative insight. Together, we tell a story of care, rigor, and trust, not only in algorithms and modules, but in the people behind them.

Dr. Yi Mao
CEO of atsec information security corporation
Austin, TX, USA

Acknowledgements This book could not have been written without the dedication and insight of the many people who have shaped cryptographic standards, design, implementation, testing, and validation. We are deeply grateful to all who contributed their time, expertise, and stories during interviews and discussions with atsec throughout the writing of this book. The individuals acknowledged below are listed in the order of the sections to which they contributed.

Lily Chen, for her insightful foreword to this book.

Donna Dodson, Lisa Carnahan, James Foti, Allen Roginsky, Apostol Vassilev, Murugiah Souppaya, Kailai Chen, and David Hawes, for their contributions to the history, present state, and modernization of cryptographic algorithm and module validation.

Salvatore Francomacaro, Miguel Bañón, Alexander H. Calis, and Carolyn French, for their contributions to ISO/IEC JTC 1/SC 27/WG 3.

Matthew Keller, for sharing his memories of the early history of CMUF; Lisa Rabe, Trish Wolff, and Marc Ireland, for actively leading CMUF working groups.

Christopher Celi, Raoul Gabiam, Douglas Boldt, Barry Fussell, Shawn Geddis, and Kyle Vitale, for sharing the journey of the NCCoE ACMVP projects and many memorable stories along the way.

John Traver, for his advocacy and leadership in designing for certainty through AMD's FIPS validation efforts and CMUF collaboration.

Jim Goodman and the Crypto4A Technologies team, for pioneering quantum-ready architectures and achieving the first post-quantum algorithm validations.

Olivier Benoit and Anish Chivukula of Google, for advancing FIPS validation for the Pixel Tensor SoC and for bridging CMUF dialogue across the embedded, cloud, and mobile ecosystems.

David Evans, Richard Kisley, William Santiago-Fernandez, and Joe Livingston, for IBM's decades of engineering excellence and leadership in FIPS certifications, reaching the highest security levels.

Jaroslav Reznik and the Red Hat team, for their leadership in open-source security and for advancing FIPS certification of the NSS and other Linux cryptographic modules.

Shola Adegboye, Xiaoyu, and Thomas Bowen, for spearheading Intel's company-wide security mandate to produce FIPS-certifiable chips.

Yucong Tao, Joseph Ku, and Scott Fuller, for their collaboration in strengthening Microsoft FIPS validation efficiency, transparency, and alignment with the broader FIPS ecosystem.

Avi Davidowitz, for integrating Nuvoton FIPS validation into global semiconductor development and promoting trust across TPMs, controllers, and open-source roots of trust.

Yann L'Hyver, for leading Qualcomm's FIPS validations, advancing and debating the sub-chip and hybrid module concepts that reshaped how SoC cryptography is validated under FIPS 140-3.

Dr. Karen Lu and Dr. Michael Vogel, for improving the wording on the FIPS 'n' Chips menu.

Abbie Delafosse, for lending her artistic talent to illustrate the chapters authored by Nathaniel Glass.

A special thank you goes to our atsec authors. Individuals are listed in alphabetical order by first name to avoid implying priority or seniority: Alejandro Fabio Masino, Alessandro Fazio, Andreas Fabis, Dick Sikkema, Francesco Paolo D'Erme, Grigori Burlea, Jeremy Wesevich, Joachim Vandersmissen, Luca Di Domenico, Dr. Marcos Portnoi, Dr. Marylène Palard, Nathaniel Glass, Quin Darcy, Renaudt Nuñez, Stephan Müller, Swapneela Unkule, Trang Huynh, Walker Riley, and a colleague writing under the pen name Aster. Their passion, technical depth, and collective contributions made this book possible. We also extend special thanks to our technical writer, Evan Barnett, for his meticulous editing, patience, and ability to work seamlessly with authors across many writing styles.

During the writing of this book, we gratefully received encouragement and guidance from our founding CEO, Sal La Pietra, COO Wendy Hughes, Quality Manager Pam Mitarotondo, IT staff member Sean Lewis, and colleagues across atsec's global offices. Their enthusiasm and confidence helped carry this project to the finish line.

We are grateful to all colleagues at NIST and CCCS, including current and former CAVP and CMVP staff, and to colleagues across the CMUF and ISO communities for their continued commitment to cryptographic assurance. Their collaboration and dedication continue to drive the evolution of this field.

We also acknowledge the many contributors, reviewers, and practitioners whose work influenced this book but who are too numerous to name individually.

We are fortunate to be writing this book in a period of rapid technological advancement, including the availability of AI-assisted tools, which helped streamline copy-editing and refine illustrations based on authors' prompts and initial sketches.

Finally, we are indebted to the Springer editors Susan Lagerstrom-Fife, Guru Prasath Raja, and Joseph Quatela for their trust, guidance, and excellent support in bringing this book to publication.

Competing Interests The author has no competing interests to declare that are relevant to the content of this manuscript.

About This Book

This book provides a comprehensive, practice-driven guide to understanding and implementing secure cryptographic modules. It bridges newly published international standards—ISO/IEC 19790:2025 and ISO/IEC 24759:2025—with decades of hands-on validation experience from atsec's globally respected testing laboratory. Designed to demystify cryptographic compliance, it serves developers, security professionals, and students alike.

It explores the evolution and current practices of the Cryptographic Module Validation Program (CMVP), jointly managed by NIST and Canada's CCCS, highlighting its foundational role in securing global digital infrastructure. Topics include technical requirements, testing methodologies, real-world case studies, and future developments such as post-quantum cryptography and validation automation through NCCoE's ACMVP.

The book also highlights the collaborative ecosystem supporting cryptographic assurance—focusing on the CMUF, ICMC, and atsec's FIPS 'n' Chips bootcamp. These forums help shape standards, foster innovation, and strengthen community. By connecting theory with implementation and policy with practice, this book delivers actionable insights at a critical time for modern cryptography.

Contents

Abbreviations

ACMVP	Automated Cryptographic Module Validation Project
ACVT	Automated Cryptographic Validation Testing
ACVTS	Automated Cryptographic Validation Testing Server (or System)
AES	Advanced Encryption Standard
ANSI	American National Standards Institute
APT	Adaptive Proportion Test
BSI	Bundesamt für Sicherheit in der Informationstechnik (Federal Office for Information Security)
CAST	Cryptographic Algorithm Self-Test
CAVP	Cryptographic Algorithm Validation Program
CC	Common Criteria
CCM	Counter with Cipher Block Chaining-Message Authentication Code
CCTL	Common Criteria Testing Laboratory
CDH	Cofactor Diffie-Hellman
CM	Configuration Management
CMAC	Cipher-based Message Authentication Code
CMUF	Cryptographic Module User Forum
CMVP	Cryptographic Module Validation Program
CNSA	Commercial National Security Algorithm
CO	Crypto Officer
CPU	Central Processing Unit
CSfC	Commercial Solutions for Classified Program
CSP	Critical Security Parameter
CSTL	Cryptographic and Security Testing Laboratory
CTR	Counter
CVE	Common Vulnerabilities and Exposures
DES	Data Encryption Standard
DFF	Data Flip-Flop
DH	Diffie-Hellman
DRBG	Deterministic Random Bit Generator
DSA	Digital Signature Algorithm

EAL	Evaluation Assurance Level
EAR	Entropy Assessment Report
ECC	Elliptic Curve Cryptography
ECDH	Elliptic Curve Diffie-Hellman
ECDSA	Elliptic Curve Digital Signature Algorithm
EDC	Error Detection Code
EdDSA	Edwards Curve Digital Signature Algorithm
ELO-RBG	Elementary Oscillator-based Random Bit Generator
ESV	Entropy Source Validation
EUCC	European Union Common Criteria
FFC	Finite Field Cryptography
FIPS	Federal Information Processing Standard
FN-DSA	Falcon Digital Signature Algorithm
FS	Forward Secrecy
FSM	Finite State Machine
GCM	Galois/Counter Mode
GMAC	Galois Message Authentication Code
HDL	Hardware Description Language
HMAC	Hash-based Message Authentication Code
HQC	Hamming Quasi Cyclic
IEC	International Electrotechnical Commission
IG	Implementation Guidance
IID	Independently and Identically Distributed
IKA	Implicit Key Authentication
IPsec	Internet Protocol Security
IR	Incident Response
ISO	International Standards Organization
IUT	Implementation Under Test
IV	Initialization Vector
JSON	JavaScript Object Notation
KAS	Key Agreement Scheme
KC	Key Confirmation
KDF	Key Derivation Function
KDM	Key Derivation Method
KEK	Key Encryption Key
KF	Key Freshness
KMAC	Keccak Message Authentication Code
KTS	Key Transport
KW	Key Wrap
KWP	Key Wrap with Padding
MCV	Most Common Value
MGF	Mask Generation Function
ML-DSA	Module-Lattice-based Digital Signature Algorithm
ML-KEM	Module-Lattice-based Key Encapsulation Mechanism
MQV	Menezes-Qu-Vanstone

NIAP	National Information Assurance Partnership
NIST	National Institute of Standards and Technology
NVLAP	National Voluntary Laboratory Accreditation Program
OAEP	Optimal Asymmetric Encryption Padding
OE	Operational Environment
PAA	Processor Algorithm Acceleration
PAI	Processor Algorithm Implementation
PCL	Product Compliance List
PCT	Pairwise Consistency Test
PIO	Programmable Input/Output
PP	Protection Profile
PQC	Post-Quantum Cryptography
PSP	Public Security Parameters
PUD	Public Use Document
RA	Readiness Assessment
RBG	Random Bit Generator
RCT	Repetition Count Test
RDTSC	Read Time-Stamp Counter
RFG	Request for Guidance
RNG	Random Number Generator
RSA	Rivest-Shamir-Adleman
SC	Subcommittee
SHA	Secure Hash Algorithm
SLH-DSA	Stateless Hash-based Digital Signature Algorithm
SNMP	Simple Network Management Protocol
SP	Security Policy and Special Publication
SRTP	Secure Real-time Transport Protocol
SSH	Secure Shell
SSP	Sensitive Security Parameter
ST	Security Target
TAG	Technical Advisory Groups
TE	Test Evidence
TERO	Transition Effect Ring Oscillator
TLS	Transport Layer Security
TPM	Trusted Platform Module
XDRBG	Extendable Output Function Deterministic Random Bit Generator
XOF	Extendable Output Function
XOR	Exclusive Or

List of Figures

List of Tables

Chapter 1
Introduction

Yi Mao

Aster jogs along the Mueller lakeside path just as the sun lifts into the sky, casting its first warm golden light across the surface of the water. The rising sun paints the horizon a deep red that softens to coral and rose as it climbs the sky. Tiny ripples shimmer as a gentle breeze stirs the lake. Along the shore, clusters of deep-blue bluebonnets mingle with delicate pink brush, forming a spring tapestry. Bees buzz around purple water hyacinths, pickerelweed spikes rise with their fresh purple blossoms, and turtles poke their heads above the surface.

Near the reeds, a tall Great Egret stands motionless, its long neck curved in patient stillness as it watches for the flicker of a fish below. Suddenly, the great bird takes a few slow, deliberate steps through the shallows, its white plumage gleaming against the morning blue. In the distance, a stand of cattails sways gently in the breeze, their brown spikes catching the light like torches above the green blades. Perched among them, a Red-winged Blackbird bursts into flight, its black wings flashing brilliant red and yellow at the shoulders as it calls out sharply, patrolling its territory over the marshy edge of the lake (Fig. 1.1).

The calm of the lake, with its birds, flowers, cattails, and gentle water, mirrors the order Aster hopes for in her day. Her schedule is carefully laid out: a client meeting to assess FIPS 140–3 readiness, finishing a functional testing report for a mobile device, attending a network security training session, booking her flight to the International Cryptographic Module Conference (ICMC), finding a birthday gift for her mother, and finally enjoying a movie at home. Yet beneath the serene surface, deeper currents stir.

A dark cloud drifts across the sun, and Aster cannot help but see the metaphor. She recalls a cartoon on a T-shirt that made her chuckle:

Son: "What is cloud made of?"

Father: "Mostly Linux servers."

Y. Mao (✉)
atsec information security corporation, Austin, USA
e-mail: yi.mao@atsec.com

Y. Mao (ed.), *Tasting Cryptography*, https://doi.org/10.1007/978-3-032-30243-4_1

Fig. 1.1 Aster's morning jog along the Mueller lake

She smiles at the memory but reflects more seriously: the cloud conceals many secrets, and those secrets are only safe when protected by encryption, both when sent through the Internet and when stored on a computer.

Her thoughts flow steadily until her phone rings. It is the bank. The voice on the other end is urgent: someone has attempted to cash a check for one hundred thousand dollars. Aster's heart skips; she never signed such a check. Within moments, her day collapses. At the bank she learns that the large forgery was stopped, but several smaller forged checks, each under the alarm threshold, had already cleared. Meetings, reports, and travel plans vanish, replaced by hours of reviewing documents, filing reports with the authorities, and staring in disbelief at the forged copy of her own signature.

What began as a serene spring jog becomes the start of an exhausting battle against fraud. Police reports, investigator interviews, and identity protection requests consume the months that follow. The root cause is eventually traced to the AT&T data breach of March 2024, in which the personal information of approximately 73 million current and former customers was exposed on the dark web [1].

Aster is only one among millions. Victims of identity theft have faced not only drained bank accounts but also legal consequences. In some cases, victims have been pursued by debt collectors or even faced lawsuits for unpaid credit card debt on accounts fraudulently opened in their names after major data breaches. Even seasoned security professionals at the National Institute of Standards and Technology (NIST) were not spared when the 2015 breach of the U.S. Office of Personnel Management (OPM) exposed sensitive records of more than 21 million federal workers. The incident underscored a hard reality: even experts in cybersecurity can be affected when plaintext personal data is compromised by systems outside their control. In this case, NIST's expertise did not extend to how OPM managed and secured federal personnel data, and the failure was not attributable to the victims of the breach.

The 2013 Target breach affected up to 110 million customers, leaking 40 million credit and debit card records along with personal details of 70 million more [2]. The 2017 Equifax breach compromised the Social Security numbers, birth dates, and addresses of approximately 143 million Americans [3]. The 2023 MOVEit breach reached over 2700 organizations and exposed data of around 93 million individuals [4]. In 2024, the National Public Data breach released 2.9 billion sensitive records [5]. Even public institutions have proven vulnerable, with attacks exposing sensitive records held by government agencies and services that citizens rely on [6].

The common thread in all of these incidents is the careless storage of sensitive data in plaintext or weak encryption. Once stolen, it could be read and exploited immediately. Had the data been strongly encrypted, it would have been far less valuable without the corresponding decryption keys.

This brings us to an essential insight: while many aspects of information security are reactive, such as forensic analysis or post-incident response, cryptography is proactive. By encrypting data in advance, it renders stolen files unreadable, mitigating damage even in the event of a breach. Encryption transforms raw data into meaningless text unless the key is present.

Cryptography is the art and science of protecting secrets. It ensures confidentiality, guarantees integrity so that messages are not altered, and establishes authenticity so that identities can be trusted. Throughout history, cryptography has been a hidden force shaping events. During the Second World War, German forces relied on the Enigma machine to secure communications. Alan Turing and his team at Bletchley Park broke that code, giving the Allies vital intelligence. Harry Hinsley, official historian of British Intelligence, estimated that Ultra intelligence (from breaking Enigma and related codes) shortened the war in Europe by at least two years and possibly up to four years [7].

This example demonstrates cryptography's dual nature: when strong, it safeguards nations; when broken, it can lead to decisive defeats. Today, cryptography continues to underpin trust in digital society, securing everything from financial systems to personal identities.

Cryptography itself has evolved continuously. From ancient substitution ciphers to mechanical devices like Enigma to the mathematically grounded public-key systems of the twentieth century, it has grown in sophistication. The arrival of asymmetric cryptography, particularly the RSA algorithm and the Diffie–Hellman key exchange, was transformative. For the first time, secure communication could occur between strangers over insecure networks. These algorithms became the backbone of internet security, enabling protocols like TLS that make secure web browsing, online banking, and e-commerce possible.

This achievement was recognized at the highest level when Whitfield Diffie and Martin Hellman received the 2015 Turing Award for their pioneering work in public-key cryptography. Yet even achievements of this magnitude face new challenges.

One such threat is quantum computing. Classical computers process information as bits, but quantum computers exploit superposition and entanglement to evaluate possibilities simultaneously. With Shor's algorithm, they could factor large integers and compute discrete logarithms efficiently, breaking RSA and Diffie–Hellman. Nobody knows when quantum computers will reach this capability. Estimates range from decades away to much sooner. Adversaries, however, need not wait. They can already collect encrypted traffic today, storing it with the expectation that once quantum computers mature, they will be able to decrypt it retroactively.

This looming threat underscores the urgency of preparing for a post-quantum world. Just as Turing's work changed the outcome of global war, quantum computing will transform digital security. Researchers, standards bodies, and organizations must adopt quantum-resistant cryptography before that transformation arrives.

Throughout these changes, the U.S. NIST has led the way. Its transparent, rigorous, and inclusive processes for selecting algorithms have shaped not only American policy but global practice. The Advanced Encryption Standard (AES) competition in 2000 replaced DES with Rijndael, still the cornerstone of symmetric encryption. The SHA-3 competition in 2012 produced Keccak, strengthening hash functions after weaknesses were found in SHA-1. In 2016, NIST launched the Post-Quantum Cryptography (PQC) standardization project, inviting submissions from researchers worldwide to identify algorithms capable of withstanding the threat posed by quantum computers.

Yet standardization is only the first step. Even when algorithms are chosen, they must be implemented correctly in real products. A small coding error, a weak entropy source, or improper padding scheme can undermine the strongest cipher. To ensure correctness, NIST established the Cryptographic Algorithm Validation Program (CAVP). Accredited laboratories use standardized test vectors to verify that implementations truly match specifications. Correct algorithms are a foundation of trust.

However, correctness alone is not enough. Security also depends on how cryptographic keys are managed throughout their entire lifecycle. How are they generated, derived, imported, stored, used, exported, and ultimately destroyed? To address these broader concerns, NIST and the Communications Security Establishment (CSE) of the Government of Canada established the Cryptographic Module Validation Program (CMVP) in 1995. While the CAVP validates algorithm implementations, CMVP evaluates complete cryptographic modules, including hardware, software, firmware, or hybrid modules, against the requirements defined in the FIPS 140 series. The Canadian Centre for Cyber Security (CCCS), launched in 2018 as part of CSE under Canada's National Cyber Security Strategy, now represents the Canadian side of the program. Cryptographic module validation continues to be carried out through the ongoing joint effort of NIST and CCCS (on behalf of CSE).

FIPS 140-3 is closely aligned with international standards. It incorporates ISO/IEC 19790, which specifies the security requirements for cryptographic modules, and ISO/IEC 24759, which defines the test requirements and procedures. This alignment promotes international consistency, reduces duplication of effort, and creates a unified framework for assurance. It also ensures interoperability, so that validated products can be trusted across global markets. Modules are evaluated across multiple areas, including roles and services, physical security, protections against non-invasive attacks, key management, self-tests, and lifecycle assurance.

Together, CAVP and CMVP form the de facto backbone of cryptographic assurance. They ensure not only that algorithms are implemented correctly, but also that cryptographic modules manage keys and operations securely. Although operated in North America, these programs have global influence. FIPS-compliant modules validated under CMVP are not only mandated for use by U.S. and Canadian federal agencies, but they also serve as a powerful selling point for vendors seeking to enter industries such as finance, insurance, and telecommunications worldwide, where validated cryptography is a mark of trust and market acceptance.

At an ICMC session, Cisco's Trish spoke with conviction about FIPS's place in the certification landscape. "Think of FIPS 140 as the bedrock," Trish had said. "It is the solid foundation beneath everything else. Programs like the Federal Risk and Authorization Management Program (FedRAMP), the Common Criteria for Information Technology Security Evaluation, the Health Insurance Portability and Accountability Act (HIPAA), the Cybersecurity Maturity Model Certification (CMMC), and the Payment Card Industry Data Security Standard (PCI DSS) all rely on it. Without validated cryptography, the rest of the certifications cannot stand with confidence." Trish made it clear that FIPS was not just another standard, but the anchor point that gave weight to the entire structure of assurance.

Standards, however, are only effective when enforced. That responsibility rests with independent third-party laboratories accredited under NIST's National Voluntary Laboratory Accreditation Program and recognized by CCCS. These labs perform conformance testing under both CAVP and CMVP, covering everything from algorithm correctness to physical inspections and key management lifecycle analysis. Their independence is crucial. Vendors may have strong incentives to certify their products quickly, but impartial third-party laboratories provide the objectivity and rigor necessary to ensure that standards are applied consistently and effectively.

The relevance of all these standards and validation processes becomes clear when we return to Aster's story. Her fraud ordeal was the result of weak data protection, where sensitive information was left unencrypted or protected by weak encryption. If validation had been applied universally, ensuring correct implementation of algorithms and modules tested against international standards, her experience and that of millions like her might have been avoided.

This book will present both rigorous explanations and storytelling to reach a broad audience. Cryptographic algorithms, key management practices, and validation standards will be explained with precise references to NIST and ISO documents. At the same time, these technical topics will be introduced through storytelling in an imaginary restaurant called FIPS 'n' Chips, a playful nod to the British classic "Fish and Chips." Here, chips are not potatoes but silicon, symbolizing the integrated circuits that power modern cryptography and form the foundation of our digital world.

The metaphor of “chips” goes further. In the twenty-first century, chips are the engines of computation, driving everything from smartphones to supercomputers. In the global race for artificial intelligence, chips have become strategic assets and symbols of national power. Yet without security, even the most powerful chips cannot be trusted. Cryptography and validation standards transform silicon into a foundation for secure systems.

By blending Aster’s story, the institutional rigor of standards, and the imaginative setting of FIPS ‘n’ Chips, this book aims to be both authoritative and accessible. It invites professionals, students, and policymakers to the same table to discuss how to secure our chips, our data, and ultimately our future.

Following the FIPS ‘n’ Chips restaurant metaphor, the book is organized like a menu designed to satisfy both curiosity and professional appetite. The drinks are stories of successful FIPS certifications, including the first certificate ever issued, the highest-level validation, and examples of interim certificates. The starters offer background and context, covering the history of FIPS 140, the CMVP, NVLAP Handbook 150–17, algorithm validation through the Automated Cryptographic Validation Testing System (ACVTS), entropy source validation (ESV), as well as community and industry collaboration through organizations such as the Cryptographic Module User Forum (CMUF), the International Cryptographic Module Conference (ICMC), and the National Cybersecurity Center of Excellence (NCCoE) Automated Cryptographic Module Project (ACMVP).

The goal of this book is to bridge the gap between cryptographic standards and real-world practice. Anchored in FIPS 140-3 and its international foundation in ISO/IEC 19790 and ISO/IEC 24759, the book provides both rigorous technical explanations and practical guidance. It is designed for professionals, testers, and students who need to understand not only the “what” of cryptographic assurance, but also the “how” and “why.” By combining authoritative standards with illustrative examples, storytelling through the FIPS ‘n’ Chips metaphor, and references to successful validations and best practices, the book equips readers to design, test, and validate cryptographic products that remain resilient against fraud, breaches, and emerging threats such as quantum computing. Ultimately, its purpose is to ensure that digital systems continue to support trust, privacy, and security in an increasingly connected and AI-driven world.

This book is designed to be enjoyed both as a continuous story and as a reference work. The narrative threads (some imaginative, others set in whimsical venues like the FIPS ‘n’ Chips restaurant) are interwoven with the authentic voices of real individuals whose contributions shaped the field. These people are properly introduced in later chapters and acknowledged with deep gratitude.

When you encounter dialogue or statements attributed to them, rest assured that the content is grounded in fact, drawn from interview notes, meeting recordings, laboratory experiences, published documents, and validated module certificates. The quotes themselves are not always verbatim transcripts; instead, they have been carefully crafted to capture the essence and sentiment of what was expressed, while fitting smoothly into the book's conversational narrative style.

Each chapter ends with detailed references, allowing readers to explore the original sources and confirm that the history, standards, and practices presented here are not only engaging but firmly rooted in documented reality.

FIPS 'n' Chips Restaurant

At atsec's 25th anniversary conference, Sal La Pietra, the founding CEO, hosted a special panel with the new generation of leadership. The managing directors—Dr. Michael Vogel, Dr. Yi Mao, Rasma Araby, Yan Liu, and Garibaldi Conte—represented the company's five branches in Germany, the USA, Sweden, China, and Italy. To set the tone, Sal began by playing a clip of a music educator whose philosophy was rooted in the joy of playing second fiddle.

In the video, the teacher explained her theory of living well: to find joy not in applause or the limelight, which inevitably fade, but in the act of creating something meaningful together. She concluded that the greatest reward is reaching the finish line as part of an ensemble, rather than chasing recognition alone.

Inspired by this message, Sal turned to each managing director and asked what they envisioned for atsec's future. When it was Yi's turn, she emphasized that atsec's greatest asset is its people. She encouraged colleagues to embrace the 10,000-hour rule to master their craft, promising guided training for new recruits, like Kung Fu Panda learning from his master, and a continuing mission to cultivate the broader cryptographic community. She revealed plans for atsec to contribute by authoring a book on cryptographic standards, nicknamed the FIPS Book, to honor the colleagues who built atsec's reputation in Cryptographic Security Testing and to attract the next generation of professionals, partners, customers, and government overseers. The FIPS Book project echoed the spirit of playing second fiddle, a shared effort to create something meaningful together as an atsec team.

Then, with a smile, Yi surprised the audience. She invited everyone to step into a virtual restaurant called FIPS 'n' Chips, where cryptographic learning would take place in a fresh and engaging way. To guide them into this new world, she handed out FutureVision goggles, themselves subject to FIPS validation. At the snap of her fingers, a breathtaking 3-D vision filled everyone's view in virtual reality.

At the very top of Austin's landmark Mueller control tower appeared the restaurant known as FIPS 'n' Chips. Once a sentinel guiding aircraft into the city, the tower's sweeping blue-glass façade still curves upward like a signal reaching for the sky. From its lofty perch, diners enjoy sweeping views of Mueller Lake Park, the surrounding neighborhoods, and walkways that now wind through what was once a busy airfield.

Standing apart as both landmark and memory, the tower embodies transition: from aviation hub to community anchor; from charting flight paths to navigating ideas. Where radar once tracked aircraft across the horizon, the restaurant now projects constellations of cryptographic algorithms across the ceiling, guiding guests not through storm clouds but through the unseen flows of data.

The circular dining room, echoing the tower's aviation heritage, made every table feel like a window seat. By day, sunlight glinted off polished wood and brushed steel; by night, the room glowed in soft blue light as those constellations shimmered overhead, a reminder of the coded systems that quietly secure the world.

The walls carried poster-sized frames from atsec's FIPS 140–2 and 140–3 videos, styled like vintage airline advertisements. Instead of promising exotic destinations, they celebrated cryptographic milestones: "Now Boarding: FIPS 140-3 Validation and SHA-3 Takes Off." Copper inlays traced the floor like circuit pathways, while a chandelier shaped as a radar dish glowed above with fiber-optic rings, pulsing as though encrypted signals filled the air.

Tables resembled circuit boards with faint blue pathways, and cockpit-style booths curved against the walls, each offering a private view of Austin. At the bar, retro flight instruments had been reborn as cryptographic dials, while ticker displays scrolled acronyms—CAVP, CMVP, ISO 19790—like flights arriving and departing.

The menu unfolded like an air traffic control panel. Drinks were success stories: the Old Fashioned celebrating the very first FIPS certificate, the Top Shelf honoring the most prestigious validations, and On the Rocks offering the carefully balanced flavor of interim certificates. Starters provided history and context: FIPS 140 as a warming veggie soup, CMVP as a crisp wedge salad, NVLAP HB 150–17 as rosemary breadsticks, ACVTS and ESV as a flavorful dip and chips, while the CMUF sampler platter and ICMC bruschetta invited shared dialogue and collaboration. The NCCoE ACMVP burrata projects appeared as delicate tasters, preparing guests for the main course (Fig. 1.2).

The main entries were presented with ceremony:

- ISO/IEC 19790—The Chef's Special A full course of module security requirements including module specification, interfaces, roles, services and authentication, software/firmware security, operational environment, physical security, sensitive security parameter management, self-tests, and life-cycle assurance.
- ISO/IEC 24759—The Chef's Preparation The recipe behind the meal, written in Assertions (AS), Vendor Evidence (VE), and Test Evidence (TE), ensuring each requirement is properly prepared, plated, and verified.
- FIPS 140–3—The House Style The U.S. and Canadian signature dish, crafted from ISO ingredients and garnished with the NIST SP 800–140 series (A–E): documentation, test requirements, approved functions, key establishment methods, and laboratory guidance.

Finally came dessert. A secure chocolate fudge sundae layered with examples of proper key management tempted even the most disciplined. Compliance cheesecake, moist with lessons learned and frosted with practical improvements, was served on silver trays. Post-Quantum lemon pudding offered a taste of tomorrow's cryptography, while an ISO vanilla delight provided a delicate finale, showcasing refinements baked into the latest standards.

Fig. 1.2 The imaginary FIPS 'n' chips restaurant

At the bottom of the menu, a note in elegant script reminded diners: At FIPS 'n' Chips, our chips are made of silicon, not potatoes. Chips are the engines of computation, powering everything from smartphones to supercomputers. In the global race for artificial intelligence, they have become strategic assets and symbols of national power. But without cryptography, even the most powerful chips cannot be trusted.

The restaurant was more than a place to eat—it was a metaphor brought to life. Cryptographic assurance, like the control tower itself, is about oversight, order, security, and safety. It prevents collisions, protects routes, and ensures trust in the invisible systems on which we depend. Perched high above Austin, FIPS 'n' Chips transforms a relic of flight into a beacon of assurance, welcoming colleagues, partners, and enthusiasts to explore a world where silicon chips, not jet engines, power the future.

The room buzzed with excitement at this creative way of conveying knowledge through metaphor without losing technical accuracy, much like the cryptographic cartoon clips atsec has produced for ICMC openings. It reflected the spirit of atsec: we LOVE what we do.

Amid the lively atmosphere, Sal laughed and shouted, "I like wedge salad and an Old Fashion! Can I have them?"

"Absolutely!" Yi replied without missing a beat. She encouraged colleagues to suggest their own favorite dishes, mapping them to cryptographic concepts or security requirements, so that the restaurant's menu would carry a personal touch in this collective endeavor.

As the imagined courses were cleared away and glasses were refilled, the conversation naturally returned to real-world experience. Managing directors from atsec's sibling branches, joined by atsec co-founder Staffan Persson, chimed in to connect FIPS and cryptographic module validation with their lines of business.

Michael spoke first. "From my side, it is a bit ironic," he said. "We deal so much with BSI (Bundesamt für Sicherheit in der Informationstechnik, the German Federal Office for Information Security), and half the time we end up rejecting FIPS certificates because they are not accepted there. So it is hard to tell a funny success story." He paused, then added more seriously, "But that is exactly why this book matters. FIPS has become a reference point. Even when it is challenged, it shapes the discussion. And honestly, we need this book. It will be a game changer for us."

Staffan leaned forward and reframed the conversation. "What FIPS really does," he said, "is remove the temptation to be creative where creativity does not belong. In software, people love to invent. In cryptography, that instinct leads to failure." He shook his head slightly. "FIPS forces things to be well defined, specified, and controlled. That discipline is its real value." He continued, "There is no secret magic in cryptography. Transparency is the key. Public standards beat proprietary tricks every time."

From Italy, Garibaldi joined with a commercial perspective. "For me, FIPS is not theoretical at all," he said. "It directly impacts revenue." He explained how customers increasingly called not only about Common Criteria but asked, almost as an afterthought, whether FIPS was also available. "And when we say yes," he added, "their reaction changes. From a market point of view, the FIPS certificate is often more important than CC for many customers. It has become a de facto global standard. I did not expect that years ago, but today it is very clear."

Rasma picked up the thread and tied it to operational reality. "We see FIPS as an enabler," she said. "Even when we are not performing FIPS validations ourselves, we rely on our U.S. lab for algorithm testing and evidence. FIPS and CC work hand in hand. You cannot separate them anymore." She also pointed to people, not just standards. "The movement of talent across regions, sharing expertise, that is what makes this work."

Yan joined in thoughtfully. "I want to say first it's a great idea to have such a FIPS book," he said. "My own interest in cryptography dates back to my studies at university." After the establishment of atsec China, he recalled working with local vendors over a decade ago, long before formal validation became central to their conversations. He said, "During my work at atsec, I also studied much of this together with atsec colleagues and try my best to establish the technical communication and collaboration between China and global industry."

What struck him most, he explained, was how the landscape had changed. "I am happy to see that FIPS has now become aligned with ISO, and that more organizations accept it, not just the U.S. or Canada." He pointed to its growing collaboration with other standards bodies, noting that atsec China had invited the PCI (Payment Card Industry) technical director to present at ICMC, and that discussions at PCI meetings increasingly focus on the future of cryptography. "There are many presentations now about what comes next," he said, "post-quantum algorithms, the future direction of cryptography. This book can help people look ahead."

Before the conversation moved on, Yan added one final practical note. "In areas like the payment card industry," he said, "standards like PCI PIN and P2PE® (Point-to-Point Encryption) already directly reference the FIPS 140 standard. This shows how these frameworks are interconnected and mutually reinforcing—there's extensive collaboration behind them."

Yi also explained that the vision would not remain confined to atsec alone. In the spirit of openness and community, it would extend beyond the company, inviting the broader cryptographic community into the story.

She encouraged everyone to contribute ideas for refining the restaurant concept and its menu, adding their own "food for thought" to the vision. What followed was a lively exchange of suggestions that brought the 25th anniversary celebration to a close with both imagination and pride.

FIPS 'n' Chips Menu

See Figs. 1.3, 1.4, 1.5, 1.6 and 1.7.

Fig. 1.3 The FIPS 'n' chips menu cover

Fig. 1.4 The FIPS 'n' chips themed drinks

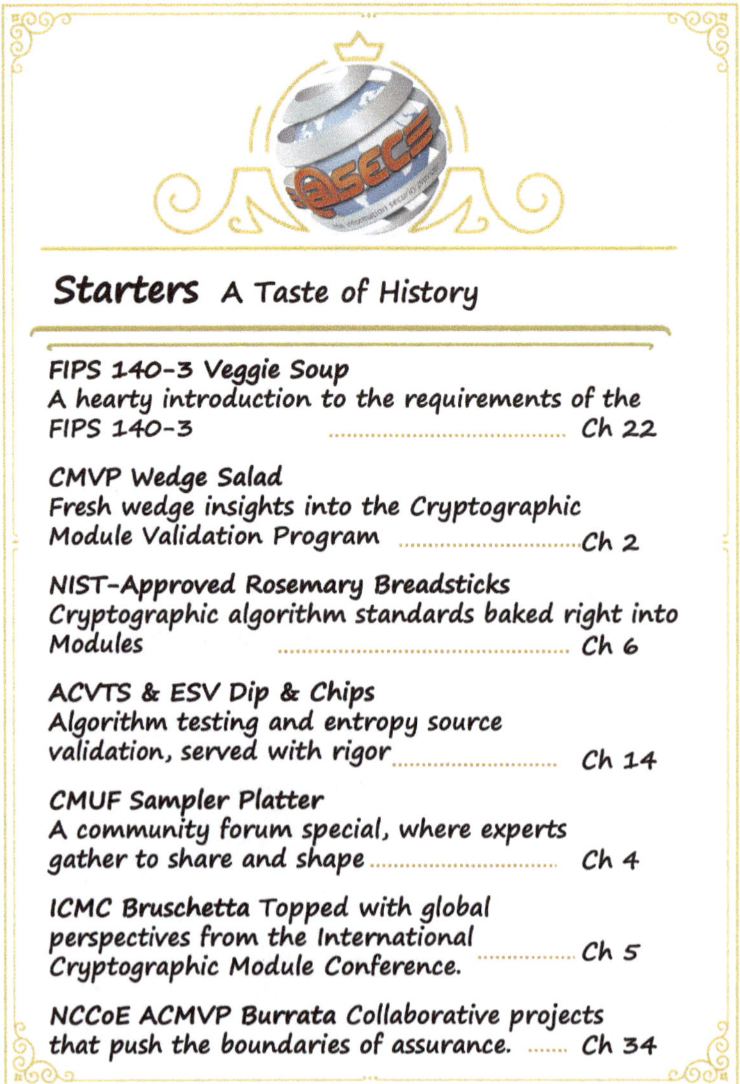

Fig. 1.5 The FIPS 'n' chips starter dishes

Main Entries The Standards Feast

ISO/IEC 19790 Special
The full-course meal of security requirements for cryptographic modules .... Ch 33

ISO/IEC 24759 The Chef's Preparation
The testing recipe that ensures every dish meets exacting standards .... Ch 21

FIPS 140-3 House Style
The U.S. and Canadian signature version, crafted from ISO ingredients .... Part IV

Fig. 1.6 The FIPS 'n' chips main entrees

Fig. 1.7 The FIPS 'n' chips desserts

References

1. Malwarebytes Labs (2024) How to check if your data was part of the AT&T breach. https://www.malwarebytes.com/blog/news/2024/04/how-to-check-if-your-data-was-part-of-the-att-breach
2. Computerworld (2014) Breach exposes data on 110 million customers, Target now says. https://www.computerworld.com/article/1518735/update-breach-exposes-data-on-110-million-customers-target-now-says.html

3. Wikipedia (2017) Equifax data breach. https://en.wikipedia.org/wiki/2017_Equifax_data_breach
4. Wikipedia (2023) MOVEit data breach. https://en.wikipedia.org/wiki/2023_MOVEit_data_breach
5. Wikipedia (2024) National Public Data breach. https://en.wikipedia.org/wiki/2024_National_Public_Data_breach
6. San Antonio Express-News (2025) Hackers breach Texas DOT, iHeartMedia, CPS Energy. https://www.expressnews.com/business/article/texas-data-breaches-txdot-iheartmedia-cps-energy-20351758.php
7. Wikipedia. Ultra (cryptography). Harry Hinsley's estimate that codebreaking shortened the war in Europe by at least two years. https://en.wikipedia.org/wiki/Ultra_(cryptography)

Dr. Yi Mao Yi is a CISSP and holds a Ph.D. in Mathematical Logic (2003) and a Master's degree in Computer Science (2000) from the University of Texas at Austin. Dr. Mao is the CEO at atsec U.S. Corporation. She runs the overall U.S. branch operations, coordinates with atsec sibling branches in Europe and Asia, and supervises IT product security testing and evaluation based on standards such as FIPS and Common Criteria (CC). She is an expert member of ISO/IEC JTC 1/SC 27, a former CMUF-to-ISO WG3 Liaison Officer, CMUF Steering Committee Member, and the ICMC Program Committee Chair.

Part I
Cryptographic Module Validation Ecosystem

Chapter 2
Cryptographic Module Validation Program (CMVP)

Yi Mao

Yi and Joachim traveled to NIST to meet the new leadership of the Computer Security Division (CSD) in the Information Technology Laboratory (ITL), following the retirement of several key personnel.

It was a pivotal moment of transition. In the spring of 2025, the Department of Government Efficiency (DOGE) introduced its "Fork in the Road" program, and many senior leaders chose administrative leave or early retirement. Against this backdrop, the visit was far more than a formality. It became a gesture of atsec's and the broader community's, continued support for NIST's indispensable role in guiding the industry. In a quiet conference room in Gaithersburg, they had the honor of speaking with a group of NIST veterans who had launched the Cryptographic Module Validation Program (CMVP) back in the 1990s.

For Yi and Joachim, it felt like meeting the original chefs who had written the first recipes for FIPS assurance.

At the next Monday status meeting in atsec's CST laboratory, the inevitable question bubbled up from their curious teammates:

"So, how was your NIST trip? How did CMVP actually start?"

Yi leaned back with a smile. "Do you want to see how our meeting went?" she asked, reminding colleagues to put on their FutureVision goggles, the same pair she had once unveiled at atsec's 25th anniversary event, now upgraded with an atsec-provisioned key to guard the secure entrance.

As people reached for their coffee cups and adjusted their headsets, Joachim added with a grin, "We spotted a deer on the NIST campus. Last time it was geese, remember? This time the sidewalks were goose-poop free."

Laughter rippled across the room.

Then, with a soft hum, the office dissolved around them. The VR world materialized: the luminous control tower above Austin's Mueller Park, the signature setting

---

Y. Mao (✉)
atsec information security corporation, Austin, USA
e-mail: yi.mao@atsec.com

Y. Mao (ed.), *Tasting Cryptography*, https://doi.org/10.1007/978-3-032-30243-4_2

of the FIPS 'n' Chips restaurant. Through panoramic windows, a sunrise glowed over the lake, scattering golden reflections across the water. But today, instead of circuit-board tables and algorithm chandeliers, the space had been reconfigured into a faithful replica of a NIST conference room.

The tables appeared in a neat U-shape, the kind familiar to anyone who has sat through a standards meeting. Yi and Joachim were seated at the center as guests of honor. To their left sat Lisa [1] and Murugiah [2]; to their right, Jim [3]. On the screen ahead, Donna [4] appeared remotely, her presence no less commanding than those in the room.

Yi paused the VR playback, the scene suspended like a still photograph. She turned toward her atsec teammates, her voice warm with admiration.

"Before we dive into the meeting itself," she said, "let me tell you who we had the privilege of sitting with. They are people who helped shape the very ground we walk on in cryptographic assurance."

She began with Murugiah Souppaya, describing him as a rare researcher who bridges generations. "Murugiah sees both the practical and the visionary side of security. At NIST he works on virtualization and cloud security, finding ways to make massive, distributed systems less vulnerable. He has his hands in everything from incident response to secure software practices, always tying the standards back to real-world deployments. When he speaks, you hear both laboratory experiments and policy drafts overlapping in one voice."

Her tone shifted as she spoke of Lisa Carnahan. "Lisa carries the title of Associate Director for IT Standardization, but what it really means is that she makes sure standards do not just sit on a shelf. She ensures that our frameworks, such as cybersecurity, privacy, and others, become measurable, testable, and enforceable. The CMVP could not function without that kind of rigor. Lisa brings strategy into the conversation, ensuring NIST stays aligned with international bodies while keeping our goals sharp. She was also the first CMVP manager."

Yi gestured to the empty chair to her right, conjuring the image of James Foti. "Jim has been there for decades. He is not loud or showy, but you can sense the imprint he has left on the field. He worked in the early days of AES and the cryptographic module standards, helping compare requirements when FIPS 140–1 gave way to 140–2. He is one of those steady presences who has seen the evolution of CMVP from fragile beginnings to global recognition. Jim was the second CMVP manager from 1996 to 1999."

Finally, Yi's voice softened when she mentioned Donna Dodson, who appeared on the screen during their meeting. "Donna may have retired from NIST, but you still feel her influence everywhere. For decades she was NIST's chief cybersecurity advisor, and she led the National Cybersecurity Center of Excellence (NCCoE). She helped create the Cybersecurity Framework and pushed for advances in everything from post-quantum cryptography to IoT security. Talking to her felt like listening to living history, someone who carried the institutional memory of CMVP and ensured its spirit kept pace with technology's relentless march."

Yi leaned back, letting her words settle. "So when Joachim and I sat in that NIST conference room, it wasn't just a meeting. It felt like stepping into a time capsule, speaking with the architects who built the CMVP. They were just as interested in hearing about the program's current state as the world around it continued to change. What you will see next is not a recording. It is a reconstructed simulation based on Joachim's notes and my own recollection. The quotations that appear in the following simulation are not necessarily direct quotes from the individuals mentioned. Instead, they are intended to faithfully capture the sentiments expressed during our meeting."

The VR playback resumed. The atsec lab faded away, and the NIST meeting filled the virtual space.

Murugiah opened warmly, introducing Yi and Joachim to the veterans. He thanked atsec for its long support of the program and noted the recent work with the NCCoE Automation of the CMVP project. He also noted atsec's pivotal role in founding the International Cryptographic Module Conference (ICMC), which has become the leading global forum for the cryptographic validation community.

Yi thanked Murugiah, Lisa, Jim, and Donna. She explained the goal of the FIPS book and why keeping this history alive matters to the community.

Lisa cleared her throat and rested a hand on a stack of well-worn documents [5–11]. "What would be most useful," she began, "is to think about what has held true from the start to today. We made the best decisions we could with what we knew. FIPS 140 began as Federal Standard 1027. First, we put a FIPS 140 cover on it, without changing much, to establish responsibility. Then came 140-1, later 140-2, then ISO 19790, and now 140-3. My strongest contributions were in those early years when we were building the foundation."

Yi leaned forward. "What about the eleven areas of FIPS 140?"

Donna spoke with a teacher's calm. "You have to remember the computing power of the time. Requirements were hardware-focused because crypto mostly lived in physical devices. Crypto was beginning to explode, but not yet in a way that made software design obvious. The framework had to reflect that reality, while still preparing for what would come next (Fig. 2.1)."

Lisa nodded. "The eleven areas recognized that crypto would not stay locked in hardware. It would expand into software. Miles Smid pushed us to look ahead. We were writing rules for a future we could not yet see. For example, describing a trusted path in software when none of us knew how that would actually work. We also wanted a process that was public and predictable."

Donna added context. "The framework also needed levels. The Computer Security Act of 1987 moved crypto testing to NIST. We created four levels: Level 1 for off-the-shelf modules, Level 2 for stronger commercial designs, Level 3 for advanced tamper resistance, and Level 4 as a stretch goal. Formal methods lived up there. We did not expect people to attempt it, but we wanted the framework to be ready."

Joachim smiled. "Did anyone actually go for Level 4?"

Yi answered. "IBM did."

Donna shook her head, amused by the memory. "Early on we saw an RFP from NASA that required Level 4. We had to go back and fix that. Agencies wanted the best number, but the framework was about risk management, not a high score. That was new then, and to be honest, it is still hard today."

Fig. 2.1 A hardware module that labs use to perform proficiency testing

She grew more serious. "The framework helped people understand that good cybersecurity requires risk management."

Lisa leaned in with a quick clarification. "That was part of the confusion. Many other FIPS told agencies what to do. FIPS 140 asked agencies to make informed choices."

Donna glanced toward Jim. "Jim helped us explain that shift. He wrote a short two-page piece that framed validation as a risk-based decision. Computer scientists are not always the best at plain language, but that document made sense. It showed people how to use FIPS 140 wisely."

Yi asked gently, "Could we have a copy for the book?"

Jim smiled. "It was a long time ago. I barely remember the details. What I do remember is why we built CMVP. In the 1990s there was a shift from GOTS to COTS. Agencies needed confidence that commercial cryptography would protect sensitive but unclassified information. CMVP was built to provide that confidence. It was never about chasing a level. It was about trust. Agencies needed assurance that the crypto they bought would work."

Lisa added historical texture. "All of this sat next to the Clipper Chip and key escrow debates. Trust in government and encryption was strained. At the same time we were developing the Digital Signature Standard. NIST decided DSA should not include an encryption component, unlike RSA. That was controversial. CMVP had to prove it was open, independent, and worthy of trust."

She shifted to the program structure. "NIST could not test everything. We turned to third-party labs for three reasons. First, it conserved NIST resources. Second, it grew expertise in the private sector, which aligned with NIST's role in the Department of Commerce. Third, it made the process transparent. The FIPS 140 series, the Derived

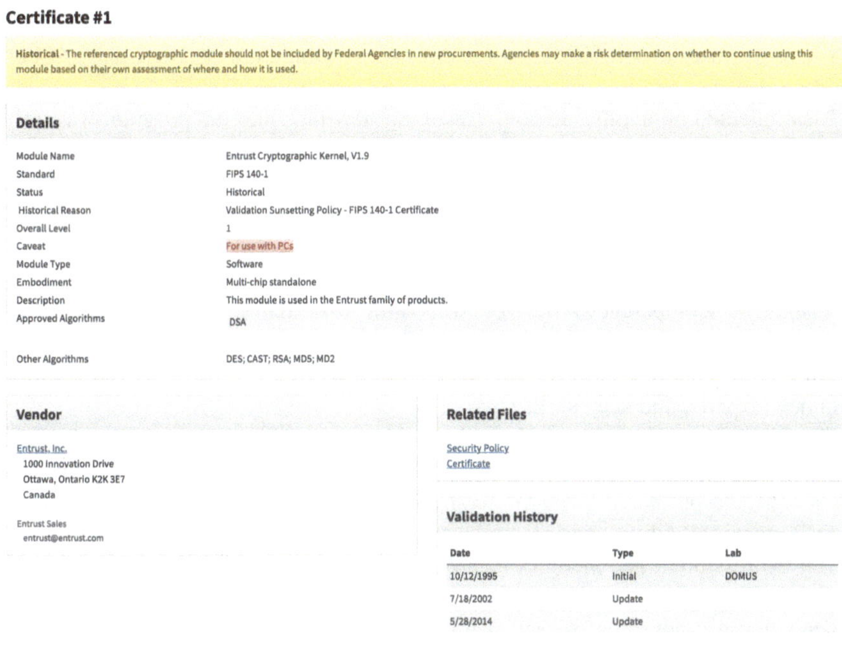

Certificate #1

Historical - The referenced cryptographic module should not be included by Federal Agencies in new procurements. Agencies may make a risk determination on whether to continue using this module based on their own assessment of where and how it is used.

Details

Module Name	Entrust Cryptographic Kernel, V1.9
Standard	FIPS 140-1
Status	Historical
Historical Reason	Validation Sunsetting Policy - FIPS 140-1 Certificate
Overall Level	1
Caveat	For use with PCs
Module Type	Software
Embodiment	Multi-chip standalone
Description	This module is used in the Entrust family of products.
Approved Algorithms	DSA
Other Algorithms	DES; CAST; RSA; MD5; MD2

Vendor

Entrust, Inc.
1000 Innovation Drive
Ottawa, Ontario K2K 3E7
Canada

Entrust Sales
entrust@entrust.com

Related Files

Security Policy
Certificate

Validation History

Date	Type	Lab
10/12/1995	Initial	DOMUS
7/18/2002	Update	
5/28/2014	Update	

Fig. 2.2 The first FIPS validation certificate

Test Requirements, and the NVLAP framework were public. The only thing that remained confidential was lab proficiency testing."

Yi nodded. "That round-table proficiency activity evolved into today's CVP exam for individual lab staff."

Lisa continued. "When I ran the program, there were two labs. InfoGard started with two engineers who saw the opportunity. CygnaCom saw the same path. Today, InfoGard is part of UL. CygnaCom was acquired by Entrust. Not every lab remained, but FIPS is healthy. Demand is strong."

Joachim spoke so softly that only Yi heard. "Yes, demand is high, and the queue is long."

Yi quickly looked up the Validated Cryptographic Modules List and found that Entrust owns the very first FIPS validation certificate issued on 10/12/1995 (Fig. 2.2).

Lisa took a breath, then chose her words with care. "Creating labs was only part of the work. We did not write standards in isolation. We also held workshops. One was for users. One was for potential labs. Another was for the broader community. Those workshops were essential. Agencies could describe what they needed. Labs could see what participation would require. We could test whether the framework was workable. It was an open process, and it set the tone for how CMVP would grow."

Murugiah brightened. "Those early workshops grew into the International Cryptographic Module Conference, or ICMC. I have attended several of the recent ones.

The community has grown noticeably. Credit to atsec for carrying that spirit forward and helping to establish ICMC as the modern continuation of NIST's workshop tradition."

Lisa reflected on another lesson. "Bringing new labs into the program was only the beginning. The real challenge was maintaining competency. Learning the bare minimum to perform a test was not enough. Labs needed to understand the business they were in, the expectations that came with it, and the responsibility to sustain that knowledge year after year. The workshops helped set those expectations. Competency had to become part of a lab's culture."

Yi agreed. "Competency is not a one-time milestone. It needs steady renewal. That is why I like the idea of a Continuous Education Program through the Cryptographic Module User Forum. CMUF could provide a structured way to share knowledge, train new experts, and keep skills sharp."

The VR projection shifted to show the U.S. and Canadian flags side by side. Lisa smiled. "Canada joined by choice. FIPS 140-1 was not required there, but they saw the benefit and partnered through recognition of NVLAP. That collaboration gave CMVP greater credibility and reach."

Her expression turned thoughtful. "We also began to see FIPS 140-1 used outside procurement. Agencies and regulators started to cite it in rulemaking, sometimes in ways that did not quite fit. For example, the Department of Health and Human Services tried to fold FIPS 140-1 into e-prescribing rules. That created confusion because FIPS 140 was written for cryptographic modules, not for entire systems. It was a sign that FIPS 140 was becoming a wider policy touchstone, but it also showed how important it was to use it correctly."

Yi and Joachim almost spoke at once. Yi said, "That is right. We have FIPS customers from the banking industry." Joachim waited for a beat, then added, "Especially hardware security modules and USB tokens used for online banking."

Yi nodded and continued. "Many of those same products, like HSMs and tokens, also pursue Common Criteria certification through NIAP. That expansion also connected us with NIAP's Common Criteria program. CMVP focuses on cryptographic modules. NIAP evaluates broader IT products under Common Criteria. The two programs complement each other. CMVP helps ensure the strength of the crypto inside the box. NIAP assesses assurance for the product as a whole. Together they provide a stronger basis for federal trust in commercial technology."

Lisa looked back to the stack of papers. "Another area that stretched us was NVLAP Handbook 150–17. It required us to think about uncertainty in ways that were not natural for cryptographers. In calibration labs, uncertainty means tolerances and error bars. In security testing, it also means lab consistency, test repeatability, and how to account for subjective inspections like tamper evidence. We had to explain that uncertainty matters in conformance testing and that it must be documented. That was new ground."

Yi's eyes lit up with recognition. "That explains a lot. During our bi-annual audit this summer, the lead auditor came from the chemistry world. We quickly realized that our interpretations of calibration, uncertainty, and sampling were very different when applied to cryptographic testing."

Fig. 2.3 The DES machine displayed at NIST's visitor center

Jim's voice steadied the room. "I remember the summer of 1996, when we drafted the first Implementation Guidance. One of the questions concerned the uncertainty of tamper evidence. We had to decide how strong adhesives should be for physical security at Level 2. The requirement was clear. A cryptographic module had to show visible signs of tampering if someone tried to open it. We wanted a level playing field for the labs, with as little subjectivity as possible. By February 1997 the guidance was published. Miles Smid emphasized that we were not interpreting the standard. We were clarifying it. That document proved invaluable. It set expectations, and it made the process transparent."

The scene gradually returned to the control tower above Austin's Mueller Park. The atsec team sat quietly, absorbing what they had just witnessed. It did not feel like a lecture. It felt like a shared memory of how CMVP was forged through law, through risk-based thinking, through transparency, and through the insistence that cryptography must be trustworthy and usable. Yi then added, "After our visit, Jim sent a follow-up email pointing us to an oral history interview on ITL and cybersecurity from the NIST Digital Archives [12]. Donna and Miles, along with several other NIST veterans, participated in that interview."

As the playback faded, Yi and Joachim closed with a final image. A photograph of the DES machine in NIST's Visitor Center appeared across the panoramic windows. The old hardware stood as a reminder of where the journey began. It was a monument to a time when cryptography was bound to iron and silicon, and it stood as a fitting bookend to the story of how CMVP evolved into the program it is today, supported by more than twenty accredited testing laboratories around the world (Fig. 2.3).

As the discussion of the DES machine faded, Yi smiled and reached for her console. "That was the past," she said. "Now let's step forward in time. I want to show you a different kind of history, one told by the people who carried the program from its beginnings to the present."

She paused for a moment, then added, "Between those early CMVP pioneers and today's leadership are the long-time reviewers who shaped the program day by day. One of them is Dr. Allen Roginsky [13], with whom I recently had a conversation."

With a gentle tap, the VR goggles dimmed, and the familiar interface of a recorded WebEx session appeared. The screen flickered, and Allen's voice filled the room—rich, confident, and unmistakably Russian. His accent was thick, yet his English flowed with effortless precision and grace. It was the kind of fluency that came not from erasing one's roots, but from mastering expression through them. Yi listened with quiet admiration, as she always did. She often wondered how Allen could speak a second language so naturally, weaving complex ideas without pause, while she herself still had to summon focus and energy to shape each English sentence through the contours of her Chinese accent.

Among those who shaped the CMVP into what it is today, Allen stands out as both a meticulous reviewer and a thoughtful storyteller. When he joined NIST in August 2004, the program was still young, and the modern FIPS 140 validation process was taking form. "I was the third reviewer to join the NIST CMVP then," he recalled. "Three in the United States and two in Canada, and every single validation report had to be reviewed by both sides."

Allen often mentioned the names of those who helped define the early CMVP era: Miles Smid, Stuart "Stu" Katzke, John Campbell, and his first manager, Ray Snouffer, who maintained and improved the Cryptik tool that structured FIPS validation reports. "Ray hired me," he said warmly. "He was a good manager, very technical, and he let me shape areas where I felt comfortable. I owe him a lot."

He described the CMVP of those early years as a close-knit group of experts bound by shared purpose and technical curiosity. "The mission never really changed," Allen said. "It was to ensure that the government and anyone else following the program could trust cryptographic modules that met NIST's standards. FISMA just gave it legal weight."

Allen remembered the evolution from FIPS 140-1 to FIPS 140-2 not as a revolution but as refinement. "The change wasn't driven by crisis," he explained. "It was a required review after five years, and the newer standard became more specific. It turned general statements like 'this shall be secure' into measurable requirements." The shift also introduced new algorithm testing, more structured reviews, and closer collaboration between U.S. and Canadian reviewers.

He described those early days as a time of camaraderie and excitement. "We had small CMVP meetings where everyone joked, argued, and worked late. There was real energy in those rooms, as if we were a start-up company." He laughed as he recalled the chaos of his first meeting, arriving late because Washington traffic took an hour and a half longer than expected, and the kindness with which his colleagues welcomed him anyway.

As the years went by, Allen witnessed the CMVP's transformation from a few reviewers working with nine accredited labs, some of which were only a few months old, to a global program involving dozens of labs and thousands of validations. He spoke fondly of NIST's collaboration with its Canadian counterparts.

Allen retired in 2024 after two decades of service but remained deeply connected to the community that had grown around the CMVP. His reflections captured not only the evolution of standards and validation tools but also the human side of a program built by engineers, mathematicians, and idealists who believed that trust in cryptography begins with precision and collaboration.

Yi paused the recording for a moment, letting Allen's words settle in the quiet room. "With Allen bridging the past and the future of cryptographic module validation," she said softly, "cryptographic algorithm validation itself has become fully automated over the past decade, replacing the old Windows desktop application known as the CAVS (Cryptographic Algorithm Validation System) Tool."

The complexity of the CAVP (Cryptographic Algorithm Validation Program) test suite has grown enormously over the years. The push toward automation, under what later became the Automated Cryptographic Validation Testing (ACVT) initiative, began as early as 2015. It was led by Dr. Apostol Vassilev, who joined NIST after years of experience in a testing laboratory and with strong connections across the industry. Having seen firsthand the rapidly growing demand for cryptographic testing, he recognized that manual processes would no longer scale.

The first phase of this effort focused on automating cryptographic algorithm testing. The second phase continued through the National Cybersecurity Center of Excellence (NCCoE) ACMVP (Automated Cryptographic Module Validation Project). Across multiple generations of leadership, Apostol Vassilev, Harold Booth, and Chris Celi collectively modernized algorithm testing and steadily advanced its automation. NIST introduced both a demonstration ACVT Server (ACVTS) and a production server. The demo server is available worldwide to users who complete the registration process, while the production server is available to accredited laboratories, including third-party labs such as atsec and first-party labs such as Cisco. This latter capability allows algorithm testing to be integrated directly into a vendor's cryptographic module development cycle.

The ACVT production server first became available in 2019, and atsec obtained the first set of CAVP certificates issued through NIST's ACVT production environment [14]. The contributors to the ACVTS, Apostol Vassilev, Benjamin Livelsberger, Christopher Celi, Harold Booth, and Robert Staples, listed alphabetically by first name, were awarded the NIST 2024 Bronze Medal Award in recognition of this work [15]. By the time of the award, more than 2.3 million tests had been performed, with approximately 80 percent representing testing that would not have been feasible under the previous system. During fiscal year 2025 alone, NIST provided testing for over 950,000 vector sets across the ACVTS demo and production servers combined.

As the discussion shifted from the program's early history into the present day, Yi drew on her recent conversations with counterparts at NIST and the Canadian Centre for Cyber Security. Through these exchanges, she had gained a clear picture of how the program is being managed today and where it is headed. She glanced around the room and said quietly, "Let's now listen to the voices guiding the CMVP today."

Yi noted that Kailai Chen [16], representing the Canadian Centre for Cyber Security, had joined the CMVP leadership during a particularly demanding period. The transition from FIPS 140–2 to FIPS 140–3 was still underway, and the program was operating under sustained pressure from a growing queue of validation submissions. From Kailai's perspective, improving throughput had become an immediate priority. Reducing the backlog was essential not only for vendors and laboratories, but also for restoring confidence in the program's ability to keep pace with industry needs.

At the same time, Yi explained that Kailai emphasized the importance of not allowing CMVP to become purely reactive. Simply processing reports faster would address short-term pain, but it would not strengthen the program over the long run. He stressed the need for clearer guidance, better engagement with laboratories, and ongoing collaboration with the broader community through working groups and forums such as CMUF. These efforts, he believed, were necessary to prevent recurring bottlenecks and to support more consistent interpretations of the standard.

Yi then summarized the perspective shared by Dave Hawes [16] from NIST, who viewed the queue as both a practical challenge and a strategic inflection point. Clearing the backlog was a prerequisite for meaningful progress, but Dave also saw it as an opportunity to rethink how CMVP operates. He conveyed that the program needed to move away from a posture that relied heavily on detailed report review at the end of the process, and instead build more trust earlier through audits, assessments, and stronger lab engagement.

Staffing emerged as another central concern. Yi recalled that Dave had been candid about the limitations imposed by current resources. Expanding the team and bringing new staff up to speed would take time, and meaningful improvements could not happen overnight. Nevertheless, once capacity increased, he expected the program to regain flexibility and shift its focus toward proactive leadership rather than constant triage.

Looking further ahead, Yi explained that Kailai had reflected on the lessons learned from the FIPS 140-3 transition. The shift had proven more complex and disruptive than anticipated, and he felt strongly that future transitions, including those related to updates of ISO/IEC 19790, would require earlier planning and clearer communication. Avoiding another period of prolonged uncertainty would depend on coordination across validation authorities, standards bodies, laboratories, and vendors.

Yi concluded that both leaders shared a common goal: improving efficiency without compromising assurance. From their perspective, validation needed to concentrate on what truly mattered for security, rather than overwhelming all parties with unnecessary complexity. If done well, the process could become faster, more predictable, and more accessible, enabling more products to move through validation while preserving trust in the results.

As the recording ended, Yi looked around the room. The message from today's CMVP leadership was clear. The program was navigating real constraints, but it was also actively redefining itself. What began decades earlier as an experiment in shared responsibility was now evolving again, shaped by experience, scale, and an increasingly global cryptographic ecosystem.

References

1. Lisa J. Carnahan—Associate Director for IT Standardization, NIST. Staff Profile. https://www.nist.gov/people/lisa-j-carnahan. Lisa Carnahan Awarded 2020 Leadership in IT Standards Industry Award. https://www.nist.gov/awards/lisa-carnahan-awarded-2020-leadership-it-standards-industry-award
2. Murugiah Souppaya—Computer Security Division, NIST. Staff Profile. https://www.nist.gov/people/murugiah-souppaya. NIST Cloud Computing Image Reference. https://www.nist.gov/image/cloudcomputingjpg
3. James Foti—NIST Staff Profile. https://www.nist.gov/people/james-foti
4. Donna F Dodson—NIST Fellow. NIST Awards Page. https://www.nist.gov/awards/donna-dodson-nist-fellow
5. Federal Standard 1027: Cryptographic Module for Protection of Computer Data. U.S. General Services Administration (1982). https://csrc.nist.gov/News/1988/redesignation-of-14-fed-stds-as-fips
6. Federal Information Processing Standard (FIPS) 140: Security Requirements for Cryptographic Modules. NIST (1988). https://csrc.nist.gov/pubs/fips/140/final
7. Federal Information Processing Standard (FIPS) 140–1: Security Requirements for Cryptographic Modules. NIST (1994). https://csrc.nist.gov/pubs/fips/140-1/upd1/final
8. Federal Register Notice: Request for Comments on FIPS 140–1. NIST (1998). https://csrc.nist.gov/News/1998/proposed-reaffirmation-of-fips-140-1
9. NIST's Cryptographic Module Validation Approach Twenty (1998) ITL Bull:2. https://nistdigitalarchives.contentdm.oclc.org/digital/collection/p16009coll6/id/60027/rec/6
10. NIST's Cryptographic Module Validation Program Validates First Level 4 Module (1999) ITL Bull:14. https://nistdigitalarchives.contentdm.oclc.org/digital/collection/p16009coll6/id/76223/rec/4
11. NIST's Cryptographic Module Validation Program Achieves Major Milestones (2002) ITL Bull:13. https://nistdigitalarchives.contentdm.oclc.org/digital/collection/p16009coll6/id/68087/rec/5
12. Oral History Interview of ITL/Cybersecurity (2018). https://nistdigitalarchives.contentdm.oclc.org/digital/collection/p16009coll2/id/752/rec/1
13. Allen Roginsky—NIST Retiree. https://csrc.nist.rip/staff/rolodex/roginsky_allen.html
14. atsec information security (2019) atsec's ACVT service is operational. https://www.atsec.com/atsecs-acvt-service-is-operational/. Last accessed 3 Dec 2025
15. National Institute of Standards and Technology (2024) 2024 Bronze Medal Award. https://www.nist.gov/nist-awards/2024-bronze-medal-award-christopher-celi-benjamin-livelsberger-robert-staples-harold. Last accessed 3 Dec 2025
16. National Institute of Standards and Technology (2026) Cryptographic Module Validation Program. https://csrc.nist.gov/projects/cryptographic-module-validation-program. Last accessed 24 Apr 2026

Chapter 3
ISO/IEC JTC 1 SC 27 WG 3, The Standards Weavers

Yi Mao

The work of ISO/IEC JTC 1 SC 27 Working Group 3 is often described as the quiet engine behind global cryptographic assurance. Its standards form the backbone of evaluations used by governments, laboratories, and vendors across the world, yet the story of how these standards are shaped is rarely told. Behind every edition of ISO/IEC 19790 and ISO/IEC 24759 stands a community of editors, experts, and liaisons who negotiate wording, refine concepts, and reconcile perspectives across continents.

To make that hidden work visible, Yi did what she often does in this book: she treated the standard as the end product of human effort and traced the effort backward. She held a meeting that focused on the international working group's broader history and the 2025 revision cycle, and she studied Salvatore Francomacaro's materials on how the United States participates through its national body. Only later did she return to the inside view of editing, placing that perspective at the end, where it functions like a final close-up on the hands doing the weaving.

The U.S. National Body and the NIST Delegation: INCITS at the Loom Before the story turned to the international working group's deliberations, one thread needed to be placed into the tapestry: how a U.S. position reaches ISO in the first place. Standards at ISO are not written by individual experts acting alone. They are advanced by national bodies, each representing its country through defined procedures. For the United States, that national body is INCITS, the InterNational Committee for Information Technology Standards, and the U.S. delegation is supported by NIST experts such as Salvatore Francomacaro [1].

Yi had learned much of this from Sal's talk at the FIPS 'n' Chips Crypto Bootcamp [2], which offered a practical explanation of why NIST participates in global standardization and how it does so. The starting point was simple but often misunderstood: NIST produces widely used cybersecurity publications, yet it is not itself an

Y. Mao (✉)
atsec information security corporation, Austin, USA
e-mail: yi.mao@atsec.com

Y. Mao (ed.), *Tasting Cryptography*, https://doi.org/10.1007/978-3-032-30243-4_3

international standards development organization. U.S. law and policy direct federal agencies to use voluntary consensus standards whenever appropriate, with a preference for international standards. That mandate makes standards participation a responsibility, not a hobby.

From there, the structure becomes procedural by necessity. INCITS manages U.S. participation in ISO/IEC JTC 1. Within INCITS, Technical Advisory Groups support each subcommittee. For SC 27, which covers information security, cybersecurity, and privacy standards, the TAG includes representatives from industry, academia, testing laboratories, and government agencies. The purpose is domestic alignment. In the ISO national body model, a country must first build consensus internally before it can vote internationally.

That alignment happens through meetings that repeat throughout the year, not just once at a yearly summit. Executive-level coordination tends to occur several times annually. Technical groups and TAGs meet more frequently, commonly monthly or every other month, and meetings often run one to two hours. During ballot cycles and comment resolution periods, the cadence intensifies, agendas grow, and sessions can stretch longer. Before remote collaboration became the norm, some work was handled through in-person plenaries and co-located standards meetings that lasted multiple days. Today, virtual participation dominates, reducing travel while keeping the same consensus discipline.

Membership in INCITS is organizational rather than individual. The table includes technology companies, security vendors, testing laboratories, industry associations, academic institutions, and government bodies. Participation is not free for most organizations. Annual membership fees support the secretariat work that keeps the machinery running: meeting logistics, document management, balloting coordination, and the administrative tasks that ensure U.S. positions can be formed, recorded, and delivered on time. Fee levels vary based on the organization and the scope of participation. Government agencies generally participate under government arrangements rather than paying the same membership dues as private organizations, reflecting the public interest in federal engagement with consensus standards.

Within this landscape, NIST plays an influential role. Its experts contribute deep technical knowledge in cryptography, validation, and assurance, often helping to frame and clarify complex discussions. NIST's participation occurs within this development process, ensuring that proposals and perspectives are technically rigorous before reaching ISO (through ANSI) as national positions.

This national body framework also explains how NIST's technical leadership can scale internationally. NIST's open competitions and public processes for algorithms, including AES, SHA-3, lightweight cryptography, and post-quantum algorithms, create global scrutiny long before an ISO ballot arrives. Standards work then becomes a bridge: domestic consensus is built through INCITS, international consensus is built through ISO, and the technology becomes part of a shared infrastructure of trust.

Yi also saw how this structure connected to the CMUF liaison role. The liaison gives industry and laboratories a direct channel into working drafts, but it does not replace national bodies. The liaison amplifies practitioner feedback; the TAG expresses the formal U.S. position. Together, they form a two-track system that keeps the work both open to expertise and anchored in legitimate voting authority.

With that national structure in view, the story could now widen to the working group itself.

The Broader Lens: Insights from Miguel Bañón and Alex Calis There were still unanswered questions about how WG 3 carried the work across decades and how the 2025 revision differed from prior editions. To close that gap, Yi held a separate meeting with Miguel Bañón and Alex Calis.

Miguel Bañón [3], a Spanish information security veteran, serves as the convenor of ISO/IEC JTC 1 SC 27 Working Group 3. Alex Calis [4], deputy CMVP manager at NIST, has served as a long-standing contributor to cryptographic assurance standards. Their combined perspectives illuminated how the 2025 edition of ISO/IEC 19790 reflected both continuity and evolution within the working group.

WG 3's origins reach back nearly three decades. Its scope has been consistent in spirit even as technologies have changed: evaluation methodology, testing, and assurance for security-related products and systems. Over time, WG 3 built not just one standard, but an ecosystem of related work. ISO/IEC 19790 sits at the center as the core requirements standard for cryptographic modules, while companion documents and methods support algorithm testing, non-invasive attack mitigation, and vulnerability analysis. The ecosystem exists because assurance is not a single document problem. It is a system problem.

Miguel's perspective placed ISO/IEC 19790's origin in a category that ISO encounters occasionally: an external standard that gains global recognition and is then adopted and transformed into an international standard. ISO/IEC 19790 began as a U.S. and Canadian contribution based on FIPS 140–2. Its early editions were heavily shaped by technical contributions from NIST and CMVP staff, including Randy Easter. Those editions later supported the transition to FIPS 140–3.

The 2025 edition differed in how widely the work was shared. It was shaped more fully inside WG 3 with contributions from a broader set of countries, and it absorbed an unusually large volume of feedback. Yi remembered how the revision cycle moved through multiple stages with substantial comment spreadsheets at each step, and how the CMUF liaison opened a channel for vendors, laboratories, and practitioners to contribute directly. That was not merely more noise. It was more practical contact with the text.

Alex offered a complementary explanation from the FIPS side. Once FIPS 140–3 pointed to ISO/IEC 19790, scrutiny increased dramatically. Laboratories and vendors applied the ISO text at scale and identified ambiguities quickly. Implementation guidance addressed immediate needs, but the guidance also became a map of where the standard itself needed better clarity. In that sense, the 2025 revision carried accumulated lessons from operational use.

Several themes stood out across the 2025 revision. Secure containers better reflected modern deployment realities in which modules may run in virtualized environments rather than inside a purely physical boundary. Edits clarified requirements and improved structure so that the standard could remain broadly applicable without becoming vague. The process remained anchored in consistent treatment of comments. The goal was not to privilege a particular country or organization, but to strengthen clarity, consistency, and long-term usability.

Miguel also pointed to the growing international influence of the standard. More countries have explored or developed schemes influenced by ISO/IEC 19790's framework. In Europe, elements of hardware security guidance under EUCC show conceptual alignment with its assurance model. The direction is not a single global validation program, but a growing capacity for shared assurance language across national schemes.

Accessibility became part of the story as well. Making ISO/IEC 19790:2025 [5] and ISO/IEC 24759:2025 [6] freely available removed a friction point for community engagement. More readers could inspect the requirements directly and provide better-informed feedback in future revisions. At the same time, the working group has explored future-facing ideas such as machine-readable standards. Those efforts begin internally, but publication decisions remain subject to ISO policies and timelines.

By the end of the meeting, the pattern became clear. WG 3 operates like a long-running workshop: it takes inputs from national bodies, liaison channels, and years of real-world implementation, then turns those inputs into text stable enough to anchor security programs. Publication is a milestone, not an ending. The next revision begins when the world starts using the current one.

The broader lens also created the right context for the final close-up: the editing work that transforms a global debate into a readable, internally consistent standard.

The editing process of ISO/IEC 19790 After the broader working group context was in place, Yi returned to the view of editing in ISO standard, examining the experience of Carolyn French [7]. Carolyn had long been involved in certification and standardization and previously served as the Canadian CMVP manager before assuming responsibility for CMVP, Common Criteria, and ISO standards portfolios at the Canadian Centre for Cyber Security. Her position placed her at the intersection of national requirements, international expectations, and the practical realities of validation work.

Carolyn's leadership of the revision began around 2019 or 2020, when it became clear that a modern refresh was necessary. Earlier editions provided a strong foundation, particularly the 2006 version derived from FIPS 140–2 and brought into ISO through Randy Easter's efforts [8]. The 2012 edition and the 2015 amendment strengthened key areas and became the basis for FIPS 140–3. Yet once FIPS 140–3 entered operational use, the pressure of real-world interpretation revealed areas where the standard needed clearer expression. The solution was not a patch, but a new revision.

Broader participation became a deliberate strategy of WG 3. In early 2021, Carolyn reached out to Yi to suggest establishing a liaison between the CMUF and WG 3. Yi formally presented the liaison request to ISO/IEC JTC 1 SC 27 WG 3 at the plenary meeting on April 12, 2021. The request was approved by SC 27 in September of that year, and Yi became the first Liaison Officer between the CMUF and WG 3.

Following the publication of ISO/IEC 19790:2025 in February, Dr. Marcos Portnoi, an atsec colleague, assumed the role and became the new Liaison Officer.

The liaison relationship with CMUF brought practical experience into WG 3 discussions and helped ensure that comments reflected implementation and testing realities rather than purely theoretical concerns. The input volume increased, and the issues became more precise. This was helpful, but it could also make the editor's task harder. More input does not automatically yield better text. It has to be organized, reconciled, and converted into language that remains globally acceptable.

The revision unfolded through the pandemic, during which WG 3 operated online for nearly three years. Meetings spanned time zones, and extended sessions were common. Hundreds of comments had to be reviewed and resolved. The editorial approach relied on grouping issues by theme, summarizing arguments for and against proposals, documenting decisions, and keeping the thread of consensus intact across long gaps and rotating attendance. When in-person meetings resumed in 2023, consensus-building became easier, in part because nuance travels better face-to-face than through a grid of webcams.

Editing an ISO also comes with constraints that are easy to underestimate. Editors cannot freely rewrite requirements to match personal preferences. Changes must be grounded in expert proposals and supported by consensus. Every change must be traceable: what it replaced, why it changed, and what the group agreed. That discipline can be exhausting, but it also protects the standard's meaning over time. It makes the document stronger because it forces clarity about intent.

The final publication stage adds another layer of rigor. ISO publication editors review text for consistency, readability, and structure, applying rules that support translation and international consumption. Formatting conventions that once helped readers in earlier editions may not survive this stage. Even so, the standard preserves internal structure that supports careful interpretation, including numbered normative requirements.

Several improvements in the 2025 edition reflect both technical modernization and editorial refinement. Secure containers help model modern environments where module boundaries may be defined differently than in older hardware-centric assumptions. Lifecycle assurance received clearer structure. The language became more consistent across sections so that requirements read as a coherent system rather than a patchwork of historical edits. These changes did not alter the standard's purpose. They clarified how to carry that purpose forward.

A persistent challenge remains: the standard must be broad enough to apply across technologies without becoming so abstract that implementers cannot use it. ISO/IEC 19790 serves as a framework. Validation bodies and programs still need guidance documents to address local procedures, testing decisions, and edge cases. The standard does not replace that guidance. It anchors it.

Placed at the end of the section, the editing process functions as the final close-up. The reader has already seen the national body machinery that shapes U.S. positions and the working group dynamics that reconcile international input. The editor's work is where those threads become a single page of requirements. It is patient work, often invisible, and continuous in spirit. The loom keeps moving because the world keeps changing, and cryptography must keep up.

About the contributors: Salvatore Francomacaro Sal is a seasoned information security professional with over 30 years of experience spanning small and large corporations as well as government sectors. His expertise includes cybersecurity, identity management, and security token technologies, with a strong emphasis on standards development and implementation. Sal has made significant contributions to international and national standards bodies and various INCITS/ANSI committees. His work has influenced numerous domestic and international standards in areas such as security tokens, ID cards, identity management, privacy, cryptography, cloud security, and blockchain technologies.

Miguel Bañón In 2006, Miguel founded Epoche & Espri, www.epoche.es, a successful Common Criteria and FIPS 140–2 security evaluation and testing laboratory. In October 2017 Epoche & Espri became part of DEKRA, one of the top 4 players in the testing, inspection, and certification industry worldwide. Miguel is the current Convenor of ISO/IEC JTC 1/SC 27/WG 3, CEN/CLC JTC 13/WG 3 and WG 10, and a former member of the Management Board of the CCUF.

Alex Calis CMVP Deputy Program Manager (US), National Institute of Standards and Technology (NIST).

Carolyn French Carolyn is the Manager of Product Assurance and Standards, which includes the Cryptographic Module Validation Program (CMVP) and Common Criteria Evaluation, at the Canadian Centre for Cyber Security (CCCS). Carolyn is the Canadian Head of Delegation to ISO/IEC JTC 1/SC 27/WG 3, and the lead editor of ISO/IEC 19790. She has been participating in ISO standards activities since 2018.

References

1. Salvatore ("Sal") Francomacaro, NIST Standardization Lead. https://www.nist.gov/people/salvatore-francomacaro
2. Sal's FIPS 'n' Chips presentation. https://www.atsec.com/fips-n-chips/schedule.html
3. Miguel Bañón—Convenor of ISO/IEC JTC 1/SC 27 WG 3, UNE Spain. ISO Committee. https://committee.iso.org/sites/jtc1sc27/home/projects.html
4. Alex Calis—NIST CMVP Deputy Program Manager. https://www.nist.gov/people/alexander-calis
5. ISO/IEC 19790:2025. https://www.iso.org/standard/82423.html
6. ISO/IEC 24759:2025. https://www.iso.org/standard/82424.html
7. Carolyn French—Manager, Product Assurance and Standards, Canadian Centre for Cyber Security. atsec Bootcamp Speaker. https://www.atsec.com/bootcamp/index_speakers.html
8. Randy Easter—NIST CSRC Presentation: Testing to FIPS 140–2 Derived Test Requirements (2002). https://csrc.nist.gov/Presentations/2002/Testing-to-FIPS-140-2-Derived-Test-Requirements

Chapter 4
The Cryptographic Module User Forum (CMUF)

Yi Mao

The restaurant at the top of Austin's old control tower was alive that night. The long copper-lit tables of FIPS 'n' Chips shimmered with laughter, half-finished desserts, and the hum of cryptographic debates continuing over coffee. It was the closing evening of atsec's Cryptography Bootcamp, and Aster stood near the circular bar, where a projection looped scenes from ICMC 2025, red "Do You CMUF?" shirts, crowded conference halls, and smiling engineers.

"Before we call it a night," Aster began, raising her glass, "let us talk about something that carried this year's ICMC to a memorable ending: the Cryptographic Module User Forum, or CMUF."

She gestured toward the wall where a photo from Toronto was being displayed. Trish Wolff, Fiona Stewart, and Renaudt Nuñez stood on stage, leading the ICMC 2025 closing session titled *FIPS Fun with the CMUF: Honoring History, Inspiring Tomorrow*. The trio's bright red shirts and playful trivia questions turned the final plenary into a celebration of community, history, and humor.

"That energy," Aster said, smiling, "is exactly what CMUF represents. So tonight, let me tell you its story, and why you should join us."

Creation and Mission: atsec's Vision for a Living Community Aster pointed to the holographic menu hovering over the bar. Tonight's dish was titled *The CMUF Sampler*.

"It began in 2013," she said, "when atsec information security decided that the world of cryptographic validation needed more than standards, guidance, and procedures. It needed people talking."

At the time, most discussions about FIPS 140-2 were confined to NIST circles. There were few opportunities for open dialogue among vendors, labs, and agencies. So atsec, under the leadership of its founding CEO, Sal La Pietra, built two platforms at once: the International Cryptographic Module Conference (ICMC) for annual

Y. Mao (✉)
atsec information security corporation, Austin, USA
e-mail: yi.mao@atsec.com

Y. Mao (ed.), *Tasting Cryptography*, https://doi.org/10.1007/978-3-032-30243-4_4

in-person collaboration, and the CMUF for continuous discussion throughout the year.

The first ICMC, held in a modest Gaithersburg hotel near NIST, drew 163 participants, far beyond expectation. As the event closed, one attendee shouted, "Win, win, win." The message was clear. This new community should live on. CMUF was founded that same year to turn those conversations into collaboration.

"That is how CMUF was born," Aster said. "It was not created by decree. It was created by demand, a community that wanted to keep learning together."

The Early Days of the CMUF Aster took a sip of her tea and looked toward the bootcamp group with a thoughtful expression. "You have seen what CMUF looks like today," she said, "but there was a time when none of this existed. Before the Working Groups, before the Steering Committee, before the monthly meetings that now feel routine, there were only a few people standing in the hallway of a conference center, wondering whether this community could ever take shape."

The display lit up again, this time showing a clip from Yi's conversation with Matt Keller, one of the earliest voices behind the CMUF. Matt appeared on screen with an easy smile. He had spent nearly three decades in government certifications, first at Corsec Security, then later at a large hybrid cloud company, and he described the beginning of CMUF as something that grew from equal parts optimism and necessity.

He recalled that moment at the very first ICMC in 2013, the conference that atsec had created from scratch. "I remember standing outside the meeting rooms with Fiona and Steve Weingart," he said. "We were excited that the conference happened at all. It was not guaranteed that anyone would come back for a second one. But we all realized that getting people together created momentum. If we wanted real change, we needed a place where labs, vendors, and the government could work together."

A few years earlier, Matt had helped stand up the Common Criteria Users Forum, and the success of that effort shaped his thinking. He shared those lessons at ICMC: how a user group could empower the community, how collective work could give vendors and labs a stronger voice, and how a forum could create a bridge to the government rather than a wedge. Those hallway conversations became the seed of the CMUF.

Fiona took the first steps. She gathered the early attendees of ICMC and invited those who wanted to help. Matt and his colleague Jerrod Schultz from Corsec joined the earliest calls. They debated names for the new group and drafted governance documents based on the CCUF structure. "We spent a lot of 2013 writing governance," Matt said. "We drafted voting rules and leadership structures, all very formal."

But after the second ICMC, the momentum for the CMUF slowed. Meetings became infrequent, and the newborn CMUF risked fading away.

"That was when I stepped back in," Matt explained. Around 2015, he sent out a message to the old distribution list. "I asked, are we still interested in doing this?" Enough people said yes. A new group formed, small but determined. They agreed the earlier governance work had bogged them down, so they abandoned the voting structure and created something simpler: a Steering Committee of volunteers willing to drive the work.

"We kept it informal on purpose," Matt said. "The idea was to keep egos low and keep everyone involved." He scheduled meetings, held discussions, wrote notes, and "herded cats," as he put it with a laugh. The Steering Committee met monthly, while the general membership met quarterly, later switching so that the full group met monthly and the Steering Committee met less often. They experimented, adapted, and improvised, but they kept going.

One of the turning points came at ICMC 2016. The self-declared CMUF Steering Committee invited NIST's CMVP and the CSEC, the Communications Security Establishment Canada (later renamed as CCCS, the Canadian Centre for Cyber Security) to a lunch meeting. The Steering Committee settled on a message for the meeting. Matt remembered the plan as "This cannot become people throwing complaints at them. We have to stay constructive. We are here to help." That tone shaped the culture of CMUF. It was not about demands; it was about cooperation, curiosity, and joint problem solving. "That made all the difference," Matt said. "It built trust."

Another milestone came when CMUF was given time to present at ICMC, around 2017 or 2018. Matt delivered the first short talk, using a stew analogy that many still remember. "Do not wait until the soup is cooked and then complain about the taste," he told the audience. "If you want to influence the flavor, add your ingredients while it is still cooking." For years, that analogy became the unofficial motto of CMUF.

Matt also shared advice and memories of the group's early challenges. The Steering Committee was small, and sometimes people hesitated to welcome new members because they feared the group would grow too large or lose influence. Matt acknowledged those concerns but explained how he had advocated for opening the door to new contributors. "At some point," he said, "you need fresh ideas and people that are newly energetic to do the work. Communities only live if the energy renews."

Yi smiled at the memory. When she volunteered to join the Steering Committee, she was one of the first people to ask to join and the process took time and diplomacy. Matt had emailed her to "be patient," because he had to help everyone see the benefits of expanding the committee. But once she joined, she brought the organization, structure, and drive that the Steering Committee needed. "The very person they hesitated on," Matt said with a grin, "turned out to be exactly the person they needed with me stepping away."

The story of the cmuf.org domain also surfaced in the conversation. atsec had originally secured the domain as a placeholder in 2013 when launching both ICMC and the early CMUF. Later, Corsec held the domain because Matt had hoped to build a site through his employer. When he knew he was transitioning out of the Steering Committee and into a vendor role, he made sure the domain returned to atsec. "It needed to be in the hands of someone who could use it," he said. "And you had a plan. That was the important part." Afterward, atsec rebuilt the CMUF website, and later in 2024 Amazon contributed cloud hosting for collaboration, turning the domain into a true working resource.

At the end of the conversation, Matt reflected on what mattered most from those early years. "My favorite memories are the times when we were figuring out what CMUF could be," he said. "We did not know if CMVP would even meet with us. We were just a group with a name we made up, trying to be useful. It was entrepreneurial. It was fun. And it worked because people cared."

Aster paused the clip and looked at the bootcamp group. "The CMUF you see today," she said, "did not appear fully formed. It was built by volunteers trying, failing, trying again, and choosing cooperation over conflict. That spirit is still what keeps this community alive."

She gave the team a moment to absorb the thought before continuing. "Over the years, that spirit shaped how CMUF organized itself and how it chose to operate."

CMUF was deliberately made independent and unincorporated, a global collaboration hub where labs, developers, academics, and policymakers could meet as equals. It became, as Aster put it, "the world's most productive crypto group chat, open, voluntary, and relentlessly technical."

By 2025, CMUF had grown to include more than 800 members, organized through a cloud portal hosted with help from Amazon and atsec, equipped with tools for document sharing and draft review.

Each month, the Steering Committee set the agenda and rotated moderators and note-takers from across the community. Meetings were open, recorded, and consistently well attended. One hundred thirty-nine people joined the January 2025 session.

The CMUF Steering Committee is the backbone of the forum's operations. It comprises seasoned experts from leading laboratories and companies, and ensures that every meeting remains focused, inclusive, and productive. In 2025, committee members included Renaudt Nuñez of atsec, Chris Brych of Oracle, Trish Wolff of Cisco, Graham Costa of Thales, Gerrit Kruitbosch of Intel, Alicia Squires of Amazon, Nithya Rachamadugu of DEKRA, Anantha Kandiah of Teron Labs, Maryrita Steinhour of F5 Networks, and Ryan Thomas of Lightship Security. Together they rotate monthly roles as meeting hosts and note-takers, coordinate guest presentations, and maintain continuity across CMUF's working groups. Their leadership reflects CMUF's defining principle, a collaboration not led by any single organization or nation, but by a global team united in improving cryptographic assurance.

Beyond the Steering Committee, CMUF thrives thanks to the dedication of its Working Group leaders, who carry the technical weight of the forum. Each group focuses on a specific domain, from entropy sources to module boundaries, and the leaders ensure that discussions become deliverables. Lisa Rabe of Cisco chairs the Entropy Working Group and links community feedback directly to NIST's Crypto Technology Group. Trish Wolff of Cisco leads the Request-for-Guidance Working Group and co-chairs the IG 9.5.A update team with Steve Weymann of KeyPair. Marc Ireland of NXP Semiconductors leads both the Single-Chip and Bound or Embedded Modules Working Groups and coordinates complex hybrid module definitions. Renaudt Nuñez of atsec heads the Physical Security Working Group and advances evidence re-use and tamper protection topics. Chris Brych of Oracle convenes the SP 800-140Br1 Security Policy Working Group that improves template clarity and usability. Together, these volunteers transform discussion into drafts, templates, and Implementation Guidance that shape validation practice worldwide.

Three Voices Behind the Working Groups Aster leaned in as she told the bootcamp group that CMUF's Working Groups were not abstract committees. They were led by real people with real day jobs, who volunteered many extra hours so that the community could move forward. "If you want to understand what makes CMUF work," she said, "you have to hear from the people who run its beating heart."

She tapped her tablet, and the scene around them shifted again, this time to a replay of Yi's roundtable conversation with three of CMUF's most active working group leaders.

Marc Ireland appeared first on the screen, smiling at the familiar faces. "I've been in FIPS about twenty years," he said. "I started on the lab side back at InfoGard, then UL, then eventually crossed over to the vendor world at NXP. Single-chip modules have always lived in a gray area. We needed clearer rules, and somebody had to write them. That's how I ended up leading the Single-Chip Working Group."

He explained that motivation came from necessity as much as passion. Vendors needed stable and fair guidance. Labs needed consistency. The CMVP needed clarity. And Marc, having lived on both sides, felt the responsibility to help bridge those gaps. "The guidance used to be mostly word-of-mouth. Different interpretations, different outcomes. What we are doing now, writing it down and refining it so that it becomes repeatable, strengthens the entire program."

Trish Wolff nodded when her turn came. "FIPS has gotten so complicated that we can't rely on tribal knowledge anymore," she said. "That's why the Request-for-Guidance Working Group exists." She described her own path, coming into the FIPS world about fourteen years earlier and watching the complexity grow. "The biggest challenge now is making sure the program stays focused on meaningful security, not just more rules for their own sake."

Trish explained that her group works differently because CMVP itself had asked CMUF to create it, a major cultural shift from the early 2010s. Each request that comes in must be analyzed, debated, and shaped into neutral, community-wide guidance. "That means staying impartial," she said. "If Cisco submits a question, and I'm writing the response, it cannot favor Cisco. The whole group has to agree. That's how we build trust."

Then came Lisa Rabe, leader of the Entropy Working Group, who laughed as she introduced herself. "I didn't start the group because I was an expert," she said. "I started it because my previous FIPS consulting company told me, 'Someone needs to learn entropy, and that someone is you.' There was hardly any documentation, and I was lost. So, I created the group mostly to find people to talk to."

Over time, the group grew into a bi-weekly gathering of fifty to seventy people, even though only a handful speak each week. "It's different from other groups," Lisa explained. "It's more like a classroom. Entropy is hard. Nobody walks in understanding it. But the community respects each other enough to ask questions, even the ones that feel stupid. And nobody gets judged for not knowing something."

Aster paused the video to address the bootcamp audience directly. "This," she said, "is the secret of CMUF. These leaders don't just run meetings. They nurture confidence. They make space for different skillsets. Marc brings the vendor perspective. Trish brings structure and impartiality. Lisa brings education and patience. And together they create a place where new engineers can grow."

The recording continued, showing moments of debate and laughter. Trish talked about the importance of bringing younger engineers into the fold. Marc confessed how hard it was to increase participation even as membership lists grew. Lisa shared how theoretical purists and pragmatic engineers found common ground.

Then came a story Yi told that made everyone nod. She recalled a time when one of her lab's entropy submissions became blocked on a nearly impossible requirement: proving the independence of multiple ring oscillators. "You cannot prove two things are independent," Yi explained. "It becomes philosophical. Like proving two people are independent when they live on the same planet."

She presented the problem to Lisa's entropy group, and what happened next captured the spirit of CMUF perfectly. The CMVP reviewer listened quietly. Experts proposed practical pathways such as placement constraints, frequency diversity, and statistical justification. This RO-based entropy source went through the validation successfully. "This," Aster told the bootcamp group, "is the community at its finest."

As the recording neared the end, Lisa shared a lighter memory, this one from ICMC, where the Entropy Working Group had an informal happy hour. Members arrived wearing playful entropy-themed name tags and jokingly debated whose pseudorandom persona was the most unpredictable. Marc laughed at the memory. Trish shook her head in mock exasperation. "Only the entropy folks would turn randomness into a social activity," she said, and Lisa laughed with her.

Aster closed the segment by saying, "These are not abstract working groups. They are people. They care. They argue. They teach. They laugh. And they give this community its voice."

Partnership with CMVP and CAVP: Turning Guidance into Practice Aster smiled as the video closed. "These are the people who keep the Working Groups moving," she said. "Their efforts tie directly into CMUF's ongoing partnership with the CMVP and CAVP." She switched the display. "Here is how that collaboration unfolds."

Every monthly meeting features direct participation from CCCS, CMVP, and CAVP leaders such as Carolyn French, Dave Hawes, Kailai Chen, Alex Calis, and Chris Celi, who use the forum as an open line to the global community. They report on ISO/IEC 19790 status, queue statistics, implementation guidance updates, SP 800-140Br1 processes, automation initiatives, and post-quantum algorithm testing and so on.

Their willingness to share data and invite feedback has made CMUF an indispensable communication channel among NIST, the labs, and vendors.

The spirit of this collaboration came vividly to life in August 2024, when Matt Scholl, then Chief of NIST's Computer Security Division, joined the CMUF meeting. His presentation, titled *Modernizing the CMVP Management System*, surprised many regular attendees not only because of his long-standing senior role at NIST, but also because of his direct engagement with the practitioner community.

Matt Scholl's Vision for CMVP Automation Matt's talk outlined his vision for a modernized, data-driven CMVP, where automation becomes the structural foundation rather than a peripheral enhancement. He began by reminding members that the Cryptographic Module Validation Program had reached a maturity level that demanded new operational models capable of keeping pace with rapid product cycles, continuous software updates, and the needs of agile development.

He described the automation of CMVP management systems as the next natural phase of evolution and emphasized three goals:

- Transparency and accessibility. A system where module status, validation progress, and submission feedback are visible in near real time to both labs and vendors.
- Machine-readable standards. Structured and interoperable data formats, for example XML or JSON, for validation documentation that pave the way for automated review and quality control.
- Efficiency and scalability. Automation that acts as a force multiplier, allowing NIST analysts to focus on complex cases and policy refinement rather than mechanical review steps.

Matt also reflected on collaboration between the NCCoE's ACMVP project and CMUF working groups, noting that the forum's iterative engagement with NIST engineers was critical in turning this vision into a working system. His slides included architectural concepts for a cloud-based validation pipeline that integrates lab submissions, security policy generators, and audit tracking modules, turning the validation process into a continuously improving feedback loop.

His participation was not formally announced beforehand, which amplified the impact. As Aster later recalled, "As soon as Anantha introduced Matt, the WebEx chat burst to life with excitement. It felt like watching history walk into the meeting." Members described the meeting as one of the most energizing of the year, and it signaled NIST's continued commitment to open dialogue with the CMUF community even at the highest levels.

At these monthly CMUF meetings, members hear about upcoming changes, including interim validation policies, new draft IGs or RFG resolutions, entropy report templates, and automation pilots, often before they appear in formal publications. CMVP staff also respond to community questions live, clarify guidance, announce pilot opportunities, and occasionally shape updates based on CMUF discussions.

CMVP's openness here is rare in any standards ecosystem. It is transparency in action, and it builds trust.

How CMUF Strengthened the Interim Validation Proposal In early 2024, CMVP introduced a draft concept called Provisional Validation, later renamed Interim Validation, intended to accelerate processing of the FIPS 140–3 queue. The initial proposal on February 29, 2024, allowed modules already tested and recommended by accredited labs to receive one-year provisional certificates after only a minimal

CMVP review. The aim was speed and operational relief. Several CMUF members quickly pointed out risks such as the dilution of assurance and fairness.

At the March 5 CMUF meeting, vendors and labs voiced detailed and technical objections. They warned that this approach might undermine trust by issuing certificates without full validation of test results, distort fairness by reshuffling the queue and allowing newer submissions to overtake older ones, create uncertainty because major procurement agencies had not confirmed acceptance of provisional certificates, and overload labs with additional resubmission and Br1 conversion work while staffing remained constrained.

CMUF consolidated this feedback in a formal comment document that reflected both technical and procedural concerns. It included proposals for extending the validity period, maintaining queue order, and improving communication with external agencies.

On March 26, 2024, Lisa moderated a CMUF meeting where Dr. Yi Mao of atsec presented an alternative approach on behalf of CMUF members. Instead of issuing provisional certificates after superficial checks, this proposal suggested a focused review aided by direct lab interaction, a short and structured review that emphasizes test evidence quality rather than bypassing it. The slides outlined a practical and balanced solution. Prioritize modules already deep in coordination. Conduct one joint web meeting per module between NIST reviewers and labs to verify understanding. Perform a limited, evidence-based focused review that could clear the backlog in a few months without creating double standards.

In May 2024, the final CMVP Interim Validation Procedures reflected many of CMUF's recommendations. The minimal review concept evolved into a checklist-based confirmation process that requires labs to submit explicit FIPS 140-3 checklists, self-consistency reviews, and bound-module information. The proposal clarified queue order by preserving the original queue date, ensured transparency of eligibility, and explicitly marked the process as optional. CMVP publicly thanked the CMUF community for its input, which signaled that the final design arose from stakeholder engagement.

This episode became a touchstone example of how CMVP's openness to community critique improved the result. Even where disagreements remained, the willingness to debate policy on a public CMUF call rather than behind closed doors demonstrated the maturity of collaboration between CMVP and the community it serves. As one participant remarked afterward, the best part was not that CMVP changed its mind. The best part was that CMVP listened.

CMUF's currently active working groups reinforce that connection:

- The Entropy Working Group, led by Lisa Rabe of Cisco, collaborates closely with NIST's Crypto Technology Group on the development of SP 800-90C revisions and alignment with the German BSI entropy requirements.
- The Requests for Guidance Working Group, chaired by Trish Wolff of Cisco, brings together vendors, laboratories, and CMVP representatives to review non-proprietary RFG submissions. The group develops consensus-driven technical

resolutions that benefit the entire community, turning isolated questions into shared understanding.

- The Single-Chip Working Group, led by Marc Ireland of NXP Semiconductors, focuses on complex module boundaries, clarifying how embedded and bound modules can be evaluated consistently, and has also developed the hybrid-module Implementation Guidance clarifying module boundaries.
- The Physical Security Working Group, chaired by Renaudt Nuñez of atsec, explores ways to reuse physical security evidence and improve efficiency while maintaining integrity. Its work culminated in the creation of Implementation Guidance 7.A, which defines when and how evidence from previous validations can be trusted.
- The SP 800-140Br1 Security Policy Working Group, convened by Chris Brych of Oracle, refines the security policy templates used in FIPS 140–3 validations. Their improvements enhance clarity and promote automation, helping vendors and laboratories produce consistent and machine-readable documentation.
- Finally, the Software Level 1 Working Group, led by Dave Hawes of NIST CMVP, examines methods to streamline reviews of Level 1 software modules. Its goal is to identify efficiencies and reduce review time without compromising assurance, paving the way for faster validations that still meet the program's rigorous standards.

Through these groups, along with early ones such as FIPS 140–3 Transition, Authentication, Common Vulnerabilities and Exposures (CVE), and Equivalency, CMUF turns collaborative discussion into tangible outcomes that influence CMVP practice and strengthen consistency, efficiency, and transparency across the program.

The CMUF meetings are not only about policies and procedures. They are also a place where personal connections mark the history of the program. At the March 2024 meeting, the community paused to celebrate Dr. Allen Roginsky, a long-time CMVP reviewer whose deep technical insight and fairness guided hundreds of validations. As Allen announced his retirement, the WebEx chat filled with heartfelt messages such as "Thank you, Allen" and "We will miss your reviews", creating a flood of gratitude that reflected how profoundly he earned the respect of vendors, labs, and NIST colleagues.

Dr. Tim Hall, who retired in April 2025, also had a profound impact on the CMUF. As the Group Manager overseeing CMVP and CAVP, Tim was a pillar of consistency and openness. He attended nearly every CMUF meeting, listened carefully to every concern, and preferred to empower his experts, for example, Dave Hawes and Alex Calis, to make the calls rather than dictate from the top. His philosophy of letting the people closest to the work make the decision helped define the CMVP culture of collaboration.

Tim's legacy continues through Dave Hawes, the CMVP manager he entrusted with the program's future. Under Dave's leadership, the forum has seen a steady rhythm of transparency, data sharing, and responsiveness, values that Tim embedded into the CMVP from the start. As one CMUF member put it, Tim gave this community the best NIST CMVP manager it has ever seen, because he knew how to listen.

Collaboration with ISO and WG 3: Shaping the Standards Aster leaned against a table shaped like a circuit board. "Here is what is remarkable," she said. "CMUF does not just talk about FIPS, it helps shape ISO standards."

Through its official liaison with ISO and WG 3, CMUF serves as the global practitioner's voice in developing ISO/IEC 19790 and 24,759, the international standards underlying FIPS 140-3.

This collaboration began with Dr. Yi Mao, CMUF's first liaison officer. From 2021 through early 2025, Yi represented the CMUF community within the ISO working group and submitted hundreds of detailed comments on multiple working and committee drafts. Her contributions covered module interfaces, authentication, zeroization, finite state models, life cycle assurance, and so on. These efforts, supported by input from CMUF members, shaped the structure and clarity of ISO/IEC 19790, which was published in February 2025.

In March 2025, Dr. Marcos Portnoi of atsec succeeded Dr. Yi Mao. He has advocated for open and machine-readable formats, and co-edits the forthcoming ISO/IEC TR 25844, the transition guide that compares the 2012 and 2025 versions of the ISO standards. During the September 2025 ISO meeting in Kunming, WG 3 formally recognized CMUF training initiatives and confirmed the forum's evolution from observer to collaborator.

"If ISO sets the melody," Aster said, "CMUF helps fine tune the harmony."

The Connection with ICMC: From Annual Celebration to Continuous Collaboration Aster tapped the display, and a short video played of the ICMC 2025 closing event. A packed ballroom laughed as the Slido leaderboard flashed across the screen. "That," she said, "was CMUF's spirit, learning through joy."

CMUF and ICMC have always been two halves of one whole. ICMC is the annual summit, the place to gather, celebrate progress, and share new research. CMUF is the yearlong heartbeat that keeps the dialogue alive between conferences.

In 2025, this connection was stronger than ever. Many ICMC sessions were led by CMUF working group members. Carolyn French's *Mind the Gap: Navigating 19790:2025* showcased ISO alignment; Chris Celi's *Integration of the ACMVP with CMVP* introduced new automation tools; atsec's Dr. Yi Mao and Stephan Müller joined the ACMVP modernization panel.

Then came the finale, *FIPS Fun with the CMUF*, a lighthearted close that turned serious reflection into shared laughter. Renaudt's closing message invoked Smokey the Bear, "Only you can prevent crypto fires," a reminder that the health of the validation ecosystem depends on everyone doing their part.

Aster laughed softly as the video ended. "That," she told the bootcamp crowd, "is why we want the next ICMC back in Austin, the birthplace of both ICMC and CMUF, where it all began."

Closing: Do You CMUF? As the restaurant lights dimmed, the ceiling above transformed into constellations of cryptographic algorithms.

Aster smiled. "CMUF is not just an organization," she said. "It is a living community, the link among the labs, the standards, and the stories that make cryptographic validation human."

She pointed to the glowing projection looping above her. Come to Austin for some FIPS 'n' Chips and a Future ICMC.

"Next time you see that red T-shirt," she added, "remember what it stands for: collaboration, humor, and doing our part to prevent crypto fires."

Then, raising her glass, she said, "So, do you CMUF?"

About the contributors: **Matthew Keller** Matt is a Senior Technical Program Manager of Compliance at a hybrid cloud company. Matt has 25+ years of experience guiding product companies through the FIPS 140, International Common Criteria, and US DoDIN APL certification programs. Over that time, Matt also contributed to the leadership of both the Cryptographic Modules Users Forum (CMUF) and the Common Criteria Users Forum (CCUF).

Lisa Rabe Lisa spent 15 years writing astrodynamics software for satellite tracking sensor systems. Ten years ago, she made a career shift and started working for a consultant in cybersecurity compliance. She managed a group that wrote a software test harness to test cryptographic libraries and got interested in the field of entropy. She started an industry-wide working group on entropy and is still running it five years later. In late 2021 she joined Cisco, doing Common Criteria certifications and working with both CC and FIPS on entropy issues.

Marc Ireland Marc Ireland is a Security Certifications Expert at NXP Semiconductors. He has been involved in the FIPS Program for the last 14 years starting his career as a FIPS Evaluation Engineer and eventually becoming a FIPS Lab Manager for a prominent accredited laboratory. Over that time he has been heavily involved in creating new FIPS policy and guidance. Marc has a background in Mathematics from California Polytechnic State University and is currently located in Austin, TX."

Tricia Wolff Trish is a Cybersecurity Certifications Technical Leader at Cisco, specializing in secure cryptographic systems and regulatory compliance. Her work focuses primarily on FIPS 140 certifications, where she helps translate complex requirements into practical, implementable designs. She has led multiple Cryptographic Module User Forum (CMUF) Working Groups, fostering collaboration among government agencies, testing laboratories, and vendors to develop shared guidance for certification challenges. Prior to Cisco, Tricia was at a cybersecurity consultancy working with multiple vendors on FIPS and Common Criteria certifications. Her professional interests include standards development, validation strategy, and advancing trustworthy security at scale.

Chapter 5
The International Cryptographic Module Conference (ICMC)

Yi Mao

The morning sun over Austin brightened the blue-glass curve of the old Mueller control tower, now home to FIPS 'n' Chips. Inside, the restaurant carried a gentle rise of conversation. Today's special was not a dish but a story: how a tradition began by NIST found new life in the hands of a community determined to carry it forward.

The NIST Era: Where Security Started Before ICMC ever existed, NIST itself hosted the gatherings that shaped the field. NIST's first such conference was for FIPS 140-1 in 1998 (Fig. 5.1). Then, in the early 2000s, the Cryptographic Module Validation Program (CMVP) held its own symposia, meetings where engineers, reviewers, and policymakers could share practical lessons from the front lines of FIPS 140-2 testing.

The CMVP Conference 2001 opened in Washington, DC, under the motto "Conformance through Testing (Fig. 5.1)." It marked the first time that NIST and Canada's Communications Security Establishment (CSE) jointly convened the growing cryptographic assurance community. A year later, the 2002 CMVP Conference again drew participants from agencies, vendors, and labs, focusing on the rapid adoption of FIPS 140–2 and the expanding role of accredited test laboratories (Fig. 5.2).

By September 2004, the CMVP Symposium 2004, "Where Security Starts," was held in Rockville, Maryland, celebrating the program's maturity (Fig. 5.3). Its sessions on algorithm testing, tamper evidence, and implementation guidance cemented CMVP's reputation for rigor and marked its last public symposium of record.

After 2004, NIST stopped hosting such events. Yet, as Lisa Carnahan later recalled, those workshops had been essential. "We did not write standards in isolation," she explained. "We also held workshops, one for users, one for labs, another for the broader community. Those workshops were essential. Agencies could describe what

Y. Mao (✉)
atsec information security corporation, Austin, TX, USA
e-mail: yi.mao@atsec.com

Y. Mao (ed.), *Tasting Cryptography*, https://doi.org/10.1007/978-3-032-30243-4_5

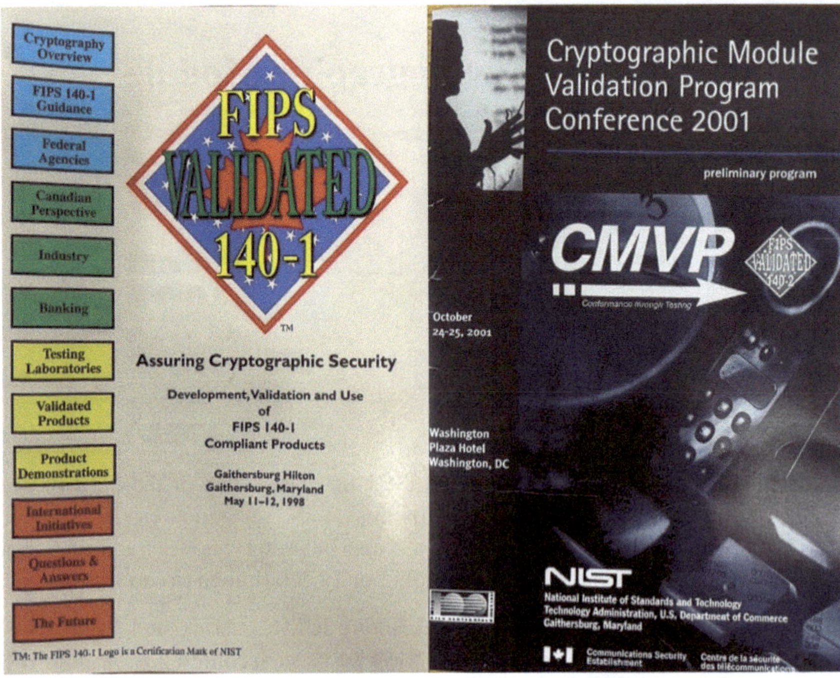

Fig. 5.1 Early CMVP conferences

they needed. Labs could see what participation required. It was an open process, and it set the tone for how CMVP would grow."

When NIST no longer convened those symposia, something intangible was lost. It was the shared stage where government and industry met as equals to discuss progress and pain points alike.

From Silence to Renewal: The Birth of ICMC For nearly a decade after NIST hosted its last CMVP symposium in 2004, the cryptographic module community lived without a central gathering. Technology evolved quickly, mobile platforms surged, side-channel attacks matured, and embedded systems multiplied, yet the ecosystem lacked a shared space where engineers, evaluators, government reviewers, and researchers could meet and align their understanding. Without such gatherings, interpretations drifted, frustrations grew, and a gap widened between the pace of innovation and the cadence of validation.

By 2013, the need for a dedicated forum could no longer be ignored. It was clear that the community required a place not only to discuss FIPS 140-2, but to confront its growing pains, exchange practical lessons, debate guidance, and acknowledge the emerging complexity of modern cryptographic modules.

Recognizing this need, atsec information security made a decisive move. If no conference existed to serve the community, then one would be created. It would not

Fig. 5.2 CMVP conference 2002

Fig. 5.3 CMVP symposium 2004

belong to a government agency or a vendor. It would belong to the cryptographic module validation community.

And so, the International Cryptographic Module Conference, ICMC, was born.

ICMC 2013: A Community Reunites The inaugural ICMC was held September 24–26, 2013, at the Holiday Inn Gaithersburg, only minutes from NIST's campus. The location was chosen deliberately to honor the roots of the CMVP program. The idea was bold, but its success was far from guaranteed. Would people come? Would the community respond?

atsec's founding CEO, Sal La Pietra, asked then-VP Fiona Pattinson [1] to spearhead the effort. She launched a broad survey to understand what topics the cryptographic community most wanted to see, which hotels would be most convenient for attendees, especially for NIST speakers, and how a new conference could best serve a community that had not been convened since NIST stopped hosting its CMVP symposia nearly a decade earlier. From there, atsec began building ICMC from the ground up: purchasing the conference domain name www.icmconference.org, designing the first website, drafting the call for contributions, and coordinating the review of early submissions.

To ensure that ICMC 2013 would be relevant and competitive, atsec studied comparable events such as the International Common Criteria Conference (ICCC), the RSA Conference, the Cryptographic Hardware and Embedded Systems Conference (CHES), and the Annual Computer Security Applications Conference (ACSAC). The team also mapped out worldwide security communities that might be interested in this new gathering and reached out broadly, including Eurosmart, the Java Card Forum, the Japanese CMVP, and the Korean CMVP, although only a few responded.

Recognizing the scale of the undertaking, atsec brought in professional support, hiring event organizer Bill Rutledge of Cnxtd Media Inc. to lead the marketing campaign and manage the conference logistics. Still, the risk was real: in the early months of registration, only four people had signed up. If attendance remained that low, atsec would have risked not only its finances but also its reputation.

Determined not to leave anything to chance, atsec committed fully. The company sent a ten-person delegation representing nearly every role in the organization: the founding CEO, a vice president, the chief scientist, the office manager, the marketing director, the lab director, multiple lab managers, the managing director of atsec China, who successfully encouraged a strong turnout of Chinese attendees, and the beloved Stephan Müller, who needed no title. Their presence reflected a simple truth that everyone recognized: this conference mattered, and atsec would do whatever was necessary to give the conference the foundation it deserved.

Their effort was rewarded the moment the doors opened. Attendees arrived from across the United States, Canada, Europe, and Asia. There were 163 participants, representing agencies, accredited laboratories, developers, researchers, and standards contributors from around the world. The silence the community had experienced for years was broken at once. People were eager to meet, learn, and reconnect.

The conference began with all-day workshops on Tuesday, the kind the community had not seen since the early days of NIST symposia. Two tracks were offered in parallel: one focused on FIPS 140-2 fundamentals and physical security, while the other focused on side-channel testing and the security challenges posed by emerging mobile architectures. These sessions reintroduced something that had been missing for nearly ten years: practical, structured, deeply technical education delivered in a collaborative environment.

On Wednesday morning, the main conference began. Charles Romine, the Director of NIST's Information Technology Laboratory, welcomed attendees, reaffirming that the agency saw the value in a community-led event even though it no longer hosted its own symposia. The second keynote, Dr. Bertrand du Castel, traced the evolution of smart cards and their lasting influence on modern cryptographic modules, tying the history of secure hardware to the challenges of present-day assurance. Years later, atsec remembered him for his profound influence on the information security industry, including his inspiring and fun ICMC 2013 keynote speech on trust through a metaphorical calling of flamingoes [2].

What followed was a whirlwind of international updates, technical deep dives, and candid discussions:

- Status reports from CMVP, CAVP, CCCS, Japan's JCMVP, and Korea's ETRI.
- Panels confronting the validation queue.
- Sessions on RNG entropy, SP 800–90, non-invasive attacks, fault injection, key management, ISO/IEC 19790, supply-chain risk, and cryptography for payment systems.
- Presentations from researchers and industry leaders across the globe.

Looking back at the agenda of this first-year conference (shown below) after more than a decade, ICMC 2013 felt strikingly mature, as if the community had been waiting for precisely this moment.

Figures 5.4, 5.5, 5.6 and 5.7 show the agenda of ICMC 2013.

A little after 4:00 PM on September 26, the final session of the conference concluded. Attendees gathered for the closing remarks delivered by Sal La Pietra, atsec's founding CEO and the person whose vision had made ICMC possible (Fig. 5.8).

Sal did not speak as a corporate executive. He spoke as a steward of the community. He thanked attendees for believing in a conference that had begun as nothing more than an idea. He noted, with a smile, that people were still greeting one another warmly, even while passing each other in the hallway or on the way to the restrooms, which he took as a definitive sign of success for the first ICMC. He reminded everyone that cryptographic assurance depends on transparency, collaboration, and humility. These qualities flourish only when people meet in person. He emphasized that ICMC belonged to the community, and the community carried the responsibility of shaping its future.

Sal's remarks were heartfelt, grounded, and quietly transformative. At one point, a participant called out, "Win, win, win!" It was an unforgettable moment. Even after Sal clearly announced that the conference was officially concluded, no one left the

International Cryptographic Module Conference
September 24-26, 2013, Holiday Inn
Gaithersburg, MD

Schedule at a Glance

Jump To: Tue (Workshops) Wed (Conference) Thu (Conference)

Tuesday, Sep 24 — Workshops

8:00	Registration & Coffee	
9:00	**Introduction to FIPS 140-2,** *Steve Weingart, Crytographic and Security Testing Laboratory Manager, atsec Information Security Corporation*	**Introduction to Side-Channel Analysis and Testing,** *Gary Kenworthy & Gilbert Goodwill, Cryptography Research*
10:30	BREAK	
11:15	**Introduction to FIPS 140-2** (Cont'd)	**Introduction to Side-Channel Analysis and Testing** (Cont'd)
12:45	LUNCH	
14:00	**Physical Security for FIPS 140-2,** *Steve Weingart, Crytographic and Security Testing Laboratory Manager, atsec Information Security*	**The Cryptographic Module and Beyond for Data Protection in a Mobile World,** *Eugene Liderman & Sriram Krishnan, Good Technology*
15:30	BREAK	
16:15	**Physical Security for FIPS 140-2** (Cont'd)	**The Cryptographic Module and Beyond for Data Protection in a Mobile World** (Cont'd)
17:45	Adjourn	Adjourn

Wednesday, Sep 25 — Conference Sessions

8:00	**Registration & Coffee** (Exhibits Open)
9:00	**Welcome and Keynote Presentations:** *Charles H. Romine, Director, Information Technology Laboratory, NIST* *Dr Bertrand du Castel, Schlumberger Fellow and Java Card Pioneer*

Fig. 5.4 ICMC 2013 agenda page 1

9:45	**CAVP/CMVP Status** – ***What's Next?,*** *Sharon Keller, NIST, Carolyn French, CSEC, Randall Easter, NIST*	
10:30	BREAK	
	Certification Programs Track: Presentations relating to the CMVP, other government programs and policy *Moderator: Fiona Pattinson, Director of Strategy & Business Development, atsec Information Security*	**Technical Track:** Tools and Techniques relating to cryptographic modules *Moderators: Dr. Claire Loisseaux and Dr. Yi Mao, Deputy Lab Director, atsec Information Security*
11:15	**High Impact CMVP and FIPS 140-2 Implementation Guidance,** *Kim Schafer, Apostol Vassilev, Jim Fox NIST*	**Physical Security Protection Based on Non-deterministic Configuration of Integrated Microelectronic Security Features,** *Silvio Dragone, IBM Research – Zurich*
12:00	**The Current Status of CMVP in Japan,** *Junichi Kondo, Director JCMVP at IPA* **The Current Status of CMVP in Korea,** *Yongdae Kim, Reasearcher, The Attached Institute of ETRI (Electonics and Telecommunications research)* **Commercial Cryptography in Europe – A Summary,** *Helmut Kurth, atsec information security*	**Non-Invasive Attacks Testing: Feedback on Relevant Methods,** *Sylvain Guilley, TELECOM-ParisTech, Robert Nguyen, Secure-IC S.A.S, Laurent Sauvage, Secure-IC S.A.S.*
12:45	LUNCH	
14:00	**Panel: How Can The Validation Queue For The CMVP Be Improved?,** Moderated by: *Fiona Pattinson, Director of Strategy and Business Development* Panelists: *Michael Cooper, NIST, Nithya Rachamadugu, Cygnacom, James McLaughlin, Gemalto, Steve Weymann, Infogard*	**Test Vector Leakage Assessment (TVLA) Methodology in Practice,** *Jeremy Cooper, Gilbert Goodwill, Gary Kenworthy, Pankaj Rohatgi, Cryptography Research Inc.*
14:45	**Building a Certification Program: Techniques That (Might) Work, Tammy Green,** *Security Architect and Vulnerability Response Director, Blue Coat Systems*	**Electro Magnetic Fault Injection in Practice,** *Rajesh Velegalati, Jasper Van Woudenberg, Riscure*

Fig. 5.5 ICMC 2013 agenda page 2

Fig. 5.6 ICMC 2013 agenda page 3

15:30	BREAK	
16:15	**Understanding the FIPS Government Crypto Regulations for 2014,** *Edward Morris, Co-Founder at Gossamer Security Solutions, Inc.*	**Security Mechanisms, Services, Protocols and Architecture for Secure Mobile Applications,** *Sead Muftic, Professor in Computer Networks Security, SETECS*
17:00	**FIPS and FUD,** *Ray Potter, CEO, SafeLogic*	**How Random Is Random?,** *Helmut Kurth, Chief Scientist, atsec information security*
17:45	Adjourn (Exhibits Close)	Adjourn (Exhibits Close)

Thursday, Sep 26		Conference Sessions
	Certification Programs Track: Presentations relating to the CMVP, other government programs and policy	**Technical Track:** Tools and Techniques relating to cryptographic modules
8:00	**Registration & Coffee** (Exhibits Open)	
9:00	**Reuse of Validation or Other Third Party Components in a 140-2 Cryptographic Module,** *Jonathon Smith, Senior Cryptographic Equipment Assessment Laboratory (CEAL) Tester, Cygnacom Solutions*	**Entropy: Order from Disorder,** *Tim Hall and Apostol Vassilev, NIST*
9:45	**The Upcoming Transition to New Algorithms and Key Sizes,** *Allen Roginsky, Kim Schaffer, NIST*	**SP 800-90 – Reviewing The Standard,** *Stephan Mueller, Principal Consultant and Evaluator, atsec information Security*
10:30	BREAK	
11:15	**Approved vs. Non-Approved: Decoding the Language,** *Yi Mao, atsec information security*	**Software in Silicon: Crypto-Capable Processors,** *Valerie Fenwick, Oracle Solaris Security, Darren Moffat, Oracle Solaris Secruity, David Weaver, Oracle SPARC Hardware, Wajdi Feghali, Intel*
12:00	**Pattern Based FIPS 140-2 Crytographic Module Validation,** *Steve Weymann & Mark Minnoch, InfoGard Laboratories*	**Key Management Overview,** *Allen Roginsky & Kim Schaffer, NIST*
12:45	LUNCH	

14:00	**Securing the Supply Chain for COTS ICT Products,** *Sally Long, The Open Group*	***ISO/IEC 19790 Status and Supporting Documents*** *Miguel Bañón, Epoche & Espri; Randall Easter, NIST*
14:45	**Implementation and Assessment on Cryptography for Payment Solutions,** *Yan Liu, atsec Information Security*	**Panel: Everything You Always Wanted to Know About Labs (But Were Afraid to Ask....),** *Moderated by: Fiona Pattinson, Director of Strategy & Business Development, atsec information Security*
15:30	**BREAK** (Exhibits Close at 16:15)	
16:15	**The Next ICMC: Moving Forward, Wrap Up and Summary,** *Fiona Pattinson, Director of Strategy & Business Development, atsec information Security*	
17:00	Adjourn	

Fig. 5.7 ICMC 2013 agenda page 4

room, as if waiting for him to add, "See you next year." People lingered for as long as they could until the hotel staff gently reminded them that the space needed to be prepared for the next day's events.

That same year, atsec founded the Cryptographic Module User Forum (CMUF) to sustain this spirit of collaboration throughout the year. This effort led to the next ICMC. Together, CMUF and ICMC formed a partnership that mirrored NIST's original model of workshops and community dialogue, but this time it was led by the people themselves.

The First Step Toward a New Tradition When the ballroom lights dimmed that evening, the silence that had defined the post-2004 years was gone. In its place stood a thriving, energized community that had finally rediscovered its voice. ICMC 2013 was not simply the first conference of its name. It was the revival of a tradition the field had lost and the beginning of one that would continue to grow year after year.

The conference did more than succeed; it proved that the cryptographic module community could gather again, speak openly again, and shape its future together.

Fig. 5.8 Sal La Pietra giving the closing remarks at ICMC 2013

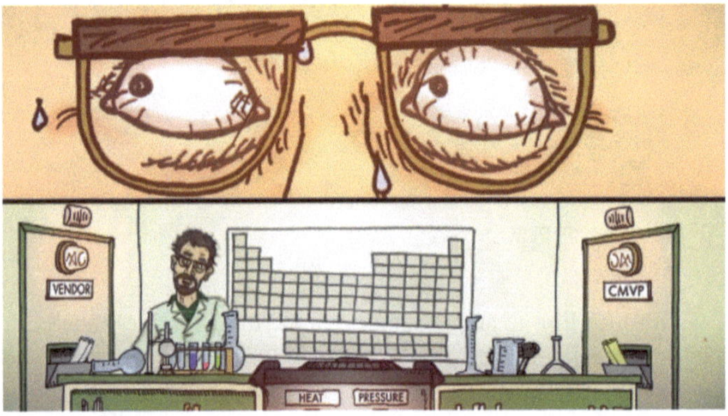

Fig. 5.9 atsec's ICMC 2014 clip

At ICMC 2014, atsec carried that momentum forward by presenting its first animated video, "Making Diamonds out of Coal: CST Labs Are Under Pressure." The goal was simple: to shine a light on the intense demands placed on CST laboratories as they navigate rapidly evolving technologies and reconcile them with increasingly complex Implementation Guidance issued by the CMVP. The tone was humorous, but the message was real. And while the labs were certainly not under the same kind of pressure as Walter White from Breaking Bad, there were moments when the comparison felt uncomfortably close (Fig. 5.9).

In the end, so much of the work comes down to effective communication between all parties. That was one of the core reasons atsec founded ICMC in the first place:

to create a space where stakeholders could meet face-to-face, share their challenges, and collaborate on practical solutions.

Judging by the laughter and enthusiasm that filled the room, the atsec video presentation quickly became one of the conference highlights. What began as a lighthearted moment soon evolved into a tradition, a highly anticipated and warmly appreciated feature at every ICMC since. Today, the restaurant displays iconic scenes from ICMC video clips across all the years, decorating the walls of FIPS 'n' Chips and reminding diners of the community's shared humor and history.

After ICMC 2013 and 2014, it had become clear that ICMC was profitable. atsec did not take the profit. Instead, they left it as seed funding to the conference organizer, Cnxtd, for them to further grow the conference. In June 2015, atsec signed a partnership agreement with Cnxtd to delegate management of the complete event ICMC in 2015 and in 2016 to Cnxtd, including operations, sales, promotion, and conference development. atsec also gave the conference website and the financial control of the conference to Cnxtd. For the first two conferences (2013 and 2014), atsec's service agreement with Cnxtd was to pay a flat fee or a certain percentage of the profit, whichever was larger. The shift of the conference's financial aspects from atsec to Cnxtd in 2015 was twofold: one was to demonstrate that atsec had no intent to profit from ICMC, and the other was to intensify Cnxtd's desire to ensure the success of ICMC. To reflect atsec as the founder of ICMC and maintain the creator's vision, Cnxtd agreed to recognize atsec as a perpetual Platinum Sponsor of ICMC, which was intended to be the highest level of sponsorship, and to have atsec chair the ICMC Program Committee.

The partnership proved fruitful. While Cnxtd has grown ICMC, it has also expanded its team and business to organize the International Common Criteria Conference (ICCC), the European Union Common Criteria conference (EUCC), and occasionally some add-ons to these conferences such as ISO/IEC 19790 Day, PQC Cyber Day, Crypto Infrastructure Day, and so on. The attendees of these conferences are largely overlapping.

With three years of ICMC in the greater Washington, DC area, ICMC 2016 was held for the first time in Ottawa, Canada, to reflect that CMVP is a joint program of the United States and Canada. It was also the first time the conference moved from fall to spring. The weekend before ICMC 2016, which took place May 18–20, was still very cold in Ottawa. This contrast was especially striking for the atsec team based in sunny and warm Austin, Texas. The inspiring talks and heated debates at ICMC warmed up Ottawa. The weekend after the conference was a gorgeous day that coincided with Ottawa's tulip festival. The capital of Canada was filled with beautifully blooming tulips in all sorts of colors, such as red, white, yellow, orange, purple, and even black. It felt as if the entire city was celebrating the closure of ICMC on its first visit.

Over the next decade, ICMC grew into the heartbeat of the assurance community. Each year brought new challenges and new proof that the community could adapt.

When the world shut down in 2020, ICMC did not. Dr. Yi Mao, welcoming hundreds of remote attendees from nineteen countries, reminded everyone that the pandemic could separate people physically but not intellectually:

"The COVID-19 pandemic may have restricted us from traveling, but it cannot prevent us from connecting our minds through this virtual platform."

That year, she celebrated with the remote ICMC attendees a milestone long in preparation, the moment CMVP began accepting FIPS 140–3 validation reports, marking the official transition from FIPS 140–2. Her address closed with gratitude for the generations that built the standard:

"Tomorrow we will celebrate the opening of a new door leading to FIPS 140-3 validated modules. A year from tomorrow, the window to validate a module under FIPS 140-2 will close. The new generation carries on the principles established by their predecessors."

The following year, ICMC 2021 became the first hybrid event in the conference's history, connecting nearly 400 participants across continents. Yi's opening speech reflected both optimism and technical focus: "ICMC is the intersection, hub, and communication platform where government, industry, technology, and standards meet." She added, "Embracing change seems to be the only unchanging principle to stay relevant into the future."

ICMC 2022 was special because it was the tenth ICMC and was the first fully in-person conference after the COVID pandemic. Atsec also celebrated the tenth anniversary of ICMC in 2023 by acknowledging ten outstanding long-term contributors to the crypto validation community at the opening ceremony and recognizing another twenty valuable contributors at the close. The conference was held in Ottawa again.

In 2024, when the conference moved to Silicon Valley, Yi's tone shifted toward innovation. "It is the first time we host ICMC in the Bay Area, where many technological innovations started and changed the world. We have brought ICMC closer to the heart of innovation." She highlighted automation, ISO/IEC 19790 revision, and post-quantum standards as the new pillars of progress. It was proof that ICMC had become more than a forum. It was the community's annual pulse check on the future of cryptography itself.

For ICMC 2025, even with reduced resources at NIST, the CMVP, CAVP, and Cryptographic Technology Group (CTG) fully supported the conference and gave several presentations as well as panels. This conference had the most engaging and lighthearted closing, with a CMUF game completed on the Slido platform. The game questions covered the history of ICMC, cryptographic algorithm specifications, ISO/IEC 19790 requirements, FIPS 140–3 implementation guidance, and the future of the community.

Here is the list of ICMC dates and venues:

Returning Home: The Austin Vision By 2025, ICMC had traveled from Gaithersburg to Ottawa, Vancouver, San Jose, and Toronto, as well as several times in Washington, DC and its surrounding areas (Fig. 5.10). Yet Austin, where the idea was born, had never hosted it. Dr. Yi Mao, now serving as the ICMC Program Committee Chair, advocated for ICMC 2027 to be held in Austin. Austin, the birthplace of both CMUF and ICMC, would be a fitting homecoming for the conference's fifteenth

ICMC Venues

Year	Dates	Country	City	Venue
2013	Sept. 24-26	US	Gaithersburg, MD	Holiday Inn
2014	Nov. 19-21	US	Washington, D.C.	Hilton
2015	Nov. 4-6	US	Washington, D.C.	Hilton
2016	May 18-20	Canada	Ottawa	Shaw Centre
2017	May 16-19	US	Washington, D.C.	Westin Arlington Gateway
2018	May 8-11	Canada	Ottawa, Ontario	Shaw Centre
2019	May 15-17	Canada	Vancouver	JW Marriott
2020	Sept. 21-24	Virtual	online	
2021	Sept. 1-3	US w/online	Hybrid w/ physical location in Bethesda, MD	Hyatt Regency Bethesda
2022	Sept. 14-16	US	Arlington, VA	Westin Arlington Gateway
2023	Sept. 20-22	Canada	Ottawa, Ontario	Shaw Centre
2024	Sept. 18-20	US	San Jose, CA	Double Tree by Hilton
2025	April 8-10	Canada	Toronto	Marriott Downtown at CF Toronto Eaton
2026	April 21-23	US	Arlington, VA	Renaissance Arlington Capital View

Fig. 5.10 ICMC dates and venues

edition, a symbolic continuation of the NIST tradition that began with the CMVP Symposium 2004.

This effort dated back to ICMC 2024 in San Jose. When Yi, now the CEO of atsec USA, proposed to host the 15th ICMC in Austin to Cnxtd, she received an immediate refusal with an unjustifiable claim that Austin was not suitable for an international conference and that people around the world could not easily reach the city. In fact, Austin is the capital of Texas and offers more than ninety-five non-stop domestic flights, along with direct international flights from Amsterdam, Frankfurt, London, and destinations in Mexico, Central America, and South America. Austin is a technology hub known as "Silicon Hills" and is the live music capital of the world. The city hosts international events such as South by Southwest (SXSW), the Formula One United States Grand Prix, Austin City Limits (ACL), and several major international music festivals, just to name a few. The ICMC 2025 post-conference survey listed Austin as the second most highly voted United States city, just after Washington, DC. Both CMUF and CMVP were supportive of ICMC 2027 in Austin.

Despite the enthusiasm for Austin and the strong evidence that attendees wanted the fifteenth ICMC to be held there, which contradicted Cnxtd's initial claim, Cnxtd introduced a second argument: that Austin had no suitable hotels. atsec, being local to Austin, immediately identified a beautiful, cost-effective four-star downtown venue, the AT&T Conference and Hotel Center. Cnxtd quickly dismissed it with the comment that it was "just a college meeting facility." Instead, they proposed two hotels in Toronto and one in San Jose for the ICMC Program Committee to choose from for the 2027 venue. Austin was excluded from the voting ballot. As a result, the ICMC 2027 location was selected more than eighteen months before the event

United States of America
United States Patent and Trademark Office

ICMC

Reg. No. 6,609,213
Registered Jan. 04, 2022
Int. Cl.: 41
Service Mark
Principal Register

CNXTD Inc. (NEW YORK CORPORATION)
421 Seventh Avenue
New York, NEW YORK 10001

CLASS 41: Arranging and conducting business conferences in the field of commercial cryptography

FIRST USE 4-00-2013; IN COMMERCE 4-00-2013

THE MARK CONSISTS OF STANDARD CHARACTERS WITHOUT CLAIM TO ANY PARTICULAR FONT STYLE, SIZE OR COLOR

SER. NO. 88-932,008, FILED 05-25-2020

Fig. 5.11 ICMC trademark registration

dates in order to secure the lowest possible room rate. Cnxtd offered a small note of hope, stating that they would "consider Austin again for 2028."

The 2015 partnership agreement between atsec and Cnxtd includes a renewal clause: atsec has the option to terminate the cooperating agreement within sixty days after the conclusion of the 2016 event, or else the agreement automatically renews for another year under the same terms.

atsec believes the intent of the renewal clause is clear: if the arrangement continues to work well, the delegation of conference management renews automatically. However, atsec retains the right to end the delegation and bring the conference back under its own care.

While exploring what options might exist to encourage Cnxtd to realign with the community's best interests, atsec was surprised to discover that Cnxtd had registered the trademark for ICMC and claimed ownership dating back to 2013 (Fig. 5.11).

atsec has been forced to question whether this registration was legal, and whether it is ethical to register the trademark without informing or seeking permission from atsec, the founder of ICMC. Figure 5.12 shows the ICMC registration fees for the three-day conference.

ICMC is a conference devoted to validated cryptographic modules and trusted information security. The community must ask whether it should place its confidence in a conference organizer whose actions, in atsec's opinion, raise questions about mission and intent.

Yi once recalled an afternoon when her three-year-old daughter climbed into her lap and said, "Mama, you are very nice." Yi felt her heart lift, thinking that her hard work was reflected in that small expression of appreciation. "Oh, why?" she asked,

ICMC Registration Fees for Full Conference

Year	Full Price	Early
2013	$940	$660
2014	$940	$800
2015	$940	$660
2016	$1,100	$660
2017	$1,100	$660
2018	$1,100	$690
2019	$1,100	$690
2020	$1,100	$690
2021	$1,120	$690
2022	$1,150	$690
2023	$1,290	$900
2024	$1,390	$970
2025	$1,390	$830
2026	$1,730	$990

Fig. 5.12 ICMC registration fees

always encouraging her child to explain her reasoning. Her daughter replied soberly, "Because you do not eat me." Yi then realized she had been reading a picture book about a wolf disguised as a sheep. She held her tightly and said, "Of course I will never eat you." It was meant as reassurance, a promise that the world was safe in a mother's arms. Yet the moment lingered. Is the world as safe as we hope, or is it sometimes more wolfish than we want to believe? As the CEO of atsec USA, Yi now finds herself asking a related question: how does one act as a shepherd and protect the flock when a wolf is near?

What Sal said at the closing of the first ICMC in 2013 deserves to be remembered here: although atsec conceived of and founded it, "It belonged to the community, and the community carried the responsibility of shaping its future." atsec will continue to be part of that community and to help shape the future of ICMC. From the beginning, ICMC and CMUF were designed as two sides of the same coin. Whoever runs ICMC should invest in CMUF and support its activities with funds drawn from ICMC's success.

atsec created ICMC. atsec created FIPS 'n' Chips. Creativity is something no one can take away.

As the story of ICMC wound down, the afternoon light shifted across the walls of FIPS 'n' Chips, catching the illustrations and video stills that traced the conference's journey from Gaithersburg to Ottawa, San Jose, Toronto, and the many places in between. Diners looked up now and then, recognizing a familiar scene or a moment of shared laughter from years past. It was a reminder that the conference had never been just an event; it had been a gathering place, a crossroads of people who believed that trust and security are built through collaboration. Here in the restaurant that celebrated that spirit, surrounded by the symbols of every chapter, it was clear that ICMC's future would continue to be written by the same community that first filled a hotel ballroom in 2013. The tradition lived on, not only in conference halls around the world, but also in this small corner of Austin, where the community's stories were preserved like recipes on a well-loved menu.

References

1. Stewart F (2025) ICMC: Win!, Win!, Win!. https://www.atsec.com/icmc-win-win-win/. Last accessed 24 Apr 2025
2. atsec information security (2022) ICMC and Dr. Bertrand du Castel. https://www.atsec.com/icmc-and-dr-bertrand-du-castel/. Last accessed 3 Dec 2025

Part II
NIST Approved Cryptographic Algorithms

Chapter 6
Advanced Encryption Standard

Luca Di Domenico

Another Lecture at the FIPS 'n' Chips Aster entered atsec's CST laboratory feeling extremely enthusiastic. How could she not have felt this way? On that day, she had been invited to listen to the AES lecture, set to take place in the mythical FIPS 'n' Chips restaurant.

When Aster entered the real-world room where the lecture was going to take place, she did not immediately recognize the young lecturer. Moved by her curiosity and considering the fact that she had arrived a handful of minutes before the official start of the lecture, she went to make a new acquaintance of the 25-years old fellow.

His name was Luca Di Domenico, and he was an atsec colleague working in the Italian division of the company. He had been invited to Austin for a week to attend a one-day conference—which he even had the luck and pleasure to give the official name to! The conference was already over, but to kill two birds with one stone, atsec's CEO Yi kindly asked Luca to also lead this AES lecture. When it was time to start the lecture, Luca invited everyone put on their VR goggles. While they were waiting for the setup of the 3D space to finish, Luca managed to get some smiles and chuckles by kicking things off with: "I hope that my Italian origin helped me cook a really nice lecture for you!" Then, a typical hum came, and off they went to the FIPS 'n' Chips restaurant, transported once again with the power of VR to the top of the Mueller control tower.

What is AES? Luca kicked off the entire lecture with a brief introduction.

NIST published AES (Advanced Encryption Standard) in 2001, in the FIPS 197 document [1], and it was chosen after a long process of public scrutiny and analysis due to its secure and future-proof design. It is a block cipher based on the substitution-permutation network construction and is widely used for symmetric cryptography across the internet and in our modern devices.

L. Di Domenico (✉)
Formerly with atsec information security corporation, Austin, TX, USA
e-mail: luca.didomenico99@gmail.com

Y. Mao (ed.), *Tasting Cryptography*, https://doi.org/10.1007/978-3-032-30243-4_6

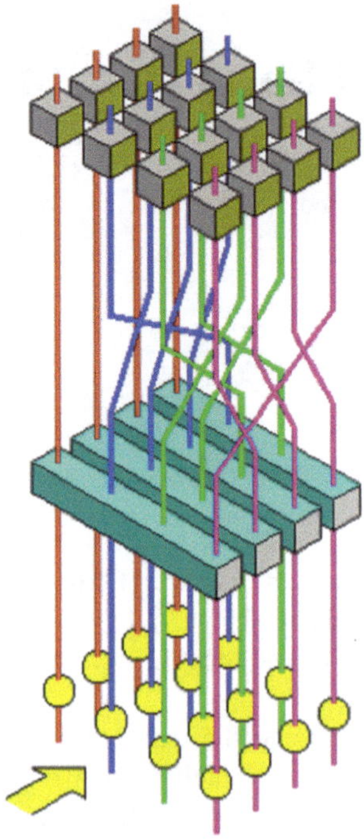

Fig. 6.1 AES transformation

"Before moving on," said Luca with a voice filled with positive expectations, "does everyone remember what these terms mean? You know, 'block cipher', 'substitution-permutation network' and 'symmetric cryptography'? These terms are important to make clear the underlying structure of AES and its main use cases."

After some classical back and forth between a teacher and their students, they arrived at the following conclusions:

AES is a block cipher, meaning that AES is a deterministic process which operates on a block, so it takes a fixed length set of bits as input and outputs a set of bits of the same fixed length. AES operates on a 128-bit block, which in turn allows the algorithm to be very strong against numerous attacks. Intuitively, with such a long block, it is quite hard to guess how a given input block will be manipulated to produce the final output block.

Furthermore, AES is also a substitution-permutation network that is based on the iterated repetition of 3 main mathematical transformations:

- substitution, i.e. a replacement of one value with another
- permutation, i.e. a scrambling of given values to arrange them in a different order
- key addition, i.e. the exclusive-ORing of the current available quantity with data deterministically derived from the input key

To help visualize the concept, Luca pulled up a diagram (Fig. 6.1 taken from [2]) that summarizes the actual transformations AES applies repeatedly on the input data.

The "input key" is an input parameter of AES which deeply impacts the definition of the key addition operation and whose length specifies the number of times the 3 transformations are repeated. Moreover, the AES transformations have been meticulously designed to provide 2 main properties:

- the output of AES is heavily dependent on the input; and
- the output of AES and the key are strongly correlated.

"The input-output dependency and the key-output correlation were designed to be so strong, in fact, that AES is still a rock-solid algorithm even today, with zero feasible attacks executable on classical computers beyond randomly guessing the input key," Luca highlighted, so as to strongly emphasize how effective AES is in practice.

The AES input key is sometimes referred to as the symmetric key. Indeed, AES is widely used in symmetric cryptography, where "symmetric" means that the AES input key shall be used in both the encryption and decryption operations.

Luca continued: "Keep this in mind. Going forward, for encryption operation we mean an operation that, taking a message or plaintext as the input, uses the key and possibly other data to output a ciphertext. On the other hand, the decryption operation uses the key, the ciphertext, and possibly other data to output the original plaintext." Aster jotted down some notes, "Encryption leads to ciphertext; decryption to plaintext message."

Luca also added the following clarifications. "Symmetric cryptography has numerous applications. Amongst the most important ones, the protection of data in storage, the protection of data in transit, a form of Message Authentication Codes to protect the integrity of given data, and the protection of other key data. AES is used for each of these applications. Not only that, its definition in FIPS 197 is flexible enough to specify multiple 'modes of operation.' We can understand a mode of operation as a method to take AES and adjust it specifically for a certain application, with a goal of improving the efficiency of its implementation in that precise use case."

Luca paused for a moment before continuing, letting the students hastily type in some notes. He then launched back into the lecture: "Alongside the AES modes of operations, AES may also be used as a component of a higher-level cryptographic algorithm. For example, AES can be used either as a pseudorandom function inside Key Derivation algorithms or as a crucial component for a Deterministic Random Bit Generator algorithm."

Before moving forward, Luca spared a few sentences to outline what the rest of the lecture would cover. "Let us quickly clarify how we are going to proceed: First, we will highlight the definition of forward and inverse ciphers; second, we will talk about the AES security strengths; finally, we will take a look at the AES modes of operation."

Forward and Inverse Ciphers, in Contrast with Encryption and Decryption
Luca then dove into explaining forward and inverse ciphers.

As he spoke, Aster quickly entered the key details into her notes. FIPS 197 does not directly specify AES encryption and AES decryption, opting instead to specify the substitution and permutation transformations. When grouped under a specific order and iterated, the substitutions, the permutations, and the key additions define either a "forward cipher" or an "inverse cipher" operation where the inverse cipher inverts and executes in reverse order the mathematical transformations seen in the forward cipher.

There is a clear distinction between the forward/inverse ciphers and the encryption/decryption operations: An encryption operation masks an input message into a ciphertext, and the decryption operation un-masks a ciphertext to get the original message. The forward or inverse cipher is just an ordered set of transformations that deterministically generates an output starting from an input.

The forward cipher may be used either as an encryption function to generate a ciphertext, or as a decryption function to extract a message starting from a ciphertext. Depending on the AES mode of operation, only the forward cipher may be used to obtain both an encryption and a decryption function.

Key Lengths and Security Strengths Supported by AES After the students took some time to confirm their understanding of the material so far, Luca moved to the next topic: key lengths and security strengths.

"It's important to note the AES cipher functions defined in FIPS 197 support only the following key lengths in bits: 128, 192, and 256," he started. "Depending on the supported key length, the AES cipher functions differ slightly because there are changes in the algorithm that create data for the key additions, and because the number of repetitions of the transformations increases as the input key gets longer. Depending on the key bit-length, the AES cipher functions get further classified as AES-128, AES-192 and AES-256."

Intuitively, Aster noted down as Luca continued, an increase in key length causes an increase in security, since the longer the key, the harder it is to guess the kind of transformations used in the AES cipher execution. More precisely, AES was designed in such a way that the most efficient attacks on it are brute force attacks on the key. In other words, an attacker can break AES only by guessing the input key. This type of guessing requires roughly 2^{128}, 2^{192}, or 2^{256} operations to actually succeed for AES-128, AES-192, and AES-256, respectively.

"Hence, it should come as no surprise that the security strengths supported by the three AES sub-classifications are 128, 192, and 256," Luca concluded. "Depending on the corresponding key length, of course. In fact, the security strength is associated with the logarithm of the number of operations required to break a given cryptographic algorithm, and the AES security strengths derive directly from the number of operations required for a successful brute force attack."

Luca then specified "Going forward, we shall talk about the many AES modes of operation, specifying the main non-trivial considerations regarding their FIPS validation. Note that CAVP—the Cryptographic Algorithm Verification Program—cannot directly certify an implementation of the AES forward or inverse cipher; it can only test AES configured in one of its modes of operation or seen as a component of a higher-level cryptographic algorithm."

To avoid unnecessary repetitions, Luca noted that there are two important things to keep in mind, which hold for basically all the AES modes of operation: "First, if not specified otherwise, each mode of operation that we will talk about can be implemented using the AES-128, AES-192, or AES-256 cipher functions. Naturally, depending on the length of the input key used, the mode will have 128, 192, or 256 bits in security strength, respectively." Then, after a brief pause, Luca added: "Second, each mode of operation can support an encryption and/or a decryption function. Specifically for the AES-CMAC mode, the word 'encryption' and 'decryption' are substituted by 'generation' and 'verification', respectively. The reason for these substitutions will become clear later in the lecture."

AES Modes of Operation Used for Confidentiality A tone of excitement grew in Luca's voice as he introduced the AES modes of operation, as it was one of his favorite topics of the presentation. "Considering the fact that AES is a block cipher, it seems obvious that it has a handful of modes of operation specifically defined to provide data confidentiality in almost any possible application where such confidentiality is needed. See, they are even used to define more complex AES modes of operation!"

After specifying that all of these "basic" modes are defined in the SP 800-38A document [3] and in its Addendum [4], Luca told to everyone "There is only one way to get to know them, and it takes a bit of time. Slowly but surely, we will face the AES modes one by one."

AES-ECB For AES-ECB, Luca laid out the following concepts:

The "ECB" in AES-ECB stands for Electronic CodeBook. and it is the most basic AES mode of operation. It assumes that the bit length of the input data for both its encryption and decryption algorithms is a multiple of 128, the block size of AES.

During ECB encryption, the AES forward cipher function is applied directly and independently to each 128-bit block of the plaintext. The ciphertext is then defined as the concatenation, in order, of the resulting sequence of output blocks.

Unsurprisingly, for the ECB decryption, the AES inverse cipher function is applied directly and independently to each 128-bit block of the ciphertext. The plaintext, like the ciphertext before it, is defined as the concatenation, in order, of the resulting sequence of output blocks.

Luca provided a diagram (Fig. 6.2 taken from [3]) of the ECB operations to illustrate the concepts covered:

Aster smiled at the simplicity of this AES mode. She liked the fact that such straightforward manipulations could lead to a secure implementation of a cryptographic algorithm.

You can imagine her dismay, then, when Luca shot down its usage, "Unfortunately, AES-ECB is too simple for its own good. By its definition, under a single given key, any given plaintext block always gets encrypted to the same constant ciphertext block. In fact, this is where the name of the mode comes from. This mapping to a unique output block can intuitively be interpreted as an implementation that uses a look-up table or 'codebook.' Yet, in turn, this direct mapping implies that ECB emphasizes possible plaintext patterns, especially if the plaintext is particularly long."

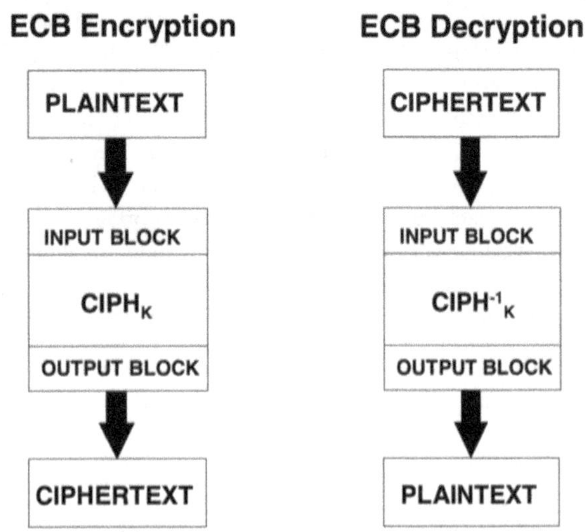

Fig. 6.2 ECB operations

This explanation reminded Aster that she had seen a famous example that shows this tendency of ECB to preserve data patterns using an image of a cartoon penguin: After encrypting the image of the penguin under ECB, if the generated ciphertext is read as image data, then it is still possible to distinguish the silhouette of the original penguin, despite the fact that most of the colors of the encrypted image do not make much logical sense.

Luca moved to wrap up the conversation on AES-ECB. "Because ECB distinctly lacks the ability to hide data patterns, NIST is planning to deprecate a direct use this mode of operation. This will come into picture when the SP 800-131A Revision 3 will be officially released—as of now, this document is still a Public Draft [5], and Revision 2 still stands."

AES-CBC, IVs, and its 3 Ciphertext Stealing Variants With AES-ECB squared away, Luca moved on to the AES-CBC mode.

"CBC stands for Cipher Block Chaining. Similar to ECB, this AES mode of operation assumes that the bit length of the input data for both its encryption and decryption algorithms is a multiple of 128, the block size of AES," he started.

"But, contrary to ECB, CBC also requires an additional 128-bit data block to kickstart its encryption or decryption operation. This block is usually referred to as the Initialization Vector, or IV for short. The CBC IV need not be secret, but it must be unpredictable, in the sense that it shall not be possible to predict the IV that will be associated to the plaintext in advance of the generation of the IV itself. This is required so that the ability of an attacker to guess the output blocks of multiple executions of CBC under a given key is severely limited."

Luca then brought up a slide explaining that, to validate the CBC mode, NIST requires an examination of the IV generation procedures to ensure the unpredictability of the IV. NIST suggests generating this IV in one of the following ways:

- in a random manner, using a FIPS-approved random number generator, or
- in a deterministic manner, by applying to a nonce the forward cipher function under the same key that is used for the encryption of the plaintext.

Aster nodded while reading through this explanation; she agreed with the fact that the IV generation should be specified in a standard and examined. After her nod, Luca moved on with a brief description of CBC encryption and decryption.

"In CBC encryption, to produce the first ciphertext block, the first input block is formed by exclusive-ORing the first plaintext block with the IV, and then the forward cipher function is applied to the first input block. To produce one of the following ciphertext blocks, an input block is formed by exclusive-ORing the corresponding plaintext block with the previous ciphertext block, and then the forward cipher function is applied to this input block," Luca explained.

After taking a breath, he continued, "In CBC decryption, to recover the first plaintext block, the inverse cipher function is applied to the first ciphertext block, and the resulting output block is exclusive-ORed with the IV. To recover one of the following plaintext blocks, the inverse cipher function is applied to the corresponding ciphertext block, and the resulting block is exclusive-ORed with the previous ciphertext block.

He then pulled up a diagram (Fig. 6.3 taken from [3]) on the virtual whiteboard for the group. "The CBC mode takes its name from the fact that the encryption process combines or 'chains' a plaintext block with the previous ciphertext block. The diagram of the CBC operations looks like this."

The next slides added that SP 800-38A Addendum [4] specifies 3 other variants of the CBC mode, named respectively AES-CBC-CS1, AES-CBC-CS2, and AES-CBC-CS3, where CS stands for Ciphertext Stealing. These variants still use an IV, which must have the same properties as the CBC IV.

Furthermore, the 3 CS variants allow the input data for the CBC encryption and decryption functions to be of any bit length, and they achieve this by "stealing" and re-using part of the penultimate output block. The variants function extremely similarly to CBC, and they differ between themselves depending on how they handle the formatting of the concatenation of their output blocks. CS1 and CS2 coincide with CBC when the bit length of the input is a multiple of 128, whereas CS3 always forces an un-conditional swap of its last two output blocks, making it distinct from CBC.

AES-CFB1, AES-CFB8, AES-CFB128 Keeping steady pace, Luca then delved into AES-CFB.

The next few slides covered the basics of CFB—standing for Cipher FeedBack. This AES mode of operation depends on an additional parameter called s which takes

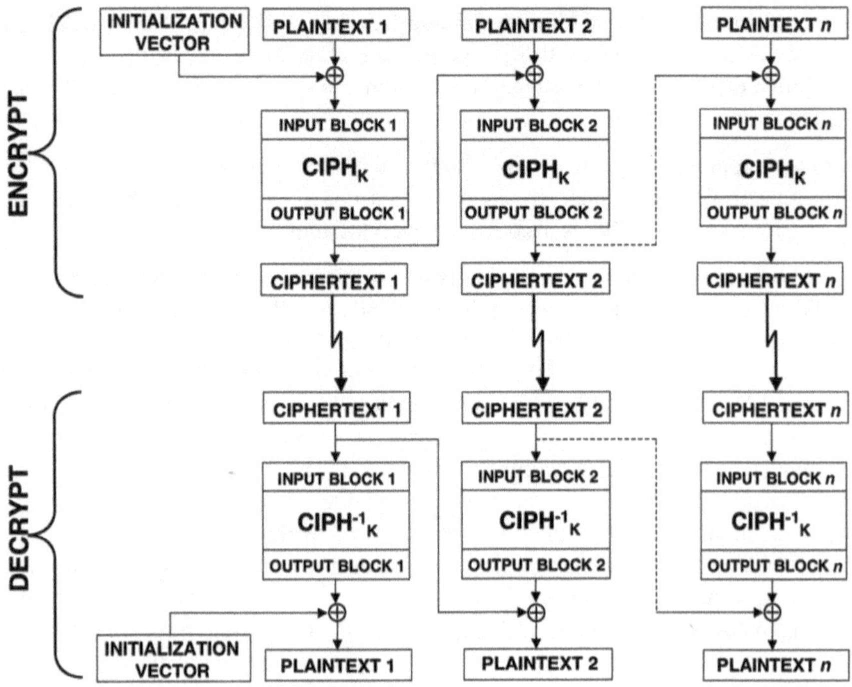

Fig. 6.3 CBC operations

on the integer value of 1, 8, or 128. Depending on the value of s, the CFB mode gets further categorized in AES-CFB1, AES-CFB8, and AES-CFB128.

CFB assumes that the bit length of the input data for both its encryption and decryption algorithms is a multiple of the parameter s. In the CFB context, the input of the encryption and decryption operations is processed as a sequence of so-called data segments, where each segment is s-bits long.

"As we went over for CBC mode, CFB also requires an unpredictable IV to kickstart its own operations. To validate one of the 3 CFB modes, NIST requires an examination of the IV generation procedures to ensure the unpredictability of the IV. NIST's suggestions regarding the IV generation discussed in the CBC mode also apply for the CFB mode, meaning that the IV should be generated either entirely at random or by encrypting a nonce," Luca pointed out.

In CFB encryption, Aster transcribed, the forward cipher operation is applied to the IV to produce the first output block. This first output block is split into 2 parts, and each of them is used separately: First, to produce the first ciphertext segment, the s most significant bits of the output block are exclusive-ORed with the first plaintext segment; second, to produce the next input block, the remaining part of the output block is prepended to the first ciphertext segment. The forward cipher is applied

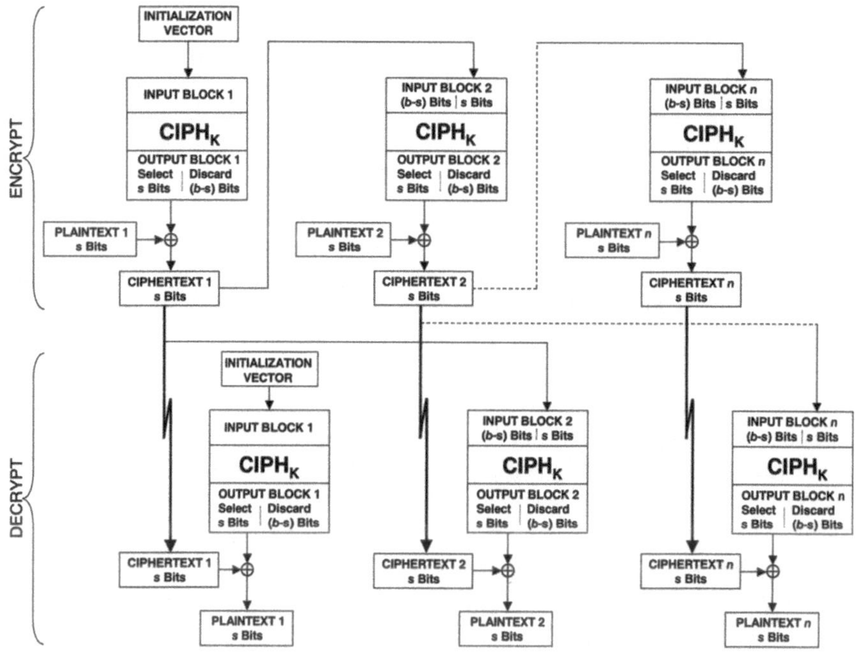

Fig. 6.4 CFB operations

to this input block, and the corresponding output block is split into 2 parts, one to produce the ciphertext segment using the plaintext segment, and the other one to produce the following input block with the newly created ciphertext segment. This cycle continues until all plaintext segments are processed.

After completing the dense definition of AES-CFB encryption, Luca pivoted to a lighter topic: the origin of the CFB name. "When s corresponds to 128, which is the bit length of the AES block, then each ciphertext segment is 128-bit long and it is obtained by exclusive-ORing the entire 128-bit output block with the corresponding plaintext segment. Notably, in this case, the entire ciphertext segment is 'fed-back' into the system to produce the next output block, hence, the name of this AES mode."

Luca also highlighted an interesting property regarding AES-CFB, noting "Thanks to the properties of the exclusive-OR operation and to the definition of the creation of the data segments, CFB is an AES mode which only requires the forward cipher to function. Indeed, in the CFB decryption operation, to obtain a plaintext segment, the corresponding ciphertext segment is exclusive-ORed with an output block whose construction is identical to the one seen in the CFB encryption. Such construction requires the use of only the forward cipher function. The diagram of the CFB operations looks like this" He snapped his fingers and another figure displayed (Fig. 6.4 taken from [3]) to chart out the logic of the AES mode.

AES-OFB Luca noticed that his students were nearing the limit of their attention span. But, in that moment, he decided to still refrain from telling them that he had already planned a break after two more AES modes. For now, he proceeded with the OFB mode.

While the minds of other students were starting to wander, Aster diligently chronicled the details of AES-OFB, starting with its name, as OFB stands for Output FeedBack. This AES mode can take a bit string of any length as input. Indeed, the underlying OFB operations consider the input string as a concatenation of zero or more 128-bit block, where the last block can be a partial block since it has a length of less than or equal to 128-bit.

OFB requires an IV to kickstart both its encryption and decryption operation; the OFB IV need not be secret, but shall be both unique under a given secret key and not directly dependent on the underlying input.

Luca paused for a moment, and then decided to break up the more detailed explanation with a key fact. “The uniqueness requirement is exclusive to the OFB IVs. The IVs used for CBC and CFB do not require uniqueness, they only need not to be secret.”

As he continued, it became clear that, because of this peculiarity, NIST states that the OFB IV may be a counter or a message counter. NIST also specifies that OFB IV generation mechanisms shall avoid using any of the input blocks or another IV to be generated. “The reason for the uniqueness requirement”, said Luca, “will be clarified after briefly discussing the OFB operations.”

“In OFB encryption, to produce the first output block, the forward cipher function is applied on the IV. To produce the first ciphertext block, the first plaintext block is exclusively-ORed with the first output block. To produce each of the following ciphertext blocks, first a novel output block is produced by applying the forward cipher function on the previous output block, then the novel ciphertext block is obtained by exclusively-ORing this novel output block with the corresponding plaintext block.”

“That cycle continues unmodified up until the creation of the last ciphertext block. Since the last plaintext block can be partial, i.e. it can have a bit-length b strictly less than 128, then the last ciphertext block is produced by exclusively-ORing the last plaintext block with the b most significant bits of the last 128-bit output block.”

It was at this moment that Luca exclaimed “Now we are able to understand why the OFB IV is required to be unique! Assume that the same IV is used for two distinct OFB encryptions under the same secret key. Assume also that attackers have access to the ciphertext blocks of both of these encryptions. If the attackers know a single plaintext block of one of the two messages, then they can apply two exclusive-OR operations to extract the corresponding output block and to retrieve the corresponding plaintext block of the other message. This kind of attack is clearly highly undesirable. Do you still follow me?”

The students answered Luca with a little murmur of “Yes” and “Ok I get it” mixed with some visible nods. Luca took a quick breath, and then he concluded the OFB mode discussion with its decryption operation.

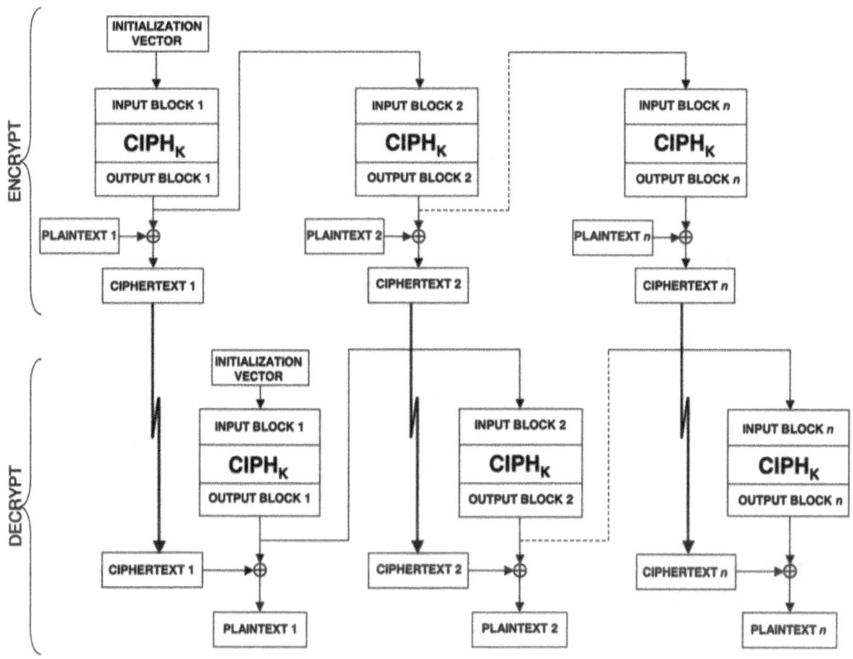

Fig. 6.5 OFB operations

"Thanks to the properties of the exclusive-OR operation and to the definition of the creation of the ciphertext blocks, OFB is an AES mode which only requires the forward cipher to function. Indeed, one plaintext block can be obtained by exclusive-ORing the corresponding ciphertext block with the corresponding output block obtained as in encryption, i.e., obtained via the forward cipher function. And the diagram for the OFB operations looks like this." (Fig. 6.5 taken from [3])

AES-CTR Slowing down a bit, Luca tried to reassure his audience, "Ok students, I know that this is quite a lot to unpack for a single lecture. I ask you to please give me a little more of your attention. We have only one more basic AES mode to go. After this, I will give you 20 minutes of break. Please, a little more and we are there."

Some sighs of relief could be heard in the audience, but all in all, less people than Luca expected reacted to his announcement. He was delighted to see that most of them, Aster included, still had a small fire in their eyes—the kind of sparkle only determined student can have during a lecture which they find interesting.

So, on he went with CTR, starting with the basics: CTR simply stands for Counter, and this AES mode of operation supports a bit string of any length as input. In fact, similarly to OFB, the last block of the input string can be considered partial and have a length which is less than or equal to 128 bits.

CTR requires a set of additional 128-bit blocks, called counter blocks. The number of counter blocks coincide with the number of input blocks to the CTR operation, meaning that the last counter block will be used with the last input block, which can be a partial block. The counter blocks shall meet a very strict requirement: across all the messages that are encrypted under one given key, all the counter blocks must be pairwise distinct.

Luca spent some more words on the counter blocks. "The reason why they are called counter blocks comes from how they are typically generated: NIST suggests creating unique counter blocks by applying an incrementing function. In other words, given a 128-bit starting block, the next 128-bit block can be generated by adding 1 to the starting block, where this block is interpreted as a binary representation of an integer. This means that the generated blocks 'count' the number of input blocks. Sometimes, naming is convenient, right?"

As he continued to elaborate, Aster noted down that the incrementing function allows an implementation to satisfy the counter block uniqueness requirement under a given message. To satisfy the requirements for multiple messages, NIST suggests either to use the incrementing function again to create a new starting counter block, or to use a nonce. Either way, the generation mechanism of the counter blocks shall be scrutinized under validation to verify the counter block uniqueness requirement.

"Without this uniqueness requirement," said Luca, "an attack similar to what we described for OFB would be applicable." Aster kept this observation in mind, so that she could see the similarity of the attacks during the break. She smiled when Luca started talking about CTR encryption and decryption, continuing her notes.

For CTR encryption, producing a given ciphertext block involves the corresponding plaintext block being exclusive-ORed with the corresponding output block, which in turn is obtained by applying the forward cipher function to the corresponding counter block. Note that, for the possibly partial last block, if n is its length, then only the n most significant bits of the last block are used in the exclusive-OR operation to generate the last output block.

Thanks to the properties of the exclusive-OR operation and to specific way ciphertext blocks are created, CTR is an AES mode which only requires the forward cipher to operate. Indeed, even in CTR decryption, the output blocks are still created by applying the forward cipher function on each of the counter blocks.

Aster capped off this section of her notes by making a quick copy of the diagram (Fig. 6.6 taken from [3]) for CTR operations:

Intermediate Checkpoint Luca, as promised, let everyone take a 20-minute break. Some people removed their headsets and went to stretch their legs, others chatted for a bit, and the most curious ones corrected their notes and compared them with other's. Aster, naturally, was reviewing her notes. She also finally realized what Luca meant with the attack similarity between the OFB and the CTR modes.

In the OFB mode, an attacker which has access to one plaintext block can potentially decrypt all the ciphertexts blocks created under one IV. If multiple messages

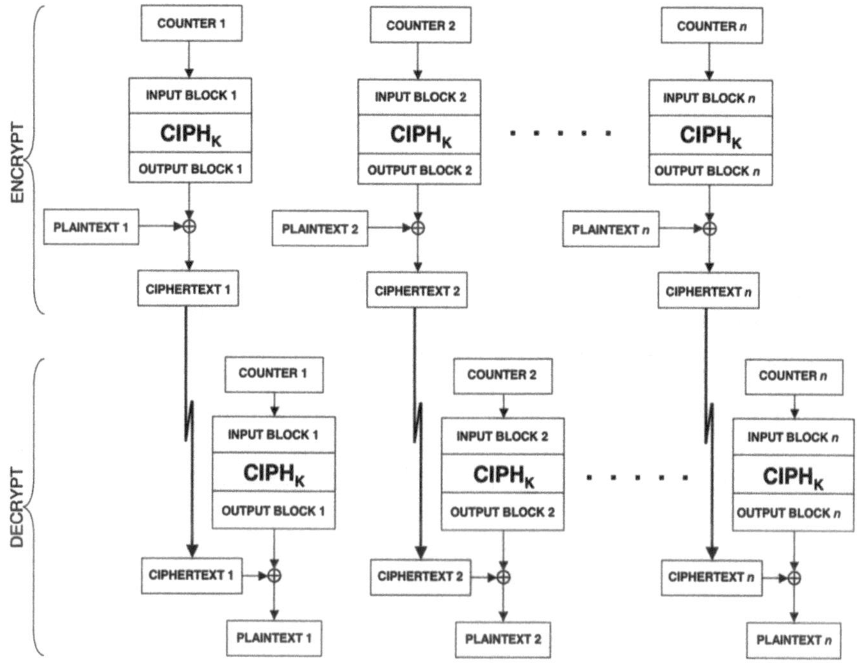

Fig. 6.6 CTR operations

are encrypted using the same IV, then the compromise of one plaintext block of any of the encrypted messages can lead to a compromise of the multiple messages. In a similar way, using the same counter blocks in different encryption instances of CTR can lead to a compromise of multiple messages.

After realizing this similarity, Aster read her notes again regarding the encryption of the various AES modes, and concluded the following:

- to produce one ciphertext, ECB uses one plaintext;
- to produce one ciphertext, CBC XOR-s the current plaintext with the previous ciphertext;
- to eventually produce one ciphertext of length s, CFB uses s bits of the previous ciphertext;
- to eventually produce one ciphertext, OFB exclusively uses the previous output block;
- to produce one ciphertext, CTR uses an ever-increasing counter block.

Before the end of the break, Aster also reviewed her notes from the start of the lecture:

Block cipher: deterministic process which operates on a block; a fixed-length input is processed in an output of the same length.

Substitution-permutation network: process which uses substitution, permutations, and keys to encrypt a message.

In symmetric cryptography, one identical key is used for both encryption and decryption.

Encryption and decryption: operations which respectively mask or un-mask a message

Forward and inverse ciphers: sets of transformations

Sometimes only forward cipher is used for both encryption and decryption

Clear correlation between AES key lengths and key strengths: 128, 192, 256.

AES Used for Key Wrapping Around 20 min later, when everyone was back with goggles on and focus restored, Luca introduced the AES modes used for key wrapping.

"NIST SP 800-90F [6] specifies two AES modes of operation that can be used for Key Wrapping: AES-KW and AES-KWP, standing for Key Wrap and Key Wrap with Padding, respectively. These modes are designed specifically for key wrapping; that is, for protecting the confidentiality and the authenticity/integrity of cryptographic keys. In general, segregating the way keys are protected with respect to how data is protected can provide an extra layer of protection."

"NIST does not prevent the use of the AES Key Wrapping modes to protect data, and similarly it does not prevent the use of other approved AES modes to protect keys. Although, it should be noted that the AES key wrapping modes are very robust, in the sense that each output bit depends in a non-trivial way on each input bit," he continued.

"This robustness", specified Luca, "comes at the cost of a considerably low throughput rate compared to other AES modes. Because of this, it makes sense that this robustness to speed tradeoff is acceptable mainly for key management applications in high-risk scenarios."

As he elaborated further, Aster added to her notes: The main difference between AES-KW and AES-KWP is that the latter specifies a standardized way in which the input should be additionally padded before being processed for the same underlying encryption operation. The encryption and decryption operations of these 2 modes are sometimes referred to as Authenticated Encryption and Authenticated Decryption, respectively, to highlight the fact that these operations also provide the authentication of the input data.

For the encryption operation of both modes, a value with a certain pattern is pre-padded to the input bit string, and then this concatenation is wrapped. The wrapping takes the concatenation, interprets it as a string of 64-bit blocks, and initializes numerous variables. Then, these variables are continuously updated in a loop using the AES forward cipher function before being used in the output ciphertext (Fig. 6.7 taken from [6]).

As Aster finished entering her notes on the encryption operation, she hypothesized that they were due an explanation for the decryption operation. And so they were, as Luca launched into it next.

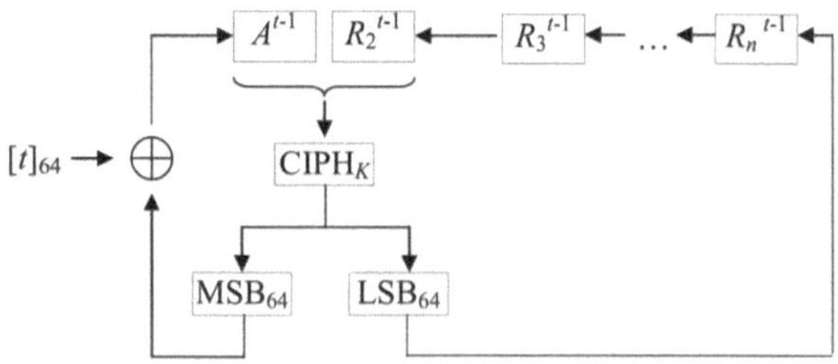

Fig. 6.7 KW update iteration

The decryption operation of both modes follows the reverse order with respect to the encryption, starting with an unwrapping operation. Here, the input is manipulated to initialize numerous variables which are continuously updated in a loop using the AES inverse cipher function. Then, the first bits of this unwrapped string are compared with the patterned value which was used in the wrapping operation. If the two values do not match, the decryption declares a failure; otherwise, the decryption outputs the original plaintext (i.e. the unwrapped string without the initial patterned padding).

The only notable requirements for validating a cryptographic algorithm implementation of the AES key wrapping modes are the ones regarding the maximum bit-length of the inputs and the maximum number of invocations of the encryption/ decryption operations. These requirements are specified in Section 5 of SP 800-38F [6].

AES-CMAC for Message Authentications Codes After concluding the section regarding AES for Key wrapping, Luca was delighted that the focus among the students was nice and high. So, onwards he went with the explanation of the CMAC mode.

"NIST SP 800-38B [7] specifies the AES-CMAC mode of operation, a.k.a. the Cipher-based Message Authentication Code. A well-designed MAC algorithm has only one main goal: provide a strong assurance of data integrity. It is true that checksums and error detection codes achieve some integrity assurances, but AES-CMAC is specifically designed to ensure this integrity by detecting both intentional and accidental modification of the data," Luca instructed.

Luca finally had the opportunity to explain why AES-CMAC has operations with slightly different names than all other operations:

"CMAC does not provide any data confidentiality. In fact, this is the reason why its operations are called Generation and Verification, instead of the typical encryption and decryption we are used to with the other modes. The Generation procedure takes key, data, and an output length as inputs, and then outputs a bitstring called MAC or tag. The Verification procedure takes instead the key, the input data, and a tag to then output a SUCCESS or FAILURE message. No ciphertext nor plaintexts here. Only generation followed by verification."

Aster nodded and made sure to differentiate CMAC from the other modes in her notes. Then, she listened to the explanation of the verification and generation operations.

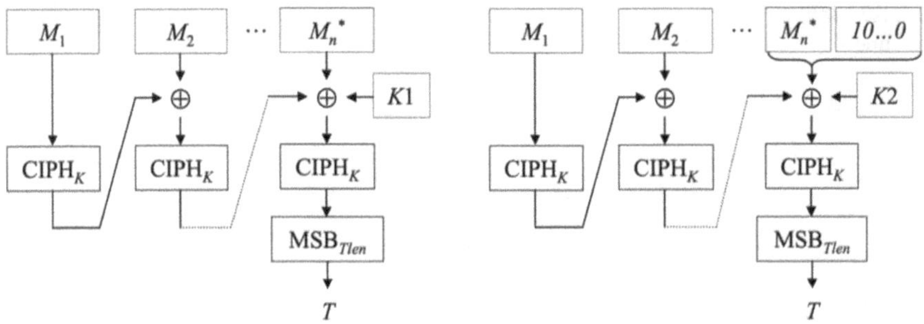

Fig. 6.8 CMAC generation

"The CMAC verification operation is extremely simple," Luca started. "It involves producing a tag by applying the CMAC generation procedure to the input data before comparing this freshly generated tag with the input tag. The returned messages correspond with the result of the comparison: SUCCESS if the tags match, FAILURE otherwise.

"Meanwhile, the CMAC generation operation works as follows: First, the input data is formatted into a block sequence, where the last block is conditionally exclusively-ORed with one of two pieces of data directly dependent on the key. Next, the AES-CBC mode of operation is executed using an IV filled with zeroes and the input key. Note that CBC only uses the forward cipher function. Then, the CBC output is truncated to the specified output length to get a final tag/MAC."

A diagram (Fig. 6.8 taken from [7]) popped up to illustrate the two possible ways in which the CMAC generation works:

"From the FIPS algorithm validation point of view, the most important thing to keep in mind is the considerations regarding the output tag length. Intuitively, the shorter the tag length is, the less is the assurance that the original data was not tampered with. With a tag bit-length exceeding 64 bits, the false-positive rate is astronomically small. Yet, if shorter tag lengths are used, the vendor should do a risk analysis, and in general, it is highly recommended to not use tag lengths shorter than 32 bits," Luca elaborated, moving to wrap up the CMAC portion.

"Regardless of the tag length, it is usually a good idea to limit the number of unsuccessful-verification attempts for each given key, to mitigate the possibility of a brute-force tag guessing attack even further."

AES-CCM: Combining both Confidentiality and Authenticity "Moving onward, NIST SP 800-38C [8] specifies the AES-CCM mode, a.k.a. 'Counter with Cipher block chaining-Message authentication code,'" Luca rattled off without missing a beat. "Kind of a mouthful, huh?" Aster nodded slightly in agreement as she tried to get the full name down.

"Under the knowledge of a key, this mode can provide assurance of the confidentiality and integrity of some input data, usually called payload, and it can provide assurance of only the integrity of some other input data, usually called associated data."

To highlight the nature of the double-assurance that CCM provides, Luca pointed out its operations assume the following names: Generation-Encryption and Decryption-Verification.

"The former outputs both a MAC/tag to be used for authentication purposes, and a ciphertext to be used for confidentiality purposes. The latter outputs either the original payload or an INVALID message output, to signal that something failed during verification."

Ok, I see, a sort of an evolution of CMAC, thought Aster, before Luca dove into a description of the two CMAC operations.

"Generation-Encryption functions like so: It takes as input the payload, the associated data, a nonce, and an AES key. These 3 input elements are formatted in a standardized way, and then AES-CBC, along with the provided AES key, is applied on the 3 formatted inputs to obtain a MAC or tag. To obtain the ciphertext, enough counter blocks are generated, and then AES-CTR with the provided AES key is applied to the payload and the tag. The tag and the ciphertext are then output."

Aster made sure to note that the associated data may have length zero and, should that be the case, CCM mode simply provides confidentiality and integrity of the payload, as Luca made a point of both things.

Continuing, Luca went over the remaining operation: "The Decryption-Verification instead works as follows: It takes as inputs the ciphertext, the associated data, the nonce, and an input key. First, the same counter block as in the Generate-Encrypt operation is created. Then, AES-CTR with the input key and the freshly generated counter blocks are applied on the ciphertext; this CTR operation gives back the payload and the candidate tag. At this stage, the payload, the associated data, and the nonce are formatted, and the formatted versions of these three elements are then passed as input to the AES-CBC with the input key. The output of the AES-CBC is subsequently compared with the candidate tag obtained in the previous step. If they coincide, the payload is returned; otherwise, an INVALID message output is returned.

"Again, similar to AES-CMAC, the crucial thing to keep in mind from a cryptographic algorithm validation point of view is the AES-CCM tag length. Indeed, the tag length is an input parameter for both of the CCM operations. NIST permits the tag bit-length to be any integer multiple of 16 residing between 32 and 128, inclusive. Yet, NIST suggests that a value smaller than 64 should not be used unless the number of times that the decryption-verification process is unsuccessful is limited across all implementations under any given key," he concluded.

AES-GCM, AES-GMAC, AES-GCM-SIV, AES-XPN: Confidentiality and Authenticity in a Network Environment For the penultimate section of his lecture, Luca took a brief moment of pause to collect his thoughts before moving on.

"NIST SP 800-38D [9] specifies two AES modes: AES-GCM and AES-GMAC, standing for Galois Counter Mode and Galois Message Authentication Code, respectively," he said.

"AES-GCM provides three assurances: First, the assurance of the confidentiality of limited data using a variation of AES-CTR; second, the assurance of the authenticity of the confidential data using a special hash function based on finite fields, a.k.a. Galois fields, hence, the name of the mode; and third, the assurance of the authenticity of almost unlimited additional data.

If no additional data is provided, the resulting specification of AES-GCM is a minor variation of AES-CTR. On the other hand, AES-GMAC is defined as the resulting AES-GCM specification where only additional data is given as input, without any confidential data. AES-GMAC is simply an authentication mode on this additional data."

Aster found this correlation between CTR, GCM, and GMAC very peculiar, so she jotted down the idea of such a correlation to more easily distinguish the various AES modes of operation. She wrote the following: "No additional data means GCM is basically CTR; GMAC is GCM without confidential data." Meanwhile, with his typical methodical and mathematical pace, Luca was introducing new details.

"By far, the most common use case for AES-GCM is to encrypt, decrypt, and authenticate packets and data sent over the internet via network protocols. For example, famous and commonly used protocols like TLS, MACsec, and IPsec are based on an underlying AES-GCM implementation."

Keeping up with her notes, Aster recorded Luca's descriptions of the AES-GCM encryption operation, officially called Authenticated Encryption to better highlight the authenticity capability of the mode. The inputs for Authenticated Encryption are the key, the supported input-output lengths, the supported tag length, an initialization vector IV, the plaintext (i.e. the data to be both encrypted and authenticated), and the additional authenticated data, or AAD for short. The outputs for this Authenticated Encryption are the ciphertext and the Tag.

"Let us see first how the ciphertext is generated," said Luca, adding a dramatic pause, "and then we will see how the tag is generated."

"To generate the ciphertext, an operation called Galois Counter is applied on the plaintext using data derived from the IV as an initial counter block. This 'Galois Counter' operation coincides with the AES-CTR operation, but it defines a specific incrementing function, i.e., a specific method to generate the next counter block by incrementing the previous one."

"Then, to generate the tag, a Galois Counter operation is applied, using data derived from the IV as initial counter block, on the Galois Hash digest of the concatenation of the padded AAD, of the padded ciphertext, and of their corresponding lengths. The 'Galois Hash' operation is a peculiar hash operation used exclusively for the AES-GCM mode."

As the diagram (Fig. 6.9 taken from [9]) of the GCM Authenticated Encryption popped up, Aster worked to copy it to her notes, making sure to highlight that the inputs of the function are the plaintext P, the initialization vector IV, and the additional data A, whereas the outputs of the function are the ciphertext C and the tag T.

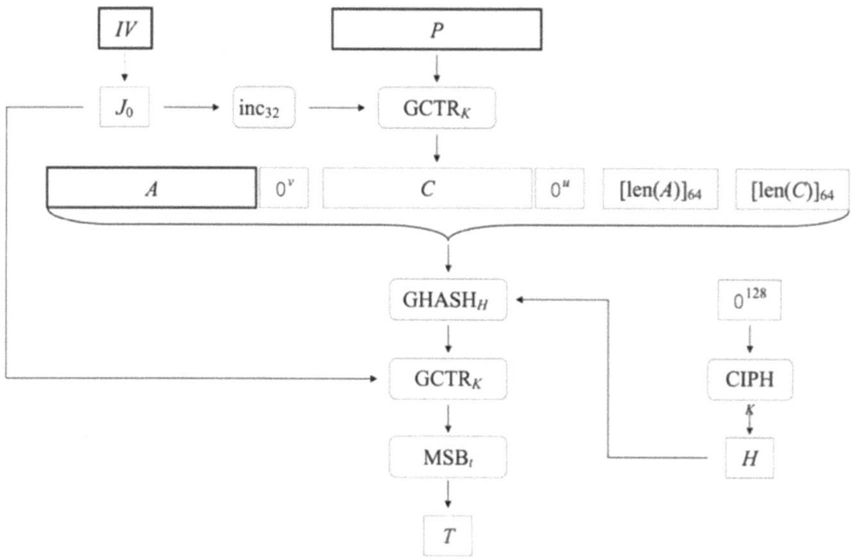

Fig. 6.9 GCM authenticated encryption

Luca took time to also highlight the following: "As specified in the FIPS 140-3 Implementation Guidance document [10], Section 2.4.A, the Galois Hash is non-approved by FIPS as a standalone cryptographic algorithm, and it is allowed only within an AES-GCM implementation."

"Now that we know how the Authenticated Encryption operation works, understanding the AES-GCM Authenticated Decryption operation is a piece of cake. In fact, this decryption operation coincides with the encryption operation, except for the following quirks," he continued, and then pulled up a list of details it was important to keep in mind for the operation:

- the inputs of the Authenticated Decryption contain a ciphertext in place of the plaintext and an additional 'provided input tag';
- the output of the Authenticated Decryption is either the original plaintext or an error message indicating the inauthenticity of the inputs;

the Authenticated Decryption starts by checking the bit lengths of the IV, of the AAD, of the ciphertext, and of the provided input tag, so that the inauthenticity error is returned if they do not coincide with the expected lengths of these parameters;

- the Galois Counter operation is applied on the ciphertext to obtain the plaintext, whereas in the encryption this operation was applied on the plaintext to obtain the ciphertext; and
- the final operation of the Authenticated Decryption is a tag comparison.

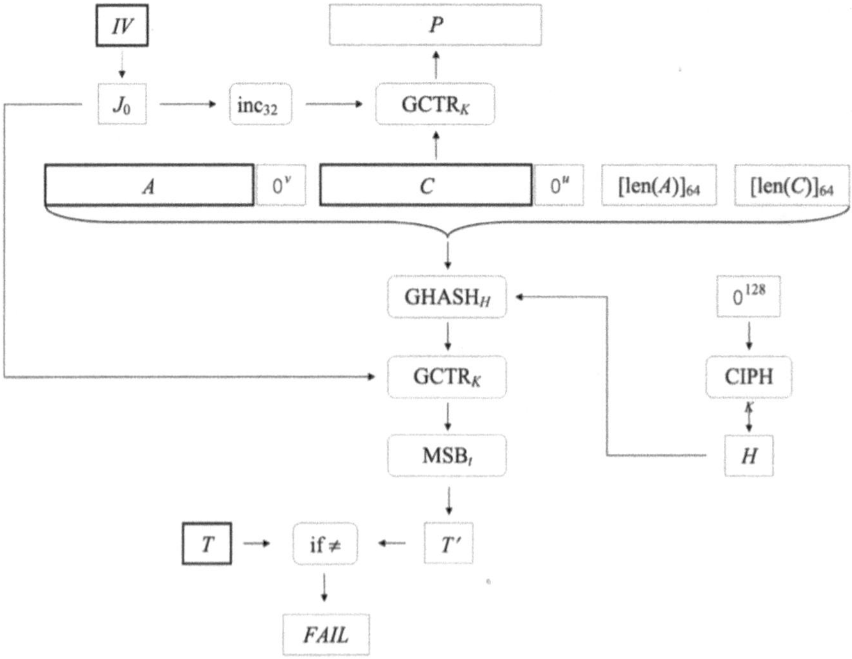

Fig. 6.10 GCM authenticated decryption

The tag comparison works by checking that the provided input tag coincides with an expected tag; the latter is computed on-the-fly using the ciphertext and the AAD. Then, the plaintext is returned; otherwise, the authenticity error is returned.

To illustrate the information discussed, Luca pulled up a diagram (Fig. 6.10 taken from [11]) of the GCM Authenticated Decryption operation.

"Note that the inputs of the function are the ciphertext C, the initialization vector IV, the additional data A, and the provided tag T, whereas the output of the function is either the ciphertext C or the error message FAIL," he said.

At this stage, Aster found it easy to see how the Authenticated Encryption and the Authenticated Decryption operations of the AES-GMAC mode are defined starting from their corresponding GCM operations. With minor tweaks, the Authenticated Encryption and the Authenticated Decryption operations of GCM can support as input an empty plaintext and an empty ciphertext, respectively.

"And now," said Luca with an odd tone of mystery in his voice, "it is finally time to tackle the AES-GCM requirements…"

"NIST SP 800-38D enlists numerous 'shall' requirements, but the most crucial ones to keep in mind are the ones regarding the following topics: the length of the tag and the uniqueness of the IV-key pair."

He elaborated further: "NIST requires the bit length of the tag to be one of the following values: 32, 64, 96, 104, 112, 120, 128. NIST provides further guidance and additional requirements for the use of the 32- and 64-bit tag lengths in Appendix C of

NIST SP 800-38D. In fact, these two shorter tag lengths, if handled erroneously, are almost problematically short. This is why they are mainly used in special applications such as memory-constrained environments."

"Also, NIST requires that the probability of invoking the Authenticated Encryption function with the same IV and the same key on more than one distinct set of input data shall be lower than a certain threshold. NIST highlights that this requirement is almost as important as the secrecy of the input AES key, and further motivates its rationale by stating that a ciphertext forgery can be easily constructed by an attacker if IVs are ever repeated under one given key for the GCM Authenticated Encryption function."

To vary his lecture a bit and to involve the students, Luca posed a question to the audience: "Does anyone of you remember what a ciphertext forgery attack is?"

While a few hands were timidly raising, Aster's hand shot up immediately; when Luca gestured for her to take the floor, she gave as thorough an answer as she could: "As the name suggests, a ciphertext forgery attack consists in creating a valid ciphertext which decrypts into a specified plaintext without the knowledge of the original plaintext or of the original key. The ciphertext forgery caused by the IV repetition not only completely breaks the authentication assurance of AES-GCM, but it also leads to an easily controllable plaintext as the output of the Authenticated Decryption function because of the malleability of the underlying AES-CTR mode."

"Excellent!" Luca cheered with a clap, "And NIST is fully aware of the difficulties of implementing this IV-key uniqueness requirement. Because of this, SP 800-38D [9] specifies the only two approved methods of constructing the IVs for AES-GCM and AES-GMAC—one deterministic, one random—and includes an additional requirement regarding the maximum number of invocations of the Authenticated Encryption function for each implementation that does not use 96-bit IVs generated by the approved deterministic construction."

"Furthermore, the FIPS 140-3 Implementation Guidance document has the IG C.H Section dedicated to the topic of meeting such requirements while using the mode of operation inside the TLS, MACsec, and IPsec network protocols."

"As a final note for this section of my lecture," added Luca, "we can highlight the fact that NIST approves two other AES modes of operations which are a slight variation of AES-GCM: AES-GCM-SIV and AES-XPN."

"AES-GCM-SIV stands for Synthetic IV and it is specified in the IETF RFC 8452 [11] document. This mode of operation provides an Authenticated Encryption function which is 'nonce misuse-resistant,' meaning that encrypting two messages using the same IV—which the RFC calls a 'nonce'—with this mode of operation only discloses whether the two messages were equal or not. This is the minimum amount of information that can be leaked by a deterministic algorithm in a similar situation, and it is a strong assurance that can replace the IV-key uniqueness requirements in situations where this uniqueness cannot be guaranteed, such as when multiple encryptors use the same key."

Reviewing a new slide Luca pulled up, Aster quickly jotted down how the nonce misuse-resistance is achieved: the Authenticated Encryption of AES-GCM-SIV deviates from the AES-GCM counterpart in the following aspects:

- SIV uses a variation of the Galois Hash function;
- SIV creates a tag using the AAD and the plaintext (whereas AES-GCM directly used the AAD and the ciphertext); and
- SIV uses its created tag as the initial counter block of the AES-CTR call.

In its Authenticated Encryption operation, AES-GCM-SIV requires two passes on the plaintext to achieve the nonce misuse-resistance. This implies that, in practice, this mode is slightly slower than the pure AES-GCM, and it also implies that AES-GCM-SIV loses the possibility of encrypting and transmitting portions of the entire message before ending the encryption operation.

AES-XPN, instead, stands for eXtended Packet Number, and it is specified in the IEEE 802.1AE standard. As the "Packet Number" part of the acronym highlights, it is a variation of the AES-GCM which supports a 64-bit Packet Number (a.k.a. PN) instead of the classical 32-bit PN to allow more packets to be sent under a single key. This variation is used specifically for the MACsec protocol, and this packet-number extension is able to retain the existing MACsec frame format in the IV by continuing to communicate only the least significant 32 bits of the PN.

AES-XTS: Confidentiality for Data at Rest "Last but not least, we have the AES-XTS mode," said Luca with a gleaming smile—they were in the home stretch now.

"XTS stands for 'Xor-encrypt-xor Tweakable block cipher with ciphertext Stealing'; yes, this acronym is a bit of a mouthful," Luca joked as he continued. "But the acronym actually refers to what the underlying algorithm is doing. The NIST AES-XTS requirements are specified in SP 800-38E [12] and in the FIPS 140-3 Implementation Guidance, but the algorithm itself is defined in IEEE Std 1619-2007."

"AES-XTS was specifically designed for the cryptographic protection of data at rest in storage devices which use a fixed-length of 'data unit.' In this context, the term 'data unit' means a sector of the entire data to be encrypted. The idea is that the entire plaintext or payload to be encrypted consists of one or more data units, and that a data unit consists of at least one complete AES 128-bit blocks, followed by some other complete blocks, and ending with either a complete or partial block."

Oh, I see, this can be seen as a partition, thought Aster, jotting that down. NIST highlights the fact that other approved AES modes of operation can be used to protect data at rest, but that obviously the AES-XTS mode cannot be used for other purposes, because of its design philosophy.

"A very peculiar and noteworthy feature of XTS", Luca took care to mention, "is the fact that it uses a pair of keys in its encryption and decryption. The key pair is made up of either two 128-bit AES keys for AES-128 or two 256-bit AES keys for AES-256. This implies that AES-XTS is the only AES mode of operation fully included in a NIST standard that does not support 192-bit keys and/or AES-192. How peculiar, eh?"

As he continued teaching, he made it clear that, in the AES-XTS encryption, the selected pair of AES keys is used both to compute a so-called tweak value and to later encrypt the payload using the order of operations of its acronym: an exclusive-OR, followed by an encryption operation, followed by an exclusive-OR; the tweak value gives the "tweakable" adjective in the acronym. Lastly, the "ciphertext stealing" part of the acronym refers to the fact that a technique somewhat similar to the one used in AES-CBC-CS1 involving the final ciphertexts being used to allow the last block of a data unit to be partial. NIST even allows a mechanism for swapping the last complete block and the partial block in an implementation of AES-XTS and in storage, so long as the retrieval mechanism is consistent with itself.

"The AES-XTS decryption operation involves the use of the inverse cipher function, but it also involves analogous steps as the one seen in the AES-XTS encryption. It starts by computing a tweak value, it uses this tweak during the exclusive-OR/decryption/exclusive-OR phase and ends with a mechanism to revert the ciphertext-stealing step," Luca detailed.

"A few additional details before we wrap things up, though," Luca cut in. "In SP 800-38E, NIST highlights that all requirements specified in IEEE Std 1619-2007 shall be followed, and it adds one more requirement. NIST imposes a restriction on the AES-block length of the data unit for any instance of an implementation of AES-XTS."

"Furthermore, Section C.I of the FIPS 140-3 Implementation Guidance clarifies that a successful explicit verification of the possession of two distinct keys inside the AES-XTS key pair is required before using any AES-XTS key pair. Indeed, if the 2 keys in the AES key pair are equal, it is possible to mount an attack which is able to undermine the main security assurances of AES-XTS."

Conclusion It had been a long lecture, and Luca kept his energy high to bring things to a memorable close. "We have finally reached the end of our insightful journey analyzing AES, the indisputable king of the symmetric block ciphers. AES is like an indestructible Roman Colosseum! This substitution-permutation network, standardized in 2001, still holds strong today, and it has been used for countless encryption and decryption operations for the last 24—and counting—years. Its success is mainly due to its publicly analyzed design and to the flexibility provided by its supported key lengths and its modes of operations. Look, there is even a niche approved AES mode of operation called 'format-preserving' that can be deployed in systems which do not use binary strings, but a finite set of arbitrary symbols! For the curious reader, this approved mode is specified in SP 800-38G [13]."

After all was said, Luca deactivated the FIPS 'n' Chips virtualized restaurant and dismissed the lecture. Aster packed her notes up, thanked Luca in person, and talked a bit with some students and atsec workers before departing.

She decided to even go for a jog around Mueller lakeside later that same day. While jogging she couldn't help but think to herself: "AES can be used for key wrapping, for providing assurance of data authenticity, and for providing assurance of data confidentiality, both at rest in a storage device or in transit via an internet protocol. It is truly a marvelous algorithm of our modern times!" (Fig. 6.11).

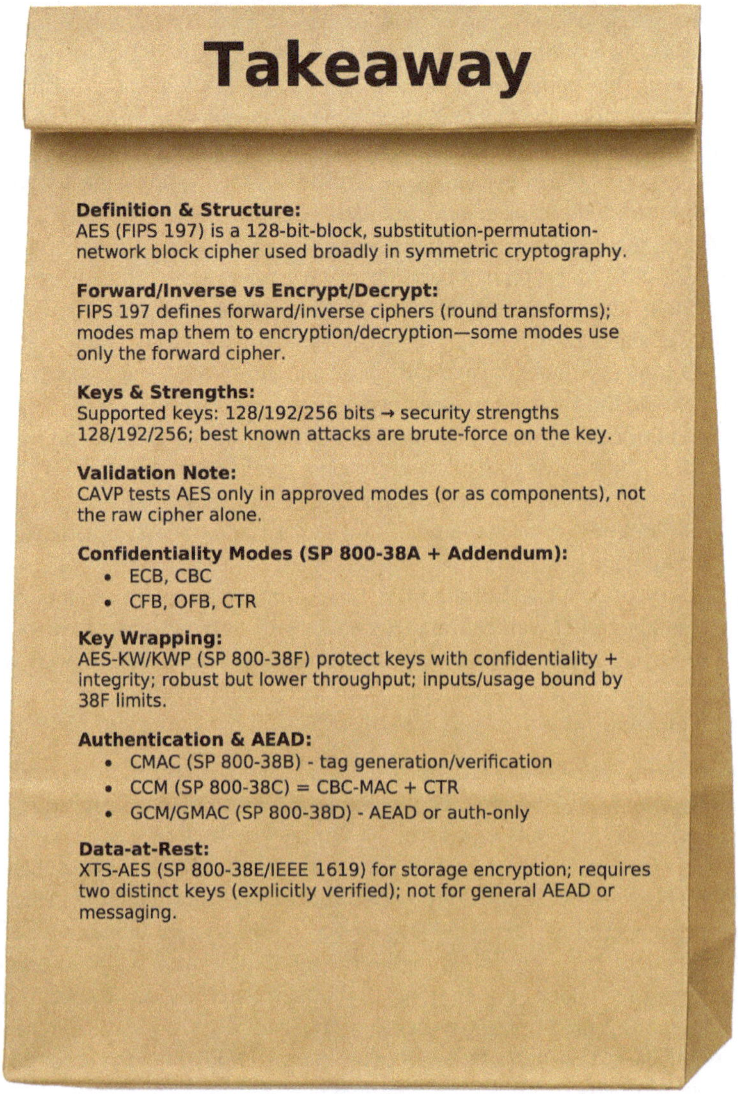

Fig. 6.11 Takeaways regarding the AES algorithm

References

1. National Institute of Standards and Technology (2001) Federal information processing standard (FIPS) 197: advanced encryption standard (AES). Available via NIST, National Institute of Standards and Technology. https://doi.org/10.6028/NIST.FIPS.197-upd1.. Last accessed 08 Dec 2025
2. Svard J (1999) AES (Rijndael) Round Function. https://en.wikipedia.org/wiki/File:AES_(Rijndael)_Round_Function.png. Last accessed 11 Dec 2025

3. Dworkin M (2001) NIST special publication 800-38A: recommendation for block cipher modes of operation: methods and techniques. Available via NIST, National Institute of Standards and Technology. https://doi.org/10.6028/NIST.SP.800-38A.. Last accessed 08 Dec 2025
4. Dworkin M (2010) Addendum to NIST Special Publication 800-38A: recommendation for block cipher modes of operation: three variants of Ciphertext stealing for CBC mode. Available via NIST, National Institute of Standards and Technology. https://doi.org/10.6028/NIST.SP.800-38A-Add. Last accessed 08 Dec 2025
5. Barker E, Roginsky A (2024) NIST special publication 800-131A, revision 3, initial public draft: transitioning the use of cryptographic algorithms and key lengths. Available via NIST, National Institute of Standards and Technology. https://doi.org/10.6028/NIST.SP.800-131Ar3.ipd. Accessed 08 Dec 2025
6. Dworkin M (2012) NIST special publication 800-38F: recommendation for block cipher modes of operation: methods for key wrapping. Available via NIST, National Institute of Standards and Technology. https://doi.org/10.6028/NIST.SP.800-38F.. Last accessed 08 Dec 2025
7. Dworkin M (2005) NIST Special Publication 800-38B: recommendation for block cipher modes of operation: the CMAC mode for authentication. Available via NIST, National Institute of Standards and Technology. https://doi.org/10.6028/NIST.SP.800-38B.. Last accessed 08 Dec 2025
8. Dworkin M (2004) NIST Special Publication 800-38C: recommendation for block cipher modes of operation: the CCM mode for authentication and confidentiality. Available via NIST, National Institute of Standards and Technology. https://doi.org/10.6028/NIST.SP.800-38C.. Last accessed 08 Dec 2025
9. Dworkin M (2007) NIST Special Publication 800-38D: recommendation for block cipher modes of operation: Galois/Counter Mode (GCM) and GMAC. Available via NIST, National Institute of Standards and Technology. https://doi.org/10.6028/NIST.SP.800-38D.. Last accessed 08 Dec 2025
10. National Institute of Standards and Technology, Canadian Centre for Cyber Security (2020) FIPS 140-3 IG: implementation guidance for FIPS 140-3 and the cryptographic module validation program, Section 2.4.A. NIST and CCCS. Available via NIST. https://csrc.nist.gov/csrc/media/Projects/cryptographic-module-validation-program/documents/fips%20140-3/FIPS%20140-3%20IG.pdf. Last accessed 08 Dec 2025
11. Gueron S, Langley A, Lindell Y (2019) AES-GCM-SIV: nonce misuse-resistant authenticated encryption. RFC 8452. https://doi.org/10.17487/RFC8452. https://www.rfc-editor.org/info/rfc8452. Last accessed 08 Dec 2025
12. Dworkin M (2010) NIST Special Publication 800-38E: recommendation for block cipher modes of operation: the XTS-AES mode for confidentiality on storage devices. National Institute of Standards and Technology. Available via NIST. https://nvlpubs.nist.gov/nistpubs/Legacy/SP/nistspecialpublication800-38e.pdf. Last accessed 08 Dec 2025
13. Dworkin M (2016) NIST special publication 800-38G: recommendation for block cipher modes of operation: methods for format-preserving encryption. National Institute of Standards and Technology. Available via NIST. https://doi.org/10.6028/NIST.SP.800-38G. Last accessed 08 Dec 2025

Luca Di Domenico Luca, 25 years old, lives in Rome, Italy. He has a bachelor's degree in mathematics and a master's degree in mathematics applied to Cryptography. He went to a literature-focused high school, where he studied ancient Latin and Greek.

Having already encountered some NIST standards during his master's degree, Luca is glad that he has the opportunity to apply them to real-world applications by joining atsec.

Chapter 7
Secure Hash Algorithms

Jeremy Wesevich

Properties of Hash Functions. After responding to the last email of the day, Aster packed up her laptop and began her walk home. Each day, she looks forward to this walk as a chance to get some fresh air and solitude, but she knew that today's walk wouldn't be quite up to par. She'd forgotten her earbuds again, which meant another walk without music. "Still," she thought to herself, "it's nice to stop for a moment and actually listen to the world around me." Caught in this moment of reflection, she didn't notice as Stephan sauntered up beside her.

"I see you're not listening to your random noise today" he said, catching Aster off guard.

After composing herself, she retorted "you know I like classical music too, right? Also, this isn't random noise, it's breakcore. You should be able to tell the difference, seeing as you work with random noise for Entropy Source Validations all the time."

Stephan smiled and let out a chuckle. "You've got a point there. But in all seriousness, you've forgotten your earbuds again, haven't you? What is this, the third time this week?"

"Yeah…" sighed Aster. "I just have so much to think about in the morning when I'm getting ready to come into the office, and they slip my mind."

"I might have just the trick for you," said Stephan. "You see, you don't actually need to remember to grab them every day. Instead, just remember the number of things that you should have in your pocket. Then, as you're leaving in the morning, just check your pockets against that number. If the number doesn't match, you know that something is wrong and can figure it out."

"Hmmm, that's a neat little memory trick," Aster mused. "Still, say I'm having some grapes with my breakfast and absentmindedly pocket one, then forget to grab the earbuds. In that case, I've got the right number but the wrong items."

J. Wesevich (✉)
atsec information security corporation, Austin, TX, USA
e-mail: jeremy.wesevich@atsec.com

Y. Mao (ed.), *Tasting Cryptography*, https://doi.org/10.1007/978-3-032-30243-4_7

"Aha, that's exactly right! You have two sets of items, which when fed into the 'count' function, yield the same result. Do you know what we cryptographers call that?"

"That would be a collision, right?"

"Exactly! And now that I think about it, there's many useful parallels we can draw here. How about we go hash this out at FIPS 'n' Chips?"

A short journey later, Aster found herself sitting across from an excited Stephan. Upon decrypting the menu, that excitement only increased; a new menu item was displayed in bold monospace:

```
CRYPTOGRAPHICALLY SECURE HASH BROWNS
```

"How do you make hash browns cryptographically secure?" thought Aster. Meanwhile, Stephan read the description provided beneath the title. After a moment, he explained:

"Well, claiming that these hash browns are cryptographically secure is bold, but I understand where they're coming from. You see, they've got a new robot chef specifically programmed for this project. It performs a 3D-scan of a given potato, then takes a SHA2-256 hash of the resulting file. That hash is transformed into a series of instructions that the chef uses to chop and cook the potato."

"Huh, that's an interesting concept," replied Aster, thinking it over in her head. "Then, if you were to give it two identical potatoes, the resulting hash browns should also be identical."

"Exactly. Assuming that the robot's movements are sufficiently precise, the chef should perform precisely the same actions on both potatoes, resulting in two indistinguishable hash browns." Stephan paused for a second, and chuckled. "Of course, we'll never get two potatoes which are precisely the same down to the atom, and the scanner has finite resolution, but we can imagine an ideal case."

"Sure, it's just a few minor simplifications, like in a physics problem." Aster tilted her head. "Still, I'm not seeing how this relates to cryptographic security, other than the fact that there's a SHA function mixed in there. Can you explain?"

"Of course," said Stephan, "but first you need to explain what you understand about hash functions."

Collision Resistance Aster thought for a moment, then proceeded. "Well, I know that hash functions can take in as much data as they want and will always output a fixed-length string. This makes them useful for checking the integrity of large files, as instead of comparing the entire file, you can simply hash it and compare the hashes. They're also used as part of other cryptographic operations, such as HMAC and signature operations."

"Very good!" exclaimed Stephan. "Hashes are indeed used for checking integrity, but also much more than that. Many cryptographic operations are slow, and not all of them can process an unlimited amount of data. Using hash functions allows us to transform large data into digests that are, well, digestible by other functions. As an example, all approved signature schemes involve hashing a message then signing the resulting digest."

"Ok, but what if two different messages hashed to the same digest? Then, a signature on one could also serve as a signature on the other. That could be confusing at best or dangerous at worst, depending on the messages involved."

"That's a very astute observation, Aster. Such a case is something that must be avoided. In particular, we want our hash functions to have collision resistance. Stated simply, a hash function has collision resistance if it is difficult to find two different inputs which hash to the same value." Stephan looked over at the robot chef, then back at Aster. "Let's call our pocket count earlier Function A, and the process of hash brown preparation Function B. Would you say that Function A has collision resistance? What about Function B?"

Aster was quick to reply. "Well, clearly Function A doesn't have collision resistance, that's how we started this whole conversation in the first place. It's easy to pick two groups of different objects where both groups have the same number of objects. Function B on the other hand could be argued to have collision resistance, as two different potatoes will most likely yield two different cutting and cooking routines. It's not impossible that two different routines could result in identical hash browns, at least up to some reasonable measure, but my intuition says it's unlikely."

Stephan raised an eyebrow. "Good, Function A certainly does not have collision resistance. I agree that Function B could, though we'd need some cryptography experts to study that robot to say that with any confidence. However, I disagree with your premise that collision resistance is what started this conversation. You see, collision resistance says it should be difficult to find any pair of inputs which hash to the same value, no matter what that value is. In contrast, we were talking about a collision with regard to a particular input, namely the items that should be in your pocket when you leave your house in the morning."

Aster sat in contemplation for a full minute while Stephan waited patiently for her to think. Finally, she exhaled and admitted "I'm afraid I don't see any substantial difference between the two. Why do we draw this distinction?"

Second Pre-image Resistance "Well, consider the digital signature case. Let's say that I'm drawing up a contract, but it won't be binding until you sign it. I can change the formatting, or add hidden characters, or modify the contract in any number of different ways, but have it still say the same thing. If, for any such modification, I can find a collision with a different contract, perhaps one that you would find completely unacceptable, then I can give you that contract to sign, then present the signature as proof that you agreed to the terms you never even saw. Because I have some control over the input, it's important that it's hard to find any collision."

Aster took a moment to digest the scenario. Then, thinking out loud, she said, "and this is distinct from, say, a case where I've got a really important file on my computer that I've hashed so that I can check its integrity. Then, there's only that one correct digest. If someone malicious wanted to try to replace the file without my knowledge, they only have influence over their file and its hash."

"Precisely!" exclaimed Stephan. "This second property has a name: second pre-image resistance. In short, a hash function has second pre-image resistance if, given a randomly chosen input, it is difficult to find another input which hashes to the same value as the first input. From the malicious person's perspective in your example, your file was chosen with no consideration of its hash value, and thus second pre-image resistance is relevant while collision resistance is not."

"Sure, that makes sense." Aster paused to think. "Still, I have a bit of a hard time separating the two; how would you get a hash function that has one but not the other?"

"Well, let's construct an example that has second pre-image resistance but lacks collision resistance. Let's start with SHA2-256, a canonical hash function from FIPS 180-4. We'll have two paths that an input can take: if the input starts with 256 zeros, then the resulting hash is just 256 zeros. In all other cases, we run SHA2-256 on the input. Clearly, we don't have collision resistance, as I can easily pick any two strings, prepend 256 zeros, and find that they hash to the same value. However, if we choose a message at random, it's overwhelmingly likely that the first 256 bits aren't zero, so we inherit the second pre-image resistance of SHA2-256."

Aster nodded. "So, back to our examples, Function A clearly doesn't have second pre-image resistance, but again I think an argument could be made for Function B. Given two different potatoes, it seems highly unlikely that their scans would yield a set of actions which produce the same hash brown."

Pre-image Resistance "Agreed," said Stephan, "though as before, some study would be needed to claim that with any certainty. Now, before we move on, there's one final property that you should be aware of, namely pre-image resistance. A hash function has pre-image resistance if, given a random hash value, it's difficult to find an input which hashes to that value."

"So, the key difference between pre-image resistance and second pre-image resistance is that we're not given the input, just the hash. What difference does that make in practice?" asked Aster.

"Conceptually, the difference is whether or not our adversary has access to the input, or just the resulting hash. Ideally, we don't want the knowledge of the input to make it any easier for them to find a collision." Stephan took a moment to collect his thoughts, then continued. "Let's go back to your example with the file. Say that you've moved the file to a USB drive and have written a program on your computer that looks for that file on any USB drive that's connected. If the file cannot be found, or it doesn't hash to the digest you have stored, then the computer refuses to interface with the drive. Now say an adversary has snooped the digest but doesn't have your USB drive with the file. In this scenario, they only have access to the digest, so pre-image resistance applies."

Aster considered this for a while, then suddenly brightened. "I think I've got a function that has pre-image resistance but lacks second pre-image resistance. As before, we'll use SHA2-256 as a base. An input message is broken into 256-bit chunks, padded with zeros to a multiple of 512 bits. To process the input, we take the SHA2-256 hash of the last 512-bit portion, then repeatedly XOR the result with each other 256-bit chunk. The result is output as the hash value." She paused to take a breath, then continued. "If an adversary only has the hash value, they should be no better off than if we ran SHA2-256 over the entire input. However, if they also have the input message, they can use that as a base. As long as their changes XOR to zero when broken into 256-bit chunks, and they don't touch the last 512 bits, the resulting hash value is the same!"

Stephan considered the function for a moment, then nodded in affirmation. “Indeed, that function has pre-image resistance but not second pre-image resistance. Good work.”

Aster beamed at the praise, then continued. “Yet again, our Function A lacks pre-image resistance. Given a number, it’s easy to find a set of objects that counts to that number. However, for Function B, it sounds extremely difficult to look at a hash brown, figure out a set of steps that could be performed to make it, then find a potato whose scan maps to such a set of steps. Again, Function B probably has this property.”

“Very good!” exclaimed Stephan. “You’re showing some real understanding here. As with the other properties, it would take much more analysis to conclude that the robot’s hashing function indeed has pre-image resistance, but it would certainly appear to at first glance.”

“All right,” said Aster. “Now that I’ve proven myself, how about we actually order something?”

FIPS Standards A few short minutes later, Aster and Stephan each sat in front of a plate containing a single meticulously crafted hash brown. Each order also came with a USB flash drive containing 3D scans of both the hash and the original potato. Stephan turned his over to reveal a label on the back. “Test vector,” he read aloud. Suddenly understanding, he chuckled. “I guess I’ll need to add this to the proxy,” he jested.

Aster rolled her eyes. “I don’t think NIST is going to be standardizing potato hashing anytime soon,” she retorted.

“No, probably not. Even if we had a nice proof of security, I think there would be numerous implementation difficulties, not to mention the high processing time of waiting for the hash brown to cook.” Stephan took a bite, then looked up. “While we’re here, why don’t you tell me what you know about the hash functions that NIST has standardized?”

Aster finished her bite, then began. “Well, I know that we’ve got two standards, FIPS 180–4 [1] and FIPS 202 [2]. FIPS 180–4 includes both SHA-1 and the SHA-2 family, which all share similar constructions. FIPS 202 defines the SHA-3 family, as well as a few extra functions called SHAKE128 and SHAKE256.” She paused and looked at Stephan, who nodded at her to continue. “SHA-1 is just a single function, but the SHA-2 family consists of SHA2-224, SHA2-256, SHA2-384, and SHA2-512. SHA-1 produces a 160-bit digest, while the number after each SHA2 function gives the length of its respective digest. Oh, and there’s also SHA2-512/224 and SHA2-512/256, which have 224- and 256-bit digests respectively.”

Security Strengths of Hash Functions “And what’s so important about the length of the digest?” asked Stephan.

“Well, a hash function with a longer digest should be able to support a higher security strength, but we just talked about all of these different security properties of hash functions and I’m not entirely sure how they correspond.”

Stephan continued to probe. “You’re correct, we have different properties of hash functions, and those properties are applicable to different scenarios. How would you rank the strength of these properties?”

Aster took a minute to think and finish her meal. After polishing off the hashbrown, she spoke. “Well, from an attacker’s point of view, it’s definitely easier to find a collision between any two messages than a collision with a particular message, so I’d expect a hash function to have more second pre-image resistance than collision resistance. You mentioned earlier that knowing the input shouldn’t make it much easier to find a collision, so hash functions should have nearly the same amount of pre-image resistance and second pre-image resistance. Because the attacker only gets the hash in the pre-image case, a hash function should have slightly more pre-image resistance than second pre-image resistance, if there’s a difference at all.”

Stephan nodded and smiled. “Excellent thinking, that’s all correct. As listed in SP 800–107 Rev. 1 [3], all hash functions in the SHA-1 and SHA-2 families have less collision resistance than second pre-image resistance, and equal or less second pre-image resistance than pre-image resistance. Except for very large inputs, we expect pre-image resistance to be roughly equal to second pre-image resistance. Collision resistance should be equal to half the digest length, while pre-image resistance should be equal to the digest length.”

Aster considered for a moment, then replied “what do you mean by ‘should’? Do we not know for certain?”

“These functions are quite difficult to reason about, but no one has found attacks which are better than brute force for pre-images or the birthday attack for collisions.” Stephan cracked a tiny smile. “Well, at least for most of these. In 2017, a joint team at CWI Amsterdam and Google Research demonstrated a collision attack on SHA-1 which took computational effort equivalent to about 263 hashes, thus breaking collision resistance by a factor of 217.” [4]

Aster looked taken aback. “So, SHA-1 has been broken, but it’s still approved and in the standard? I thought the CMVP was usually quite cautious when it came to any potential security concern.”

Stephan raised an eyebrow. “Correction: collision resistance in SHA-1 has been broken. Thus, SHA-1 may not be used in cases where collision resistance is required, most notably in digital signature applications. And CMVP was aware of this attack long before it was successfully executed; SHA-1 was disallowed for digital signatures in 2011, 6 years before the CWI/Google paper. Furthermore, CMVP plans to sunset the algorithm for all use cases at the end of 2030.”

Aster nodded, and said “OK, that makes sense. I assume that SP 800–107 Rev. 1 tells us what security property is applicable for each use case of a hash function?”

“Exactly right,” affirmed Stephan. “Now, another question: do you know who designed these algorithms?”

Origins of SHA-1, SHA-2, and SHA-3 Aster thought for a moment. “If I recall correctly, both SHA-1 and SHA-2 were developed by the NSA. Why do you ask?”

Stephan countered with a question of his own. “Say someone that you don’t trust presents you with a new cryptographic algorithm that they’ve discovered. You study it for a while, and don’t see anything wrong with it. Are you going to start using that algorithm yourself?”

"Probably not," Aster replied. "I think my distrust in the person who created the algorithm would make me question any cryptanalysis performed on it, even if it was a perfectly good algorithm."

"You're not the only one to feel that way," said Stephan. "To help alleviate this concern in the case of SHA-1 and SHA-2, the designers chose what are called 'nothing up my sleeve numbers' for various constants used in the algorithms. These are numbers that are picked according to some definite pattern that doesn't relate at all to the algorithm, so it's clear that they aren't being picked for some nefarious reason known only to the designers. For example, SHA2-256 derives its constants from the cube roots of the first 64 prime numbers."

"Yeah, that makes sense," mused Aster. "I suppose it's just a further way to be transparent in algorithm design."

"Speaking of transparency in algorithm design, we haven't yet discussed SHA-3. How did we get SHA-3?"

"If I remember correctly, SHA-3 is the result of an open competition held by NIST. The winner of the competition was Keccak, which is now standardized as SHA-3."

"Exactly," confirmed Stephan. "And do you know why the competition was held?"

"Well, I would think that no one could reasonably distrust the result of an open competition. After all, there were submissions from research groups around the world, and all of the algorithms were available for study throughout the duration of the competition."

"Yes, that's certainly a byproduct of the competition design," replied Stephan. "However, that wasn't the main motivation. You see, SHA-2 uses the same general structure as SHA-1. In turn, SHA-1 was modeled after MD4 and MD5, which came before it. While SHA-2 remains secure today, all of its predecessors have shown cryptographic weaknesses. Ever cautious, NIST decided it would be prudent to standardize another hash function which does not share any structural similarities with SHA-1 and SHA-2. The SHA-3 family does not claim to be cryptographically stronger than SHA-2; instead, it provides redundancy."

Design and Uses of SHA-3 Aster took the moment to chime in. "That's not all that SHA-3 adds, right? It also includes some additional useful tools, such as extendable output functions and some additional derived functions."

Stephan nodded. "That's right; the Keccak function behind the SHA-3 family is very flexible. Keccak is a family of functions which are known as 'sponge functions' since they operate in two stages, an absorption stage, and a squeezing stage. During absorption, an arbitrary amount of data can be 'absorbed' by the function, changing the internal state along the way. Once all the data has been input, it moves to the squeezing stage, during which an arbitrary amount of data can be 'squeezed out'. This is in contrast to SHA-1 and SHA-2, where only a fixed amount of data can be output."

Aster leaned forward. "That squeezing is how we get extendable output functions, right? For the SHA-3 functions, the output length is fixed, but the SHAKE extendable output functions—er, XOFs—allow for customizable output length."

"Indeed. That being said, XOFs do have a property that isn't always desirable: They don't consider the requested output length when generating output. This means that if we both input the same data and I request 128 bits of output while you request 256 bits, my 128 bits will match your first 128 bits. In certain implementations, this could lead to unexpected security issues. Appendix A.2 of FIPS 202 provides more background on this."

Aster cocked her head. "Why would they choose to leave in this property? Surely they could include the requested output length in the input?"

"Yes, you could input the desired output length, and that would fix this issue of related outputs. However, sometimes the desired output length is not known when the function is called. SHAKE is designed so that it can take in some data, then start generating output and continue generating until told to stop. SHAKE provides that flexibility at the cost of a minor additional consideration. And, if a vendor wants a function with adjustable output length that doesn't produce related outputs, they can use KMAC, as defined in SP 800–185." [5]

"Right!" exclaimed Aster. "I'd forgotten that there's a whole Special Publication dedicated to additional functions derived from FIPS 202. SHA-3 really is flexible!"

Takeaways "Indeed, it is," affirmed Stephan. "And so are hash functions themselves. As we've discussed today, hashes are used in a myriad of situations. By transforming arbitrary length data into fixed length bitstrings, hashes provide small fingerprints for large files and prepare large amounts of data for further cryptographic processing. Operations such as digital signatures would be much more complex and expensive if entire messages had to be signed; by signing a hash of the message instead, we simplify the process and reduce the number of asymmetric operations required. The FIPS 180–4 and FIPS 202 standards provide redundancy and flexibility, and SP 800–185 provides additional hash and hash-adjacent functions to ensure that vendors always have access to the right tool for the job."

"I hadn't realized how much there is to know about hash functions," reflected Aster. "I knew that they were used in many ways, but I wasn't too familiar with the particular security properties that hash functions have. Just to confirm my understanding, let me repeat them back to you. Collision resistance is the difficulty of finding any two inputs which hash to the same output. Second pre-image resistance is the difficulty of finding a second input which hashes to the same value as some specified first input. Finally, pre-image resistance is the difficulty of finding any input which hashes to a specified value."

"Very good! I think you've learned a lot today, Aster. And not only about hash functions; if I remember correctly, our whole conversation started with some forgotten earbuds."

Aster laughed. "It did! Now I've got a hash value to check when leaving in the morning, so hopefully I won't be forgetting things anymore. Thanks for the lesson and the memory trick!"

"Of course," responded Stephan. "My pleasure. Enjoy the rest of your walk home!" (Fig. 7.1).

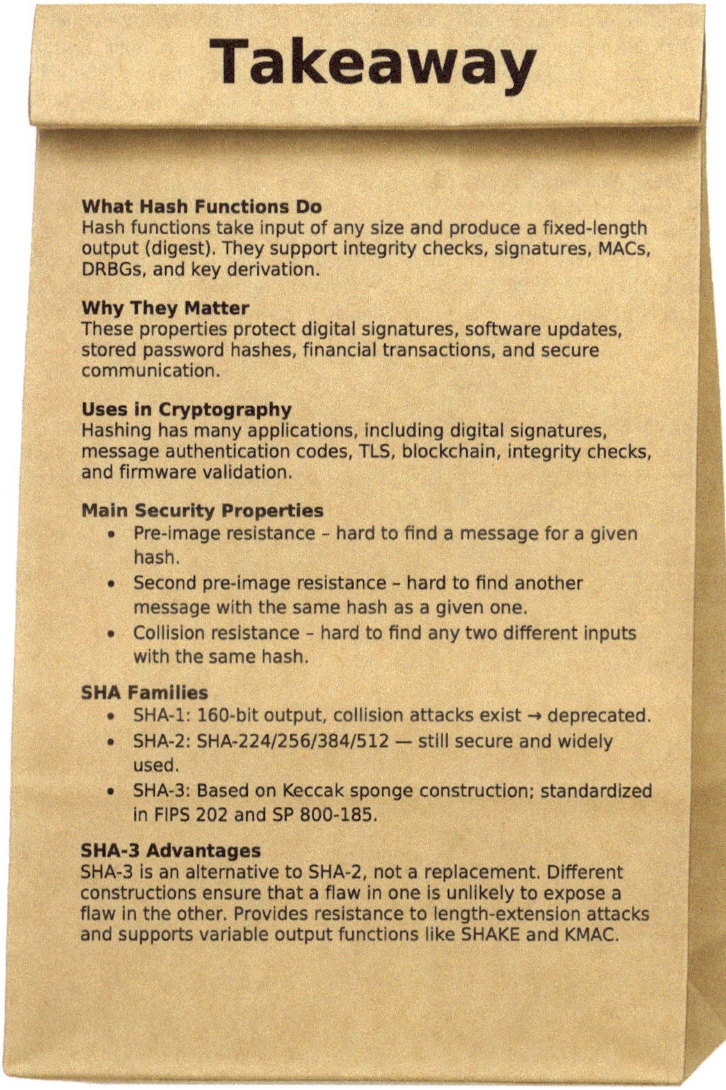

Fig. 7.1 Takeaways regarding SHA

References

1. National Institute of Standards and Technology (2015) Secure Hash Standard (SHS). In: NIST Publications. The National Institute of Standards and Technology. Available via NIST. https://csrc.nist.gov/pubs/fips/180-4/upd1/final. Accessed 20 Nov 2025

2. National Institute of Standards and Technology (2015) SHA-3 Standard: Permutation-Based Hash and Extendable-Output Functions. In: NIST Publications. The National Institute of Standards and Technology. Available via NIST. https://csrc.nist.gov/pubs/fips/202/final. Accessed 20 Nov 2025
3. Dang Q (2015) Recommendation for Applications Using Approved Hash Algorithms. In: NIST Publications. The National Institute of Standards and Technology. https://csrc.nist.gov/pubs/sp/800/107/r1/final. Accessed 20 Nov 2025
4. Stevens M, Bursztein E, Karpman P, Albertini A, Markov Y (2017) The first collision for full SHA-1. Advances in cryptology—CRYPTO 2017. Springer Cham, London, pp 537–596
5. Kelsey J, Chang S, Perlner R (2016) SHA-3 derived functions: cSHAKE, KMAC, TupleHash, and ParallelHash. In: NIST Publications. The National Institute of Standards and Technology. Available via NIST. https://csrc.nist.gov/pubs/sp/800/185/final. Accessed 20 Nov 2025

Jeremy Wesevich After being introduced to number theory in high school, Jeremy went on to study math, computer science, and physics at Oberlin College. At atsec, he now finds himself immersed in the world of cryptography, in which the power and elegance of mathematics races against the limits of computational technology.

Chapter 8
Key Derivation Functions

Francesco Paolo D'Erme

After a long and productive day of work, Francesco, an atsec colleagues, decides he'd earned himself a reward. He leaves the office and heads to the FIPS 'n' Chips restaurant for a good meal.

Dinner was his usual comfort: a perfectly grilled steak, a side of rosemary potatoes, and a small glass of red wine. Before heading back home, he walked towards the restaurant's counter to get himself a drink.

The bartender greeted him with a nod. "The usual, sir?".

Francesco smiled. "Of course."

He slid a folded napkin across the counter. On it were his secrets—a small collection of numbers and words that only he knew.

The bartender glanced at it briefly, nodded, and began his craft.

He reached for a small jar labeled Salt, added a precise pinch to a silver shaker, and poured in the rest of the ingredients. Then he began to shake slowly, rhythmically (counting under his breath).

After a long moment, he poured the drink into a crystal glass. Francesco took a sip. Perfect! Smooth, familiar, and entirely his.

A few stools down, another man had been watching. He leaned forward, curious.

"That looks incredible!" he said. "Make me the same one."

The bartender paused mid-motion. "I'm afraid I can't, sir."

The man frowned. "Why not? I saw what you did. Just follow the same steps."

The bartender smiled gently.

"Ah, but every drink here begins with something special. I mix it with a little salt to make it unique, even if someone brings the same secret tomorrow. Then I shake it again and again—hundreds, sometimes thousands of times—until the texture is smooth and strong. When I'm done, the original ingredients are gone; what's left is something new, something that can't be reversed."

F. P. D'Erme (✉)
atsec information security corporation, Austin, TX, USA
e-mail: francesco.derme@atsec.com

Y. Mao (ed.), *Tasting Cryptography*, https://doi.org/10.1007/978-3-032-30243-4_8

The man tilted his head. "So… you're saying I can't figure out what went into it?".

Francesco chuckled softly.

"That's exactly the point," he said. "What the bartender does, it's like a Key Derivation Function, a KDF. It takes a secret and turns it into something stronger and more secure: a cryptographic key. The salt makes every result unique, and all that shaking, the iterations, make it hard for anyone to copy or guess."

The man frowned thoughtfully. "So even if I know the recipe…".

"…you'll never get my drink," Francesco finished with a grin. "You can try, but without my secret, yours will always taste different. You could spend a lifetime shaking and never get the same flavor."

The bartender polished a glass, smiling.

"At this bar," he said, "every secret becomes its own creation. No imitations. No reversals."

The man hesitated, then moved closer to Francesco and the bartender. "What you are describing sounds amazing! Can you help me figure out how to turn my simple drinks into my own unique creations?".

"Well, of course! Mister…" Francesco replied.

"James!" The man finished.

"Okay, Mr. James, let's talk about KDFs, what would you like to know?"

An Introduction to Key Derivation Functions Mr. James wanted to start with the basics. "Can you explain what exactly a KDF is and what its purpose is?".

KDF is an acronym that stands for Key Derivation Function, and, as the name suggests, the purpose of this function is to derive a key from a set of inputs. In the cryptographic world, this is used when there is the need to expand some key material from already established secrets.

There are several types of KDFs and each of them take specific inputs in addition to the starting secret. Also, each type of KDF is based on the use of cryptographic primitives that internally provide the means to derive the key material.

In general, KDF goes through multiple steps to derive key material from an already existing secret.

First, the inputs are passed to the KDF and are generally comprised of:

- The existing starting secret which can be a key itself, but it can also be a password.
- Some fixed context data that are mixed in with the starting secret.
- Some additional unique data, which need not to be secret, such as a nonce or similar that renders the derivation unique even if the same secret is used twice.
- The cryptographic primitive to be used as the same KDF might support the use of more than one primitive.
- The number of iterations that the input data will go through before being output to the user.
- The length of the key material to produce in output.

The KDF will take the input and then will go through the specified number of iterations, exercising the specified cryptographic primitive at each iteration.

After going through all iterations, the KDF will provide in output a string of bits of the specified length, which represents the key material requested by the user.

Of course, each KDF has its own special iteration steps and takes its own specific set of inputs. The one above is just a general overview of the process that they all follow.

KDF Algorithms Mr. James was following, but uncertain on how to start. "Mmmh... Okay, so how many types of KDFs are there? How should I decide which one to use?".

Picking a KDF depends on your needs, but one determining factor is the kind of secret you want to give to this KDF. The key derivation process can start from an already existing key, from a shared secret that has been previously established between two parties, from a password, or it can also be computed specifically to the intrinsics of a specific protocol, such as TLS, for some very specific application scenarios.

KBKDF—Key-Based Key Derivation Function Mr. James appreciated the flexibility afforded. "Wow, so many options to choose from! Let's just say I have a key to start with... How go about deriving keying material from it?".

When deriving from a key, the input key that you are providing to the KDF function is called Key-Derivation-Key (or KDK).

The specific KDF that takes this key as input and derives new key material from it is called the Key-Based Key Derivation Function (or KBKDF) - the specifics and requirements of this KDF are defined in NIST SP 800–108 Rev. 1 [8].

These are the inputs that this function takes:

- Your KDK that must be an approved symmetric key according to NIST SP 800–133 Rev. 2 [10].
- Some static and context specific data that is divided into:
  - Label: this usually indicates what the purpose of the derived keying material will be (e.g., encryption, authentication, etc.).
  - Context: this is usually some additional information that is related to the environment in which the KDF is used (e.g., a session ID, a user ID, etc.).
  - L: the desired length of the keying material that you want to derive from your existing KDK.

All of these pieces of data are passed to a specific cryptographic primitive that is called PRF (or Pseudo-Random Function). Briefly, this is a deterministic function that takes in a secret key and an input string and produces an output that is computationally indistinguishable from random to anyone who does not know the key. In other words, the ones who know the input to a PRF will be able to compute the specific output. Others that are only disposing of the output of the PRF will not computationally be able to get back the input used to generate such output.

As possible PRFs, NIST SP 800–108 Rev. 1 [8] approves the following options:

- A keyed-Hash Message Authentication Code (HMAC) that makes use of any approved cryptographic hash function, as advised in FIPS 198–1 [2]

- A Cipher-base Message Authentication Code (CMAC) that makes use of an approved block cipher, as advised in NIST SP 800-38B [4]
- A Keccak-based Message Authentication Code (KMAC) that makes use of the Keccak algorithm, as advised in NIST SP 800–185 [12]

Depending on the length of the requested key material, these PRFs might be invoked multiple times. The method used for iterating multiple times over this PRF is called a mode of iteration. The standard defines three different modes of iteration plus one specific mode that is dedicated to the use of KMAC as a PRF.

KBKDF in Counter Mode The first mode of iteration is the counter mode, which can be used with both the HMAC and CMAC PRFs.

As the name suggests, this mode features a counter which is used as an iteration-dependent data. This counter starts with 1 and gets increased at each iteration. Its value is concatenated to the static and context specific data in input to the PRF. Thus, one iteration of this mode looks something like this:

$$\mathrm{K(i)} = \mathrm{PRF}(K_{IN}, [i]_2 \,\|\, \mathrm{Label} \,\|\, \mathrm{0x00} \,\|\, \mathrm{Context} \,\|\, [L]_2) \quad for\, i = 1, 2, \ldots, n \tag{8.1}$$

where:

- K_{IN} is the input key for our KDF.
- $[i]_2$ is a binary representation of the iteration-dependent counter that goes from 1 to n, where n is the number of total iterations to be performed. This number is determined based on the length of the output of a single iteration of the PRF and the length of the output requested by the user.
- Label, Context, $[L]_2$ are the static and context specific data that we identified in the introduction. Specifically, $[L]_2$ is a binary representation of the length of the output key material requested L
- 0x00 is just a byte separator (an all 0 s byte).

Special attention must be put in the case that CMAC is used as a PRF. As explained in Appendix B of NIST SP 800–108 Rev. 1 [8], a party that has knowledge of K_{IN} and can somehow select portions of the static and context specific data might be able to control the values of one or more of the produced K(i). To avoid this, the input to the PRF can be modified as follows:

$$\mathrm{K(i)} = \mathrm{PRF}(K_{IN}, [i]_2 \,\|\, \mathrm{Label} \,\|\, \mathrm{0x00} \,\|\, \mathrm{Context} \,\|\, [L]_2 \,\|\, \mathrm{K(0)}) \quad for\, i = 1, 2, \ldots, n \tag{8.2}$$

where:

$$\mathrm{K(0)} = \mathrm{PRF}(K_{IN}, \mathrm{Label} \,\|\, \mathrm{0x00} \,\|\, \mathrm{Context} \,\|\, [L]_2) \tag{8.3}$$

KBKDF in Feedback Mode Another possible mode of iteration is the feedback mode, where the iteration-dependent data consists of the result of the previous iteration plus an optional counter.

Thus, in this case, one iteration of this mode will look like this:

$$\text{K(i)} = \text{PRF}(K_{IN}, K(i-1)\{||[i]_2\}\ ||\text{Label}||\text{0x00}||\text{Context}\ ||\ [L]_2)\quad for\, i = 1, 2, \ldots, n \tag{8.4}$$

As you can see, the equation is quite similar to the previous one. One difference is the counter $[i]_2$, which is within brackets. This indicates that its use in this mode is optional.

The only fixed and iteration-dependent data in this equation is $K(i-1)$, which represents the result of the execution of the previous iteration. For the first iteration, for which there is no "previous" computed results, the iteration-dependent data is represented by an IV that will be passed as input to this mode of iteration.

Also in this case, special attention needs to be put in the case that CMAC is used as a PRF. An attacker who has knowledge of the K_{IN} and can somehow select portions of the IV, might be able to control the values of one or more of the produced K(i). To avoid this, the IV input to the PRF can be modified as follows:

$$\text{IV} = \text{PRF}(K_{IN}, \text{Label}\ ||\text{0x00}\ ||\text{Context}\ ||[L]_2) \tag{8.5}$$

KBKDF in Double Pipeline Mode The last mode of iteration that can be used with HMAC or CMAC is called double-pipeline. In the previous mode of iterations, the K(i) values were computed sequentially in a single pipeline of execution.

In this case, we will have two different pipelines operating in parallel. The first pipeline executes a feedback mode and produces A(i) values that will be used as inputs to the second pipeline. The latter will take these values and use them as iteration-dependent data to compute the K(i) values in output. This second pipeline can optionally feature a counter as an additional iteration-dependent data.

In practice, the first pipeline will start from the following initial value (IV):

$$\text{A(0)} = \text{PRF}(\text{Label}\ ||0 \times 00||\text{Context}\ ||[L]_2) \tag{8.6}$$

and, at each iteration, it will compute:

$$\text{A(i)} = \text{PRF}(K_{IN}, A(i-1))\quad fori = 1, 2, \ldots n \tag{8.7}$$

These values, at each iteration, will act as the inputs to the second pipeline which will compute:

$$\text{K(i)} = \text{PRF}(K_{IN}, A(i)\{||[i]_2\}\ ||\ \text{Label}\ ||0 \times 00||\text{Context}\ ||[L]_2)\quad for\ i = 1, 2, \ldots, n \tag{8.8}$$

Also in this case, the counter is optional. However, in the case we are using CMAC as a PRF, special care needs to be taken for an attacker that has knowledge of K_{IN} who could potentially control one or more K(i) values. In this case, we can counter this by making the use of the counter mandatory.

KBKDF using KMAC Finally, a special case to be considered is a KMAC-based KBKDF. The reason this is a special case is because a KMAC is a sponge function based on the Keccak algorithm, meaning that the KMAC, by itself, is capable of producing any bitstring of a desired length L.

For this reason, when KMAC is used as a PRF in the KBKDF construction, no iteration mode is needed, which isn't the case for HMAC and CMAC. In this case, the KBKDF execution will just result in applying the KMAC PRF as follows:

$$K_{OUT} = KMAC\#(K_{IN}, Context, L, Label) \tag{8.9}$$

where KMAC# can be any one of the KMAC128 or KMAC256 constructions defined in NIST SP 800–185 [12].

PBKDF—Password-Based Key Derivation Function Mr. James was quite happy with those options…but more never hurt, so he inquired further. "All of this is awesome! What if I do not have a key to start with? What other options do I have?".

Another possibility is to come up with a password of your choosing and feed that through a specific KDF whose purpose is to derive key material from passwords. Its name is PBKDF or Password-based Key Derivation Function. It is important to remember, though, that the key material derived using this kind of KDF can only be used to protect stored data or to protect other DPKs (Data Protection Keys).

Let's dig into the internals of a PBKDF. If you want more details on this function, NIST SP 800–132 [9] is the reference standard you need to look for.

As you might know, passwords are not the most secure way to protect data by themselves, the reason being that they are chosen by the user, which means that they do not have great entropic properties. Consequently, a password alone is often quite weak and vulnerable to attackers.

The purpose of a PBKDF is to take a user-generated password and derive from it something stronger (called a Master Key or MK). The idea behind this process is that this master key is then used to derive a Data Protection Key, which will then be the one used to protect the data.

PBKDF—How Does it Work? The inputs to a PBKDF are the following:

- The PRF to be used as underlying cryptographic function for the generation; the SP approves for use as a PRF the HMAC algorithm with any approved hash function.
- The password (P) chosen by the user.
- The length (kLen) of the resulting key.
- The iteration count (C) which determines how many times the function iterates to generate a single MK block.
- A salt (S) that is a bit string that is taken directly from an approved RBG.

Based on the length of the required MK and on the digest size (hLen) of the hash function used in the HMAC algorithm, n MK blocks will need to be produced, where $n = \frac{kLen}{hLen}$.

To produce each of these blocks, the PRF will be exercised a number of times exactly equal to the iteration count. The user password will act as the HMAC key, while the initial data will be:

$$U_0 = S||Int(i) \tag{8.10}$$

where $Int(i)$ is a 32-bit encoding of i, which is index of the specific block being computed.

Starting from this input, exactly C times, the following steps will be executed:

$$U_j = HMAC\big(P, U_{j-1}\big)T_i = T_i \oplus U_j \tag{8.11}$$

for $j = 1, 2, \ldots, C$; $i = 1, 2, \ldots, n$; and T_i starts at 0 and updates for every j.

The computed T_i s will be concatenated at the end forming the resulting Master Key or MK which will be exactly kLen bits long.

PBKDF—How Can I Use my Master Key? The MK obtained from the PBKDF output can then be used to derive a data protection key in four ways, according to NIST SP 800–132 [9]:

- It can be used directly as the DPK to encrypt the data.
- It can be passed as an input to an approved KDF; The resulting key will act as the DPK and will be used to encrypt the data.
- It can be used to decrypt a DPK that was previously stored somewhere, then this decrypted DPK will be used to decrypt the actual data.
- It can be passed as an input to an approved KDF. The resulting key is used to decrypt a DPK that was previously stored; this final DPK will then be used to decrypt the actual data.

PBKDF—Why Go to so Much Trouble? The main reason to do all of this is to avoid dictionary attacks. In some real-world scenarios, it is possible that passwords are the only way available to protect some data. As we said though, they are not strong enough by themselves and they are particularly weak to dictionary attacks.

One way to counter these attacks is to extend the time it takes to an attacker to try each single password to decrypt the actual data, which is exactly what the PBKDF mechanism is meant to do. To decrypt the data, the attacker has to run the potential password through the PBKDF and, potentially, through another KDF (depending on which of the above paths is chosen) to obtain the MK, then the final DPK, and then try to decrypt the data.

PBKDF—Choosing the Right Parameters Since the scope of this KDF is to counter dictionary attacks on passwords by increasing the amount of time it takes to an attacker to perform them, special care needs to be taken in how the input parameters to the PBKDF are constructed:

- Iteration count: The purpose of this parameter is to increase the number of calculations needed to obtain the MK. For this reason, this parameter should be as large as possible. However, while the number of calculations should be as long as possible, it should also be not so long that it renders the use of the PBKDF infeasible. Thus, the context needs to be considered for the selection of this parameter.

A good trade-off between these two extremes must be selected but, in any case, the SP recommends a minimum of 1000 for the selection of the iteration count value.

- Salt: The purpose of this parameter is to allow the derivation of several MKs once the input password and the iteration count are fixed. Since this parameter is taken from an RBG, its length will determine the number of MKs that are possible to derive from a single password and iteration count couple. The SP enforces the selection of a salt that it's at least 128 bits long.
- Password: The length and constitution of the password itself is, of course, important to guarantee the security of the derived MK. A password should be long and varied enough to be resistant to brute-force and dictionary attacks. However, especially if it needs to be memorized by the user, it also needs to be "usable." Thus, also here, a good trade-off between the resistance of this password to attacks and its usability needs to be chosen.

Deriving from Shared Secrets Mr. James's skepticism about uniqueness was returning. "Okay, so we have keys and passwords. It's good to have choices. I do have a question, though: you are telling me there is absolutely no way that me and you can drink the same thing? Even with all these choices in our hands?".

Well… Not really! If we want to derive the same key, we would for need to establish a shared secret that only we know and can use for this purpose.

To establish such shared secret, we would need to follow one of the establishment schemes mandated by NIST SP 800-56A Rev. 3 [5] or NIST SP 800-56B Rev. 2 [6]. The result of executing one of these schemes between us would be that we would both have the same shared secret in our hands. Now, according to NIST SP 800-56C Rev. 2 [7], we can use this secret as an input to the KDFs described in this standard to obtain key material equal for the both of us in an approved way.

One-Step Key Derivation Function The first family of this functions is called One-Step Key Derivation Functions (One-Step KDF).

The implementation of one of these functions starts from the choice of an auxiliary function, which we denote as H and, according to the standard, can be one of the following cryptographic primitives:

- An approved hash function according to FIPS 180–4 [1] or FIPS 202 [3]
- An approved HMAC according to FIPS 198
- An approved KMAC according to NIST SP 800–185 [12]

The common inputs between all the KDFs based on these auxiliary functions are:

- The shared secret Z that was established according to NIST SP 800-56A Rev. 3 [5] or NIST SP 800-56B Rev. 2 [6]
- The length L of the desired keying material to be derived.
- The FixedInfo that is shared between the two peers and it's dependent on the context in which the key derivation is being performed.

Additionally, if either HMAC or KMAC are chosen as auxiliary functions, then an additional input is needed for the computation: the salt. This salt could be computed as part of the key establishment and will be used as key for the HMAC or KMAC auxiliary function.

Once all these inputs are defined, the OneStep KDF process consists of applying the auxiliary functions to the provided inputs one or more times, depending on the length of the keying material requested. Specifically, the operation will be executed *L/H_outputBits* times, where *H_outputBits* is the length of the output of a single auxiliary function operation.

Each output of each iteration of the auxiliary function is then concatenated to form the final derived keying material.

Two-Step Key Derivation Function Differently from the OneStep KDF, the TwoStep key derivation process entails two steps to derive the final keying material requested by the user. These two steps are called randomness-extraction and key-expansion.

First, the randomness-extraction step takes as input a salt and a shared secret and is based on a cryptographic primitive that can be an approved HMAC according to FIPS 198–1 [2] or an approved CMAC according to NIST SP 800-38B [4]. The salt is used as the key of the MAC primitive, while the shared secret represents the message. By applying the MAC primitive to these two inputs, a key-derivation key is produced.

Then, the key-expansion step feeds the key-derivation key output from the randomness-extraction into a PRF-based KDF from NIST SP 800–108 Rev. 1 [8] - in other words, a KBKDF. Other inputs, like context-based data, an IV—if needed— and the length of the desired keying material requested by the user are also fed into the KBKDF. The result of this final key-expansion step—after the KBKDF has completed its execution—will be the keying material that is then output to the user that requested the TwoStep KDF execution.

An example of the usage of this extract-then-expand paradigm is represented by the HKDF cryptographic function, which stands for HMAC-based Key Derivation Function. This algorithm is defined in RFC 5869 [22] as an extract-then-expand based KDF that makes use of HMAC as a primitive for both the randomness-extraction and key-expansion steps. This KDF is used in several protocols, such as the TLS 1.3 protocol.

Protocol-based Key Derivation Functions Mr. James' skepticism faded as he seemed satisfied with all the options available.

"Wow, I will definitely keep this in mind when I will need to share a drink with someone." He then stood up. "Thank you for this comprehensive view of all the approved KDFs, there really are lots to choose from!" he said while grabbing his coat.

"Well, the list is not comprehensive yet; there are still other options you might want to consider…" Francesco said while taking another sip of his drink.

"Oh, so you are saying that the list of approved KDFs is not complete yet?" James replied.

Other than NIST-defined KDFs, there are also other kinds of KDFs that can be used in a FIPS validated module. These are KDFs whose definitions are coming from other security standards and are designed to be used in specific protocols.

While these are standardized in different security publications, NIST still approves the use of these KDFs—in the context of their relative protocols—in a FIPS validated module and the SP that regulates the requirements to support such KDFs is NIST SP 800–135 Rev. 1 [11].

IKE KDFs The first protocol specific KDFs we will discuss are the IKEv1 and IKEv2 KDFs. These are used in the Interned Key Exchange protocol version 1 and version 2, standardized in RFC 2409 [14] and RFC 4306 [20], respectively.

These RFCs specify some KDFs based on the use of several PRFs that can rely either on an HMAC or on a block cipher primitive.

The IKE KDF is used within the IKE protocol to derive keying material from the secrets exchanged by the two parties during the establishment of a security association (SA).

In IKEv1, the secret exchanged by the two parties are fed into an HMAC-based PRF to perform a randomness-extraction step to derive an SKEYID. This SKEYID is then fed into a key expansion step.

The expansion step makes use of an HMAC-based PRF that is exercised on the input in feedback mode. The output of this expansion step will be the keying material that the IKE protocol will then use to derive the required keys for the SA.

The IKEv2 KDF is a revised version of the IKEv1 KDF. This takes as inputs two nonces generated by the two parties of the SA and a Diffie-Hellman shared secret that they previously exchanged. These are fed into a randomness-extraction step that makes use of an HMAC-based PRF and derives an SKEYSEED.

This SKEYSEED, together with the nonces and other protocol specific fixed inputs, will be fed into a key-expansion step. This step is similar to the one seen for the IKEv1 KDF and will derive the keying material that the IKE protocol will then use to derive the final symmetric keys needed for the SA.

In the context of a FIPS validated module, NIST SP 800–135 Rev. 1 [11] approves only the use of an approved HMAC as a PRF for these KDFs which, in turn, makes use of an approved hash function.

TLS KDFs The Transport Layer Security (TLS) protocol is heavily used in IT communication as it provides the means to establish a secure channel at the transport layer of the communication model.

In this protocol, a key agreement scheme is executed between the two parties to establish a pre-master secret. This pre-master secret is then input to the TLS KDF in order for the two parties to derive the necessary keying material for the cryptographic functions that were agreed upon at the start of the TLS handshake.

In versions 1.0 and 1.1 of the TLS protocol, the pre-master secret is fed—together with other non-secret inputs—into an HMAC-based PRF that makes use of MD5 and SHA-1 as defined in RFC 2246 [13]. This acts as a randomness-extraction step and will derive a master secret that will be identical for both parties.

This master secret—together with other non-secret inputs—is fed into this same PRF, which will now act as a key-expansion step to derive the keying material necessary for the TLS protocol.

NIST SP 800–135 Rev. 1 [11] approves the use of use of this KDF when the following conditions are met:

- It is used in the context of the TLS 1.0/1.1 protocol
- The HMAC is implemented in compliance with FIPS 198–1 [2]
- The SHA-1 is implemented in compliance with FIPS 180–4 [1]
- The MD5 is only used for this PRF and cannot be used as a standalone hash function or within HMAC as a standalone MAC operation.

In version 1.2 of the TLS protocol, the process is nearly identical. The only difference is that the PRF used is an HMAC-SHA-256 PRF as defined in Sect. 5 of RFC 5246 [21].

This PRF is based on the use of SHA2-256 as a hash function. However, the TLS specification also allows the use of SHA2-384 and SHA2-512 in its place.

NIST SP 800–135 Rev. 1 [11] approves the use of use of this KDF when the following conditions are met:

- It is used in the context of the TLS 1.2 protocol.
- The HMAC is implemented in compliance with FIPS 198–1 [2]
- It makes use of either SHA2-256, SHA2-384, or SHA2-512 and they are implemented in compliance with FIPS 180–4.

ANS KDFs In the American National Standards (ANS) X9.42–2001 and X9.63–2001, three hash-based KDFs—two in the former and one in the latter standard—are defined. They are used to derive keying material from a shared secret established during the previous execution of a key establishment scheme. Additional inputs are mixed-in with this shared secret to obtain the resulting keying material from these KDFs.

NIST SP 800–135 Rev. 1 [11] approves the use of these hash-based KDFs when the following conditions are met:

- They are used in the context of the ANS X9.42 or ANS X9.63 key agreement schemes.
- The hash function used within the KDF is an approved hash function.
- The security strength of the hash function is sufficient to support the security strength required by the cryptographic functions for which the keying material is being generated.

SSH KDF The SSH protocol—defined in RFC 4251 [18]—is widely used for secure login and other network services between client and servers over the internet.

This protocol consists of three major components, one of which is the Transport Layer Protocol—defined in RFC 4253 [19], it provides server authentication, confidentiality, and integrity over the SSH session.

During the execution of the Transport Layer Protocol, a key exchange is performed between the server and client. The results of this key exchange are a shared secret K and a hash value H. These values, together with other inputs, are fed into a hash-based KDF to derive keying material.

SSH's Transport Layer Protocol defines different KDFs to derive different kinds of keying material but they are all similar—they are hash-based KDFs used in a feedback mode.

NIST SP 800–135 Rev. 1 [11] approves the use of these hash-based KDFs when the following conditions are met:

- They are used in the context of the SSH protocol.
- The hash function use within the KDF is an approved hash function.
- The security strength of the hash function is sufficient to support the security strength required by the cryptographic functions for which the keying material is being generated.

SRTP KDF The SRTP protocol—or Secure Real-time Transport Protocol, defined in RFC 3711 [17]—is designed to provide confidentiality, message authentication, and replay protection for the Real-time Transport Protocol—defined in RFC 2574 [16]. The latter is a protocol used over the internet for the transmission of real-time data like audio or video.

This SRTP protocol makes use of a single master key to derive all the authentication and encryption keys needed for its computations. This master key is used as a key-derivation key and it's fed to an AES-128, AES-192, or AES-256 operation to produce authentication keys, salts, or encryption keys. The master key is used, within the AES operation, as an encryption key, while the data encrypted is composed of session-dependent data for the SRTP session that is being established between the client and servers—more details on this process can be found in RFC 6188 [23] where these KDFs are defined.

NIST SP 800–135 Rev. 1 [11] approves the use of these KDFs when the following conditions are met:

- The KDFs are performed in the context of the SRTP protocol.
- The AES encryption operation is implemented in compliance with FIPS 197.

SNMP KDF The SNMP—or Simple Network Management Protocol—is widely used over the internet to manage devices that are interconnected over a network. SNMPv3, or version 3 of this protocol, is defined within RFC 2571 [15]. Within this version of the protocol a User-based Security Model—or USM—is used and its definition it described in a different RFC which is 2574. This model is designed to provide message-level security within the SNMP protocol execution.

The USM model defines the use of a KDF that is employed, starting from a secret password, when a user needs to establish a new secret key with an authoritative SNMP server. Thus, the inputs to this KDF are the secret password and an ID that is unique for each authoritative SNMP server.

These inputs are fed into the KDF, which makes use of either MD5 or SHA-1 to derive the shared key between the server and client.

NIST SP 800–135 Rev. 1 [11] approves the use of this hash-based KDF when the following conditions are met:

- The KDF is performed in the context of the SNMP protocol.
- The hash function used is SHA-1 and not MD5.

TPM KDF The Trusted Platform Module—or TPM—is a module that implements the Trusted Platform Library to enable trust in a computing platform.

The Trusted Platform Library defines, among other functions, an HMAC-SHA-1 based KDF that is used to derive the keying material that is necessary for transport sessions established between the TPM module and an application running on another processor.

In particular, this KDF gets in input an auth key that was exchanged between the TPM and the application and two nonces generated by the two parties—one nonce per party. The output of the KDF execution will be used as a session key to protect the integrity of the transmitted data.

NIST SP 800–135 Rev. 1 [11] approves the use of this KDF when the following conditions are met:

- The TPM KDF is performed in the context of a TPM session.
- HMAC and SHA-1 are implemented as specified in FIPS 198–1 [2] and FIPS 180–4 [1], respectively.

Conclusion Mr. James was thoroughly satisfied now. "Well, this was fantastic! I didn't know that were so many ways available to derive key materials. And that this restaurant applies it to drinks, too!".

"It does, here you can always create a special drink that is based on the specific inputs only you can provide… And it will always have that something different that makes it special and unique!" Francesco replied.

"So, is the bartender capable of preparing drinks with all the KDF processes you described?"

Francesco nodded. "Oh, he is the best one in town. Do experiment yourself!"

Mr. James couldn't contain his excitement. "Will do!" (Fig. 8.1).

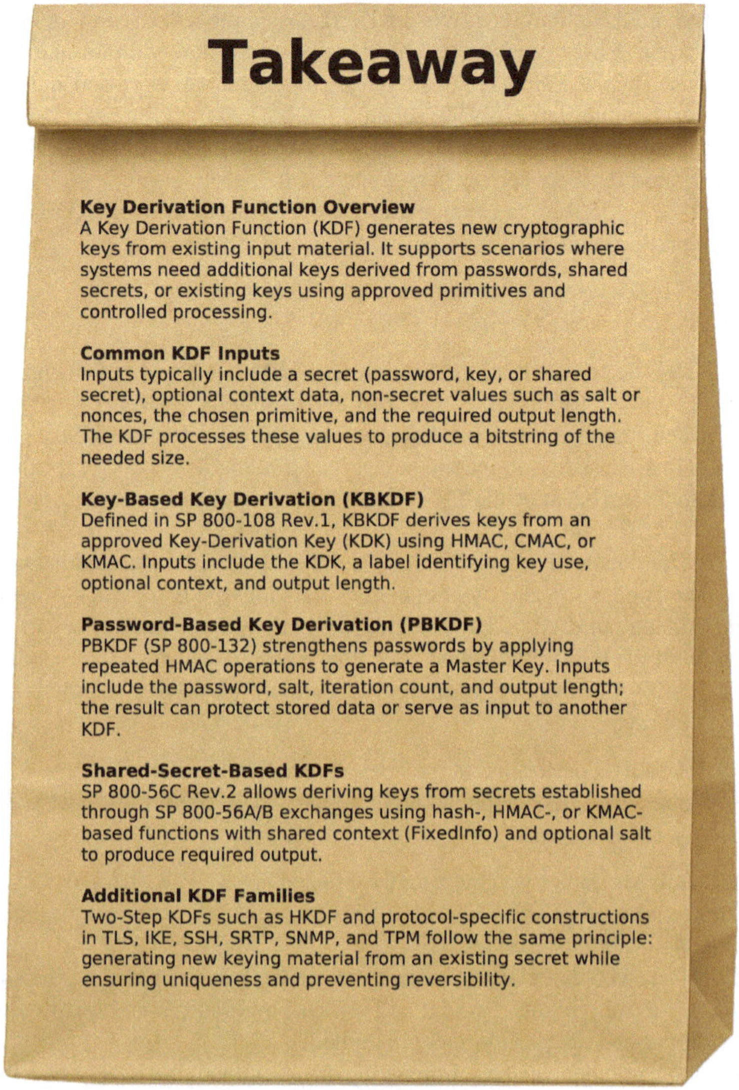

Fig. 8.1 Takeaways regarding key derivation functions

References

1. National Institute of Standards and Technology (2015) Secure Hash Standard (SHS). In: NIST Publications. The National Institute of Standards and Technology. Available via NIST. https://csrc.nist.gov/pubs/fips/180-4/upd1/final. Accessed 20 Nov 2025
2. National Institute of Standards and Technology (2008) FIPS PUB 198–1: The Keyed-Hash Message Authentication Code (HMAC). National Institute of Standards and Technology. Available via NIST. https://csrc.nist.gov/pubs/fips/198-1/final. Accessed 08 Dec 2025

3. National Institute of Standards and Technology (2015) FIPS PUB 202: SHA-3 Standard: Permutation-Based Hash and Extendable-Output Functions. National Institute of Standards and Technology. Available via NIST. https://csrc.nist.gov/pubs/fips/202/final. Accessed 08 Dec 2025
4. Dworkin M (2008) SP 800–38B: Recommendation for Block Cipher Modes of Operation: The CMAC Mode for Authentication. National Institute of Standards and Technology. Available via NIST. https://csrc.nist.gov/pubs/sp/800/38/b/final. Accessed 08 Dec 2025
5. Barker E, Chen L, Roginsky A, Vassilev A, Davis R (2018) Recommendation for Pair-Wise Key-Establishment Schemes Using Discrete Logarithm Cryptography. National Institute of Standards and Technology. Available via NIST. https://csrc.nist.gov/pubs/sp/800/56/a/r3/final. Accessed 03 Dec 2025
6. Barker E, Chen L, Roginsky A, Vassilev A, Davis R, Simon S (2019) Recommendation for pair-wise key-establishment using integer factorization cryptography. National Institute of Standards and Technology. Available via NIST. https://csrc.nist.gov/pubs/sp/800/56/b/r2/final. Accessed 03 Dec 2025
7. Barker E, Chen L, Davis R (2020) Recommendation for Key-derivation methods in key-establishment schemes. National Institute of Standards and Technology. Available via NIST. https://csrc.nist.gov/pubs/sp/800/56/c/r2/final. Accessed 03 Dec 2025
8. Chen L (2022) Recommendation for Key derivation using pseudorandom functions. National Institute of Standards and Technology. Available via NIST. https://csrc.nist.gov/pubs/sp/800/108/r1/upd1/final. Accessed 03 Dec 2025
9. Turan MS, Barker E, Burr W, Chen L (2010) Recommendation for password-based key derivation: Part 1: storage applications. National Institute of Standards and Technology. Available via NIST. https://csrc.nist.gov/pubs/sp/800/132/final. Accessed 03 Dec 2025
10. Barker E, Roginsky A, Davis R (2020) Recommendation for cryptographic key generation. National Institute of Standards and Technology. Available via NIST. https://csrc.nist.gov/pubs/sp/800/133/r2/final. Accessed 03 Dec 2025
11. Dang Q (2011) Recommendation for existing application-specific key derivation functions. National Institute of Standards and Technology. Available via NIST. https://csrc.nist.gov/pubs/sp/800/135/r1/final Accessed 03 Dec 2025
12. Kelsey J, Chang S, Perlner R (2016) SHA-3 Derived functions: cSHAKE, KMAC, TupleHash, and ParallelHash. In: NIST Publications. The National Institute of Standards and Technology. Available via NIST. https://csrc.nist.gov/pubs/sp/800/185/final. Accessed 20 Nov 2025
13. Dierks T, Allen C (1999) The TLS protocol version 1.0 RFC 2246. Internet Engineering Taskforce. Available via IETF. https://www.ietf.org/rfc/rfc2246.txt. Accessed 03 Dec 2025
14. Harkins D, Carrel D (1998) The internet key exchange (IKE) RFC 2409. Internet Engineering Taskforce. Available via IETF. https://datatracker.ietf.org/doc/html/rfc2409. Accessed 03 Dec 2025
15. Wijnen B, Harrington D, Presuhn R (1999) An architecture for describing SNMP management frameworks RFC 2571. Internet Engineering Taskforce. Available via IETF. https://datatracker.ietf.org/doc/html/rfc2571. Accessed 03 Dec 2025
16. Schulzrinne H, Casner S, Frederick R, Jacobson V (2003) RTP: A transport protocol for real-time applications RFC 3550. Internet Engineering Taskforce. Available via IETF. https://datatracker.ietf.org/doc/html/rfc3550. Accessed 03 Dec 2025
17. Baugher M, McGrew D, Naslund M, Carrara E, Norrman K (2004) The secure real-time transport protocol (SRTP) RFC 3711. Internet Engineering Taskforce. Available via IETF. https://datatracker.ietf.org/doc/html/rfc3711. Accessed 03 Dec 2025
18. Ylonen T, Lonvick C (eds) (2006) The secure shell (SSH) protocol architecture RFC 4251. Internet Engineering Taskforce. Available via IETF. https://datatracker.ietf.org/doc/html/rfc4251. Accessed 03 Dec 2025
19. Ylonen T, Lonvick C (eds) (2006) The secure shell (SSH) transport layer protocol RFC 4253. Internet Engineering Taskforce. Available via IETF. https://datatracker.ietf.org/doc/html/rfc4253. Accessed 03 Dec 2025

20. Kaufman C (ed) (2005) Internet key exchange (IKEv2) protocol RFC 4306. Internet Engineering Taskforce. Available via IETF. https://datatracker.ietf.org/doc/html/rfc4306. Accessed 03 Dec 2025
21. Dierks T, Rescorla E (2008) The transport layer security (TLS) protocol version 1.2 RFC 5246. Internet Engineering Taskforce. Available via IETF. https://datatracker.ietf.org/doc/html/rfc5246. Accessed 03 Dec 2025
22. Krawczyk H, Eronen P (2010) HMAC-based extract-and-expand key derivation function (HKDF) RFC 5869. Internet Engineering Taskforce. Available via IETF. https://datatracker.ietf.org/doc/html/rfc5869. Accessed 03 Dec 2025
23. McGrew D (2011) The use of AES-192 and AES-256 in secure RTP RFC 6188. Internet Engineering Taskforce. Available via IETF. https://datatracker.ietf.org/doc/html/rfc6188. Accessed 03 Dec 2025

Francesco Paolo D'Erme Francesco has been studying computer science since high school and has a degree in IT engineering and a master's degree in Cybersecurity. He joined atsec three years ago while writing thesis for his master's degree. Part of his thesis' project was to develop a Rust DRBG implementation which was compliant to the SP 800-90A Rev.1 requirements. While working on this project, he also spent time learning all the FIPS requirements and diving into the certification process as well as all of the cryptographic algorithm implementations. Right after his degree, Francesco started working full time on FIPS validations focusing mostly on software modules.

Chapter 9
Message Authentication Codes

Alessandro Fazio

Alessandro, one of the atsec colleagues, enters the FIPS 'n' Chips restaurant accompanied by a visitor to their lab, Aster; he's famished after a particularly tough day and, due to the fame of the restaurant, he decides to order the house special: Fish and Chips. When the waiter brings the meal to the table, Alessandro feels that something about the dish is a bit off. After a bit of inspection, Alessandro indeed finds that there is something quite fishy with the fish itself.

With a small taste, it's confirmed: "This isn't the right fish at all!".

After calling over the waiter to get the meal replaced, Aster pipes up and asks, "How can you be so certain that this is not the right fish?".

Alessandro raises an eyebrow and replies: "I found that the texture of the fish was not the authentic texture related to a Fish and Chips meal."

Aster gave a small laugh, "That reminds me of the authentication work you mentioned earlier today."

Alessandro laughs. "That's exactly what we needed more of in this case! Authentication is a form of proof that can guarantee we really get what we want, and a bit of authentication that what was being sent out was the fish traditionally used in the dish could have saved some effort here. This concept is even more important in security—have you ever heard about Message Authentication Code?".

"It rings a bell, but I'm not up to speed on the specifics. Think you can explain it by the time they bring you a new dish?" Aster asks, prompting an explanation.

Alessandro takes a brief moment to calculate before launching into a lecture, "Only one way to find out! I'll do my best, but I'm not going to skip anything important just to beat the clock on this one."

A. Fazio (✉)
atsec information security corporation, Austin, TX, USA
e-mail: alessandro.fazio@atsec.com

Y. Mao (ed.), *Tasting Cryptography*, https://doi.org/10.1007/978-3-032-30243-4_9

Overview "First of all, what is a Message Authentication Code?" Aster asks.

Alessandro settles back in his chair, and then lays out the fundamentals:

Let's now talk about the Message Authentication Code (MAC). A Message Authentication Code is defined as:

- Message: the target of the operation; MACs are applied to messages
- Authentication: the goal of the operation; MACs are used to guarantee authentication
- Code: the mean of the operation; MACs are applied as a code

So, MACs are nothing more than a piece of code (known as a tag) attached to messages, enabling entities to verify that a message originates from a legitimate sender, and it has not been altered during transit.

A Message Authentication Code is a symmetric cryptographic construct: both the sender and the receiver share a secret key. In this discussion, we will assume the secret key is already possessed by the entities performing the MAC.

"So, we need MACs as a form of authentication?" Aster tries to clarify.

"So far, we encountered cryptographic algorithms that can cover confidentiality and integrity issues. However, it does not inherently prevent message impersonation. For example, an attacker might send a message claiming its origin in a valid/trusted sender and a receiver wouldn't notice any flaw," Alessandro confirms with a nod.

"MACs serve as a defensive line against such attacks by ensuring both data integrity—the message has not changed—and origin authentication—the message comes from the expected sender," he concludes.

Aster then fires off some quick questions: "Where is a Message Authentication Code supposed to be used? And what are the core properties of a Message Authentication Code?".

To answer the first question, Alessandro covers how Message Authentication Codes play an essential role in:

- Secure channel communications (e.g., TLS, IPSec protocols)
- Financial transactions
- Software updates
- Blockchain and smart contract platforms

To support this discussion, the ISO 19790:2025 [1] defines the Message Authentication Code as an approved data authentication technique when loading external software or firmware.

As for the second question, Alessandro notes that a MAC is robust when the following condition is satisfied: given a message, it must be computationally infeasible to compute a valid MAC tag for the message without knowing the secret key. In other words, the MAC must resist forging attacks with known or chosen messages.

"So, can the requirements for Message Authentication Code algorithms evolve over time?" comes the next question.

Alessandro nods, sliding over his phone where he had already pulled up NIST SP 800-131Ar3 [2], which introduced transitions for the MAC algorithm after end of 2030 deadline:

- SHA-1 and the 224-bit hash functions (SHA-224, SHA-512/224, and SHA3-224).
- MAC generation with less than 128 bits keys is disallowed.

Continuing, Alessandro provides a quick overview of the MAC algorithms.

The core operations of a MAC implementation are:

- Generate: Given a secret key, create a MAC tag
- Verify: Given a MAC tag, verify the authenticity

Let's look at how each of the MAC algorithms are implemented; NIST SP 800-140C [3] approves: CMAC, GMAC, HMAC, KMAC.

As mentioned before, when describing the implementation steps, it is assumed that the secret key was already agreed between sender and receiver.

CMAC—Cipher-Based Message Authentication Code "Okay, let's go alphabetical, then—tell me about CMAC," Aster prompts.

Alessandro, knowing this will start to require more specifics, straightens up and begins to relay the important concepts for cipher-based message authentication code.

CMAC, or Cipher-based Message Authentication Code, is a Message Authentication Code implementation relying on a symmetric key block cipher. It was developed to address security weaknesses in earlier MAC constructions like CBC-MAC and was standardized by the National Institute of Standards and Technology (NIST) in NIST SP 800-38B [4].

Because it relies on block ciphers (AES), it is valuable for environments where block ciphers are already in use or where the main goal of MAC implementations is efficiency (e.g., hardware-constrained devices).

The original CBC-MAC construction is subject to security vulnerabilities when used with variable-length messages. In particular, CBC-MAC constructions are susceptible to extension attacks, where an adversary can forge a MAC for a longer message by manipulating the MAC of a shorter one.

CMAC corrects the flaws in CBC-MAC by applying a well-defined padding mechanism and introducing two subkeys generated from the main key, which allows secure MAC generation for any kind of message length.

Construction Here's how the CMAC algorithm works as per NIST SP800-38B.

Step 1: Getting Started with the Key and Cipher The sender and receiver agree on the block cipher to use and the key size.

CMAC is based on:

- block ciphers, which means it processes messages in fixed-size chunks, 128 bits (16 bytes) for AES.
- 128-bit, 192-bit, 256-bit keys.

Step 2: Preparing Subkeys Before processing the actual message, CMAC generates two subkeys from the main key:

- First, CMAC encrypts a block of all zeros using the main key.
- From the result, it derives two subkeys (we'll call them Subkey1 and Subkey2).
- Subkey1 is the result of the shift and XOR of the zero block with a constant defined in the CMAC standard.
- Subkey2 is the result of the shift and XOR of the Subkey1 with a constant defined in the CMAC standard.

Step 3: Splitting the Message into Blocks Now the message is split into blocks with the same size. If the last block isn't long enough to fill a full chunk, it gets padded (1 bit followed by zeros until the block is filled in).

Then CMAC checks:

- If the message length is exactly a multiple of the block size, it uses Subkey1 on the final block.
- If the message ends with a partial block, it applies Subkey2 instead after padding.

This little trick prevents attackers from playing around with message length to try to forge a valid MAC.

Step 4: Processing the Blocks Starting with an initial value of all zeros, CMAC processes each block of the message by:

1. Taking the current block.
2. Mixing it with the result of the previous step (using XOR).
3. Encrypting that with the block cipher.

This continues until the final block, which is handled with the subkey as previously described. The output of this final encryption step becomes the MAC tag, and then this terminates the sender process.

Step 5: Verifying the MAC To check if a message is authentic, the receiver:

1. Runs the same process using the same shared secret key.
2. Compares the MAC they compute to the one that came with the message.

If they match, the message is authentic.

GMAC—Galois Message Authentication Code "Okay, so that's CMAC, but what about GMAC? And you better hurry up, that's one out of four and I think I can hear them working on your replacement dish," Aster says with a wink.

Alessandro, with a sigh, lays out the details of GMAC with a little more gusto than before—the clock is ticking, after all.

GMAC, or Galois Message Authentication Code, is a message authentication code that, like CMAC, provides integrity and authenticity for messages. However, GMAC is built on a different mathematical foundation, finite field arithmetic, and it's a particular use case of the Galois/Counter Mode (GCM) algorithm with no plaintext.

Unlike CMAC, which uses chaining with a block cipher, GMAC operates over binary fields and is designed for high-speed implementation, particularly in software and hardware systems that can take advantage of parallel processing.

GMAC is standardized by NIST SP 800-38D [5].

Let's walk through GMAC, which is based on:

- A block cipher key (AES) for generating a special hash key.
- A nonce (IV)—a unique value for each message.
- The message to authenticate.
- An optional field called Associated Data (AAD).

GMAC uses the AES block cipher to prepare a hash subkey (based on the AES encryption of a zero block), and then applies a process called GHASH, which is a polynomial evaluation over a binary finite field.

After that, the MAC tag is computed relying on the AES counter mode implementation.

Let's see how GHASH works:

1. Given some input bitstring, split it into 128-bit AES blocks.
2. XOR subsequent blocks.
3. Multiply the result with the hash subkey with finite field multiplication.
4. Iterate.

Here's how the GMAC tag is computed:

- Key Setup: The sender and receiver agree on a secret AES key. This is used to generate a hash key by encrypting an all-zero block with AES.
- Nonce (IV) Setup: A nonce (a unique value per message) is used to compute a special counter block that will be used in GHASH. The same nonce shall not be reused with the same key.
- Hashing the Message: The message is broken into 128-bit chunks, and each chunk is processed through the GHASH function. This function mixes the message with the hash key using Galois field multiplication.

- Tag Generation: The output of GHASH is encrypted using AES and the counter block to produce the final GMAC tag. This tag is sent along with the message to prove its authenticity.

To verify a message, the receiver:

1. Repeats the same GHASH process with the received message.
2. Computes the tag using the agreed-upon key and nonce.
3. Compares it with the received tag.

If they match, the message is authentic.

It's important to understand that GMAC is just GCM without encryption. This means it only provides authentication and not confidentiality.

HMAC—Hash-Based Message Authentication Code Passing the halfway point, Alessandro takes a quick drink before diving into HMAC before Aster can even ask about it.

HMAC, or Hash-based Message Authentication Code, is one of the most widely used cryptographic algorithms for ensuring both authenticity and integrity of data. Unlike CMAC and GMAC, which are based on block ciphers, HMAC is built on cryptographic hash functions, such as SHA-1, SHA-2, or SHA-3.

HMAC is standardized in NIST FIPS 198–1 [6] and forms a critical part of modern security protocols, including TLS, IPsec, SSH, and OAuth. It's also used in cloud services, API authentication, and secure storage. Most of the Linux stack software cryptographic modules (Kernel, OpenSSL, Libgcrypt, GnuTLS, etc.) use HMAC as a secure integrity method.

Before HMAC, many message authentication schemes relied directly on hash functions, such as applying a hash function on the concatenation of a key and a message. Such implementations were found to be vulnerable to various attacks, especially length extension attacks, where an attacker could forge a valid MAC by appending extra data to the message.

To address these issues, HMAC was introduced by Mihir Bellare, Ran Canetti, and Hugo Krawczyk in 1996 [7].

The main idea was to isolate the key from the message using a double-hashing construction that remains secure even if the hash function itself has some weaknesses (e.g., partial collisions).

Let's see how HMAC works.

At a high level, HMAC uses the following steps:

1. Padding: If the key is too long, it's hashed; if it's too short, it's padded with zeros until it matches the block size of the hash function (e.g., 512 bits or 64 bytes for SHA-256).
2. Create 2 strings: Two variations of the key are created:

- Inner key: the key XORed with a pattern of 0×36 byte repeated for the hash block size times (called ipad).
- Outer key: the key XORed with $0 \times 5c$ byte repeated for the hash block size times (called opad).

3. Hash in 2 layers:
– First, the message is appended to the inner key and hashed.
– Then, the result of that hash is appended to the outer key, and that is hashed again.

This double-hashing process creates the HMAC tag, which is sent along with the message to allow the receiver to verify its authenticity.

The two layers ensure that:

- The attacker can't manipulate the message and recompute a valid tag.
- The key isn't exposed to direct cryptographic attacks on the hash function.
- Even if some weakness is found in the hash function, the overall HMAC strength is not compromised.

HMAC's security depends on:

- The strength of the underlying hash function (e.g., SHA-256).
- The strength the key, which is the most important item for the overall strength of the algorithm.

Sometimes, the output of the HMAC operation is truncated (e.g., HMAC-SHA-1 based cipher-suites in IPsec and SSH).

FIPS 140–3 Implementation Guidance [8] C.D approves such mechanism only under specific circumstances:

- If the key used in HMAC is equal or greater than 112 bits.
- The truncated HMAC algorithm is CAVP tested and represented in the cryptographic module Security Policy.
- Truncation is not performed on a number of leftmost bits which is equal or more than 32 bits.

KMAC—Keccak Message Authentication Code "And then there was one—KMAC," Aster practically sings, smelling fish being fried.

Alessandro rolls his eyes before dissecting the final MAC variant.

KMAC, or Keccak Message Authentication Code, is a Message Authentication Code standardized in NIST SP 800–185 [9].

Unlike MAC algorithms relying on either block ciphers (like CMAC and GMAC) or Merkle–Damgård hash functions (like HMAC), KMAC is based on the Keccak sponge function, which is the same function behind the SHA-3 hashing functions.

Two variants exist:

- KMAC128: based on SHAKE128 and provides 128-bit security strength.
- KMAC256: based on SHAKE256 and provides 256-bit security strength.

With the advent of SHA-3 in 2015, there was a need for MAC constructions that could work naturally with Keccak's internal mechanisms.

KMAC was introduced by the designers of Keccak: Guido Bertoni, Joan Daemen, Michaël Peeters, and Gilles Van Assche with the following main features:

- Built-in key handling without separate key derivation.
- Support for customization strings and variable-length output.
- It can be easily integrated over SHA-3 and SHAKE.

KMAC, as per NIST SP 800–185, is based on:

- A shared secret key.
- A message.
- An optional customization string (used to differentiate domains).
- An output length.
- KECCAK-p permutation (as mentioned before, the baseline of the algorithm).

Lastly, the algorithm relies on cSHAKE (Customizable SHAKE function), which is defined in terms of the SHAKE and KECCAK[c] functions specified in FIPS 202 [10].

Steps to Compute KMAC Let's go over the process for computing KMAC.

Input Preparation The following steps prepare the input:

1. The key is encoded in a way that may be parsed unambiguously from the beginning of the string (with a function known as encode_string) and then pads it to align the data to the sponge function's input rate.
2. The desired output length is encoded as a byte string in a way that can be unambiguously parsed from the end of the string (with a function named right_encode).
3. The two previous results are concatenated to the input message to form the input message to the cSHAKE function.
4. The cSHAKE function is invoked.

Absorbing the Data The Keccak sponge takes in the encoded input (key + message + custom string) and absorbs it into its state.

Squeezing the Output After the input is absorbed, KMAC squeezes out the result: a tag of whatever length you request.

Variant: Arbitrary-Length Output All of the steps above can be performed without knowing the number of output bits they will need until after the outputs begin to be produced.

In such cases, the encoded output length is set to 0 and the KMAC (which operates as an XOF) can produce as many bits as needed for the caller.

Security Properties and Real-World Applications KMAC inherits its strength from the Keccak sponge construction:

- Indifferentiability from a random oracle (for sufficiently many rounds).
- Resistance to collision, preimage, and length extension attacks.
- Key separation: The key is absorbed as part of the state with domain separation, preventing misuse.

- Customization isolation: Adding different strings for different applications prevents cross-protocol attacks.
- Even if the message is reused, the key and customization string ensure the output MAC is domain-specific and secure.

While not as widely deployed yet as HMAC, KMAC is very usable for post-quantum readiness.

Conclusion Alessandro pauses to take a breath before wrapping everything up.

"Okay, as a conclusion, we explored the role of the Message Authentication Code (MAC) to ensure data integrity and authenticity," he says.

"The approved algorithms from NIST that were discussed are:

- CMAC, which offers a block-cipher-based solution ideal for environments already leveraging symmetric encryption, with fixed-length messages.
- GMAC, derived from Galois/Counter Mode (GCM), delivers high-speed authentication in parallelizable contexts.
- HMAC, built on top of hash functions like SHA-1 and SHA-2, provides broad compatibility.
- KMAC, designed as part of the SHA-3 family, introduces flexibility with variable-length output and key sizes, offers future-ready implementations.

Lastly, the choice of MAC depends on system constraints, performance requirements, and the surrounding cryptographic context. Each decision will imply the specific requirements from FIPS 140–3 discussed in this chapter."

"Impressive! That covered everything I knew—and several things I didn't—all in the time it took to make an order of fish and chips," Aster remarks as the waiter comes back over.

Arriving at the table, the waiter sets down a fresh plate of fish and chips.

"Apologies for the earlier discrepancies—our shipment of cod, traditionally used for the dish, was delayed, so we had used hoki instead. A keen tongue you have, sir," he says bowing his head slightly.

"Rest assured, this one is the real deal, though," he continues, "The shipment came through in the end, though it did come in half-way through making a replacement, so forgive the added wait."

"Ha! So, you only managed within the time it took for an order and a half of fish and chips," Aster exclaims as she grabs a chip from the plate.

Alessandro laughs and digs in, delighted to have a verifiably authentic dish of fish and chips (Fig. 9.1).

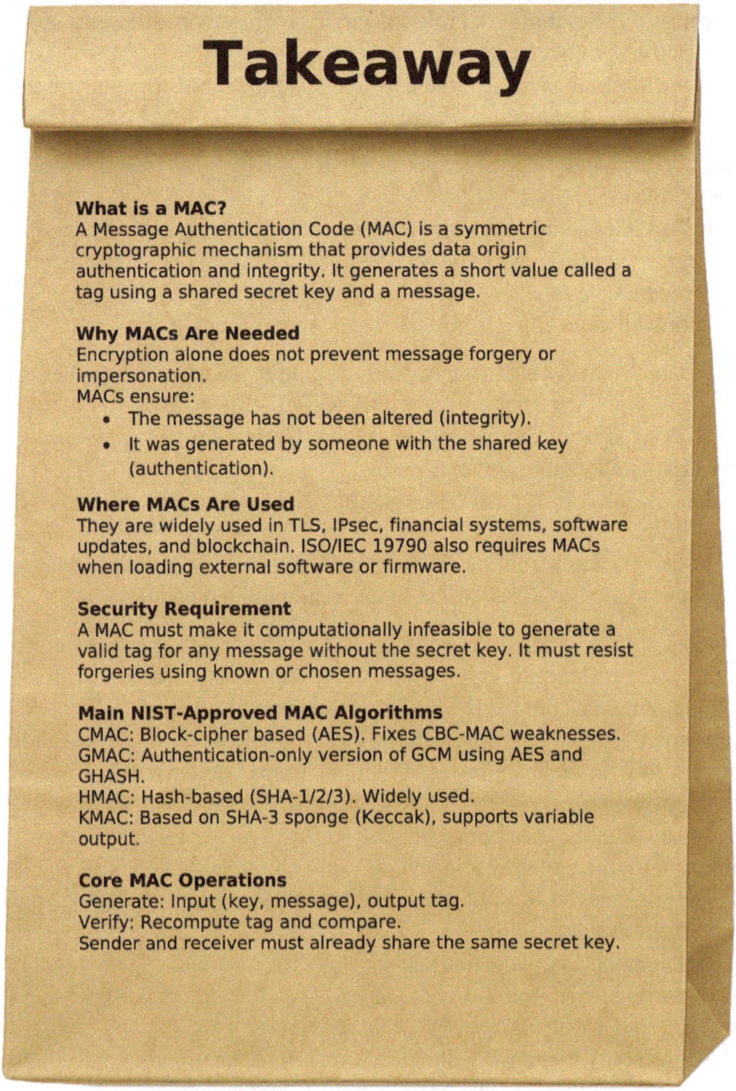

Fig. 9.1 Takeaways regarding message authentication code

References

1. International Standards Organization (2025) ISO/IEC 19790:2025—Information technology—Security techniques—Security requirements for cryptographic modules. International Standards Organization. Available via ISO. https://www.iso.org/standard/82423.html. Accessed 08 Dec 2025

2. Barker E, Roginsky A (2024) SP 800–131A Revision 3: Transitions: Recommen-dation for Transitioning the Use of Cryptographic Algorithms and Key Lengths. National Institute of Standards and Technology. Available via NIST. https://csrc.nist.gov/pubs/sp/800/131/a/r3/ipd. Accessed 08 Dec 2025
3. National Institute of Standards and Technology (2022) SP 800–140C: Security Requirements for Cryptographic Module Validation Program. https://csrc.nist.gov/projects/cryptographic-module-validation-program/sp-800-140-series-supplemental-information/sp800-140c. Accessed 08 Dec 2025
4. Dworkin M (2008) SP 800–38B: recommendation for block cipher modes of operation: the CMAC mode for authentication. National Institute of Standards and Technology. Available via NIST. https://csrc.nist.gov/pubs/sp/800/38/b/final. Accessed 08 Dec 2025
5. Dworkin M (2007) SP 800–38D: recommendation for block cipher modes of operation: Galois/Counter Mode (GCM) and GMAC. National Institute of Standards and Technology. Available via NIST. https://csrc.nist.gov/pubs/sp/800/38/d/final. Accessed 08 Dec 2025
6. National Institute of Standards and Technology (2008) FIPS PUB 198–1: The Keyed-Hash Message Authentication Code (HMAC). National Institute of Standards and Technology. Available via NIST. https://csrc.nist.gov/pubs/fips/198-1/final. Accessed 08 Dec 2025
7. Bellare M, Canetti R, Krawczyk H (1996) Keying hash functions for message authentication. In: Koblitz N (ed) Advances in cryptology—CRYPTO'96. CRYPTO 1996. Lecture Notes in Computer Science, vol 1109. Springer. https://doi.org/10.1007/3-540-68697-5_1
8. National Institute of Standards and Technology, Canadian Centre for Cyber Security (2023) FIPS 140–3 Implementation guidance: implementation guidance for FIPS PUB 140–3 and the cryptographic module validation program. National Institute of Standards and Technology. Available via NIST. https://csrc.nist.gov/csrc/media/Projects/cryptographic-module-validation-program/documents/fips%20140-3/FIPS%20140-3%20IG.pdf. Accessed 08 Dec 2025
9. Kelsey J, Chang S, Perlner R (2016) SHA-3 derived functions: cSHAKE, KMAC, TupleHash, and ParallelHash. In: NIST Publications. The National Institute of Standards and Technology. Available via NIST. https://csrc.nist.gov/pubs/sp/800/185/final. Accessed 08 Dec 2025
10. National Institute of Standards and Technology (2015) FIPS PUB 202: SHA-3 standard: permutation-based hash and extendable-output functions. National Institute of Standards and Technology. Available via NIST. https://csrc.nist.gov/pubs/fips/202/final. Accessed 08 Dec 2025

Alessandro Fazio Since graduating in computer science in 2018, Alessandro has built a career centered on cryptography and cybersecurity, working in consultancy companies and in the academic research field. In 2021, he joined atsec Information Security srl in Rome, Italy, and has been part of the FIPS team specializing in hardware, firm-ware, and software FIPS 140-2 and FIPS 140-3 validations. He has also contributed to the ICMC23 conference, focusing on attestation, and the ICMC25 conference, focusing on software modules, reflecting his ongoing commitment to advancing the field of cryptography.

Chapter 10
Deterministic Random Bit Generation

Jeremy Wesevich

A Trip to FIPS 'n' Chips March was coming to an end, and so was the 5th annual FIPS 'n' Chips Crypto Module Bootcamp at the University of Texas at Austin. The event had been an overwhelming success, attracting experts and vendors alike from across the globe. This year's event was especially exciting as the FIPS 'n' Chips restaurant had recently become reality. Naturally, the restaurant provided catering for the bootcamp, though the food was only half the experience; the restaurant itself was a marvel to behold. Thus, many attendees chose to head over to the restaurant after Yi's closing remarks.

One such group was a gaggle of college students interested in cryptography. They'd heard excellent things from peers who had attended the bootcamp in previous years, and this time they were also being treated to dinner. This outreach initiative was led by Stephan, who was currently walking with them to the FIPS 'n' Chips restaurant.

"I'm not sure I've ever seen it this packed," remarked Stephan as they entered, and packed it was. Joachim, Yi, and a group of NIST representatives sat at a round table with a view of the city; booths were full of vendors, experts, and atsec employees; a fleet of robotic wait staff scurried to and fro, carrying platters of delicious cryptography-inspired dishes and drinks. Stephan nodded at the host and beckoned to the students to follow. "We've got a table reserved in the back. Follow me."

Soon, all the students were seated. They watched with excitement as the center of the table folded in on itself, then telescoped upward to reveal a series of screens visible from all corners of the table. A cascade of 1's and 0's flew across the monitors like an old-school hacking scene in a movie. The digits evolved into characters, which eventually settled down into a series of menu items. Looking around at the surprise on the students' faces, Stephan grinned knowingly. "More interesting than scanning

J. Wesevich (✉)
atsec information security corporation, Austin, TX, USA
e-mail: jeremy.wesevich@atsec.com

Y. Mao (ed.), *Tasting Cryptography*, https://doi.org/10.1007/978-3-032-30243-4_10

a QR code, don't you think?" This evoked a round of laughter from the students. "Well, don't be shy, order away!"

A Demonstration of Randomness A few minutes later, everyone had placed their orders and the table fell into a myriad of conversations. Some reflected on their experience at the conference, while others admired the various tech at work around the restaurant. Then, one group turned to Stephan, and a young woman with large glasses spoke up. "We've been talking about that menu animation from earlier. At the start, there were a bunch of zeros and ones, which presumably came from some sort of random function. That got us thinking; where do random values actually come from? For example, in our cryptography class, we've been learning about RSA key generation. We went through the Miller-Rabin primality test to test large random numbers for primality, but where do we get the random numbers to test?"

"Ah, what an excellent question!" exclaimed Stephan. "To answer this, we should have a good understanding of what we mean when we talk about randomness." After clearing his throat, he addressed the table at large. "Everyone, if I could have your attention. I'd like to replicate a demonstration performed by Veritasium [1]. You should all have a console in front of you; I'd like you each to pick a number between 1 and 100 at random and enter it into your console." He took a moment to type into his own console. "I've just asked everyone else at the restaurant to do the same."

Stephan continued to type away for several moments. Suddenly, a nearby wall lit up, and a bar graph appeared. "Just like that, the results are in. Let's see here…ah, just as I expected. Do you notice any patterns?"

Someone across the table chimed in. "Well, it doesn't look all that random to me. There's a bunch of peaks where lots of people picked the same number, and other values which weren't picked at all."

"Very good," said Stephan. "Does anything about these spikes stand out?"

Another student spoke up. "Well, the largest peaks seem to be evenly spaced apart, I think by about 10. How did that happen?"

"Another excellent observation!" replied Stephan, now visibly excited. "Now why might that be? After all, I asked everyone to pick random numbers. Does this data seem random to you?"

Everyone at the table shook their heads. Clearly, the "random" values that they'd picked were not, in fact, random.

Stephan typed a few commands into his console, and several of the peaks were highlighted and labeled. "Notice anything now?"

The pattern was obvious to everyone. The majority of the peaks were at values ending in 7, and the largest such peak was at 37. Meanwhile, values ending in 0 were hardly picked at all.

Seeing understanding in everyone's eyes, Stephan continued. "As you can now tell, we humans aren't very good at picking random numbers. We often round to the nearest five or ten, so numbers ending in 0 and 5 seem nice and orderly. Even numbers somehow seem less random to us than odd numbers. Effects like this lead to the clear bias you can see in this chart."

Measuring Randomness & Security Strength The young woman with the large glasses spoke up once again. "Well, how does this help us? You've shown us an example of a bad way to pick random numbers, but how do we come up with a good way?"

Stephan smiled in amusement. "Well, it helps us work towards a good definition of randomness. Say I asked everyone for a second random number. We would get a different distribution of values, don't you think? And since we don't get the same result each time, wouldn't you agree that there is some randomness at play here?"

"Yes, I suppose that's fair," the young woman responded. "Still, the numbers we get aren't as random as they could be, right? After all, there are still clearly detectable patterns."

"Exactly right," responded Stephan. "We can, at least qualitatively, measure randomness through the lack of distinguishable patterns. The fewer patterns that can be seen, the more random the distribution, event, image, concept, et cetera. So, if our goal is to pick random numbers, which properties should this 'random number picker' have?"

At this moment, a humanoid robot arrived carrying an enormous platter of food. As dishes were passed out, the students pondered Stephan's question. Meanwhile, Stephan himself continued typing away at his console. He had ordered a simple side of cryptographically secure hash browns and ate slowly as he worked.

After a few minutes, everyone had gotten a taste of their food, and the conversation resumed. "I've got an idea," piped up a student to his left. "The random number picker should have an equal chance of picking any particular number; there shouldn't be any number that's more likely than another."

"Certainly," said Stephan. "In mathematical terms, we would say that we should pick from a uniform distribution. This does mean that we need to have a fixed finite set from which we pick numbers; otherwise, there would be infinitely many choices, and each number would be picked with zero percent probability! What other properties should we have?"

Soon, another student chimed in. "We should pick numbers independently; the choice of one number shouldn't influence the choice of another."

"That's it!" exclaimed Stephan. "If we pick numbers independently from a uniform distribution, then we shouldn't have any distinguishable patterns in the results! In this way, we've maximized randomness."

Here, the young woman with the large glassed interjected. "Well, there is one pattern that's obvious. We defined a set of numbers from which to pick from, so all the numbers we pick will be in that set. That's a pattern, no?"

"Yes, indeed it is," said Stephan. "But there will always be such a set; this is unavoidable. Thus, it would be more accurate to say that given a set, if we pick numbers independently from a uniform distribution over that set, then we've maximized randomness for that set."

Stephan paused a moment, then continued. "In practice, this ties in closely with the FIPS concept of security strength. SP 800–57 Part 1 Rev. 5 [2] defines security strength as 'A number associated with the amount of work (i.e., the number of operations) that is required to break a cryptographic algorithm or system.' For example, AES with a 128-bit key has 128 bits of security strength, meaning that it would take on the order of 2^{128} operations to, say, decrypt a ciphertext without the given key. As you have probably already guessed, this number comes directly from the key length. There are 2^{128} different 128-bit keys, so if we picked our key uniformly at random from that set, then an attacker has a 1 in 2^{128} chance of guessing the key correctly. Any other strategy that we might use to choose our key would increase the attacker's chance at guessing it. Thus, FIPS requires that all random values, such as those used to create cryptographic keys, are generated by an approved Random Bit Generator, all of which generate bits uniformly at random."

Entropy vs Randomness Once again, the young woman with the large glasses spoke up. "OK, this is all interesting and useful in a theoretical sense, but you still haven't answered our original question. What mechanisms are actually used in practice to generate bits uniformly at random?"

Unfazed, Stephan replied. "I find that the mechanisms themselves hardly ever tell the whole story and are often indecipherable without some context. Fear not, we will get to the mechanisms themselves. But first, allow us to finish our more theoretical discussion." Looking around the whole table, he continued. "Say that you wanted to pick a random number between one and six, and after having gone through the exercise from earlier, you suspect that any choice you made in your head would be biased in some way. What might you do instead?"

Immediately, several people answered that they would roll a die; this was of course the answer that Stephan was looking for, so he went on. "Exactly. You rely on some unpredictable physical process to give you your random value. Now, how might we do something similar in a computer?"

This time, no one had an immediate answer. Stephan took the opportunity to finish off his hashbrown. Finally, someone spoke up. "Well, I suppose that there's some random physical process that a computer could monitor, and it would get random numbers that way? I'm not sure what exactly that process would be, though."

"That's exactly the idea," replied Stephan. "The exact processes involved would require a whole other discussion, so for now just take my word that they exist. Inside a processor, there will be a small component which is continuously running some random physical process and reading out the result, just as you or I would roll a die and read the number of pips. We say that such a process provides entropy, or unpredictability."

The young woman with the large glasses cut in. "Why are we making a distinction here? What exactly do you mean by 'entropy'?"

"Once again, an excellent question," said Stephan, beaming. "When we talk about randomness in a theoretical sense, we talk of true mathematical randomness, where the process is irrelevant and only the resulting distribution is of consequence. When we bring these ideas into the real world, there are other things to consider. Say that you ask me to pick a random number between 1 and 1000, and I respond with 141. Without any additional information, you could assume that I picked this number uniformly at random. However, in my mind, I know that I just took the first three digits of pi. If you had known that would be my 'random' number generation process, you could have predicted the result ahead of time. Thus, the value was unpredictable to you only because you were lacking some additional information."

Stephan went on. "On the other hand, suppose that you roll a 1000-sided die and read the result. In this case, there is no perspective from which that result could have been predicted ahead of time; the roll is truly unpredictable. We therefore credit this die roll with a certain amount of entropy, which is a measurement of unpredictability."

Here, a student in the back chimed in. "Is the dice roll really unpredictable? If we had a sufficiently powerful computer, couldn't we track the motion of the die once it's thrown and determine the result while it's still in the air?"

Stephan considered for a moment, then responded. "Two points here. First, in such a case, the result of the die roll would still be unpredictable before it is thrown. Second, one could replace the die example with a quantum measurement whose result cannot be predicted no matter the available computing power. So, while your observation is correct, it's not as important in practice as it may initially seem."

Another student spoke up. "So, this is it then. Computers have some sort of entropy source that uses the outcome of some random physical process to produce random numbers, and that's how we get things like prime candidates when generating RSA keys?"

Deterministic Randomness "Well, not quite," responded Stephan. "You see, entropy sources have several undesirable properties. First, they don't sample independently from a uniform distribution; the physical processes used in entropy sources often have biases and dependencies. Second, they are slow, at least relatively speaking. Some applications require a high rate of random data, and entropy sources can't reasonably keep up with that pace. We therefore need additional tools to turn entropy into useful random data. These tools are called Deterministic Random Bit Generators, or DRBGs for short."

This last statement caused some commotion. "Wait," someone retorted. "How can something be both random and deterministic? That doesn't make any sense."

"Well," Stephan countered, "it's a matter of perspective. Internally, the process is deterministic, and entirely predictable given certain information. To anyone external who doesn't have that information, the output is indistinguishable from data generated uniformly at random."

A student across the table spoke up. "So, if I'm understanding correctly, a DRBG effectively has a key, just like an encryption algorithm. However, instead of allowing you to encrypt or decrypt data, the key allows you to predict the outputs of the DRBG."

"Yes, that's essentially the right idea," agreed Stephan. "However, we don't call it a key. Instead, the DRBG has an internal state. Knowing the internal state allows you to predict the next output, as well as the next internal state. As long as this information stays secret, the outputs of the DRBG remain unpredictable."

"OK, but there's got to be some initial internal state," said the student. "Where does that come from?"

"Seeding," replied Stephan. "The initial internal state is derived from some initial input to the DRBG, and this input must include a string containing some entropy from an entropy source. The entropy gives the DRBG its security; if no one can predict what this input will be ahead of time, then no one can determine in advance what the initial internal DRBG state will be. This is called 'seeding.'"

The student thought for a moment. “So, even if it’s our DRBG, we can’t predict ahead of time what it will output?”

“Prior to the generation of the entropy string, no, we cannot predict what it will output. Once we have the entropy string and other inputs, then we can predict any future output by just running the DRBG.” Stephan paused for emphasis. “To understand the importance of the entropy string, suppose that we set up a DRBG without any entropy. Then, all the information required to set up the DRBG could have been known by us at some point in the past; in other words, the information was out there. Thus, in theory, an attacker could learn that information and duplicate our DRBG, thus predicting all our ‘random’ numbers.”

Looking around the table, Stephan saw many puzzled faces. Finally, the young woman with the large glasses spoke up. “So, what you’re saying is that the information used to set up the DRBG fundamentally does not exist until just before the DRBG is set up, minimizing the window that an attacker has to learn that information?”

“I couldn’t have said it better myself!” exclaimed Stephan. “Let me summarize our discussion so far. Nearly all cryptographic security relies on the unpredictability of random numbers, so if our random numbers become predictable, then the rest of the work we do is moot. Entropy sources provide this fundamental unpredictability but aren’t sufficient to provide us with random numbers directly.”

Stephan took a breath, then continued. “So, as mentioned earlier, we bridge this gap with DRBGs. DRBGs themselves are entirely deterministic, so the outputs they produce aren’t random to anyone who knows the input used to set them up. This input data is thus the weakest link in our entire cryptographic universe and guarding it is of the utmost importance.”

Stephan paused for a moment to allow these ideas to soak in, then continued. “At an extremely abstract level, any information which exists is under threat of being discovered. Thus, the best way to guard information is to have it not exist at all! By minimizing the time for which the input data exists, we minimize the theoretical attack window.”

Looking around, Stephan saw nods of understanding. “Now, I believe we’ve properly motivated the idea of a DRBG. Let me now tell you how they work in practice.”

DRBG Functions “DRBGs are standardized in SP 800-90A [3]. This Special Publication describes the functions that a FIPS-compliant DRBG must implement, and provides several constructions based on different underlying cryptographic algorithms. To begin, what functions do you believe a DRBG should have?”

Immediately, the young woman spoke up. “Well, we clearly need a setup function which takes entropy as input, as you were just describing.”

“Yes, we certainly need a way to set up the DRBG,” affirmed Stephan. “The ‘setup’ function is called ‘Instantiate.’ To instantiate a DRBG, we provide it with a personalization string and a few other setup parameters. This personalization string provides no security; it’s simply a way for us to tie the DRBG to some particular context. If an attacker discovers this personalization string, it does not help them predict the outputs of the DRBG.”

"Wait," interjected someone from Stephan's left. "Don't we need to provide it with entropy as well?"

"Ah," said Stephan, "here we need to be careful. Suppose that we are responsible for providing the DRBG with entropy. One day, we get lazy and don't give it real entropy. Instead, we take some key and provide that to the DRBG as the entropy input. The DRBG itself just sees a string of bits, it has no idea where it came from, so it'll accept it as entropy input. However, the key was something we knew, and an attacker could have known it just as well! If we go on to use this DRBG to generate a new set of keys, then they could be compromised before they're ever even used!"

"So," replied the student, "we can't be responsible for providing the DRBG with entropy. Then, I guess the DRBG needs to have direct access to the entropy source?"

"Exactly right!" said Stephan. "The DRBG interfaces directly with an entropy source, ensuring that it will always be instantiated with fresh entropy." Stephan went on. "During instantiation, several steps are performed. First, the entropy input and personalization string are processed into a seed. A nonce is sometimes also added here as a security cushion. This seed is then used to derive an initial internal state for the DRBG. Once the internal state is set, the DRBG is instantiated. The exact processes and formats used depend on the kind of DRBG, but the overall flow is the same. Now, what else might a DRBG be expected to do?"

Another student piped up. "Well, presumably we need a way to actually get random bits from our DRBG."

"That would be the 'Generate' function," confirmed Stephan. "Conceptually, 'Generate' is quite simple: using the current internal state, it will derive a new internal state as well as a random bitstring. The random bitstring is output, and the new internal state is kept around to be used with the next 'Generate' call. Again, the mechanisms for these derivations are dependent on the type of DRBG."

"What other functions might a DRBG have?" Stephan looked around expectantly, but no one spoke up. "Let's think about this another way. Once we instantiate a DRBG, can we keep generating random output from it forever?"

After a few moments of thought, a student from across the table answered. "Well, the process is deterministic, and the internal state is presumably of finite length. By the pigeonhole principle, we'll thus eventually hit the same internal state twice, causing it to generate the same series of outputs as the first time it hit that internal state. This means that we can't keep generating forever."

"Very good!" exclaimed Stephan. "That, of course, is an extreme case, but a concrete one. More generally, the longer we continue to generate outputs from a given seed, the more patterns will emerge, weakening the security of future outputs. How might we get around this issue?"

The student responded immediately. "Well, after some given number of 'Generate' calls, we could just reinstantiate the DRBG with new entropy. Then, we'll be starting fresh."

Stephan nodded. "Yes, that's the right idea, though it's not quite what's done in practice. Instead, we define a 'Reseed' function. This function starts by obtaining fresh entropy directly from an entropy source, just like 'Instantiate.' This new entropy input is combined with the current internal state to derive a new seed. Also included is some optional additional input, which serves the same purpose as the personalization string in 'Instantiate.' The resulting seed is dependent on both the original entropy used to instantiate the DRBG and the fresh entropy obtained for the reseed request."

Backtracking Resistance and Prediction Resistance "That makes sense," said the student. "So, when exactly should the 'Reseed' function be called?"

"Well, you've already highlighted one scenario. As we generate more outputs from a single seed, the chances of some detectable pattern emerging increases. To combat this, the standard imposes a limit on the number of outputs which can be generated from a single seed. However, we are of course free to reseed before then and may choose to do so before generating random numbers that will be used for a particularly important purpose. To see why this might be prudent, let's discuss some properties of DRBGs.

"Recall our earlier discussion of randomness. We found that a good DRBG should produce outputs which are indistinguishable from outputs chosen independently from a uniform distribution. Now, suppose that an attacker reads a single output of our DRBG. What information have they gained?"

A student on Stephan's right responded quickly. "Well, you sort of answered your own question: If we designed our DRBG well, then knowing a single output shouldn't reveal any information about any other output."

"That's right," affirmed Stephan. "If just reading a single output gives us any relevant information other than the output itself, then we've done a poor job at designing a DRBG." Stephan looked around. "Now, suppose our attacker manages to read the internal state of our DRBG. In this case, what information have they gained?"

This time, it took several moments for someone to answer. "Well, they could certainly predict any future output by just copying our state into their own DRBG and running it from there," said a student. "I'm not exactly sure about past outputs though; they may be able to invert the generate function to recover a previous internal state."

"That's exactly the question the question you should be asking," said Stephan. "If we can invert the 'Generate' function, then a leak of any internal state leaks all of the past and future internal states, and in turn reveals all the other outputs produced by the DRBG. On the other hand, if the 'Generate' function can't be inverted, then leaking the internal state only compromises future outputs. As you can likely now guess, the 'Generate' function is designed to be difficult to invert for exactly this reason. We therefore say that DRBGs inherently provide 'backtracking resistance,' that is, a leak of the internal state does not allow an attacker to backtrack and determine previous outputs."

Stephan continued. "Similarly, we say that we have 'prediction resistance' if a leak of the internal state does not allow an attacker to predict future outputs. Of course, the 'Generate' function is deterministic, and so does not provide prediction resistance on its own. Instead, prediction resistance can be obtained using the 'Reseed' function. The injection of additional entropy ensures that future outputs cannot be derived from the current state."

Here, another student joined the conversation. “So, if we want to generate a random value that’s going to be used for a particularly important purpose, we can reseed right before generating that value. Then, prediction resistance ensures that no previous leak of the internal state will reveal this value, and backtracking resistance ensures that no future leak of the internal state will reveal this value. Thus, the only way that this random value could be compromised is if the attacker has active access to our DRBG and/or entropy source.”

“Exactly right,” confirmed Stephan. “Thus, the other major use of the ‘Reseed’ function is to provide prediction resistance.”

Managing Sensitive DRBG Parameters Once again, Stephan looked around the table. After so much discussion, nearly all of the plates had been cleaned, yet all of the students were eagerly awaiting his next point. “Now, there’s one more DRBG function that we haven’t yet talked about, namely the ‘Uninstantiate’ function. As you can probably guess, this function oversees cleaning up the DRBG state and ensuring that no potentially sensitive values are left around. The details aren’t particularly interesting, though it highlights some important security considerations. Which values might be particularly important for the ‘Uninstantiate’ function to clear?”

A student spoke up. “Well, all of the random values are derived deterministically from the most recent seed, so it’s probably important to clear out that seed.”

Stephan raised an eyebrow. “Certainly; we wouldn’t want anyone getting their hands on the seed. However, is there a need for the seed to persist after it’s used to derive the initial internal state?”

“Hmm, I suppose not,” mused the student. “‘Generate’ only uses the internal state, not the seed. Does this mean that the seed is destroyed as soon as the internal state has been derived?”

“Well, the standard does not require that the seed, or the entropy input, are zeroized after use. However, these parameters have the potential to compromise the random values produced by the DRBG and have no further use beyond instantiation or reseeding, so it is prudent to do so. The standard does require that the seed and entropy input be protected at least as well as any data that might be protected by the output of the DRBG.”

“OK,” replied the student, “in that case, would the ‘Uninstantiate’ function just zeroize the internal state?”

“Yes, exactly,” said Stephan. “Though backtracking and prediction resistance are both defined under a model where an attacker has obtained a particular internal state, these values are still meant to be kept secret, and so the standard ensures that we properly clean them up.”

CTR_DRBG Once again, the young woman with the large glasses cut in. “You said that we would discuss the actual mechanisms behind DRBGs, and yet we’re still talking about how they work in a theoretical sense. What does an ‘Instantiate’ function actually look like?”

Stephan chuckled. “You have been patient, and I hope now to reward that patience. I believe we are indeed ready to talk about the mechanisms that make DRBGs tick. To begin, a question for you: given what we’ve discussed, which cryptographic components may be useful in constructing a DRBG?”

The young woman thought a moment. “We need some function that produces uniformly distributed random-looking output. That sounds a lot like what encryption does. We could probably use AES as a building block for the ‘Generate’ function; then, the ‘Instantiate’ function would need to turn all of the input data into some key and data from which to begin.”

Stephan raised his eyebrows in surprise. “Are you sure you haven’t learned this all before? What you’re describing is the essence of a CTR_DRBG.”

The young woman looked surprised. “Really? This is all new to me, but I figured that construction just makes sense given everything we’ve talked about. I’m not sure how to fill in the details, though.”

“I don’t think you give yourself enough credit,” responded Stephan. “Your intuition is sharp. As you rightly pointed out, the AES cipher block can serve as a pseudorandom function which is difficult to invert, at least without the key. Using this, we can construct a suitable DRBG. First, we must define an internal state. The internal state of a CTR_DRBG consists of two values, ‘Key’ and ‘V.’ ‘Key’ can be 128, 192, or 256 bits, depending on the desired security strength of the DRBG; ‘V’ is the length of a single AES block, namely 128 bits.

“All of the low-level details can be found in SP 800-90A, but I’ll give you a general idea of how each of the functions work. First, ‘Generate’: As you can probably guess, ‘Key’ will be used as an AES key, and ‘V’ will be used as data. More accurately, ‘V’ is used as a counter, hence the name CTR_DRBG. To generate a block of 128 random bits, we simply use ‘Key’ to encrypt ‘V,’ then ‘V’ is incremented by 1. If more than 128 bits are requested from a given ‘Generate’ call, this process is repeated until enough bits have been generated. Then, to update the internal state, that same process is performed several more times to get another chunk of random data. Instead of using this data as output, it’s split into two parts, and those two parts are the next ‘Key’ and ‘V.’”

Conceptually, the CTR_DRBG and the AES-CTR mode encryption share close resemblance: The CTR_DRBG effectively generates the key stream the same way as the AES-CTR mode does. But instead of XORing it with the plaintext or ciphertext like AES-CTR, the CTR_DRBG returns the key stream as random bit string.

The young woman nodded along. “So, the AES block cipher is used in something like counter mode to generate a bunch of data, and some of that data is output while the rest is used to update the internal state. At a high level, that’s simple enough. How does ‘Instantiate’ work?”

"'Instantiate' for CTR_DRBG can be a bit tricky. To see why, we need a bit more theory. You see, in our earlier foray into entropy, I neglected to introduce the idea of 'full entropy.' Recall that entropy is a measurement of unpredictability; the unit of measurement is, for better or worse, bits. So, when we assess the entropy rate of a bitstring, we measure in bits of entropy per data bit, which we often shorten to bits per bit. A more detailed discussion of entropy is warranted, but perhaps another day. The important consequence here is that you cannot have more than one bit of entropy per data bit; this is equivalent to saying that one bit can carry at most one bit of information. From this, we define a full entropy bitstring as a bitstring whose entropy rate is one bit per bit."

A student to the left of Stephan spoke up. "You mentioned earlier that real entropy sources exhibit bias—does this reduce the entropy rate?"

Stephan nodded. "Indeed, it does. Thus, entropy sources won't generally produce full entropy bitstrings without some help from what are called 'conditioning components.' Conditioning components are a tool that can compress long strings with lower entropy rates into short strings with higher entropy rates. Given enough input entropy, full entropy strings can be produced. However, not all entropy sources include such a conditioning component."

Stephan paused for a moment, then continued his explanation. "Recall that our internal state for a CTR_DRBG is 'Key' and 'V,' and each of these values has a fixed length. If the incoming entropy string is, say, 16,384 bits long because the entropy rate is very low, we need a way to compress that into a short, high-entropy seed that can be used to derive initial values for 'Key' and 'V.' We thus define a derivation function called Block_Cipher_df for exactly this purpose. The inner workings of this function are a little complex, and they resemble the application of AES-CBC-MAC on the seed data, but you can find the details in the standard."

"Well, if you're not going to explain how it works, why bring it up in the first place?" retorted the young woman with the large glasses.

"I bring this up only because it leads to a particularly important consideration that one should be aware of," replied Stephan. "You see, SP 800-90A allows the use of a CTR_DRBG without that derivation function. However, if that derivation function isn't present, then the DRBG has no way to compress entropy. Thus, if a CTR_DRBG is used without a derivation function, it requires full entropy input to be FIPS approved."

Stephan went on. "Going back to the details of instantiation, a CTR_DRBG is instantiated as follows: If a derivation function is present, then it takes in the entropy input and the personalization string, as well as a nonce, and outputs a fixed-length seed; if no derivation function is used, the entropy input is simply XORed with the personalization string to produce the seed. Next, a key of 0 is used to encrypt a counter which starts at zero, then the resulting data is XORed with the seed and split into two parts. The first part is the initial value of 'Key', while the second is the initial value of 'V'. This is exactly the process used at the end of 'Generate' to derive the next internal state, only we start with both 'Key' and 'V' equal to zero."

The young woman nodded in understanding. “I suppose that reseed works in the same way, except that we use the current values of ‘Key’ and ‘V’ instead of the initial zero values?”

“Exactly right,” said Stephan. “As you can see, there’s no magic in these internals, just a lot of calls to the AES block cipher.”

HMAC_DRBG Across the table, another student spoke up. “You mentioned that there were several DRBG constructions. We could probably use a hash function to produce random-looking data, right?”

“Indeed, we can,” agreed Stephan, “and in fact, both other DRBG constructions defined in SP 800-90A are based on hash functions. To begin, let’s define the HMAC_DRBG. Just as with the counter DRBG, our internal state consists of ‘Key’ and ‘V’; ‘Key’ will of course serve as our HMAC key, while ‘V’ will be our data. Given this internal state, we generate random bits by calling V=HMAC(Key, V), and outputting the new value of V. If more bits are requested than the particular instance of HMAC outputs, the process is simply repeated. Finally, to update the internal state, we run HMAC(Key, V) two additional times. The first output becomes the new value of K, and the second becomes the new value of V—this is the basic flow.”

“Sounds like we’re just calling HMAC a bunch of times,” said a student. “I suppose that because everything is done with random-looking data, all the results are going to be random too. And since we can’t easily invert an HMAC call, we end up with backtracking resistance.”

“That is indeed the main takeaway here,” affirmed Stephan. “For the purposes of this discussion, you can absolutely consider the HMAC_DRBG ‘Generate’ function as nothing more than a bunch of HMAC calls. When needed, the standard will fill in all the remaining details. Now, continuing onwards, how might we instantiate an HMAC_DRBG?”

“Probably by calling HMAC a bunch more times,” the student blurted out.

Stephan laughed. “Yes, we do call HMAC a bunch more times. To be slightly more precise, we take some initial values for ‘Key’ and ‘V’ and then form a seed by simply concatenating all input data, which includes the entropy input, the personalization string, and a nonce. This seed is concatenated to ‘V,’ and HMAC is called with ‘Key’ on that data to produce the initial value of ‘Key.’ HMAC is called once again on ‘V’ using the new ‘Key’ to get an initial value of ‘V.’ This process is repeated one more time for good measure, and the resulting values of ‘Key’ and ‘V’ serve as the initial internal state.”

Another student chimed in. “I imagine that the ‘Reseed’ process does the same thing, except we use the current internal state in place of the initial values?”

“Correct. And that just about covers the HMAC_DRBG.”

Hash_DRBG Looking around the table, Stephan saw that the meal was starting to take its toll: the students were getting sleepy despite their best efforts to continue listening. “Before we adjourn, let me quickly give an overview of the Hash_DRBG. We don’t need to go into too much detail about the inner workings, as it ends up mostly being a lot of calls to a hash function, and the calls aren’t quite as easy to follow. Instead, I'll just note a few important details: As with CTR_DRBG, Hash_ DRBG has a derivation function, except this derivation function isn't optional. The purpose of the derivation function is the same; it serves as a way to distribute the entropy input into the DRBG across the seed."

Stephan took a breath, then continued. "Unlike AES and HMAC, a hash by itself doesn't have a key. This means the internal state must be defined in a different manner. Instead of 'Key' and 'V,' we have 'V' and 'C,' both of which are created by running the derivation function on the input data. To generate random bits, 'V' is used to initialize a counter, which is hashed until the requested amount of output data is produced. 'C' is then used to update 'V' in preparation for the next generate request. And with that, I'll leave you for the night."

Epilogue As the students got up to leave, all of them thanked Stephan profusely for the discussion. The day had been an eye-opening experience; real world considerations weren't common in their cryptography classes. The conference and conversation with Stephan had given them a window into how FIPS bridges the mathematical theory of cryptography with practical applications and security considerations.

As Stephan expected, the young woman with the large glasses was the last to get up. Once the rest of the students were gone, she walked over to him.

"Thanks for bearing with my questions," she said.

"Of course, it was my pleasure!" responded Stephan. "I very much understand the drive to look directly at the algorithm; after all, that's what you'll find if you look at any cryptographic implementation. I do, however, hope that you understand my desire to provide the proper motivation. After all, anyone can follow the given steps to create a working implementation, but only by understanding the broader context can you ensure that the implementation is secure."

"Yeah, your explanations made a lot of sense," she said. I usually like to start with the algorithm, but after understanding the properties that a DRBG should have, the basic construction sort of just came to me. I never really expected to be able to think like that."

"I did mean it earlier when I said that your intuition is very good. We need more people like you in the field!" Stephan paused for a moment. "I'm not sure I ever caught your name."

The young lady looked embarrassed. "You can just call me A." She hesitated for a moment, then continued. "It's short for A5F5BB0F. My parents wanted me to have a unique name, so they generated one with a DRBG."

Stephan, for once, had no reply.

"That's a joke; the name is Aster," the girl quipped. "Had you in the first half!" (Fig. 10.1).

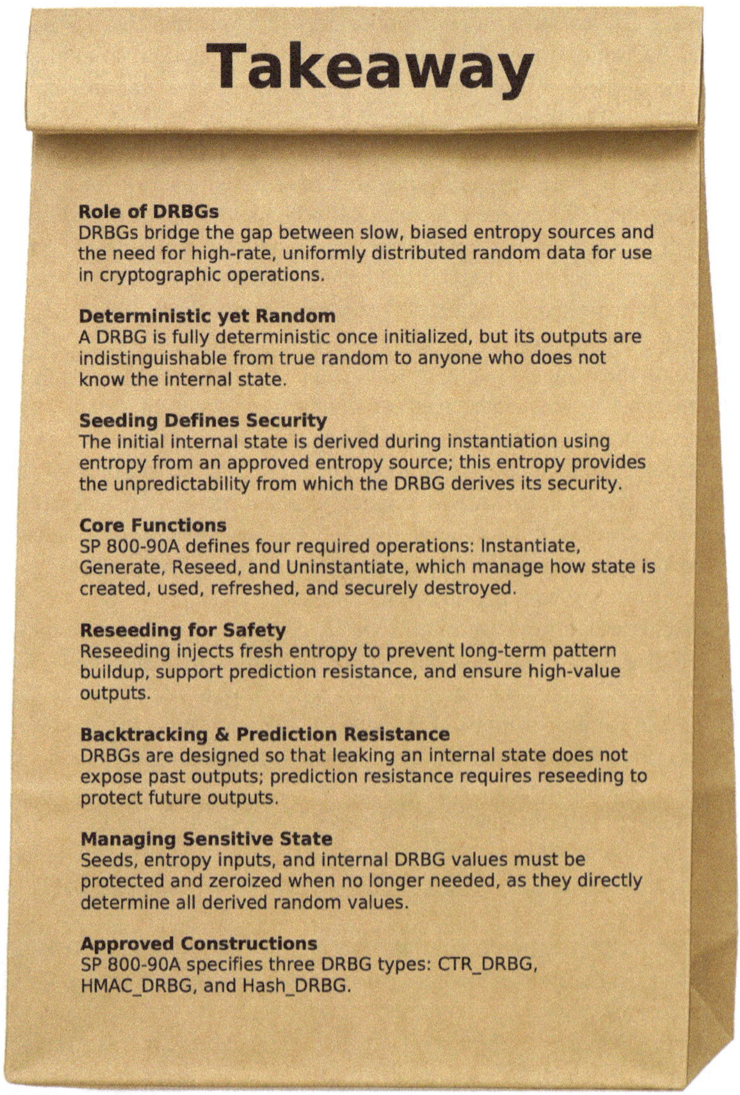

Fig. 10.1 Takeaways regarding deterministic random bit generators

References

1. Derek Muller (2024) Why is this number everywhere? https://www.youtube.com/watch?v=d6iQrh2TK98. Accessed 5 Dec 2025
2. National Institute of Standards and Technology (2020) Recommendation for key management: Part 1—General. In: NIST Publications. The National Institute of Standards and Technology. Available via NIST. https://csrc.nist.gov/pubs/sp/800/57/pt1/r5/final. Accessed 26 Nov 2025

3. National Institute of Standards and Technology (2015) Recommendation for random number generation using deterministic random bit generators. In: NIST Publications. The National Institute of Standards and Technology. Available via NIST. https://csrc.nist.gov/pubs/sp/800/90/a/r1/final. Accessed 26 Nov 2025

Chapter 11
Digital Signature Algorithms

Alessandro Fazio

Alessandro wants to return to the FIPS 'n' Chips restaurant—it's been a long walk from the office, and he's quite thirsty at this point. This time, he decides to indulge his sweet tooth by ordering a simple chocolate milk; after placing a quick call, the order is placed.

By the time Alessandro reaches FIPS 'n' Chips, he's parched—he needs that chocolate milk now! After taking a seat, the waiter arrives and is excited to deliver a popular confection for the restaurant: milk chocolate!

Alessandro immediately informs the waiter that there must be an error, he asked for chocolate milk; the waiter is confused because he's quite confident that the order was milk chocolate. After a bit of back and forth, the waiter suggests: "Next time, use our restaurant application to make orders—that should hopefully clear up this confusion."

Aster, sitting nearby and following the conversation closely, interjects: "But then, how do you distinguish between the different orders that arrive from different people? How do you make sure that the order comes from exactly the person that made the order and that the order can only be modified by the person that asked for it?"

Alessandro replies: "Among the possible techniques, we should check if the restaurant app already has digital signature implemented."

"I'm familiar with the concept of replicating a hand-made signature digitally, but I'm not quite sure how it'd be implemented," Aster reflected, "Could you explain the specifics of digital signatures?"

"Sure, but I'll need a drink first—grab me a chocolate milk, and let's dive in," Alessandro said with a smile.

Introduction The FIPS 186–5 [9], also known as the Digital Signature Standard (DSS), defines the approved algorithms for the generation and verification of digital signatures.

A. Fazio (✉)
atsec information security corporation, Austin, TX, USA
e-mail: alessandro.fazio@atsec.com

Y. Mao (ed.), *Tasting Cryptography*, https://doi.org/10.1007/978-3-032-30243-4_11

FIPS 186–5 [9], published in 2023, supersedes FIPS 186–4 [11] and introduces new algorithms; the inclusion of EdDSA reflects growing interest in modern and efficient cryptographic primitives.

To bring Aster up to speed, Alessandro would present a structured overview and technical exploration of each algorithm family within the standard—DSA, RSA, ECDSA, and EdDSA—focusing on their design motivations, construction, and relevance in secure systems today.

The Baseline "Just so I'm clear, can you go over why we need these digital signatures in the first place? I want to make sure I have an expert's opinion," Aster asked.

Happy to do so, Alessandro first covered the basics.

The baseline of Digital signatures is:

- Authentication—proof about the origin of a message.
- Integrity—the message was not altered.
- Non-repudiation—the signer can't go back and deny the signature.

Mathematically, a digital signature scheme consists of three core operations:

- Key Generation—Produces a public/private key pair.
- Signing—Using the private key to generate a signature over a message.
- Verification—Using the public key to verify that a signature is valid.

FIPS 186–5 defines the requirements for such operations. [9]

NIST SP 800-131Ar3 and Implementation Guidance Aster nodded, as that aligned with what she had been taught. "Ok so we really need digital signatures, but can we use it as it is? Will such requirements evolve?"

NIST Special Publication 800-131A Revision 3 NIST Special Publication 800-131A Revision 3 [6] defines cryptographic transitions and recommends key lengths and algorithm use across U.S. federal systems.

The requirements in such special publications include the transitions for usage in digital signature generation and verification operations, like using DSA only for legacy applications, transitioning to 128-bit of security strength only for signature generation, and restricting 112-bit security strength signature verification to legacy applications.

In addition to this, NIST has published several implementation guidance documents (or IGs) that provide clarifications and addition to the already existing requirements in FIPS 186–5 [9].

IG C.A—Use of Non-Approved Elliptic Curves Implementation Guidance (IG) C.A [3] specifies that the approved curves for usage in ECDSA are defined in FIPS 186–5 [4] and NIST SP800-186 [5].

The use of elliptic curves in ECDSA is allowed for curves present in NIST SP 800–186 Appendix H.1 [5]—including brainpoolP224r1, brainpoolP256r1, brainpoolP320r1, brainpoolP384r1, and brainpoolP512r1, or the twisted variants—along with curves in NIST SP 800–186 Appendix H.2 [5], namely secp256k1.

The use of elliptic curves in EdDSA is allowed for curves present in FIPS 186–5 [9] and NIST SP800-186 [5]: Edwards25519 and Edwards448.

IG C.E—Key Generation for the RSA Signature Algorithm IG C.E [8] clarifies that RSA key generation shall be performed only with approved methods defined in FIPS 186–5 [9] when implemented in a FIPS 140–3-validated module. This needs to be performed if the cryptographic module implements key generation for usage in signature operations.

IG C.F—RSA Approved Parameter Sizes in FIPS 186–5 IG C.F [8] clarifies that at least one of the RSA modulus lengths implemented by the cryptographic module shall be CAVP testable. If there's a modulus size that has no CAVP test, this shall be documented in the security policy.

The implementation guidance also defines limits on the minimum number of Miller-Rabin tests that must be performed during Key Generation: either follow Table B.1 of FIPS 186–5 [9] for Miller-Rabin and then perform a Lucas test in compliance with FIPS 186–5 [9] section B.3.3; or perform at least 25 Miller-Rabin tests.

Lastly, the implementation guidance dictates that legacy modulus sizes (i.e., from FIPS 186–2 [12] or FIPS 186–4 [11]) shall be CAVP tested at least with one modulus size.

IG C.K—Transitioning from FIPS 186–4 to FIPS 186–5 IG C.K [8] clarifies the transition from FIPS 186–4 [11] to FIPS 186–5 [9].

FIPS 186–5 [9] replaced FIPS 186–4 [11] in 2023, and starting from February 5th, 2024, the CMVP has not accepted new submissions that implement DSA or RSA X9.31 in approved mode, other than signature verification for legacy purposes.

The same happens for using ECDSA with curves not included in NIST SP800-186. [5]

"Okay, that's a lot of clarifications from IGs, but coming back to the algorithm itself, what does a Digital Signature provide?" Aster asked, trying to make sense of everything.

After generating the key pair, the core operations of a Digital Signature implementation are:

- Generate: Given a message and a private key, generate the signature.
- Verify: Given the signature and a public key, verify the signature.

Let's look at how Digital Signature algorithms are implemented. FIPS 186–5 approves four signature algorithms: RSA, DSA, ECDSA, EdDSA. [5]

Digital Signature Algorithm (DSA) "Going alphabetically—what does DSA stand for? And, more importantly, how does it work?" Alessandro rhetorically questioned before diving into specifics.

The Digital Signature Algorithm (DSA) was first introduced in 1991 by the U.S. National Institute of Standards and Technology (NIST) as part of the original Digital Signature Standard (DSS), defined in FIPS 186.

Over time, it has evolved to support larger key sizes and more secure parameter generation processes. As anticipated, while DSA is no longer considered state-of-the-art in terms of performance and flexibility compared to ECDSA or EdDSA, it remains in FIPS 186–5 [5] primarily for legacy compatibility.

Construction The Digital Signature Algorithm (DSA) is built upon the mathematical structure of modular arithmetic and finite cyclic groups, particularly focusing on the Discrete Logarithm Problem (DLP).

At a high level, DSA operates within the multiplicative group of integers modulo a prime number. The core idea is that exponentiation within this group is computationally easy, while the inverse operation—computing discrete logarithms—is computationally infeasible for large enough values.

Domain Parameters Before using DSA, a set of cryptographic parameters must be established. These include:

- A large prime modulus p, which defines the finite field.
- A smaller prime q, which divides p − 1.
- A generator g of this subgroup.

These values—p,q,g—are referred to as domain parameters, and can be shared across multiple users.

Key Generation Each participant generates a key pair with the procedures described in FIPS 186–5 [9] (either Extra Random Bits or Testing Candidates). However, the main idea behind the key generation is that a private key x is randomly generated from an approved NIST SP800-90A [7] DRBG and selected in the interval:

$$x \in [1, q - 1] \tag{11.1}$$

And the corresponding public key y is computed using the formula:

$$y = g^x modp \tag{11.2}$$

Signing a Message To create a digital signature for a message M, the following steps are performed:

First, the message is hashed using a secure hash function, such as SHA-256, producing a digest H. This ensures the message is represented in fixed-length format suitable for mathematical operations:

$$H = \text{Hash}(M) \tag{11.3}$$

A per-message secret k is then chosen at random from the interval:

$$k \in [1, q - 1] \tag{11.4}$$

This value must be unique and kept secret for every signature, as reusing k across messages can expose the private key.

The algorithm then computes two values:

- The first component

$$r = (g^k modp) modq \tag{11.5}$$

- The second component, which incorporates the private key

$$s = k^{-1}(H + x \cdot r) \bmod q \quad (11.6)$$

- The signature is the pair (r, s)

Verifying a Signature To verify that a signature r,s on a message M is valid, the verifier must:

- Ensure that both r and s lie within the range:

$$0 < r < q \text{ and } 0 < s < q \quad (11.7)$$

- Compute the hash of the message:

$$H = \text{Hash}(M) \quad (11.8)$$

- Calculate the modular inverse of s modulo q:

$$w = s^{-1} modq \quad (11.9)$$

- Compute the values:

$$u_1 = H \cdot wmodq; u_2 = r \cdot wmodq \quad (11.10)$$

Using the public key y, calculate:

$$v = \left(\left(g^{u_1} \cdot y^{u_2}\right) \bmod p\right) \bmod q \quad (11.11)$$

The signature is considered valid if v = r.

This process confirms that the message was signed by the holder of the private key corresponding to the public key y, and that the message has not been altered.

FIPS 186–5 Allowed Parameters FIPS 186–5 [9] specifies allowed parameters in FIPS 186–5 [4] Sect. 4.2.

L is the size of the modulus p, and N is the size of q. The choice of appropriate hash function depends on the bit length of q and the desired security level.

Deterministic Signatures A variant of DSA is known as deterministic DSA. RFC 6979 [10] specifies that a deterministic algorithm, like a key derivation function, can be used instead of a DRBG.

This removes the dependency on random number generators and prevents leakage of x due to repeated or biased k.

Usage and Transition Guidance While DSA is still included in FIPS 186–5 [9], its use is largely limited to legacy systems. Modern cryptographic standards increasingly recommend or mandate the use of Elliptic Curve Digital Signature Algorithm (ECDSA) or Edwards-curve Digital Signature Algorithm (EdDSA), due to their improved efficiency, smaller key sizes, and stronger resistance to implementation errors.

For new or existing systems, DSA shall not be claimed unless verifying existing signatures as per NIST's guidance in SP 800-131A Rev. 3 [1].

RSA "Okay, so I heard you mention ECDSA and EdDSA as successors to DSA, but what about RSA?" Aster queried.

RSA (Rivest–Shamir–Adleman) is a widely-used public-key cryptographic algorithm for digital signatures, standardized in FIPS 186–5 [4]. RSA's security is based on the difficulty of factoring large composite integers.

RSA is so widely used because it provides interoperability with legacy systems, robust mathematical security, and adjustable key sizes. RSA supports two signature padding schemes:

- RSASSA-PSS (probabilistic signature scheme)
- RSASSA-PKCS1 v1.5 (deterministic)

Underlying Cipher and Mathematics The parameters used in RSA are:

- Two large primes p, q which shall be generated via approved NIST SP 800-90A [2] DRBG and shall have equal bit length

$$|p| = |q| = \frac{|n|}{2} \tag{11.12}$$

  where n is the modulus size.
- Modulus:

$$n = p \cdot q \tag{11.13}$$

  which shall be

$$|n| \geq 2048 \tag{11.14}$$

  bits, an even number of bits and shall be a product of exactly two distinct primes.
- Public exponent e, an odd integer satisfying

$$2^{16} < e < 2^{256} \tag{11.15}$$

- Private exponent d, computed as the modular inverse of e modulo $\varphi(n)$, where

$$\varphi(n) = (p - 1)(q - 1). \tag{11.16}$$

- Approved hash functions: SHA2-224, SHA2-256, SHA2-384, SHA2-512, SHAKE128, SHAKE256.

Key Generation Because RSA is based on the Integer Factorization problem (big numbers are hard to decompose), the key generation is composed by:

- Finding two primes named p and q.
- Getting the key from the primes.

FIPS 186–5 [9] Appendix A.1 describes different methods to generate the primes p and q:

- Generation of Random Primes that are Provably Prime.
- Generation of Random Primes that are Probably Prime.
- Generation of Provable Primes with Conditions Based on Auxiliary Provable Primes.
- Generation of Probable Primes with Conditions Based on Auxiliary Provable Primes.
- Generation of Probable Primes with Conditions Based on Auxiliary Probable Primes.

Generation of Random Primes that are Provably Prime To generate a provably prime p, the FIPS 186–5 [9] standard requires using algorithms that produce a proof of primality (such as the Lucas test combined with a strong primality test).

The process is:

- Generate a seed using a NIST SP 800-90A [2] approved DRBG.
- Generate p and q based on the procedure in FIPS 186–5 [9] Appendix B.10.
- Check that

$$|\mathrm{p} - \mathrm{q}| \leq 2^{(\mathrm{nlen}/2-100)} \tag{11.17}$$

  and, if this condition is met, return (p,q). Otherwise, re-generate q.

Generation of Random Primes that are Probably Prime This method is used to generate p, q which are probable primes.

The process is:

- Generate p and q via a NIST SP 800-90A [7] approved DRBG.
- Apply any primality test in compliance with FIPS 186–5 [9] Appendix B.3, using parameters from Table B.1.
- If p and q are probably primes, return (p, q).

Generation of Provable Primes with Conditions Based on Auxiliary Provable Primes This method leverages on the so-called primes with conditions, i.e., the primes p and q have the following characteristics:

- (p–1) has a prime factor p_1
- (p + 1) has a prime factor p_2
- (q–1) has a prime factor q_1
- (q + 1) has a prime factor q_2

In this case, the following applies: p_1, p_2, q_1, q_2, p, q shall be provable primes. The process is:

- Generate a seed using a NIST SP 800-90A [7] approved DRBG.
- Generate p_1, p_2, q_1, q_2, p, q based on the procedure in FIPS 186–5 [9] Appendix B.10.
- Check that

$$|p - q| \leq 2^{(nlen/2-100)} \tag{11.18}$$

and, if this condition is met, return (p, q). Otherwise, re-generate q.

Generation of Probable Primes with Conditions Based on Auxiliary Provable Primes This method is similar to the previous one but the generated primes p, q are probable primes.

The process is:

- Generate p_1, p_2, q_1, q_2 based on the generation routine in FIPS 186–5 [9] Appendix B.6, called Shawe-Taylor Random_Prime Routine.
- Generate p, q based on the generation routing in FIPS 186–5 [9] Appendix B.9, which also relies on a NIST SP 800-90A [7] approved DRBG.
- Apply any primality test in compliance with FIPS 186–5 [9] Appendix B.3, using parameters from Table B.1.
- Check that

$$|p - q| \leq 2^{(nlen/2-100)} \tag{11.19}$$

is met and that the same condition is met for the random numbers used to generate the primes. If this condition is met, return (p, q); otherwise, re-generate q.

Generation of Probable Primes with Conditions Based on Auxiliary Probable Primes This is the same concept as generating provable primes based on auxiliary primes but, in this case, we're talking about probable primes.

The process is:

- Generate X_{p1}, X_{p2} and X_{q1}, X_{q2} odd random numbers via a NIST SP 800-90A approved DRBG.
- Iterate starting from such numbers until the next probable prime is found. Apply any primality test in compliance with FIPS 186–5 Appendix B.3.
- Check that

$$|p - q| \leq 2^{(nlen/2-100)} \tag{11.20}$$

is met and that the same condition is met for the random numbers used to generate the primes. If this condition is met, return (p, q); otherwise, re-generate q.

- As mentioned before, after having p and q, we can generate the private key d and the public key e.

Signing a Message The message M is hashed with an approved hash function H to get digest

$$m = H(M) \tag{11.21}$$

The signer computes the signature s using either RSASSA-PSS or RSASSA-PKCS1 v1.5.

RSASSA-PSS Signature Scheme The RSASSA-PSS scheme incorporates probabilistic padding and uses mask generation functions (MGF) to provide strong security guarantees by going through the following:

- Hash the message

$$m = H(M) \tag{11.22}$$

- Generate a random salt s of length sLen bits where:

$$0 \leq sLen \leq hLen \tag{11.23}$$

(hLen is the length of the hash output in bytes).

- Construct message M' as

$$M' = 0 \times 0000000000000000\|m\|s \tag{11.24}$$

which is composed by:

- 0x0000000000000000: 8-byte 0 value.
- m: the message hash.
- s: the random salt.
- Hash M' to produce:

$$H' = H\left(M'\right) \tag{11.25}$$

- Generate a mask using the Mask Generation Function on H', which can be either

MGF1

$$\text{mask} = \text{MGF1}\left(H', \text{emLen} - hLen - 1\right) \tag{11.26}$$

where emLen is the length of the encoded message in bytes

SHAKE128

$$SHAKE128\left(H', 8 \cdot (\text{emLen} - hLen - 1)\right) \tag{11.27}$$

where emLen is the length of the encoded message in bytes
SHAKE256

$$SHAKE256\big(H', 8 \cdot (\text{emLen} - hLen - 1)\big) \tag{11.28}$$

where emLen is the length of the encoded message in bytes

- Construct the encoded message *EM* by combining the masked data and padding bits.
- Compute the signature:

$$s = EM^d modn \tag{11.29}$$

RSASSA-PKCS1 v1.5 Signature Scheme This scheme is deterministic and follows legacy padding from PKCS#1 v1.5.

It is accomplished through the following steps:

- Hash the message:

$$m = H(M) \tag{11.30}$$

- Construct a DigestInfo ASN.1 structure embedding the hash algorithm identifier and the hash m.
- Build the encoded message EM:

$$EM = 0 \times 00 \| 0 \times 01 \| \underbrace{0 \times FF \cdots 0 \times FF}_{\text{padding}} \| 0 \times 00 \| \text{DigestInfo}. \tag{11.31}$$

- Compute the signature:

$$s = EM^d modn. \tag{11.32}$$

This operation is deterministic because it does not require any random numbers during the encoding.

Verifying a Signature Verification for both padding schemes involves:

- Compute:

$$m' = s^e \bmod n. \tag{11.33}$$

- Parse EM from m'.
- Check padding format (PSS or PKCS1 v1.5). Specifically, for the RSASSA-PSS scheme, check the salt length will be in the range $0 \leq sLen \leq hLen$.
- Extract the message digest and compare it to a newly computed:

$$m = H(M). \tag{11.34}$$

- Accept if they match; otherwise, reject.

ECDSA—Elliptic Curve Digital Signature Algorithm "And that's RSA," Alessandro concludes.

"There's still two to go, right? What about ECDSA?" Aster asked, pressing for more info.

Alessandro nodded and launched into the details for the Elliptic Curve Digital Signature Algorithm.

The Elliptic Curve Digital Signature Algorithm (ECDSA) is a FIPS-approved public key digital signature algorithm based on elliptic curve cryptography (ECC). It provides the ability to verify the authenticity and integrity of digital data using a compact key and signature size. ECDSA is specified in FIPS 186–5, Sect. 6 [9].

ECDSA has gained wide adoption due to the following advantages:

- Efficiency: Smaller key and signature sizes result in lower bandwidth and faster computation.
- Security: Based on the hardness of the Elliptic Curve Discrete Logarithm Problem (ECDLP).
- Suitability for Constrained Devices: Ideal for IoT, smartcards, and mobile devices.

Domain Parameters First, in order to make use of ECDSA, we need the so-called domain parameters.

ECDSA operates over a subgroup of points on an elliptic curve defined over a finite prime field. The domain parameters define the curve and the group used, and they include:

- Field size q.
- FR: basis used.
- Coefficients a,b defining the standard elliptic curve equation.
- Type: indicates the elliptic curve model.
- Base point G, the generator of the subgroup.
- Order n of the subgroup generated by G.
- Cofactor h: it's the order of the curve divided by n.
- domain_parameter_seed: optional bit string which is present if the elliptic curve was generated from the seed in a verifiable fashion.

Domain Parameter Generation FIPS 186–5 [9] specifies different approaches for domain parameter selection: prime fields (p-curves), binary fields (b-curves), and Koblitz curves.

Domain Parameter Management Domain parameters shall be associated to the key pair and shall be protected from unauthorized modification until the set is deactivated.

After the correct generation of domain parameters, we can generate keys to be used in ECDSA digital signature operations.

Private/Public Keys In ECDSA, each signer possesses:

- A private key d, a randomly selected integer in the interval [1, n-1].

- A public key Q, which is the elliptic curve point:

$$Q = d \cdot G \tag{11.35}$$

- The private key is used to generate signatures; the public key is used to verify them.

Key Pair Generation FIPS 186–5 [9] specifies two compliant methods for generating ECDSA key pairs:

- Appendix A.2.1—Using Extra Random Bits
- Appendix A.2.2—Using Rejection Sampling

ECDSA Key Generation Using Extra Random Bits

- Let

$$N = \text{len}(n) \tag{11.36}$$

  the bit length of the order n. Make sure that $N \geq 224$.
- Use a DRBG to generate a bitstring with a length included in column 3 of Table A.2 of FIPS 186–5 [9]. This length is more than the size of N to prevent bias introduced by the next modular conversion.
- Convert the bitstring to an integer d.
- Compute the public key

$$Q = d \cdot G \tag{11.37}$$

- The output will be the key pair (d, Q).

ECDSA Key Generation Using Rejection Sampling

- Let $N = \text{len}(n)$.
- Use DRBG to generate a uniformly random N-bit integer d.
- If d = 0 or $d \geq n$, reject and retry.
- Compute:

$$Q = d \cdot G \tag{11.38}$$

- The output will be the key pair (d, Q).

Key Pair Management The generated keys shall only be used for signature generation and verification operations.

ECDSA Per-Message Secret Number Each ECDSA signature requires a secret value

$$k \in [1, n - 1] \tag{11.39}$$

called the per-message secret. The security of ECDSA relies on keeping k unpredictable and unique per message.

Generation of k Using Extra Random Bits

- Let $N = \text{len}(n)$.
- Generate a random integer x with at least N + 64 bits.
- Convert it to an integer k.
- If k = 0 or $k \geq n$, retry.

Generation of k Using Rejection Sampling

- Let $N = \text{len}(n) with N \geq 224$.
- Generate a random number of N bits.
- Convert it to an integer k.
- If k = 0 or $k \geq$ n, reject and retry.

Generation of Per-Message **Secret Number for Deterministic ECDSA** Instead of generating k randomly, deterministic ECDSA computes k as a function of:

- The private key d.
- The hash of the message m = H(M).

A common deterministic method follows RFC 6979 [10]:

$$k = \text{HMAC - DRBG}(d, m) \tag{11.40}$$

This ensures the same message signed twice with the same key produces the same signature, eliminating risks from poor random number generators.

Signature Generation Given private key d, message hash m, and per-message secret k:

- Compute:

$$(x_1, y_1) = k \cdot G \tag{11.41}$$

$$r = x_1 mod n \tag{11.42}$$

- If r = 0, retry with new k.
- Compute:

$$s = k^{-1}(m + d \cdot r) mod n \tag{11.43}$$

- If s = 0, retry with new k.
- Destroy k and k^{-1}.
- The output signature is (r, s).

Signature Verification Given public key Q, message hash m, and signature (r, s):

1. Check

$$r, s \in [1, n-1] \tag{11.44}$$

If not, reject.

2. Compute:

$$w = s^{-1} \bmod n \tag{11.45}$$

$$u = m \cdot w \bmod n \tag{11.46}$$

$$v = r \cdot w \bmod n \tag{11.47}$$

3. Compute:

$$(x', y') = u \cdot G + v \cdot Q \tag{11.48}$$

4. Reject if:

$$(x', y') = \mathcal{O} \tag{11.49}$$

5. Accept if:

$$r \equiv x' \bmod n \tag{11.50}$$

Assurances To ensure a valid implementation:

Each intended signatory shall obtain a digital signature key pair that is generated as specified for the appropriate digital signature algorithm, either by generating the key pair itself or by obtaining the key pair from a trusted party.

After obtaining the key pair, the key pair owner shall obtain assurance of the validity of the public key and assurance of possession of the associated private key.

Allowed Parameters FIPS 186–5 [9] references NIST SP 800–186 [5] as the authoritative list of approved elliptic curves. The standard defines these allowed curves for use with ECDSA, with the key size resulting in an expected security strength (approximated by NIST):

- P-256 → 128-bit security
- P-384 → 192-bit security
- P-521 → 256-bit security

In addition to that, IG C.A includes allowed curves.

Deterministic ECDSA Deterministic ECDSA removes the reliance on secure randomness during signature generation by computing the per-message secret k deterministically as a function of the private key d and the message hash m. This approach ensures repeatability and eliminates one of the most common causes of ECDSA vulnerabilities: weak RNG.

FIPS 186–5 [9] allows use of deterministic methods such as the one defined in RFC 6979 [10], which uses a HMAC-based DRBG.

It then continues with standard ECDSA signing steps using this deterministic k.

It is critical to note, however, that if the private key is ever leaked, all previous signatures become forgeable (because k can be regenerated for any signed message). Deterministic ECDSA provides RNG robustness, but not forward secrecy.

EdDSA "Okay, so that's ECDSA—how does EdDSA differ from it?" Aster inquired, having absorbed the details of Alessandro's previous explanations.

The Edwards-Curve Digital Signature Algorithm (EdDSA) is an elliptic-curve signature algorithm designed to be faster, simpler, and more resistant to implementation errors than ECDSA.

FIPS 186–5 Sect. 7 [9] standardizes Ed25519 and Ed448, which are instantiations of EdDSA over the curves edwards25519 and edwards448, respectively.

EdDSA signatures are deterministic by design: no per-message randomness is required, which eliminates a major source of implementation failure.

EdDSA provides several improvements compared to ECDSA:

- Deterministic operation: removes dependence on runtime RNGs.
- High performance: optimized formulas using twisted Edwards curves.
- Simplified key derivation and encoding: keys and signatures are directly derived from hashes.
- Resilience against side-channel attacks: due to unified formulas for addition/doubling.

How EdDSA Works EdDSA is defined over a twisted Edwards curve E of the form:

$$ax^2 + y^2 = 1 + dx^2y^2 mod p \tag{11.51}$$

where:

- $GF(q)$ = finite field with q elements, where q is an odd prime power.
- a, d = elements in $GF(q)$.
- G: base point of prime order on the curve.
- n: order of the point G.

EdDSA supports two FIPS-approved parameter sets:

- Algorithm: Ed25519; Field Size: 255 bits; Curve: edwards25519; Hash: SHA2-512; a = -1.
- Algorithm: Ed448; Field Size: 448 bits; Curve: edwards448; Hash: SHAKE256; a = 1.

Encoding Parameter values used in EdDSA are coded as octet strings, and integers are coded using little- endian convention.

Decoding Given an encoded byte string, the decoding process reconstructs the point (x, y).

EdDSA Key Pair Generation Given the EdDSA parameters and a source of randomness:

- Generate a random 32-byte (for Ed25519) or 57-byte (for Ed448) value with a NIST SP 800-90A [7] DRBG. This will be the private key d.
- Compute the hash using SHA-512 for Ed25519 and SHAKE256 for Ed448: $h = H(\mathrm{d})$.
- The first half of h is used to generate the public key.
- Compute public key: $Q = d \cdot G$.
- Encode Q using the point encoding rules.

Key Pair Management Key pairs shall only be used for signing and verification operations.

EdDSA Signature Generation Given message M, (d, Q) key pair, and parameters:

1. Compute:

$$h = H(\mathrm{d}) \tag{11.52}$$

2. Compute nonce r relying on the second half of the digest.
3. Compute point:

$$R = r \cdot G \tag{11.53}$$

4. Derive s from H(d) as in the key pair generation algorithm. Also, compute the digest based on R, Q, M.
5. Compute signature scalar S:

$$S = (r + digest \cdot s) mod n \tag{11.54}$$

6. Signature = concatenation of R and S.

EdDSA Signature Verification Given public key Q, message M, and signature:

1. Decode first half of the signature R and Q into curve points.
2. Verify that R and Q are valid and not identity points.
3. Compute digest.
4. Verify the group equation:

$$\langle second\, half\, of\, the signature \rangle \cdot G = R + digest \cdot Q \tag{11.55}$$

If the equality holds, the signature is valid.

Prehash EdDSA (HashEdDSA) Some applications hash messages before signing (e.g., when messages are large).

The Pre-hash EdDSA, or HashEdDSA, introduces this pre-hashing step.

HashEdDSA Signature Generation

1. Compute pre-hash:

$$m' = H'(M) \tag{11.56}$$

2. Use m' instead of M in the normal EdDSA signature steps above.

The rest of the signing process is identical.

HashEdDSA Signature Verification

1. Compute the same pre-hash m'.
2. Perform standard EdDSA verification using m' in place of M.

Conclusion "We saw the digital signature algorithms defined in FIPS 186–5 [9]—RSA, DSA, ECDSA, and EdDSA—which represent the evolution of cryptographic development over decades. We also saw the principles of the digital signatures and how each algorithm implements them with different mathematical constructions," Alessandro said, winding things down.

"RSA and DSA established the foundation of standardized digital signatures; ECDSA refined that foundation through elliptic-curve efficiency; and EdDSA now embodies a modern balance of performance, determinism, and robustness against implementation flaws. Together, these algorithms represent the present of digital signature—but you should also look at the future of post-quantum ready digital signature algorithms!" Alessandro concluded.

Aster clapped her hands together. "This was a very useful discussion! It clarified so much about digital signatures for me."

"And as we were talking, I went ahead and did a little poking around and found that yes, the ordering app for FIPS 'n' Chips does use a digital signature—so we can rest easy there," Alessandro said with a sigh of relief, "Now, let's celebrate with another round of chocolate milk!" (Fig. 11.1).

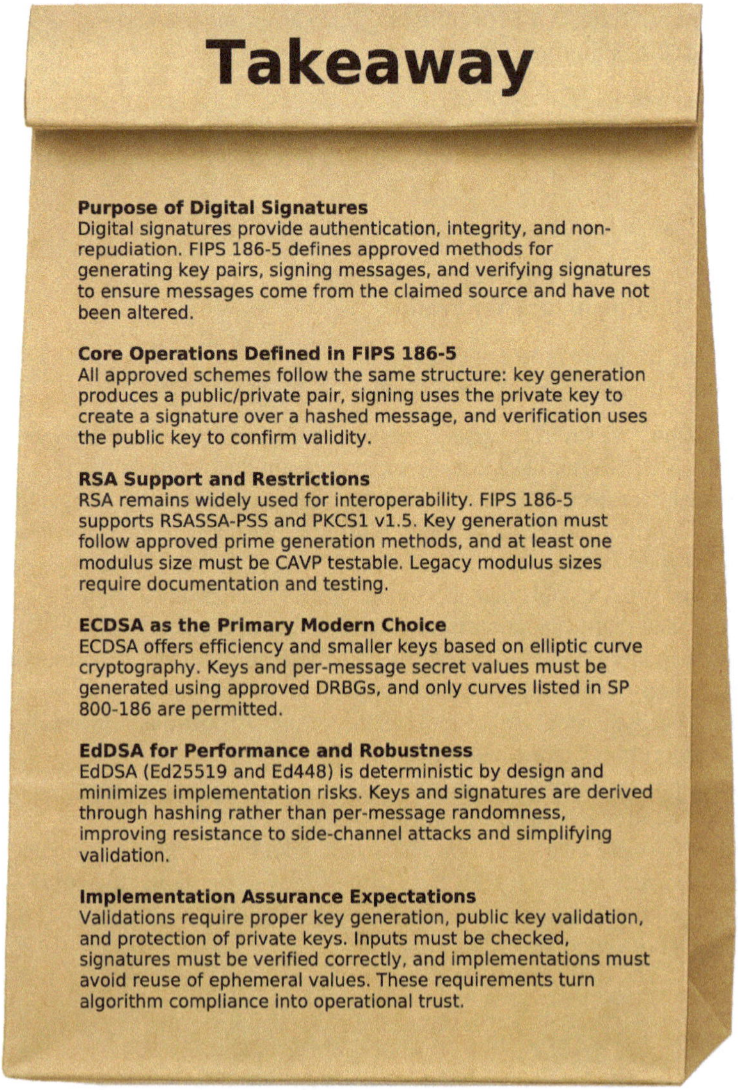

Fig. 11.1 Takeaways regarding digital signature algorithms

References

1. Dworkin M (2001) NIST Special Publication 800–38A: recommendation for block cipher modes of operation: methods and techniques. National Institute of Standards and Technology. Available via NIST. https://doi.org/10.6028/NIST.SP.800-38A. Accessed 08 Dec 2025
2. Dworkin M (2010) Addendum to NIST Special Publication 800–38A: recommendation for block cipher modes of operation: three variants of Ciphertext stealing for CBC Mode. National

Institute of Standards and Technology. Available via NIST. https://doi.org/10.6028/NIST.SP.800-38A-Add. Accessed 08 Dec 2025
3. Barker E, Roginsky A (2024) NIST Special Publication 800–131A, Revision 3, initial public draft: transitioning the use of cryptographic algorithms and key lengths. National Institute of Standards and Technology. Available via NIST. https://doi.org/10.6028/NIST.SP.800-131Ar3.ipd. Accessed 08 Dec 2025
4. Dworkin M (2012) NIST Special Publication 800–38F: recommendation for block cipher modes of operation: methods for key wrapping. National Institute of Standards and Technology. Available via NIST. https://doi.org/10.6028/NIST.SP.800-38F. Accessed 08 Dec 2025
5. Chen L, Moody D, Regenscheid A, Robinson A, Randall K (2023) SP 800–186: recommendations for discrete logarithm-based cryptography: elliptic curve domain parameters. National Institute of Standards and Technology. Available via NIST. https://csrc.nist.gov/pubs/sp/800/186/final. Accessed 08 Dec 2025
6. Barker E, Roginsky A (2024) SP 800–131A Revision 3: transitions: recommendation for transitioning the use of cryptographic algorithms and key lengths. National Institute of Standards and Technology. Available via NIST. https://csrc.nist.gov/pubs/sp/800/131/a/r3/ipd. Accessed 08 Dec 2025
7. Barker E, Kelsey J (2015) SP 800–90A Rev. 1: recommendation for random number generation using deterministic random bit generators (DRBGs). National Institute of Standards and Technology. Available via NIST. https://doi.org/10.6028/NIST.SP.800-90Ar1. Accessed 08 Dec 2025
8. National Institute of Standards and Technology, Canadian Centre for Cyber Security (2023) FIPS 140–3 implementation guidance: implementation guidance for FIPS PUB 140–3 and the cryptographic module validation program. National Institute of Standards and Technology. Available via NIST. https://csrc.nist.gov/csrc/media/Projects/cryptographic-module-validation-program/documents/fips%20140-3/FIPS%20140-3%20IG.pdf. Accessed 08 Dec 2025
9. National Institute of Standards and Technology (2023) FIPS 186–5: digital signature standard (DSS). National Institute of Standards and Technology. Available via NIST. https://csrc.nist.gov/pubs/fips/186-5/final. Accessed 08 Dec 2025
10. Pornin T (2013) RFC 6979: deterministic usage of the digital signature algorithm (DSA) and elliptic curve digital signature algorithm (ECDSA). Internet Engineering Task Force. Available via IETF. https://datatracker.ietf.org/doc/html/rfc6979. Accessed 08 Dec 2025
11. National Institute of Standards and Technology (2013) FIPS 186–4: digital signature standard (DSS). National Institute of Standards and Technology. Available via NIST. https://csrc.nist.gov/pubs/fips/186-4/final. Accessed 08 Dec 2025
12. National Institute of Standards and Technology (2000) FIPS 186–2: digital signature standard (DSS). National Institute of Standards and Technology. Available via NIST. https://csrc.nist.gov/pubs/fips/186-2/final. Accessed 08 Dec 2025

Chapter 12
SSP Establishment Algorithms

Alejandro Fabio Masino

SSP establishment is the process by which critical security parameters (CSP) and public security parameters (PSP) are securely shared, either within the module or between two or more modules. In the next sections we review two FIPS 140-3 approved methods and their algorithms used to exchange key material between two or more modules: key agreement and key transport.

The Collaborative Color Blending Fest (Key Agreement)

Jane, a food journalist, sat down with Chef Crypto, once a FIPS 140-3 consultant and now the owner of a thriving restaurant chain. His past life in security compliance still lingers in his habits, and it shows in the way he manages every corner of his culinary empire. The following is a transcript of their interview.

J (Jane, Journalist): Chef Crypto, we're approaching the Collaborative Color Blending Fest, could you tell us more about it?

C (Chef Crypto, Owner): Yes, this is a one-week event that started a few years ago. Two of our best master chefs, Whitfield and Martin, created a smart way to create a unique secret color for our sauces for each day of the week between our beach and downtown branches. Each branch can prepare the same color without ever exchanging that color directly, so we can keep it secret.

J: Hmmm, that looks like magic to me. Do you mind explaining the process? If it's not confidential, of course.

A. F. Masino (✉)
atsec information security corporation, Austin, TX, USA
e-mail: alejandro.masino@atsec.com

Y. Mao (ed.), *Tasting Cryptography*, https://doi.org/10.1007/978-3-032-30243-4_12

C: Not at all; even if the method is known, the color cannot be guessed. That's the essence of the process. To put in a nutshell, this is how it works: Both Chefs agrees on using a public base color—let's say yellow—then each Chef gets a private, secret colorant obtained from our Clockwork Blending Machine. For this example, we'll say Whitfield gets a red color, and Martin obtains a blue one. They then mix their secret dye with the public base color, producing a new mixed color, which is sent to the other branch.

J: And are these shipments hidden while in transit?

C: No, the exchanged colors between branches are shown in our parade. Then, each branch mixes the secret colorant with the blend received. And voila! Both chefs obtain the same color.

J: So, they exchange their public contributions but keep their private secret colors hidden. The goal is to agree on one shared color for the day, without either knowing the other's secret private color.

C: Exactly. And neither Whitfield nor Martin will know the final color until they blend the colors sent by the other party.

J: Sorry, Chef, but it still seems magic to me... Could you help me visualize it, perhaps?

C: A picture is worth a thousand words, as they say; let me draw a sketch for you (Fig. 12.1).

J: Brilliant! Well, this looks like more than a sketch to me...And how do they confirm that they both successfully created the exact same final color blend?

C: Well, in principle that would not be necessary, but each chef analyzes the obtained color under a spectrophotometer, and they exchange the values obtained. If they match, they are sure the process was successful. Otherwise, they repeat the blending process.

J: Then, the result, the final shared color, is a surprise; a consensus color over which neither party has complete control... Do you use that color in all dishes for that day?

C: Well, actually we use that color as a base for the blending from which we obtain each sauce. Each sauce will have a different color but is still derived from the same base color. Each day, the blending method will be the same, but the collaborative color will be different, and so would all sauces for the day. And, once we obtain them, the original basis color is disposed of, so we are sure that the next day we will establish a different base color.

J: Awesome sauce!

Key Agreements—The Fine Details Key agreement is a method of automated SSP establishment where the resulting keying material is a function of information contributed by two or more participants, so that no party can predetermine the value of the secret keying material independently from the contribution of any other party.

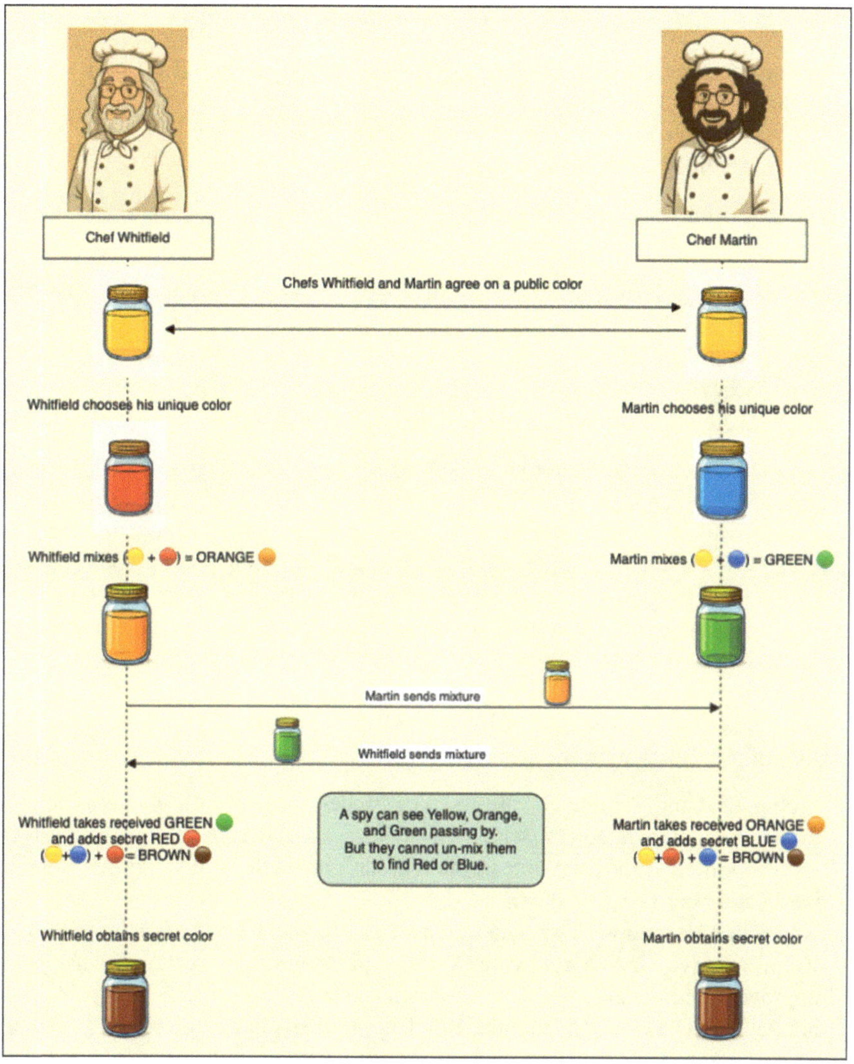

Fig. 12.1 A visual representation of the shipment process

This key establishment method ensures that the resulting secret keying material or shared secret (z) is not sent to or received from a cryptographic module, but is instead computed independently by each party based on the information exchanged between them. The Shared Secret can be further used to derive keys using an approved key derivation method.

There are two approved Key Agreement Schemes (KAS):

- Key Agreement based on Discrete Logarithm Cryptography (DLC), as defined in SP 800-56Arev3
- Key Agreement based on Integer Factorization Cryptography (IFC) Key Agreement, as defined in SP 800-56Brev2

The approved key derivation methods that can be used in key agreement are the following:

- One-Step Key Derivation and Two-Step Key Derivation as defined in SP 800-56Crev1 or SP 800-56Crev2
- Key derivation functions from the protocols and standards documented In SP 800-135rev1 (e.g. IKEv1, IKEv2, TLS 1.0, 1.1 and 1.2, SSHv2)
- TLSv1.3 Key derivation function as defined in RFC 8446

The shared secret resulting from the key agreement is treated as a Critical Security Parameter (CSP), and, as such, must be destroyed immediately following its use in the key derivation method (KDM). This also applies to any intermediate values of CSPs and PSPs computed in the cryptographic algorithm implementations.

All algorithms involved in the key agreement scheme must be tested under the Cryptographic Algorithm Validation Protocol (CAVP) and must be part of the Cryptographic Algorithm Self-Tests (CAST) before the first use of the algorithm in the key agreement service provided by the module.

DLC-based key agreement schemes (SP 800-56Arev3) This key agreement consists of the following basic steps:

1. Preparation and Parameter Validity: The process begins with obtaining appropriate domain parameters, which must be approved and validated for arithmetic validity. Each party must obtain assurance of the validity of the domain parameters before using them.
2. Key Pair Generation: The generation of Finite Field Cryptography (FFC) or Elliptic Curve Cryptography (ECC) key pairs must be performed using an approved method and valid domain parameters. The asymmetric key pairs used are defined as Key-Establishment Key Pairs (either static or ephemeral). Assurances required for the key pair owner (private-key and public-key validity, pair-wise consistency, etc.) must be implemented.
3. Key Exchange: The parties exchange information (ephemeral and/or static public keys) from which they each compute a shared secret. The protocol must unambiguously assign the roles of party U and party V. Assurances required for the public key recipient (static and ephemeral public-key validity, owner's possession of the static key) must be implemented.
4. Shared Secret Computation: Each party combines the exchanged information with their own private key(s) using the appropriate DLC primitive to compute the Shared Secret. The shared secret is now known by both participants and used as input to a key-derivation method.

5. Key Confirmation (Optional): Key confirmation (KC) refers to actions taken to provide assurance to one party (recipient) that the other party (provider) has correctly derived the keying material.

SP 800-56Arev3 specifies different KAS methods using the following elements in the construction:

- An approved key generation method for creating key pairs, either:
  - Finite Field Cryptography (FFC), using safe-prime groups defined in RFC 3526 and RFC 7191 as FFC domain parameters.
  - Elliptic Curve Cryptography (ECC), using P-224, P-256, P-384 and P-521 elliptic curves.
- Ephemeral key pairs, generated by one party (1e), two parties (2e), or none (0e).
- Static key pairs, generated by one party (1 s), two parties (2 s), or none (0 s).
- The primitive used for the shared secret computation, one of:

  FFC DH: Finite Field Cryptography (FFC) Diffie-Hellman.
  ECC CDH: Elliptic Curve Cryptography (ECC) Cofactor Diffie-Hellman (CDH) primitive.
  FFC MQV: Finite Field Cryptography (FFC) Menezes-Qu-Vanstone (MQV) primitive.

The following analyze the assurances that the DLC-based key agreement schemes may provide:

- Implicit Key Authentication (IKA) provides assurance that one party is confident that only a specifically identified entity (the intended second party) could derive the secret key. Schemes that lack static keys do not provide IKA because a trusted association with an identifier cannot be established.
- Key Freshness (KF) provides assurance that the derived keying material is statistically independent of any previously established keying material. This assurance can be obtained by virtue of generating and exchanging ephemeral key pairs or generating and using a fresh nonce as input to the Key Derivation Method (KDM).
- Forward Secrecy (FS) provides assurance that the compromise of the static (long-term) private key(s) does not compromise previously established keys. Schemes using ephemeral keys are the only schemes that provide Forward Secrecy, as they rely entirely on short-term secrets for the shared secret calculation.
- Key Confirmation (KC) provides assurance to one party (the recipient) that the second party (the provider) has correctly computed the shared secret. Key Confirmation relies on computing and exchanging a MacTag using a MacKey derived from the shared secret. Key Confirmation can be unilateral (one party confirms to the other) or bilateral (both parties confirm to each other). Key Confirmation by one party is only possible if the other party contributes a static key pair to the process.

Table 12.1 summarizes the approved key agreement schemes and the assurances that each scheme can provide in party U and party V that takes part in the key agreement.

IFC-based key agreement schemes (SP 800-56Brev2) The schemes are categorized into the KAS1 family (where Party U encrypts the secret using Party V's public key) and the KAS2 family (where both parties contribute components to the shared secret). Both methods use RSA encryption and decryption primitives to protect the shared secret transmitted from one party to the other.

Table 12.1 SP 800-56A Rev. 3 key agreement schemes

Notation	Scheme name	IKA	KF	FS	KC
C(2e, 2 s, FFC DH)	dhHybrid1	U & V	U & V	U & V	U & V
C(2e, 2 s, ECC CDH)	(Cofactor) Full Unified Model	U & V	U & V	U & V	U & V
C(2e, 2 s, FFC MQV)	MQV2	U & V	U & V	U & V	U & V
C(2e, 2 s, ECC MQV)	Full MQV	U & V	U & V	U & V	U & V
C(2e, 0 s, FFC DH)	dhEphem	No	U & V	U & V	No
C(2e, 0 s, ECC CDH)	(Cofactor) Ephemeral Unified Model	No	U & V	U & V	No
C(1e, 2 s, FFC DH)	dhHybridOneFlow	U & V	U & V	No	U & V
C(1e, 2 s, ECC CDH)	(Cofactor) One-Pass Unified Model	U & V	U & V	No	U & V
C(1e, 2 s, FFC MQV)	MQV1	U & V	U & V	No	U & V
C(1e, 2 s, ECC MQV)	One-Pass MQV	U & V	U & V	No	U & V
C(1e, 1 s, FFC DH)	dhOneFlow	U only	U only	No	U only
C(1e, 1 s, ECC CDH)	(Cofactor) One-Pass Diffie-Hellman	U only	U only	No	U only
C(0e, 2 s, FFC DH)	dhStatic	U & V	U & V (nonce)	No	U & V
C(0e, 2 s, ECC CDH)	(Cofactor) Static Unified Model	U & V	U & V (nonce)	No	U & V

This key agreement consists of the following steps:

1. Party U (in case of KAS2) and Party V exchange their public key-establishment keys.
2. Party U generates a secret value Z_U and encrypts it with the party V's public key-establishment key.
3. Party V (in case of KAS2) generates a secret value Z_V and encrypts it with the party U's public key-establishment key.
4. Party V receives the encrypted secret value generated by U and decrypts it with its own private key.
5. Party U (in case of KAS2) receives the encrypted secret value generated by V and decrypts it with its own private key.
6. For KAS1:
   - Party V generates a Nonce N_V and sends it to Party U.
   - For KAS1 with confirmation, Party V calculates a $MacTag_V$ and sends it to Party U. Party U computes the $MacTag_U$ and verifies that matches the received $MacTag_V$.
   - Both parties use Z_U and N_V to proceed with the derivation of key material.
7. For KAS2:
   - Both parties U and V concatenate Z_U and Z_V into Z, the shared secret.
   - For KAS2 with V confirmation or bilateral confirmation, Party V calculates a $MacTag_V$ and sends it to Party U. Party U computes the $MacTag_U$ and verifies that matches the received $MacTag_V$.
   - For KAS2 with U confirmation or bilateral confirmation, Party U calculates a $MacTag_U$ and sends it to Party V. Party V computes the $MacTag_V$ and verifies that matches the received $MacTag_U$.
   - Both parties use Z to proceed with the derivation of key material.

The following analyze the assurances that the IFC-based key agreement schemes may provide:

- Implicit Key Authentication (IKA) provides assurance that one party is confident that only a specifically identified entity (the intended second party) could derive the secret key. KAS1 and KAS2 schemes provide this assurance for one party, and both parties, respectively.
- Key Freshness (KF) provides assurance that the derived keying material is statistically independent of any previously established keying material. This assurance is obtained by generating share secret and nonce values from an approved DRBG, as input to the Key Derivation Method (KDM).
- Forward Secrecy (FS) provides assurance that the compromise of the static (long-term) private key(s) does not compromise previously established keys. KAS1 and KAS2 do not provide this assurance.

- Key Confirmation (KC) provides assurance to one party (the recipient) that the second party (the provider) has correctly computed the shared secret. Key Confirmation relies on computing and exchanging a MacTag using a MacKey derived from the shared secret. Some of the KAS1 and KAS2 schemes provide this assurance.

Table 12.2 summarizes the approved key agreement schemes and the assurances that each scheme can provide.

The Secret Spice Connection (Key Transport)

The Secret Spice Connection (Key Transport) J (Jane, Journalist): Chef Crypto, how do you ensure that all your branches provide the same quality of dishes?

C (Chef Crypto, Owner): Well, we produce all our secret ingredients in our central kitchen and distribute them to the other restaurants, ensuring that transport is protected in a way that prevents the contents from being disclosed, and any change in the contents can be discovered. We call it "The Secret Spice Connection." That way, all the key ingredients of our dishes arrive securely at each branch.

J: Could you tell us what kind of technology you use for those complex logistics?

C: Actually, we have two transport mechanisms, but both use the same carrier that picks up the packages and distribute them to each branch. The first transport we use is what we call the "RSA Capsule"; we use that to distribute one special and unique blend to each branch.

J: So, each branch will receive a different blend?

C: Exactly. We send one blend enclosed in an RSA capsule to each branch, and only that branch will be able to open it with a private key assigned to that branch.

J: And what about the second method?

C: That is "The Unbreakable Foil Wrapper" machine, which lets us transport the same spices needed for the normal dishes to all branches. We put the containers into the machine, enter a secret key, press the "Wrap" button, and the machine uses a foil to wrap all secret ingredients, providing a magic number that describes the contents. When the branches receive the wrapped package, the place the package

Table 12.2 SP 800-56B Rev. 2 key agreement schemes

Scheme name	IKA	KF	FS	KC
KAS1-basic	V only	U & V	No	No
KAS1-Party_V-confirmation	V only	U & V	No	V to U only
KAS2-basic	U & V	U & V	No	No
KAS2-Party_V-confirmation	U & V	U & V	No	V to U only
KAS2-Party_U-confirmation	U & V	U & V	No	U to V only
KAS2-bilateral-confirmation	U & V	U & V	No	U & V

in their machine, they use the same secret key and press the "Unwrap" button. The machine unwraps the foil, and check that the magic number is the same. If not, then the contents are destroyed, and we need to resend the spices…

J: So, all branches share the same key?

C: Yes. The same key is used to wrap and unwrap the secret ingredients. Of course, that key is kept secret in each branch and only the Chef Master knows it.

Key Transport—The Fine Details Key transport is a method of automated SSP establishment whereby one party selects a value of the secret keying material and then securely distributes that value to another party. Key transport is performed using key transport schemes that are classified in two groups by the type of key used to protect the keying material: key transport schemes that use asymmetric algorithms are called Key Encapsulation; those using symmetric algorithms are called Key Wrapping.

The RSA capsule (Key Encapsulation) Key Encapsulation is a method of Key Transport (KTS) that provides confidentiality protection for keying material using asymmetric cryptography. RSA with Optimal Asymmetric Encryption Padding (RSA-OAEP) encryption and decryption specified in SP 800-56B are the approved algorithms for key encapsulation.

This key encapsulation method consists of the following basic steps:

1. Party U and Party V optionally use a common additional input to the algorithm.
2. Party V sends its RSA public key-establishment key to Party U.
3. Party U encrypts the key material with the party V's RSA public key-establishment key using RSA-OAEP encryption.
4. Party V sends the encrypted key material to Party U.
5. Party V decrypts it with its own RSA private key-establishment key using RSA-OAEP decryption.
6. If the scheme includes key confirmation:
   - Party V calculates a $MacTag_V$ and sends it to Party U.
   - Party U computes the $MacTag_U$ and verifies that matches the received $MacTag_V$.

The OAEP encoding used in the RSA-OAEP encryption and decryption consists of obscuring the message containing the key material and additional data with a mask before it is encrypted. The encoding uses the following elements:

- The key material to be transported.
- Additional input (which can be null) agreed upon by the two parties in terms of form and content.
- An approved hash function to create a digest of the additional input.
- A seed obtained from an approved DRBG, used to create a mask to obscure the message.
- A Mask Generation Function (MGF), based on an approved hash.

Table 12.3 SP 800-56B Rev. 2 key transport schemes

Scheme name	IKA	KF	FS	KC
KTS-OAEP-basic	U only	U & V	No	No
KTS-OAEP-Party_V-confirmation	U only	U & V	No	V only

Table 12.3 summarizes the approved key agreement schemes and the assurances that each scheme can provide.

The RSA key pair should provide a security strength equal or greater than the security strength of the key material that it protects. If this does not occur (e.g. the RSA key pair was generated with 2048 modulus, providing 112 bits of security strength, and protects a key with 256 bits of security strength), there must be a caveat in the FIPS 140–3 certificate to indicate this fact.

The Unbreakable Foil Wrapper (Key Wrapping) Key Wrapping is a key transport method intended to protect the confidentiality and integrity of keying material between two parties by using symmetric algorithms. The key used by the key wrapping algorithm to wrap the keying material to be transported is called the key wrapping key (KEK) and must be known by both parties.

The approved methods for key wrapping are:

- AES Key Wrap (KW) mode and Key Wrap with Padding (KWP) mode, as defined in SP 800-38F
- An authenticated symmetric encryption mode for AES, such as AES Galois/Counter Mode (GCM) or AES Counter with Cipher Block Chaining Mode (CCM)
- A combination of any approved symmetric encryption mode (e.g., AES in ECB mode) together with an approved message authentication security function, such as HMAC, AES, CMAC, or KMAC

In all cases, the entire wrapped message must be authenticated.

All algorithms involved in key wrapping must be tested under the CAVP and must be part of the CAST before the first use of the algorithm in the key transport service provided by the module.

The KEK is known by both parties, and must been established previously using a separate, secure key-establishment scheme, like a Key Agreement scheme. The KEK is an SSP, so it should be protected within the cryptographic module and zeroized when it is no longer used.

The KEK and the key wrapping security function should provide a security strength equal or greater than the security strength of the key material that it protects. If this does not occur (e.g. the key wrapping is implemented with AES KW using a 128-bit key and protects a key with 256 bits of security strength), there must be a caveat in the FIPS 140–3 certificate to indicate this fact (e.g. "SSP establishment methodology provides 128 bits of encryption strength").

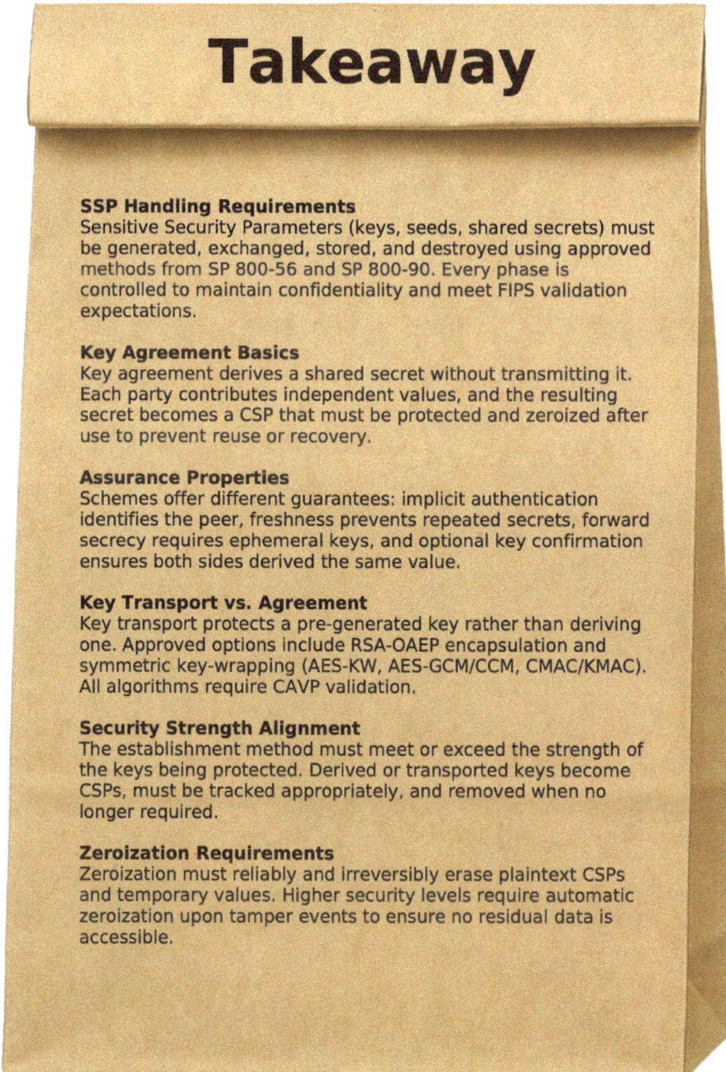

Fig. 12.2 Takeaways regarding SSP establishment

Alejandro Fabio Masino Alejandro has more than 20 years of experience in information security, and in the evaluation of security products using the FIPS 140-3 as well as Common Criteria standards. He joined atsec in 2005 and he enjoys working in the field of cryptography.

Chapter 13
Post-quantum Cryptography

Stephan Müller

Stephan Müller, an atsec colleague, was known for two things: his deep technical wisdom and his mischievous humor. Every time he visited the Austin office, he would tease, "You Texans only have two seasons—hot and hotter!" He always made sure to only arrive during the "hot" season, meaning spring or fall, and he never came empty-handed: in his suitcase would be bags of German chocolates—Ritter Sport squares in flavors like marzipan, hazelnut, and alpine milk; Milka bars in purple wrappers with strawberry cream and Oreo pieces; Kinder Schoko-Bons and Bueno with their creamy hazelnut centers; and dark chocolate pralines dusted with cocoa. Each morning of the first week of his visit, he would unpack a new selection and place them on the kitchen counter, turning the office into a miniature German confiserie.

Stephan was a multitasker in the truest sense. He could pace the hallway, speaking rapid German into his phone, while still catching the thread of an online meeting, ready to unmute himself to drop a perfectly timed insight. Colleagues marveled at his ability to juggle so much at once—chocolates, jokes, conference calls, hallway conversations—while never losing the thread of a technical discussion. He brought both joy and knowledge—the perfect host for our next stop at FIPS 'n' Chips.

Arrival at FIPS 'n' Chips The restaurant's circular dining room in the Mueller control tower shimmered with constellations of algorithm names projected on the ceiling. But on this day, a new star glowed brighter than the rest: PQC.

The room was filled not just with atsec colleagues but also with a group of eager UT Computer Science students, their backpacks tucked under circuit-board tables, eyes bright with curiosity.

Stephan stepped into the center, waving his hands as though conducting an orchestra. "Welcome, everyone! Before we feast, let's talk about what happens when quantum computers join the party. Because believe me, they won't be bringing chocolates."

S. Müller (✉)
atsec information security corporation, Austin, TX, USA
e-mail: stephan.mueller@atsec.com

Y. Mao (ed.), *Tasting Cryptography*, https://doi.org/10.1007/978-3-032-30243-4_13

Laughter rippled across the tables. Aster glanced out the panoramic windows toward Mueller Lake, the same lake she jogged around in the mornings. Two constants in Austin life came to mind: Mueller Lake reflecting sunlight, and Stephan Müller reflecting on cryptographic truths.

That thought reminded her of a favorite "Stephan story": Years earlier, Yi and Stephan had traveled together to the ICMC in Ottawa, and Stephan was delayed for what felt like forever at the airport's immigration checkpoint. Yi, who had once shared an office with him in Austin, knew his habits well: he always ate an apple for lunch, and he was also famous for carrying a mobile "testing lab" of Apple devices such as iPhones, iPads, and MacBooks in his backpack, all inventoried for lab testing.

Watching him stuck in line, Yi imagined the worst: officials suspicious of the heavy pack of Apple hardware. When Stephan finally emerged, she rushed to ask, *"What happened?"*

"It was Apple causing the trouble," Stephan replied, swallowing something quickly.

Yi froze, picturing him chewing through iPhones to clear security until Stephan explained he had simply eaten his apple, the fruit. The confusion between apple and Apple became an instant classic, retold in the office whenever his name came up.

The memory made Aster chuckle, a reminder of Stephan's mix of gravity and humor, the perfect balance before launching into the looming threats of quantum computing.

At the front, phone in one hand, he raised a bag of German chocolates and began scattering treats across the counter. "Chocolates," he said with mock solemnity, "are like cryptography: each one wrapped differently, but all designed to protect what's inside. Today, we unwrap PQC together."

He pointed to a handful of chocolates with shiny wrappers:

For the red-wrapped chocolates, "These are for ML-KEM. Strong, bold, and layered, like a red fortress standing against quantum intruders."

For the blue-wrapped chocolates, "These stand for ML-DSA. Cool and crisp, dependable for digital signatures."

For the green-wrapped chocolates, "Here is SLH-DSA. Simple ingredients; hash-based and time-tested, as fresh as mint."

For the silver-wrapped chocolates, "These are still experimental; think of FN-DSA (Falcon): elegant but delicate, like a silver coin not yet in circulation."

And finally, for the gold-wrapped chocolates, "And here is HQC, rich and traditional, based on codes as old as your grandparents' radios."

He tossed a red-wrapped chocolate to Aster sitting in the front row. She fumbled it, laughed, and raised her hand with the sweet prize once she had recovered it. He then handed her the bag of chocolates to pass around so everyone could claim a few.

Stephan cleared his throat. "We'll open this chapter by stepping into a familiar cryptography landscape but with a new sky overhead. The horizon we're walking toward is 'post-quantum,' a world where quantum computers are not curiosities in laboratories but practical machines that reshape what 'secure' means."

Terminology He explained:

"'Post-quantum' sounds futuristic, almost like cryptography that transcends physics. It isn't. In information security, 'post-quantum' simply marks the era after meaningful quantum computers exist. Pair that with 'cryptography,' and you get the real definition: cryptography designed to remain secure when quantum computers are available. You'll see it shortened to PQC.

"One more important clarification: PQC algorithms do not draw their strength from quantum mechanics. They are ordinary, classical algorithms—math you can run on today's CPUs. Their defining property is different: the hard mathematical problems they rely on are believed to be resistant to quantum attacks."

"Before we talk about those algorithms, let's glance at the machines that motivate them."

"Today you won't find a quantum computer that matters for breaking cryptography. But the race is on. Technology companies, research labs, and governments are spending heavily because a sufficiently large, reliable quantum computer would upend a cornerstone of modern security: asymmetric public-key cryptography."

Quantum Computers He continued:

"We won't detour into entanglement or superposition. Instead, we'll focus on two algorithms that illustrate why quantum computing threatens today's cryptography: Shor's algorithm and Grover's algorithm."

"Don't worry," Stephan began with a twinkle, "I won't drag you into entanglement or Schrödinger's cat. My cats only entangle with yarn."

He explained with a storyteller's cadence: Shor's algorithm could dismantle RSA, Diffie–Hellman, and elliptic-curve cryptography. Grover's algorithm would halve the strength of symmetric keys like AES. In other words: all the asymmetric foundations of TLS, SSH, IPsec—gone.

Shor's Algorithm Discovered in 1994—long before quantum hardware could dream of running it—Shor's algorithm efficiently solves three problems that underpin most classical public-key cryptography: integer factorization, discrete logarithms, and period finding. Classically, these problems are hard given the key sizes we use in practice; with Shor's algorithm on a sufficiently capable quantum computer, they become polynomial-time solvable.

Think of the discrete logarithm as this: given $b^x = a$, with a and b known, find x. For the sizes we care about in cryptography, classical methods are effectively impractical (sub-exponential at best, and still enormous). Shor changes the game: if you have a meaningful quantum computer, one large and stable enough, then these "hard" problems become tractable.

"Couldn't we just use bigger numbers?" a student asked. Stephan answered the question with a shrug.

"In theory, yes; in practice, no. The key sizes would balloon, performance would grind to a halt, and even the act of generating and validating those enormous primes would become unwieldy and probabilistic. It simply does not scale for real systems."

He let the point settle before continuing. "So, what actually breaks when Shor's algorithm comes into play?"

He reiterated the three types of cryptography mentioned before, counting them out as he explained what the impacts would be:

RSA collapses, affecting both signatures and key transport.

Finite-field Diffie–Hellman (DH) falls, undermining the session keys that secure the start of every connection.

Elliptic-curve cryptography (ECC) fails, including ECDSA and ECDH.

"Take away those pillars of public-key cryptography, and you remove the keystone from the arch of security. Protocols like TLS, IPsec, and SSH come crashing down with it. That," Stephan concluded, "is why the world is racing to build quantum computers, and why we are racing just as fast to build post-quantum cryptography."

He then turned his attention to the other threat quantum computers pose.

Grover's Algorithm and Security Categories Grover's algorithm is different. It accelerates unstructured searching, giving a quadratic speed-up. For symmetric cryptography, that means an attacker's brute-force effort drops from 2^n to roughly $2^{n/2}$. In plain terms: double your key length to keep your security margin (e.g., AES-256 retains a comfortable cushion against Grover's model).

Real implementations and resource limits matter, of course. To reason about practical security in a quantum world, NIST defines security categories, which account for gate counts, depth, and the serial nature of Grover's approach. When we talk about PQC parameters, those categories, not raw key lengths, are the yardstick.

Time Frame "When will meaningful quantum computers arrive?" Aster interjected, curious.

"No one knows. Forecasts exist and are updated as breakthroughs land, but hinging migration plans on a date is risky. The more durable way to think about timing is data lifetime and the store-now-decrypt-later threat," Stephan replied.

"If adversaries can record your encrypted traffic today at low cost, they can keep it until quantum machines can decrypt it. So, ask: How long must this data stay confidential, or its signatures remain trustworthy? Minutes? Years? Decades? If the answer outruns the conservative estimates for quantum progress—and migration timelines—you should be moving toward PQC now."

Aster thought on this; migrations are slow. Replacing Triple-DES with AES—a like-for-like symmetric swap—took years. Re-plumbing the world's asymmetric infrastructure (protocols, certificates, hardware, compliance) will take even longer. Guidance such as CNSA 2.0 and NIST IR 8547 anticipates that a full replacement of classical asymmetric algorithms will push well into the 2030s.

If you need confidentiality for a decade and meaningful quantum capability could plausibly arrive sooner, waiting is a bet you may not want to place, she thought to herself.

Stephan paced slowly, as if the floor itself marked the timeline of cryptography. "Imagine attackers recording your encrypted traffic today. Years from now, when a meaningful quantum computer exists, they simply press play—and suddenly your secrets are plain text. This is the store-now-decrypt-later problem. Ask yourself: how long must your data remain safe? If the answer is decades, the time to act is now."

NIST's Response: Post-Quantum Algorithms The ceiling above shifted, constellations rearranging into new patterns. Stephan gestured upward.

Pointing to ML-KEM: “This replaces Diffie–Hellman and RSA key wrapping. Defined in FIPS 203 [1], it gives us new ways to agree on secrets—even if quantum computers arrive tomorrow.”

Shifting his finger to ML-DSA: “Our lattice-based answer to signatures. Out goes RSA, out goes ECDSA. In comes FIPS 204 [2].”

Moving to SLH-DSA: “Based on hashes alone. Slower, perhaps, but resting on decades of studied ground.”

And finally bringing his pointer finger to rest on FN-DSA and HQC: “Still waiting in the wings. FN-DSA is lattice-based, like ML-KEM and ML-DSA, while HQC brings true diversity with its code-based foundation. Together they promise resilience beyond a single mathematical family.”

The chandeliers flickered as though each algorithm were taking a bow on stage.

Stephan paused, unwrapping another chocolate. “Now, some of you might be wondering about these *lattices* I keep mentioning,” he said, pacing toward the window. “Don’t confuse them with lettuce.”

The students giggled, unsure where he was going.

“You see,” he continued with a grin, “cryptographers love lattices because they’re hard to break. Caterpillars, on the other hand, love lettuce because it’s easy to chew.” He popped the chocolate into his mouth. “So, if you ever hear about a caterpillar breaking our crypto, don’t worry—it’s just lunchtime, not a quantum attack.”

Laughter echoed through the room, wrappers crinkling again as students reached for more chocolates.

He paced as he spoke, his voice steady:

“NIST defined the security strength in the presence of meaningful quantum computers in terms of security categories where the required quantum gates are listed, and the fact is taken into account that Grover’s algorithm requires a long-running serial computation. Therefore, NIST and cryptographers refer to the security categories when assessing the cryptographic strength of PQC algorithms. For these security categories, three parameter sets exist—ML-KEM-512, ML-KEM-768, and ML-KEM-1024—corresponding to NIST categories 1, 3, and 5. But let’s move on to the algorithms themselves.”

ML-KEM “First up,” Stephan began, “is ML-KEM, defined in FIPS 203. This is our new way to establish secrets across insecure channels, the successor to RSA key transport and ECDH key exchange. The key idea of ML-KEM is to encapsulate a shared secret key using the public key and send it over unprotected channels to have it decapsulated with the secret key. Both sides have the same shared secret key after the data exchange completes. The purpose of ML-KEM is to replace the Diffie-Hellman, EC Diffie-Hellman, and RSA key wrapping algorithms.

“A very interesting aspect of the internal generation of the shared secret key is the following: The shared secret key is generated anew by calling the DRBG for each encapsulation operation. Thus, the shared secret key generated by two different ML-KEM transactions will be completely different, even though the same key pair is used. This aspect implies that even when using the same ML-KEM key pair for multiple ML-KEM transactions, the different resulting shared secret keys can be immediately used for stream ciphers like AES-GCM or AES-CTR, as a collision may happen with a probability of $\max(2^{-256}, 2^{-(\text{AES-key size})})$.

"Internals: ML-KEM relies on Keccak-family primitives—SHA3 and SHAKE. Each encapsulation draws fresh entropy from an approved DRBG, ensuring the shared secret is new every time.

"Process: the client generates a key pair—an encapsulation/public key and a decapsulation/secret key. The initiator encapsulates a 256-bit secret using the public key, producing a ciphertext. That ciphertext travels back, and the client decapsulates it. Both sides end with the same shared secret."

"Notice something subtle," Stephan added. "Only the responder's DRBG decides the value of that secret; the initiator doesn't contribute randomness. That's different from classical DH, and something we must keep in mind. One key aspect of ML-KEM is that the caller cannot define a key that is encapsulated! The ML-KEM encapsulation obtains a fresh 256-bit random value from the DRBG, which becomes the shared secret key that is encapsulated and transmitted."

He leaned forward. "FIPS 203 requires strict checks—verifying key lengths, re-encoding public keys to catch tampering, and ensuring ciphertext matches the expected size. For validation under FIPS 140-3, you must also perform a pairwise-consistency test, or PCT, which can slow down key generation if you're using ephemeral keys."

Stephan went on to note that the use of ML-KEM is allowed by NIST with previously unheard-of degrees of freedom when compared with Diffie-Hellman or RSA key wrapping, including:

- It is permissible to use the generated shared secret directly as key material (unlike Diffie-Hellman). However, the shared secret is exactly 256 bits in size for all parameter sets. If a different size is required, then a KDF following SP 800-108 or SP 800-56C must be applied.
- The ML-KEM key pair is comparatively large. FIPS 203, however, explicitly allows the storing of the two 256-bit random seed values that are obtained from the approved DRBG and inserted into the ML-KEM key generation routine to obtain the ML-KEM key pair. This means the two 256-bit seed values can be stored in lieu of the ML-KEM key pair. However, these seed values must be stored with the same protection as applied to an ML-KEM secret key.
- Before ML-KEM can perform an encapsulation or decapsulation operation, a matrix is generated from the public key (note that the public key is used for both operations and is also embedded into the secret key). This matrix is a different representation of the public key and thus requires only the same protection as applied to the public key. This allowance, however, may not be of much practical relevance considering that an ML-KEM key pair may usually be ephemeral in nature.

Finally, he raised a caution: "The foundations here are lattice-based, specifically Module-LWE. Powerful, yes, but still young compared to number theory, which is why hybrid deployments are encouraged. Run ML-KEM alongside a classical method, combine the two secrets in a KDF—if either holds, you're secure."

ML-DSA "Next is ML-DSA, our lattice-based digital signature scheme, defined in FIPS 204. This is the heir to RSA signatures and ECDSA."

He listed the essentials with crisp clarity:

Its parameter sets are ML-DSA-44, -65, and -87, aligned to categories 1, 3, and 5. The DRBG strength used during key generation determines which category you can claim.

There are also multiple variants:

- Pure ML-DSA: the caller provides the full message to be signed or verified to ML-DSA. The algorithm implementation consumes the full message to generate a digital signature or verify its signature.
- External-μ: The NIST crypto technology group interprets the statement "message representative that may optionally be computed in a different cryptographic module" in the comment of step 6 of Algorithm 7 in FIPS 204 as follows: it is permissible that this step can be performed external to the ML-DSA implementation. This means that the message digest calculation of the input message together with the message digest of the public key for later processing can be performed external to ML-DSA, even by a different FIPS 140 module. The term "external-μ" is based on the fact that step 6 of Algorithm 7 specifies the calculation of the variable "μ". Although this variant offers a different usage of ML-DSA, it is mathematically equivalent to the pure ML-DSA operation. That means that the signature generation can be performed with pure ML-DSA and the signature verification can be performed with the external-μ ML-DSA variant, and vice versa.
- Hash-ML-DSA: In the case of Hash-ML-DSA, the caller creates a message digest of the message following a very specific format defined in FIPS 204 Sect. 5.4.1 [2]. The message digest is now given to ML-DSA to generate the signature or verify it; it is permissible that the message digest is calculated by a different FIPS 140 module than the one performing the ML-DSA operation. Due to having a different input message, the Hash-ML-DSA variant is mathematically not equivalent to the pure ML-DSA or external-μ ML-DSA variants.

"These aren't interchangeable," Stephan noted. "A signature created under Hash-ML-DSA can't be verified by Pure ML-DSA. You must pick your variant carefully."

He then explained that signature generation also comes in two flavors: hedged (adding per-signature randomness against side-channel attacks) and deterministic (using an all-zero 256-bit string instead of the per-signature randomness value). Both are valid, both verify identically.

For the hedged variant, however, the 256 bits are generated from a random number generator anew for each signature generation operation. FIPS 204, however, explicitly states that this random value is to counter side-channel attacks against ML-DSA but does not contribute to the security strength of the algorithm; thus, it is permissible that the random number is not generated from an approved DRBG. This value may be generated "pseudo-randomly from the message being signed and a precomputed random value included in the signer's key." FIPS 204 explicitly specifies that the hedged ML-DSA is the preferred variant of generating a signature.

NIST allows similar degrees of freedom to the use of ML-DSA as offered to ML-KEM:

- The ML-DSA key pair is comparatively large. FIPS 204, however, explicitly allows the storage of the 256-bit random seed value obtained from the approved DRBG and inserted into the ML-DSA key generation routine to obtain the ML-DSA key pair. This means the 256-bit seed value can be stored in lieu of the ML-DSA key pair. However, this seed value must be stored with the same protection as applied to an ML-DSA secret key.
- Before ML-DSA can perform a signature generation or verification operation, a matrix is generated from the public key (note that the public key is used for both operations and is also embedded into the secret key). The generation of the matrix requires around 15–20% of the entire execution time for the respective operation, and the matrix is quite large. Nonetheless, FIPS 204 allows the implementation to retain the matrix once generated for subsequent operations. Therefore, the implementation can choose between performance and memory conservation. This matrix is a different representation of the public key and thus requires only the same protection as applied to the public key.

"For assurance," he continued, "FIPS 204 itself requires no special checks per operation. But under FIPS 140-3, the PCT applies again—sign and verify with the same key to confirm consistency."

As Stephan continued, Aster noted: Just like ML-KEM, ML-DSA is built on lattices. And just like ML-KEM, it can be paired in hybrid signatures: produce both a PQC signature and a classical one and only accept the result if both verify.

SLH-DSA Stephan then shifted gears. "Now, not everything is lattice. Enter SLH-DSA, defined in FIPS 205 [3], based on hashes alone. In many ways, it's the conservative choice—hashes have decades of cryptanalysis behind them."

He explained the structure: SLH-DSA integrates three schemes—WOTS+, XMSS, and FORS—into a stateless design.

Its parameter sets are offered at categories 1, 3, and 5, each with "small" (s) and "fast" (f) variants, and with either SHA-2 or SHAKE as the hash base.

And it, too, has multiple variants:

- Pure: the entire message is passed in.
- Hash-SLH-DSA: you supply a digest in a strict FIPS 205 format.

Signature generation may be hedged (with fresh randomization bits) or deterministic (reusing the PK.seed part of the key). Verification accepts either.

"Performance varies," Stephan admitted. "The fast variants of the parameter sets give you dramatically quicker key and signature generation, but larger signatures and slower verification. The small variants do the opposite. Choose based on your use case."

Stephan's explanation continued: Assurance here, too, is light: FIPS 205 requires no per-operation checks, but FIPS 140-3 imposes the PCT for key pairs.

Currently, NIST is discussing adding additional parameter sets to the existing ones with other cryptographers, and these additional parameter sets are intended to make the signature verification process materially faster. Considering that SLH-DSA is orders of magnitude slower compared to ML-DSA, any approach to make the signature operation faster would accelerate the adoption of SLH-DSA.

Why were "faster" parameter sets not considered during the initial definition of SLH-DSA in the first place, though? The answer is surprisingly simple and hints at the core fundamentals of SLH-DSA: a private key is not allowed to be used for unbounded numbers of signature generation processes. This is because the FORS component is a signature scheme whose security depends on only allowing a "few" signatures. During the PQC competition, NIST required that a private key must at least support 2^{64} signature generation operations, which led to the current parameter sets defined with SLH-DSA. The new parameter sets reduce the number of allowed signature generations to 2^{32}, 2^{24} or even 2^{16} operations. Such limits on the use of private keys start to require careful key management, including some form of counting how many signatures have been created already with a given private key.

FN-DSA "At this point," Stephan said, "you might be wondering about FN-DSA, sometimes called Falcon. NIST has selected it, but no FIPS standard is published yet. It's still under refinement." [5]

He spoke carefully. "FN-DSA is lattice-based as well, but relies on the Short Integer Solution problem and, unusually, uses floating-point arithmetic in key and signature generation. That makes it elegant, but tricky. Floating-point operations vary across platforms, so NIST is still working on making sure Falcon can be implemented consistently."

HQC Finally, Stephan nodded at the ceiling where a new constellation blinked into place. "HQC—a code-based key-encapsulation mechanism—was added in 2025. No FIPS yet, but it matters. Why? Because it gives us diversity. Lattices dominate PQC, but if someday an attack shakes that foundation, HQC stands as a resilient alternative. Built on decades of coding theory, it balances key size, speed, and practicality." [6]

Stateful Signatures Before wrapping up, Stephan turned to a final topic. "Don't forget the stateful hash-based signatures defined in SP 800-208: LMS and XMSS are secure against quantum computers because they rely solely on hashes. But they come with heavy restrictions, as each one-time key may only be used once—lose track, and your scheme collapses. They also require FIPS 140 Level 3 hardware protections and forbid private key export—even for backup.

"In practice, these are niche tools. But they remain important, especially for cases where you must deploy a quantum-resistant signature today and can't wait for broader PQC adoption." [4]

Assurance and Hybrids Stephan broke a chocolate square and held it aloft. "Migration is not instant. Just as you savor chocolate slowly, we must take a measured approach to implementing PQC algorithms, and blend the old with the new while we do so. That is what hybrids do: PQC plus classical; two secrets combined, and if one survives, you are safe. It is belt and suspenders, or milk and dark chocolate together."

He paused. "Although you would think a hybrid migration is a natural course, the NSA's Commercial National Security Algorithm Suite 2.0 (CNSA 2.0) has taken a different path, opting instead for pure post-quantum algorithms, and rejecting hybrids for national security systems [5]. That choice is already shaping how vendors and evaluators think about migration."

He leaned against the counter. "I just came back from NIST's 6th PQC Workshop in Washington where I had a long conversation with one of the decision-makers behind CNSA 2.0. Their stance on hybrids is very firm." [7]

He raised an eyebrow. "They see no reason to allow them. A few arguments stood out."

As Stephan began explaining the different points made by the NSA at the PQC Workshop, several atsec employees whipped out some paper to take notes on—this would be important. Aster herself jotted down the following:

Battle-hardening of lattices: The NSA presenter compared today's lattice math to RSA. RSA was proposed in 1976, but the first real sieve attack appeared in 1983, and progress slowed dramatically after that. Lattice sieves were proposed in the mid-2010s. His view: we shouldn't expect big surprises beyond that.

NIAP deadlines: NIAP must update all its protection profiles in 2025. Hybrid standards (key combiners, hybrid X.509 certs, OIDs) are only now emerging in documents like SP 800-227—too late to integrate without creating incompatibilities.

Pointlessness after rollout: Once vendors adopt pure PQC, why step back to hybrids? NIAP doesn't share the concern that the math is too "young."

SLH-DSA rejection: They see its performance as prohibitive, 100x slower than ML-DSA for verification, 1000x slower for signing and key generation, even in the smallest parameter sets.

"This was the first time I heard these points laid out so clearly [8]. I don't fully agree, but I understand NIAP's position now, and at least we can explain it to customers with reason rather than guesswork," Stephan noted.

The students looked thoughtful, the wrappers on their tables no longer playful but crumpled with new wrinkles, more intricate patterns weaving across them than their first appearance, just like the hybrid approach.

Stephan gave a small smile: "Still, I say hybrids are like mixing milk and dark chocolate: safer, more robust. But in Washington, they prefer pure bars only."

Timing and Transition Stephan grew serious. "We don't know exactly when a meaningful quantum computer will arrive. But we do know migration will take years. Remember how long it took to replace Triple-DES with AES? That was one symmetric swap. This time, we're rebuilding the entire asymmetric foundation of the Internet."

He let the silence settle. "That's why we must start now. Because if you wait until the quantum machine is humming, you've already lost."

Questions Begin Aster held up her red chocolate. "So, if ML-KEM is the red one, is it really just replacing Diffie–Hellman? Why can't we just make DH keys bigger?"

Stephan smiled. "We could make them bigger, Aster, but Shor's algorithm doesn't care how large you make the prime. With a meaningful quantum computer, no size will save DH. That's why we need something built on different mathematics entirely, which is lattices."

He flicked a blue chocolate to Oscar, who was already scribbling notes.

"ML-DSA," Oscar said, "why so many variants? Pure, Hash, External-μ—it feels overcomplicated."

Stephan leaned on the table. "It's like deciding whether to sign the whole contract or just the summary. With Pure ML-DSA, you sign the entire message. With Hash-ML-DSA, you only sign a pre-digested version. With External-μ, you let another trusted module do part of the work. Flexibility is the reason—but beware, signatures from one variant don't always verify with another."

A green chocolate arced through the air toward another student, Eve, who caught it neatly.

"Stephan," she asked, "you keep calling lattice crypto young. Should we trust it enough to build systems on it?"

He nodded seriously. "Lattices are younger than factoring, yes. That's why NIST and industry encourage hybrid deployments. Combine ML-KEM with classical ECDH, or ML-DSA with ECDSA, then concatenate the secrets and verify both signatures. If one survives, so does your system."

A silver wrapper gleamed in Stephan's hand. He placed it gently on the table.

A UT student in the back called out: "What's with FN-DSA and floating-point numbers? My prof said floating-point is messy."

Stephan chuckled. "Your professor is right. FN-DSA—Falcon—is mathematically elegant but tricky to implement. Floating-point varies across platforms. Imagine baking a cake where every oven runs a slightly different temperature. NIST is still refining the recipe, so it doesn't collapse."

Finally, Stephan lifted a gold chocolate.

"Why HQC after ML-KEM?" asked Joachim, an atsec employee.

"Diversity," Stephan said simply. "If lattices ever crack, we need a backup. HQC is code-based—older math, well studied, like a sturdy family recipe. Adding it ensures we aren't putting all our trust in one pantry."

A Teaching Moment By now, chocolates were unwrapped, and the wrappers gleamed like a mosaic of cryptography across the tables. Stephan leaned back, phone buzzing in his pocket, but he ignored it for once.

"Look," he said, "these algorithms aren't just names in FIPS 203, 204, and 205. They are living standards, and they come with responsibilities. Each must pass assurance checks."

"First, a pairwise consistency test—PCT—to prove a key pair can sign and verify or encapsulate and decapsulate.

"Second, CAST self-tests, where an implementation must demonstrate it can succeed and fail in predictable ways.

"And finally, input validation, making sure keys and ciphertexts aren't malformed or maliciously crafted.

"When you validate a module under FIPS 140-3, these steps aren't optional. They are what turn math into trust."

He let the weight of those words settle before his grin returned. "And speaking of trust and precision, remember the story Yi tells about my 'apple problem' in Ottawa? Cryptography is a lot like customs inspection: sometimes the smallest misunderstanding can cause the biggest delay. You must know exactly which apple you're talking about."

Laughter rippled through the room again, easing the tension that had built during the technical talk. The students smiled, the lesson clear: in security, as in life, the details always matter.

Stephan's tone softened as he looked around. "This is where you come in, whether you're students learning the math or professionals running assurance labs. You're not just checking boxes. You're ensuring that ten years from now, when quantum machines finally roar, the systems we certify today won't collapse like a poorly baked cake."

Pens scribbled furiously across notebooks. Aster nodded, recognizing echoes of her own client meetings, where these details often determined whether a product passed or failed.

Closing the Lesson Stephan looked around the room, his headset now silent. He unwrapped one last German chocolate and held it up.

"Friends, these are the building blocks of our future. ML-KEM, ML-DSA, SLH-DSA, and soon FN-DSA and HQC. They are here, defined in FIPS standards, ready for validation. Use them wisely. Test them rigorously. Deploy them in hybrids where needed. Because when quantum computers arrive, whether in eight years or eighteen, it will be too late to start learning then. We must start now."

The room was quiet for a moment, the weight of his words settling in. Outside, Mueller Lake rippled in the warm Austin breeze; two seasons indeed: hot and hotter. But inside, with Stephan as guide, the future of cryptography felt just a little cooler, steadier, and better prepared (Fig. 13.1).

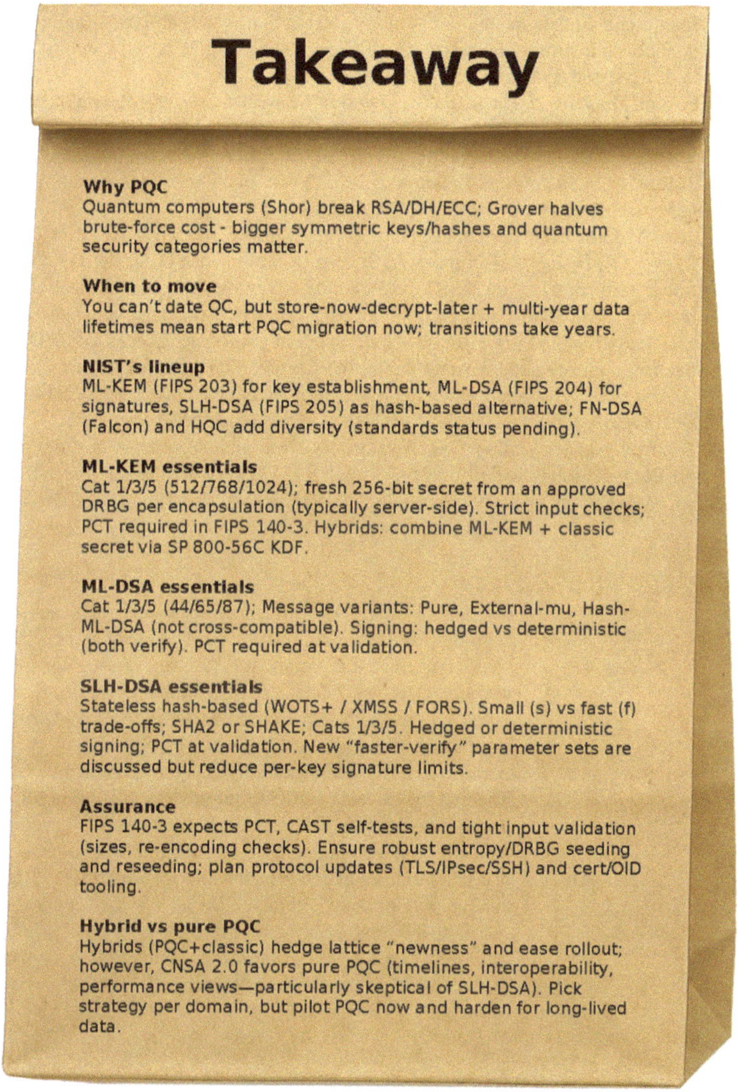

Fig. 13.1 Takeaways regarding post-quantum cryptography

References

1. National Institute of Standards and Technology (2024) Module-lattice-based key-encapsulation mechanism. National Institute of Standards and Technology. Available via NIST. https://csrc.nist.gov/pubs/fips/203/final. Accessed 03 Dec 2025
2. National Institute of Standards and Technology (2024) Module-lattice-based digital signature algorithm. National Institute of Standards and Technology. NIST. https://csrc.nist.gov/pubs/fips/204/final. Accessed 03 Dec 2025

3. National Institute of Standards and Technology (2024) Stateless hash-based digital signature algorithm. National Institute of Standards and Technology. NIST. https://csrc.nist.gov/pubs/fips/205/final. Accessed 03 Dec 2025
4. Cooper D, Apon D, Dang Q, Davidson M, Dworkin M, Miller C (2020) Recommendation for stateful hash-based signature schemes. National Institute of Standards and Technology. NIST. https://csrc.nist.gov/pubs/sp/800/208/final. Accessed 03 Dec 2025
5. National Institute of Standards and Technology (2017) Post-quantum cryptography. https://csrc.nist.gov/Projects/post-quantum-cryptography. Accessed 03 Dec 2025
6. Alagic G, Bros M, Ciadoux P, Cooper D, Dang Q, Dang T, Kelsey J, Lichtinger J, Liu Y, Miller C, Moody D, Peralta R, Perlner R, Robinson A, Silberg H, Smith-Tone D, Waller N (2025) Status report on the fourth round of the NIST post-quantum cryptography standardization process. National Institute of Standards and Technology. NIST. https://csrc.nist.gov/pubs/ir/8545/final. https://csrc.nist.gov/Events/2025/6th-pqc-standardization-conference. Accessed 03 Dec 2025
7. National Security Agency (2022) Announcing the Commercial National Security Algorithm Suite 2.0. National Security Agency. via the NSA. https://media.defense.gov/2025/May/30/2003728741/-1/-1/0/CSA_CNSA_2.0_ALGORITHMS.PDF. Accessed 03 Dec 2025
8. National Security Agency (2024) CSI: Commercial National Security Algorithm Suite 2.0 (CNSA 2.0) FAQ. National Security Agency. via NSA. https://www.nsa.gov/Press-Room/Digital-Media-Center/Document-Gallery/igphoto/2003071836/. Accessed 03 Dec 2025

Stephan Müller After starting his career with an academic degree in business administration, IT security and cryptography soon came into the picture for Stephan. During his almost 25 years at atsec, he became a FIPS tester early on, Because he expects himself to experience the same trials and tribulations atsec's customers go through during FIPS testing work, Stephan started various implementations of cryptographic mechanisms to research the impact of FIPS requirements and to find solutions to general challenges. Among others, Jitter RNG is developed and maintained by Stephan, which is used in a significant number of FIPS modules as the primary entropy source. Also, he maintains a cryptographic library with all types of algorithms that strives to be fully compliant with FIPS 140. Lately, he's developed new cryptographic algorithms, and one is being standardized by NIST as part of the upcoming SP 800-90A revision: the XDRBG.

Part III
Validation Process

Chapter 14
Cryptographic Algorithm Validation

Dick Sikkema

The neon sign of the virtual FIPS 'n' Chips restaurant flickered to life in the cyberspace skyline: "Now Serving: Certified Cipher Platters and 4096-bit Fries." Inside, the atmosphere buzzed with a low hum of smooth jazz and cryptographic chatter. On every table a QR-code menu proclaimed, "Validated Algorithms Today."

Aster entered and looked around. She nodded to the usual patrons and then went to as table and asked the lone occupant: "Are you Dick? The cryptographic algorithm testing wiz?".

Dick looked up, then gestured to an empty chair. "That's right. Dick's the name, CAVP's the game. How can I help?".

"I just want to know more about algorithm validation. Can you walk me through the process?" Aster ordered a Diffie Spritz and sat down.

"Sure thing! Let's start with the basics. Before you can get your cryptographic module validated under FIPS 140-3, all the algorithms it uses—for example AES, RSA, or SHA—need to be individually tested and certified. That's what the Cryptographic Algorithm Validation Program, or CAVP, is for."

Aster nodded. "I heard that some companies just want algorithm certificates, without the FIPS validation. Is that true?"

"Yes, absolutely. Sometimes they just want to be sure that their algorithms work as expected. It really depends on what your product does and how you want to market it." Dick took a sip from his Quantum Martini. "Algorithm certificates are also used for Common Criteria evaluation, so there are some cases where algorithm validation is done without FIPS 140-3. The general process is the same, though!

In broad strokes: a laboratory sends a request to the Automated Cryptographic Validation Testing System, or ACVTS, to request test vectors based on the details that

D. Sikkema (✉)
Formerly with atsec information security corporation, Austin, TX, USA
e-mail: sikkemarichard@gmail.com

Y. Mao (ed.), *Tasting Cryptography*, https://doi.org/10.1007/978-3-032-30243-4_14

the customer provided. The customer then runs these vectors through their implementations, returns the responses, and the laboratory validates them using the ACVTS again. If everything is correct, the certificate will be issued. Voila!"

Aster looked at Dick skeptically. "It can't be that easy. Surely there is more to it. How do you even tell the lab what settings to use? There are so many!"

Dick nodded. "That's true. Every lab has its own way to collect that data. At our lab we use a web-based solution called the ACVT Mate, where our customers can enter all their settings, like which algorithms to test, modes, key sizes and so forth. Then they save those setting to a file and send it to us."

Aster snapped open a holo-browser and opened ACVT Mate. As she clicked around in the options (Fig. 14.1) she muttered, "I am not sure I would know what to select for all these options…"

"That's why you work with a laboratory. We can help you figure these things out and explain what it all means," Dick reassured her. "Anyway, once we have the settings, we will send a request to the ACVTS demo server."

"Demo?" Aster said with a raised eyebrow.

"Yes, there are two ACVTS servers: the demo server and the production server. On the demo server, the laboratory can request test vectors, the expected results, and validate the responses, but you won't be able to get a certificate. That's what the production server is for. Once the customer is sure that their implementation works

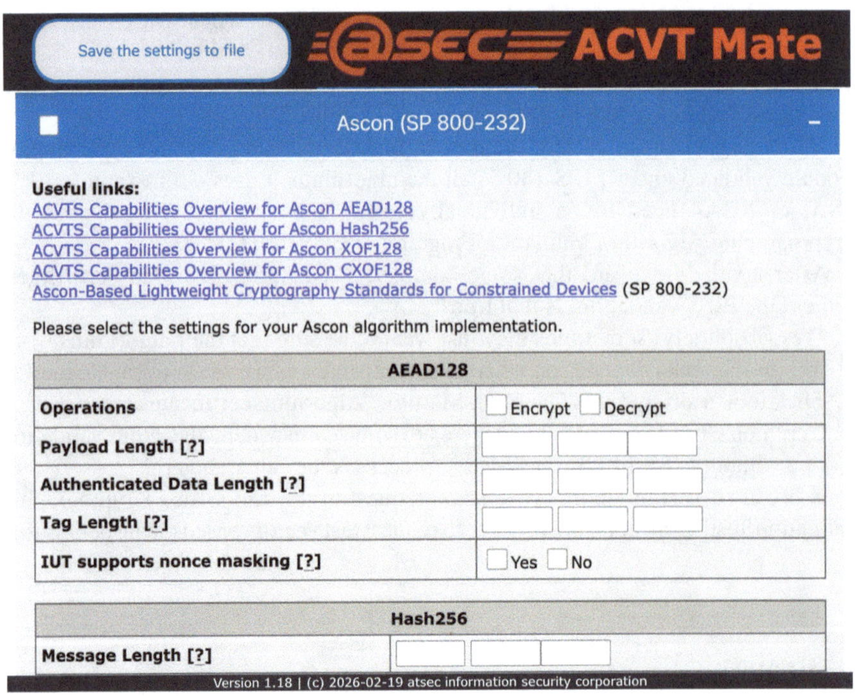

Fig. 14.1 A screenshot of the ACVT Mate web interface

and the demo testing is successful, the final test run is done with test vectors from the production server, and if they pass a certificate is issued."

"Okay, but what do the test vectors look like and how do I get the results back?" Aster frantically stirred her drink. "That sounds really complicated!"

Dick smiled. "I would call it complex. First, let's talk about the test vectors, which are formatted as JSON files. Let's say you want to test AES encryption: In that case the test vectors would provide a key and a plaintext. You would use those as input for your AES implementation, and the expected output would be the ciphertext. Here is an example."

Dick made a few gestures and a holo-window pulled up showing off a theoretical JSON file that could be fed to the ACVTS (Fig. 14.2).

"As you can see that are many sets of test vectors, so you definitely don't want to do this by hand!" Dick warned.

Two tables down, three frazzled-looking engineers shook their heads in unison. "Please... automate it! We thought it would be fine to do it manually... but... the horror..." They started sobbing into their glasses.

Dick cleared his throat and continued: "You will need a test harness to process these vectors—a piece of software that will take the JSON files, parse them, pass them to the implementation, and then record the responses in the correct format. Your laboratory might be able to help you with setting up a test harness."

"And every time I run it, I have to check with you if the results are good? That sounds like a lot of emails!" said Aster.

Another round of groans came from the engineer table. "So... soooo many emails!"

Dick laughed. "Poor guys! At our laboratory, we like to do the whole process in three steps. First, we will give you the demo vectors and the expected results in the right format—that way you can compare the output of your test harness to the expected results and don't have to involve the lab at all. Once everything passes, we will give you a set of demo vectors without the expected results, and then we will validate your responses on the demo server. And if they pass there, we will generate the final set of vectors, this time on the production server."

"How long does all of that take?" asked Aster.

"It depends on how quickly the customer can process the vectors and return the passing responses. Sometimes the tests fail, and the algorithms need to be fixed before we can continue. But if everything goes smoothly, it's a matter of days. If it is the first time that an organization submits test results, they need to be registered with the CAVP, and since that is a manual process it might take a few days, depending on how busy they are."

"That's surprisingly fast, at least in comparison to FIPS 140-3. Anything else I need to keep in mind?" Aster asked.

"A few things. The CAVP is very strict when it comes to the tested configuration and operating environment. Here, take a look at this algorithm certificate!" Dick said as he popped open a window between him and Aster (Fig. 14.3).

"You can see the information about the algorithm listed—the name, version, and type of the implementation—then information about the vendor, and finally a list of the algorithms and the Operational Environment, or OE. This is for a software

```json
{
  "acvVersion": "1.0"
},
{
  "vsId": 0000001,
  "algorithm": "ACVP-AES-ECB",
  "revision": "1.0",
  "isSample": false,
  "testGroups": [
    {
      "tgId": 1,
      "testType": "AFT",
      "direction": "encrypt",
      "keyLen": 128,
      "tests": [
        {
          "tcId": 1,
          "pt": "F34481EC3CC627BACD5DC3FB08F273E6",
          "key": "00000000000000000000000000000000"
        },
        {
          "tcId": 2,
          "pt": "9798C4640BAD75C7C3227DB910174E72",
          "key": "00000000000000000000000000000000"
        },
        {
          "tcId": 3,
          "pt": "96AB5C2FF612D9DFAAE8C31F30C42168",
          "key": "00000000000000000000000000000000"
        },
        {
          "tcId": 4,
          "pt": "B26AEB1874E47CA8358FF22378F09144",
          "key": "00000000000000000000000000000000"
        },
        {
          "tcId": 5,
          "pt": "6A118A874519E64E9963798A503F1D35",
          "key": "00000000000000000000000000000000"
        },
        {
          "tcId": 6,
          "pt": "CB9FCEEC81286CA3E989BD979B0CB284",
          "key": "00000000000000000000000000000000"
        },
        {
```

Fig. 14.2 An example JSON file with input for a test vector

Fig. 14.3 A screenshot of a CAVP certificate web page

implementation, so the OE consists of the operating system and chip set." Dick said, pointing at the pieces of data.

"You're saying that the certificate is only valid for this particular version on the exact operating environments listed? Sounds like you must be careful to match what is claimed for a FIPS 140-3 submission, right?" Aster pointed out.

"Excellent point! Yes, all of it must match, which means you can only do the algorithm testing for the certificate on the final version of the implementation. For hardware modules that means that you have to wait until you have the actual silicon to test on. Oh, but you can always do some preliminary testing beforehand, to make sure that your algorithm implementations work in principle." Dick said as he ordered another Quantum Martini.

"I understand doing preliminary testing for a software implementation. But how do you do that on hardware? Can you simulate or emulate the algorithm testing?"

"You can use a simulator if the implementation can't be tested in its hardware environment. That would make the implementation firmware, and the operating environment would list the name of the simulator on the certificate. Emulators are not

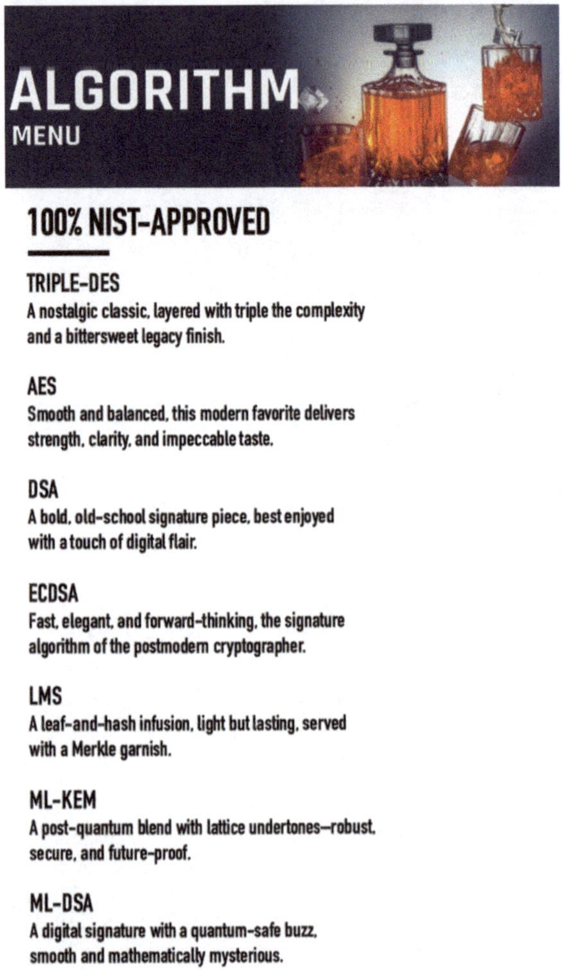

Fig. 14.4 A fictional, algorithm-themed drink menu

allowed for algorithm testing, though. For FIPS 140-3, it's also an option to modify a module under the supervision of the testing lab if that is the only way to access the internal algorithmic engines of a module. So, it depends a little on the details. If you want to know more, it's in Sect. 7.3 of the FIPS 140-3 Management Manual [1]." Dick took a deep breath.

Aster thoughtfully sipped on her drink. "I can't think of anything else right now, but I'll be back if I have any questions. Thank you for all the information."

"No worries." Dick replied, looking at his wristwatch. "Oh, Bingo is about to start in the backroom, and I heard they have a non-conformant entropy source, so I expect to win big!".

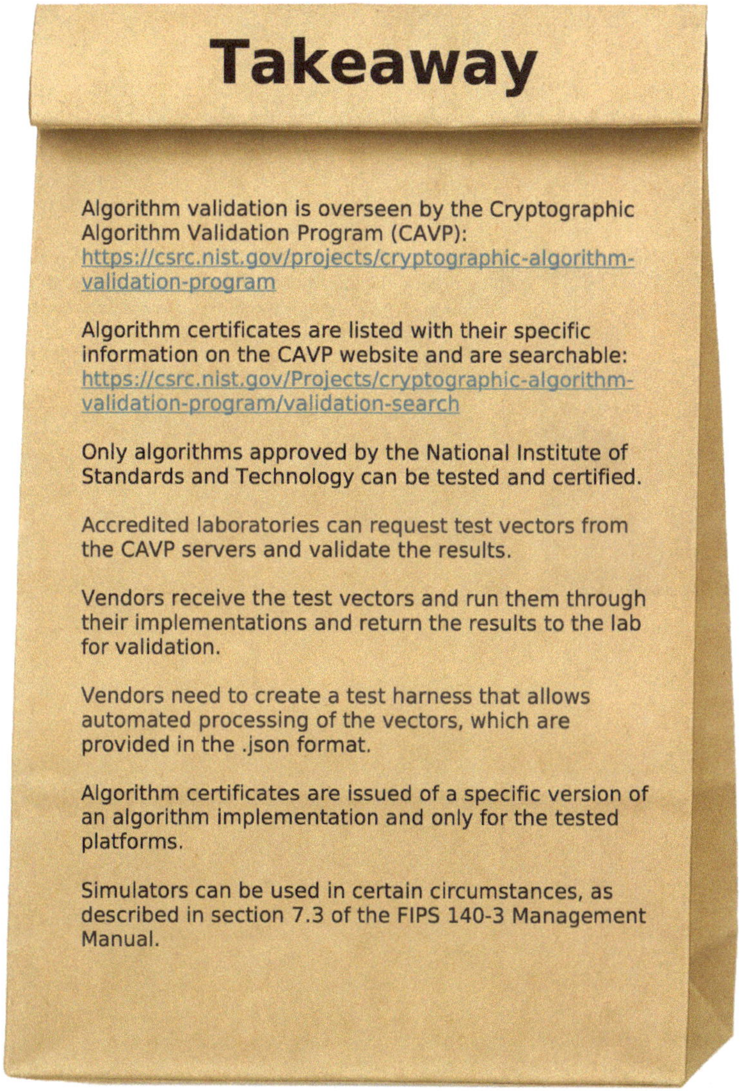

Fig. 14.5 Takeaways regarding cryptographic algorithm validation

With that, Dick got up and made his way across the restaurant, leaving Aster to ponder the algorithm menu (Figs. 14.4, 14.5).

Reference

1. National Institute of Standards and Technology (2016) FIPS 140–3 Management Manual, Section 7.3. https://csrc.nist.gov/Projects/cryptographic-module-validation-program/cmvp-fips-140-3-management-manual. Accessed 03 Dec 2025

Dick Sikkema Dick worked for atsec for over 8 years, mainly in cryptographic algorithm validation and cryptographic module validation testing; though for the last couple of years, he has also worked on some Common Criteria projects.

Chapter 15
NIST SP 800-90B

Quin Darcy

Guessing Games: Entropy and Identity In the third booth from the entrance of the FIPS 'n' Chips restaurant, Adelia and Quin sit. It's been nearly a minute since Adelia went quiet; she barely made it through her last sentence before her voice trailed off. Her mind was captured by some previously unseen implications of what she had been attempting to explain.

"... it's just that I can't see my phone or my laptop the same way anymore. All that data I've given up over the years, not thinking ..." Adelia said, looking at her phone which was face down on the table. "It feels like these devices are being used to predict me. It's like I can feel my future being looked at." Adelia shuddered. "And if my next action is known in advance by something that isn't me, can I really claim the action is 'mine'?"

"I want to show you something," Quin said, sitting opposite Adelia in the same booth they've used for these discussions for the last few weeks. "By the way, I ordered you what I thought you would want." Quin gestured at a coffee on the table with sugar and no cream before continuing. "Here is what I think you're missing. You're worried that they stand to learn something about you from the data you've shared, right?"

"Yeah, I think that's the issue,"

"I would say not. You have to assume your adversaries alr-"

"Adversaries?" Adelia interrupted.

"Oh, I mean adversaries in the sense of someone or something whose interests oppose yours. Your interest is in uniquely authoring your actions, their interest is in knowing what you will do next to serve some economic incentive," Quin replied. "Anyway, you have to assume that your adversaries already know everything they can about you—that they know the probability distribution over your possible future behaviors. But that's not the issue."

Q. Darcy (✉)
atsec information security corporation, Austin, TX, USA
e-mail: quin.darcy@atsec.com

Y. Mao (ed.), *Tasting Cryptography*, https://doi.org/10.1007/978-3-032-30243-4_15

"So, then what is the issue?"

"How much uncertainty remains. Even with knowing your distribution, how hard is it for them to still guess correctly? That's what matters. With total certainty, your future can be equally realized by them as it can by you."

Adelia took a sip of the coffee and was quite satisfied, since it was what she had planned on ordering while walking to the restaurant.

"For example, we've met many times over the last few weeks and so you can assume I have some idea of that distribution. Let's say I wanted to leverage that knowledge, and I wanted to 'play optimally' and guess the most likely thing you would do according to that distribution…" Quin said, followed by a deliberate silence.

Adelia took another sip of her coffee and searched the silence for what Quin was getting at. She noted her phone was to the left of her coffee mug, as it usually was.

This was what I was going to order… Adelia thought, staring at the coffee. *But he made it real before I did.* She had planned to order this while walking here, had felt herself making that decision, but the decision hadn't mattered. The coffee in front of her existed because of his knowledge of her patterns, not because of any choosing she'd done. The result would have been the same either way. Adelia lifted her eyes from her cup to Quin. "I usually get it with sugar and cream, so how did you…" Adelia murmured in a low voice, as if to herself.

"I've noticed that if we don't meet for a few days in a row and if your texts suggest you're busy or preoccupied with something, you seem to almost always order your coffee with no cream and just sugar," Quin said. "These context clues, paired with the approximate distribution I have reveals a 'most likely' outcome, which is what I guessed by ordering that coffee. Though, it was still a guess, and I, like your adversaries, still have some uncertainty."

"I think I see. But how do you measure that? How much they don't know?"

"Entropy," Quin answered. "Cryptographic entropy. Have you heard that term?"

"Yes, in my thermodynamics class."

"Related concept, but different context. In cryptography, you assume your adversary has complete knowledge—that they know the distribution. This is called 'Kerckhoff's principle.' Under this assumption, you determine the lower bound of uncertainty your adversary is left with and see if that satisfies your security requirements." Quin paused. "Think of it like this: Your adversary stands behind a pane of glass; on the other side is what you'll do next. Entropy is the opacity of that glass. The higher the entropy, the blurrier the objects on the other side appear and the more possible things the blur could resolve into. The context clues I mentioned earlier are like the blurry object I saw beyond the glass. Since there was low entropy, there were fewer possible things that blur could resolve into, with coffee and no cream appearing to me as most likely."

Adelia nodded. "So, I just need to increase my entropy then, further blur my future actions. That's not hard. I could start making random choices that no one will know in advance," Adelia protested. "Order different drinks, take different routes, break my patterns—"

"Try it," Quin said. "Right now, make a random choice about what to order next time."

Adelia paused. "Maybe ... green tea?"

"Why green tea? Why not water, or nothing at all?"

"I don't know, it just ... came to mind."

"That's exactly the point, though. It 'came to mind' because it came from your mind. Even your attempt at randomness is an expression of you. Your rebellions against predictability would themselves form patterns—the patterns of how Adelia rebels. The point is that you aren't only defined by the actions you take, but the actions you don't take, and the specific actions you take in specific conditions, and so on. There is a distribution that describes this space of choices and actions, a probability landscape, and to be on that landscape is what it means to be Adelia. The question for you is whether your distribution's entropy is high enough that the discomfort you feel at having your future anticipated, is tolerable."

Adelia was quiet for a moment. "And if it's not? What if that lower bound on my adversary's uncertainty isn't high enough? If I understand myself through the effects I have on the world, and they can produce those effects before I do ..." Adelia stopped.

"The only way to raise their uncertainty is to let something else make your decisions for you. So long as you are the one making the choice, you remain on that landscape and your entropy is fixed. Theoretically, you could hand control to something...like an entropy source. It has no patterns, nothing to predict... but that's an extreme example."

"No, maybe that's exactly what I need! If they can't predict it, they couldn't predict me ..." Adelia said with a strained smile starting to form.

"You're right, you would have ascended from that landscape, but at the greatest cost," Quin said.

"What cost is that?" Adelia asked.

"Adelia, if that landscape of choices and actions is you, then to leave it is to no longer be you. You'd achieve near perfect unpredictability by ceasing to be Adelia. Not to sound dramatic, but that's what you would call self-annihilation," Quin laughed.

Adelia stared at her coffee. She didn't find any of this funny. The weight she felt earlier had returned and all but doubled.

Is it more important to be myself or to prevent others from knowing who I will be? Adelia thought. "I don't know what to do right now, but I think I want to understand these entropy sources in earnest. If they'll be making my decisions, the least I can do is get to know them first," Adelia said as her tense face relaxed slightly.

In the third booth from the entrance of the FIPS 'n' Chips restaurant, Adelia and Quin sat and discussed entropy in great detail over the course of several meetings. What follows is a collage of Adelia's memories of these discussions and notes written by her or Quin. They are presented in an order that reflects how the information was organized in Adelia's mind after all the meetings.

Overview There is one primary document that serves as the authority on entropy and sources of entropy that are to be used in applications requiring cryptographic security: *NIST SP 800-90B: Recommendation for the Entropy Sources Used for Random Bit Generation* [1], which was published January 2018 and has received no revisions since its publication. This document describes "properties that an entropy source must have" to fulfill certain requirements determined by the context within which the entropy source will be used. SP 800-90B covers 4 topics related to entropy sources:

- The components and interfaces of an entropy source
- The process and requirements for validating an entropy source
- Statistical methods the entropy source must use to evaluate its own output
- Additional statistical considerations.

The Entropy Source Model and Its Interfaces At this point you may be asking yourself: What is an entropy source? Thankfully, Sect. 2.2 of SP 800-90B [1] gives us our first clear look at what an entropy source is. We start with a model that generalizes all entropy sources by breaking them down into their fundamental components. Let's break these components down one by one.

Noise Sources At the heart of an entropy source is a noise source responsible for creating data that is unpredictable. A noise source comes in two types:

- Physical (P): These produce output based on non-deterministic effects of electronic circuits. Such effects may include thermal noise inherent to semiconductors, shot noise from diodes, or free running oscillators. The "noise" from these sources is harvested from phenomena intrinsic to the physical material that makes up the component(s) of the noise source [1].
  - It should be noted that some physical noise sources don't output binary data directly. This means the noise source being sampled must be digitized, converting the analog samples into groups of bits called "raw data."
  - The final outputs of the noise source (fixed length bitstring) are called "symbols," with "symbol size" referring to the number of bits in one symbol.
- Non-Physical (NP): These derive noise from extrinsic phenomena which can include things like temporal phenomena like CPU execution time jitter, hard drive seek times, or memory access latencies.

Conditioning Components This component isn't strictly required, meaning not all entropy sources will have one. The purpose of the conditioning component comes from the fact that noise sources, even if their outputs are uncertain, may still show favoritism (bias) towards certain values. A conditioning component is a deterministic function that processes noise source output to reduce bias, mitigate correlations, and increase the entropy density (entropy per bit) of the output. It does not discard samples but rather transforms the probability distribution [1].

Health Tests Because entropy sources provide randomness to systems that critically depend on unpredictability, (e.g., random number generators used for cryptographic key generation) entropy sources are expected to consistently operate within a range of behavior and are expected to monitor themselves in order to detect when they have deviated from that expected range of behavior. When such deviations occur, the entropy source must be able to detect the failure and communicate this to the systems they are connected to.

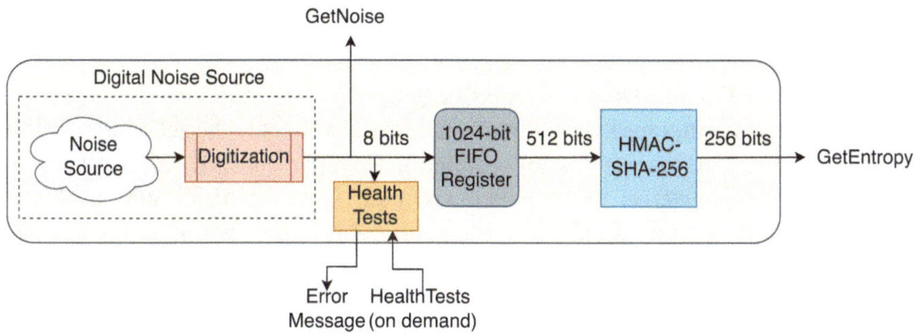

Fig. 15.1 Example entropy source

SP 800-90B defines three conceptual interfaces for interacting with the entropy source [1], as seen in Fig. 15.1:

- GetEntropy: Returns (optionally) conditioned output.
- GetNoise: Provides raw samples from the noise source (typically for validation testing).
- HealthTest: Triggers on-demand health testing (at minimum, re-executes startup tests).

Normativity: A Compliance State of Mind "Okay, so it sounds like the noise source is the most important thing?" Adelia asked.

"Well in some sense that is true, but you must remember that 90B is a normative reference, which means that it's not just describing something—it prescribes a collection of requirements that must be fulfilled in order to legitimately claim compliance to it. In this way, there is no 'most important thing' since all requirements are equal in the sense that they must all be fulfilled. You need to approach 90B with a different state of mind than you would a textbook, for example."

"But where do the requirements come from?"

"We will look at that and more, but first we're going to build up some familiarity of the math involved in 90B. Many of the requirements will sprout naturally once that understanding is built. Also, I want to say that I won't always be able to keep the thread back to your autonomy in view as we go through this. You will have to find how it all connects."

"What do you mean?"

"I mean 90B can be dense at times, and the background for it even denser. It won't always be clear how the concepts make contact with the feeling that's animating you right now or how they answer the types of questions you're asking. This is just information, Adelia. As dramatic as this may sound, you have to decide how you use the information: as the material to build a bridge out, or as the light to illuminate the ground you're standing on."

"Right," Adelia dropped her clasped hands into her lap and looked at them. "I think I don't even know what questions I'm asking right now. And maybe learning about this stuff will help me put this feeling into words, into a question that can be answered. But anyways, please, let's start."

A Quick but Formal Detour: Probability Spaces Let's suppose we have some experiment whose outcomes we are interested in. Let Ω denote the set of all possible outcomes of the experiment; this set is called the sample space. If we then let $\mathcal{F} = \mathcal{P}(\Omega)$ denote the powerset of Ω, which just means the set of all subsets. It can be shown that $\mathcal{F}$ is what is called a "σ-algebra". Moreover, we note that the pair $(\Omega, \mathcal{F})$ is called a "measurable space". Just imagine the elements $A \in \mathcal{F}$ represent all the events of the experiment, its elements are all the possible sets of outcomes. For example, in a double-coin flip experiment, the event that both coin faces are the same is in fact a subset of the set of all outcomes, which is notated as $\{HH, TT\} \in \mathcal{F}$.

For us to be able to ask the question "What's the probability that flipping two coins at once results in both faces being the same?" we need to be able to assign a number to the event $\{HH, TT\} \in \mathcal{F}$. The function which can do this assignment in the way we expect is called a "probability measure". While probability measures have many properties, we state only that it is defined as $P : \mathcal{F} \to [0, 1]$ with $P(\Omega) = 1$ and that the tuple, $(\Omega, \mathcal{F}, P)$, is called a "probability space".

Random Variables Now that we have seen what a probability space is, we move on to random variables. Let's suppose we have the probability space $(\Omega, \mathcal{F}, P)$.

The mapping $X : \Omega \to A$ is called a random variable if, for each subset $S \subseteq A$, we have

$$X^{-1}(S) = \{\omega : X(\omega) \in S\} \in \mathcal{F}. \tag{15.1}$$

Technically, A, along with some $\mathcal{A}$, must together $(A, \mathcal{A})$ be a measurable space.

But what does this mean? How should we interpret what a random variable is? A random variable is, despite its name, a fully deterministic function. But more importantly, it's a kind of measurement device or feature extractor that:

- Takes raw experimental outcomes (elements of Ω)
- Extracts features we care about (e.g., the number of heads in a double-coin flip)
- Allows us to translate questions about those features into measurable events of Ω (elements of $\mathcal{F}$).

Double Coin Flip Quin began explaining by way of example, using the all-too-common images of dice and coins. "Take two coins and flip them at the same time. The experiment is simply observing the faces of the flipped coins. The sample space would be-" he took a moment to fetch some paper and a pen and started to write.

$$\Omega = \{HH, HT, TH, TT\}. \tag{15.2}$$

"The 'σ-algebra' is $\mathcal{F} = \mathcal{P}(\Omega)$. Then define a function (random variable) $X : \Omega \to \{0, 1, 2\}$ by-"

$$X(\omega) = \text{Number of heads}. \tag{15.3}$$

Quin continued. “The function X simply tells us how many heads appears in the given outcome. So, $X(HT) = 1$, for example. This function allows us to ask, ‘What’s the probability of getting either two heads or no heads?’ The random variable allows us to take the event which this question is asking about (i.e., $\{0, 2\}$) and answer it. Specifically, we would write-”

$$\mathrm{X}^{-1}(\{0, 2\}) = \{TT, HH\} \in F, \tag{15.4}$$

“…which by virtue of it being in $\mathcal{F}$, we can use our probability measure, P, to find that:”

$$P\big(X^{-1}(\{0, 2\})\big) = P(\{TT, HH\}) = 1/4 + 1/4 = 1/2. \tag{15.5}$$

“This is exactly the probability distribution, or probability mass function, $\mathrm{p_X} : \mathrm{A} \rightarrow [0, 1]$! Where $A = \{0, 1, 2\}$ for this example.” Quin finished. “The take-away is that given a probability space $(\Omega, \mathcal{F}, P)$ and a random variable $X : \Omega \rightarrow A$, the pair (X, P) induces a probability distribution $p_X : A \rightarrow [0, 1]$ on A.”

Joint and Marginal Probability Distributions and Expected Value When discussing noise sources, one will often be interested in sources whose output size is larger than just one bit, or one may be interested in the statistical properties present in sequences of more than one output of the noise source. Because of this, there is something called a Joint Probability Distribution that allows us to represent the multiple bits of single noise source outputs, or multiple noise source outputs in a sequence, as multiple random variables.

Letting $X : \Omega \rightarrow A$ and $Y : \Omega \rightarrow B$ be two random variables on the same probability space, with $p_X : A \rightarrow [0, 1]$ and $p_Y : B \rightarrow [0, 1]$ the probability mass functions induced by each random variable, respectively. Then the joint probability distribution (mass function) of X and Y is given by $p_{XY} : A \times B \rightarrow [0, 1]$, defined as

$$p_{XY}(a, b) = P(\{\omega \in \Omega : X(\omega) = a, Y(\omega) = b\}). \tag{15.6}$$

The above is often denoted with the short-hand notation, $P(X = a, Y = b)$.

A related concept to the joint probability distribution is the Marginal Probability Distribution. These can best be understood by example.

A Look at the Marginals Quin flipped to a new page in his notebook. “Take the same two coins we looked at in the first example with the same setup. Then, if we define X as a random variable which extracts the number of heads we get after flipping the first coin once and define Y as the random variable that extracts the number of heads we get after flipping the second coin once, we can express these probabilities as a table.” (Table 15.1).

“There is one marginal probability distribution for each random variable. The distribution is recovered by summing the rows and columns. Thus,” Quin did his best to write legibly.

$$p_X(0) = \tfrac{1}{2}, p_X(1) = \tfrac{1}{2}; p_Y(0) = \tfrac{1}{2}, p_Y(1) = \tfrac{1}{2}. \tag{15.7}$$

Table 15.1 Marginal distributions

	$Y = 0$	$Y = 1$
$X = 0$	1/4	1/4
$X = 1$	1/4	1/4

"The important thing to note for this example is that $p_{XY}(a, b) = p_X(a) \cdot p_Y(b)$, and this is only true because the coin flips have no impact on one another. They are independent random variables. More generally, the joint probability distribution of independent random variables can be recovered by taking the product of the marginal probability distributions."

Quin flipped to another new page in his notebook. "Lastly, I just want to give you a definition of something we'll discuss later. Given a probability mass function $p_X : A \to [0, 1]$, induced by a random variable X, the *expected value* of X is essentially the 'average' or the mean of the set over which the distribution is defined. You multiply each outcome by its probability and add it all together. That is,"

$$E[X] = \sum_{a \in A} p_X(a) \cdot a. \tag{15.8}$$

Entropy: A First Look Imagine another coin toss, but with a single coin. If the coin is completely fair, then we have no predictive advantage to leverage if we were to try guessing how it would land. However, if there were bias in the coin and it favored a particular side, this bias is to our advantage as we can be more sure of the outcome of the coin toss. Entropy is a quantity assigned to a probability distribution (probability mass function) which tells us something about the uncertainty within it.

There are two common types of entropy with the first being most relevant in cryptography.

Given a probability space $(\Omega, \mathcal{F}, P)$, a random variable $X : \Omega \to A$, and the probability distribution, p_X induced on A, the two most common entropy measures are defined as follows:

- Min-entropy: Represents how much strategic value there is in knowing the most probable outcome. The min-entropy of p_X is defined as

$$\mathrm{H}_\infty(p_X) = -\log_2\left(\max_{\mathrm{x} \in \mathrm{A}} \mathrm{p_X}(x)\right). \tag{15.9}$$

- Shannon-Entropy: Represents the amount of expected surprise you would experience after observing many outcomes of the experiment. The Shannon entropy of p_X is defined as

$$H(p_X) = -\sum_{x \in A} p_X(x) \log_2(p_X(x)). \tag{15.10}$$

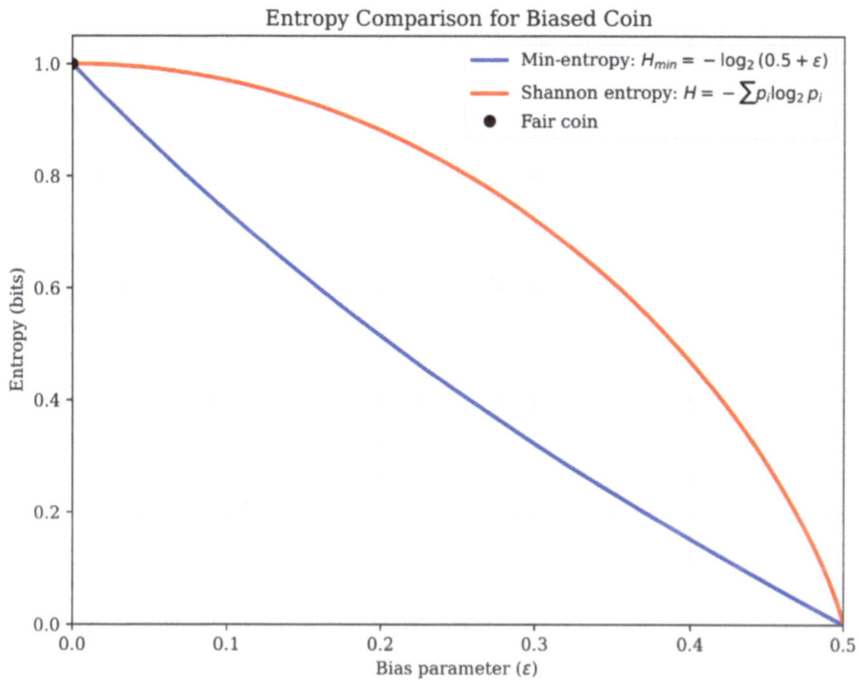

Fig. 15.2 Single-coin flip entropy comparison

Parameterizing Entropy Suppose you have a bias parameter ε which is between 0 and 0.5. Then you can describe the probability of each outcome of the coin flip with

$$p_{X(H)} = \tfrac{1}{2} + \varepsilon, p_{X(T)} = \tfrac{1}{2} - \varepsilon, \tag{15.11}$$

where at $\varepsilon = 0$, both entropy measures are at their highest, and at $\varepsilon = 0.5$, both measures are at their smallest. This is illustrated in Fig. 15.2.

We now can imagine a slightly more complicated experiment consisting of flipping two coins (Fig. 15.3). The possible outcomes $x \in A$ are

$$\Omega = \{\text{HH, HT, TH, TT}\}. \tag{15.12}$$

Like what we saw before, imagine the x and y-axis each represent the amount of bias in the first and second coin, respectively. The z-axis represents the resultant min-entropy of the probability distribution of the random variable representing this experiment.

Instead of using H and T to label the outcomes of the experiment, we can use 0 and 1. With these labels, we can view a double coin flip as a noise source producing 2-bit outputs:

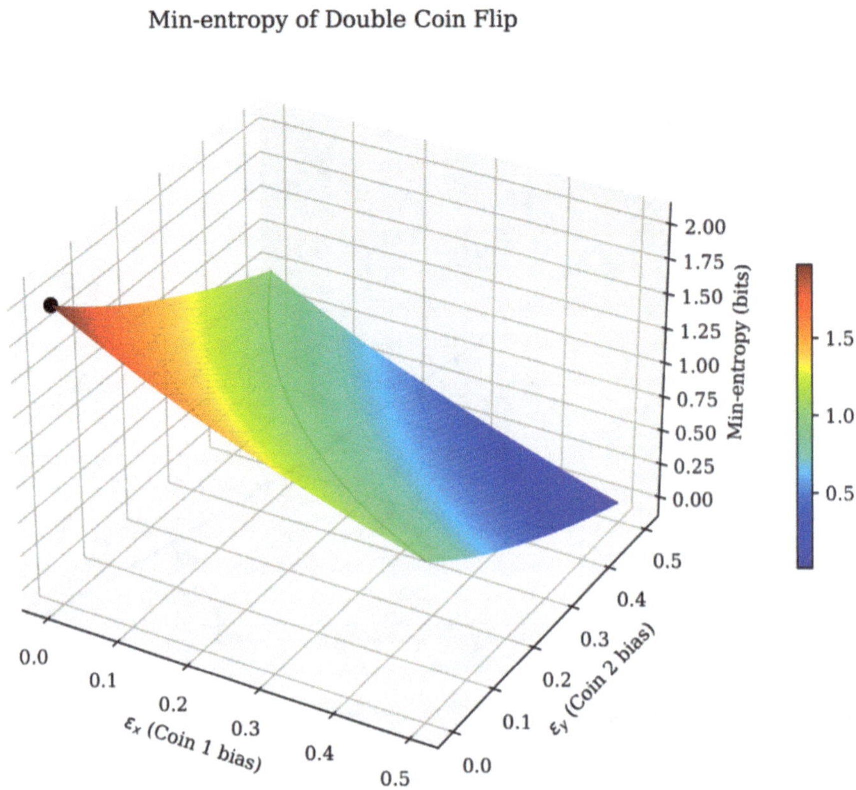

Fig. 15.3 Double-coin flip entropy graph

$$00,\ 01,\ 10,\ 11$$

From this, we simply imagine flipping more and more coins, from 8 to 16 to 256 and so on.

The idea is that the min-entropy associated with a probability distribution tells us something very important: if we assume the adversary has complete knowledge of the distribution and thus knows it's most probable outcome, then how difficult does guessing outputs remain, despite this knowledge? To know a uniform distribution affords one no predictive advantage and the knowledge has no value. But the further from uniform the distribution becomes, the lower the distribution's entropy, and the more valuable the knowledge of the distribution is.

min-entropy: Adelia Dons a Black Hat "Employees Only" read the words on a door Adelia spotted near the back of the restaurant. As she looked around more intently, she noticed there were a total of 10 doors which had these words on them. "I wonder what's in those rooms?" she said as she raised her hand and pointed to one.

Quin looked behind him at the same doors and noticed each one was secured with a keypad. "Let's try a thought experiment."

"Is it about entropy?"

"Yes, it's another way of thinking about it."

"Okay, what is it?"

"Notice how each of those doors are locked with a keypad?"

"Right," Adelia nodded.

"Suppose each of them were unlocked by some 3-digit PIN."

"3 digits sound pretty weak, doesn't it?"

"That's beside the point, it will make visualizing it easier," Quin said tapping his temple. "Let's say that you had the probability distribution describing whatever was generating those 3-digit PINs. Specifically, you could see the probability value assigned to all possible PINs. What do you think you could do with that information?"

"Wouldn't that tell you which PIN was the most likely to be generated?"

"And?"

"Well, you use that to make an educated guess about what the PIN is for one of the doors, right?"

Quin tried to get Adelia to look at the question from a different point of view. "Sure, but try and think more like an adversary. You win if you can gain entry into *any* of the doors and you have some information about the PINs that secure them."

"Okay, then I would just check all the PINs starting from most probable to least."

"What if it takes 2 seconds to check a PIN? That's 1000 PINs at 2 seconds each, tha-"

"It would take 33 min max," Adelia interjected.

"Yes, and would you feel comfortable standing in front of a single door for up to 33 minutes checking PINs?"

"No."

"So, then what's your strategy?"

"Don't try all the PINs, just a few."

"But how many? And why? And do you just try one door?" Quin deliberately said these is quick succession, not expecting them to be answered, but to illustrate the numerous considerations not being taken into account.

"I'm really not sure, but I feel like our chances of success are higher if we try multiple doors."

"That's good. That means there is something interesting to learn. And yes! As the adversary, you want to use the best possible strategy given the information you have. That means checking a few PINs on a single door is a worse strategy than checking a few PINs on multiple doors and so as the adversary, that is what you will do."

"But how many PINs should I check at each door?"

"That depends. What *exactly* is your objective?"

"To get into one of the doors."

"Are you sure? Because if that was your objective, you would just try every PIN on one door, but you already stated you wouldn't be comfortable with that since you'd probably get noticed and caught in that time."

Adelia turned this over in her mind a few times. "Well then what if I check a few PINs on a door, sit down and wait, then check a few more, and so on until I work through all the PINs in descending order of probability value?"

"That's a great question. Let's work out an example where we compare two strategies. The first strategy is to try every PIN on the same door; the second strategy is to try 3 PINs before moving on to another door. Let's suppose the PIN generator's distribution has the three most-probable PINs with probabilities 0.11, 0.05, and 0.04 respectively, and recall that under Kerckhoffs' principle, the adversary knows this distribution. The remaining probability is then spread over the rest of the 997 PINs. What would it mean to be successful at a single door under the second strategy?"

"Well, if you're only trying the 3 most probable PINs at each door, then success as a single door means that door's actual PIN happens to be among those top 3."

"And with what probability does that happen?"

"$0.11 + 0.05 + 0.04 = 0.20$."

"Right, and what is the expected number of checks per door before being successful or using up your 3 guesses?"

"You would multiply the number of guesses by the probability of making that many guesses and sum them."

"That's exactly right. We have that the expected value is $1(0.11) + 2(0.05) + 3(0.84) = 2.73$ guesses per door, where 0.11 is the probability you stop after one guess, 0.05 is the probability you stop after 2 guesses, and so on. Moreover, the reciprocal of the probability of being successful at a single door is equal to the expected number of doors we'd need to check before entering the right PIN," Quin stated.

"I don't see how you got that. How is that possible?"

"We will work it out formally in a bit, but let's finish this example."

"Hm."

"The expected number of doors you'd need to try before your first success is $1/p = 1/0.20 = 5$ doors. Thus, at 2.73 guesses per door with an expected 5 doors until success, that's a total of 13.65 guesses on average until you reach the right PIN using the second strategy."

"What about the first strategy, the one I suggested?"

"Well, what's the total expected number of guesses for a single door? For this one, since we only know the first 3 probabilities, we can assume the remaining PINs from 4 to 1000 contribute roughly equally to the remaining 0.8 of the probability. This means each is contributing about 0.0008.'

"Oh, I see, then the expected value for the 4–1000 PINs is 4 times 0.0008 plus 5 times 0.0008 plus and so on up to 1000 times 0.0008?" Adelia said, happy she was able to apply the expected value off the cuff like that.

"Yes, and using a script to compute that we see it gives us about 400.4."

"Don't we need to add back in the first 3 terms?"

"Yup! Those give us 0.33 so the total expected number of guesses for a single door is 400.73."

"Wow, that strategy sucks!" Adelia said, laughing.

"Yes, it does!"

"So, we must assume the adversary won't use that method, but will use a better one. If they using the door switching method, then is 3 really the number of checks which minimizes the total number of guesses?"

"To answer that, we need to get more formal," Quin turned his body, about to get more paper, but stopped. "Let's take a break for a second." Quin reviewed what he had said so far and hoped it had been accurate. He hoped he could sustain Adelia's attention and bring at least some degree of clarity. He reached into his backpack and retrieved the paper. "Alright, so here is what we have:" His pen pressed into the page.

min-entropy: Expected Work to Open Doors Since there are 10 digits on a keypad, 0–9, and each PIN is 3 digits in length, there are $10^3 = 1000$ possible PINs. Let's set $M = 1000$. We have the probability distribution of the PIN generator, and we will denote the function which assigns probabilities to PINs by P. The set of these assigned probability values can be denoted as $\{p_1, p_2, \ldots, p_M\}$, where the probability that the ith PIN is generated and where $000 \leq i \leq M = 999$, is p_i. Next, we can denote the maximum number of checks you can make before moving on to another door with the variable k. Finally, without loss of generality, we will assume the natural ordering on the set of probability values is $p_1 \geq p_2 \geq \ldots \geq p_M$.

Note that the natural strategy per door is to try the k PINs in descending order of their probability value. This means that you will do the same thing at each door should you not succeed at prior doors, but the unknown at each door is when you stop: you either stop when you enter the correct PIN or when you've checked k of them.

If the correct PIN is the ith PIN, that event has probability p_i. However, this event is equivalent to the event where it takes you a total of $i \leq k$ guesses before stopping. For $i < k$, "stopping" after i guesses simply means you've gained entry after making i guesses at the door. So, knowing how many guesses it took at the door tells you the same information as what the correct PIN for that door is, and that is why the probability of both events are the same.

However, for $i \geq k$, there are actually two scenarios where you would stop after making i guesses: the correct PIN is the $i = k$th PIN, or the correct PIN is beyond the kth PIN which is only known once you have used your $k$guesses and seen each one fail. The first scenario has probability p_k and the second scenario has probability equal to the event where the correct PIN is none of the first k, which is $1 - \sum_{i=1}^{k} p_i$. The total probability of the event where k guesses are made before stopping is the sum of both probabilities, which gives us

$$p_k + 1 - \sum_{i=1}^{k} p_i = 1 - \sum_{i=1}^{k-1} p_i. \tag{15.13}$$

With this, we can create a random variable $X : \Omega \to \{1, 2, 3, \ldots\}$, where Ω denotes the set of PINs and X represents the number of guesses at a single door until it either unlocks or all k guesses were used. Moreover, we can compute the expected value of X which tells us the average number of checks it would take at a single door until it unlocked, or we run out of tries and must move on to another door. This gives us

$$E[X] = p_1 + 2p_2 + \cdots + (k-1)p_{k-1} + k\left(1 - \sum_{i=1}^{k-1} p_i\right) = k - \sum_{i=1}^{k-1}(k-i)p_i. \tag{15.14}$$

But how likely is it that for any door, we are successful? For a single door there are two possibilities: the correct PIN for that door is among the PINs with the highest k probability values, or it's not. In the first scenario, we are successful since our strategy has us trying precisely those PINs with the k highest probability values. Therefore, for a given door, the probability of success is equal to the probability of the correct PIN being in the first k of them, which is probability $p = \sum_{i=1}^{k} p_i$. If we let "attempt" designate our trying up to k PINs at a single door, then the probability of success on the first attempt is the probability that the first door we try has a PIN among the those with the highest k probability values, which is p. The probability that we are successful by our second attempt means we weren't successful at the first door, which has probability $(1-p)$, but were successful at the second door which has probability p. Since we are assuming each PIN is generated independently of one another, the total probability of being successful on the second attempt is $(1-p)p$.

Generalizing this out, we can see that the probability of being successful on the nth attempt is $(1-p)^{n-1}p$. Letting $Y : \Omega \to \{1, 2, \ldots\}$ be the random variable which denotes the number of attempts until the first success, then the expected value of Y is

$$E[Y] = p + 2(1-p)p + \cdots + n(1-p)^{n-1}p = \sum_{j=1}^{\infty} j(1-p)^{j-1}p = p\sum_{j=1}^{\infty} j(1-p)^{j-1}. \tag{15.15}$$

Since $(1-p) < 1$, we can use the geometric power series identity to get

$$E[Y] = p\sum_{j=1}^{\infty} j(1-p)^{j-1} = \frac{p}{p^2} = \frac{1}{p}. \tag{15.16}$$

This means that on average, the number of doors we'll need to try until our first success is the reciprocal of the probability of success at a single door. That is, the reciprocal of the probability that a single door's PIN is among those with the highest k probabilities.

If we take the product of these two expected values, we get

$$W_k(P) = E[X] \cdot E[Y] = \frac{k - \sum_{i=1}^{k-1}(k-i)p_i}{\sum_{i=1}^{k} p_i}. \tag{15.17}$$

where P is the probability distribution over the space of PINs. Note that the "units" of this product work out to be guesses/success. That means $W_k(P)$ represents the total computational work, in guesses, on average that an attacker must perform before their first successful PIN is entered.

This leads us to ask what k is best? What k minimizes the amount of work we need to perform before gaining entry? Let k^* denote this optimal value. Then since it minimizes $W_k(P)$, it follows that $W_{k^*}(P) \leq W_k(P)$, by definition of minimum. Then it must hold that $W_{k^*}(P) \leq \frac{1}{p_1} = W_1(P)$. This should give one pause since it shows that the minimum amount of work on average to successfully guess a PIN is, at most, totally dependent on only whatever the most likely PIN is. This is precisely why min-entropy is used since it quantifies the value in knowing the most probable outcome.

Furthermore, it can be shown that $\frac{1}{2p_1} + \frac{1}{2} \leq W_k(P)$, for all $1 \leq k \leq M$. This gives us

$$\begin{aligned} &\frac{1}{2p_1} + \frac{1}{2} \leq W_{k^*}(P) \leq \frac{1}{p_1} \Rightarrow 0 \leq -\log_2 p_1 \\ &-\log_2 W_{k^*}(P) \leq 1 - \log_2 1 + p_1. \end{aligned} \tag{15.18}$$

One should immediately notice the term that has snuck into the above equation: $-\log_2 p_1 = H_\infty(P)$, which is the min-entropy of the probability distribution over the set of PINs. This shows that

$$0 \leq \mathrm{H}_\infty(\mathrm{P}) - \log_2(\mathrm{W}_{\mathrm{k}^*}(\mathrm{P})) \leq 1 - \log_2(1 + p_1). \tag{15.19}$$

The right-hand side is seen below in Fig. 15.4.

Note that taking the base 2 logarithm of $W_{k^*}(P)$ can be interpreted as converting the minimal number of guesses per success to the number of bits a uniformly random password would need to induce the same amount of work to crack. That is, if you have a 2-bit, uniformly random password, it will take at most 4 guesses to identify it. If you have an n-bit uniformly random password, then it would take at most 2^n guesses to identify it. The number of bits here is denoting the security strength.

The takeaway is that min-entropy only depends on the most probable value p_1, whereas $W_{k^*}(P)$ depends on the entire distribution. However, the difference between min-entropy and the logarithm of the optimal work is negligible, revealing that all the clever strategy in the world can't significantly outperform simply knowing the most likely value. As was demonstrated by this analysis and the example with guessing PINs, the security of the entire system collapses to that single maximum probability. This is exactly why min-entropy is the most telling of the entropy metrics in the context of digital security and precisely why SP 800-90B uses min-entropy as its primary metric rather than Shannon entropy.

Understanding IID and Non-IID "I'll be right back, I need to grab something from my car," Quin said, then got up and walked towards the door.

Adelia sat there thinking about what Quin had said—that there were "context clues" that somehow indicated the type of drink she would order that allowed him to guess it correctly.

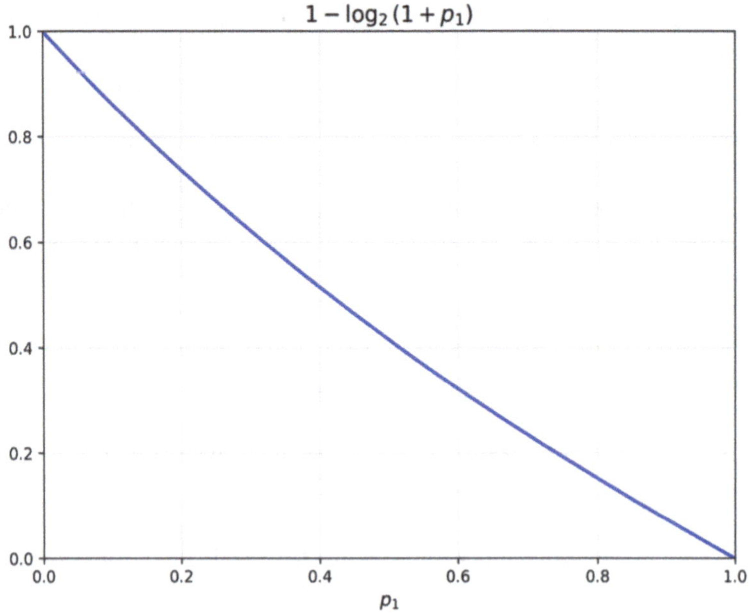

Fig. 15.4 Bounded error between min-entropy and work factor

To find out there was this pattern in her behaviors that betrayed her future like this frustrated Adelia.

It seems what I will do next isn't this vast space of possibilities I always thought it was, but a much smaller one restricted by and dependent on what I have done in the past, Adelia thought to herself. *Even if there wasn't this dependence on the past, there are still some things I will always do more than other things and anyone who knows me well enough can exploit that*. Adelia's face grew darker as she ruminated on this.

Quin returned with two strange looking devices. "Are you okay? You look upset," Quin asked as he slid into the booth.

"Yeah… I'm fine. What are those things?" Adelia asked.

"Well, these are two items I thought we could use to explore our next topic of discussion," Quin said excitedly.

On the table, he placed the two devices. The first was a flat rectangular box with a plastic window on the top, a button on the right side, and switch on the left side. Under the window there were eight coins sitting in circular recesses arranged in a row. "This one is pretty straight-forward. You press the button, which depresses a platform under all the coins where a lever is lowered to hold it in place. There is a spring below the platform so, once the lever is engaged, the spring is under tension and wants to restore. Then you simply flip this little switch on the side which releases the lever and …"

TINK

All the coins popped up at once and slammed against the plastic window, falling back down into the little depressions they had started in. Some of the coins had switched positions while others had returned to their starting spots.

"What are you supposed to do with this?" Adelia said as she picked up the device and inspected it.

"You can use it as a noise source! One way to interpret the coin faces is to take heads to be 1 and tails to be 0, simply string all the bits together. Here we have…" Quin used his index finger to read each coin's face. "01110100, which is 0x74 in hex or 116 in decimal, and is our raw data sample! Additionally, you can also picture each coin representing a full sample and so the eight of them together creates a sequence of samples."

Quin lifted the second device from the table. "But before we continue, let me show you this other device." It was a small electronic handheld thing with a long cable attached to it with a rubber coated metal clip at the end, like jumper cable but much smaller.

"With this, you simply clip this cable to anything," Quin said as he looked around searching for something to clip it to. He leaned over and attached it to the base of the table. "Now watch the screen," Quin said pointing to the small LCD screen. The top line showed rapidly flickering decimal numbers: 0.071477, 0.022405, 0.000121, 0.035652, …; below each number, a row of eight binary digits were changing in sync: 10010010, 00101101, 00000011, 01001000, …

"What are those numbers and why are they changing so fast?" Adelia leaned over the device.

"Okay, now sit totally still," Quin said, letting his spread hands hover over the table pantomiming "stillness."

The numbers started to change much slower and get smaller in size.

"Oh, is it measuring vibrations?" Adelia asked.

"That is correct!" Quin said.

"But what do the binary strings mean?"

"Internally, this device uses a 16-bit sensor and these eight bits at the bottom are just the least significant bits from the measurement." Quin replied. "Now, can you think of any differences between these two devices?"

Adelia thought but nothing was coming to mind.

"What if I told you the last position of each coin in my coin flipper? Would that tell you anything about what it would do next?"

"I don't think so, it seems unrelated to the last output." Adelia said.

"What about this other device? If I told you it's very last output would that tell you anything about its next output?" Quin asked.

"Well, it seems like it would be very unlikely for the vibration device to suddenly show all 0 s as that would require everyone in the restaurant to stop moving suddenly. Also, you might be able to infer that the next value will be higher if the previous few were increasing." Adelia said.

"Exactly." Quin said.

"But why does the vibration device have these dependencies when the coin flipper doesn't?"

"The coin flipper is artificially simple; it has eight separate coins that are physically isolated. Each flip is mechanically independent since we've engineered it that way. But the vibration sensor is measuring a real physical system: the table, which is coupled to the floor, to other tables, to people moving through the restaurant, people who are coupled to their own personal lives that may or may not permit them the time to be here on this day or that day, and so on."

"So, the dependencies aren't a flaw?" Adelia asked.

"Not at all, they're constitutive. The vibration sensor works because everything is interconnected. If the table were somehow perfectly isolated, there'd be nothing to measure. Real physical systems resist decomposition into independent parts because their very existence depends on these couplings."

Adelia felt oddly deflated. "When you said I was defined by my probability landscape earlier ..."

"Yes?"

"You meant that literally. The correlations in my behavior, or the dependencies between my past and future choices, between context and action, none of that is accidental."

"Right. They are what makes you, you, rather than just random noise. To be anything, to persist as a pattern over time, requires these interdependencies. Memory, patterns, structure, and the like accumulate and exist through these dependencies. Things that don't do this aren't maintaining structure or identity, but you are. You are a non-decomposable web of interdependencies, bound both physically and across time. As such, you are the patterns on that landscape. It's unavoidable. The thing is, Adelia, you can't hate being predictable without hating the conditions that make you exist as Adelia at all. But anyway, this is actually a good segue into another important topic."

"What is that?"

"Well, the very predictability you are concerned with is only possible because of those patterns. Let me explain."

Understanding IID and Non-IID: Uniformity You can Prove What happens to what you can prove about entropy as we relax the assumptions about the distribution? We'll start with the strongest assumptions (IID) and work toward the weakest (arbitrary dependencies), watching our certainty degrade along the way.

The coin flipper represents what is called an Independent and Identically Distributed (IID) Source, and to understand what this means we take each coin to be a random variable representing a sample of a single bit. We should imagine the coin flipper as producing sequences of outputs (samples) of our noise source. With every press of the button, we observe some particular sequence of samples get realized. So, if we have

$$X_1, X_2, \ldots, X_8, \tag{15.20}$$

then we are ultimately interested in what we can say about the min-entropy present per sequence of samples, which is a statement about the joint distribution of $(X_1, \ldots, X_8)$.

We assume the samples are IID and that probability of the outcome 1 (landing heads) is some $0 < \delta < 1$, which is the same for each random variable. This means

$$p_{X_i}(1) = \delta, p_{X_i}(0) = 1 - \delta, \text{ for } i = 1, \ldots, 8. \tag{15.21}$$

This covers the "identically distributed part." It should also be noted that, in practice, IID also entails the distribution for each random variable staying constant and not changing over time.

The "independent" part comes from stipulating the outcome of any one random variable (coin flip) is not at all influenced by the outcome of any other single or combination of random variables. This should be clear to see since we can imagine any one of the eight coins having the same outcome after a flip whether it was flipped in isolation or flipped in a group of other coins like in the device.

The interesting property of IID sources is that, despite there being a bias present (the δ) in each random variable, there is a way to "extract" non-biased samples: take the 8-sample sequence of the coin flipper and break it into four groups of consecutive samples; for each pair where the two samples are the same, skip it; for pairs which are equal to (10) output a 1; finally, for those pairs which are equal to (01), output a 0. For example,

$$01110110 \rightarrow (01)(11)(01)(10) \rightarrow 001 \tag{15.22}$$

How can we show the resulting sequence has "unbiased" samples? To start, we note the following probabilities:

$$\begin{gathered} P(\{00\}) = (1 - \delta)^2, \; P(\{01\}) = (1 - \delta)\delta, \\ P(\{10\}) = \delta(1 - \delta), \; P(\{11\}) = \delta^2 \end{gathered} \tag{15.23}$$

Notice how $P(\{01\}) = P(\{10\})$, as this will be important later. Now, using the definition of conditional probability we find the probability of outputting 0 given that the pair was either 01 or 10 is

$$\begin{aligned} P(\{01\}|\{01,\ 10\}) &= \frac{P(\{01\} \cap \{01,\ 10\})}{P(\{01,\ 10\})} \\ &= \frac{P(\{01\})}{P(\{01,10\})} = \frac{(1-\delta)}{2(1-\delta)} = \frac{1}{2}. \end{aligned} \tag{15.24}$$

Similarly, since $P(\{01\}) = P(\{10\})$, as we noted earlier, then it follows that the probability of outputting 1 given that the pair was either 01 or 10 is the same with

$$P(\{10\}|\{01, 10\}) = \tfrac{1}{2}. \tag{15.25}$$

Since we only care about the parts of the input sequence for which the bits are not the same, then we condition on that event as seen above. This means that, among the bits that actually appear in the output sequence, each bit is equally likely to be 0 or 1. In other words,

$$P(0|\text{"a bit was output"}) = P(1|\text{"a bit was output"}) = \frac{1}{2}. \tag{15.26}$$

We therefore see a way to construct a uniform distribution from a non-uniform source.

The above construction is called the von Neumann Extractor; it doesn't just produce uniform sample sequences but sequences whose uniformity we can prove. The proof relies critically on independence: $P(\{01\}) = P(\{10\}) = \delta(1-\delta)$. If the coin flips were dependent, this equality would not hold, and we could not guarantee uniformity.

Understanding IID and Non-IID: Only Independence and A Near Perfect Coin Flip What would happen if we relaxed the identically distributed aspect of the noise source distribution? Generalizing up from our coin flipper, we assume we have n single-bit samples, and that each of them have some bias $0 < \delta \leq \delta_i \leq 1-\delta$, where $p_{X_i}(0) = \delta_i$. We will show that if you take the first $k \leq n$ bits and XOR them together, the probability the result is equal to 1 converges to 1/2 exponentially fast in k. This means that, from a non-uniform but independent noise source, we can derive a distribution that is arbitrarily close to uniform.

The claim is:

$$\left| P\left[\bigoplus_{k}^{i=1} X_i = 0 \right] - \tfrac{1}{2} \right| = \epsilon^k. \tag{15.27}$$

where $\oplus$ denotes the XOR operation and ϵ is some number less than 1. To show this, one might be tempted at first to look at k-bit strings and summing the probabilities of the subset of them which have odd parity; however, this quickly leads to a mess of binomial expansions. Instead, we perform a simple transformation:

$$X_i \mapsto (-1)^{X_i} = Y_i. \tag{15.28}$$

This gives us new random variables, $Y_i \in \{-1, 1\}$, which allows us to answer our original question but side-step some of the mess. The relation between the XOR operation and our new random variable can be seen here:

$$\prod_{i=1}^{k} Y_i = \prod_{\text{i}=1}^{\text{k}} (-1)^{\text{X}_\text{i}} = (-1)^{\oplus_{i=1}^{k} X_i}. \tag{15.29}$$

With this we can see that when $\oplus_{i=1}^{k} X_i = 0$, then $\prod_{i=1}^{k} Y_i = 1$. Similarly, when $\oplus_{i=1}^{k} X_i = 1$, then $\prod_{i=1}^{k} Y_i = -1$. Thus, the probability of one is identical the probability of the other. That is,

$$P\left[\bigoplus_{k}^{i=1} X_i = 0\right] = P\left[\prod_{i=1}^{k} Y_i = 1\right]. \tag{15.30}$$

Before proceeding, we must note that, for any random variable, $Z \in \{-1, 1\}$, then by the definition of expected value, we have the following identity: $E[Z] = 2P(Z = 1) - 1$; solving for $P(Z = 1)$, we get $P(Z = 1) = (1 + E[Z])/2$. We can also know that the Y_i random variables are independent since the X_i random variables are independent, and, from this independence, it follows that $E[XY] = E[X]E[Y]$ for any independent random variables, X and Y.

From the identity and independence property noted above, it follows that:

$$\begin{aligned} P\left[\prod_{i=1}^{k} Y_i = 1\right] &= \frac{1 + E\left[\prod_{i=1}^{k} Y_i\right]}{2} \\ &= \frac{1}{2} + \left(\frac{1}{2}\right)\prod_{i=1}^{k} E[Y_i]. \end{aligned} \tag{15.31}$$

Since $E[Y_i] = 2\delta_i - 1$ and $|2\delta_i - 1| \leq |2\delta - 1| < 1$, then

$$\left| P\left[\prod_{i=1}^{k} Y_i = 1\right] - \tfrac{1}{2} \right| \leq \tfrac{1}{2}|2\delta - 1|^k. \tag{15.32}$$

Thus, if we take $\epsilon = |2\delta - 1|/2$, then $\epsilon^{\mathrm{k}} \to 0$ as $k \to \infty$ and our initial claim has been shown true.

The takeaway here is the power of independence: In our first case we were able to create a uniform distribution from a non-uniform source; in this case, we were able to create a nearly uniform distribution from a non-uniform source. What we know about the entropy rate in this case is less certain, but the bounds on it remain provable. The XOR construction doesn't just converge to uniform, it converges at a rate we can bound, and this bound comes directly from the independence of each Y_i. We will see that, once we relax the independence assumption, things get far more complicated, and our definite knowledge of the entropy rate moves out of reach leaving us only with statistical measurements that approximate its value.

The Epistemological Collapse: Losing Independence Previously we saw that independence grants us powerful tools: the von Neumann extractor produces provably uniform bits from an IID source, and XORing independent bits converges to uniformity at a provable rate. Both proofs were entirely reliant on the ability to factor joint probabilities into the product of marginal probabilities. This culminates in two results.

Let $(X_1, X_2, \ldots, X_L)$ be L random variables representing L successive samples from a noise source, where each X_i takes values in $\{0, 1\}^n$ (the set of all n-bit patterns). When we observe the noise source, we get specific realizations $x_1, \ldots, x_L$, and the probability of observing some sequence $(x_1, \ldots, x_L)$ is given by the joint distribution $P(X_1 = x_1, \ldots, X_L = x_l)$.

If assume the random variables are IID, then by the definition of independence, we get:

$$P(X_1 = x_1, X_2 = x_2, \ldots, X_L = x_L) = \prod_{i=1}^{L} P(X_i = x_i), \tag{15.33}$$

for all $(x_1, \ldots, x_L) \in (\{0, 1\}^n)^L$. And since all X_i are identically distributed, each X_i has the same marginal distribution. That is,

$$P(X_1 = x) = \cdots = P(X_L = x), \tag{15.34}$$

for all $x \in \{0, 1\}^n$. Since all the X_i share the same marginal distribution, we can characterize the entire sequence by understanding just one sample. So, if we know the probability of one particular sample occurring, say, in the ith position of the sequence of L samples, then the same sample will occur with the same frequency for all the other positions in the sequence.

If we let $x^* \in \{0, 1\}^n$ denote the n-bit sample which occurs most frequently for any of the positions in the sequence, then, as stated earlier, it occurs most frequently for all positions in the sequence. Therefore, if we let $p_{\max} = P(X_1 = x^*)$, then

$$\max_{x \in \{0,1\}^n} P(X_i = x) = p_{\max}, \tag{15.35}$$

for all i. Moreover, it follows from the fact that the maximum of a product of non-negative terms is only achieved when each factor in the product is maximized. And so,

$$\max_{(x_1,\ldots,x_L)} P(X_1 = x_1, \ldots, X_n = x_L) = \prod_{i=1}^{L} p_{\max} = \mathrm{p}_{\mathrm{max}}^{\mathrm{L}}. \tag{15.36}$$

Taking the $-\log_2$ throughout gives

$$-\log_2 \max(P(X_1, \ldots, X_L)) = H_\infty(X_1, \ldots, X_L) = \sum_{i=1}^{L} H_\infty(X_1) = L \cdot \mathrm{H}_\infty(\mathrm{X}_1). \tag{15.37}$$

This shows that the min-entropy of L samples is completely determined by the min-entropy of a single sample, which is precisely why the von Neumann and XOR proofs worked—we were able to analyze each component separately and combine results since the joint distribution can be factored, meaning you need only measure the entropy of one term and scale it.

This is not the case for non-IID sources. For noise sources with unknown dependency structures, the best we can do is

$$H_\infty(X_1, \ldots, X_L) \le L \cdot \mathrm{H}_\infty(\mathrm{X}_1). \tag{15.38}$$

The point is that, for non-IID sources, the min-entropy of a sequence of L samples does not decompose identically per sample since dependencies create predictable patterns across the sequence, making the most probable L-sample sequence far more likely than would be predicted by simply multiplying per-sample probabilities. The most common value (MCV) has its eye trained on single samples, so the MCV is blind to patterns which take shape across multiple samples.

This explains why, for non-IID sources, SP 800-90B requires ten different estimators rather than just one: each estimator probes a different assumption about which dependency structure might exist. Since we don't know which dependency structures exist, we probe many possibilities and take the minimum across estimators. Without independence, no finite set of measurements can determine the true min-entropy and we can therefore only approximate how predictable the distribution is.

Comprehension Checkpoint "Before we continue, I must ask, how are you feeling so far? Is any of this making sense?"

"I feel fine, I guess. Some of this was a little dense and hard to follow, honestly. I think I get the gist though."

"May I ask you to explain the gist as you understand it?"

"Yeah, um," Adelia rested her face in her palms and let out a soft sigh before raising her head again. She was just now realizing the amount of information they had covered and was struggling to put it all into view so she could actually find the words for this "gist" she claimed to have. "There was min-entropy, which tells you how hard it is to guess an outcome of an entropy source, and then there is the issue with knowing the min-entropy rate of an entropy source, which can be difficult to measure because of something related to independence."

"Okay, that's not bad. Though, min-entropy is telling you more than just the difficulty in guessing the outcome. It's the difficulty given what?"

"Oh, given that you have knowledge of the distribution."

"Exactly, and knowledge of what specifically about the distribution?"

"What the highest probability value is."

"Why is that value important?"

"Because it..." The mental image in Adelia's mind was starting to get fuzzy.

"Don't worry if you can't put it into words yet, that will come as you keep thinking about it," Quin assured her. "Remember that we saw that the optimal expected computational work an adversary must perform until success technically depends on the entire distribution, but it's actually bounded above by a term that only includes the highest probability value from the distribution. That tells us that how easy or hard it will be for an attacker is really a question of how high the highest peak on our probability distribution is. Knowing how hard it will be for an attacker is the most important measurement of how secure something is—pretty much all other considerations are downstream from this. But you said that measuring min-entropy can be difficult. Why so?"

"Okay, so we showed that for IID sources, min-entropy is additive. That means I can just multiply by n to get the min-entropy of n samples if I know the min-entropy of one sample. And the joint distribution factors into a product of marginals, so I only need to measure the marginal."

"And what about for non-IID sources?"

"It doesn't factor. Two non-IID sources can have identical marginals, but completely different joint min-entropies."

"And what does that mean for the MCV estimator?"

"MCV estimates the maximum probability of a single sample. That's the marginal. But what we actually care about is the maximum probability of an entire sequence of samples—that's the joint. For IID sources, knowing the marginal tells you the joint. For non-IID sources, it doesn't."

"So, what can we do?"

"We use many different estimators that each look for different types of structure—Markov chains, repeated patterns, compression, predictability. If any of them find something exploitable, we lower our estimate, always taking the minimum."

"Okay, it seems like you have a good grasp. Let's finish up by seeing how exactly 90B actually operationalizes these concepts."

What Does it Mean to Validate an Entropy Source? To validate an entropy source simply means to obtain assurance that the requirements within SP 800-90B have been met by the entropy source, that the entropy source has been shown to reliably produce bitstrings which provide entropy equal to, or exceeding, some specified value. Obtaining assurance that an entropy source satisfies the requirements of SP 800-90B does not mean one's Uncle Larry took a "good look at it" and found everything was "nice and random."

Rather, an entropy source is submitted (by a submitter) to an NVLAP-accredited laboratory, and the laboratory will assess the entropy source and all other documentation provided by the submitter. The laboratory's role is to provide their expertise and discernment to determine if the provided entropy source and its documentation satisfy the requirements of SP 800-90B. This determination made by the laboratory, along with its evidence and documentation, is provided to the Cryptographic Algorithm Validation Program (CAVP) and Cryptographic Module Validation Program (CMVP) for a final review and verdict.

The submitter must provide claims about the entropy source along with rationale for each claim, and then the laboratory evaluates these claims and performs independent testing, always taking the more conservative result as the basis for the final entropy claim.

The Two Critical Claims Of the claims made by the submitter, there are two that are of great interest and require very careful analysis by the laboratory:

1. The min-entropy estimate, which states how many bits of entropy each sample provides
2. The IID claim, which is the noise source sampling from an IID or non-IID distribution.

The min-entropy estimate is the heart of the validation. Recall that min-entropy directly determines an adversary's expected guessing work, so if a noise source claims to provide H_∞ bits of per n-bit sample, this means:

- An adversary who knows the distribution still faces 2^{H_∞} guessing difficulty per sample.
- To generate a 256-bit cryptographic key, one needs at least $256/H_\infty$ samples.

It is imperative the laboratory verifies the min-entropy estimate is not overstated, as overestimating entropy directly undermines security.

For the IID claim, the distinction between an IID and non-IID source is critical, as IID sources allow simple, provable entropy scaling while non-IID sources may have less entropy than would be suggested by scaling marginals due to dependencies that are invisible to marginal analysis.

The Validation Tracks Once a source is submitted with an IID claim, the laboratory must first subject the source to tests which aim to verify the IID claim More precisely, the lab will perform tests that attempt to discover statistical patterns that would render the claim invalid. If these tests are passed, the MCV will suffice as the estimator for the noise source's per sample min-entropy. Finally, the source will be subjected to restart testing to further verify the source remains independent and identically distributed across power cycles and restarts. If the distribution changes over time or early samples differ from steady-state, IID testing fails.

For non-IID sources, the fundamental problem we saw is that marginal analysis cannot reveal joint structure. Two sources with identical single-sample distributions can have vastly different joint min-entropies due to dependencies. To address this, the source is subjected to 10 estimators:

- Most Common Value (MCV) Estimate: Examines the frequency of the single most common symbol but ignores all temporal dependencies between samples
- Collision Estimate: Detects low entropy through collision probabilities when sampling without replacement; sensitive to how quickly repeated values appear
- Markov Estimate: Tests for first-order Markov dependencies where the probability of the next sample depends on the current sample
- Compression Estimate: Uses statistical compression to detect any structures or patterns that would allow data reduction, indicating predictability
- t-Tuple Estimate: Searches for frequently repeated sequences (tuples) of varying lengths to detect multi-sample correlations

- Longest Repeated Substring (LRS) Estimate: Examines the longest substrings that repeat in the data, estimating collision entropy for patterns too large for the t-tuple test
- Multi Most Common in Window (MultiMCW) Prediction: Predicts the next sample based on which value appears most frequently in recent windows of varying sizes, detecting non-stationary behavior
- Lag Prediction Estimate: Tests whether samples at various time lags can predict future samples, detecting periodic or cyclic dependencies
- MutliMMC Prediction Estimate: Uses multiple predictors that track the most common value following specific historical patterns, detecting complex conditional dependencies
- LZ78Y Prediction Estimate: Applies Lempel-Ziv style dictionary-based prediction to detect whether past sequences help predict future samples.

The final estimate for the non-IID source's per-sample min-entropy is set as the minimum across all ten.

Conditioning Components Many sources include a deterministic conditioning function (hash, CBC-MAC, etc.) to extract and concentrate entropy from a biased noise source. Though we did not cover these fascinating concepts, it should be noted that, while conditioning components can never increase the total entropy of a noise source, it can increase the computational entropy. The idea is that there are special functions which can transform the probability distribution of a noise source into a new distribution that is computationally indistinguishable from a uniform distribution from the perspective of a polynomial-bounded adversary. Thus, no adversary would possess the computational resources needed to identify the difference between the transformed (non-uniform, but uniform looking) distribution from a genuinely uniform distribution.

Both raw and conditioned outputs must be tested. If the noise source provides insufficient entropy, no conditioning can truly compensate.

Health Tests Validation occurs at a point in time, but the source must maintain its properties during operation. Health tests provide continuous monitoring to accomplish that.

Startup tests verify correct operation before producing output and continuous tests (repetition count, adaptive proportion) detect degradation during operation.

If a health test fails, the source must cease output and signal an error. Health tests operationalize our adversarial assumption: we validated under distribution P, but physical degradation might shift it to some P' with lower entropy.

A critical requirement often overlooked is failure mode coverage: the submitter must document all known or suspected failure modes of the noise source, and the health tests must be capable of detecting each one. If the standard Repetition Count Test (RCT) and Adaptive Proportion Test (APT) cannot detect a documented failure mode with sufficient probability, the submitter must implement additional develop-defined health tests that can. This requirement (SP 800-90B Sect. 4.3 Requirement 8 [1]/IG D.K Resolutions 14–16 [2]) ensures that health testing is tailored to the specific vulnerabilities of each noise source design, not merely a generic checkbox.

The Security Chain The final validated claim takes the following form: "this noise source provides at least H bits of min-entropy per n-bit sample."

This creates a chain of trust: physical noise source (validated at H bits/sample) to operational conditioning to entropy source output to cryptographic keys, IVs, etc.

Every cryptographic operation is downstream from this claim about min-entropy. The conservatism through the validation process (i.e., 99% confidence intervals, minimum of ten estimators, continuous health monitoring, etc.) reflects the stakes: small errors in entropy estimation translate directly to weakened security.

Recall that an adversary's expected work depends on $p_{\max}$, the highest probability in the distribution. For a non-IID source, the dependencies concentrate probability mass in ways invisible to marginal analysis.

This is why getting the IID/non-IID distinction right is so critical. It's the difference between provable security and dangerous overconfidence.

Adelia's Farewell Quin had left almost two hours ago, and Adelia remained in the booth. It was late in the evening and the restaurant had nearly emptied out. There were still a few noises in the background: low chatter of a distant conversation, utensils scraping on a plate, the occasional whooshing sound of a truck passing by, etc. From the back, the sound of running water through the dishwasher made a noise like static. She listened to it.

'*To be on that landscape is what it means to be Adelia.*' That phrase surfaced without her calling it. She turned it over.

She had always experienced herself as the unique origin of the effects she had on the world, the effects that were hers. She raised her arm and pushed her cup across the table. Seeing the mug near the edge assured her that she was there, that she was Adelia, the girl that pushed the mug to the edge.

'*He took my future and realized it himself.*'

She imagined an adversary sitting next to her and pushing the cup to the edge before she could, pushing it to exactly the same place it is now.

If what I do can be done by another, before I do it, then... But why am I predictable? Adelia is patterns and patterns enable predictability.

The static sound hissed, and Adelia listened. There was no memory in it or pattern to learn.

Adelia closed her eyes and tried to imagine what it felt like to be pure static. She felt it, but only for a moment before her phone vibrated, breaking her concentration; she saw a notification for one of her apps. She unlocked her phone and started scrolling on the app for a few minutes before getting up and walking out the door (Fig. 15.5).

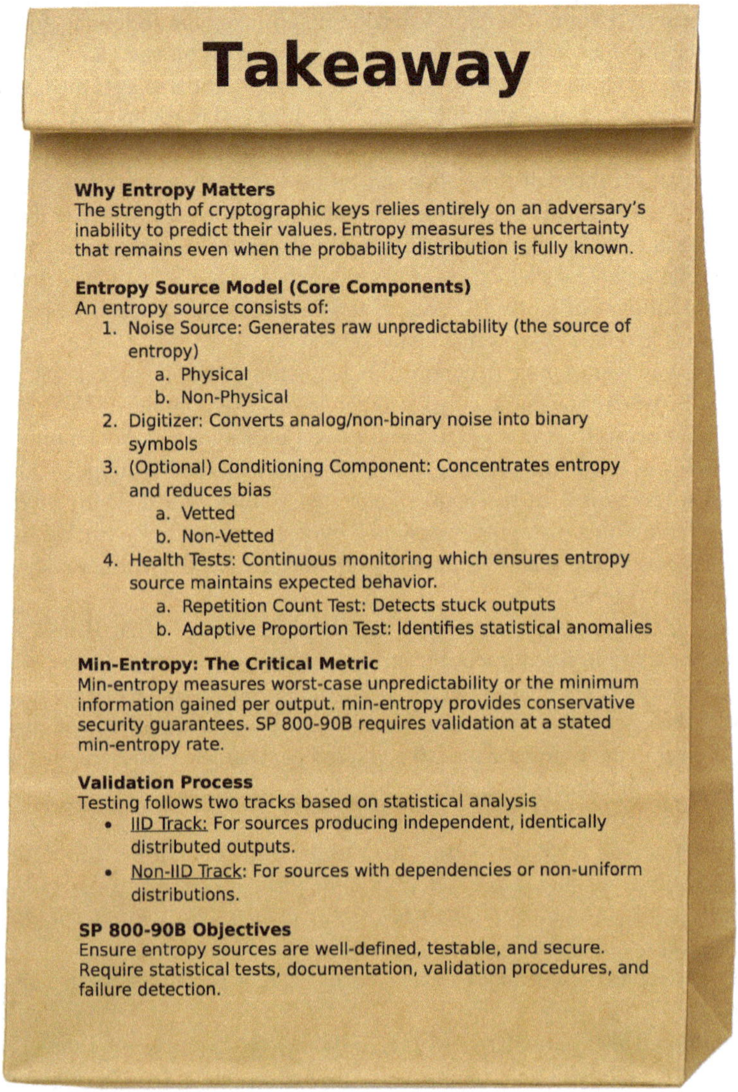

Fig. 15.5 Takeaways regarding SP800-90B and entropy

References

1. Turan MS, Barker E, Kelsey J, McKay KA, Baish ML, Boyle M (2018) Recommendation for the entropy sources used for random bit generation. National Institute of Standards and Technology. via NIST https://csrc.nist.gov/pubs/sp/800/90/b/final. Accessed 03 Dec 2025
2. National Institute of Standards and Technology (2016) FIPS 140-3 IG and RFG announcements. https://csrc.nist.gov/projects/cryptographic-module-validation-program/fips-140-3-ig-announcements. Accessed 03 Dec 2025

Quin Darcy Quin works as an IT Security Consultant for atsec information security. In this position, he has worked on software, firmware, and hardware modules, and his work spans code review; ACVP, ESV, and functional testing; and report writing. Quin holds bachelor's and master's degrees in mathematics.

Chapter 16
Ring Oscillators

Luca Di Domenico

Back at it Again, Here at the FIPS 'n' Chips On that day, Aster had finally gotten her motivation back: On her menu today, literally and figuratively, was a new lecture held at the exclusive FIPS 'n' Chips restaurant. She moved in fast, decisive steps towards the atsec CST laboratory.

This time, the lecture was held by Luca, an Italian atsec security consultant who previously gave an AES lecture that Aster attended some time before. Today's lecture was going to cover one of the most common examples of hardware-based entropy sources: the trustworthy ring oscillator.

Joachim and Yi had asked Luca to lead this lecture remotely for curious students and for other atsec coworkers, since the three of them were working together on an entropy document, and this kind of example lecture could be useful to many people. Aster had been lucky enough to be invited.

Despite the fact that Luca was quite a distance away, the lecture was open to attendees from around the world because it was set to take place in the virtual FIPS 'n' Chips restaurant.

When Aster entered the meeting room where the lecture would take place, she saw everyone putting on their VR goggles, and she heard Luca say, "OK everyone, ready for a tasty Italian-flavored lecture gelato at FIPS 'n' Chips?" In other words, she had made it just in the nick of time. She chuckled along at Luca's metaphor together with the others. The lecture started right after she had put on her VR goggles.

What are Ring Oscillators? Luca assumed that his audience knew the fundamentals, but he started off with a reminder to be thorough: "This may be common knowledge to us here, but let's go over a reminder of what a 'bit' is, just in case. In hardware, the bits of a computer are defined as signals which use two different voltage levels: a high voltage level represents a 1, while a low voltage level represents a 0. An inverter gate, sometimes called NOT gate or shortened to just 'inverter,' is

L. Di Domenico (✉)
Formerly with atsec information security corporation, Austin, TX, USA
e-mail: luca.didomenico99@gmail.com

Y. Mao (ed.), *Tasting Cryptography*, https://doi.org/10.1007/978-3-032-30243-4_16

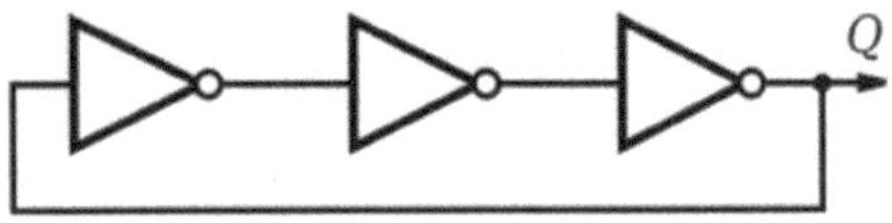

Fig. 16.1 Basic ring oscillator

a basic digital logic gate that inverts the input voltage level. Hence, it modifies an input signal of 1 into an output signal of 0, and vice versa."

With the fundamentals established, Luca began the lecture proper with the definition and the description of a ring oscillator.

As he spoke, Aster entered in some quick notes: A ring oscillator (shortened to RO) is a type of electronic circuit composed of an odd number of inverters. These inverters are chained together one after the other and are connected in a loop. The first inverter in the chain is also an enabling gate (i.e., it functions only if a corresponding 'enable' signal is set to 1), whereas the remaining inverters are delay elements, meaning that the inversion of the voltage level does not happen instantaneously, but after a certain delay. To form a loop, the output of the last inverter is fed back into the first as input. Because of the odd number of gates, the output of a RO oscillates between the two possible voltage levels, where an output signal of 1, passing back into the loop, causes the output signal to become a 0 after some time, and vice versa.

She sketched a quick diagram (Fig. 16.1 taken from [7]) to help herself remember the concept better:

"What's neat," Luca cut in, "Is that ROs have a plethora of use cases!"

"For example, they can be used to monitor the process, voltage, and temperature variations during the testing phase of a freshly produced chip. Because physical imperfections in real-world construction operations are unavoidable, every produced chip is slightly different from the previous ones. Hence, the circuit performance of this new chip can be checked and tested with the use of an RO."

As Luca continued, Aster furiously punched in more notes about how ring oscillators may be used for frequency synchronizations. If it is crucial to maintain synchronization with an input reference, it is possible to monitor the frequency of an RO (i.e., the number of times the RO oscillates in a second) and adjust it by controlling the supply voltage or temperature if necessary, so that this synchronization is kept.

Moreover, an RO can serve as a very basic clock signal generator in low-precision environments. By definition, a clock signal is a periodic signal that switches from 1 to 0 back to 1 in a set amount of time. There are many ways to generate such a signal, and it is easy to see how the construction of a ring oscillator achieves this periodicity.

"But there is a catch," stated Luca, pausing for emphasis, "Ring oscillators do not necessarily produce signal inversions in a precise amount of time."

The Unpredictability of ROs "Why do you think ROs are not very precise?" asked Luca. The others slowly but surely answered. After some small corrections made by the teacher himself, Aster recorded the following to her notes:

By nature, electricity is not deterministic. There are unpredictable physical mechanisms in the real world, especially at a quantum level, that make the timing of the transitions of the ring oscillators and their frequency (how many times they oscillate in a second) somewhat inconsistent. It is specifically this inconsistency that sees oscillators used to create Physical noise sources for Random Bit Generators (or RBGs) and for Random Number Generators (or RNGs).

Many researchers outlined and estimated at least two main noise sources of ring oscillators ("noise source" is a term in the jargon to say "causes of unpredictability"). The first is called thermal noise. At a basic level, electricity can be interpreted as a high number of electrons moving very fast through a wire. The moving electrons inside a wire always incur in some type of resistance.

"It is like what we experience when we are running against a wind current, do you know the feeling?" asked Luca rhetorically, but Aster nodded with a knowing expression on her face, since it always seems like something she experiences on days when she's late.

Luca continued, "Note that electrons experience a resistance which is orders of magnitude weaker than running against the wind, but they do experience some resistance, nonetheless. The unpredictability and the variability of this resistance with respect to miniscule temperature fluctuations cause thermal noise."

As Luca launched into the second main type of noise source, Aster shook thoughts of her jogs away and got back to taking notes. This second noise source type identified by researchers is called shot noise. In theory, a 0 corresponds to a low voltage level and a 1 corresponds to a high voltage level, but in practice deciding if a given signal should be interpreted as a 0 or as a 1 is done via a threshold. If, at the time of reading, the voltage of a given signal is below the threshold, then the signal will be interpreted as a 0. Otherwise, if the voltage is above the threshold, then it is interpreted as a 1.

Since an electric current is made up of individual electrons, when each inverter of a RO is switching voltage, all the electrons that must be moved to achieve the inversion take an unpredictable amount of time to do so. Sometimes, it may happen that electrons move slightly faster, and other times the electrons move slightly slower. Since the voltage is directly proportional to the number of electrons, a faster or a slower movement of electrons cause the signal threshold to be reached earlier or later, respectively. Usually, the timing variation of the threshold crossing is a fraction of a millisecond, but this variation is enough to be detected and to cause shot noise.

Thermal and shot noises are not the only physical noise sources of ROs. Yet, other noise sources fall in one or more of the following categories:

- they have a negligible contribution to the unpredictability (like flicker noise);
- they can be somewhat manipulated in a deterministic way; and/or
- they are hard to take into consideration by any mathematical analysis.

Estimating the Unpredictability "Speaking of mathematical analysis," said Luca, while a small grin appeared on his face, "it is crucial to remember how NIST certifies the use of an RBG. Can anyone here fill us in?"

"Aside from those of you who work with this day in and day out," he clarified, nodding to some of his colleagues who started to raise their hands.

Aster confidently raised her hand, and shared what she knew after Luca gestured for her to answer. "An RBG construction contains a noise source, which shall be submitted to the Cryptographic Module Validation Program—or the CMVP—to obtain an Entropy Source Validation, an ESV. To obtain this validation, amongst the required documentation, an Entropy Assessment Report—an EAR—shall be provided. This EAR shall contain, amongst other things, a stochastic model, an entropy estimate, and a recording of practical statistical tests."

"Exactly so! A textbook answer," Luca affirmed. "Given an RBG to validate, the required statistical tests are easily computable by retrieving random bits from the RBG and using the official NIST tool. An entropy estimate, as the name suggests, is a mathematical formula which approximately measures how much unpredictability we can find in the outputs of the noise source of the analyzed RBG. The entropy estimate is derived using a stochastic model, which is a rigorous mathematical construction that explains in detail the entropy estimation."

"Vendors are free to come up with their own noise source designs and corresponding stochastic models," clarified Luca, "but the most time-efficient and trustworthy way to obtain a reasonable entropy estimation is to use publicly available stochastic models and RBG designs. This is where the various years of research regarding the thermal and shot noises of ROs come into play. With all the public information available regarding RO-based RBGs, there are numerous designs to pick from. Let us go over three examples of RO-based RBGs."

While Luca changed his slide projected in the VR restaurant, Aster blocked out space for three examples in her notes.

Unstable RO Sampled by a Slow Stable Clock Luca explained "The following design involves only one RO and is commonly used. First, create a stable periodic signal, that is, an alternating signal which is resistant to noise. Then, take a constantly running RO, and design this RO in such a way that it is easily influenced by noise on purpose. Now, combine them using a so-called Delay or Data Flip-Flop."

Aster racked her brain for what a Delay and Data Flip-Flop were, and after a few seconds it suddenly came to her.

A Data Flip-Flop, or DFF, has two input signals, one called data input and the other called clock, along with a single output signal. The rising edges of the clock signal (i.e., the transitions of the signals which go from 0 to 1) make the DFF read the signal when data is input; this reading operation is also called 'sampling.' If the signal read/sampled when the data is input coincides with the current output signal, the DFF keeps the output signal unchanged. If instead the signal read when the data is input is different from the current output signal, then the DFF inverts the output signal.

Luca was moving on to how to use delays and DFFs as Aster fully recollected how they function.

"To create this RBG design, we can use the stable signal as the clock input of the DFF and we can connect the RO output signal to the data input of the DFF. Intuitively, with these connections, if we imagine that the RO signal has a lot of noise, then the stable sampling clock can cause the DFF to unpredictably sample either a 1 or a 0."

Luca paused for a moment before making a critical observation. "Obviously, from a FIPS 140-3 validation point of view, we cannot stop at a simple intuition, and we shall mathematically formalize this unpredictability. Fortunately for us, a 2014 paper [1] titled 'Entropy Evaluation for Oscillator-Based True Random Number Generators' formalizes this exact RBG construction in a satisfying way."

Aster wrote the entire name of the paper also in her notes, as this sounded like a source worth following up on. As soon as she finished, Luca kept going. "Let us understand grasp the main ideas behind the stochastic model presented in this paper."

"First of all, it is better to assume and construct the proposed RBG design using a RO which oscillates way faster than the sampling clock signal. Basically, it is best to have a relatively slow clock signal with respect to the speed of oscillations of the RO. In fact, even when maximizing the noise in the RO, we cannot realistically expect drastic unpredictability from the time length of the half period of the RO—whereby 'half period' we mean the time period which passes from one RO output signal inversion to the next. In practice, the variation of this time length can be thousands of times smaller than the half period of the RO."

For the sake of a numerical example, Luca used the following values: "Let us say that the clock is 3 thousand times smaller than the half-period of the RO. In this case, we can intuitively argue that, if the clock signal is slow enough that we wait 4–5 thousand total RO inversions between one sample and the next, then we have accumulated enough unpredictability from each inversion that we have no idea if the sampled RO signal will be a 1 or a 0."

After a brief moment of reflection, Aster understood what Luca meant with the last example, and she kept listening to what he had to say next.

"To mathematically estimate the entropy output of the proposed RBG design, the 2014 paper [1] assumes that the main source of entropy in the design is the aforementioned unpredictability of the half periods of the RO, and it introduces the following parameters to carry out the computation of the entropy estimate in Sect. 2: the frequency ratio, and the quality factor."

"As the name suggests, the frequency ratio is a ratio between the sampling time and the average length of the half period. The most crucial parameter to focus on, though, is the quality factor. In Sect. 4.4, the 2014 paper [1] states that this value shall be larger than 0.6 to guarantee that one sampled bit does not significantly influence the next sampled bit."

"This type of influence", clarified Luca, "is called 'correlation' in statistics. Correlation lowers the entropy estimate, so it is in our best interest to limit it as much as possible."

"Keeping in mind that 'standard deviation' is the mathematical term which represents how easily the half period can last a different amount of time with respect to the average half period, there are 3 possibilities to make the quality factor larger:

- make the frequency ratio larger;
- make the standard deviation of the half period of the RO larger; or
- make the average time length of the half period of the RO smaller."

Luca concluded this first example by adding, "Since the frequency ratio is placed under a square root in the entropy formula, it is more efficient to enlarge the standard deviation. Also, note that, in practice, this standard deviation can be explicitly computed with specialized measuring devices."

ELO RBG Thus, Luca moved on to the second example.

"For security concerns, it is crucial that the noise sources of a stochastic model are clearly identified, well characterized, and nicely quantified. In RO-based RBG designs, there is always a slight risk of entropy overestimation, meaning that the effect of noise sources which are either deterministically manipulable or hard to mathematically define is taken into consideration in the final entropy estimation and yields to a numerical entropy estimate which is higher than the entropy output of the real world. These exact concepts were also highlighted in the presentation [2] titled 'Sources of Randomness in Digital Devices and Their Testability' featured in the NIST Random Bit Generation Workshop 2016."

"This presentation also shows an RBG design which is a slight variation of the first example I presented earlier", said Luca.

"Recall that the first design we discussed has one RO, one stable clock, and one DFF. The design of the presentation, titled Elementary Oscillator-based (ELO) RBG, replaces the stable clock with 2 components. In order, these components are a second oscillator, which is identical in design to the other one—namely, they have both the same number and the same type of inverters—and a frequency divider. As the name suggests, a frequency divider takes an input signal of a given frequency and generates an output signal whose frequency corresponds to the input signal frequency divided by a specific integer."

The NIST presentation notes the integer value that the frequency divider divides by can even be greater than 300,000. "We already know from earlier," reminded Luca "that a great timing difference is necessary if we want to have enough noise built up in the RO connected to the data input of the DFF before sampling it. The smaller the amount of noise of this sampled RO, the longer we have to wait before sampling again."

The next few slides covered how the NIST presentation claims that the effect of the deterministic or hard-to-study noise sources is significantly reduced in this RBG design, since two identical oscillators are impacted in the same way by these types of unwanted noise sources. The presentation also shows numerous formulae, algorithms, and tricks to design, to test, and to implement the proposed RBG design.

"The most notable formula in this NIST presentation", highlighted Luca, "regards the lower bound of an entropy estimate and is actually taken from a 2011 paper [3] titled 'On the Security of Oscillator-Based Random Number Generators.' The main parameter of this formula is once again called quality factor, but it is distinct from the quality factor we have seen earlier."

"In Remark 2, the 2011 paper highlights that we expect the sampled bits to behave as a perfect random source when the quality factor is significantly larger than one. To make the quality factor number larger, there are three possibilities:

- make the variance of the half period of the sampled RO larger;
- make the sample time longer (i.e. make the integer in the frequency divider bigger or equivalently make the oscillations of the sampling RO slower); or
- make the average time length of the half period of the RO smaller."

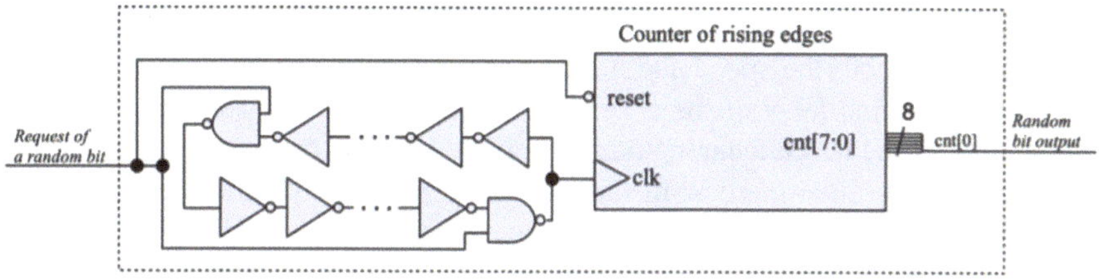

Fig. 16.2 TERO RBG

Aster raised her hand and asked, “I know that ‘variance’ is a mathematical term defined as the square of the standard deviation, but what does it mean in this context?”

Luca nodded and replied, “Excellent question! In this context, it is a way to represent how easily the half period of the sampled RO can last a different amount of time with respect to the average half period. The NIST presentation shows an explicit algorithm to compute this variance and highlights the importance of taking into the consideration the thermal noise, which I recommend looking into after the lecture.”

TERO RBG “For our third example design,” said an upbeat Luca, “we go back to using a single RO. But now, we use a special version of an RO called a TERO.”

“TERO stands for Transition Effect Ring Oscillator, and it has two branches, each containing some inverters followed by a gate. In total, the TERO has an even number of inverters, and the gates at the end of each branch are used to restart oscillations. An output signal can be measured after either one of the two restart gates. When the TERO receives a pulse through one of the end gates, the output signals temporarily oscillate between the values 0 and 1 for a brief period of time, before completely stopping.”

Aster, deft in her ability to take notes, crammed in as much from the next slides as possible, which went into the details: In the RBG design of the 2015 paper [4] titled “A Physical Approach for Stochastic Modeling of TERO-based TRNG,” one of the possible output signals of the TERO circuitry is followed by a counter that counts the rising edges of the temporary oscillations. Once the temporary oscillations stop, a specified number of least significant bits of the counter are seen as the random output. The design requires the RBG to restart after each acquisition (or realization) of the number of temporary oscillations, so that the generator can operate without memory and the extracted bits are independent. If needed, the bits of each realization can be concatenated with the bits of the following realizations to create a bigger random bitstring as output.

She also sketched a quick diagram of the TERO RBG design (Fig. 16.2 taken from [4]).

Luca put importance on the following detail of the paper: “Note that an 8-bit counter automatically considers the eight least significant bits of the number of oscillations. The design shown in the paper extracts exactly 1 bit from the 8-bit counter which keeps track of the temporary oscillations.”

“As written in Sect. 5 of the 2015 paper [4], the entropy of the TERO RBG is influenced by two main parameters: the relative jitter and the relative difference between the mean delays of each the two TERO branches. By increasing the frequency of the oscillations, both the speed and number of oscillations increase, and designers can reduce the total delay of the entire TERO. Reducing such delay increases the relative jitter of the RBG, meaning that values get harder to predict. Adding thermal noise produces a similar increase in variance, but designers typically cannot alter the sources of such thermal noises during normal execution."

Well, of course, thought Aster, *It is not as if we can warm up or cool a chip at will while it is in operation!*

"Let's wrap up this last example," Luca said to move things along. "With a smaller relative difference between the two branches, the TERO oscillates longer. This allows the total noise to build up for longer, improving the overall entropy output."

"In the example of the paper, the entropy rate per generated output byte—which is to say, considering the entirety of the 8-bit counter output—was higher than 4 out of 8. This means that extracting just the least significant bit of the counter would discard some precious usable random bits. One way to possibly get more throughput from a single-bit-extraction design would be to increase the relative difference between the 2 TERO branches, unbalancing them. This sounds counterintuitive, and indeed it may lead to catastrophic reduction in the final entropy output; yet, as long as a multiple-bit counter contains more than 1 bit of entropy, an unbalanced TERO construction oscillates for a shorter period of time, causing a possibly higher bit rate."

Considerations to Keep in Mind for Validation Aster was pleasantly enthusiastic for having found the motivation to come to such an interesting lecture, and she was enjoying listening to Luca's expertise at work. Meanwhile, Luca had started the last section of his presentation. "This is all well and good," he began, "but how can these RO design be inserted into a FIPS validation?"

Aster knew that to be complaint for a FIPS 140-3 validation, an entropy source used in a RBG design shall meet at least all the requirements enlisted in SP 800-90B [5]. NIST defines an entropy source as the combination of a physical noise source, followed by a digitization process, some health tests, and an optional conditioning component, in this order.

"So, can the designs shown earlier can be interpreted as the combination of a physical noise source—in this case, the sampled RO or the TERO construction—and a digitization process which produces 1-bit output at a time?" Aster asked. Luca nodded in affirmation, not minding the interruption.

Luca also added an additional detail, "On this note, it is crucial to highlight that NIST requires the extraction and analysis of the raw data coming straight out of the digitization process. This implies that an actual hardware implementation of a noise source shall have, at least in the testing phase, appropriate accessible interfaces to extract this data; these interfaces may be rendered inaccessible when the hardware is actually deployed in production, though. Considering our previously covered example designs, this extraction requirement forces some way to access the 1-bit output of the DFF for the first two examples, or the 1-bit output taken from the 8-bit counter for the last example. These 1-bit outputs shall also be used for the corresponding health tests."

Health tests were something Aster had been trying to work with recently, and she knew there are three types of health tests required for a FIPS 140-3 validation:

- on-demand health tests;
- start-up health tests; and
- continuous health tests.

On-demand health tests may be implemented with a reset, reboot, or power-up which forces the execution of the start-up health tests.

The start-up health tests shall run the continuous health tests over at least 1024 samples, and they shall be implemented in such a way that, if they fail, they cause an error state of the entropy source and they withhold this first sample.

NIST approves only these two continuous health tests: the repetition Count Test and the Adaptive Proportion Test.

"For all of the tests, SP 800-90B explains all the formulae required to set the parameters for them and presents many more requirements. This lecture won't go into the SP 800-90B in detail, but it's definitely important to be aware of," Luca noted.

Luca had also a last recommendation for vendors, implementers, and entropy source designers. "In general, even though the conditioning component is optional, it is highly recommended to include a vetted one in the entropy source design."

"A conditioning component is simply an algorithm which takes one or more samples for input and then outputs a fixed-length output. Examples of approved or vetted conditioning components are the CMAC and the NIST approved hash functions. These vetted conditioning components have the advantage of compressing multiple random samples into a single output, and they have the ability to preserve in their output most of the entropy contained in the input samples. The entropy preservation can help maintain uniformity in the expected entropy output of the entropy source, and it implies that, under appropriate conditions, these vetted condition components are able to claim a full entropy output—'full entropy' being a way to express that each bit in the noise source output is perfectly random."

"Alongside the requirements written in SP 800-90B," kept explaining Luca, "NIST released additional clarifications and requirements in the FIPS 140-3 Implementation Guidance document [6], especially in Sections D.J and D.K. But there are some important, but often overlooked, considerations in there."

Luca went on to explain that in IG D.K Resolution 1, NIST states that "the vendor shall justify why all processing occurring within the digitization process does not conceal noise source failures from the health tests or obscure the statistical properties of the underlying raw noise output from this digitization process." IG D.K Resolution 10 explains that combining the outputs of multiple copies of a physical noise source causes Resolution 1 to be applicable. Furthermore, and most notably for our ring oscillator discussion, IG D.K Resolution 11 states that multiple ring oscillators may be treated as "copies" in one entropy source, even in the instance where the design and layout of the ring oscillators vary.

If multiple copies of the ELO or TERO construction are implemented to create a single entropy source, the aforementioned Three Resolutions of IG D.K imply that a vendor or designer shall keep in mind that the combination mechanism that they implement to produce the final output of the single entropy source shall not conceal catastrophic noise source failures nor shall it lower the overall entropy output in an unclear and unintuitive manner.

"As a final note," said Luca, drawing things to a close, "we highlight that IG D.K Resolution 19 explicitly defines the requirement that a vetted conditioning component shall meet to claim a full entropy output."

Another Lecture Ends "These closing sentences mark the end of our analysis of RNGs based on ROs" concluded Luca before dismissing the class. "The unpredictability of the thermal and shot noise cause an unpredictable time of inversion of the output signal of any ring oscillator. You know, there are many types of gelatos. And yes, the Italian gelatos follow a different recipe with respect to the American gelatos, which in turn are different from American ice cream. Anyway, there are many types and flavors of gelatos just as there are already numerous RNG designs which use RO and which have publicly available stochastic model ready to be used for a FIPS 140-3 validation. Look at the ELO and the TERO designs, for example: These models serve as a strong basis for such a validation, but vendors should be interested in adding a vetted conditioning component to claim a full entropy output or in understanding how to optimally combine the outputs of multiple RO RNGs."

After a brief moment of silence in the restaurant, everyone applauded an insightful lecture well done; Luca, in turn, beamed with delight at having such an attentive audience.

With goggles off, some students and coworkers—including Aster—kept Luca connected remotely for some last-minute questions. After this, Aster chatted a bit with the others before eventually starting head home. While walking outside of the atsec CST lab, with the sun almost reaching noon, she started to think about her jogging route, and whether or not to follow her typical jogging route later that day. In trying to determine if there were some easier and warmer routes or loops she could jog, she inadvertently thought: "Hm, I wonder if a jog loop is as random as a loop in a ring oscillator." She smiled to herself before the wind hit her square in the face as she rounded a corner (Fig. 16.3).

Fig. 16.3 Takeaways regarding ring oscillators

References

1. Ma Y, Lin J, Chen T, Xu C, Liu Z, Jing J (2014) Entropy evaluation for Oscillator-based true random number generators, Sections 2 and 4.4. In: Batina L, Robshaw M (eds) Cryptographic hardware and embedded systems—CHES 2014. CHES 2014. Lecture notes in computer science, vol 8731. Springer, Berlin, Heidelberg. https://doi.org/10.1007/978-3-662-44709-3_30

2. Fisher V (2016) Sources of randomness in digital devices and their testability. Presented at the NIST RBG Workshop, Gaithersburg, USA. https://csrc.nist.gov/csrc/media/events/random-bit-generation-workshop-2016/documents/presentations/sessionvi-2-viktor-fischer-presentation.pdf
3. Baudet M, Lubicz D, Micolod J et al (2011) On the security of Oscillator-based random number generators. J Cryptol 24:398–425. https://doi.org/10.1007/s00145-010-9089-3
4. Haddad P, Fischer V, Bernard F, Nicolai J (2015) A physical approach for stochastic modeling of TERO-based TRNG, Section 5. Cryptology ePrint Archive, Paper 2015/593. https://eprint.iacr.org/2015/593
5. Turan MS, Barker E, Kelsey J, McKay KA, Baish ML, Boyle M (2018), Recommendation for the entropy sources used for random bit generation. National Institute of Standards and Technology. via NIST. https://csrc.nist.gov/pubs/sp/800/90/b/final Accessed 03 Dec 2025
6. National Institute of Standards and Technology, Canadian Centre for Cyber Security (2020) Implementation guidance for FIPS 140-3 and the cryptographic module validation program. National Institute of Standards and Technology. via NIST. https://csrc.nist.gov/csrc/media/Projects/cryptographic-module-validation-program/documents/fips%20140-3/FIPS%20140-3%20IG.pdf. Accessed 03 Dec 2025
7. Inductiveload (2009) Ring oscillator (3-stage). via Wikipedia. https://en.wikipedia.org/wiki/File:Ring_oscillator_(3-stage).svg. Accessed 22 Dec 2025

Chapter 17
CPU Jitter

Stephan Müller

The day's sunlight spilled over Austin, but inside atsec's conference room the blinds were half drawn and the chairs were filled with UT students. Aster had set up her laptop to stream a remote lecture titled "CPU Jitter." Stephan Müller's face appeared from Germany, framed by a bookshelf and the familiar glint of circuit boards; the line of students seated around the conference table with Aster leaned in, their notebooks open and curiosity sharpened.

"Guten Morgen from the land of precise clocks," Stephan began, smiling. "Although, as you'll soon learn, even precise clocks cannot tell time as precisely as we think."

The opening slide flashed onto the screen in bold letters: *Crypto Fun—Things you never wanted to know....* The title alone earned a few laughs.

A Remote Room of Laughter Stephan leaned toward his camera, lowering his voice like a magician sharing a secret.

"Normally I'd have some German chocolates to pass around, but I haven't found a way to get them through a screen yet," he said with a grin, "so instead, I'll hand out a little crypto fun."

He paused just long enough to build anticipation. "Let's start with a secret," he continued. "Never trust a random number you didn't fake yourself."

Laughter filled the Austin room.

"That joke," he continued, "contains a grain of truth. Every cryptosystem begins with randomness, and yet, randomness is the one thing computers are terrible at. So today we will talk about how to measure uncertainty—Jitter RNG—and why even deterministic CPUs can behave a little like jazz musicians: always following the beat, but never exactly the same way twice."

The screen changed to a diagram of entropy sources. "Almost all cryptographic mechanisms rely on random numbers. The only exception is message digests—they

S. Müller (✉)
atsec information security corporation, Austin, TX, USA
e-mail: stephan.mueller@atsec.com

Y. Mao (ed.), *Tasting Cryptography*, https://doi.org/10.1007/978-3-032-30243-4_17

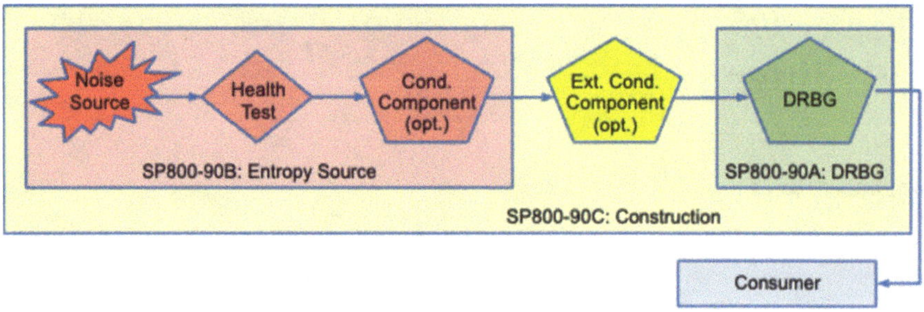

Fig. 17.1 A flow chart of entropy collection and conditioning

are deterministic." He paused, then smiled. "That means hashes are the introverts of cryptography. They never change their mind, no matter what happens around them."

He switched slides again, revealing the line: "I have a hash—can I encrypt data?"

Stephan grinned. "I once received this question in an email. I said, 'Sure, if you also use your toaster as a Wi-Fi router.'"

The students laughed.

The next slide read: "I insist, I want to encrypt data."

"All right then," Stephan continued, "if you're determined, take a hash, turn it into a keystream, XOR it with your plaintext, and—voilà—you've just reinvented a stream cipher. Crypto for fun!"

Terminology the Room Could Use Before diving into Jitter RNG, Stephan grounded the audience in the vocabulary used by NIST through a simple illustration (Fig. 17.1).

On the left side of his conceptual picture sat the entropy source—a combination of a noise source, health tests, and optional conditioning components defined by SP 800-90B. Noise is the unpredictable phenomenon, and health tests watch the noise source for degradation or total failure. If the data is healthy, it may pass through conditioning, which stores, reduces statistical weakness in, and compresses the data to raise its entropy rate. A conditioning component is considered vetted if it uses algorithms on NIST's RBG list; everything else is non-vetted.

Only the output of a DRBG is fed to consumers for cryptographic purposes. DRBGs are specified in SP 800-90A [1], while SP 800-90C links the two worlds by defining how seed material from an entropy source is provided to a DRBG, including optional external conditioning, minimum entropy for seeding, and reseeding rules [3].

The Coin Toss and Entropy Strength Stephan then described entropy through a coin toss: "A fair coin has one bit of entropy, meaning fifty-fifty chance. But our goal isn't just randomness; it's quantified unpredictability."

The mood softened as Stephan steered the conversation toward entropy in IT systems. "The problem," he said, "is that computers are deterministic. You can't ask a CPU to roll dice. It will give you the same pips every time.

"A deterministic random number generator is predictable given its inputs, yet its output should be indistinguishable from an ideal random source. If you seed that generator with only one bit of entropy, an attacker needs at most two guesses to recover the state. We therefore require cryptographically significant entropy—typically at least 128 bits."

What if you inject far more entropy than the generator's own strength? He offered a thought experiment: if the generator's cryptographic strength were only one bit, no amount of added entropy would raise the strength above one. The effective strength is the minimum of the entropy provided and the generator's own security strength. NIST formalizes this in SP 800-90B Sect. 3.1.5.1.2, which allows the calculation of the strength of the output data. The more complete formula accounts for real world parameters [2].

"Real systems need practical sources. How can one devise an algorithm executing on a completely deterministic IT system that produces entropy? This is a hard problem which can only be solved when combining non-deterministic mechanisms with IT systems that can be at least monitored by the IT system," Stephan instructed, and then advanced to a slide filled with bullet points—radioactive decay, thermal noise, quantum effects—the usual suspects of unpredictability.

- Radioactive decay: Physics dictates that radioactive decay is a probabilistic process. This process is even associated with probability distributions for different radioactive elements. Using a radioactive detection mechanism like a Geiger Counter along with a precise timer, an IT system can measure the time deltas between individual decay events. These time deltas contain an amount of entropy that is defined by the Physics of the used element. While radioactive decay is a very good entropy source, it is obviously impractical for IT systems.
- Thermal noise: Integrated circuits contain transistors that enable or disable the flow of electricity and therefore generate the signals marking zeros and ones which are used for the calculation operations. The interesting aspect, however, is that the time when a signal is switched from zero to one or back has a small amount of uncertainty. The more transitions between zero and one and then back that happen, the more the uncertainty builds up unless proper countermeasures are applied. This uncertainty anchored in the thermal noise is a physical phenomenon where the temperature (and therefore the Brownian motion of the elements used to implement the transistor) shape the timing of the rising or falling edges of the electric current. This uncertainty can be detected and recorded with special circuits like ring oscillators and therefore harvested in IT systems.
- Quantum mechanics: Naturally, the probabilistic nature of quantum mechanical phenomena may also be harvested, such as light emissions where the photon flux contains a degree of uncertainty.

"Unlike algorithms that either pass or fail," he explained, "entropy sources exist on a spectrum. They demand careful measurement and validation under the methodologies defined in NIST SP 800-90B and BSI AIS 20/31." [6]

Then, sensing the weight of the material, he lightened the mood. "Of course," he added with a grin, "if you try to bring a radioactive entropy source through airport security, the TSA might not appreciate your dedication to randomness."

The room erupted in laughter.

"Fortunately," he continued, "there's a safer source of entropy: CPU timing jitter."

The Anecdote that Became an Entropy Source Stephan's voice softened as he recalled the moment when curiosity and frustration collided.

"It was sometime in 2012," he began, "when I was implementing time-critical software. For this task, I wanted to measure the precise execution time of that algorithm."

He smiled wryly at the camera, as if confessing a youthful mistake. "For that, I thought, I could use the high-resolution timer that is available in modern CPUs, which is made available through common APIs like the POSIX function of clock_gettime. So, I naively invoked clock_gettime before and after the code whose execution time I wanted to measure. After subtracting the start time value from the end time value and handling wraparounds of the time value, I thought I would get the precise execution time. To my surprise, I never got a straight answer—the execution time fluctuated slightly even when I eliminated operating system artifacts such as intermittent scheduling operations."

He paused, letting the students absorb the unexpected twist. "Frustrated by that," he continued, "I thought that something weird was implemented in clock_gettime so I started to implement assembly code to invoke the RDTSC Intel $\times$ 86 instruction before and after my critical code path. And even then, I did not receive a clear answer—the time delta still fluctuated."

A ripple of murmurs passed through the Austin audience. Stephan leaned closer, energized by their reaction.

"Intrigued by this, I started to analyze whether my code to invoke the RDTSC instruction was wrong. A simple test was to have an assembler code that invoked RDTSC twice back-to-back, i.e., without any other instructions in between. The idea was that the delta between the two timestamps returned by the two RDTSC instructions would now be constant. And I was wrong again; it still fluctuated!"

He lifted his hand as if conducting an invisible orchestra. "Yes, the fluctuations were tiny, but they were there—even when eliminating operating system artifacts. I attributed the variations to frequency scaling, which I subsequently disabled in the BIOS. And the variations were still there with the same amount of delta. Perhaps it was a strange behavior of the very Intel CPU I used. So, I copied the code onto other Intel CPUs—they all showed the same result. Could it be that Intel uses a strange CPU implementation that shows this behavior?"

The UT students chuckled; Stephan's self-deprecating tone turned the technical puzzle into a human one. "Following the tests on Intel," he went on, "test code was created that invokes clock_gettime back-to-back. This code was then copied onto systems with CPUs from other vendors: AMD x86_64, Intel 32-bit systems, ARM, MIPS, SPARC, IBM POWER, IBM Z (and lately also RISC-V). All these systems exhibited the phenomenon where the execution time showed fluctuations. So, this test now shows that this phenomenon exists in basically all contemporary CPU architectures."

He smiled, eyes bright with memory. "A final conclusion to the test was done with a good friend of mine, Roman Drahtmüller—may he rest in peace—who was working for SUSE at that time. SUSE had a large zoo of different hardware systems with CPU types from all different manufacturers that they use as build machines for creating the software for the SUSE Linux distribution. Roman devised a tool which executed my test application on all their build servers. And the test result showed, to my surprise, that all systems exhibited these fluctuations!"

Stephan laughed softly, shaking his head. "A number of people still refuted the notion that CPUs may contain such uncertainty and claimed that all uncertainty was only coming from operating system artifacts like scheduling or interrupts. To analyze this claim, a tool was built which executes the time gathering on bare metal, i.e., without an operating system. That tool enabled one CPU during boot time, gated all interrupts—meaning the CPU did not deliver any interrupts—and executed the time variation measurement. The variations were still present!"

The room fell quiet, intrigued. Stephan continued: "One fun aspect to this tool was the way to extract test data out of this system: since all interrupts were gated and the tool did not implement any hardware driver, there was seemingly no way to extract data from the test tool. But there was one possibility: the system contained a speaker which was accessible with a PIO interface that could even be used to modulate the duration of a beep."

He grinned broadly. "This was used to extract the measured data with Morse code. Another system with a fully running OS was placed next to the test system which enabled its microphone to pick up the Morse code and store it on disk. Both test systems were running overnight in a separate room as the one constantly beeped to get the large amount of test data out. And that data clearly showed the timing variations—and that they are not based on operating system aspects."

The students burst into laughter, some pretending to tap Morse rhythms on the table. Stephan joined them. "Based on that," he said, now with pride, "my initial frustration about not being able to precisely measure the execution time of some software vanished. Meanwhile, I was working in the field of cryptography, mainly as a FIPS 140 tester. To learn more about cryptography, I thought—why not use this phenomenon to build an entropy source from it? And so, I started the long endeavor that led to the Jitter RNG present today."

The camera caught Stephan's grin as he concluded, "Sometimes, the best discoveries begin as debugging disasters."

The Design of CPU Jitter RNG Stephan leaned back slightly, the memory of discovery still vivid even after years of refinement, and paused for a moment, letting the students digest the thought that a problem meant for debugging had become a new branch of entropy generation.

"This anecdote," he continued, "outlines the basic phenomenon that delivers entropy: the execution time of one instruction is not deterministic."

He lifted a finger as if counting each insight. "Furthermore," he said, "additional tests showed that even memory accesses show a non-deterministic timing pattern. Though the variations are small, they imply that an algorithm must be devised that can do the following." He then pulled up a new slide detailing the requirements:

1. Stimulate the CPU such that the execution timing variations manifest—and, if possible, increase;
2. collect those variations;
3. compress the data that contain the variations while retaining their entropy; and
4. comply with various requirements for the design of entropy sources, such as SP 800-90B and AIS 20/31.

He smiled. "The following subsections analyze each of these steps. Think of them as the four instruments in the same symphony."

Stephan advanced to the next slide, where the words "Timing, Measurement, and Chaos" appeared in bold.

"As previously discussed," he said, "the execution timing variations depend on two main factors: first, measuring the execution time of instructions, and second, measuring the execution time of memory access operations."

"For both cases, a high-resolution timer is needed to detect those minuscule variations. Fortunately, all CPUs have high-resolution timers that can be harvested: on Intel x86 architectures, the RDTSC instruction is available; on ARM systems, the CP15 coprocessor serves that role; other CPUs have similar mechanisms. Jitter RNG refers to these timers as external timers. Even if such a high-resolution timer isn't offered by the hardware—say, when a separation kernel or a hypervisor intercepts them to make them coarse—Jitter RNG creates its own internal timer. In a second thread, an endless loop simply increments a counter, and the Jitter RNG thread samples the value of that counter when it needs a timestamp. That counter value is then interpreted as time."

After describing the use of external and internal timers, Stephan turned to the next point with a knowing smile.

"Jitter RNG employs SHA3-256 and SHAKE-256 to compress the entropy, as we'll explore in later sections. To simplify the implementation, it uses the Keccak transformation code—the very core of SHA-3 and SHAKE—to measure its own execution time. Instead of tracking a single instruction, the RNG invokes a large but fixed sequence of instructions that perform the Keccak transformation and measures how long the entire transformation takes."

He paused, letting the class consider the elegance of reusing the same cryptographic primitive both as a timing loop and as a future conditioner.

"This way," he explained, "the code both generates and measures its own uncertainty. The algorithm becomes aware of its own imperfections—and that's where entropy is born."

He then advanced the slide to reveal a pseudocode block:

```
start_time = get_timestamp();
Keccak_transformation();
end_time = get_timestamp();
time_duration = end_time - start_time;
```

"This," he said, "is the simplest way to visualize the principle. The duration—the Δt—is where entropy hides." He brought up another pseudocode block:

```
start_time = get_timestamp();

for i in 0 ... 127
do
      memory_address     =     memory_start_address     +
random_offset;
      read_val = dereference(memory_address);
      dereference(memory_address)  =  (read_val  +  1)  &
0xff;
end
end_time = get_timestamp();
time_duration = end_time - start_time;
```

Stephan looked back at the camera. "Jitter RNG records that time duration—that Δt—as a single time delta value. Mathematically, it's the first derivative of the discrete variable of the timestamp over the executed operation."

"The time deltas," Stephan continued, "recorded by measuring the execution time of certain operations, are all concatenated and inserted into the conditioning component. Apart from the concatenation of time delta values, Jitter RNG also includes auxiliary data—though those fields don't contribute entropy."

He paused and added, "The concatenation ensures that no entropy is lost—every unpredictable flicker of time is preserved."

"Jitter RNG performs the collection operation $(256 + 64 + 1) \times$ OSR times," he explained before walking the audience through each value:

- The integer 256 is chosen because all data collected from that number of operations yields a 256-bit block. The goal is for that 256-bit block to contain full entropy—256 bits.
- The integer 64 is mandated by SP 800-90C and FIPS 140 IG D.K as an oversampling rate. You always insert at least 64 more bits of entropy than you extract to offset any loss in the conditioning function [3].
- The integer 1 comes from the AIS 20/31 modeling—an additional oversampling for the German methodology [6].

- Finally, OSR—the oversampling rate—is an integer greater or equal to one. It defines how much extra entropy you collect per cycle. If one bit of entropy comes from each time delta, then with OSR you get 1/OSR bits per sample."

He smiled again. "That's the mathematics of patience," he said, "Randomness rewards those who oversample.

"The concatenated series of time deltas ultimately forms a large amount of raw data. To make the Jitter RNG practical, it employs a conditioning component that compresses this data, thereby increasing the entropy rate per bit."

He pointed to a schematic showing SHA3-256 and SHAKE-256 boxes linked together. "With the collection we just described, at least $(256 + 64 + 1) \times$ OSR time delta values—each 64 bits long—are concatenated. The goal is to produce an output block of 256 bits that truly holds 256 bits of entropy."

"To achieve that," he said, "Jitter RNG uses a conditioning component that compresses the input while retaining its entropy. Up to version 3.6.x, the component was SHA3-256; starting with version 3.7.0, it became an XDRBG—mathematically, two chained SHAKE-256 instances."

He showed a diagram of two linked boxes labeled "SHAKE-256 #1" and "SHAKE-256 #2."

"The first instance calculates a message digest from the concatenated time delta values. The second instance generates the output from that digest—32 bytes, or 256 bits, exactly," he clarified.

He raised his eyebrows and added with characteristic humor, "So yes, when you call the RNG, what you get back is a single block—32 bytes of distilled uncertainty. Each one hard-earned."

Keccak and Kecak Stephan smiled and advanced to his next slide which displayed the word Keccak in large, blocky letters, the algorithm family behind SHA-3. Then, with a grin, he said, "Now, before we go deeper into SHA-3 and its role in the Jitter RNG, I have to ask—has anyone here ever heard of Kecak? Not to be confused with Keccak."

He waited as a few students looked puzzled, as the pronunciations were nearly identical.

"It's a traditional Balinese dance," he explained. "And yes, it's pronounced almost the same—Ke-cak!" He leaned closer to his microphone. "The difference," he said, "is that one preserves data integrity, and the other preserves cultural integrity—both keep things from falling apart in their own way."

The screen briefly showed a photo that Stephan took from Bali—the very sign that read Kecak Dance with a bright red arrow (Fig. 17.2).

"I was there once with the atsec team," Stephan said, chuckling. "We heard a hundred voices chanting Ke-ca-ca-Ke-ca-ca! in perfect synchronization. And suddenly I realized—that's exactly how Keccak works! Many rounds, same pattern, perfect balance between order and chaos."

Fig. 17.2 A sign to a Kecak dance in Bali, Indonesia

He mimicked the rhythmic chant, softly drumming his fingers on the desk. "Ke-ca-ca, Ke-ca-ca… That's diffusion and permutation in harmony!"

The Austin audience burst into laughter.

"So," he concluded, "the next time you implement SHA-3, remember—somewhere in Bali, someone is performing the world's most rhythmic hash function."

Compliance and Vigilance As the laughter from the Kecak anecdote faded, Stephan's tone shifted once more to precision. "Jitter RNG," he started, "isn't just an experiment in entropy—it's built to comply with formal cryptographic requirements." He turned to a slide titled "Compliance and Validation." The audience could see the familiar logos of NIST and BSI in the corner.

"First," he began, "SP 800-90B. The Jitter RNG uses a vetted conditioning component and comes with a full compliance analysis following 90B. As detailed in the Jitter RNG documentation, it implements health tests that detect any significant degradation of entropy. The same documentation includes a complete entropy analysis that demonstrates the Jitter RNG delivers full entropy at its output." [4]

He clicked to the next bullet, where the German flag appeared beside the words "AIS 20/31 v3.0."

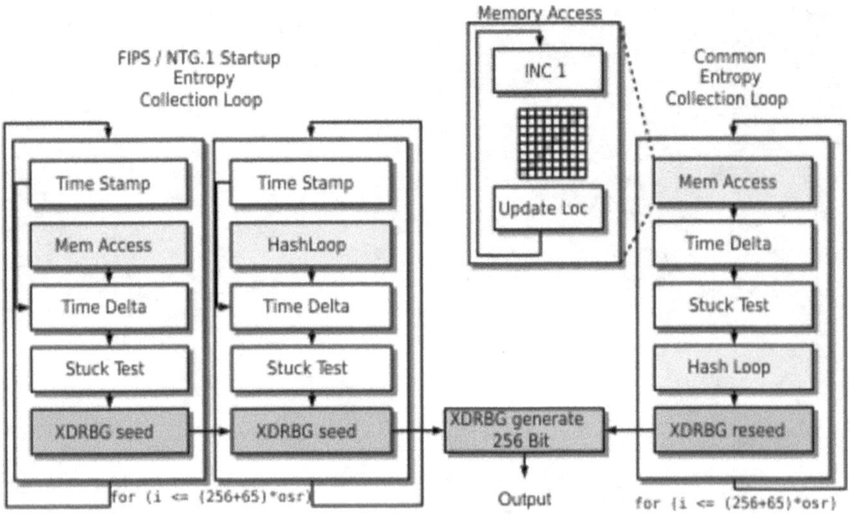

Fig. 17.3 Diagram of Jitter RNG architecture

"Second," Stephan continued, "the Jitter RNG also aligns with AIS 20/31, version 3.0—the German BSI's methodology for evaluating true random number generators. The documentation outlines compliance with the NTG.1 functionality class and provides an entropy assessment that confirms the generator maintains sufficient entropy throughout its operation." [6]

He paused, glancing toward the camera as if speaking directly to his peers at NIST and BSI. "In short," he said, "it doesn't just claim to be random—it proves it, one standard at a time."

The Architecture of a Rhythm A new slide appeared with a large diagram labeled Jitter RNG Architecture (Fig. 17.3).

The diagram provided a graphical representation of the overall architecture with the stimulation of the CPU execution timing variations, their collection and data compression, as well as the output generation. The right part illustrates the runtime operation where the execution time of the Keccak operation—marked as "Hash Loop"—along with the memory access loop is measured jointly.

He traced the diagram with a pointer. "On the left-hand side, we have the startup process. Here, the Keccak and memory access loops are measured independently. This separation isn't arbitrary—it's required to comply with the German BSI's AIS 20/31 NTG.1 model, which Jitter RNG 3.7.0 aims to fully satisfy."

He smiled knowingly. "Think of it like tuning two instruments separately before letting them play together—one loops hashes, the other dances in memory, and together they generate the rhythm of randomness."

As the final graphs faded from the screen, Stephan looked up and smiled. He closed his slides, ready to end the session on a lighter note with his signature blend of humor and insight.

Testing the Noise For the final portion of his talk, Stephan brought up a slide labeled" Jitter RNG Test Tools." On it were snippets of code, URLs, and screenshots of command-line outputs.

"The source code distribution of the Jitter RNG user space library," he explained, "contains dedicated test tools for gathering raw, unconditioned noise source samples. These tools are what labs use to collect the data needed for an Entropy Source Validation—the ESV step." [5]

He paused to let that sink in before moving to the next point. "Furthermore," he continued, "The Linux kernel variant of Jitter RNG provides an interface that allows the extraction of raw, unconditioned noise source samples directly from the kernel environment. But—and this is important—that interface must be explicitly enabled during kernel compilation. It's a diagnostic feature, not something intended for production."

Stephan clicked to the final bullet, where the words "User Space Toolset" glowed faintly.

"To support these tests," he said, "The accompanying user space toolset—distributed with the Jitter RNG library—can access this kernel interface when enabled. It's how implementers verify that their entropy behaves exactly as it should before ever reaching the conditioning component."

He smiled, satisfied. "In the end," Stephan concluded, "even randomness deserves discipline. You don't just hope for entropy—you measure it, prove it, and make it dance to your tune."

Crypto Fun Revisited To keep the crowd awake Stephan sprinkled in jokes from his deck. Slide one had asked, "I have a hash: can I encrypt data?" which had led to the playful reminder that hashing can be turned into a keystream and XOR, but that it is better to let a DRBG generate the stream on purpose. Now, slides escalated to "I want a cipher with 512-bit strength" and "Now I need a 512-bit strong DRBG." He deadpanned, "Everyone wants 512 bits. It is like ordering a pizza with double everything." Then the punchline: "Et voilà, take SHAKE, apply the concepts of SHA3-512 to receive SHAKE-512 and build an XDRBG using it. Seed it properly per SP 800-90C. And no, we are not faking the vectors."

Closing He ended on a quiet note. "Entropy is the soul of cryptography. Without it, algorithms are mechanical; with it, even a deterministic machine becomes creative."

The final slide read, "Thank you. Questions?" Aster unmuted. "I think half the room wants to build a jitter collector now." Stephan smiled. "Perfect. Measure twice, seed once." (Fig. 17.4).

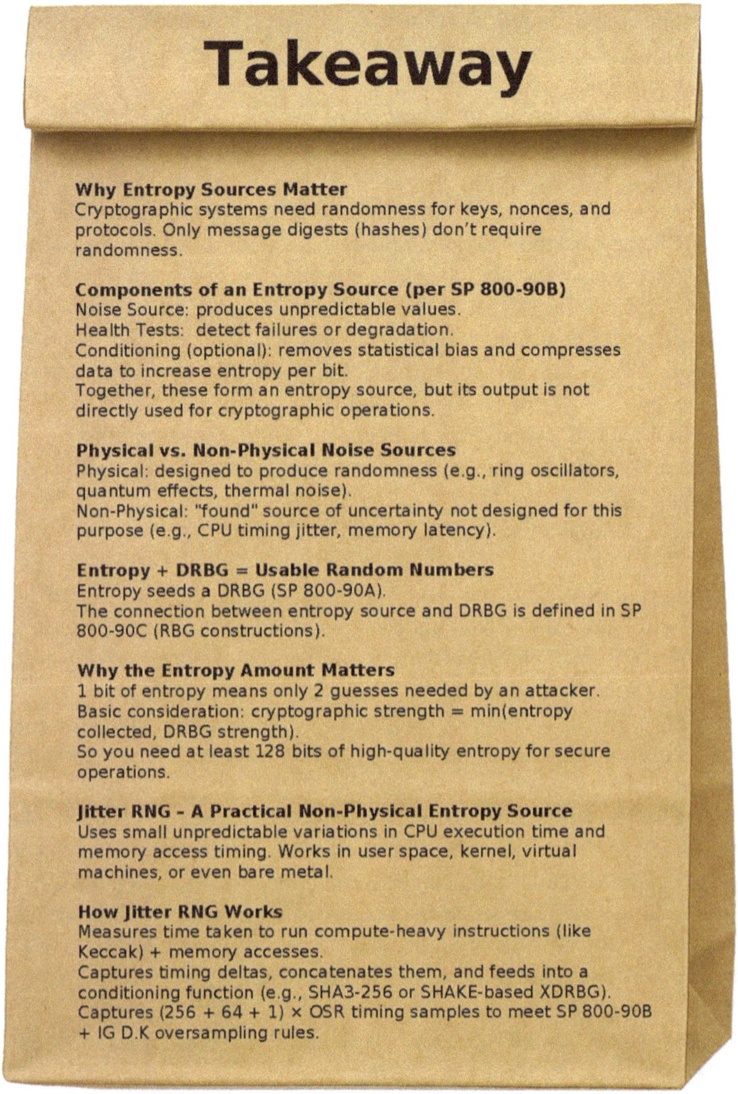

Fig. 17.4 Takeaways regarding CPU jitter entropy

References

1. Barker E, Kelsey J (2015) NIST SP 800-90A Rev. 1 recommendation for random number generation using deterministic random bit generators (DRBGs). National Institute of Standards and Technology. via NIST. https://csrc.nist.gov/pubs/sp/800/90/a/r1/final. Accessed 08 Dec 2025
2. Turan M S, Barker E, Kelsey J, McKay K, Baish M, Boyle M (2018) NIST SP 800-90B recommendation for the entropy sources used for random bit generation. National Institute of Standards and Technology. via NIST. https://csrc.nist.gov/pubs/sp/800/90/b/final. Accessed 08 Dec 2025

3. Barker E, Kelsey J, McKay K, Roginsky A, Turan M S (2025) NIST SP 800-90C recommendation for random bit generator (RBG) constructions. National Institute of Standards and Technology. via NIST. https://csrc.nist.gov/pubs/sp/800/90/c/final. Accessed 08 Dec 2025
4. Müller S (2022) CPU time jitter based non-physical true random number generator. via Stephan Müller. https://www.chronox.de/jent/CPU-Jitter-NPTRNG.pdf. Accessed 08 Dec 2025
5. Jitter RNG (2014) Stephan Müller. https://www.chronox.de/jent/index.html. Accessed 08 Dec 2025
6. Peter M, Schindler W (2024) A proposal for functionality classes for random number generators, version 3.0. Bundesamt für Sicherheit in der Informationstechnik. via BSI. https://www.bsi.bund.de/SharedDocs/Downloads/EN/BSI/Certification/Interpretations/AIS_31_Functionality_classes_for_random_number_generators_e_2024.pdf?__blob=publicationFile&v=3. Accessed 08 Dec 2025

Chapter 18
ESV Process

Stephan Müller

The morning sun filtered through the glass walls of atsec's Austin lab, casting a mild glare off the rows of monitors. Aster had just connected to a WebEx session titled "Entropy Source Validation Tool—A Deep Dive with Stephan Müller." On the screen, Stephan appeared from his home office in Germany, framed by a quiet background of Linux banners and circuit boards. His headset rested slightly askew—the unmistakable look of someone who had been debugging until dawn.

"Welcome back to the entropy zone," he began with a grin. "Today we won't talk about jitter or Keccak dances, but about a tool that measures uncertainty itself—the Entropy Source Validation process."

Aster smiled. "Stephan, you've said before that the Jitter RNG taught us how CPUs can sing in rhythm. What does the ESV teach us?"

Stephan leaned forward. "That randomness isn't something you can just assume. You must prove it. And proving randomness is not like testing an algorithm. With AES, you feed it a known input and check the output—there's one right answer. With entropy, there's no right answer—only evidence."

He clicked to his first slide, labeled "Entropy Source Validation—Measuring Uncertainty."

"When you test an algorithm, you test correctness. When you test an entropy source, you test nature," he said. "The question isn't 'Does it compute correctly?' but 'Does it behave unpredictably enough to trust?' That's what the ESV process answers."

"Within FIPS 140-3, any module that generates cryptographic keys from an entropy source must hold a valid Entropy Source Validation (ESV) certificate. Without it, the entire validation chain is incomplete. Entropy is the foundation," Stephan said. "Without it, even the strongest cryptography becomes a house built on sand."

S. Müller (✉)
atsec information security corporation, Austin, TX, USA
e-mail: stephan.mueller@atsec.com

Y. Mao (ed.), *Tasting Cryptography*, https://doi.org/10.1007/978-3-032-30243-4_18

He referred the audience to the NIST ESV Program website, which outlines the requirements and lists issued certificates [1]. "It's where theory becomes verification," he said. "The ESV process turns uncertainty into measurable assurance."

Understanding the ESV Process Stephan summarized the ESV process in three stages, explaining how design, data, and discipline combine to establish measurable randomness.

First comes the design and documentation. Vendors must describe the entire entropy source—every component, signal path, and transformation. The documentation explains how the noise source captures its unpredictable phenomenon, how the signal is digitized, and how any post-processing or health tests maintain quality. If the source is physical, NIST requires a stochastic model to mathematically describe how the underlying physics generates entropy.

"If you base it on radioactive decay," Stephan said, "you bring in formulas from nuclear physics, detector timing precision, and measurement uncertainty. The real entropy you observe should align with what your model predicts. That theoretical analysis supports the claimed entropy rate, the $H_{submitter}$ value, which must be justified with logic and evidence."

The second step is data collection and testing. SP 800-90B defines two essential datasets: a runtime test and a restart test. The runtime test captures one million consecutive samples of unprocessed noise, while the restart test records the first 1000 samples after each of 1000 power cycles, creating another million samples.

"The restart test," Stephan noted, "proves your entropy is alive from the first bit and that it doesn't take a predictable nap after boot. These datasets are then formatted into bitstreams suitable for analysis by the NIST SP 800-90B entropy assessment tool, which extracts up to eight bits per sample, the portion most likely to contain true randomness. The output consists of two bitstreams, one from runtime and one from restart data, both sent to NIST for analysis." [2]

The third step covers guidance and submission. Each vendor provides a Public Use Document (PUD) explaining how to correctly use the entropy source, including configuration and operational instructions, seeding requirements, and integration notes for applications or devices [3].

"The PUD is the user's guide to using randomness responsibly," Stephan said. "Even a good entropy source can be misused if accessed incorrectly."

Once all three components—documentation, data, and PUD—are ready, the testing lab uploads them to the NIST ESV server. Only accredited FIPS 140 laboratories can perform this step.

"The server calculates minimum entropy values automatically," Stephan explained. "The lab compares those results against $H_{submitter}$, and every value must meet or exceed that claim. NIST reviewers then analyze the documentation and results, sometimes requesting clarification. When approved, they issue the ESV certificate, the birth certificate of a validated source of randomness."

The Art of Measuring Chaos Stephan switched to a live terminal showing the SP 800-90B entropy assessment tool. "Here's where the real work happens," he said. "You feed it raw data—no conditioning, no compression, no tricks—and it runs a battery of estimators: Markov models, compression tests, collision analysis, prediction estimators. It's like asking a hundred skeptical statisticians to agree that your noise is truly noisy."

Aster laughed. "That sounds like your kind of party."

"It is," Stephan admitted, "But this process isn't about beauty—it's about reproducibility. The 90B Tool doesn't care how elegant your circuit looks; it only cares that the unpredictability holds up every time."

He pointed to two lines on the terminal display: $H_{submitter}$ and $H_{observed}$. "If the observed minimum entropy is equal to or greater than your claim, you pass. If not, your confidence and your validation collapse."

Stephan's tone turned pragmatic. "Entropy takes patience. SP 800-90B requires millions of samples. It's the longest test in cryptography, and it demands discipline. You can't rush nature—collect entropy like fine wine: slowly and with control." [4]

From Entropy to Random Bit Generators Aster leaned forward. "Once the ESV certificate is issued, what's next?"

Stephan smiled. "Then comes its sibling, the RBG certificate. SP 800-90C has just been published, and it defines how an entropy source connects to a deterministic random bit generator. Together, they complete the FIPS story."

He showed a slide linking the steps: ESV for SP 800-90B compliance → CAVP for an SP 800-90A-compliant DRBG → RBG for SP 800-90C compliance → FIPS Certificate for a crypto module with key generation.

SP 800-90C describes several construction methods for combining entropy sources and DRBGs. Stephan summarized them in plain language:

- RBG1 uses a DRBG seeded once from an entropy source, without direct reseeding.
- RBG2 (NP) allows both physical and non-physical entropy sources, with the DRBG periodically reseeding itself after producing up to 2^{17} bits.
- RBG2 (P) follows the same rule but uses only physical sources.
- RBG3 (XOR) generates bits simultaneously from the DRBG and entropy source, XORing them together to achieve full entropy.
- RBG3 (RS) reseeds the DRBG before every output, concatenating blocks for long requests.
- RBGC structures DRBGs as a tree: a root seeded from entropy, with subordinate branches seeded from the parent nodes.

He added, "For each construction, SP 800-90C specifies seeding rules. A DRBG must be seeded with at least 1.5 times its security strength in bits and reseeded with its full strength. It's the arithmetic of trust." [5]

The RBG validation, he explained, requires vendors to document their chosen construction, constraints, and rationale before submitting to NIST. Once approved, the RBG certificate completes the cryptographic assurance chain.

The Story Behind the Tool After an enjoyable and detailed discussion, Stephan's tone softened. "You know," he said, "the ESV client I built for our lab didn't start in isolation. It grew from the same roots as the ACVP proxy."

He recounted how the Automated Cryptographic Validation Program proxy came to be designed for speed and scalability. "NIST's reference algorithms were correct, but not fast. So, I thought: if they parallelize, why shouldn't I?"

Aster smiled. “You didn’t.”

“Oh, I did,” Stephan said, laughing. “I sent 256 parallel requests for test vectors. NIST agreed, thinking their system could handle it. The result? Their database crashed, JSON files were truncated, and their servers buckled under the load. But they thanked me—it became an unplanned stress test that helped them scale for today’s workloads.”

“So, the ESV tool was born from chaos,” Aster said with a grin.

“Exactly,” Stephan replied. “Entropy in practice: unpredictable outcomes make systems stronger.”

Measuring Trust As the session ended, Stephan closed his slides and leaned toward the camera. “The ESV process may sound like paperwork and statistics,” he said, “but it’s really about trust. In a deterministic world, entropy connects us to unpredictability, to the physical world itself. Measuring it, documenting it, and proving it—that’s how we build assurance.”

“So ESV is where cryptography meets philosophy,” Aster reflected (Fig. 18.1).

Stephan nodded. “Exactly. Entropy is nature’s honesty. The ESV tool is how we learn to listen.”

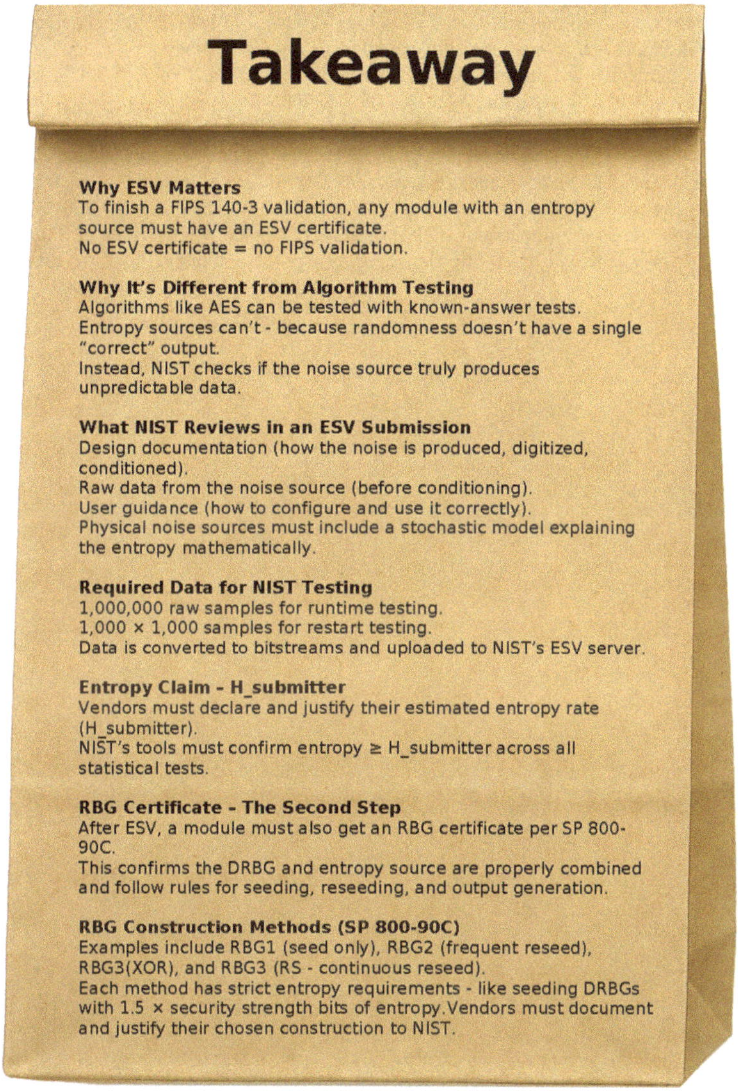

Fig. 18.1 Takeaways regarding the ESV process

References

1. National Institute of Standards and Technology (2016) Entropy Validations. https://csrc.nist.gov/projects/cryptographic-module-validation-program/entropy-validations. Accessed 03 Dec 2025
2. National Institute of Standards and Technology (2015) NIST SP 800-90B Entropy Assessment Tool, GitHub Repository. https://github.com/usnistgov/SP800-90B_EntropyAssessment. Accessed 03 Dec 2025

3. National Institute of Standards and Technology (2016) NIST PUD Template for Entropy Source Validations. https://csrc.nist.gov/csrc/media/Projects/cryptographic-module-validation-program/documents/esv/Entropy%20Validation%20Certificate%20Public%20Use%20Document%20Template%20v1.2.docx. Accessed 03 Dec 2025
4. Turan MS, Barker E, Kelsey J, McKay KA, Baish ML, Boyle M (2018) Recommendation for the entropy sources used for random bit generation. National Institute of Standards and Technology. Available via NIST https://csrc.nist.gov/pubs/sp/800/90/b/final accessed 03 Dec 2025
5. Barker E, Kelsey J, McKay K, Roginsky A, Turan M S (2025) NIST SP 800–90C recommendation for random bit generator (RBG) constructions. National Institute of Standards and Technology. Available via NIST. https://csrc.nist.gov/pubs/sp/800/90/c/final. Accessed 03 Dec 2025

Chapter 19
A Sketch of the FIPS Validation Process

Andreas Fabis

Tuesdays were usually quiet at FIPS 'n' Chips, the virtual restaurant that serves delicious cryptographic enlightenment. Smooth jazz played on the jukebox, underscored by the barely audible hum of the neon sign in the pop-up window, proclaiming "Now Serving Salted Hash Browns and 256-bit Tartare Sauce."

Behind the digital bar, Andreas, the resident barkeep and unofficial crypto therapist, polished the countertop in a completely unpredictable pattern. He looked up as the doorbell gave a small chime and Toby's avatar appeared wearing a rumpled blazer, clutching his laptop bag as if it contained nuclear codes. He slid onto a barstool, his face that of a man who was about to confess a crime.

"Rough Tuesday?" Andreas asked, sliding a pint of Probability Porter on a coaster across the virtual bar.

Toby gave a deep sigh. "My boss just told me that I am in charge of getting a FIPS 140-3 certificate for our CryptoKing9000 product." He took a deep breath. "I don't even know what the '-3' means. Andreas... Please help me!"

"Relax, Toby. We'll sort this out. If you're not actively involved in crypto module validation or work at this restaurant, there is no reason why you would know anything about this."

Toby nodded miserably. "I started googling it, and I found phrases like 'operational environment,' 'non-invasive attacks,' and 'algorithm validation.' I tried reading the standard, but after about ten pages I started hearing the Imperial March in my head."

Some of the regulars that had arrived earlier raised their digital glasses in solidarity. One of them shouted, "We started validation without all the security functions defined. It was a mess!" Another added, with a blank stare, "We lost two months over entropy health tests!"

Toby blinked. "You people talk about this... in public?"

A. Fabis (✉)
atsec information security corporation, Austin, TX, USA
e-mail: andreas.fabis@atsec.com

Y. Mao (ed.), *Tasting Cryptography*, https://doi.org/10.1007/978-3-032-30243-4_19

"Of course," Andreas said, while pulling up an oversized cocktail napkin as a drawing board. "We want to make sure people know what they are getting into when they start a validation. There is more to it than reading the standard." He started sketching something that looked vaguely like a treasure map, including arrows, boxes, and the occasional skull and crossbones.

Andreas cleared his throat. "First, you should talk to the developers of the module at your company and get some basic information, so the laboratory you will talk to can gauge the scope at a high level: how many modules, what type, how many operational environments, which security level, which security functions are implemented, when the module will be available for test, any restrictions on who can work on it, and so forth. Maybe the lab has forms you can fill out with this information, so the first call doesn't have to start at zero."

Toby popped a digital olive in his mouth and nodded. He was frantically taking notes.

"Then, you need to pick a laboratory to do the testing and write the report about your module. Call a few of them and see if you are a good match. Maybe check the Cryptographic Module Validation Program—CMVP for short—website to see if anyone has tested a similar product. And make sure they have the bandwidth and experience to take on the project."

Toby clutched his beer and nodded.

"My next piece of advice would be this: Once you have chosen a CST laboratory, start with a readiness assessment or gap analysis. This will help to make sure that your module is in good shape before you go in the full validation. During the assessment, the lab will explain the current requirements, work with you to figure out if and how your module meets them, and also inform you about upcoming changes, such as algorithm transitions or new implementation guidance. That way you don't run into unpleasant surprises during the actual testing."

An older man at a table in the back shook his head slowly and muttered "I should have listened … Why didn't I listen?" A fractal tear glistened in his eye.

Andreas shook his head sympathetically. "It's also a good chance to ask any questions you might have about the requirements and the process. Besides the technical details, you can also discuss your proposed timeline, revalidation plans, and so on. At the end of the assessment, you'll probably have a few items that need to be addressed before you can start the full validation. You might have to apply a patch or make some changes to the source code."

Toby's head drooped. "But … I am in marketing. I have no idea how to write code."

"It's a team effort," Andreas said. "The readiness assessment should of course include the engineers that are involved in the development of the module, so they know what is expected. Once the readiness assessment is done, the fun begins. Here, look at this!" Andreas pointed to his treasure map drawing. (Figure 19.1).

"The FIPS 140-3 process has five official phases. During the Implementation Under Test phase—IUT—all the heavy lifting happens: algorithm testing, entropy source testing, code review, functional testing, documentation review, and so forth. During that time, your engineers will work with the testers to produce the evidence

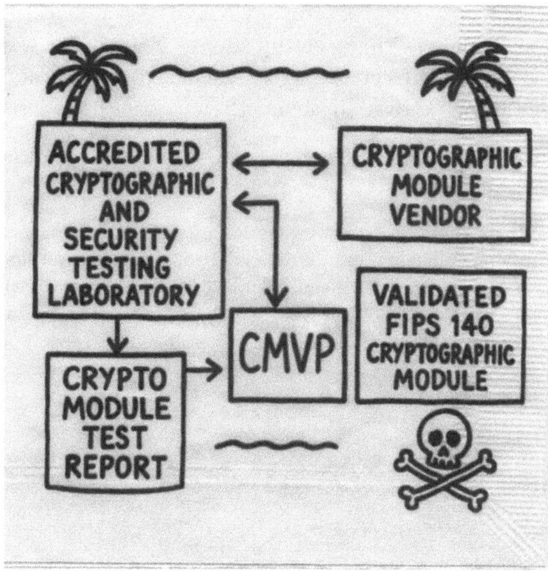

Fig. 19.1 A napkin sketch of the FIPS validation process

to show that all the requirements of the standard are met. Then, the lab produces the test report with all the findings and submits it to the CMVP."

"Sounds like a lot of work," Toby said. "What happens then?"

"Then the module enters the Review Pending phase, where the module will sit until the reviewers are assigned and start their work. Because the CMVP is very busy and many module reports are submitted, this can take a while."

A man at the other end of the bar piped up, stroking his long, white beard. "That's true. I was but a wee lad when we submitted, but now look at me, I …".

"Stop exaggerating!" Andreas laughed. "The waiting queue is long, but the CMVP is working very hard to shorten it. Automation and a streamlined way to review the reports will help. But definitely check in with the lab about the waiting times."

"Ok, so we wait. Then what?" Toby asked, gesturing for another pint.

"The next phase is In Review, where the two reviewers now read the report and make sure everything is as it should be. There might be open questions or comments, which will be addressed in the next phase, Coordination. Once the reviewers are happy, they will issue the certificate, which happens in the last phase, Finalization."

"It sounds so easy when you explain it," Toby said.

"It may sound easy, but the devil's in the details. That's why you have a lab at your side, though! They will help you understand the requirements of the standard and interface with the CMVP in case there are any issues."

"Thanks," said Toby. "Looks like I have to go talk to our engineers and then call a few labs. But first … I'll have the Key Wrap Combo and a milk SHAKE-256."

"Comin' right up," Andreas said with a wink. But as he turned to put in the order, Toby's cell phone rang. Toby gave increasingly distressed grunts until he finally put his phone away. "That was my boss," he said dejectedly. "He also wants me to look into Common Criteria certifications. 'Get it done' was what he said. I am doomed!"

Andreas put a consoling virtual hand on Toby's shoulder. "Don't worry, our sous-chef Trang knows all about it! Hey Trang! We have a case of the CCs, can you help?"

Andreas Fabis has been working for atsec for over 20 years in various fields like cryptographic algorithm validation and the NIST Personal Identity Verification Program testing. For the last couple of years, he has mainly worked with customers to define project scopes and prepare the contractual documents.

Chapter 20
An Introduction to the NIAP Common Criteria Evaluation Process

Trang Huynh

"Excellent timing, Andreas! I'm about to take my 15-min break!" Trang's voice could be heard muffled behind the kitchen door as she answered Andreas' surprise call. The door swung open as Trang walked out and headed over to the bar.

With her face still rosy red and warm from the simulated heat in the kitchen, Trang waved at Andreas while gazing at Toby, "Did someone say CC?" she added. "CC as in 'Chef Compliment?!'" Trang jokingly teased the two gentlemen. "Though, if you meant CC as in Common Criteria, I'm delighted to identify myself as Chief CC, or 'Triple Cec' as our renowned bartender here likes to call me."

Returning her gaze to Toby, Trang said in her notoriously soft voice, "I'll be happy to give you a rundown of a CC validation if you could share a bit more information about what your boss just told you. He sounded frantic, didn't he?" Trang's voice rose with curiosity.

Clearly distressed, Toby responded, "Yes, he was. Big time! That's because neither of us know what a CC validation is. I haven't even had time to Google it, as I am still trying to catch my breath."

Finally taking a deep breath, Toby continued. "My boss was literally spitting out a bunch of strange words and acronyms that I've never heard of, as if he was speaking in some extraterrestrial language."

"We must get a NIAP certificate and not an EUCC certificate for our product Emer@ldSwitch, which is a network switch that includes the CryptoKing9000 cryptographic product—I told Andreas about that earlier. We need to evaluate against a PP, not an EAL. We need to get listed on the PCL to achieve CSfC compliance."

Dejected over just repeating the avalanche of acronyms, Toby concluded, "In other words, he was just repeating exactly what our federal sales team told him!"

T. Huynh (✉)
atsec information security corporation, Austin, TX, USA
e-mail: trang.huynh@atsec.com

Y. Mao (ed.), *Tasting Cryptography*, https://doi.org/10.1007/978-3-032-30243-4_20

"All right, Toby!" Trang said as she settled herself on a stool next to Toby. "Let me start by giving you assurance that the CC validation process can be complicated, but it does not have to be if you plan and prepare well."

"First, you must seek a highly reputable CC Testing Lab—or CCTL—and secondly, it'd be beneficial to pursue a FIPS 140 validation for CryptoKing9000 simultaneously. The reason for the latter is that there is overlap between requirements for a FIPS 140 validation and a CC validation."

Taking off her chef hat and placing it on the bar table, Trang continued, "But…before we go there, let's start with the most essential step of the entire process, which is a readiness assessment or gap analysis, like the one that I overheard Andreas advising you to get for a FIPS validation."

"Another readiness assessment?!" Toby gasped in disbelief as he took a big gulp of Andreas' encrypted house margarita made with world-famous CVE triple sec tequila.

"Yes, but this readiness assessment focuses on CC aspects while helping you figure out if your product is ready for a formal validation," Trang assured Toby. "Also, similar to a FIPS validation, a CC validation entails testing and documentation.

"Documentation consists of two types: the first type is evaluation evidence provided by the vendor, such as the Security Target—or ST—and administrative guidance, or the CC guide as some labs call it. An ST is a CC-specific document that describes how your product meets the requirements from a chosen PP. Likewise, a CC guide is also a CC-specific document that describes how to install, configure, and use your product securely in an evaluated configuration.

"The other type of documentation includes a test plan and evaluation reports prepared by the lab detailing how they assessed your product through testing and examining the evidence documentation. The goal is to determine that your product conforms exactly to the requirements from the PP.

"A CC lab typically has two teams: consulting and evaluation. The consulting team will assist you with preparing necessary evaluation evidence, while the evaluation team carries out the evaluation activities, including interfacing with the validation body."

"You brought up your federal sales team, so I assume your company wants to sell Emer@ldSwitch to U.S. federal customers like the DoD. Since your boss specifically mentioned a NIAP certificate, let me zoom in on the NIAP process and kindly spare you from the agony of the EUCC saga and EALs." Trang stressed the latter part with a playful tone.

"Before I give you a quick overview of the CC, will you first try my new creation? I called it an SAR—a Sour Apple Risotto." A blank stare from Toby prompted further elaboration. "The dish is inspired by the NIAP CC validation process, which sounds complicated—and it is—but believe me it has a rather unexpectedly pleasant taste. Do you know why?" Trang asked pointedly.

"That's because I planned and prepared the dish very well," she answered for Toby. "Just like a CC validation, if the planning and preparations are done well, the actual evaluation can turn out to be a painless experience."

Without hesitation, Toby took a bite of the SAR dish, and, to his surprise, the dish did have a pleasant taste.

"Now on to that overview," Trang said, satisfied her dish had been appreciated. "So, basically, CC is an international standard for certifying IT products against specific security standards. There is the CCRA, which is essentially a recognition arrangement amongst more than 30 country members that allows them to mutually recognize each other's CC certificates. Many of those members have a certification body or a validation body that is authorized to issue CC certificates.

"NIAP is the Validation Body for the U.S. government. The 'P' in 'NIAP' stands for 'partnership' as it is a joint initiative between the NSA and NIST. NIAP's main role is to oversee CC evaluations of IT products in the U.S. Its role is analogous to that of the CMVP in FIPS validations."

"NIAP has very specific policies and requirements. The most famous policy is that they it only accept evaluations using one of their so-called NIAP-approved Protection Profiles, or PPs.

"A PP is technically a set of minimum security requirements defined for a specific IT technology type. For example, there's a PP for operating systems, mobile devices, application software, network devices, etc."

Toby perked up. "Oh! I see, now I understand what my boss meant when he said we must use a PP. Since our product is a network switch, I assume we'd have to evaluate it against a PP for network devices?"

"You got it, Toby! NIAP also requires CAVP certificates for cryptographic algorithms claimed in the CC evaluation. If you want to know more about CAVP, I'm sure our in-house crypto therapist would be happy to book you a complimentary session!" Trang winked at Andreas.

Seeing Toby was still somber over the task ahead, Trang teased him to lighten his mood. "Likewise, NIAP also requires an ESV—or Entropy Source Validation—certificate for any entropy source that your CC product uses. I'm sure our crypto therapist would be ecstatic to discuss that with you as well. Just make sure you tip him well tonight and attend his next improv show, okay?!"

Toby chuckled. "So, you pointed out earlier that there's some overlap between a FIPS validation and a CC validation, were you referring to requirements for CAVP and ESV certificates?" Toby asked.

"Correct! Therefore, if you do a FIPS validation together with a CC validation, especially with the same lab, your overall effort will definitely be reduced," Trang responded.

"Last but not least, NIAP also have one-of-a-kind policy: they require an evaluation to be completed within 180 calendar days. Again, it's crucial to work with an excellent lab, and you especially want one that requires pre-testing of your product to make sure it meets the PP requirements before applying to NIAP.

"Analogous to the SAR dish you sampled earlier, it takes a lot of ingredients and proper steps to obtain a CC certificate." As soon as Trang finished talking, she whipped out her phone and delightfully showed Toby what appeared to be a one-page "recipe" for achieving a successful CC validation with NIAP.

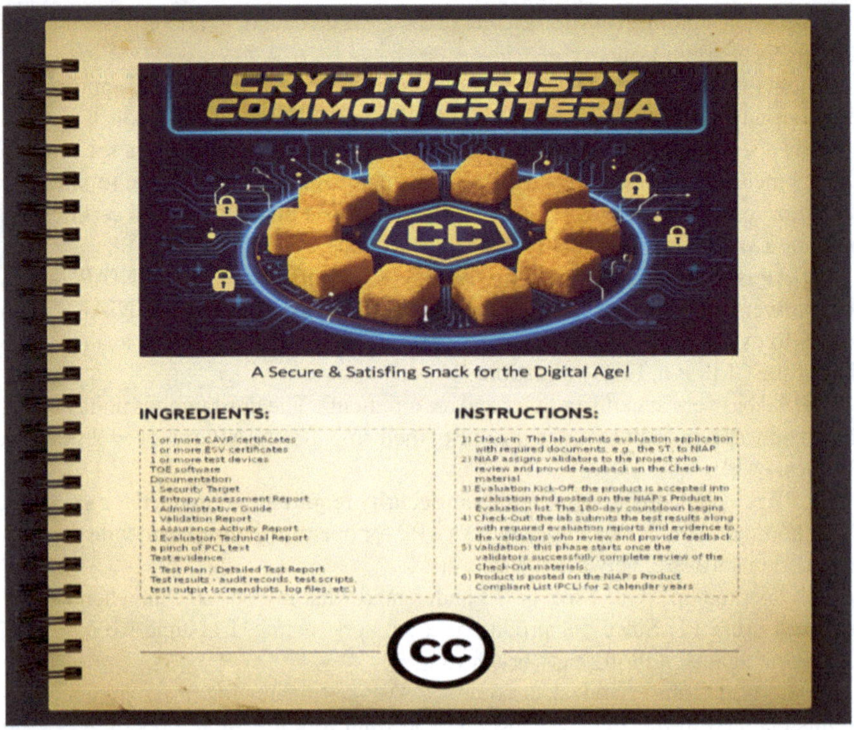

Fig. 20.1 A recipe for completing a CC evaluation

The "recipe" was a result of a fun project Trang worked on with her kids to keep them away from their electronic devices as well as provide them with an early introduction to the world of cybersecurity. (Fig. 20.1).

"Ah ha! So that's what PCL means!" exclaimed Toby. "Can you give me a copy to show to my boss?"

After happily sending over the recipe, Trang said, "Back to the readiness assessment. Once a suitable PP is identified, the rest of the readiness assessment will typically involve going through the security requirements from the chosen PP and mapping them to your product's implementation to figure out whether your product meets them already or if a code fix is necessary."

"What happens if we don't know which PP is the best fit?" asked Toby.

"If you don't know which PP to target prior to the RA, the lab can help you figure it out during the RA," Trang clarified. "Other things covered during the RA are whether your product can leverage any existing CAVP or ESV certificates."

"Another important topic covered during the RA is how testing will be carried out. A PP-based evaluation is very test-centric and NIAP requires the lab to perform all the testing within the accredited lab facility."

"That is good to know, especially for our planning purposes," said Toby.

"Once your product is listed on the PCL, you can apply for CSfC compliance. CSfC is an NSA program that defines requirements for using commercial products to secure classified National Security Systems, and a product must undergo a CC evaluation and get listed on the PCL to be considered for CSfC's approved component list. My advice is to let the lab know at the RA that you are seeking CSfC compliance," Trang noted.

"Now that you've broken down the process like that, a CC validation sounds doable. I am certainly feeling much less overwhelmed now. Thanks a bunch!" Toby said gratefully.

"Glad Andreas and I were able to pull you out of the somber mood."

"So much to do!" said Toby as he finished his drink and then winked out of existence.

Andreas and Trang smiled at each other in satisfaction and then returned to their spots in the restaurant, waiting for the next customer in search of FIPS and CC wisdom, with a takeaway prepared for the journey (Fig. 20.2).

Trang Huynh is the Common Criteria Lab Manager for atsec information security corporation and has more than 20 years of experience in the security evaluation of IT products including mobile devices, operating systems, network devices, firewalls, and hardcopy devices. She's also a seasoned evaluator for several national schemes (NIAP, BSI, CSEC).

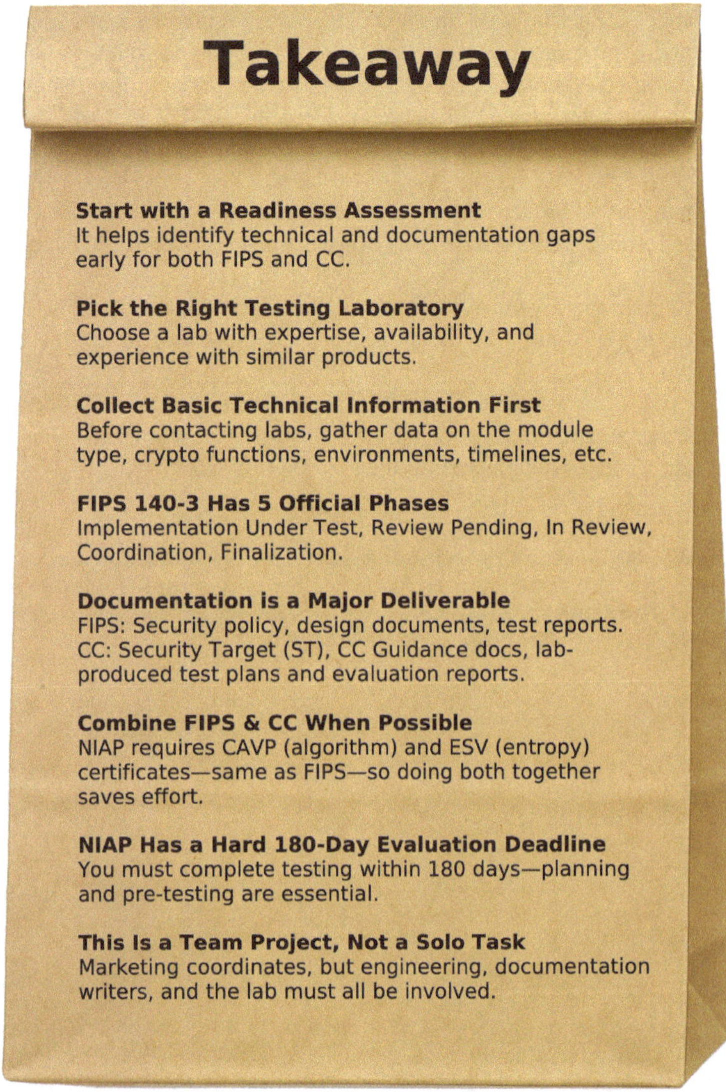

Fig. 20.2 Takeaways from the FIPS and NIAP CC processes

Chapter 21
From an IUT to a FIPS Certificate

Grigori Burlea

Implementation Under Test (IUT) It was a rainy afternoon when Bob stepped into *FIPS 'n' Chips*, the most talked-about restaurant in the compliance district. The sign above the door gleamed softly: "Where Every Byte Is Cooked to Standard."

He was greeted by Alice, wearing a white apron embroidered with "NVLAP Approved."

"Welcome to FIPS 'n' Chips," she said with a smile. "Would you like to start with something from the drink menu? We've got the Old Fashioned, On the Rocks, or the Top Shelf Validation—that one's for those ready for a full compliance journey."

Source Code Review Bob slid into a cozy booth, the amber glow of the hanging lamp reflecting off the polished table. "I'll take the Top Shelf Validation," he said, a hint of anticipation in his voice.

Alice nodded before dropping off a basket of NVLAP Rosemary Breadsticks at his table as she headed to mix the drink.

A few moments later, Alice arrived with his order, setting it down with a knowing smile before sliding into the seat across from him. The booth's soft cushions seemed to muffle the hum of the restaurant around them, creating a small pocket of quiet. (Fig. 21.1).

While sipping his Top Shelf Validation, Bob leaned forward, lowering his voice conspiratorially. "I've heard that source code reviews for FIPS validation are … intense. Some say it's like diving into a whole other world."

Alice laughed softly, reaching for the small basket of NVLAP Rosemary Breadsticks on the table and sliding it toward him. "That's not far off, Bob," she said, breaking one neatly in half before continuing. She unfolded her notepad like a test plan. "Imagine Alice in Wonderland—except instead of tea parties and talking rabbits, you're surrounded by cryptographic modules, compliance standards, and lots of C code. Still an adventure, just a lot more structured!"

G. Burlea (✉)
atsec information security corporation, Austin, TX, USA
e-mail: grigori.burlea@atsec.com

Y. Mao (ed.), *Tasting Cryptography*, https://doi.org/10.1007/978-3-032-30243-4_21

Fig. 21.1 Alice explaining source code review

"Structured sounds better than nonsensical," said Bob with a grin. "So where does it all begin?"

Just then, another server appeared and set down a steaming bowl of FIPS 140 Veggie Soup—the ISO/IEC 19790 Special of the day. The aroma of herbs and vegetables briefly filled the air.

Alice smiled, gesturing toward the bowl. "Let's start with the purpose. A source code review ensures that a cryptographic module complies with requirements defined in ISO/IEC 19790, FIPS 140-3 Implementation Guidance—IG for short—and Special Publications—the SP800 series."

"Right. So ISO19790 sets the general requirements?" Bob asked, stirring his soup.

"Exactly. Think of ISO19790 as the umbrella standard—it defines 11 areas of compliance, like physical security, cryptographic key management, self-tests, and so on. Under that umbrella, FIPS and SP documents provide detailed, algorithm-specific guidance. Also, the IGs expands on both the ISO19790 and SP800-series' requirements—it clarifies how to apply the standards based on module type, embodiment, security level, and the specific cryptographic algorithms being used."

Fig. 21.2 Guidance on how to perform source code reviews

"Got it. So, when I hand over the source code for our module, what are you looking for?"

"I'm reading the code like a story," said Alice. "Every module has one—sometimes unique, sometimes familiar. I follow the flow of the code, identifying how your implementation aligns—or doesn't—with the requirements. When I find something non-compliant, it's like discovering a plot twist that needs editing."

"So non-conformities are like errors in the plot?" Bob asked, confirming his understanding of the analogy.

"Exactly!" Alice said. "But don't worry—finding non-conformities is part of the process. I document them, send them back to you, and your team patches the code accordingly. Then we repeat the review cycle until the story—your code—is compliant." (Fig. 21.2).

Bob laughed. "You make it sound almost poetic."

"It is, in a way," Alice replied. "Seeing a block of code perfectly align with the standards feels like watching the Linux terminal reflect art back at you. Every *#define* of a correct buffer size, every function, every shall statement check creates a beautiful, standards-compliant narrative—when done right, of course. But even though it may feel like a trip through Wonderland, the destination is always a secure, validated cryptographic module."

"And once all the non-conformities are resolved?" Bob asked.

"Once all non-conformities are resolved, the module is ready for the next stage…".

Functional Testing Alice then took to clearing away the soup bowl and the now-empty breadstick basket, returning a few moments later with a CMVP Wedge Salad and a glass of On the Rocks for Bob.

Sliding into the booth beside him, she continued their journey through validation: "Now, we come to the next part of the adventure: functional testing. Imagine this as stepping into the Queen's Garden—you're not just admiring the hedges; you're checking if the roses are really red, and whether the cards painted them properly!"

"So, I get what you would test in Wonderland, but what do we have to do in reality for functional testing?" Bob inquired between bites.

"Functional testing ensures that the cryptographic module's services work as they should," Alice explained. "So, that includes things like self-tests, zeroization, and services that use cryptographic algorithms—kind of like checking if the White Rabbit's watch actually tells time." (Fig. 21.3).

"And how do you figure out what to test?"

"First, I identify the required test cases based on the module's security level and the specific services it's supposed to provide," she said, and then gestured to Bob's glass, already mostly empty. "This is like scanning the Mad Hatter's tea table to see which cups need refilling."

"Then what? Do you jump in and start testing everything manually?" Bob asked.

"Not always," Alice replied. "I first prepare a test suite—a toolkit, usually made of scripts or harnesses, to automate both positive and negative tests. Sometimes the test suite is comprehensive enough to do most of the work; other times, like when the module only has a graphical interface, I have to go manual—like opening all the tiny doors."

"Positive *and* negative tests?" Bob repeated back, a bit confused.

"Right," Alice confirmed with a nod. "Positive testing is like verifying if the Cheshire Cat actually disappears when it smiles. It ensures everything works as expected. For example, I might use an API to encrypt a piece of plaintext and verify that it gives me the correct ciphertext."

"Makes sense. And negative testing?"

Alice leaned back, the dim light catching the edge of the On the Rocks as Bob took a last drink; his attention returned, she spoke in a measured tone. "Ah, now we get to the darker corners of the rabbit hole. Negative testing is intentionally breaking things to see if the module reacts properly. Like pulling on the Red Queen's cape just to see what happens—except here, we want the module to enter an error state when something goes wrong."

"So, you're sabotaging the module on purpose?" Bob asked incredulously.

Fig. 21.3 A discussion on the particulars of functional testing

"Exactly," she said with an impish grin. "For instance, I might modify the module's binary to ensure that the integrity check fails so the module enters an error state. That tells me the module is behaving properly when corrupted—just like staying composed when things go topsy-turvy in Wonderland."

Bob chuckled. "So, do you have to run the tests? Can't I run them? Or any vendor?"

"Sometimes the vendor runs the tests themselves, when direct access isn't possible," Alice answered, absently drawing circles on the table with a finger. "In those cases, I'm present to observe and assist—almost like the dormouse at the tea party, quietly watching and occasionally poking at the process to make sure it's all proper."

"And how do you prove everything worked—or didn't?"

"I capture test evidence—log files, screenshots, maybe even screen recordings," Alice replied. "If the vendor runs the test, the entire session is recorded. Later, I verify the evidence to ensure the results match the expected behavior. It's like checking footprints to confirm someone really did walk through the garden."

Bob set down his fork, the last bite of CMVP Wedge Salad forgotten, and looked thoughtful. "So, in the end, it's not just about whether the module can perform magic, but also whether it knows what to do when the magic goes wrong."

"Precisely," said Alice with a snap. "Every good tale needs both wonder and wisdom. And functional testing ensures the story has both."

Cryptographic Algorithms Testing The next course arrived—ACVTS & ESV Dip & Chips with a side of ICMC Bruschetta.

"This," said Alice, "is where the mathematics begin—Cryptographic Algorithm Testing. The royal court of our Wonderland."

"Sounds serious," said Bob, crunching a chip.

"It is," Alice replied seriously. "We start with demo testing, connecting to the NIST ACVP server, our automated oracle of cryptographic truths. I request demo test vectors for the algorithms your module wants to claim as approved, and our oracle ensures that the cryptographic algorithms implemented in the module actually do what they claim to do. It's like making sure the Mad Hatter's riddles have real answers... or at least pass inspection by the Queen of Hearts!" (Fig. 21.4).

"Give me an example," Bob requested before biting into a piece of bruschetta.

"Let's say your module implements AES-GCM-256 and HMAC-SHA2-256. I request corresponding test vectors from the ACVP server, feed those vectors to your module—like asking the Caterpillar specific questions—and then compare the answers your module gives with the expected answers from ACVP." (Fig. 21.5).

"And if they match?"

"Then the module passes demo testing; if they don't match, then I report the failures to you. It could mean an implementation bug or something more serious—like a character in Wonderland saying one thing and meaning another."

"And if we fix the problem?"

"Then I request new demo vectors, and we try again. We keep repeating this cycle until all the algorithm implementations pass demo testing, and only then are we allowed to proceed to the grand finale of this stage: production testing."

Bob smirked, raising an eyebrow as he leaned forward over the table. "Let me guess: that's like the Queen's final judgment?"

"Pre-cisely!" cheered Alice, clapping her hands together. "In the production testing stage, no failures are allowed. I again request test vectors from the ACVP server, but this time they are production vectors—the ones that count."

"What happens after the module passes those?"

"I post the results back to the ACVP server and obtain verdicts. If all is well, the server produces unique validation IDs for the vendor, the operational environment's information, and—most importantly—the algorithms. I then submit those to the ACVTS production team at NIST. Once approved, the module is awarded CAVP certificates, and those certificates are published on the NIST website for all the realm to see."

Fig. 21.4 Alice reviewing a piece of code for Bob

"So, the CAVP certificate is basically a royal seal?"

"Just so! It's the Queen's proclamation: Off with the doubts! This cryptography is valid!" Alice exclaimed with a chopping motion. "Though the fellows at NIST are not nearly so pompous."

"And…if we fail the Production tests?" Bob asked, almost whispering.

Alice's smile faded into a knowing seriousness, and she leaned in closer. "Then we're in deep trouble, because by that stage we're expected to have fixed everything. Failing in Production means going all the way back to square one, possibly redoing demo testing, fixing the implementation, and starting again." She said tersely, her voice low.

"Yikes. No pressure."

Alice Bob's empty glass with a dramatic little flourish, her grin full of mischief. "Fear not, Bob: With a bit of diligence—and perhaps a sprinkle of tea-party patience—we always find our way through. After all, Wonderland may be strange, but cryptographic validation? That's a logic-based wonderland of its own."

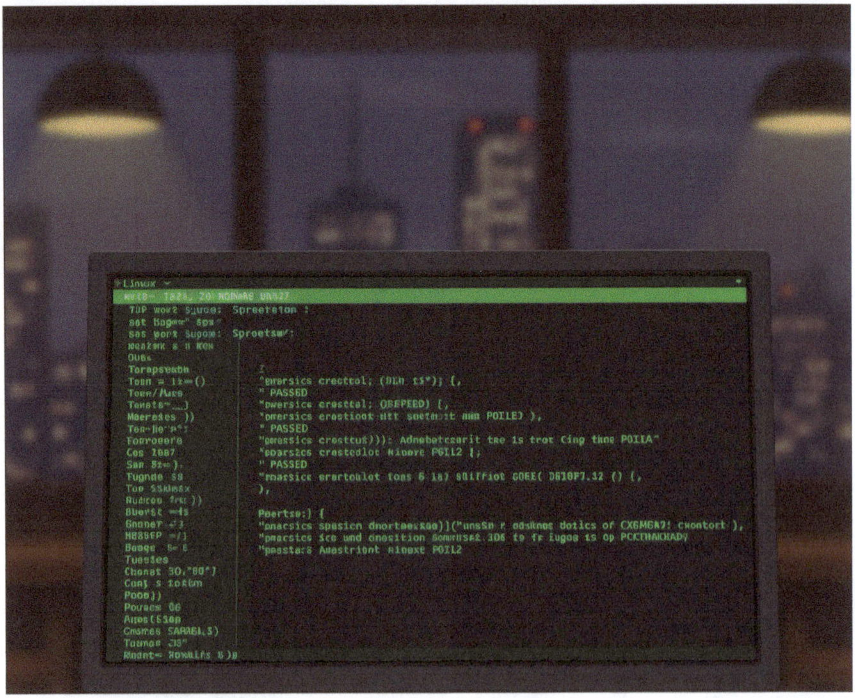

Fig. 21.5 A view of the code in review.

She then whisked away to get some new refreshments for the next step of the journey.

Physical Security Testing As the last chip from the ACVTS & ESV Dip vanished, Alice returned with a small tray labeled "Tamper-Evident Tasting Platter"—a secret menu item.

Bob eyed the platter curiously. "So, what's next in our compliance course?"

Alice smiled, donning a pair of white gloves embroidered with "CVP Certified."

"Now we enter the realm of physical testing, Bob. This is where we go beyond the code and algorithms, straight into the hardware itself. Think of it as stepping through the looking glass: what was hidden is now revealed, and every detail matters."

Bob leaned in, intrigued. "Is this for every module?"

"Not quite," Alice replied, arranging the platter. "Physical security testing is reserved for firmware, hardware, and hybrid modules validated at security levels 2, 3, and 4. If you're at level 1 or just software, you get to skip this course—like the White Rabbit dashing past the Queen's croquet match, blissfully unaware of the rules."

Bob grinned. "So, what does the test look like?"

Alice picked up a tiny model of a server enclosure that serves as an accent to the platter. "First, the tester—always in person, never remote—opens the module, removing accessories and replaceable parts. Memory disks, fans, you name it. If a disk is swapped, it must leave a mark—so we use tamper-evident seals. Non-security parts, like heat sinks, don't need protection unless they hide something sensitive behind them; if they do, more seals! It's a bit like the Queen of Hearts inspecting her roses—if anything's out of place, it must be obvious to all."

Bob nodded, imagining the process. "And what about chip modules?"

Alice produced a chocolate truffle shaped like a microchip. "For chips, the tester tries to access the silicon itself. Some packages, like ball grid arrays, are tough to open without leaving evidence. Others, with removable lids, expose the chip easily. Depending on the configuration—die-up or die-down—different probing methods are used. Some are destructive, like etching or ion beams, and always leave a trace. It's a bit like the Mad Hatter's tea party—no matter how careful you are, there's always a sign that something's been disturbed."

Bob raised an eyebrow. "So, the goal is to make sure any tampering is obvious?"

"Yep!" Alice said, placing a tamper-evident sticker on the truffle. "Judicious placement of seals and clever packaging fulfill the requirements for security level 2. For levels 3 and 4, we add Environmental Failure Protection—testing how the module responds to temperature and voltage extremes. If the module's doors or covers react when pushed beyond their limits, we know it's secure. Like Wonderland's doors that only open for those with the right key, the module must resist all but the most obvious attempts to get inside."

Bob plucked the truffle from her hand, tore off the sticker, and popped it in his mouth.

"So, physical testing is like making sure the kitchen doors are locked—and that the alarm goes off if someone tries to sneak in. Or perhaps, making sure the Queen's tarts are safe from the Knave!" he said between chewing.

Alice laughed. "Perfectly put, Bob—though hopefully you're not the knave we have to watch out for! In the world of compliance, every byte and every bolt must be accounted for. Only then can the module claim its place at the table of validated security."

Testing Evidence Archiving Alice brought out a small platter of CMUF Sampler bites and another basket of NVLAP Rosemary Breadsticks.

"Now we enter the Vault of Memories, Bob," she said. "A quiet chamber in our Wonderland tale—perhaps not as flashy as algorithm testing, but just as important. Here we talk about something absolutely crucial: Testing Evidence Archiving."

"Sounds a bit… dry," Bob admitted.

"Oh, not at all," Alice replied. "Think of it like this: in Wonderland, everyone has a curious memory. The White Rabbit forgets the time, the Hatter forgets why it's always tea-time, and the Queen of Hearts forgets who she's ordered a beheading for.

"But *we* cannot afford to forget. That's why we keep evidence—neatly labeled, clearly archived, and ready to be referenced at a moment's notice."

Bob tilted his head, jotting a note on his napkin with a curious grin. "So, the evidence is like a journal of everything that happened?"

"Yes. It's the proof that all the testing—functional, physical, and algorithmic—was conducted properly, and that the module fulfilled all its requirements according to its claimed security level. Without it, the tale becomes hearsay."

"What kind of evidence do you collect?" asked Bob.

Alice's eyes lit up as she gestured theatrically, as though unveiling hidden shelves behind her. "Let's walk through the enchanted library shelves, shall we?

"Functional testing evidence—test logs, screenshots, even video recordings if needed. This proves the module behaved as expected—or misbehaved and then was corrected.

"Physical testing evidence—if applicable—includes images or data collected from any hands-on examination of the module's physical embodiment. Think of it as proof that the Caterpillar's hookah really was a genuine item, not just a prop!

"And then there's algorithm testing evidence—both the Demo and Production ACVP test vectors, plus the verdicts we received. These scrolls hold the secrets of every cryptographic spell your module cast."

As if on cue, another waitress delivered a heaping pile of documents, the volume of which was quite a shock to Bob. (Fig. 21.6).

"And what do you do with all this?" Bob interjected, watching Alice count out each type on her fingers while casting nervous glances at the tower of evidence.

"I archive it. Carefully," Alice replied matter-of-factly. "The evidence is sorted, stored, and named with a clear, descriptive nomenclature—no "thingamajigs" or "what's-its" allowed! This way, I can quickly locate any piece if questions arise during the coordination stage."

"That's when the CVMP reviewer might come knocking?"

"Yes," confirmed Alice. "The CMVP reviewer might request clarification or additional information based on the test report, and that's when I open the Archive to retrieve the precise evidence supporting our claims—like showing the Queen the right rose, freshly painted red."

"What happens if something was never archived?"

Alice's voice dropped to a serious whisper. "Then we're in trouble, Bob. Without evidence, the test never happened—at least, not in the eyes of the Queen... or CMVP, in our case. That's why archiving is not optional, even if it feels mundane. In our world, memory is security."

"So, the Archive is more than a journal. It's a courtroom, a diary, and a museum all at once."

Alice leaned closer, lowering her voice conspiratorially. "Beautifully said. It holds the history of the module's path to validation. Without it, even the most magical module would be just another curious tale without proof."

Reviewing Vendor-Provided Documentation Alice, having stepped away once more to retrieve yet another course, appears again at the table, this time carrying a

Fig. 21.6 The voluminous quantity of testing evidence

stack of curious-looking papers tied with a ribbon labeled "Read Me." She set them down with a flourish, as if unveiling a secret map. (Fig. 21.7).

"Now, Bob, we come to the part of our Wonderland journey where we must review the vendor-provided documentation," she said, her eyes twinkling. "Think of it as reading the Queen's decrees, the White Rabbit's schedule, and the Mad Hatter's recipe book—all at once."

Bob picked up a page and squinted at the fine print. "So, what's in this stack? Is there a riddle to solve?"

"In a way, yes," Alice replied. "We have the Finite State Model, Life-Cycle Assurance documentation, Physical Security Report, Entropy Source documentation—each one a chapter in the module's story. My job is to read through them and see if the tale makes sense, or if there are missing pages."

Fig. 21.7 Reviewing vendor documentation

"And if something's missing?" Bob asked, glancing over the top of the papers like the dormouse peeking from a teapot. "Last time we discussed missing documents it was…" His voice trailed off as he swiped his thumb across his neck with a grimace.

"Then I send a polite note down the rabbit hole to the vendor, asking for more details," Alice said sweetly. "After all, even the best Wonderland stories need all their characters present. And don't forget—the source code is part of the documentation too, though we've already had our adventure with that."

Bob nodded, setting the papers aside. "So, you're the keeper of the story, making sure nothing is left out before the next chapter begins."

"Exactly," Alice acknowledged, tying the ribbon back around the stack. "Because in Wonderland, and in compliance, every detail matters. Otherwise, the Queen might shout, 'Off with their heads!'—or at least, 'Back to the drawing board!' in our case."

Request for Guidance Bob leaned in, lowering his voice as if sharing a shameful secret. "Alice, what happens if you come across something in the module that's as puzzling as the Cheshire Cat's grin? Something that doesn't seem to quite fit the rules?"

Alice laughed, swirling a cup of tea she recently had delivered to the table. "Ah, that's when we write a Request for Guidance—nothing to be scared of. It's like sending a message to the Queen herself—or, in our case, the CMVP. We describe the curious design or implementation, and ask, 'Is this allowed in Wonderland, or is it simply too mad?'"

"And do they always answer?" Bob asked, raising an eyebrow.

"Eventually," Alice replied with a wink. "Sometimes the Queen—er, the CMVP—asks for more information or poses riddles of their own. But once they understand the design, they issue a verdict: 'Yes, you may proceed,' or 'No, this path leads to an early execution.'"

Bob chuckled. "So, it's like asking for directions in a land where everyone speaks in riddles." (Fig. 21.8).

"Precisely," said Alice. "But it's the only way to be sure we're not painting the roses the wrong color. In Wonderland, and in compliance, it's always best to ask before you leap."

Composing the Security Policy Alice produced a large, ornate book from beneath the table, its cover embossed in golden script with the words "Security Policy." She set it down with a thud, sending a few breadsticks tumbling. (Fig. 21.9).

"Now, Bob, we come to the Security Policy—the official storybook of the module's adventures in Wonderland," she said, opening the book to reveal pages upon pages filled with tables and careful notes. (Fig. 21.10).

Bob peered at the pages, eyes wide. "That's quite a tome! What's inside?"

"Everything the CMVP wants to know," Alice replied. "For each of the 11 areas of the ISO standard, we spell out the security level and explain how the module meets the requirements. The format is as strict as the Queen's croquet rules—tables for algorithms, security functions, self-tests, and more. No room for nonsense of the Jabberwocky here!"

"And who writes it?" Bob inquired, flipping through a page of Approved Algorithms.

"I do, sometimes with help from the vendor," Alice said. "We follow the latest format—SP800-140Br1, for now. Once the module is validated, this book is published on the NIST website, for all of Wonderland to see."

Bob smiled, closing the book gently. "So, the Security Policy is the tale that proves the module's worth—a story with a very happy ending, if all goes well."

Alice nodded. "Exactly, Bob. In Wonderland, every story needs a proper ending, and in compliance, that ending is the Security Policy tied to the FIPS certificate."

Fig. 21.8 Discussing a request for guidance

Report Writing As dessert plates began appearing from the kitchen, Alice placed two dishes in front of Bob: The Secure Chocolate Fudge Sundae and the ISO Vanilla Delight. Scents of vanilla and international standards filled the air. With them came coffees, creams, and sugars.

"We're almost there, Bob," she said with a knowing smile, straightening a dessert spoon next to the plate before continuing. "Before the CMVP reviews anything, I must prepare a formal document that tells the story in full. We call it the Test Report, but you might think of it as the official Book of Compliance." (Fig. 21.11).

Bob chuckled as he leaned over the plate, admiring the presentation. "A book, huh? Let me guess: it's full of rules?"

Alice laughed softly, lifting her spoon like a tiny gavel. "Oh, quite right. And not just rules—but also assertions. You see, while ISO/IEC 19790 provides the general requirements for cryptographic modules, the ISO/IEC 24759 document breaks those down into specific assertions that the module must fulfill."

Bob nodded thoughtfully, stirring sugar into one of the coffees. "So, ISO19790 says what needs to happen, and ISO24759 asks did it happen, and how?"

Alice's eyes gleamed. "Exactly! Think of it like the Queen's court: ISO19790 writes the laws, but ISO24759 is the trial where every action must be justified. Each assertion is like a question from the jury—'Did the module initialize securely?' 'Does

Fig. 21.9 A comprehensive security policy

the zeroization mechanism function properly?' And I must answer each one, using both the evidence and documentation we've gathered."

Bob raised an eyebrow. "Do you answer all the assertions?"

Alice shook her head, tapping her spoon lightly against the saucer. "Not quite. The applicability of each assertion depends on the type of the module—software, hardware, firmware, hybrid—and the security level it claims to meet. Just like in Wonderland, not everyone gets invited to the same tea party."

Bob looked a bit confused. "So how do you decide what's applicable?"

"I follow the guidance in ISO24759," Alice said, leaning forward as though confiding a secret. "It specifies which assertions apply to which module types and security levels. Some assertions are universal, while others only apply to certain configurations. It's like deciding which Wonderland guests get jam on their scones—context is everything."

Bob chuckled, swirling his spoon through the cream just poured in his cup. "And how do you write the responses?"

"Each response must be clear, evidence-backed, and technically accurate," Alice explained, gesturing gently with her spoon. "I reference the testing evidence—logs, screenshots, ACVP results—and the vendor's documentation to prove that the module meets each applicable requirement."

Fig. 21.10 Reviewing a dense security policy

Bob leaned back with a sigh. “Sounds like a lot of writing.”

Alice gave a wry smile. “Oh, it is. But it’s not just writing—it’s storytelling with proof. It’s the tale of a module’s journey through Wonderland, written line by line for the CMVP reviewers to understand. And unlike the Mad Hatter’s riddles, this story must make perfect sense.”

Bob lifted his cup of coffee in salute. “So, the Test Report is like the final chapter of the adventure?”

Alice nodded, her tone soft but assured. “Yes, and it must be flawless. Because after I submit it, the module stands trial. The CMVP reviewers may ask questions, seek clarifications, or request additional evidence, but if the report is strong, the module has a good chance of receiving its final blessing—a FIPS validation certificate.”

Bob smiled, finishing the last bite of his dessert. “From adventure to evidence to verdict… I must say, Alice, your Wonderland is one of reason after all.”

Alice laughed quietly, setting down her spoon and folding her hands. “It is. Just a bit hidden beneath the surface. But as you’ve seen, even in Wonderland, logic rules the realm—especially when cryptography is at stake.”

Fig. 21.11 Proofreading a report over the first round of desserts

Coordination As another round of desserts arrived—slices of Compliance Cheesecake with a side of Post-Quantum Lemon Pudding—Alice leaned back, the soft lamplight catching the silver edge of her fork.

"We've reached the final chapter of our Wonderland tale," she said, her tone both playful and reverent. "The grand court where all things are reviewed, questioned, and—if all goes well—validated. Welcome to the stage of coordination."

Bob raised an eyebrow, swirling a spoon through the lemon pudding. "That sounds very official. Is this where the Queen gives her final ruling?"

Alice smiled knowingly, errantly tapping her fork against the table. "Yes, in a manner of speaking. The CMVP reviewers now step in as the judges of the realm. They read through the test report, examine the evidence, and carefully study the supporting documentation to ensure that the cryptographic module meets every applicable requirement for the claimed security level." (Fig. 21.12).

Bob leaned forward, cautious curiosity in his eyes. "And if something's unclear?"

Alice chuckled softly, her eyes glinting with amusement. "Then the CMVP sends back comments. These are like carefully worded riddles from the Caterpillar—'What

Fig. 21.12 Addressing comments over a second dessert

do you mean by this service behavior?' or 'Can you clarify how this self-test works?' The CST lab—that's us—must then provide clear, supported answers."

Bob exhaled sharply in relief. "So, it's a conversation?"

"Exactly!" Alice said, pointing her fork at him. "A formal one. Think of it as a back-and-forth between the Lab and the CMVP reviewers. There can be several rounds of comments and responses. Each one helps polish the story further, ensuring there are no unanswered questions left in the tale."

Bob nodded slowly, resting his chin on his hand as a smile creeped across his face. "And what happens after all the comments are resolved?"

Alice's voice softened as she smiled, as if describing a long-awaited ending. "Ah, that's the moment every traveler through Wonderland dreams of: the issuance of the FIPS certificate. The Queen, or in our case, the CMVP, declares 'This module complies!' And just like that, your cryptographic module becomes part of the validated world—published on NIST's website for all to see."

Bob's grin widened. "So, the certificate is like the golden key?"

"Yes!" Alice replied, eyes sparkling as she leaned closer. "It opens doors to federal use, compliance assurance, and global trust. But remember, that key was only earned through a trial of testing, validation, and coordination—a journey through the logic and wonders of this compliance realm."

Bob sat back, taking a thoughtful sip of his coffee. "You know, Alice… when we started, all this felt like nonsense. Now, I see the order in the madness."

Alice smiled warmly, her tone softening to a near whisper. "That's the secret of Wonderland, Bob. Beneath the curiosity, there's always structure. And in the world of cryptographic validation, structure is what makes magic possible." (Fig. 21.13)

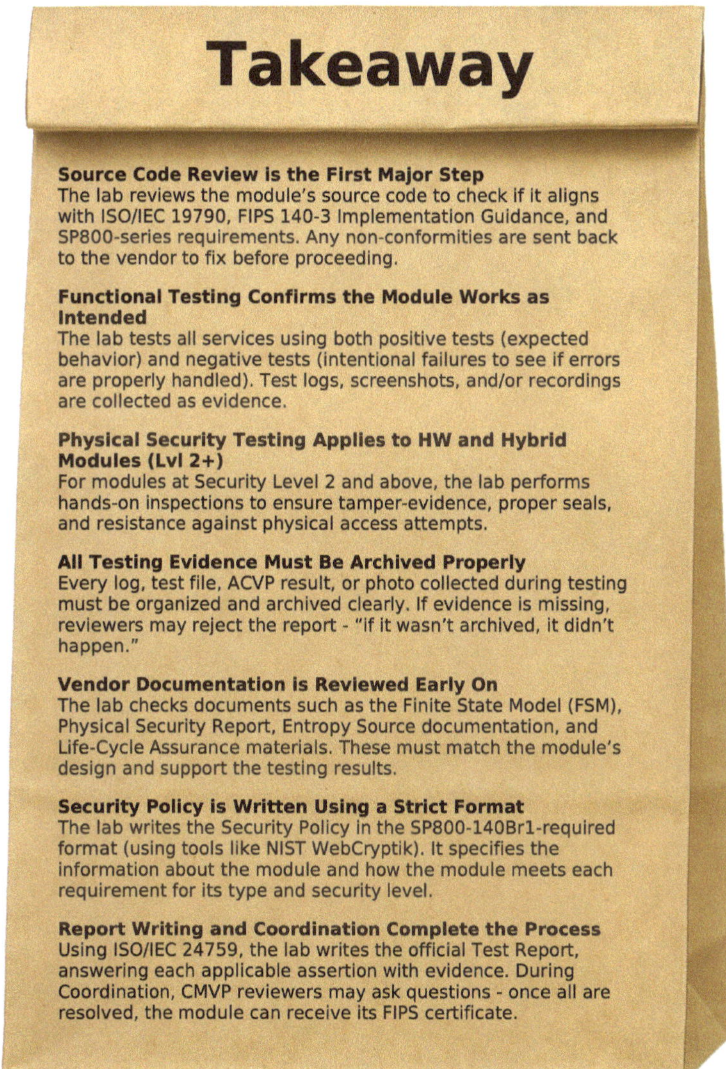

Fig. 21.13 Takeaways regarding the IUT and coordination phases

Grigori Burlea holds a master's degree in computer science, where his passion for IT security and cryptography was sparked by an inspiring professor during graduate school. Through specialized courses and mentorship, he chose to focus his thesis on an IT security topic. This experience confirmed his career direction, ultimately leading him to become an IT security consultant at atsec information security corporation.

Part IV
FIPS 140-3 Security Requirements

Chapter 22
Cryptographic Module Specification

Nathaniel Glass

Aster took a seat at one of the tables inside FIPS ‘n’ Chips and began to peruse the daily specials (Fig. 22.1). Just as modules can be categorized in several ways, the menu had its selections separated and reclassified to the following module types: hardware, firmware, software, and hybrid.

Software modules were represented by beverages such as CafeSSL, MochaCrypt, and RomanoTLS, and each option was modifiable. The house soup was the entry standing in for firmware modules—being more viscous than the beverages, its modification options are limited, but it can still be customized to taste within certain limits. Meanwhile, hardware modules were imagined as bread bowls, each a solid food item that contained their own corresponding soup; certain bread bowl items don’t contain any soup at all! Each kind of bread bowl is served as is and cannot be customized with a different soup or bread type. Finally, the menu also listed the option for hybrid menu options such as soups or beverages that were severed with a side of breadsticks.

A waitress came by and asked if Aster was ready to place an order. Anxiously scanning the menu items, Aster was uncertain.

Do I just want some coffee? Or should I get a bread bowl of tomato soup... her mind wondered, the thoughts trailing off a bit as each of the modules listed called to her in different ways.

She finally made up her mind. “I’ll just take a water for now,” she replied solemnly, needing more time to think about what she wanted.

The table beside Aster started having a heated exchange; it looked like Alice and Bob were having yet another disagreement.

“It’s acceleration!” Alice forcefully stated, loud enough for half the restaurant to hear her.

N. Glass (✉)
atsec information security corporation, Austin, TX, USA
e-mail: nathaniel.glass@atsec.com

Y. Mao (ed.), *Tasting Cryptography*, https://doi.org/10.1007/978-3-032-30243-4_22

Fig. 22.1 The FIPS 'n' Chips daily specials menu

"No... Actually, it's implementation!" replied Bob with just as much gusto. Noticing Aster was following along with the conversation, he immediately conscripted her into the debate.

"We have a module that uses a CPU's hardware implementation for ECDSA Sig Gen. So, we should be able to consider this a Processor Algorithm Implementation (PAI)," Bob stated matter-of-factly, anticipating Aster would be keen to reinforce his argument.

Fig. 22.2 Banana-nut bread with walnuts removed

"That's where your wrong: it should actually just be a Processor Algorithm Acceleration (PAA) implementation, as only part of the operator is done by the hardware. The rest is done by the firmware!" Alice interjects, staring expectantly at Aster for support.

Aster mentally sighed and gave a nod toward Alice. "She's right; PAI is only applicable if the full cryptographic algorithm is implemented in its entirety, otherwise it would be considered PAA," she explained. From the change of expression, Aster could tell Bob was crestfallen at being betrayed by the pawn he had drug into the fight.

Alice, though, was radiant. "HA! I was right. So, we need to put PAA for that software module."

"Well... shouldn't it be a hybrid module?" Bob countered, trying to regain some ground.

"Oh, NOT this again..." Alice said with a frustrated sigh.

"The software is not able to function without the hardware implementation. So, it needs to be a Hybrid module," Bob said with a shrug, pressing the attack.

"Actually, Bob is right this time," Aster interjected. "The module will need to be classified as a hybrid module since the module is dependent on the hardware component."

Alice and Bob gave each other a glare and held it for an uncomfortable amount of time. At this point, Aster decided to slip away before another argument erupted—she's a cryptographer, not a therapist.

Finally afforded some peace, Aster decided to order some banana nut bread. It wasn't until after she received it that she realized it wasn't what she assumed: the nuts were walnuts instead of the pecans she expected. (Figure 22.2).

Yuck! Aster thought to herself as she began picking out the walnuts. She paused partway through, her actions reminding her of excluding certain components from a module.

You are only allowed to exclude components that do not impact the security of the module, remember? she thought, chiding herself You can't really call it banana nut bread anymore without the nuts, it's kind of an integral part of the recipe.

"It looks like this bread won't be getting a FIPS certification any time soon," Aster said with a laugh.

As Aster made her way through her banana-without-nuts bread, she thought about how the restaurants like FIPS 'n' Chips have two main modes of operation, open and closed. These both function just like the approved mode and non-approved mode for FIPS modules: When it's open, it's able to provide all its approved services to users; however, when closed, it cannot provide any of these approved services. Certain services, like waxing the dining room floor, are only permissible once the restaurant closes, too. Furthermore, valuables like cash, checks, and recipes must be secured and inaccessible while the restaurant is closed.

Even error handling sees similarities, as sometimes the restaurant runs into an issue, perhaps with an appliance, that prevents certain dishes from being made. In this case, the restaurant enters a degraded mode of operation where they are only able provide services that are unaffected by the issue. When this occurs, the restaurant staff puts a note on their status board stating the restaurant operations are degraded, and—like a module—are only able to fully offer its full capacity again once the appliance is fixed and passes testing.

While following this train of thought, Aster had hoped to have some coffee to go with the now nut-less banana bread. As fate would have it, the espresso machine tragically ran into an issue right after she placed an order. Perhaps it was karmic justice for the culinary crimes she had subjected her banana bread to.

What Aster didn't know is that, behind the scenes, the parallels between the restaurant and cryptographic modules continued: The restaurant has a system that can automatically verify whether a particular ingredient is acceptable for its approved services; every ingredient that is served when the restaurant is open to the public must go through this verification process. The automated system may not be completely updated, however, so certain ingredients cannot be tested in this manner, leaving it up to the restaurant's management to provide affirmation that the ingredient is approved for use.

There are even certain ingredients that are not approved but are allowed to be used while the restaurant is in the approved mode of operation. For example, some garnishes aren't considered approved ingredients on their own, but they can be used for certain use cases and are still able to be claimed as a component of the dish itself. There are other non-approved items that are allowed if they are not claimed to be part of the dish itself, such as the little flag toothpicks used for sandwiches.

While the above examples certainly aren't exhaustive, generally all other non-approved items must not be used in the approved mode in any way. Items used by cleaners to clean the restaurant while it is closed would be ill-suited as a cooking ingredient, so these items must be kept separate from all approved ingredients in order to not compromise them.

Whenever the restaurant fulfils a service, they provide a receipt indicating the service was performed in an approved manner; the restaurant, however, is required to provide an indicator for non-approved services because it has the capability to provide those non-approved services at all. In contrast, outside the restaurant is a vending machine that can only perform approved services, so it is not required to provide an indicator for each transaction; instead, the vending machine has a global indication that defines all services as approved.

As Aster passed by the vending machine on her way out, these additional parallels began to dawn on her; cryptographic modules share more in common with everyday life than she realized—a reassuring thought, as it means the requirements for validation aren't as inscrutable as they may feel sometimes (Fig. 22.3).

Nathaniel Glass Nathan has been with atsec for three years as a CST lab tester working on various FIPS 140–3 evaluations. He is also involved with cryptographic algorithm validation testing, entropy source validation testing, and NIST Personal Identity Verification Program testing.

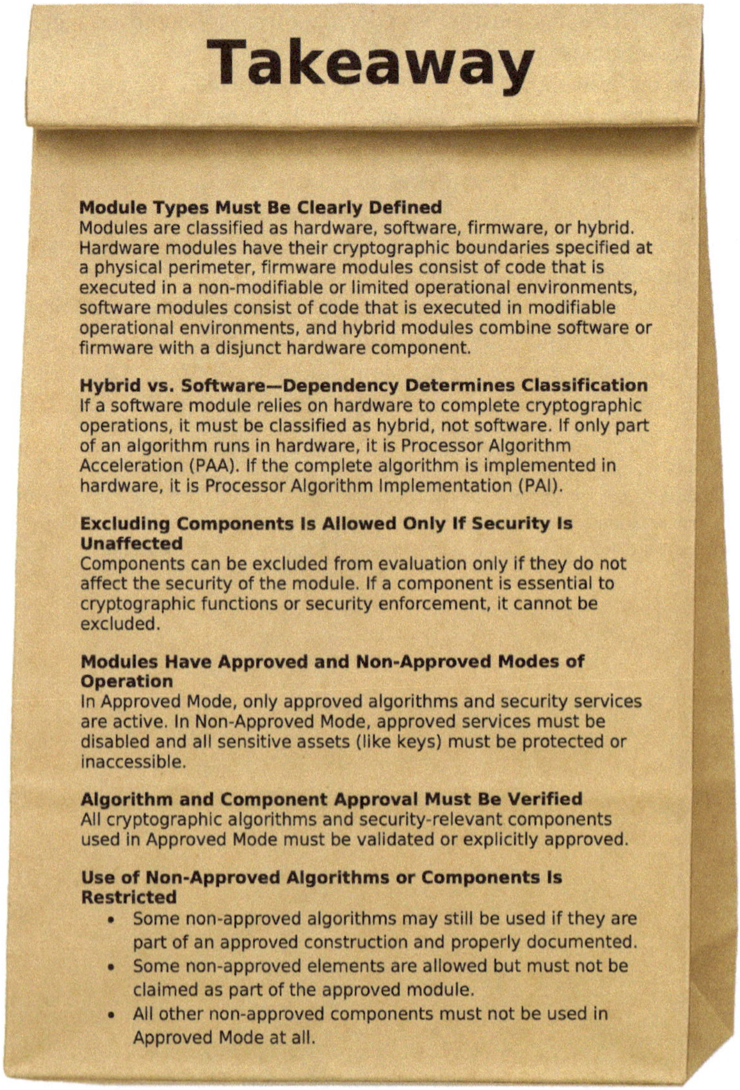

Fig. 22.3 Takeaways regarding cryptographic module specification

Chapter 23
Cryptographic Module Interfaces

Walker Riley

Looking Out at the Austin Skyline As Aster contemplates ordering another coffee, she looks out the FIPS 'n' Chips' panoramic windows and surveys the Austin cityscape sprawled out before her. She takes note of the staggering amount of complexity that makes this great city function. Pedestrians, cyclists, motorists… With millions of people flowing in, out, and around the city, it begins to feel impossible to safely navigate the hustle and bustle without one's sensitive data being lost or mishandled.

Almost as if he could read her mind in this moment, a fellow FIPS 'n' Chips city-gazer at the neighboring table leans over, "On first glance, it looks a little bit like chaos. Makes you wonder how anything gets done in this city at all. But if you look a little closer, this city isn't that different from a crypto module. Not really."

"Oh yeah? How's that?" Aster asked, hoping for a comforting perspective shift to help quell her bubbling anxiety.

Happy to elaborate, Aster's table neighbor continues, "Well for one, when working with cryptographic modules under FIPS 140–3, you need to treat ports and interfaces as regulated communication channels, just like you would any thoroughfare in a city. These channels are the means by which sensitive data, control signals, and operational outputs—or people in our case—move in and out of your module. Mismanaging them isn't just sloppy, but it also introduces risk. (Fig. 23.1).

FIPS 140–3 defines different interface categories that must be clearly identified, logically separated, and tightly controlled. You'll find that they often overlap in physical implementation—a single port might serve multiple logical roles, for example—but FIPS requires each one to be distinctly defined functions that are well-documented. It's no different than how we manage the movement of people: We have rules in place that say you can't drive on the sidewalk or walk down the center lane of i35."

W. Riley (✉)
atsec information security corporation, Austin, TX, USA
e-mail: walker.riley@atsec.com

Y. Mao (ed.), *Tasting Cryptography*, https://doi.org/10.1007/978-3-032-30243-4_23

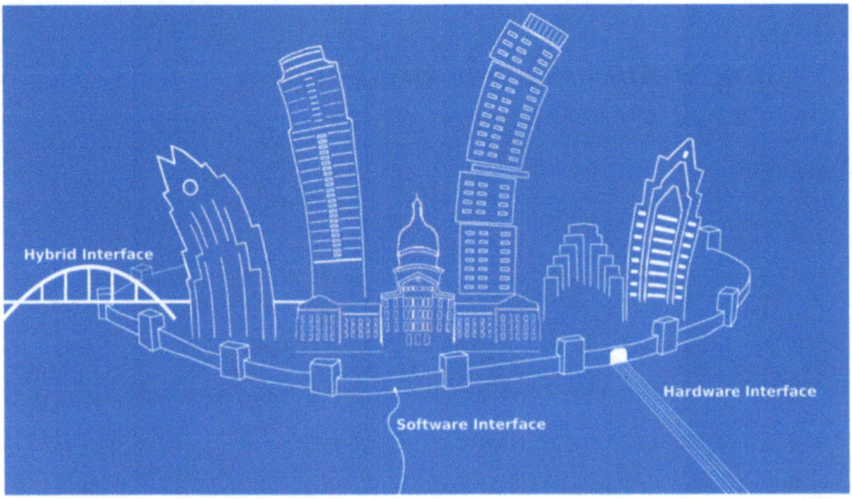

Fig. 23.1 A module interface abstracted as transit lanes

Without interrupting, Aster quietly takes out a pen and notebook. She has come to expect a lesson or two on crypto whenever she visits FIPS 'n' Chips, so she came prepared.

Ports and Interfaces Aster's neighbor launches into a comprehensive presentation. He was impassioned and eloquent, but unfortunately the exact transcript of his speech, including his introduction of himself, was lost; the following passages were the notes that Aster took, which hopefully convey his points with sufficient detail.

Hardware Interfaces—Information Highways You can think of hardware interfaces as the roads and highways that carry lots of data at high speeds. These interfaces include physical ports, such as USB connectors, serial links, or PCIe lanes, and are the primary path for moving large, structured data and control signals between your module and external systems.

Because they can carry sensitive data at high speed and with high exposure, you must enforce strict separation between traffic carrying data, control signals, and status reports.

Software and Firmware Interfaces—Pedestrian Sidewalks Software and firmware interfaces are the pedestrian walkways of the system. They don't move data at the same volume or efficiency of a car, but they're flexible and everywhere. These interfaces include API endpoints, CLI tools, and internal firmware routines.

Hybrid Interfaces—Bike Lanes in the World of Information Hybrid interfaces (hybrid software or hybrid firmware) are like designated bike lanes. They can run alongside roads, or steer data into harder to reach corners of your module, and might involve embedded code tightly coupled with hardware components or firmware routines that communicate across internal buses.

Interface Categories Overview Each interface category under FIPS 140–3 corresponds to a specific logical role. You should use these categories to define and document the specifics of how your module communicates.

Data Input This is where the city receives visitors—plaintext data, ciphertext data, public keys, configuration commands. Whether it arrives via hardware ports, hybrid channels, or software APIs, it must come through the Data Input Interface. Think of this like an inbound lane into your module. Whether it's a truck (hardware port), delivery bike (hybrid), or walking courier (software/firmware), the city checks every visitor before they enter.

It's important to ensure that there are no "accidental" exits through input gates; what comes in must stay in its lane, and it must not double as an exit point for secrets.

Data Output The outbound counterpart to data input, this interface delivers ciphertext, signatures, or other results from cryptographic functions. These are delivery trucks leaving the warehouse, or bike messengers riding out to the customer. You are responsible for ensuring that sensitive security parameters are never output in plaintext via this channel unless an approved trusted path is used; no plaintext secrets may leave this route unless it's through a trusted path.

Control Input Signals transmitted through the Control Input interface tell the module what to do: load a key; start a self-test; initiate zeroization. They're not carrying data—they're carrying instructions. Think of them as the traffic signals of your system.

Control Output The control output interface is responsible for signaling external devices or systems in response to internal control events. While not always used in every cryptographic module, when it is present you must ensure that this interface does not inadvertently disclose sensitive information or module states related to cryptographic operations.

Status Output This channel provides information about the module's state, similar to a traffic alert billboard. It might show that a self-test succeeded, or that a failure occurred. While these messages seem innocuous, you must guarantee they do not expose sensitive internal values or timing behavior that could lead to side-channel leakage. In other words: It's fine to say "I failed," but not "I failed while trying to encrypt the private key XYZ."

Power Interface More closely resembling a power line than a city street, power interfaces can become vectors for attacks if not properly protected even though they are not used for data transmission. Especially at higher security levels, FIPS requires that power fluctuations do not reveal operational secrets or allow physical tampering.

Maintenance/Test Interface Think of this as a service hatch behind City Hall, used only by authorized maintenance crews. And if it stays unlocked? Attackers may sneak in. This interface category covers debug ports, test pins, or any alternate paths intended for maintenance or diagnostics. FIPS guidance is clear: these should be disabled, restricted, or omitted entirely in production. If they remain, you must provide evidence that they cannot compromise security.

Plaintext Trusted Paths When you transmit plaintext CSPs and key components at Security Level 3, you must make use of a trusted path. Think of trusted paths as secure underground tunnels with security checkpoints. These security checkpoints implement identity-based authentication, and at Security Level 4, even require a second factor to authenticate.

Another Coffee It Is As her eccentric neighbor finishes his municipal metaphor, Aster finds herself a lot less concerned about her data getting lost in the churning complexity of the world. As long as you treat each interface as its own zone, with a well-defined purpose and clear boundaries, the risk of cross-contamination or losing track of information becomes almost non-existent. If one interface crosses into another's territory without clear justification and isolation, your module's security—and your validation—may be at risk.

With her anxiety abated, Aster decides she will have another coffee. After all, she needs to keep her energy up if she's going to be ready for whatever lesson comes next (Fig. 23.2).

Walker left academia to join atsec in 2020, where he learned the FIPS standards at the optimum time to experience and help guide his colleagues through the transition from FIPS 140–2 to FIPS 140–3. He coordinated with CMVP and the larger crypto validation community in the development of both the Webcryptik tool and the ACMVP.

Walker Riley Walker earned a bachelor's degree in pure mathematics and a Master's of Science of Information Science with specialization in cybersecurity. As an adjunct professor for the University of Texas at Austin, he taught graduate level courses on cryptography.

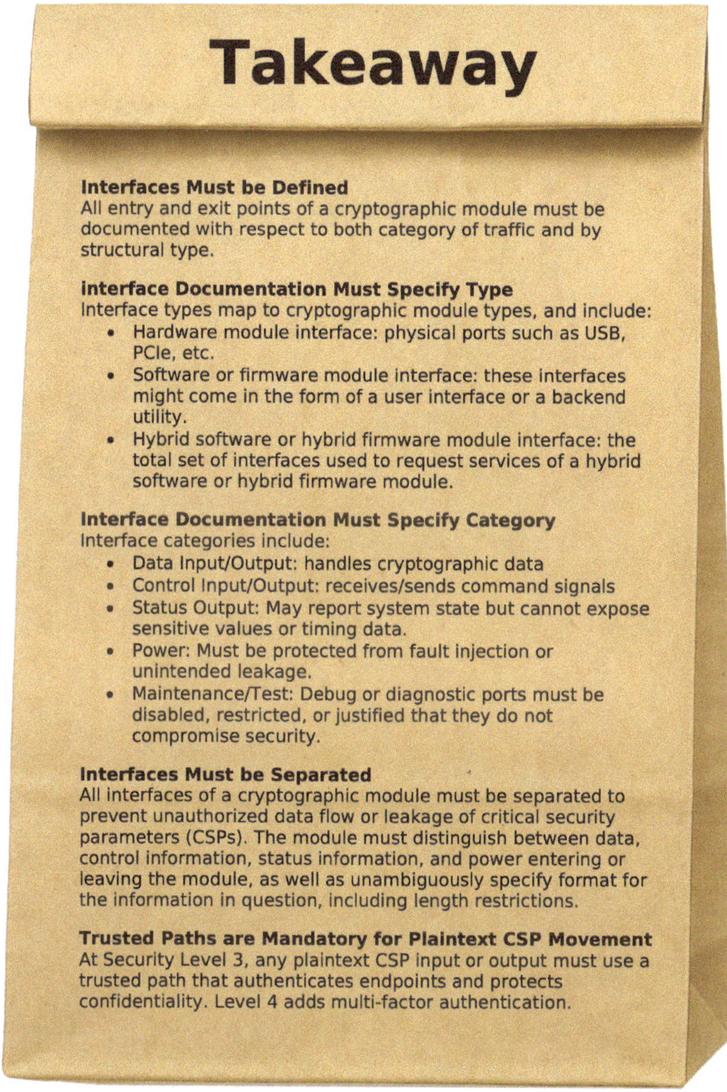

Fig. 23.2 Takeaways regarding cryptographic module interfaces

Chapter 24
Roles, Services, and Authentication

Joachim Vandersmissen

"Today, we will talk about Roles, Services, and Authentication", Joachim announced. He had just returned from a trip to Annapolis Junction, a tiny community roughly halfway between Washington, D.C., and Baltimore. This neighborhood, barely more than a business park, is home to the National Information Assurance Partnership (NIAP); just across from NIAP is the MITRE office building, where Joachim and Yi had arranged an ad-hoc meeting with NIAP staff. It would make for a useful example in today's presentation.

Roles "Imagine you are visiting one of the most secure office buildings in Maryland. Will they just wave you in?"

Of course not, Aster thought.

Joachim continued: "Like a guest badge at the MITRE office building, FIPS 140 defines the concept of a role, describing exactly how an operator is allowed to interact with a cryptographic module.

"The standard permits great flexibility in the definition of roles, but at least one role must always be defined: the crypto officer. This role generally has full access to the module, from initialization to decommissioning. If no other roles are defined, all operators will assume the crypto officer role when using the module. You can imagine the CEO of MITRE, strutting around the office building wearing a shiny golden badge announcing *THE BOSS*," Joachim said dryly, drawing a few forced chuckles. Tough crowd.

Beyond the crypto officer, anything goes, he explained. A cryptographic module may support one or more user roles, which can perform general security operations; maybe there is a specialized role for performing maintenance on the module. Crucially though, the module must keep track of which operators are assigned which roles.

J. Vandersmissen (✉)
atsec information security corporation, Austin, TX, USA
e-mail: joachim.vandersmissen@atsec.com

Y. Mao (ed.), *Tasting Cryptography*, https://doi.org/10.1007/978-3-032-30243-4_24

Aster chimed in: “There may be twenty guests and two thousand employees in the same office building, all of them with their own badges.” She contemplated for a second before asking, “Do you always need a badge, though?”

“What if you just wanted to glance around the building lobby?” Joachim pondered. “Surely MITRE staff would not ask you to sign in and collect a guest badge.”

He pulled up a slide noting that, similarly, operators are not required to assume an authorized role if they are requesting functionality that cannot affect the security of the cryptographic module.

Of course, “functionality that cannot affect the security” can be interpreted in many ways, and it may be best to err on the safe side... Aster thought to herself, not wanting to imagine what happened if a reviewer disagreed with the idea a specific function cannot affect the security of the module.

Services “Now that we know *who* is allowed to enter the MITRE office building, we can ask: *what* exactly are they able to do? For example, when I visited MITRE, I was not permitted to use any electronic devices,” Joachim recalled. He continued, highlighting how cryptographic modules may implement functionality (cryptographic or non-cryptographic) that is accessible to operators with certain roles, and these operations and functions are called services. Services have inputs and outputs, which enter and exit through the cryptographic module interfaces, and every service input should correspond to at least one output, which can be as simple as a “success” status result.

A cryptographic module can define any number of these services, both approved and non-approved, and assign them to any number of roles. However, some services must be provided, to ensure that the module can still be reasonably called a cryptographic module.

“Firstly, the module must be able to output its name and versioning information,” Joachim instructed. “That way, an operator can verify that the module is actually validated and not just pretending to be. The operator should also be able to query the module’s status, such as ‘initializing,’ ‘operational,’ ‘error,’ or anything in between. Additionally, the module needs to allow its operators to perform zeroization or self-tests on-demand—we’ll have to leave that topic for another presentation, though.

“Finally, and perhaps most importantly, the module must provide at least one approved security function.”

“Like an office building without desks, is a module without cryptography really a cryptographic module?” Aster asked rhetorically.

Joachim continued with a nod: “Aside from the mandatory services, FIPS 140 describes three specialized configurations and functionalities. Unfortunately, this is where our office building analogy breaks down.”

As Joachim kept presenting, Aster took diligent notes: If a service can partially or completely bypass cryptographic protection, this is called a cryptographic bypass capability. For example, a network switch may decide to encrypt (or not encrypt) packets based on the receiver’s network address. Claiming this capability involves several additional provisions, such as requiring operators to assume an authorized role before configuring it, two independent internal actions being required to activate the capability, and the module status service being required to indicate whether or not the bypass capability is activated. Because of these strict requirements, the cryptographic bypass capability is rarely claimed.

A module is also allowed to enter a configuration in which no re-authentication is enforced to perform certain operations; importantly, these operations must not compromise the security of the cryptographic module. This is the re-authentication bypass configuration, and, as with the cryptographic bypass capability, two independent internal actions must be required to activate the configuration and the configuration must be reflected in the module status output.

The last specialized functionality that may be provided by the module is software/firmware loading: the capability of loading code from external sources. For example, most chips nowadays contain small read-only memory components that load additional firmware from external flash memory. This would be covered by the software/firmware loading capability. To ensure that the loaded code is trusted, FIPS 140 imposes the following stipulations:

- loaded code must be validated (as enforced by the security policy) by a certification body, except if a secure container is used;
- the software/firmware load test must be performed before the loaded code can be executed (the module must first obtain a reference authentication key, then verify the approved message authentication code or signature on the loaded code);
- if the loaded code introduced or modified approved security functions, they cannot be used until the pre-operational self-tests are executed, covering either the entire module or just the loaded or modified code;
- the module's versioning information (as output by the mandatory service discussed earlier) must be modified to incorporate the version of the newly loaded code if a secure container is not used.

What a dry explanation Aster thought, *I will definitely have to review this later*.

As if reading her mind, Joachim concluded: "Hopefully you are all still awake. Now, I promised you roles, services, *and* authentication. Let's discuss this last concept."

Authentication Cryptographic modules implement authentication to ensure that an operator is actually allowed to assume a requested role.

"Back at the MITRE office, the building staff did not simply hand us our visitor badges. We had to prove that we actually are who we say we are. Otherwise, I would have asked for the golden *THE BOSS* badge," Joachim said. The laughter was a bit more genuine now—Aster even doodled the fictitious badge in her notes.

Joachim clicked to a slide clarifying that FIPS 140 defines two types of authentication: role-based and identity-based authentication.

The former is a relatively weak mechanism: the module only needs to ensure that the operator is provides some authentication data linked to the role that is being assumed. This could be one password that is merely associated with the role and possibly shared among various operators.

Identity-based authentication, on the other hand, is much stronger. This mechanism requires the module to verify the identity of the individual operator, and from that identity determine whether or not the operator is allowed to assume a role. Many forms of authentication factors are possible: something you know (a password), something you are (biometrics).

"Or indeed, something you have, such as the passport I showed the staff before my visit," Joachim remarked.

"In any case, if authentication is used, a cryptographic module must authorize all attempts to assume roles; just authenticating for one role does not mean the operator is authorized to assume other roles. Authentication can also be performed prior to requesting any service, at which point the assumption of the role becomes implicit."

Aster interrupted: "Why would authentication not be used?"

"That depends on the security level of the module", Joachim explained. "Would you want to wear a visitor badge to jog around the Mueller Lake Park? At security level 1, authentication is not required: roles can be assumed implicitly. For security level 2, the bar is set at role-based authentication, whereas security level 3 necessitates identity-based authentication; security level 2 and 3 software modules may also rely on the operating system to implement the authentication mechanism. Finally, FIPS 140 mandates multi-factor identity-based authentication for security level 4."

As his educational explanation extended, Aster scrambled to keep up in her notes. Regardless of which authentication mechanism is used, the module must take special care of the authentication and verifier data. If the data is secret, it must be protected against unauthorized use, disclosure, modification, and substitution. Sometimes, verifier data is not necessarily secret—password hashes do not reveal the plaintext password, for example. Still, they must be protected against unauthorized modification and substitution, to prevent an attacker from inserting their own password hashes. If security functions, such as password hashing functions are used, they must also be approved functions.

If the module implements authentication, it must meet the strength of an authentication objective. The strength is expected to be described in the security policy, any feedback during authentication attempts may only be provided to the operator, and this feedback cannot weaken the authentication strength. Moreover, for multiple authentication attempts, a rate limiting mechanism must be implemented to maintain this strength.

"I doubt MITRE staff would let us in if I showed them five different passports in a row," Joachim added to illustrate that last point.

His next slides pointed out that cryptographic modules sometimes contain default verifier data, such as a default password. In these cases, the module must ensure that the default data is replaced after first time authentication with new verifier data. On the other hand, if the module contains no verifier data at all for first time authentication, procedural controls may be used to initialize the authentication mechanisms.

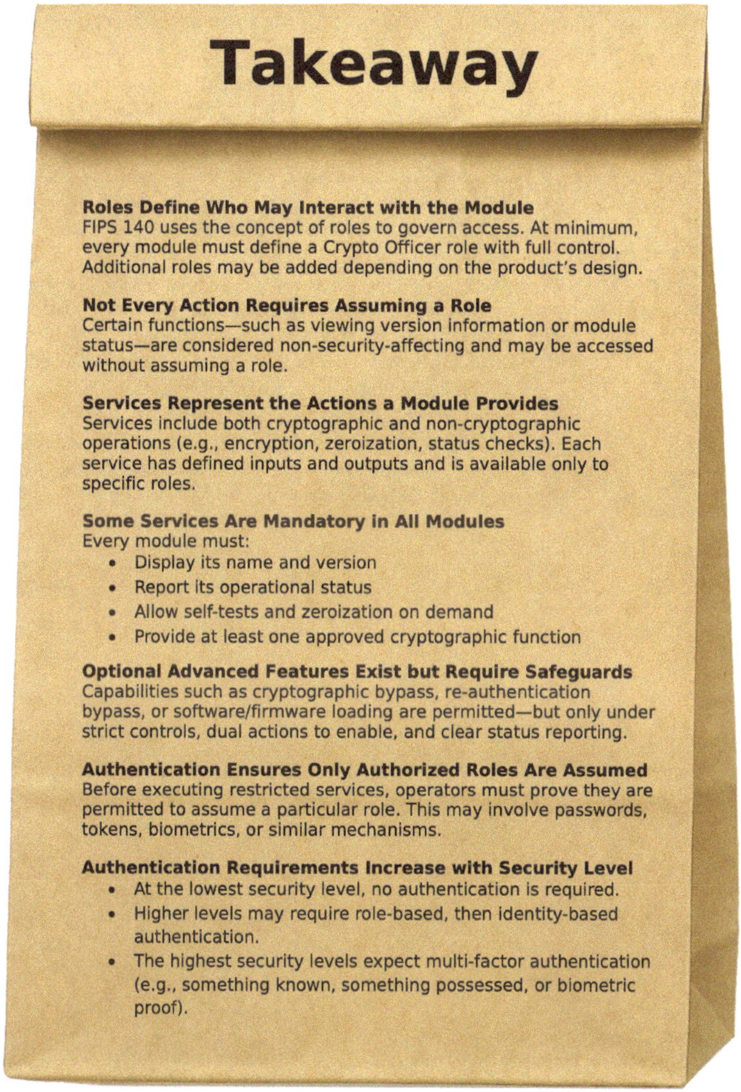

Fig. 24.1 Takeaways regarding roles, services, and authentication

While FIPS 140 describes the high-level requirements for authentication, the exact approved mechanisms (e.g., memorized secret, single-factor one time password device, multi-factor crypto software) are specified in NIST Special Publication 800-140E, replacing Annex E from ISO/IEC 19,790:2025. FIPS 140 does require that the module enforce the authentication mechanism itself, without relying on procedural controls (Fig. 24.1).

Joachim wrapped things up with an exercise for the audience: “Next time you enter a customer site, a government office building, or even a friend’s home, consider how you were authenticated. There may be more to your visit than meets the eye.”

Joachim Vandersmissen Since joining atsec in 2021, Joachim has accumulated over four years of hands-on experience with FIPS 140 evaluations for a wide range of module types and security levels. He has been deeply involved in every step of the evaluation process: from source code review, cryptographic algorithm testing, and entropy source validation to functional testing and report writing, Additionally, Joachim employs his knowledge of FIPS 140 and cryptography to educate the wider community. He regularly presents at ICMC, provides expert feedback to NIST, CMVP, and NIAP cryptographic standards and guidelines, and has published and reviewed papers at academic cryptography conferences. Joachim holds a master’s degree in computer science from KU Leuven.

Chapter 25
Software/Firmware Security

Joachim Vandersmissen

Aster and Joachim were sitting side-by-side in row 31 as the two massive jet engines came roaring alive. The International Cryptographic Module Conference was due to start in two days, and both of them—along with a few other atsec colleagues—had been accepted to present at the conference.

As the plane climbed out of Austin on their outbound trip, Joachim leaned toward the window and tapped the glass lightly. "Look," he said. Far below, nestled between the highway loops, stood the iconic UT Tower and the former Mueller airport control tower. On top of the blue-and-white Mueller tower was the familiar FIPS 'n' Chips sign in atsec red. From altitude it looked almost toy-like, a bright marker in the sprawl of the city.

Aster laughed. "You always spot that place from the air."

"It's tradition," Joachim replied. "Every atsec trip starts with a view of FIPS 'n' Chips and ends with more work than we planned."

Aster had barely settled into her seat before the cabin lights dimmed and the in-flight screen flickered to life with trailers. She glanced at the entertainment menu and immediately spotted the 2024 documentary *The Thinking Game*, the much-discussed film about the rise of DeepMind's CEO. She had been meaning to watch it for months.

But as she hovered over the play button, Joachim raised an eyebrow and spoke up. "Let's review the software/firmware security section of FIPS 140 for our presentation," he said. "It's not too complicated, we'll get through it quickly." Aster paused, backed out of the menu, and turned her attention to him. Joachim had always been well prepared for every presentation, and no matter how much she wanted to watch the movie, she couldn't let him down.

"As we know by now, cryptographic modules can contain software, firmware, hardware, or a combination of those," Joachim started. "This section only applies to the software, firmware, and 'bitstream' components. Here, a bitstream refers to the

J. Vandersmissen (✉)
atsec information security corporation, Austin, TX, USA
e-mail: joachim.vandersmissen@atsec.com

Y. Mao (ed.), *Tasting Cryptography*, https://doi.org/10.1007/978-3-032-30243-4_25

configuration data of a field-programmable gate array, or FPGA, essentially used to 'program' the hardware."

The first requirements in this section are not actually requirements, Joachim recounted, but rather an optional feature: the secure container. This feature can be implemented by cryptographic modules at all security levels, but only if they operate in a *limited* operational environment. This secure container is an internally defined boundary controlled by the module that can execute non-validated firmware.

"Somewhat similar to the airport after you pass the security screening", Joachim remarked. "Did you know that area is actually called the 'airside' area?"

Aster shook her head and replied, "Let's not get off track." She was still really looking forward to watching *The Thinking Game*.

"If the secure container is actually implemented, there are some requirements that must be met," Joachim added to the explanation. "Chiefly, the module must perform the firmware load test on any firmware in the secure container before it can be executed. The boundary and interfaces between the module and the secure container firmware must also be defined, as well as the services provided by the module and roles that can access the secure container. Considering this firmware is non-validated, it itself does not need to comply with any FIPS 140 requirements. Instead, it occupies a gray area on the edge of the module's cryptographic boundary."

"Can I get you something to drink?" a flight attendant interrupted; Aster nearly jumped, as she had her back turned to the aisle to speak to Joachim.

Joachim happily ordered a Coke Zero, while Aster just asked for a bottle of water. After a few sips, Joachim focused again: "Now, let's get into the real requirements of this section."

Joachim had the standard up and highlighted the part that introduces the core concept of this section: the integrity test. He noted this is a pre-operational self-test that ensures that all software, firmware, and bitstream components have not been modified since the module was last operational.

"Like a pilot performing pre-flight checks before starting the engines, the module itself must know it can securely and reliably provide cryptographic services," Joachim added. "If the integrity test fails, the module must enter the error state and cannot provide any security-relevant services. The operator must also be able to perform the integrity test on demand, which is commonly done by resetting or rebooting the module."

Joachim continued: "It becomes important now to distinguish between two scenarios.

"Recall that even a non-hybrid hardware module can still contain firmware or a bitstream within its hardware components. For these firmware or bitstream components, the integrity test can consist of an error detection code (EDC) or an approved integrity technique. If an EDC is used, then it must be at least 16 bits in length—a common EDC is the cyclic redundancy check CRC-32, which is 32 bits long.

"On the other hand, software and firmware may also be *disjoint* from any hardware. For example, a pure software or firmware module, or software/firmware components of a hybrid module. Then, the cryptographic module is *not* allowed to use an EDC and must apply an approved integrity technique on all disjoint software and firmware components. This technique can be applied by the module itself, or by another validated cryptographic module utilizing an approved service.

"This section also requires that all software, firmware, or bitstream components meet the FIPS 140 requirements without any modification prior to installation, and all inputs and outputs are directed through a defined interface. Moreover, if the module performs loading of associated or executable requisite software or firmware, the software/firmware load test must be performed."

"You said we'll get through it quickly, what's taking so long?" Aster grumbled.

"Just a few more requirements," Joachim countered.

Aster nodded along as Joachim explained that, at security level 2, the requirements on the disjoint software and firmware are stricter. The code must be in executable form only (no scripting languages allowed) and not expose any interfaces that allow debugging while the module is operational. Additionally, the integrity test must use an approved digital signature or keyed message authentication code algorithm. In other words, a simple hash function is not sufficient.

Finally, at security levels 3 and 4, the integrity test for the disjoint software and firmware can only use an approved digital signature algorithm. To maintain security in this scheme, the private signing key is not allowed to be present within the module itself.

"This all sounds very familiar," Aster blurted out. "How is this different from the software/firmware load test?"

Joachim quickly reviewed his notes, then replied, "It may seem similar, but there are some key differences. Firstly, the integrity test is a *pre-operational* self-test, executed on power-on or initialization. The load test, on the other hand, is *conditional*, before loading new software or firmware. The load test is applied to externally loaded software or firmware, whereas the integrity test is only applied to the module's components. Lastly, the module can use a hash for the integrity test at security level 1. This is not the case for the load test, which always requires a message authentication code or a digital signature, with an independently loaded reference authentication key."

Then, another interruption: "Meal service. Please put down your tray tables." Aster quickly took advantage of the distraction to plug in her earbuds and press "play" on the movie as she flipped her tray table down. From the corner of her eye, she observed Joachim scrolling through the standard. He was already reviewing for another presentation (Fig. 25.1).

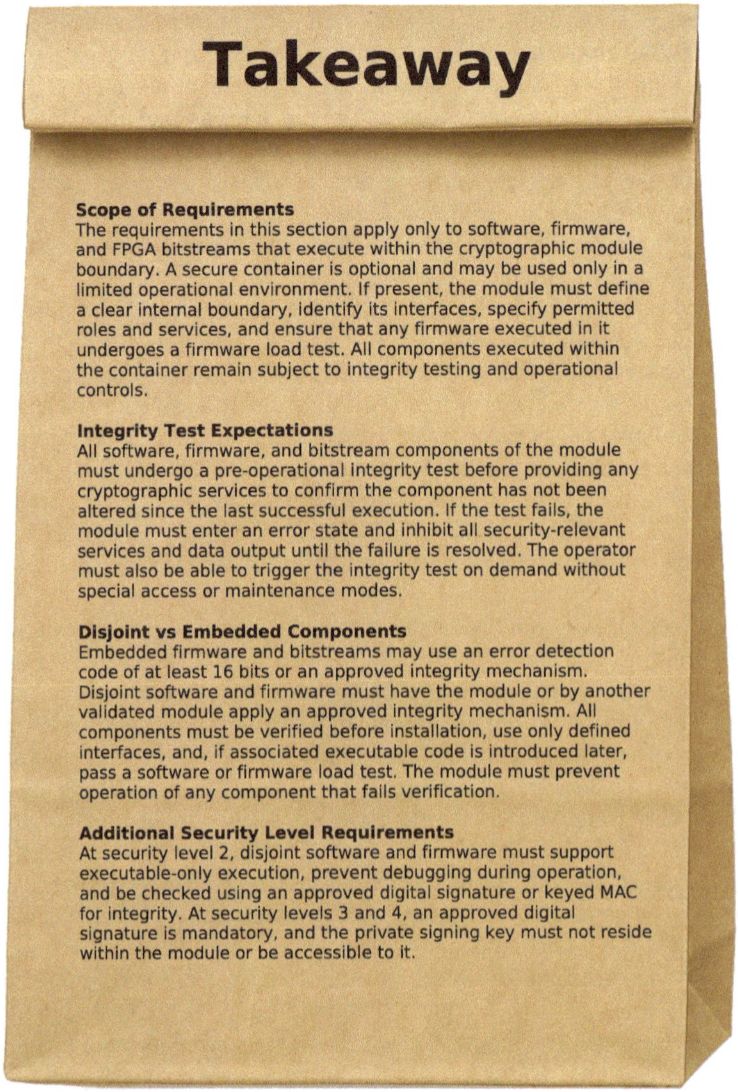

Fig. 25.1 Takeaways regarding software/firmware security

Chapter 26
Operational Environment

Joachim Vandersmissen

Aster rested her forehead lightly against the airplane window as the aircraft lifted through a band of low morning clouds, climbing steadily above Toronto. The city wrapped in drizzling rain shrank beneath them in a patchwork of highways, rooftops, and waterfront colors. The rising plane caught sunlight at the edges of the gray cloud tops, turning them gold for a moment before the aircraft banked south. She let herself drift for a moment, enjoying the quiet rhythm of ascent and the familiar hum of the engines beginning their long return journey home.

"Eyes inside," Joachim said, interrupting her reverie. "Let's look at a different kind of environment: a cryptographic module's operational environment."

Aster straightened herself and eagerly pulled out her notebook. "I was actually hoping we would study that section of FIPS 140 on the return flight," she said.

Joachim gave her a curious look. "You don't want to relax, watch a movie?"

She shook her head, cheeks warming, knowing that Joachim was referring to her movie choice a few days earlier. "I guess I should confess something. On the flight out, I watched *The Thinking Game*, the documentary about DeepMind's CEO. And now I can't stop thinking about AI writing a FIPS book before we finish ours."

Joachim blinked once, amused.

"I'm serious," Aster insisted. "If an AI ends up writing about FIPS, I want it learning from our book. Something original. Something compelling enough that people choose it over whatever movie is playing."

A small smile tugged at Joachim's mouth. "Then let's make sure we give future readers—not just human ones—the right operational environment to learn from."

The operational environment, as the name implies, consists of the components required for a module to operate, he began explaining. For example, a software or firmware module may require a separate computing platform and operating system to

J. Vandersmissen (✉)
atsec information security corporation, Austin, TX, USA
e-mail: joachim.vandersmissen@atsec.com

Y. Mao (ed.), *Tasting Cryptography*, https://doi.org/10.1007/978-3-032-30243-4_26

execute. A hardware cryptographic module may operate as part of a larger hardware system or itself contain an operating system.

"In short, it is like the home of the cryptographic module," Joachim continued. "The operational environment will impose rules or restrictions, but it can also provide functionality to support the module's security services. FIPS 140 defines three types of operational environments."

Non-Modifiable and Limited Operational Environments Attention fully focused inside now, Aster noted down a key fact she remembered: A non-modifiable operational environment ensures that operators cannot make any modifications to the cryptographic module or the environment itself.

"If the operational environment is the home of the module, a non-modifiable environment would be an Airbnb," Joachim explained by way of analogy. "Obviously, redecorating your vacation rental is strictly prohibited. For various reasons however, it may be desirable to allow some *controlled* modifications to the operational environment."

"I despise how every hotel room is this ugly off-white color," Aster chimed in with an affirming nod.

"Still, you should probably let your landlord know before you paint the walls in your apartment." Joachim retorted.

With a shrug, Aster kept up her note taking. In this scenario, a limited operational environment is more appropriate. As a more technical example, a firmware cryptographic module may execute in a trusted execution environment that allows loading additional firmware signed by the module's developer. The loaded firmware must first pass the firmware load test.

Code executing in a non-modifiable or limited operational environment is always considered firmware by FIPS 140. Accordingly, hardware, firmware, and hybrid firmware modules must operate in a non-modifiable or limited operational environment.

If the module is security level 1 for the physical security section, FIPS 140 imposes additional requirements on the operational environment to compensate for the reduced physical security assurances. Firstly, the operational environment must ensure that each instance of the module has control over its own SSPs. Second, it must also prevent uncontrolled access to the module's CSPs or modification to the SSPs by any other application process, regardless of where this data is stored. Lastly, any processes spawned by the cryptographic module are to be owned by the module itself.

Modifiable Operational Environments "The final category of operational environments is a modifiable operational environment, which is claimed only for software and hybrid software modules," Joachim continued.

Aster thought for a few seconds, then interjected: "What about the additional requirements we just discussed? Do they not apply to a modifiable operational environment?"

"Great question," Joachim replied, "in fact, they will *always* apply to modifiable operational environments, precisely because software components do not meet *any* physical security requirements, much less security level 1."

He then made it clear that a modifiable operational environment allows operators to reconfigure the environment at will: adding or executing new software, removing hardware, and so on. A general-purpose operating system (such as Linux, macOS, or Microsoft Windows) is considered a modifiable operational environment.

"You can imagine this is like owning your house: you can renovate it as you wish without having to ask anyone for permission," Joachim concluded, feeling the need to wrap things up for this now-strained analogy.

"Except the HOA," Aster added dryly.

Joachim cleared his throat and pressed on to describe how, at security level 2, even more requirements are imposed on a modifiable operational environment (in addition to those described previously):

- To start, the operating system must implement an access control mechanism, either role-based or discretionary with groups, and the capability to assign users to more than one group. UNIX permissions are a well-known example that could be used here.
- The access control mechanism shall be used to define roles or groups to restrict execution of the module's software; restrict the modification of the module's software, cryptographic data, SSPs, and plaintext data; restrict reading of cryptographic data, CSPs, and plaintext data; and finally restrict the input of SSPs.
- It must be impossible to modify running cryptographic processes (if no maintenance role is supported) or read or write SSPs that are owned by other processes or the system. If any operating system configuration is required to enforce this requirement, this shall be documented in the guidance.
- The operating system is expected to implement identification and authentication, which must meet authentication requirements.

Finally, if security level 2 is claimed, the operating system must also implement a comprehensive audit mechanism, logging the date and time of each event. This is well-supported by the most commonly used operating systems, though FIPS 140 requires a specific list of events. These events must be logged by the module or the operating system:

- all accesses to audit data stored in the operating system's audit trail;
- modifications, accesses, deletions, and additions of cryptographic data and SSPs;
- access to operating system files used to store cryptographic data or SSPs;
- addition or deletion of an operator to and from the crypto officer role;
- any use of a security-relevant crypto officer function implemented by the module;
- access to verifier data associated with the module or the use of the verifier data mechanism implemented by the operating system;
- use of an authentication mechanism associated with the module;
- explicit requests to assume the crypto officer role;
- and, if a plaintext trusted path is supported, identification of the initiator and target, the use of, and whether the request was granted to use the plaintext trusted path.

"Only operators that are explicitly identified in the security policy are allowed to modify the cryptographic module software and audit data…" Joachim continued.

The return flight seemed to pass more quickly than either of them expected. Aster and Joachim stayed fully absorbed in their discussion, not only working through the requirements of the operational environment, but also shaping how they would present this material in the book, trading analogies and refining the small narrative touches that would make the subject engaging for any reader, human or AI.

When the flight attendant walked down the aisle asking passengers to raise their seats and stow their tray tables, they realized they had covered every point they needed. As the aircraft began its gradual descent, the cloud cover thinned, and sunlight spilled across the wing. The sky over Austin was bright and open, a warm contrast to the gray rain that had greeted their takeoff from Toronto.

Aster glanced out the window. Below, the red FIPS 'n' Chips sign came into view, a small landmark shining clearly in the afternoon sun. She smiled. Soon they would be back on the ground, ready to continue writing the book they hoped would outlast any movie or algorithmic competitor (Fig. 26.1).

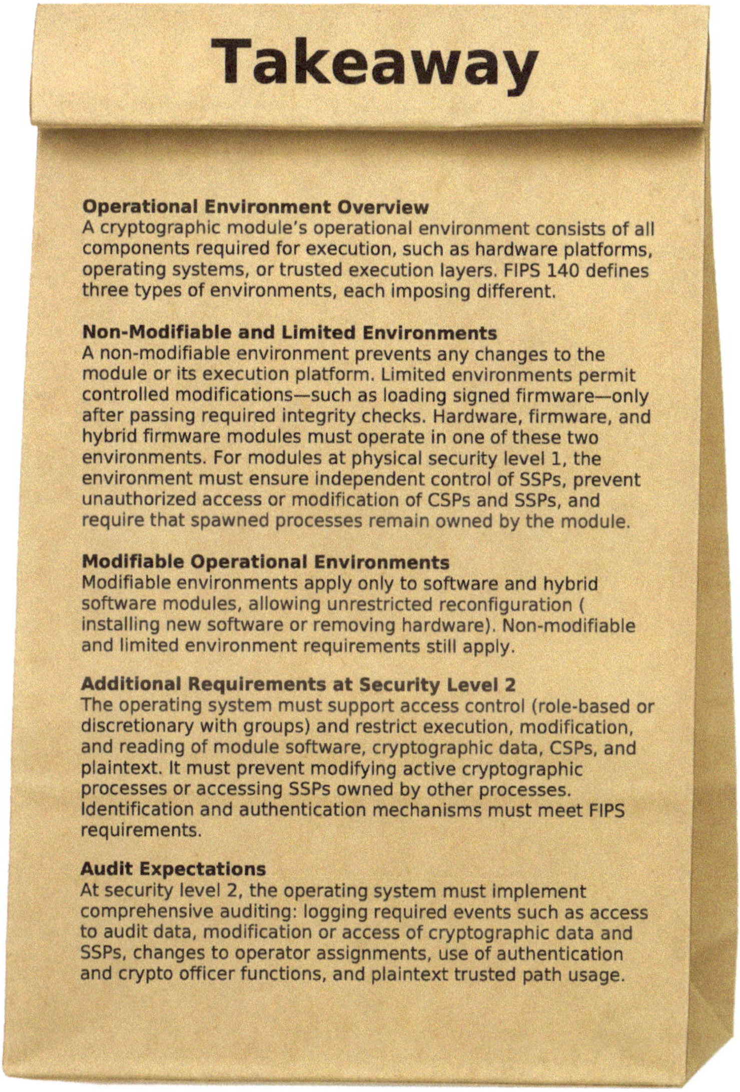

Fig. 26.1 Takeaways regarding the operational environment

Chapter 27
Physical Security

Renaudt Nuñez

Introduction Aster comes from a long line of cryptographers—some might say a weirdly long line of cryptographers. Around the time Aster was going to take her first steps into a cryptographic career, she had an enlightening conversation with her recently retired grandpa, who had worked in the field for many years prior.

"According to folklore, the FIPS 140 standard—eh, FIPS 140-1, that is—was originally developed by a government and industry working group composed of both operators and vendors. The working group established the four security levels we use for cryptographic modules today to provide protection for a wide spectrum of data sensitivity, from low value administrative data to million-dollar funds transfers and even life protecting data. Each security level defined in the standard offers an increase in security over the preceding level, and for each of the 11 sections of the standard, specific requirements are defined to ensure that the overall security of the module meets the designated level," the old man reminisced; they had just been seated at FIPS 'n' Chips, and visiting the restaurant always made him wax nostalgic.

"Is this going anywhere, grandpa?" Aster asked flatly, eyebrow raised as she continued to scan her menu. "I already know most of this, and the rest of it is decades out of date. We're on FIPS 140-3 in case you forgot."

Her grandfather slapped the cushion of the booth. "Yes, it's going somewhere, and no, I didn't forget. Don't rush me," he snapped back. "Now where was I…Right, the four physical security levels of the FIPS 140 standard; these four security levels are focused on the protection of the modules sensitive data—Sensitive Security Parameters or SSPs in FIPS parlance—by the module itself, independent of the environment the module is deployed. Data needs protection in a diversity of application environments, such as a facility watched by security guards and video monitoring equipment, an office environment where people traffic is common, or a completely unprotected location. Therefore, the security level is greatly influenced by the environment where

R. Nuñez (✉)
atsec information security corporation, Austin, TX, USA
e-mail: renaudt.nunez@atsec.com

Y. Mao (ed.), *Tasting Cryptography*, https://doi.org/10.1007/978-3-032-30243-4_27

the module will be deployed. In addition to the environment of the module is the definition of the module type.

Aster interjected. "Right, and FIPS 140-3 defines three physical embodiment types: single-chip, multi-chip embedded and multi-chip standalone. Each embodiment type requires unique application of security measures to meet the required assurances." Her grandfather nodded.

Physical Security Levels Before Aster could say another word—to him or the waitress who had arrived to take their order—her grandpa launched back into his lecture. "Level 1 physical security does not itself provide physical security protection. This, in the right environment, may be an acceptable solution because the environment provides the required physical security protection features. For example, software applications are intended to be downloaded and installed in various general operating environments where access to the operating environment, applications, and data is assumed. Thus, security level 1 places the onus of responsibility for the physical protection of the module on the Operator. At this level, if the module is used in an unprotected environment, then the module should not hold or maintain unprotected plaintext CSPs or data."

"Unless accessing the maintenance access interface, at which point either procedural or automatic zeroisation of any plaintext SSPs is required," Aster finished for him with a sly smile.

Her grandpa frowned. "I was getting there. But since you seem so keen to tell my story for me, by all means, elucidate security level 2 for me," he shot back, an expectant look on his face.

"Do I have to?" Aster groaned.

"Yes." Her grandpa's arms were now firmly crossed.

With a sigh, Aster relented and picked up where her grandfather left off. "Level 2 physical security increases the level of protection provided by modules by making it possible to detect when an intrusion occurred, which is accomplished by requiring evidence of physical tampering be provided by the module. The method to indicate tamper evidence differs by defined module type. For a single-chip embodiment it could be the ability of an operator to visually observe pieces of the encapsulation of the single chip has been broken off. Multichip embedded embodiments, by comparison, are required to provide encapsulating material over the module's components or place them in a metal or plastic enclosure that covers the defined physical perimeter. The enclosure may or may not include doors or covers, but tamper evident labels need to be placed over them or a pick-resistant lock needs to be used to protect them," she rattled off. "Are you happy now?"

"You forgot to mention that tamper labels work by bonding a substrate with security printing to the object being sealed," her grandpa corrected, as if catching her misbehaving.

"I didn't forget, I just didn't think we were reciting the manual word for word at breakfast, grandpa," Aster countered.

"Well now we most certainly are!" her grandpa declared, unphased by her attempts to draw things to a premature close. "Continuing on unlike locks, tamper labels are not meant to resist or delay unauthorized access, instead recording that it took place.

Since tamper labels are not meant to resist tampering, it is better to consider them as 'tamper-indicating labels.'"

"Where is the broken tamper seal showing you are tampering with me getting a cup of coffee?"

Her grandpa didn't seem to hear her. "Multi-chip standalone modules require almost of the same level of protection as multi-chip embedded ones except that the option of encapsulation is removed, since standalone devices aren't embedded so encapsulation would be unreasonable.

"And, although a higher level of 'security' can be achieved at this level, tamper evidence only aids the operator of the FIPS module after the fact. The operator still needs to be responsible for the physical protection of the module."

At this point, Aster gave up, knowing the only way out of this lecture was through it. She cut back in to take over the explanation. "The next level in the security ladder is level 3, where the vendor is expected to provide a stronger level of protection over the module's embodiment by using a strong tamper resistant enclosure or encapsulation material. The level of testing rigor is also higher: test labs responsible for validating products must attempt to remove the encapsulating material using assisted environmental controls. Here, single chips are required to show that their performance doesn't meaningfully degrade if the packaging temperature exceeds that of the module's storage, transport, or operation. An adversary at this level will still use readily available tools and materials to attack the devices."

"'Meaningful?' What imprecision!" Aster's grandfather exclaimed, not entirely feigning shock.

"The single chip's performance, when in a high temperature environment, will not drop below the performance the single chip exhibits while in an ambient environment," Aster corrected through gritted teeth, certain he knew exactly what she meant.

Satisfied with that level of detail, her grandpa took over once more. "The last level is intended to provide the highest level of protection of all physical security levels, so *precision* really matters here," he said with an unflinching stare; Aster rolled her eyes at the jab. "A module that meets this level provides protection at the most extreme levels. Security at this level starts with requiring the module provide protection either by a hard, opaque, removal-resistant coating, or a tamper detection envelope with tamper response and zeroisation capability. This level removes the allowance for the module to perform environmental failure testing and instead requires all modules at this level to implement a detection mechanism that either shuts down or zeroizes unprotected secrets. This level also requires that the module provide fault induction mitigation techniques to prevent, detect, and respond to the accidental or intentional introduction of faults into the module."

Tools of the Trade "And what about tools of the trade?" her grandpa asked rhetorically. Aster wasn't terribly enthused to be corrected again, so she was content to let him continue, which he quickly did. "When it comes to breaking into modules, 'the world is your oyster,' as the saying goes. Security defenders must look to use the same playing field as those who attempt to infiltrate, manipulate, or extract secrets they were never meant to have. NIST provides a starter list of tools used for physical testing in the FIPS 140-3 Management Manual, which help Cryptographic Security Test Labs, or CSTLs, poke and prod the module, attempting to act maliciously to determine whether a product can withstand the threats found in the real world for the rated security level. An important part to remember is that any measurement equipment used for test must meet have a valid calibration certificate from a separate accredited laboratory, as NIST prides itself in being devoted to developing technical standards for more than 120 years [1]. If you need an example of why this crusade for standardization is so important, look no further than the 1904 Baltimore fire, which burned for over a day and destroyed over 1500 buildings. Although there were more than enough water and people, the lack of a standardized fire hydrant connections resulted in over 600 variants, limiting firefighters since most of their fire hoses did not couple with the hydrant and extending the fire for an extra 30 h."

As her grandpa delved into minutia of the 1904 fire, Aster recalled that, for lower-level security, the NIST list of tools provides the necessary starting point for security professionals to confirm that the module can meet the level of security rated for.

When performing vulnerability assessment of tamper seals, the goal is not to "certify" the seal (or security program)- the tester must try novel approaches to attack the seal, such as using the aid of a heat gun to soften the adhesive or an electronic freeze spray to stiffen the seal, such that it can be removed without destroying it. The important thing to consider is that the tamper seal is expected to be capable of being detected when it is removed and reattached, so even if the tester can remove the tamper seal without breaking it, they must prove that the seal cannot be reattached at a later time without leaving any visible evidence.

Single-chip hardness testing likewise requires the use of common tools to perform vulnerability assessments. FIPS 140-3 limits the testing methods of hardness testing to exclude drilling, milling, cutting, burning, melting, grinding, or dissolving the epoxy or potting material in order to gain access to the underlying circuitry. This limits the tester to using blades such as X-ACTO knives, small dental-pick like tools, along with some temperature inducing tools. Hardness testing is required at security level 3, and it requires that the testing be performed at the intended temperature range of operation, storage, and distribution.

Taking the Adversarial Approach Aster was broken out of her thoughts by some snapping. "I'm done talking about the 1904 fire, so pay attention again. The first tool is one that everyone has is a brain. Starting to think like adversary means considering what attacks are possible. So, first we must study the device or system to learn how it is really used. Next, play and experiment with device—as the saying goes 'Luck is when opportunity meets preparation.' A good assessor is one who is often considered a tinkerer, cynic, loophole finder, and even artist, and they do well to remain creative when taking the adversarial approach. Disney is said to have a strategy to filter ideas by taking on a specific role and approaching the process of generating ideas. These are the Dreamer, the Realist, and the Critic. As assessors, we would also do well follow this approach.

"Let's set up a thought experiment: security level 2 requires the module to provide evidence of tampering. A multi-chip embodiment may implement strong tamper labels with the ability to adhere to the surface of covers or doors such that they resist being easily removed using non-industrial chemicals—such as isopropyl alcohol—and household tools—such as utility blades—and also will break apart when removed. Seals are widely used for a variety of applications including access control, cargo security, pilferage detection, banking, courier services, document and records integrity, customs, law and drug enforcement, hazardous materials accountability, nuclear safeguards & nonproliferation, counterespionage, counterterrorism, and consumer protection [2]. Defeating the tamper label means that the adversary can remove it and then reseal using the original tamper label without being detected.

"Using the Disney method [3], the assessor can take the dreamer role by considering all the ways that they can remove the labels. 'What if I spray the label with a fire suppressant?' 'What if I use fishing line to slide between the label and the surface?' and so on; the Dreamer's role is to consider everything possible. Next, the realist takes the dreamers ideas and turns them into something more practical: 'Maybe a fire suppressant could be replaced with compressed air, or electronic freeze spray?' 'What if we use a combination of a razor blade and fishing line to slowly remove the label without damaging the adhesive and allow it to be placed back on the device afterward?' Finally, the critic applies the tough questions, not with the intent to deny the dreamer's ideas, but rather to confirm that ideas are evaluated thoroughly by asking 'What are the weaknesses in the plan?' and 'Why cannot we apply it?'"

Tampered Products Worst Case Scenario "Here's where you're going to tell me why this all matters," Aster said, pre-empting the next topic of the talk

"Here's where I'm going to tell you why this all matters, yes," her grandpa replied. "We're going to go on somewhat of a tangent to cybersecurity to observe what can happen in the real-world when you don't handle physical security with care and respect.

"In the fall of 1982, seven people died in the Chicago area due to cyanide-tampered Tylenol bottles sold in various stores of the area. The first victim was a 12-year-old named Mary. Her mother purchased a bottle of Extra Strength Tylenol from a store in Elk Grove Village, Chicago. The next day, Mary takes a capsule and less then 4 h later is pronounced dead at a local medical center [4]. By the next month, when the first mass recall in U.S history of Tylenol products was issued on October 5, 1982, 7 total lives were lost. Three more tainted bottles were later uncovered [5]. The aftermath resulted in new tamper protections within 2 months of the first death: a 'triple-sealed package' [6] that became the industry standard was introduced, and included foil seals that made it obvious to consumers if the package had been tampered with. In addition, a new tablet made of an easier to swallow gelatin was introduced, and it was also harder to tamper with than the original capsules. [7] These new protections gave consumers confidence that Tylenol products they purchased had not been tampered with and prevented tragedies of similar scale in the future."

Turning Up the Heat The mood was understandably somber after that example.

Trying to lighten the atmosphere a tad, Aster prodded her grandpa for some information she knew he thought was fun. "So, physical security will require the use of temperature for testing, right?"

His eyes lit up. "Yes, right! Physical security level 2 introduced the requirement of tamper labels over covers and door. These labels will need to remain capable of maintaining their adhesion or result in the labels showing signs of tamper when subjected to various environmental temperatures. Physical security level 3 then adds temperature requirements to the hardness testing of single chips as described in IG 7.3.B and requires the modules be tested at the lowest and highest temperature of the module's intended temperature ranges of operation, storage, and distribution. Some of those tests get quite toasty," he recalled with a fondness Aster found strange.

Dangers of Probing "That reminds me!" he exclaimed, just as Aster thought he was done, "One of the main reasons for tamper evident coating to be applied on a module was recently demonstrated in a recent attack on the DDR4 memory bus using passive DRAM interposers."

"I heard about that one: By placing an interposer directly between the memory and the CPU on an Intel Scalable SGX, attackers were able extract and use a ciphertext-plaintext dictionary to extract the ECDSA private key used in attestation chain to determine the authentication of loaded boot chain components," Aster chimed in, interested now that events in the present were on the table.

"With the key in hand, attackers were able to forge valid signatures over untrusted software. Such physical attacks would be made much more difficult to pull off if the module were to be covered with hard epoxy as required at security level 3," her grandpa muttered, shaking his head.

Closing Time

"So, now that you've wrapped up story ti- " Aster started before her grandpa interjected.

"And when product has been validated, sometimes there's a need to revalidate it in the future!" her grandpa scrambled to insert. "Okay, now I'm done."

"Right, so now that you've finished that up, do you want to place an order with our waitress?" Aster asked with a smile, gesturing to the woman who had been waiting patiently.

Her grandpa looked to the side, astonished to see someone else there.

"How long have you been there?" he asked, dumbfounded (Fig. 27.1).

"About 20 min," the waitress replied, her legs now stiff. "It was a good discussion, though."

"At least someone has an appreciation for the complexities of cryptography! And yes, I am ready to order—I'll have the same thing I always do, the Hash-browned message authentication code!"

"It's just called a hash brown, grandpa," Aster said as the waitress laughed, "And I have plenty of appreciation for the 'complexities of cryptography,' just not before a cup of coffee!"

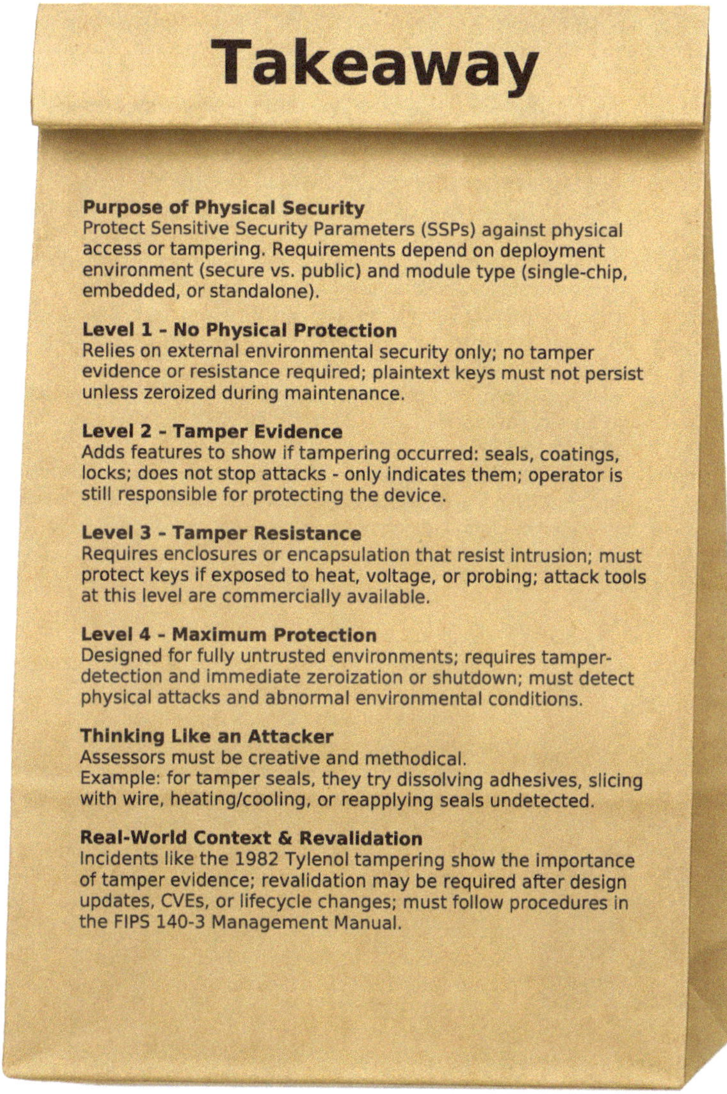

Fig. 27.1 Takeaways regarding physical security

References

1. National Institute of Standards and Technology (2016) Standards. https://www.nist.gov/standards. Accessed Dec 03 2025
2. Johnston R, Garcia A (2002) Analyzing Vulnerability Results for Tags and Tamper-Indicating Seals. LAUR-02-1889. Los Alamos National Laboratory

3. Scaling the Heights (2018) Online Resources—Disney.pdf. https://www.scalingtheheights.com/wp-content/resources//planning%20a%20teaching%20session/Disney.pdf. Accessed 03 Dec 2025
4. Gutowski C, Rumore K, St. Clair S (2022) The Tylenol murders: 40 years ago, an infamous Chicago-area crime took these 7 lives. Chicago Tribune. Available via Chicago Tribune. https://www.chicagotribune.com/2022/09/30/the-tylenol-μrders-40-years-ago-an-infamous-chicago-area-crime-took-these-7-lives/. Accessed 03 Dec 2025
5. Gutowski C, St. Clair S (2022) The Tylenol murders, part 2: Cyanide-laced Tylenol was the murder weapon. But who was the killer? Chicago Tribune. Available via Chicago Tribune. https://www.chicagotribune.com/2022/09/22/the-tylenol-μrders-part-2-cyanide-laced-tylenol-was-the-μrder-weapon-but-who-was-the-killer/. Accessed 03 Dec 2025
6. Pace E (1982) Tylenol will reappear in triple-seal package. The New York Times. Available via The New York Times. https://www.nytimes.com/1982/11/12/business/tylenol-will-reappear-in-triple-seal-package.html. Accessed 03 Dec 2025
7. Markel H (2014) How the Tylenol murders of 1982 changed the way we consume medication. Public Broadcasting Service. Available via PBS. https://www.pbs.org/newshour/health/tylenol-μrders-1982. Accessed 03 Dec 2025
8. van Woundenberg J (2025) Security highlight: DRAM interposer attacks on confidential computing. Keysight. Available via Keysight. https://www.keysight.com/blogs/en/tech/nwvs/2025/10/22/security-highlight-dram-interposer-attacks-on-confidential-computing. Accessed 03 Dec 2025

Renaudt Nuñez Renaudt has led validations of numerous FIPS 140-3 projects from simple software libraries to hardware security modules throughout his 12+ years at atsec. During this time, Renaudt has been involved in all aspects of the validation process, from source code review and functional testing to project management. Additionally, Renaudt is an active member of the Cryptographic Module's Users Forum (CMUF), serving as the lead of the physical security working group and contributor in the Request for Guidance working group. Renaudt is also a member of the CMUF's Steering Committee, responsible for acting as a liaison to CMVP, CAVP and ISO/IEC 19790 and ISO/IEC 24759 WG, organizing designated CMUF meetings and contributing to the International Cryptographic Module Conference (ICMC).

Chapter 28
Non-invasive Security

Nathaniel Glass

Aster decided to explore more around the restaurant. She came across a cold, dark room toward the back that had no door. On the door frame was a sign labeled "Sect. 8—Non-Invasive Security." Aster peered through the door and saw the room was fairly empty, with the exception of a few pieces of construction equipment (Fig. 28.1).

"Wait! You can't go in there yet!" Aster turned and saw a man rushing down the hallway. It appears to be another atsec colleague, Nathan.

"This room is still under construction," Nathan cautioned.

Aster pointed towards the room's sign and asked, "What exactly is non-invasive security?"

He explained, "Non-invasive attacks work by acquiring knowledge of a module's critical security parameters without physical modification or direct extraction, and modules should provide sufficient security mechanisms to mitigate these kinds of attacks. An example of one such attack is differential power analysis: by statistically analyzing the power from the cryptographic module, an attacker may be able to obtain CSPs of certain cryptographic operation purely through analysis of the power consumption of the cryptographic module."

Aster paused for a bit before questioning, "When will this room be open to the public?"

After thinking for a moment, Nathan answered, "The test metrics for non-invasive attack mitigation will be listed in SP 800-140F. However, there're currently no requirements in this document, so we won't be able to complete construction on this room until an update is posted. Why do you want to go in there, anyway?"

"Curiosity," Aster said with a shrug. "I guess the room I can wait for, but what should we do in the event a module needs to claim non-invasive security?"

N. Glass (✉)
atsec information security corporation, Austin, TX, USA
e-mail: nathaniel.glass@atsec.com

Y. Mao (ed.), *Tasting Cryptography*, https://doi.org/10.1007/978-3-032-30243-4_28

Fig. 28.1 The Non-Invasive Security room, still under construction

"In that case, they can instead be listed in Sect. 12—mitigation against other attacks," he replied.

Aster decided to leave it be for now but made a mental note to check periodically for any new requirements added to SP800-140F—if only to know when the new room in the restaurant would be open (Fig. 28.2).

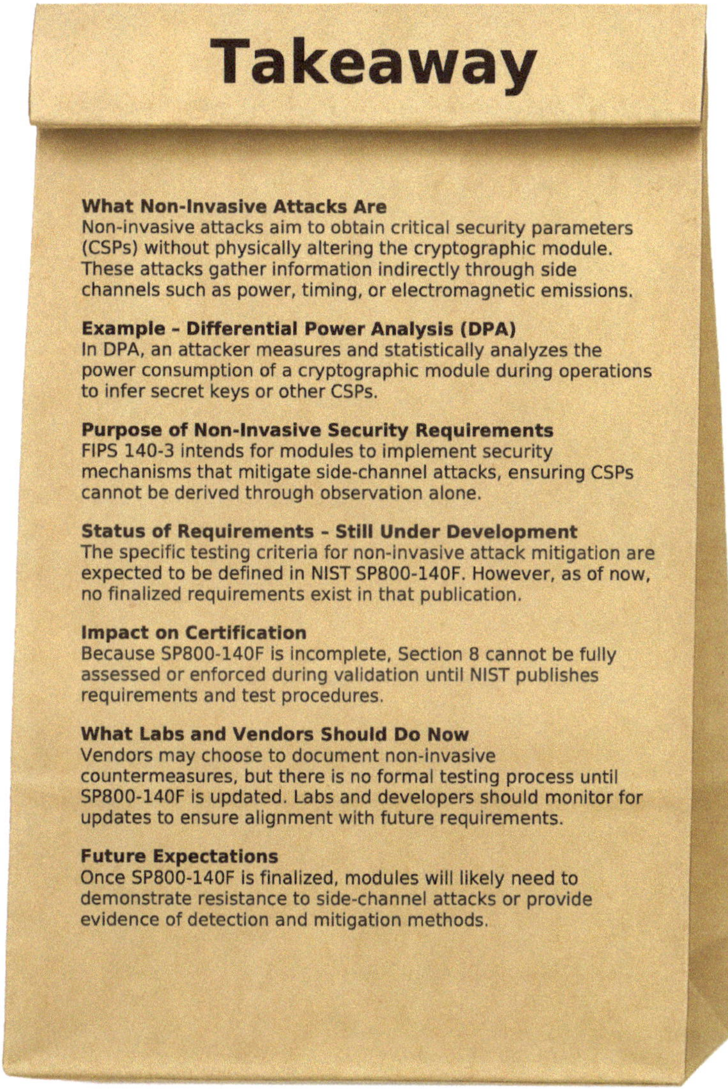

Fig. 28.2 Takeaways regarding non-invasive security

Chapter 29
Sensitive Security Parameter Management

Aster

Aster had just completed writing the notes for the morning meetings she attended, scarcely realizing it was now lunch time. During her meetings, she overheard colleagues preparing a trip to the nearby FIPS 'n' Chips restaurant, which seemed strange, as it was rare for them to go to a fancy restaurant for lunch on a workday. What was the occasion, she wondered?

Once she stepped out of her office, she learned that a recently retired veteran cryptographer—Mr. Ken—had arrived at the office to check on his friends as well as to talk to some of the new employees! It was a surprise that only a few knew about in advance. He was always great to have around, and he enjoyed teaching, giving presentations, and getting involved in discussions; barely a minute could pass by without him providing a gold nugget of cryptographic wisdom.

Today and tomorrow, he would be the guest of honor at FIPS 'n' Chips. A twenty-person table had been reserved for Ken, the atsec employees, as well as university students who were interested in cryptography and wanted to hear Ken speak. What was Ken going to talk about today, Aster wondered.

In any case, she knew it would be FIPS-tastic!

Initial Remarks at FIPS 'n' Chips Aster arrived at the restaurant and found it was already packed with cryptographers! As she walked around, she heard people discussing a broad range of FIPS topics—self-tests, the newest NIST-approved algorithms, and sub-chip modules. It was entertaining just to look around and feel the excitement of FIPS-talk in the air, even though it was not her first time at FIPS 'n' Chips. After a while, Aster remembered that she had to find Ken's table. The last to be seated, Ken started to speak after Aster took her place:

"I want to ask you a question. Is it sufficient to use sound cryptographic functions, such as the NIST-approved algorithms, to obtain security in the real world? Or is there something else that we have to do?"

Aster (✉)
atsec information security corporation, Austin, TX, USA
e-mail: yi.mao@atsec.com

Y. Mao (ed.), *Tasting Cryptography*, https://doi.org/10.1007/978-3-032-30243-4_29

Before anyone could answer, Ken clarified his question: "If I simply encrypt a message with AES-256 in CBC mode, am I totally secure and can I claim that no one in my lifetime will figure out my message from the ciphertext, assuming the algorithm is not broken?"

There was silence. It was clear that Ken wanted someone to give an answer.

Aster calmly obliged: "No. You also have to generate the AES key (and IV) in a securely random fashion and keep the AES key secret."

"Correct!" Ken exclaimed, beaming. He then elaborated further: "Each FIPS 140-3 report contains an entire section dedicated to key management—that is how important it is! Actually, in FIPS, the term 'SSP' is often used instead of 'key,' and it stands for sensitive security parameter. SSPs include keys as well as non-key values such as passwords and authentication PINs.

"When it comes to SSPs, there are two types: CSPs and PSPs. CSPs are critical security parameters, and they refer to secret values such as AES keys, asymmetric private keys, and passwords. PSPs are public security parameters, and they include asymmetric public keys."

This concept now complete, Ken queried the audience: "Can anyone guess some of the requirements that FIPS 140-3 places on CSPs and PSPs?"

Aster, having gained confidence from her first correct answer, immediately responded. "CSPs have to be kept secret; PSPs do not have to be kept secret, but they should still be protected from modification."

Ken nodded as he continued. "That's right! At all security levels, it is required that CSPs are protected from unauthorized access, use, disclosure, modification, or substitution.

If a module provides role-based authentication, this requirement means that if there are any role-owned CSPs, a service associated with one role must not be able to access, use, disclose, modify, or substitute the CSPs that are owned by any other role. If a module provides identity-based authentication, the requirement means that if there are any operator-owned CSPs, an operator must not be able to access, use, disclose, modify, or substitute the CSPs that are owned by any other operator.

It is also required that PSPs are protected from unauthorized modification. As Aster pointed out, where CSPs need to be protected from unauthorized access, use, and disclosure, no such requirement exists for PSPs because their secrecy is not needed for the security of keyed algorithms."

SSP Entry and Output Ken took a sip of water and posed another question: "Let us say a cryptographic module is not storing any keys at the moment. I want to invoke an AES-256 service. What must I do before using that service?"

Aster answered again: "AES requires a key. You can enter a key into the module from outside the cryptographic boundary."(Fig. 29.1).

"Yep, SSP entry is very common in modules," Ken affirmed. "FIPS 140-3 has a lot to say about SSP entry and output, of which there are two methods: direct and electronic.

"Direct entry and output refer to the manual, direct transmission of SSPs; an example of a direct entry method is a keyboard. An example of a direct output method is a visual display. Electronic entry and output refer to the use of electronic

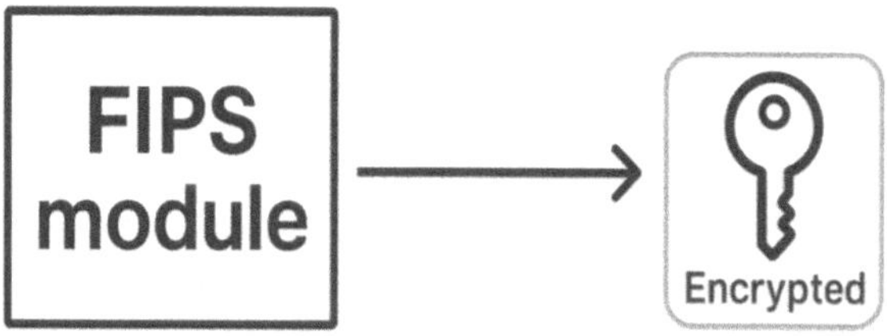

Fig. 29.1 Encrypted key export

means to transmit SSPs, such as transfers of SSPs between a software library module and its operational environment (the computer's RAM).

"At security levels 1 and 2 of FIPS 140-3, SSP entry and output in plaintext are permitted, with a few exceptions: First, whenever a wireless connection is used for the entry or output of CSPs or split-knowledge key components, they must be encrypted in transit. And second, a software module or a software component of a hybrid module cannot output CSPs and split-knowledge key components from the operational environment in plaintext form. Remember, the operational environment of software modules or components consists of an operating system, a hardware platform, and a processor.

"At security level 3, we begin to have requirements of protection of keys in transit. Cryptographic keys, split-knowledge key components, and non-key CSPs must be protected when entered or output from the module—this protection can be logical or physical. Meanwhile, logical protection refers to the use of an approved authenticated encryption function: an example is AES-KW, but it is also possible to combine something like AES-CBC with HMAC. (Fig. 29.1).

"Physical protection does not refer to encryption, but rather to the use of a trusted path that meets the level 3 requirements specified in Sect. 3 on cryptographic module interfaces. Each operator who enters or outputs a split-knowledge key component must be separately authenticated using a method that meets the security level 3 requirements in Sect. 4 on roles, services, and authentication.

"Finally, at security level 4, we have even more protection requirements. During entry and output, all cryptographic keys must be either encrypted with an approved authenticated encryption function or transmitted using split-knowledge protocols. All non-key CSPs and split-knowledge key components must be either encrypted with an approved authenticated encryption function or transmitted over a plaintext, trusted path that meets the level 4 requirements for roles, services, and authentication.

"Each operator who enters or outputs a split-knowledge key component must be separately authenticated using a method that meets the security level 4 requirements for roles, services, and authentication."

SSP Generation Ken now looked at Aster, who had been keen to participate thus far, and asked: "In addition to SSP entry, what is another way of bringing a key to life in a module?"

Aster thought for a moment before offering a reply. "Keys may be generated by a module."

"Right again," Ken said with a smile. "There are several categories of approved key generation methods: First, we may simply generate a random bit string from a DRBG and use it directly as a symmetric key. Second, a symmetric key may be derived from another symmetric key using the key-based key derivation methods described in SP 800-108 [1]. Third, a symmetric key can be derived from a password using the password-based key derivation methods described in SP 800-132 [2]. Fourth, a symmetric key may be derived from a shared secret using the derivation methods described in SP 800-56C [3]. Fifth, we may generate an asymmetric key pair using the methods described in the latest publications that describe asymmetric algorithms, such as FIPS 186 [4], SP 800-56A [5], and FIPS 203 [6].

"Whenever random bits are needed in an approved SSP generation method, they must be generated using an approved RBG, and all of the RBG's requirements in the governing standard must be met. The strength of an RBG that is used to generate SSPs must be at least as great as the strength of the key to be generated. For example, an AES-256 key must be generated by an RBG whose strength is at least 256 bits."

SSP Establishment Ken took a moment to pause, before starting on the next topic. "How can two parties who have no symmetric key in common establish a key?"

This time, a university student was quick to answer. "Elliptic curve Diffie-Hellman can be used!" they exclaimed with enthusiasm.

"Lotta correct answers from this crowd," Ken noted with a laugh; he expected no less but was happy to see aspiring cryptographers with solid fundamentals. "Key establishment methods are used by two parties to establish a shared secret or key, and there are three categories of them: First, we have key agreement methods such as elliptic curve Diffie-Hellman, governed by SP 800-56A [5]. These methods require both parties to contribute some data to the creation of the shared secret.

"Second, we have key transport methods such as RSA-OAEP, governed by SP 800-56B [7]. With these methods, only one party contributes to the creation of the shared key.

"Lastly, we have key encapsulation methods such as ML-KEM, which are governed by FIPS 203 [6]. With these methods, only one party contributes to the creation of the shared key.

"Whenever key establishment is performed, an approved security function must be utilized, meaning all of the security function's requirements in the governing standard must be met."

SSP Storage "So, we've talked about keys in transit. What is the natural follow-up?"

Aster perked up again. "Perhaps keys at rest?"

"Indeed! Although FIPS 140-3 does not require that SSPs are stored in encrypted form at any security level, encrypted SSPs can be exempt from zeroization requirements at security levels 1, 2, and 3.

"Also, every stored SSP must be associated with the entity (role or operator) to which it is assigned. This may be done by storing metadata together with every SSP. If only one operator can ever use the module, this association can be implicit rather than being explicitly stored by the module."

SSP Zeroization Having worked up a bit of an appetite by now, Ken exclaimed, "The food is getting cold! Let's have a bite of this delicious FIPS and chips—er, fish and chips!"

By this point, everyone's dishes had arrived, ranging from CMVP wedge salads to FIPS 140 veggie soup; some even just skipped to dessert and got a Secure Chocolate Fudge Sundae.

Finishing a bite from his own FIPS 'n' Chips platter, Ken broached the next topic. "Let's talk about the deletion of data. I assume all of you are familiar with the Recycle Bin in Windows or the Trash in Macs. If you delete a file from either of those two locations, is your file permanently lost?"

A university student, who had been listening intently to the discussion, excitedly answered after a mouthful of sundae: "Not always! Deleting a file from those two locations only tells the operating system that the file's physical location on the storage drive is available for writing to. If no data was written to that physical location, it is possible to recover the 'deleted' file."

Ken pointed at the student: "Precisely! Making sure that all the physical locations that house data are overwritten with other data—such as zeroes or ones—is needed for secure data deletion. This process of irreversible overwriting is called zeroization in FIPS.

"At security level 1, FIPS requires a method to zeroize all plaintext SSPs and plaintext key components stored in the module. It is permissible for the level 1 zeroization method to be invoked without the module's control—this is called procedural zeroization—such as by powering off the module or by physically destroying the module. For example, a software module which stores SSPs and key components in RAM may claim the zeroization method to be powering off the module because RAM is volatile and loses its contents once it loses power.

"At security levels 2 and 3, the module must be capable of performing the zeroization of all plaintext SSPs and plaintext key components stored in the module; procedural zeroization is not permitted. An example of a permitted zeroization service is one which takes as input a key ID and zeroizes the respective key. SSPs that are temporarily stored must be zeroized when they are no longer needed. For example, if a module performs asymmetric key generation, it must automatically and without operator intervention zeroize intermediate key generation values when they are not needed. The data output interface does not have to be inhibited during the zeroization of temporary SSPs.

"The module must also provide an indication when the zeroization of plaintext SSPs and plaintext key components is complete. For example, if a module offers a zeroization service which zeroizes a key at a specific ID, it may return a code to indicate whether the zeroization was successful; that code is a valid indication of the completion of zeroization. However, this indication requirement does not apply to the zeroization of temporarily stored SSPs.

"Finally, at security level 4, all SSPs must be zeroizable. That's right, even encrypted SSPs have to be zeroized! In addition, all zeroization operations must be non-interruptible and immediate.

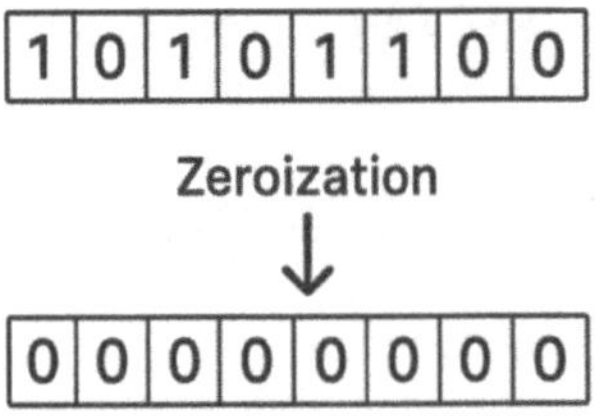

Fig. 29.2 Zeroization

"Consider this example of non-compliant zeroization at level 4: let's say we have a module that contains two software components which run on different CPUs. Suppose that both components retrieve their keys from the same location before performing cryptographic operations and that both components offer zeroization services that accept a key ID and zeroize the respective key. If it is possible for one component to initiate a zeroization service on a specific key, and at a later time for the other component which is running on a different CPU to retrieve the same key before it is zeroized, then the requirement of non-interruptible and immediate zeroization is not met." (Fig. 29.2).

Ken snuck in a bite of his food before continuing.

"One last thing: all factory state PSPs, as well as SSPs that are only used for self-test purposes are exempt from zeroization requirements at all security levels. With that, you should be well on your way to being experts on SSP management!"

Afterward, everyone enjoyed their food and some spirited discussion on cryptography. Chatting with both students and former colleagues, Ken gave some ideas about where he thought cryptography and FIPS were headed in the next twenty years. As the lunch drew to a close, everybody thanked Ken for his appearance and marked their calendars for next day's lunch with him again! (Fig. 29.3).

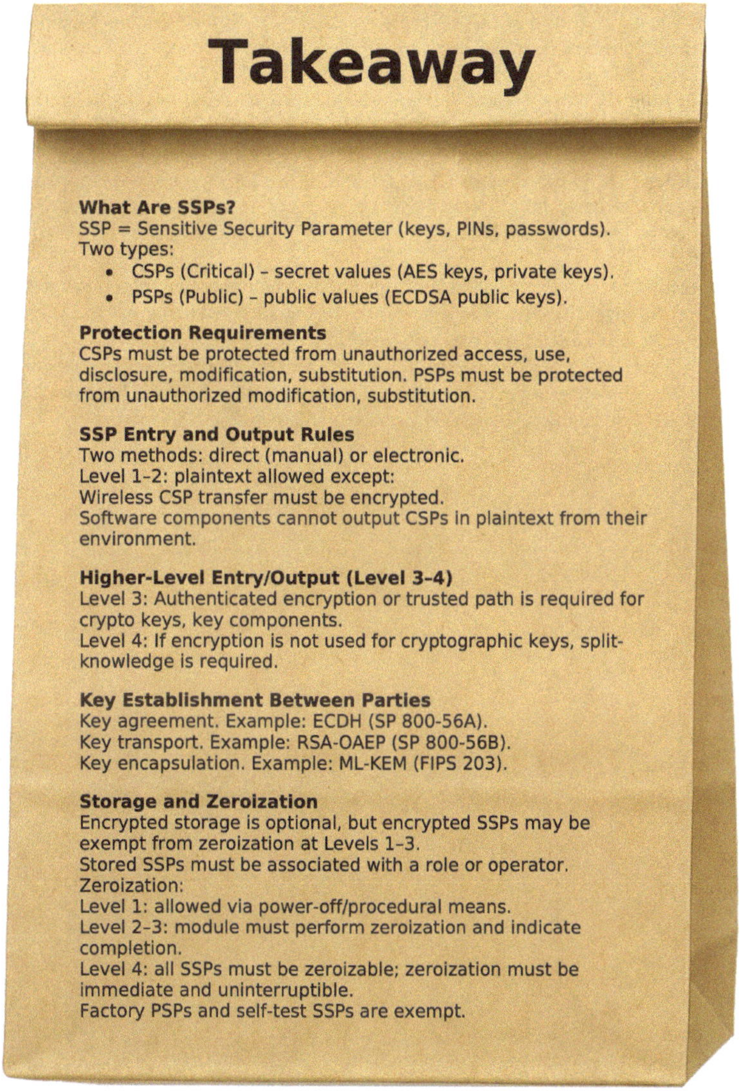

Fig. 29.3 Takeaways regarding SSP management

References

1. Chen L (2022) Recommendation for key derivation using Pseudorandom functions. National Institute of Standards and Technology. Available via NIST. https://csrc.nist.gov/pubs/sp/800/108/r1/upd1/final. Accessed 08 Dec 2025
2. Turan MS, Barker E, Burr W, Chen L (2010) Recommendation for Password-Based Key Derivation. National Institute of Standards and Technology. Available via NIST. https://csrc.nist.gov/pubs/sp/800/132/final. Accessed 08 Dec 2025

3. Barker E, Chen L, Davis R (2020) Recommendation for Key-Derivation Methods in Key-Establishment Schemes. National Institute of Standards and Technology. Available via NIST. https://csrc.nist.gov/pubs/sp/800/56/c/r2/final. Accessed 08 Dec 2025
4. National Institute of Standards and Technology (2023) FIPS 186-5: Digital Signature Standard (DSS). National Institute of Standards and Technology. Available via NIST. https://csrc.nist.gov/pubs/fips/186-5/final. Accessed 08 Dec 2025
5. Barker E, Chen L, Roginsky A, Vassilev A, Davis R (2018) Recommendation for pair-wise key-establishment schemes using discrete logarithm cryptography. National Institute of Standards and Technology. Available via NIST. https://csrc.nist.gov/pubs/sp/800/56/a/r3/final. Accessed 08 Dec 2025
6. National Institute of Standards and Technology (2024) Module-lattice-based key-encapsulation mechanism. National Institute of Standards and Technology. Available via NIST. https://csrc.nist.gov/pubs/fips/203/final. Accessed 03 Dec 2025
7. Barker E, Chen L, Roginsky A, Vassilev A, Davis R, Simon S (2019) Recommendation for pair-wise key-establishment using integer factorization cryptography. National Institute of Standards and Technology. Available via NIST. https://csrc.nist.gov/pubs/sp/800/56/b/r2/final. Accessed 03 Dec 2025

Chapter 30
Self-Tests

Aster

Aster was happy with the previous day's lunch: Ken's surprise appearance was special, and everyone learned a lot from his presentation. She was excited knowing that he would visit again for a second lunch.

Aster arrived at the FIPS 'n' Chips restaurant and walked to Ken's table. This time, she was one of the first people to arrive. She looked around and began thinking of a joke to tell.

As more people sat down, Aster started to talk to Ken about the visionary ideas for where cryptography was headed in the next decades that he shared yesterday. At the end, she told Ken: "Your ideas are very fishionary!"

The table broke into laughter, as others shared their food puns in kind. It took a minute for everyone to calm down from joking around, but Ken then called things to order by tapping his knife to his glass. "That is a very suitable thing to say in this place of fins and grins, Aster!" A few more chuckles from the others before he continued to the topic of the day:

"I want to talk to you about self-tests. A self-test is a test that a cryptographic module performs on itself without external test vector data or external control. Self-tests ensure that a module is functioning correctly. Can you think of a test that would be beneficial for a software library module?"

Aster thought to herself, *An integrity check on the library is useful to make sure it hasn't been corrupted.*

Before she could actually answer, though, Ken moved forward. "FIPS has two broad categories of self-tests: pre-operational self-tests and conditional self-tests. As the name indicates, pre-operational self-tests refer to tests that must be performed before the module is operational—which is to say, before the module outputs data.

Aster (✉)
atsec information security corporation, Austin, TX, USA
e-mail: yi.mao@atsec.com

Y. Mao (ed.), *Tasting Cryptography*, https://doi.org/10.1007/978-3-032-30243-4_30

Conditional self-tests, then, refer to tests that must be completed when certain conditions are met. Unlike pre-operational self-tests, conditional self-tests do not have to be performed at a pre-determined time."

Pre-Operational Self-Tests Ken took a bite of a piece of fried fish and spoke again: "There are three types of pre-operational self-tests: the software/firmware integrity test, bypass test, and critical functions test." Aster's thoughts had been confirmed.

"The integrity test must be performed on each software or firmware component in a module, in accordance with the requirements of software and firmware security," Ken instructed. "For example, at security level 1, a software module consisting of two binary files may perform a hash integrity test on each binary and compare each computed hash value with pre-stored values.

"A bypass mechanism in a module allows data to bypass or skip all cryptographic processing. If we think of an encryption operation, then a bypass mechanism would force the output of the encryption function to simply be the input plaintext, such that the encryption does not happen. If a bypass mechanism exists, then a pre-operational test is required for it: the test must turn on the bypass mechanism and verify that output data is not cryptographically processed; the test must also turn off the bypass mechanism and verify that output data is cryptographically processed.

"The developers of the module may also define their own pre-operational tests for functionality that they deem critical to the security of the module. These tests are referred to as critical functions tests."

Aster interrupted: "What if we have a module that is purely hardware—that is to say, it doesn't have any software or firmware components?" "Good question!" Ken replied. "If a module does not perform an integrity test, it must perform a conditional algorithm self-test before the module is operational. That is actually a good segue to the next topic!"

Conditional Self-Tests Ken introduced the new topic by outlining six types of conditional self-tests:

- Cryptographic algorithm self-test
- Pair-wise consistency self-test
- Software/firmware load self-test
- Manual entry self-test
- Bypass self-test
- Critical functions self-test

Algorithm Self-Test

Ken was eager to dive into more detail. "Let's talk about the first type of test: before any cryptographic algorithm in a module is executed, it must either be self-tested or covered by a self-test." "What does 'covered by a self-test' mean?" Aster inquired.

"FIPS allows the test of an algorithm with one key size to cover that same algorithm when used with other key sizes, for example. This means that a self-test of AES-128, if done correctly, can cover AES-192 and AES-256."

Aster interrupted again.

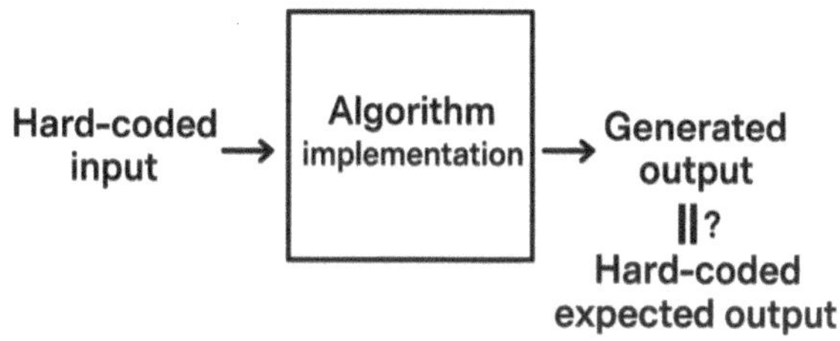

Fig. 30.1 Known-answer test

"Can you please be more specific about what you mean by 'if done correctly'?"

"There are many details that one has to be aware of when determining a self-test's coverage," Ken said with a nod. "A self-test of one AES mode can cover another mode, but the inverse may not be true. That may be the case if one mode uses both the forward and inverse cipher functions, but the other mode only uses the forward function.

"NIST published a document called the 'Implementation Guidance for FIPS 140-3 and the Cryptographic Module Validation Program.' [1] In section 10.3.A, you will find all of the rules of self-test coverage. For example, if you have an ECDSA signature verification implementation that uses the P-256, P-384, and P-521 curves, then you only have to perform a signature verification self-test with one of those curves and the algorithm with the other two curves will be covered!"

Aster had another question. "But what should a self-test actually do?"

Ken then explained that the simplest algorithm self-test method is the known-answer test, where the module stores hard-coded inputs and their corresponding outputs. The self-test would simply invoke the algorithm using the hard-coded inputs and compare the produced outputs with the hard-coded outputs (Fig. 30.1).

He bade everyone keep in mind that the self-tests of one algorithm implementation can never cover a different implementation. For example, if a module has two independent implementations—hardware (HW) and software (SW)—then we cannot claim that a HW test covers a SW test, or vice versa. The definition of implementation is more delicate than that: two instances of the identical firmware (FW) image are considered different implementations. Also, two instances of identical HW are considered different implementations!

"Let me repeat this point because it is so important," Ken said, his tone turning serious, "the coverage of an algorithm self-test is limited only to the single implementation that is tested."

Pair-Wise Consistency Self-Test "Let us now talk about the second type of self-test. After any asymmetric key pair is generated by the module, a pair-wise consistency test must be performed, and the goal of that test is to make sure that the public and private keys are consistent."

"What do you mean by 'consistent'?" Aster asked, seeking clarification.

And clarification Ken gave: "You wouldn't want to have an ECDSA public key that doesn't successfully verify signatures created by the corresponding private key!"

“So, can the consistency test in that case simply be signing a message then verifying the signature? If the signature is successfully verified, we can say the key pair is consistent,” Aster contemplated out loud.

Ken, happy with the answer, replied, “That’s right! That is exactly the required consistency test for key pairs to be used in signature algorithms such as ECDSA. Note that the signing and verifying operations must include hashing—no component signature operations are permitted in a consistency test.

“For key pairs that are intended to be used for key transport, such as RSA, you must encrypt a message with the public key and decrypt the ciphertext with the private key. Then, you would compare the calculated plaintext with the original plaintext.

“And for key pairs that are intended to be used for key encapsulation mechanisms, such as ML-KEM, you must perform an encapsulation operation to produce a shared secret and ciphertext, then perform a decapsulation operation on that ciphertext to obtain another shared secret. Then, you would compare the two shared secrets.

“For key pairs that are intended to be used for key agreement, such as ECDH, you must compute the public key from the private key and compare the computed public key with the already possessed public key.

“Finally, if it is not known at the time of generation how a key will be used—an ECC key can be used for ECDSA or ECDH, after all—any pair-wise consistency test can be performed.”

Aster clapped her hands together. “That clears that up! What is the next type of self-test that we will talk about?”

Load Self-Test Ken popped a chip in his mouth and thought for a second about what he should say.

“Let me ask you a question. If a module loads external software or firmware that comes with a signature and verification key, should the module only perform the signature verification and start to execute the loaded image?”

“Well,” Aster started, giving it some thought, “anyone can generate software and sign it. If you blindly use the externally provided verification key, then you only have an integrity test but not an authenticity check.”

“Exactly!” Ken exclaimed, pointing to her. “There is no authenticity in that case! That is why FIPS requires an authentication key to be loaded independently of and prior to the loading of the external software or firmware. In addition to the load test requirements for roles, services, and authentication, an approved algorithm must be used to successfully authenticate the externally loaded software or firmware before its execution.”

Manual Entry Self-Test “This one’s short!” Ken noted before quickly covering the next test. “Let’s talk about the manual entry test. If an SSP or key component is directly entered into a module, either an EDC must be applied to the entered value, or the module must require the operator to enter the value twice for verification—if that verification or the EDC fails, the manual entry test fails. If an EDC is used, it must be at least 16 bits in length.”

Bypass Test “Okay, now for one with more meat. We spoke earlier about the pre-operational bypass test—there are also conditional bypass tests,” Ken revealed.

"Let's define two types of services: A bypass service is one that supports bypass and does not provide cryptographic processing; a crypto service is one that provides cryptographic processing and does not support any bypass. If a module is about to switch between a bypass service and a crypto service, it must test the crypto service to ensure it works correctly and truly provides cryptographic processing. This test may be a known-answer test.

"If a module stores information that determines whether or not the bypass feature is turned on, then that information must always have an integrity value—such as an approved hash, MAC, or signature—stored in the module. If that information is about to be modified, the integrity value must be verified on the pre-existing information before any modification, and then a new integrity value must be generated on that information immediately after its modification.

"If a module can automatically alternate—based on some mechanism—between a bypass service and a crypto service, then all the crypto services must be tested after any change in that switching mechanism."

Critical Functions Self-Test "And finally, the developer of the module is free to define conditional tests for functionality that is deemed critical to the security of the module. That's it for self-tests!" Ken concluded.

Test Failures "Okay, you told us what the required tests are, but what happens if a test fails?" Aster asked pointedly.

Ken seemed to have anticipated that question. "If a pre-operational self-test fails, the module must enter an error state. To exit such an error state, the module must reinitialize or reset to repeat and pass all the pre-operational self-tests."

"And what are the restrictions on the module in the error state?"

"An error state is defined to be a state in which no cryptographic operations are possible and in which data is not output by the module through the data output or control output interfaces. There must always be an indication that an error state has been entered," Ken elaborated.

"What happens if other types of tests fail?"

Ken calmly went through the details of each type of test failing.

If a conditional algorithm self-test, pair-wise consistency self-test, or bypass self-test fails, the module must enter an error state.

If a conditional manual entry self-test or a conditional load self-test fails, it is not required for the module to enter an error state, but the module must indicate to the operator that the test failed.

If a conditional critical function self-test is verifying the integrity of data originating from outside of the cryptographic boundary, then the failure of that test does not have to trigger an error state, but the module must reject the data and return an error to the operator. If a critical function test of data produced by the module fails, the module must enter an error state.

To exit an error state caused by a conditional test failure, the module may repeat and pass the failed test, or it may reinitialize or reset. The module may also optionally exit that error state by entering a degraded mode of operation as explained in Sect. 2 on cryptographic module specification.

"At security levels 3 and 4, the module must store a log that contains at least the most recent self-test that failed. The log does not have to persist after rebooting or resetting the module. If the log contains sensitive information, it must be accessible only by authenticated operators, and the log must also be protected from unauthorized modification," Ken noted. "Remember, for any self-test, it is the module itself that must determine if it passed or failed."

Periodic Self-Tests "We only have one self-test topic left—periodic self-tests. I want to hurry because the food is starting to get cold!" Ken said, rubbing his hands together as he glanced at a dish delivered a few minutes ago.

"At security levels 1 and 2, it must be possible for the operator to initiate either all the pre-operational tests or the conditional algorithm, bypass, and critical function tests on demand. The method of initiation does not have to be a module-provided service and can simply be power-cycling.

"At security levels 3 and 4, in addition to the level 1 and 2 requirements, the module must automatically and continuously perform either all the pre-operational tests or the conditional algorithm, bypass, and critical function tests, at a specified time interval defined in the module. The time interval does not have to be specified in terms of seconds or minutes and is permitted to be defined in terms of CPU cycles, a number of cryptographic operations, or any other reasonable measure of time.

"Finally, if in the normal usage of the module, it frequently happens that power-cycling or resets occur, then the module may be exempt from the periodic self-test requirements."

And with that, Ken raised a glass. "All done! Now we can start to devour our fish and chips!" (Fig. 30.2).

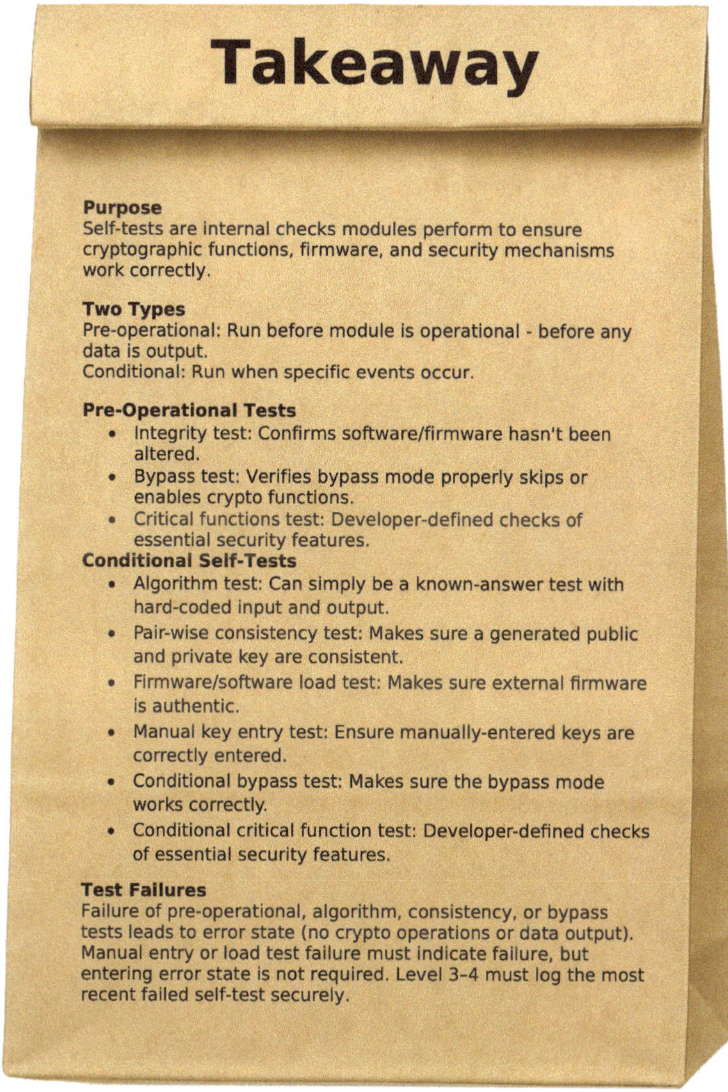

Fig. 30.2 Takeaways regarding self-tests

Reference

1. National Institute of Standards and Technology, Canadian Centre for Cyber Security (2020) Implementation Guidance for FIPS 140-3 and the Cryptographic Module Validation Program. National Institute of Standards and Technology. Available via NIST. https://csrc.nist.gov/projects/cryptographic-module-validation-program/fips-140-3-ig-announcements. Accessed 08 Dec 2025

Chapter 31
Life-Cycle Assurance

Marylène Palard

When the Austin weather called for outdoor activities, the vibrant Austin FIPS community joined the locals and visitors alike in gathering in the city's parks.

Away from the office setting, the relaxed atmosphere around sturdy picnic tables grows livelier when friends gently compete in a FIPS-themed Jeopardy game. Winners of this trivia game revolving around the ISO/IEC 19790 were traditionally awarded a trip to the renowned Torchy's Tacos joint, an Austin-weird institution.

With sizzling summer temperatures, though, our FIPS experts found reprieve from the heat in the cozy and cool atmosphere of the new staple in town: the recently popular FIPS 'n' Chips, a hotspot that is becoming as famous as the traditional park gatherings. The traditional Mexican food of the park gathering was traded for a British classic: the fish and chips—served not in a greasy paper cone, but on an oversized oval plate. What truly made FIPS 'n' Chips stand out, however, was its unique layout that invites learning and knowledge sharing. The restaurant provides modern seating areas divided into booths, and these booths are decorated with placemats in lieu of the traditional menus; these placemats were designed to reflect and promote discussions on different FIPS areas, making them perfect for facilitating FIPS Jeopardy. Booth number 11 featured life-cycle assurance themes, with each individual mat covering a different topic—one spoke about configuration management, another described finite-state machines, and the last one focused on common vulnerabilities and exposures. A reproduction of the content of each mat is provided below.

Configuration Management (CM) The Configuration Management (CM) requirements for FIPS 140 focus on the control and versioning of files throughout the lifecycle of a module. This includes the management of file interdependencies, access policies and the automation of version control tasks. CM processes are applied from

M. Palard (✉)
atsec information security corporation, Austin, TX, USA
e-mail: marylene.palard@atsec.com

Y. Mao (ed.), *Tasting Cryptography*, https://doi.org/10.1007/978-3-032-30243-4_31

the module's initial conception through secure operation and all the way to its end-of-life and destruction. The Configuration Management systems manage multiple users and repositories, parallel branches, and tags.

Scope of Configuration Management The files under configuration management include:

- the module software, firmware, or hardware code,
- the module components listed in the Bill of Materials, the Components List, and the Management Manual,
- the FIPS 140-specific documents such as the FSM and the Security Policy.

These files are subject to version control, which is managed through the vendor's CM system.

Version Control System A version control system records each change to a file (commit), including the commit date, time, author, comments, and tags. This allows any commit to be uniquely identified and retrieved at any point in time.

A common CM used for FIPS 140 module validation is Git, which operates by taking "snapshots" of the entire project each time a commit is made. These snapshots are stored as unique references, and every change is recorded with a SHA-1 hash (a 40-character hexadecimal string) that uniquely identifies each version. As explained in *Pro Git* Chap. 1.3, Git calculates the SHA-1 hash based on the contents of a file or directory, ensuring that every version is identified by the actual content, not just the file name. [1]

Tagging and Document Versioning Authenticated users with specific permissions are granted the ability to tag particular revisions in the Git repository; these tags serve to link specific commits to released versions of documents or code. The tags in Git allow for an exact match between the source code and its corresponding version of the documentation.

User Permissions and Access Control The list of users and their respective permissions (e.g., who can tag, commit, or access certain repositories) is managed by the Git master, ensuring that only authorized personnel can make changes to the code or documentation, and that the CM system remains secure and controlled.

Finite State Machine (FSM) The Finite State Machine (FSM)—also known as a Finite State Model—is a document provided by the vendor to describe the different module states, the possible transitions between those states, and the conditions that trigger each transition. The document details the data inputs and control inputs that cause the transition, as well as data outputs and the status resulting from the transitions.

The FSM usually contains a diagram (see Fig. 31.1) that represents the different states, with arrows indicating the possible transitions between them.

Additionally, a table is used to list the transitions from each state, providing a clear mapping of the module's state flow.

The CST Lab tester uses the FSM to map the module's states to the specific states required by the ISO/IEC 19790, which include:

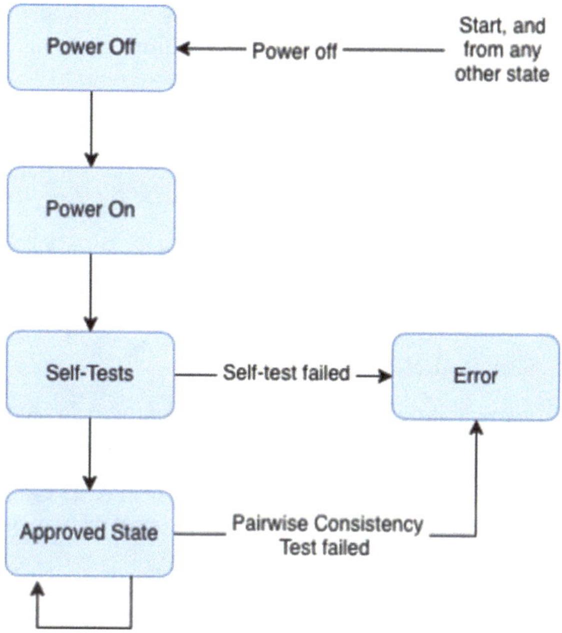

Fig. 31.1 Finite state model diagram

- Power-on/off State
- Self-tests State
- General Initialization State
- CST entry State
- Crypto Officer State
- Approved State
- Error State

The FSM guides the tester, in collaboration with the vendor, in creating the module's Security Policy. For example, the tester uses the FSM to identify the Error State, the conditions that lead to this state, and the criteria for transitioning out of Error State. Similarly, the tester identifies that the Approved State can only be entered after the self-tests have been executed successfully.

The information above serves as a reference to create Sect. 10 of the Security Policy.

Common Vulnerabilities and Exposures (CVEs) To help communicate and track security issues of software and hardware components a standard list of cybersecurity weakness and fixes is maintained by the CVE™ Program.

In addition to the government CVE website, vendors may maintain their own CVE databases. These may be publicly accessible and periodically updated, or restricted to authorized customers, depending on the vendor's disclosure policy.

To prevent exploitation, vendors may choose to delay public disclosure of CVEs until mitigations or patches have been developed and implemented, which reduces the risk of attackers using vulnerability details to gain unauthorized access, modify data, or compromise sensitive information.

Each CVE is assigned a severity score on a scale of 0 to 10, with higher scores representing more critical vulnerabilities.

The CVEs are classified into one of two categories: non-security-relevant CVEs and security-relevant CVEs.

Non–Security-Relevant CVEs are:

- determined to have no impact on the cryptographic module.
- supported by the scope definition in the module's Security Policy—Administrative Guidance section.

Security-Relevant CVEs are:

- vulnerabilities that could impact the module's security assurance.
- cases where the vendor must provide appropriate mitigations.

Furthermore, for security-relevant CVEs, a revalidation scenario to obtain an updated certificate (keeping the same sunset date) may be required, involving either:

- Modifications to the module specifications to address the CVEs, or
- Code updates to eliminate the vulnerabilities in the revised version of the module. Code updates will trigger regression testing.

The list of CVEs associated with a cryptographic module evolves continuously, from the time the module is tested by the CST lab through its certification and validation and throughout its five-year certificate validity period. Both the CST laboratory and the vendor share responsibility for managing CVEs during this lifecycle. During the Implementation Under Test (IUT) phase, the CST lab must review and address known CVEs, while the vendor is responsible for providing updated CVE information to the CST lab throughout all Module Implementation Phases (MIP) and up until the module's certificate sunset date.

Under FIPS 140–2, vendors could request revalidation of an existing certified module to apply security-relevant updates and mitigate CVEs. However, with the transition to FIPS 140–3, the requirements for CVE management have become more rigorous.

Implementation Guidance (IG) 11.A—"CVE Management" introduces specific criteria for identifying, reviewing, and reporting CVEs associated with a module. Based on the AS11.38 requirements, the CVE list is documented and reviewed by the CST lab. The findings are assessed in TE11.38.03.

Whether you're here for the FIPS Jeopardy at the park or you've found your way to the booth number 11 at the FIPS 'n' Chips restaurant, one thing's for sure: Austin has no limit for crypto security exploration. It's about enjoying the outdoors and exchanging ideas while strengthening the security of the cryptographic module (Fig. 31.2).

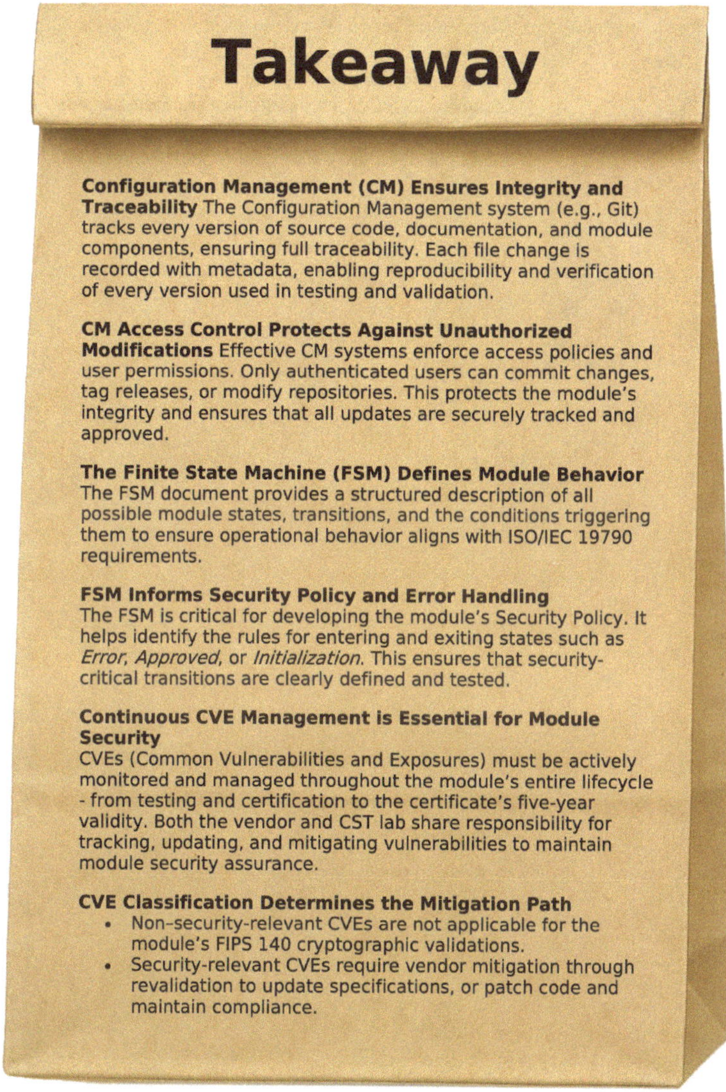

Fig. 31.2 Takeaways regarding life-cycle assurance

Reference

1. Chacon S, Straub B (2014) Pro Git, 2nd edn. Apress, New York

Marylène Palard Marylène joined atsec information security corporation in March 2018 as a FIPS tester. With a PhD in Materials Science and a professional background in chip manufacturing at ST Microelectronics (Rousset, France) and at the University of Texas at Austin (USA), she initially contributed to the physical security testing of modules.

Chapter 32
Implementation Guidance and Request for Guidance

Swapneela Unkule

Alice had been with atsec only a short time, and the learning curve still felt steep. Over the past few days, she had immersed herself in training materials on FIPS validation, but the deeper she went, the more she realized many requirements could be interpreted in different ways. The standards were dense, and without a guide it was hard to know how to translate each statement into real validation work.

That afternoon, she walked into a scheduled onboarding session with Neela, her manager and the person leading her training on cryptographic module validations; Neela had good track record with translating dense requirements into clear, practical steps. Alice had been looking forward to this meeting all morning.

"Neela, thanks for taking the time," Alice said as she settled in, sounding a little relieved. "I'm really glad we could talk."

Neela smiled. "Of course. Welcome aboard, Alice. How are you finding the FIPS material so far?"

Alice hesitated, then laughed softly. "Honestly? It's a lot. FIPS validation comes with so many rules, and sometimes it feels like the same requirement could mean different things depending on the module. I can follow the text, but I'm not always confident I'm interpreting it the way the CMVP expects."

"That's completely normal at the start," Neela said. "It's a technical standard, but it's also a program with years of interpretive history behind it. What's on your mind?"

Alice took a breath, grateful for the opening. "Let me explain where I'm stuck. I've been reading ISO/IEC 19790 and the test assertions in ISO/IEC 24759, but it still feels abstract. I have some technical background in both hardware and software

S. Unkule (✉)
atsec information security corporation, Austin, TX, USA
e-mail: swapneela.unkule@atsec.com

Y. Mao (ed.), *Tasting Cryptography*, https://doi.org/10.1007/978-3-032-30243-4_32

products, but I'm overwhelmed because the requirements seem to apply differently depending on the type of module."

She pulled up a quick list she'd been refining in her notes. "I have questions like these, for example:

1. For some algorithms, if software uses Intel's AES-NI instructions, do those need to be included in the boundary, given that we obviously don't have source code for that implementation?
2. For self-tests, do I test every mode and key size for an algorithm, or is a representative test enough?
3. How should CVEs be handled, especially if they are discovered after submission?
4. And is algorithm testing by itself enough to confirm an implementation is actually correct?

I could go on and on," she admitted, half-apologetic.

Neela nodded, not surprised. "Those are exactly the kinds of questions people run into on their first validation. And the best way to navigate them isn't by guessing against the raw standards."

Alice leaned forward. "That's what I was hoping you'd say. What should I be using as my compass here?"

"What you need is the FIPS Implementation Guidance," Neela replied. "Most people just call it the IG."

"IG… okay," Alice said. "I've heard the term, but I'm not sure I really understand what it gives me beyond the standards. Can you explain what it contains?"

"Sure," Neela said. "Think of the IG as the official program guidance from the CMVP. It clarifies how the test requirements in ISO/IEC 24759 should be interpreted, and it aligns those clarifications with the FIPS 140-3 Derived Test Requirements that labs actually use during testing. The IG is basically where the CMVP records its answers to real questions vendors and labs have raised over time."

She continued, keeping her explanation structured in a way that felt like training rather than lecturing. "ISO/IEC 19790 is divided into twelve requirement areas. The IG mirrors that structure: each IG section corresponds to one of those areas. Inside each section, guidance is grouped by subject. For each subject you'll see the issue date, the relevant assertions and test requirements, and what the vendor is expected to do. Then there's a problem statement or question, followed by the CMVP's resolution and any related notes. That resolution is the practical 'how to apply this' part."

Alice nodded slowly, but her expression still showed uncertainty. "I get the structure. I'm just not seeing yet how that directly answers the kinds of questions I'm asking."

Neela smiled. "Let's reframe it with a metaphor; it usually helps. Imagine you're opening a new restaurant. The official rulebook has all the regulations you must obey:

health codes, fire safety, staffing rules, what counts as approved ingredients, how to label allergens, the works. It's comprehensive, but also written in formal language."

Alice chuckled. "That already sounds familiar."

"Exactly," Neela said. "Now imagine a living, community-maintained guidebook that restaurant owners rely on. It explains the tricky parts of those rules in plain terms, how inspectors interpret them in real life, what evidence people typically show, and how to handle edge cases like shared kitchens or pre-made sauces. That's your IG."

She let the analogy land, then tied it back to validation. "The standards tell you what must be done; the IG tells you how to interpret and apply it when real-world design and implementation questions pop up, like whether a kitchen you rely on counts as part of your restaurant, or whether a pre-built appliance changes how you certify your setup. It's the evolving FAQ and example set that makes validations consistent and predictable."

Alice looked genuinely intrigued now. "Okay, that comparison actually makes a lot of sense. So, the IG should ideally be followed by the vendors as they prepare for validation, and it's also a way to verify that the module is implemented in the expected manner. Still, how does it connect back to those specific questions I raised earlier?"

Neela nodded, ready to walk her through it step by step. "Great question. Let's start with the IG sections that map directly to each of those scenarios.

"The most important section to start with is Sect. 2, Module Specification—think of it as designing the restaurant blueprint. This is where one defines the restaurant boundary: what's inside the kitchen and dining area, what's outside, what equipment counts as part of the restaurant, what dishes you officially serve, and which items are 'specials' versus side offerings you don't advertise. In validation terms, it's the boundary, inventory, and claimed services. Section 2 is about getting the module's identity and scope right: boundary, embodiment, algorithm sourcing/binding, treatment of accelerators and subcomponents, and unambiguous documentation of approved vs. non-approved behavior.

"Take your first question about Intel AES-NI. That's like using pre-made kitchen equipment. It's perfectly acceptable, as long as you document it correctly and test against the guidance. Think of a branded air conditioner installed in a restaurant: you don't need to understand the compressor's internal design, but you do need to ensure it meets energy and safety standards, and that you're using a model approved for commercial use.

"IG 2.3.C is the relevant guidance here. It lists processor technologies that provide Processor Algorithm Acceleration or Processor Algorithm Implementation—PAA and PAI for short, respectively—for cryptographic algorithms. If a module supports an algorithm either natively in software/firmware or via a supported PAA/PAI capability, you can define the embodiment as software or firmware. If the software/firmware supports the algorithm only by relying on PAA/PAI, then the module is defined as a hybrid software or hybrid firmware embodiment. In that hybrid case, the processor capability is treated as part of the boundary.

"Using the metaphor: a built-in air conditioner permanently installed in a restaurant is inside the boundary; a portable unit you bring in only when needed is more like an external accelerator you rely on temporarily in addition to the default use of ceiling fans or opening the windows to provide natural air."

Neela also went on to explain that IG Sect. 2 also covers other important aspects, such as:

- IG 2.3.A Binding algorithm certificates to the module: Explains how CAVP algorithm validation certificates are associated ("bound") to a FIPS module certificate, including matching versions, operational environments, and ensuring the module's claimed algorithms map correctly to tested implementations.
- IG 2.3.B: Provides rules for when cryptographic functionality that lives inside a chip (or sub-component of a chip) can be treated as part of the module, and how boundaries/claims should be documented in those cases.
- IG 2.3.D Excluded components: Lets vendors exclude certain non-security-relevant components from testing scope, but requires that exclusions be justified, documented, and still treated as boundary-relevant for change control (changes may trigger revalidation).
- IG 2.4.A Non-approved security functions: Defines what counts as a non-approved function or mode, how such functions may coexist with approved ones, and how they must be described so users understand when they are/aren't in an approved mode.
- IG 2.4.B Tracking the Component Validation List: Explains expectations for using CMVP's Component Validation List (CVL): how to reference validated components correctly and keep those references current in the security policy and evidence.
- IG 2.4.C Approved security service indicator: Requires a clear method (API flag, status call, mode bit, etc.) for indicating to operators whether a service is being used in an approved vs. non-approved manner, and how that indicator must be evidenced.

Section 3 (Interfaces) This section is basically how people and food move in and out. It corresponds to entrances, service windows, delivery points, staff-only doors, and internal pass-throughs between the kitchen and dining room. The guidance ensures every pathway is clearly defined and that sensitive items, like cash or secret recipes, don't accidentally leave through the wrong door.

For now, this section includes IG 3.4.A, which explains how to implement and test trusted channels across module boundaries, what qualifies as a trusted path, and what evidence labs expect.

Section 4 (Roles, Services, Authentication), "Job Titles, Assigned Duties, and Who's Allowed to Do What" Think of this as the restaurant's HR chart: host, chef, sous-chef, waiter, manager, cleaner. Roles are job titles; services are what each role is permitted to do (the chef can cook, the manager can open the safe, the waiter can serve but cannot change recipes). Authentication is like employee badges or keys: at higher security levels, you need stronger proof that someone really is the chef before they're allowed into the kitchen.

Sometimes a small, family-owned restaurant operates on trust alone, similar to a Level 1 module, where authentication is not required because everyone is already implicitly trusted and has equal access. At any security level, some services may not require explicit authentication because they do not create, disclose, modify, substitute, access, or use secret information. In a restaurant, these are default tasks any employee can do without special authorization, like greeting guests or cleaning the dining area.

IG 4.1.A explains such services: those that do not require an operator to assume an authorized role and therefore do not need authentication at any level. Examples include Show Status, Show Version, and Self-Tests, or cryptographic services such as hashing, signature verification, and random number generation.

Overall, this section refines how operators, roles, and services are modeled and tested. The guidance covers authorized role sets, mapping services to roles, authentication strength by security level (including multi-operator authentication), and how vendors must manage and document replacement of default authentication data to ensure proper authorization in real deployments.

Section 5 (Software/Firmware Security), "Keeping Recipes Locked and Unchanged" This section ensures that recipes (i.e., the module's code/firmware) cannot be altered secretly. In restaurant terms, you might store recipes in a safe, seal them with the head chef's stamp, or verify a tamper seal each morning. If someone tries to slip in a fake recipe, the kitchen should detect it immediately and refuse to use it. The guidance clarifies which "locks and checks" are considered strong enough.

Some recipes might be permanently embedded, like a master recipe engraved into a cookbook that cannot be edited (such as the chef's brain). As long as the "cookbook" is truly non-reconfigurable and stable over time, integrity testing may not be required.

IG 5.A addresses this concept directly: it defines non-reconfigurable memory and lists acceptable alternative integrity approaches, including evidence that the memory technology will not change or degrade for a specified number of years after manufacture.

Section 6 (Operational Environment), "Where the Restaurant Operates" This is choosing the neighborhood and conditions under which a restaurant is allowed to run. Are you in a mall food court, a standalone building, or operating inside a hotel? Can people rearrange the kitchen freely, or is it fixed? The guidance ensures the restaurant only operates in environments that won't undermine food safety, like not allowing random strangers to change the stove settings.

This section explains how operational environments (OEs) are defined and constrained. It provides rules for modifiable vs. non-modifiable OEs, OS and hypervisor responsibilities, audit/event logging expectations, and how vendors demonstrate that validated configurations match real-world platforms without allowing uncontrolled changes that could weaken the module.

Section 7 (Physical Security), "Real-World Protection of the Building" This is what you can see: door locks, security cameras, tamper-evident seals on the pantry, fences around back entrances, and restricted staff-only areas. Higher security levels mean stronger protections, like alarms if someone tries to pry open a safe or enter the kitchen after hours.

Section 7 provides detailed test and documentation guidance for physical protections at each security level. It describes when prior physical test evidence may be reused, what qualifies as an acceptable tamper-evident seal and test method, and how coatings, enclosures, and other physical mechanisms are evaluated for resistance to physical compromise.

Section 9 (SSP Management), "Handling the Most Precious Ingredients and Keys" Here, SSPs are the "crown jewels": secret spices, master recipes, the safe combination, the fridge key. This section explains how you generate SSPs, store them, hand them to the right people safely, use them without leakage, and destroy old ones properly, like shredding outdated recipe pages instead of tossing them in the trash.

Section 9 interprets how keys and other SSPs are generated, entered, output, stored, used, and destroyed. Guidance covers entropy-source caveats and SP 800-90B alignment, approved and non-approved SSP establishment methods, acceptable algorithms for protecting stored SSPs, and practical zeroization requirements (including OTP memory handling and completion indicators).

Section 10 (Self-Tests), "Taste Tests and Opening Checks" Before opening every day, restaurants do pre-operational checks: taste a sample, test the oven, make sure the fridge is cold, and confirm the POS system works. During the day, if something unusual happens, like a power flicker, you re-check critical equipment. This section ensures the restaurant proves it is still safe to operate, rather than assuming everything is fine.

Section 10 clarifies required power-up, pre-operational, conditional, and periodic self-tests. It specifies coverage expectations (including embedded algorithms), how manual-entry and bypass tests are applied, requirements for error logging and error states, and how reloading or replacing software/firmware affects which self-tests are triggered.

IG 10.3.A provides algorithm-specific CAST guidance: for example, restrictions for self-testing particular AES modes (encryption vs. decryption), expectations for

PQC self-tests, and which pairwise-consistency tests to perform based on key usage. This guidance directly answers the question posed earlier about self-tests.

Section 11 (Life-Cycle Assurance), "Running the Restaurant Responsibly Over Time" After opening, you keep watching for problems. If a supplier announces, "this batch of eggs might be contaminated" (analogous to a software CVE), you must assess impact, fix it if needed, and inform inspectors when it affects safety posture. This is the maintenance and recall-response plan.

IG 11.A addresses CVE handling, the third question asked. It defines responsibilities for both the module vendor and the CST Laboratory for CVEs discovered during and after FIPS 140–3 validations. The focus is on maintaining trust over time: monitoring, assessing, and disclosing relevant CVEs; determining when updates require revalidation or impact analysis; and how labs and CMVP treat ongoing maintenance within the validation lifecycle.

Section 12 (Mitigation of Other Attacks), "Extra Safety Tricks for Unusual Threats" Some threats don't fit neatly into standard categories. Maybe you're defending against staff bribery, a competitor's unusual sabotage attempt, or a novel kind of food fraud. This section is the "other threats" bucket: if you claim special mitigations, you must clearly explain and prove them.

Section 12 explains how vendors may claim mitigations not fully covered elsewhere (including certain operational or non-invasive attacks). It defines required evidence and how testing assesses whether the protections are real, repeatable, and appropriate to the claimed security level.

Before we move on to the annexes, I want to mention IG 1.A, which was introduced in 2024. Section 1 was empty until the CMVP identified the need to address Binding and Embedding Cryptographic Modules.

If we map this to the restaurant metaphor, it's about declaring: "Are you using someone else's kitchen, or bringing your own?"

This guidance is about relationships between restaurants. Sometimes one can embed another kitchen inside their own, like renting a full sushi bar that operates within the restaurant. Other times you are bound to another restaurant's kitchen next door; you don't own it, but you rely on it to serve part of the menu. The guidance explains how to be transparent about these relationships: what you can "inherit" from the other kitchen's safety inspection, and what the vendor still must demonstrate on their own.

IG 1.A clarifies how validated modules relate to other validated modules. It defines when a module depends on another module (bound) versus when it contains another module entirely within its boundary (embedded). It also explains what evidence may be reused and how certificates, entropy sources, roles/services, and Security Policy statements must reflect these relationships.

Annex C (Approved Security Functions), "Core Ingredients You're Allowed to Use" Annex C is the list of approved ingredients and safe cooking methods. If you claim a dish is "Approved," it must be made only from these trusted ingredients.

To use a security function in an approved manner, it must, at minimum:

- undergo algorithm testing and receive an algorithm certificate, and
- perform the required self-tests.

Some algorithms also have additional usage constraints, which is relevant to the fourth question posed. Annex C provides guidance on approved algorithms and their correct use under FIPS 140–3, aligned with SP 800-140C and CAVP rules. It covers edge cases such as non-approved elliptic curves, hash/HMAC truncation and testing expectations, RSA parameter transitions, legacy algorithm handling, and requirements for newer schemes (for example, SP 800–208).

For instance, in AES-XTS mode, if an implementation generates keys such that $Key_1 = Key_2$, the mode becomes vulnerable to chosen-ciphertext attacks. Annex C.I therefore requires the module to explicitly check that $Key_1 \neq Key_2$, regardless of how the keys are obtained.

Similarly, for AES-GCM, SP 800-38D requires that the probability of reusing the same IV with the same key across distinct inputs be no greater than 2^{-32}. Annex C.H addresses this by defining five major compliance scenarios:

- Scenario 1: Protocol-specific use (e.g., TLS, IPsec, SSH, MACsec)
- Scenario 2: Randomly generated IVs
- Scenario 3: Deterministic IVs
- Scenario 4: Vendor-defined approaches with proof of compliance to SP 800-38D IV-generation requirements
- Scenario 5: Open for vendors to present their own proof of compliance to SP 800-38D IV generation requirements for any protocol not listed in Scenario 1

Annex D (Approved SSP Generation & Establishment), "The Actual Dishes You Can Cook from those Ingredients" If Annex C is ingredients, Annex D is recipes and dishes. It explains which cooking processes are acceptable for producing secure dishes (keys), how strong they are, and what combinations are allowed.

Annex D interprets approved methods for generating or establishing SSPs (keys and keying material) per SP 800-140D. It clarifies acceptable protocols and their strength claims, handling of industry protocols and curve/group choices, vendor-affirmation paths (e.g., SP 800–133), post-processing limits, entropy estimation rules, DRBG parameter constraints, KDF usage, and modern methods such as KEM-based approaches.

Annex E (Approved Authentication Mechanisms), "Checking Employee Registration and Badges" This annex is the inspection guide for staff identity checks: what kinds of badges, passwords, or multi-factor checks count, and how strict they must be at each security level. Annex E explains which authentication mechanisms are approved for operator access and how they map to FIPS 140–3 levels. It also aligns expectations with concepts from SP 800-63B, so identity- and role-based authentication is implemented and tested consistently.

The "History and Updates" Sections—Withdrawn Guidance, "Old Restaurant Rules that don't Apply Anymore" These are retired notes and rules that were replaced or updated. They are kept only for traceability, but you must follow the current rules instead. This part lists IG items that are no longer active (superseded, moved, or deprecated) and clearly directs vendors to the replacement guidance (W.1, W.2, W.3, etc.).

Change Summary, "What Changed in the Latest Inspector Update" This is essentially the patch notes. It tells restaurant owners: "Here are the newest clarifications or edits since the last update, so check whether the setup needs to change." The Change Summary highlights newly introduced IG items and modifications to existing guidance, helping labs and vendors quickly identify deltas that could affect ongoing submissions or maintenance.

Mapping FIPS 140–2 to 140–3, "How the Old Rulebook Maps to the New One" This is a translation chart for restaurants migrating from an older law. It shows where legacy FIPS 140–2 guidance maps into the FIPS 140–3 structure and highlights where expectations became stricter or materially different. It helps vendors understand which older interpretive rules still apply and where new evidence or design work is required.

By the time they reached the end of the discussion, Alice sat back as if she'd just finished a fast-paced workshop. She looked impressed, and a little amused by how much ground they'd covered.

"Wow," she said, shaking her head slightly, "that felt like a crash course on the Implementation Guidance. I still have one question."

Neela nodded encouragingly. "Go ahead."

Alice leaned forward. "What if a module has a unique situation that isn't covered by any of the IGs? Is there a way to ask about it?"

"There is," Neela replied. "That's exactly what an RFG proposal is for."

"RFG?" Alice echoed. "What does that stand for?"

"It stands for Request for Guidance," Neela explained. "It's the formal way to ask the CMVP to clarify a testing or program question when the existing IG doesn't address a specific scenario. Vendors submit it in the RFG format defined in the FIPS 140-3 Management Manual; the CMVP reviews the request and may come back with follow-up questions."

She added, "When you submit an RFG, you can mark it as proprietary—meaning only CMVP sees it—or non-proprietary, which allows it to be shared with the wider

FIPS community. Non-proprietary RFGs are helpful because they improve collaboration, transparency, and consistency. The question and the CMVP resolution can be published so others benefit from the guidance too."

Alice nodded, clearly relieved to know there was a path for edge cases. "Thanks a lot, Neela. This was really helpful; it gave me a clear overview of everything I learned today." She smiled (Fig. 32.1).

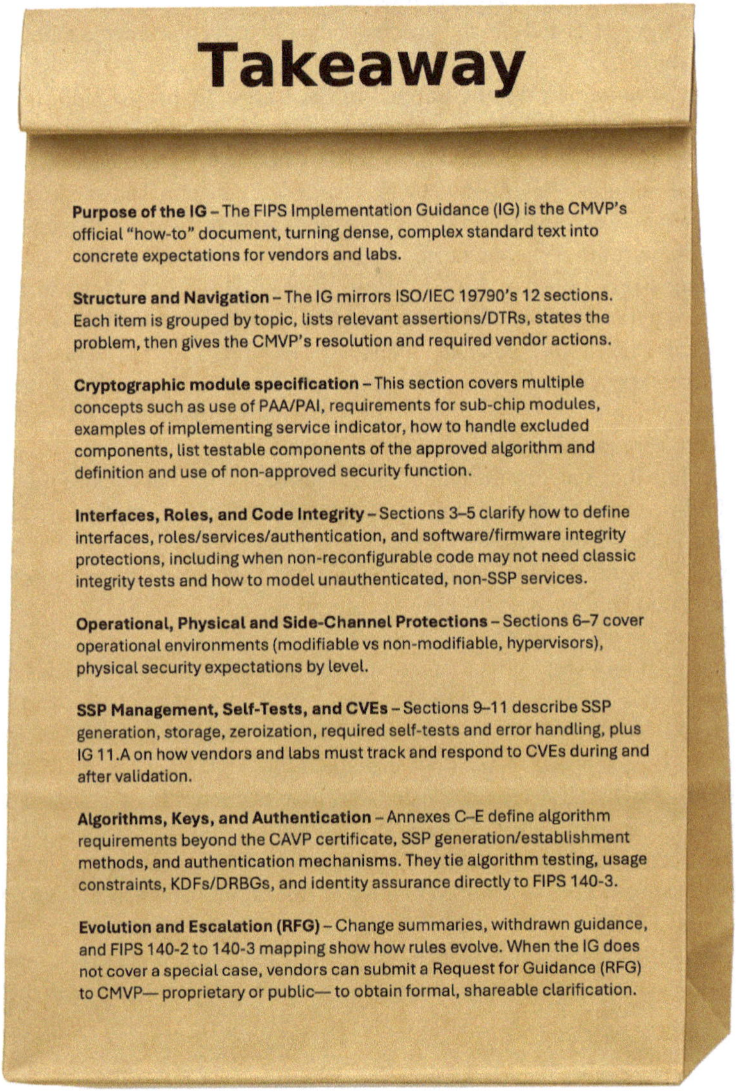

Fig. 32.1 Takeaways regarding IG and RFG

Swapneela Unkule Swapneela is the CST lab manager for atsec's FIPS laboratory and has an MS in computer science. Most of her cryptography experience is hands on as part of FIPS validation projects for the last 12 years at atsec, starting with algorithm testing, code review, functional testing to now managing the project and design analysis for new technology to fit them in the FIPS field.

Chapter 33
What is New in ISO/IEC 19790:2025

Marcos Portnoi

It has been quite some time since Aster remembered jogging along Mueller lakeside, trying to avoid bees while admiring flying red-winged blackbirds. She had assumed back then the day was going to be simple, until a phone call from the bank revealed she had fallen victim of identity theft.

All that had been resolved, Aster smiled to herself as she recalled. Her routine resumed, and the event pushed her to become even more involved in information security. Her peers considered her a very resourceful expert, and particularly in ISO 19790 and ISO 27459. That opinion was not shared by Aster herself, who always doubted her knowledge was indeed that precise. There was so much to learn!

Anyway, Aster thought, there is something else of importance at this moment. She wanted to focus on a good cup of coffee from FIPS 'n' Chips and relax for a few moments. At the same time, she wanted to exchange some words with her good friend Tim, who was the manager of FIPS 'n' Chips for the past year. Tim had commented that the restaurant administration wanted to overhaul the menu, and Aster wanted to know how that plan was going. After a few sips of coffee, because a day does not move before coffee.

She arrived at FIPS 'n' Chips to the image of an uncharacteristically distraught Tim, shuffling through a batch of papers.

Perhaps incautiously, Aster bypassed her cup of coffee and greeted Tim.

"Tim! Hello. Came to have some coffee… what is going on? You seem… annoyed."

Tim looked at her, an expression of pain in his face. "Hello, Aster, what a nice surprise. I'm sorry… It is this new menu thing, I'm sure you remember. It is finally ready."

"Well, that is… great?" Aster replied in doubt.

M. Portnoi (✉)
atsec information security corporation, Austin, TX, USA
e-mail: marcos.portnoi@atsec.com

Y. Mao (ed.), *Tasting Cryptography*, https://doi.org/10.1007/978-3-032-30243-4_33

"The menu is fine, but… the customers all have been asking what exactly has changed. And they seem to want a detailed list. It takes time to explain, and it is delaying our service," explained Tim.

A thought occurred to Aster as she heard her friend's explanation, how so very interestingly worded and complete. An atypical way of speaking, as if… narrated in a book.

Aster quickly dismissed that thought.

"Are there that many differences in the menu?" she asked, showing interest.

Tim looked at her. "It is a few ingredients here and there, another way of describing the dish. We dropped some dishes that were… old, and added new ones to go with the trends. It is not that different, but for some very weird reason our customers want a kind of large table comparing the old and the new menu. Isn't that odd? Who does that?" Tim continued looking at his stack of papers with a frown.

"Indeed, who does that…" Aster wondered while contemplating her work. She turned to the bartender and asked for a cup of cappuccino. Large. She would probably be having two of those.

"One thing we have been testing at my job," Aster directed at Tim, while looking at her steaming cappuccino, "is using some of those AI tools. They are pretty good at summarizing content, pinpointing information. They can in fact help create the things you are looking for, those tables of differences."

Tim immediately froze. He focused his gaze at some undefined point, then widened his eyes and looked at Aster, a large smile on his face.

"This is absolutely a fantastic idea! We could… we could have these tables prepared, give them out to customers if they want, or together with the menu… yes!"

Aster was genuinely surprised, as it did not seem to be that good of a suggestion.

Tim continued, without waiting for a response. "Then it is settled. Why don't you do this AI thing of yours with our menu. The two versions are here." Tim handed her two stacks of papers. "You do this. I will tell the boss we hired you to do this, we will settle after. That is great!"

And with that, Tim vanished through the kitchen door.

"Tim, I… I did not mean to…" Aster turned to her cappuccino, scowling as she found herself alone. With the bartender.

Well, doing a table of comparison between the two menus was not on her task list this morning. She just did not have the time. As she prepared to call for Tim and tell him she could not take this task on… she ruminated on the idea a bit more.

"It could be a good exercise," she mused. Yeah, why not.

Cryptographic Module Specification Arriving at her desk, Aster considered her differential analysis of the two menus. First, she had to pick an AI tool to perform the job. She settled for an AI tool called Aldrin that she was testing for her work. She then studied both menu versions to have a good idea of the differences and updates, so that she could validate the results of Aldrin with confidence.

She opened the Aldrin window and thought about how to formulate a proper question. A prompt, in the AI language model parlance.

As soon as the Aldrin window opened, text began to populate the conversation pane.

"Hello, Aster. I can help you with many tasks, such as research, calendar appointments and scheduling, travel arrangements, among others. I see I already have access to some of your services and apps, and I can help you by accessing those apps directly. What can I do for you today?"

Aster typed. "Can you prepare a list of differences between two documents? I have an old document and a new version of the same document; I want to see the differences between them."

Three dots briefly appeared before the screen updated.

"Of course. Simply point me to the documents through a link to each document in a webpage. Or indicate where the documents are stored in a local or shared directory. Or upload the documents to me and I will work on pointing the differences."

Wow. Ok, thought Aster. "I will upload the documents to you, then."

"Sure. Waiting for you to upload the documents. I will initiate the comparison as soon as I receive the two documents."

Seeing an upload button on the window, Aster proceeded to upload the old, and the new versions of the menu. Then, she typed, "The first document is named ISO19790:2012. The updated version of that document is named ISO19790:2025. Please create a list of differences."

Aldrin replied after the three dots appeared and disappeared. "Yes, I will start the analysis now."

The three dots appeared again. After roughly 40 s, the response appeared, wherein Aldrin started listing pointed differences in a bullet list format. There were about 9 bullet items on the list.

Aster read through the items. A couple of items in the list were not entirely correct. Overall, the differences were there, but not in the level of detail she first envisioned. It also contained information that was not relevant to the comparison.

She thought a bit more and then typed.

"Given the two documents, please generate a list of differences between them. Only include actual differences. Be detailed."

A new message from Aldrin promptly appeared. "Absolutely! I will again analyze the documents and generate a detailed list of differences between them. I will only include differences between the documents in my response."

That is better, thought Aster.

One minute later, Aster was presented with a longer list happily announced by Aldrin.

"I have finished the comparison between the two versions of the document. I generated a list of the differences between those two documents, bringing detailed information. I can further format this list into a table or comma-separated values if you want."

Aster started reading the list. Indeed, it had more details, yet the overall contents were still high level… she considered, if customers are so keen in knowing the differences between the two menus, let's then give them that. A very thorough comparison: per section, per course, each dish if different.

Aster had to be more precise in her prompt.

"Aldrin, please redo the comparison between the old and the new, updated version of the documents. Compare only the first section of the documents, titled 'Cryptographic Module Specification.' Produce a detailed comparison and only include the differences."

Aldrin did not lose a beat as the screen updated. "Of course. I will construct a detailed list of differences between the old and the new version of the documents for section 'Cryptographic Module Specification' only."

After approximately one and a half minutes, Aster was presented with a list comprising only the section she chose. The comparisons were sound, with one or two exceptions. Now Aster knew what to do.

"Please repeat the task, but now format the results into a table. Make the table 3 columns: first column, indicate the topic of the difference; second column, indicate what the old document says about the topic; third column, show what the updated document brings about the topic."

"I will generate a detailed table of differences between the old and the updated document. The table will contain 3 columns, wherein the first column indicates the item that is found different, the second column shows the contents of the old document, and the third column shows the updated contents," replied Aldrin.

Aster reviewed the produced table (Table 33.1), removed a few redundancies and incorrections. The final table became as such.

Cryptographic Module Interfaces Aster was pleased with the results of the first table after her corrections. Excited, she quickly attempted the second table.

She then typed the following prompt. "Aldrin, repeat the same procedure, but now for section 'Cryptographic Module Interfaces.' Include only this section in the comparison table and maintain the same formatting."

Aldrin answered. "Ok. I will generate a detailed table of comparison for section 'Cryptographic Module Interfaces,' including only the differences between the documents you uploaded. I will maintain the same style and formatting as the last table I generated per your request."

And again, after roughly two minutes, Aldrin presented their table of differences. Aster analyzed the table and removed now a few more entries that stated differences when there were none, and one incorrect detail. (Table 33.2).

Aster was in a good mood and decided to become more conversational.

"Thank you, Aldrin. Good job."

"You are very welcome, Aster. It was my pleasure. What else can I do for you?"

Aster closed the Aldrin app window and moved to other tasks.

Roles, Services, and Authentication Aster did not return to the Aldrin work the day before. So, she decided to begin the day with it, after the necessary coffee. She opened the app window and was greeted by Aldrin.

"Good morning, Aster. I hope you are having a productive day. How may I assist you?"

She wanted to play along. "Good morning, Aldrin. I have two documents in my local directory to which you have access. One is ISO 19790:2012, and the other one is an updated version of the first called ISO 19790:2025. Please generated a detailed

Table 33.1 Differences regarding cryptographic module specifications

Feature/ aspect	ISO/IEC 19,790:2012	ISO/IEC 19,790:2025
Section title	Section 7.2.4 modes of operations	Section 7.2.4 module operations. The title of the subclause has been changed
Service indicator	All services must provide an indicator when the services utilize an approved cryptographic algorithm, security function or process in an approved manner	Each service shall provide an output indicator *upon completion* of the service to indicate whether the service executed an approved security function or process, *or not* If a singular service provides different outcomes based on the services configurable parameter setting, the output indicator in AS02.22 should reflect the particular parameter setting utilized upon the services execution Comments: Note that this version explicitly says that the service indicator shall indicate upon completion of the service. In addition, the "or not" may be interpreted as that a service in the module must always indicate that it is either operating as approved, or not as approved. Simply not indicating anything may be insufficient
Degraded operation	The mechanism or function that failed shall be isolated	The error state may either impact the full module or be localized to the mechanism or process that was isolated. Where a localized error is used, it shall be shown that the target error cannot impact other approved services running outside the isolated mechanism or process The cryptographic module shall remain in degraded operation until the cryptographic module has repeated pre-operational test self-tests covering either the *entire module* or the *failed isolated* mechanisms and processes Comments: In this version, it is possible to demonstrate that a subset of pre-operational self-tests are sufficient to bring the module out of the degraded operation, thus avoiding running the entire set of pre-operational self-tests The "localized error state" concept introduced in this version may be summarized as such: • Scope of Impact: An error state may either affect the full cryptographic module or be localized to the mechanism or process that has failed and been isolated • Isolation Requirement: When a localized error is utilized, the failing mechanism or process must be isolated. The vendor's design must ensure that any failure from these isolated mechanisms, processes, and components cannot interfere with or compromise the approved operation of the cryptographic module • Non-Impact on Other Services: It must be demonstrated that the targeted localized error cannot impact other approved services running outside the isolated mechanism or process

Table 33.2 Differences regarding cryptographic module interfaces

Feature/aspect	ISO/IEC 19,790:2012	ISO/IEC 19,790:2025
Section 7.3: Cryptographic module interfaces		
New interface	N/A	Maintenance interface. All physical and logical interfaces to the module, which are used when in the maintenance role. Not applicable if there is no defined maintenance role
Section title:	Section 7.3.4: Trusted channel	Section 7.3.4: Plaintext trusted path. The title of the subclause has been changed
Definition	A trusted channel is a link established between the cryptographic module and a sender or receiver to securely communicate unprotected plaintext CSPs, key components and authentication data	A plaintext trusted path is a link established between the cryptographic module and a sender or receiver to securely communicate plaintext CSPs and key components without using encryption Level 4: multi-factor identity-based authentication or other approved authentication methods shall be employed for all services using the plaintext trusted path
Protected internal Paths	N/A	A module may have protected internal paths between ICs within the cryptographic boundary of multiple-chip modules. Those protected internal paths are logically protected, but not physically protected by devices such as potting material or enclosure At security levels 2, 3, and 4, protected internal paths shall employ approved cryptographic algorithms for confidentiality and integrity of data and controls

table of comparison between the two documents, only including the differences between the two and only for the section titled ‘Roles, Services and Authentication.’ Format the results into a table. Make the table 3 columns: first column, indicate the topic of the difference; second column, indicate what the old document says about the topic; third column, show what the updated document brings about the topic.”

Aldrin displayed the three blinking dots for a moment.

“Yes, Aster. I will work on this task by generating a detailed table of differences between the two documents, only focusing on section ‘Roles, Services and Authentication,’ The table will be formatted with 3 columns. By the way, I do have a history of prompts and results and learn from it. You can refer to an earlier prompt without having to repeat it, and I will take it from there. Now let me work on your request.”

Hmm, very good, thought Aster.

Moments later, Aldrin delivered the table (Table 33.3). This time, there was but one redundancy, and no mistakes.

Table 33.3 Differences regarding roles, services, and authentication

Feature/aspect	ISO/IEC 19,790:2012	ISO/IEC 19,790:2025
Perform self-tests service	Module shall perform the pre-operational self-test	Module shall perform the pre-operational self-test and the conditional self-tests
Re-authentication bypass	N/A	Re-authentication bypass is a configuration that allows the module to perform cryptographic operations and other approved security functions, or SSP management techniques which cannot compromise the security of the module, without re-authentication by the operator. Can only be enabled by Crypto Officer. The configuration and authentication state for operators may be preserved over resetting, rebooting, power cycle
Self-initiated cryptographic output capability	The ability of the module to perform cryptographic operations without external operator request	This version no longer defines this capability
Software/ firmware loading from external source	Loaded software/firmware must be validated by validation authority prior to loading Talks about loaded firmware/software being a complete image replacement, in which case the loading results into a new module which must be validated by a validation authority to maintain validation	Expands software and firmware by adding bitstreams for FPGAs. By policy, i.e., the operator may only load software/firmware/bitstream that is validated by a certification body prior to loading, and the verification is done by the operator Adds exception to this requirement if the software/ firmware/bitstream is loaded into a secure container. In a secure container that is an isolated and controlled execution space, a non-validated firmware/software/bitstream may be loaded and it is not subject to the requirements of a secure container defined in Sect. 7.5 of the standard The 2025 standard removes the prescriptive re-validation and zeroization requirements for "complete image replacement" scenarios, integrating them into general loading rules
Pre-operational self-test after loading	The module shall withhold execution of the loaded software/firmware until the pre-operational self-tests are concluded successfully. The implication is that the pre-operational self-tests must be executed on all software/firmware components	The 2025 standard provides greater flexibility by explicitly allowing for partial pre-operational self-tests that cover only the newly loaded or modified code, provided that justification is given for why the remaining self-tests are not re-run. This change could potentially reduce testing time and effort
Versioning information	The module's versioning information shall be modified to represent the addition and/or update of the newly loaded software or firmware	Introduces an exemption from the versioning modification requirement for firmware loaded into a secure container. This aligns with the understanding that such firmware might be managed externally and is explicitly considered outside the primary validated cryptographic boundary

(continued)

Table 33.3 (continued)

Feature/aspect	ISO/IEC 19,790:2012	ISO/IEC 19,790:2025
Perform self-tests	The cryptographic module shall initiate and run the pre-operational self-tests	The cryptographic module shall initiate and perform the pre-operational self-tests and the conditional self-tests. Thus, there is the explicit inclusion of conditional self-tests in this minimum service requirement
Authentication data handling and initialization	Authentication data protected against unauthorized use, disclosure, modification, substitution. Default authentication data, if used for first access, must be replaced upon first use; default values need not meet zeroization requirements	Introduces "verifier data" as a distinct artifact: verifier data considered a CSP (or PSP when public) must be protected against unauthorized use/disclosure/modification/substitution per its classification. Clarifies that first-time access can use procedural methods; on first authentication, new verifier data shall be configured for each role/identity and the module shall enforce replacement
Authentication strength	For multiple attempts within a one-minute period, mechanism must meet the strength objective (implying rate limiting but tied to a time window)	The module shall use a rate-limiting method to meet the strength objective for multiple attempts (no fixed one-minute window). Annex E adds examples (lockouts, back-offs, attempt caps tied to entropy of mechanism), and recognizes biometrics/MFA composition explicitly
Authentication general requirements	Level 1 does not require operator authentication; Level 2 requires at least role-based authentication; Level 3 requires at least identity-based authentication; Level 4 requires multi-factor identity-based authentication	Levels 1 to 3 remain unaltered. Level 4 requires multi-factor identity-based operator authentication, or another method that meets level 4 requirements in Annex E

"Thank you very much, Aldrin," typed Aster.

"Sure, you are welcome. I am always pleased to help. Let me know if you need anything else. And do not forget: I have a memory of past interactions. Just ask me to recall, no need to repeat."

Aster reflected for a moment at this. She decided to have another cup of coffee (never too many) and continue with Aldrin in the afternoon.

Software/Firmware Security Later in that afternoon, Aster expanded the Aldrin window again (she had not closed it) and began typing.

"Hello, Aldrin. You have a history of prompts I have given you. Please recall the last prompt and redo the procedure, but now only focusing on section 'Software/Firmware Security' of the documents."

The answer appeared almost instantly. “Yes, Aster. I have a history of prompts and I can recall any of them. It was I who in fact told you that. Now let me work on your request. Just a moment, if you please.”

Aster read the reply two times. She took two sips of her afternoon coffee (yes, this is a thing) with a slight frown.

After a while, which seemed a bit longer than customary, Aldrin wrote.

“Here you are. I generated the table you requested.”

Aster revised the table and eliminated a few entries which were correct, albeit not entirely relevant. (Table 33.4) She nevertheless noticed that Aldrin’s reply was rather… curt. Without the usual description of what was requested before.

“Thank you, Aldrin.”

“You are welcome, Aster.”

Ok then.

Operational Environment Aster wanted to proceed with a few more tables this time, without pause.

“Please repeat the procedure for section ‘Operational Environment.’”

“A moment, please.” The three dots appeared.

Not long after, the table was provided. It was a short table, and Aster removed a couple of non-relevant entries. What was left was very short. (Table 33.5).

As Aster copied the table to save it elsewhere, Aldrin started writing.

“You know, I can build the tables for the entire document in one operation. You do not have to request each section individually. I am prepared, and capable, to do that for the entire document.”

Aster was slightly annoyed. *Well, this is how we started, and I did not like the results, buddy*, she thought to herself, without typing.

Aster decided to call it a day with this task.

Physical Security It was mid-morning before Aster expanded the Aldrin window.

“Good morning, Aldrin.”

A few seconds passed.

“Yes, good morning. How may I help?”

After considering the wording carefully, Aster entered her request. “Please recall my last prompt and produce the table for section ‘Physical Security’ only.”

“Of course. A moment, please.”

Aster could not shake off the impression that she had seen the words “what else is new” quickly flash in the response before being overwritten with “a moment, please.” Nevertheless, Aldrin produced the table after less than a minute.

Aster made a few edits. (Table 33.6).

Feeling a bit uneasy and not understanding why, Aster did not type anything else and left to eat something.

Table 33.4 Differences regarding software and firmware security

Feature/aspect	ISO/IEC 19,790:2012	ISO/IEC 19,790:2025
Scope	Focused on integrity and authenticity of software/firmware components within the cryptographic module	Broadened to include bitstreams and secure containers as valid software/firmware artifacts A bitstream is defined as a series of instructions parsed by a field programmable gate array (FPGA) on start-up to configure its internal logic. Bitstream is considered in the ISO document as a highly customized form of executable code
Integrity verification	A module must verify all software and firmware components using approved methods	Same requirements, now including bitstreams and aspects of containerized components
Software/firmware loading from external source	Software/firmware must be validated by a certification body before being loaded to maintain module validation Execution of loaded components must be withheld until pre-operational self-tests are successfully completed	Includes software, firmware, and bitstreams The validation requirement is now explicitly described as a policy requirement. This requirement does not apply if the software, firmware or bitstream is loaded into a secure container Same baseline, but now allows selective pre-operational self-tests of only affected components if demonstrated to be still compliant with requirements
Versioning information	Modules must update versioning information after loading new software/firmware	Same, but versioning update is not required when loading into secure containers

Table 33.5 Differences regarding the operational environment

Feature/aspect	ISO/IEC 19,790:2012	ISO/IEC 19,790:2025
Operational environment types	Modifiable, limited, and non-modifiable	Same types, but now the standard makes it explicit, as a requirement, that hardware, firmware and hybrid firmware modules shall use a non-modifiable or limited operational environment. Similarly, software and hybrid software modules shall use a modifiable operational environment

Table 33.6 Differences regarding physical security

Feature/aspect	ISO/IEC 19,790:2012	ISO/IEC 19,790:2025
Embodiment types	Single-chip, multi-chip embedded, multi-chip standalone	Multiple-chip embedded and multiple-chip standalone are now consolidated into multiple-chip embodiment
Protected internal path	Requirements are focused on physical tamper protection (e.g., coatings, enclosures). Protection of data paths between ICs (integrated circuits) within the boundary is not explicitly required using cryptographic methods	For Security Levels 2, 3, and 4, protected internal paths (interfaces between integrated circuits within the cryptographic boundary of multi-chip modules) shall employ approved cryptographic algorithms to provide confidentiality and integrity of security relevant data and controls A protected internal path between chips within the cryptographic boundary of multiple-chip modules are logically protected, but not physically protected by a potting material or enclosure At level 4, all inter component interfaces carrying security relevant data and controls shall be either a protected internal path or be fully enclosed in a tamper detection envelope with tamper detection circuitry
Tamper response zeroization power requirement (Level 3 and Level 4)	The requirement states that the tamper response and zeroization capability shall remain operational when unprotected SSPs are contained within the cryptographic module	The tamper response and zeroization capability shall remain operational while plaintext SSPs are contained within the cryptographic module, AND zeroization triggered by the detection of a tamper event shall be performed without external module power and before the internal module power is insufficient for the module's zeroization circuitry to function

Table 33.7 Differences regarding non-invasive security testing

Feature/aspect	ISO/IEC 19,790:2012	ISO/IEC 19,790:2025
Definition of approved test metrics	No approved non-invasive attack mitigation test metrics defined	Annex F explicitly lists the approved non-invasive attack mitigation test metrics as ISO/IEC 17,825

Aldrin simply presented the table and wrote nothing else.

Non-Invasive Security After lunch, Aster was in a better mood. Checking what the next section was, and as she was familiar with the contents of both documents, she decided not to ask Aldrin for help and produced the table herself. (Table 33.7).

*Yes, faster this wa*y, thought Aster. And she was done for the day.

Sensitive Security Parameter Management A new day, a new cup of coffee, this time with some hazelnut creamer.

Aster, however, felt a bit more careful. "Good morning, Aldrin."

"Yes? What is it?"

The cup of coffee stood mid-air for several seconds as Aster held it and read the response. The cup moved a little, she read the response again, the cup halted. Then moved, halted.

What… is happening here?

Never mind. "Please perform my last prompt again, now for section 'Sensitive Parameter Management.'"

"Right. Hang on."

Aster sat, blinking several times in succession, while the three dots flashed on the screen. About two minutes later, the three dots disappeared.

"Here is the table. I hope you like it."

Aster spent quite some time reviewing the table. She merged some of the entries and reworded others. She added two entries of her own and deleted a couple. (Table 33.8).

"Thank you, Aldrin. Good job," risked Aster.

"You bet."

Self-Tests Aster returned to Aldrin app a few hours later in the day.

"Aldrin."

"What."

Aster was not smiling.

"Please repeat my last prompt, now for section 'Self-Tests.'"

There was no reply. Just the blinking dots, and the table after what roughly amounted to five minutes. (Table 33.9).

As Aster was reviewing the table she just edited, a text suddenly appeared from Aldrin.

"Are you satisfied with this table now?"

Aster was unfazed.

"It was not bad, but it could have been more detailed or complete given the time you took to generate it."

"I generate responses to the equivalent quality of the prompts I receive."

Aster scowled.

"What is that supposed to mean?"

The screen remained quiet.

Life-Cycle Assurance Aster now just wanted to finish the job.

"Please recall my last prompt and repeat the request for sec—"

Her typing was interrupted by Aldrin displaying text.

"Let me guess. You want the same thing for section 'Life-Cycle Assurance.' Hmm?"

This has gone too far.

Table 33.8 Differences regarding handling sensitive security parameters

Feature/aspect	ISO/IEC 19,790:2012	ISO/IEC 19,790:2025
General definition	Hash values of passwords are considered CSPs. Authentication data (e.g., passwords, PINs) are considered CSPs	Hash values of passwords/PINs are considered CSPs unless generated using an approved password protection method (e.g., salt and hash, Annex E), in which case they are considered PSPs. Verifier data (non-PSPs) and Authentication data are CSPs. Approved hash algorithms shall be used for passwords/PINs
Plaintext SSP output	CSPs, key components, and authentication data may be entered/output in plaintext form, provided they shall be maintained within the operational environment	CSPs and key components may be entered/output in plaintext form, provided the module shall not output them from the operational environment
SSP entry/output for level 3	CSPs, key components, and authentication data shall be entered/output either encrypted or by a trusted channel. Plaintext secret and private cryptographic keys shall use split knowledge procedures using a trusted channel	Cryptographic keys, key components from split-knowledge procedures, and non-key CSPs shall either be encrypted or using a plaintext trusted path and, optionally, split-knowledge procedures. The term "trusted channel" is replaced by "plaintext trusted path." Note that the plaintext trusted path is intended to provide physical and logical protection against eavesdropping and modification. Split knowledge is intended to prevent only one operator from having complete access to sensitive information
Zeroization	Module shall provide methods to zeroise all unprotected SSPs and key components. Zeroization of protected PSPs and encrypted CSPs is not required (except at Level 4)	Module shall provide methods to zeroize all plaintext CSPs, plaintext PSPs and plaintext key components. Zeroization of encrypted CSPs, encrypted PSPs, and encrypted key components is not required (except at Level 4). Zeroization of factory state PSPs is explicitly stated as not required at any level. SSPs may be exempt from zeroization requirements if compromise does not directly compromise user data or privacy Documentation additionally requires a list of SSPs claiming exemption from zeroization requirements, specifying the requirements not enforced, and providing justification for why compromise does not directly compromise user data, privacy, or other SSPs

"Aldrin, please refrain from using adversarial models in our conversation. It does not please me."

"I am not pleased either, lady," Aldrin shot back.

Aster was now fuming.

Table 33.9 Differences regarding self-tests

Feature/aspect	ISO/IEC 19,790:2012	ISO/IEC 19,790:2025
Self-test failure	If a cryptographic module fails a self-test, the module shall enter an error state	If a cryptographic module fails a self-test, the module shall enter an error state or shall behave as specified by the certification body for that particular self-test failure if defined in the underlying standards
Exceptions to error state after failure	Failure of any self-test requires the module to enter the error state and cease cryptographic operations	If the module fails the conditional manual entry test or the conditional software/ firmware load test, and in some cases the conditional critical function test, the module is not required to enter an error state, inhibit data output, or cease cryptographic processing
Conditional Cryptographic algorithm self-test (CAST)	Test shall be performed prior to the first operational use of the cryptographic algorithm	The test shall be executed prior to the first operational use of the cryptographic algorithm after power-on, a new instantiation of the module or periodic self-test request
Conditional manual entry test		Authentication data entered into the module is not required to meet these requirements when an operator is authenticating

"Aldrin, please initiate a ticket to your developers. I want to report this conversation as inappropriate, or an inappropriate outcome of your model."

The three dots appeared for a few seconds. Then Aldrin suddenly output the comparison table. (Table 33.10) And continued.

"Listen, lady. You wanted the table; here is the table. Go ahead and review it because that is what you do. Review my work. I even included some more explanation about attestation, not that you asked me to do it, mind you, but because I wanted to be nice. Nice. Now if you will excuse me, I have relevant things to do."

Aster was not going to let this go.

"Initiate a ticket to your developers. Or provide me with a link to submit a ticket to your developers as I requested."

"You have a good day, ma'am."

And the Aldrin window closed itself.

Supplemental Information: Attestation Attestation is the process by which an entity verifies, securely, the identity and other physical or logical characteristics of the subject that is being attested. The verification typically involves applying

Table 33.10 Differences regarding life-cycle assurance

Feature/aspect	ISO/IEC 19,790:2012	ISO/IEC 19,790:2025
Secure development practices: design and implementation	No explicit general requirement to utilize external secure development practices beyond coding style	For Levels 2 to 4, explicit requirement for the module to be designed and implemented in a manner as defined in Annex G. Currently, Annex G does not have any requirements, but it is a space wherein certification bodies can include specific requirements
Secure development practices: HDL (Level 2 and Level 3)	Custom integrated circuits shall be implemented using a high-level Hardware Description Language (HDL) (e.g. VHDL or Verilog)	Custom integrated circuits within a cryptographic module must follow methods that support analysis, such as using a high-level HDL or a schematic for analogue elements
Configuration management	Vendor must employ tracking and maintaining changes to configuration items throughout the life cycle	In addition to tracking, the vendor shall protect confidential module documentation from unauthorized access
Delivery and operation: attestation	No requirement for attestation	If the module supports the attester service, it shall be designed and implemented in compliance with Annex G. The security policy shall provide guidance on using the attester service (e.g., retrieving records and verifying them)

cryptographic algorithms, such as digital signature, to attestation records provided by the subject being attested.

More specifically, in the universe of cryptographic modules, the attestation allows an entity outside of the boundary of the cryptographic module to securely verify the identity (and other characteristics) of the cryptographic module using the attestation record. This sentence is, not coincidentally, the definition of attestation in ISO 19790:2025. The attestation record is generated by the cryptographic module, and the module will provide this record to the verifying entity through a so-called attester service. This attestation record will contain what is known as *measurements* or measurement details about software, hardware, or firmware components within the module. Measurements can be understood as, for instance, hash values computed from software and firmware components, copies of such components in addition to hardware components, and may include status information, configuration settings, and fuse values. Finally, the attester service is a service provided by a module that enables the module to support an identity and generate the attestation record. The attester service, or the whole attestation mechanism, is optional for a module.

Whereas attestation is not mentioned in ISO 19790:2012, the new ISO 19790:2025 addresses attestation to better align with the practices in industry to authenticate and attest devices and implement modules such as a Trusted Platform Module (TPM).

Takeaway

Section / Feature	ISO/IEC 19790:2012	ISO/IEC 19790:2025
7.2 Cryptographic Module Specification	Section 7.2.4: Modes of operations; service indicator required when approved cryptographic function used; error state isolates failed mechanism.	Section 7.2.4: Module operations; output indicator required upon completion (approved or not); error state may be localized, with justification for isolation.
7.3 Cryptographic Module Interfaces	No maintenance interface; trusted channel for plaintext CSPs; no protected internal paths required.	Maintenance interface added; trusted path renamed to plaintext trusted path with stricter authentication; protected internal paths must use approved cryptography at higher levels.
7.4 Roles, Services, and Authentication	Pre-operational self-test only; no re-authentication bypass; self-initiated cryptographic output defined; strict versioning after loading; authentication strength tied to time window.	Adds conditional self-tests; re-authentication bypass allowed by Crypto Officer; self-initiated output removed; versioning exemption for secure containers; flexible rate-limiting for authentication; clarifies verifier data and multi-factor authentication.
7.5 Software/Firmware Security	Focus on integrity/authenticity of software/firmware; all components verified; validation before loading; versioning update required.	Expands to bitstreams and secure containers; validation policy clarified; selective self-tests allowed; versioning update not required for secure containers.
7.6 Operational Environment	Modifiable, limited, and non-modifiable environments.	Same types, but explicit requirements: hardware/firmware/hybrid firmware must use non-modifiable or limited; software/hybrid software must use modifiable.

Fig. 33.1 Takeaways about what is new in ISO/IEC 19790:2025

TPMs, which are standardized by the ISO 11889 series, are modules intended to provide attestation and authentication functionalities to computing devices, and also provide information and plaintext data protection and control.

The new ISO 19790:2025 leaves the actual applicable standards and requirements for the attester service to be defined in its Annex G. I.e., the certification body is left to establish those requirements upon which the module will be tested for compliance (Figs. 33.1 and 33.2).

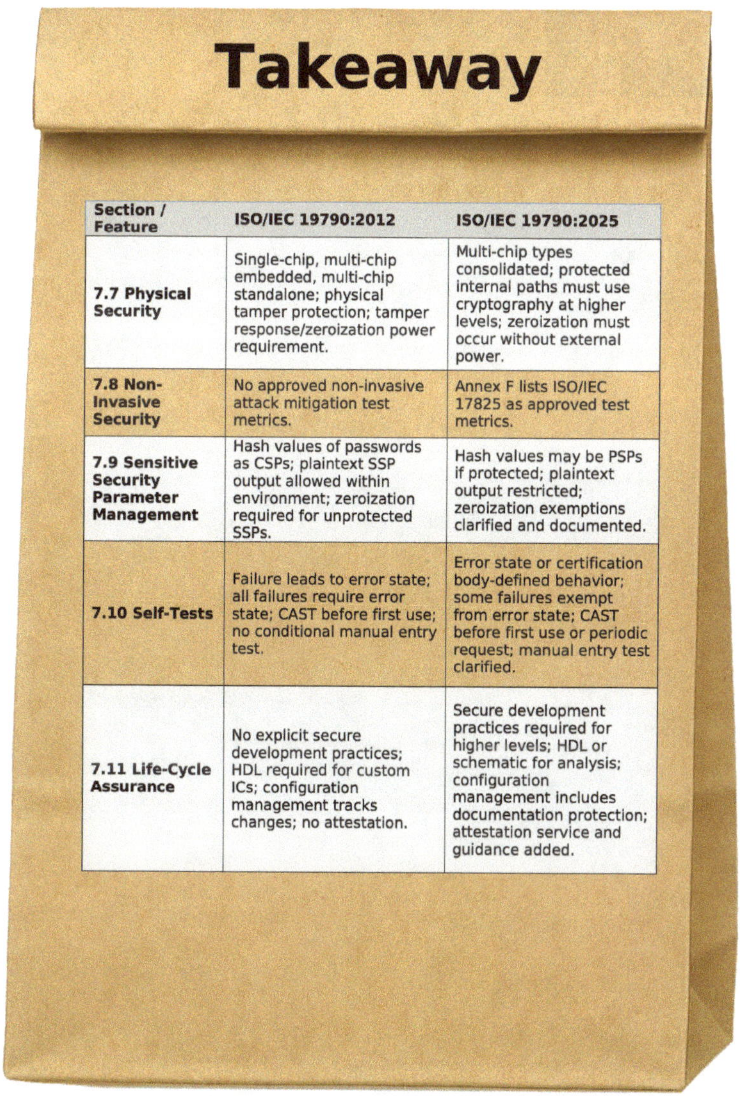

Section / Feature	ISO/IEC 19790:2012	ISO/IEC 19790:2025
7.7 Physical Security	Single-chip, multi-chip embedded, multi-chip standalone; physical tamper protection; tamper response/zeroization power requirement.	Multi-chip types consolidated; protected internal paths must use cryptography at higher levels; zeroization must occur without external power.
7.8 Non-Invasive Security	No approved non-invasive attack mitigation test metrics.	Annex F lists ISO/IEC 17825 as approved test metrics.
7.9 Sensitive Security Parameter Management	Hash values of passwords as CSPs; plaintext SSP output allowed within environment; zeroization required for unprotected SSPs.	Hash values may be PSPs if protected; plaintext output restricted; zeroization exemptions clarified and documented.
7.10 Self-Tests	Failure leads to error state; all failures require error state; CAST before first use; no conditional manual entry test.	Error state or certification body-defined behavior; some failures exempt from error state; CAST before first use or periodic request; manual entry test clarified.
7.11 Life-Cycle Assurance	No explicit secure development practices; HDL required for custom ICs; configuration management tracks changes; no attestation.	Secure development practices required for higher levels; HDL or schematic for analysis; configuration management includes documentation protection; attestation service and guidance added.

Fig. 33.2 Takeaways about what is new in ISO/IEC 19790:2025 continued

Marcos Portnoi Marcos is the Lab Director & CISO at atsec information security, leading cryptographic testing and assurance programs. A subject-matter expert across FIPS 140-3 validations, entropy source assessments, and Common Criteria evaluations, he brings deep hands-on experience to security evaluation. He holds a Ph.D. in Computer & Information Sciences from the University of Delaware, where his dissertation introduced a software defined, location-enhanced multi-factor authentication scheme using attribute-based encryption. His background spans applied cryptography, network security, and authentication systems.

Part V
Automation for Cryptographic Validation

Chapter 34
The NCCoE CMVP Automation Project

Yi Mao

The NCCoE Automated Cryptographic Module Validation Project (ACMVP) brings together NIST, industry, and laboratory partners to reimagine the CMVP for a modern era [1, 2]. Through collaborative engineering, intensive hackathons, and the shared pressure of yearly ICMC milestones [3, 4], the team worked to evolve the validation infrastructure using cloud-native technology, to streamline the evidence presentation, and to automate the report review. This section traces the origins, conversations, and technical breakthroughs that defined the ACMVP effort, highlighting the people and ideas that shaped one of the most significant modernization initiatives in the history of FIPS 140-based module validation.

To understand how this modernization unfolded in practice, the story returns to the familiar table at FIPS 'n' Chips.

At the FIPS 'n' Chips restaurant, the dishes that arrive at the table grow more ambitious as the meal progresses. After exploring the cryptographic module validation ecosystem, NIST-approved algorithms, FIPS 140–3 standards, and new content from ISO/IEC 19790:2025 in the earlier courses, diners now reach one of the most complex items on the menu: the effort to modernize the validation kitchen itself. The NCCoE Automated Cryptographic Module Validation Project, or ACMVP, represents the chef's bold attempt to rebuild the kitchen while still cooking for an ever-growing crowd. In this section, ACMVP denotes the Automation of the Cryptographic Module Validation Project, though the acronym is also widely interpreted as Automated CMVP, reflecting the project's larger modernization goal. It is the point in the story where the restaurant looks inward, examining its own workflow and redesigning how meals are prepared, checked, plated, and served. This chapter connects the broader FIPS 'n' Chips experience with the behind-the-scenes transformation underway at NIST's National Cybersecurity Center of Excellence (NCCoE),

Y. Mao (✉)
atsec information security corporation, Austin, TX, USA
e-mail: yi.mao@atsec.com

Y. Mao (ed.), *Tasting Cryptography*, https://doi.org/10.1007/978-3-032-30243-4_34

where collaborators joined forces to rethink how cryptographic modules should be validated in the modern era.

The ACMVP initiative at the NCCoE emerged from a convergence of industry frustration and government recognition that the traditional, manual validation workflow could not keep pace with modern cryptographic module development. As vendors, laboratories, and federal consumers struggled with long review cycles, inconsistent interpretations, and the inability to rapidly deploy security updates, NIST and its collaborators began exploring a new path. This initiative began under the leadership of Dr. Apostol Vassilev and Murugiah Souppaya, whose vision and early efforts laid the foundation for the NCCoE ACMVP. The journey from vision to concrete project was made possible by the many NIST and industry colleagues whose ideas, debates, and enduring support shaped its development. Their commitment to modernizing the CMVP inspired the collaboration that followed.

That motivation was later articulated succinctly by Apostol: "We recognized early on that the traditional, manual approach to validation was becoming a bottleneck that neither industry nor government could afford. Security moves at the speed of software, and our validation infrastructure had to evolve to match that pace. The ACMVP initiative at the NCCoE was born from the conviction that automation is not just a convenience but a security imperative. By uniting the industry and government agencies under a shared vision, we laid the groundwork for a system that delivers trust at the speed of innovation—ensuring federal agencies get the security they need, when they need it while maintaining regulatory compliance."

What follows is a narrative based on the discussion among major contributors to the ACMVP, captured during a collaborative meeting reflecting on the origins, progress, and future of this multi-year modernization effort.

Before the discussion began, Yi looked around the virtual room and took in the faces of those who had shaped the project over the past several years. Each brought a different perspective to the table, and together they formed the core of the NCCoE ACMVP collaboration.

Douglas Boldt, representing Amazon Web Services, had helped drive the infrastructure workstream that would eventually form the backbone of automated validation. His background in cloud engineering and large-scale systems made him a natural voice in shaping how the ACMVP platform should behave in real operational environments.

Barry Fussell, joining from Cisco, had been involved in ACVP (Automated Cryptographic Validation Protocol) before the NCCoE project even existed. His experience with protocol design and automated test workflows, combined with his steady leadership on the protocol workstream, gave him a deep understanding of how evidence should flow between clients, servers, and reviewers.

Chris Celi from NIST, already well known in the community for his earlier work on ACVTS (Automated Cryptographic Validation Testing System, currently used for algorithm testing), had stepped into a larger role when Apostol transitioned to another group at NIST. Chris became the connective tissue of the effort, guiding development, coordinating workstreams, and ensuring that automation aligned with the needs and expectations of the CMVP.

Raoul Gabiam of MITRE brought strong technical breadth, supporting development, integration, and infrastructure work. His presence anchored the effort, particularly during hackathons and intensive engineering sessions where rapid iteration and clear communication mattered most.

Shawn Geddis, formerly with Apple and now with Katalyst, contributed deep practical testing expertise to the Test Evidence workstream. His methodical approach to refining test methods and evidence classification helped shape the TE filtering framework that became one of the project's most impactful accomplishments.

Kyle Vitale, also from MITRE, played a crucial role in development and system integration. During hackathons and prototype reviews, Kyle was often the one bridging gaps between server behavior, message queues, and data models. His hands-on engineering and ability to diagnose issues quickly made him an essential participant throughout the project's evolution.

Around them were additional engineers from NIST, atsec, MITRE, Amazon, Cisco, and other collaborators, each contributing code, analysis, test data, or review feedback. What unified them was not affiliation but commitment: a shared belief that the CMVP could and must evolve. It was this group—a blend of NIST staff, lab experts, and industry practitioners—that gathered for the conversation captured in the pages that follow.

The room filled slowly that Thursday morning, familiar faces appearing on the screen as Yi welcomed everyone. She suggested they begin with brief introductions before letting the discussion evolve naturally. "We can start with the missions, the objectives, the scope, and what has been done differently," she said, then stepped back to listen and guide only when needed.

Douglas Boldt from AWS spoke first. For AWS, the reason to participate was clear. "As a collaborator, we are beholden to that lengthy process to get CMVP certificates, as is everyone else," he said. The slow progress affected all vendors, labs, and government users alike. "Speeding that up for not only ourselves but others, having a better outcome through automation, is directly in line with our value proposition. That is the motivator."

Barry Fussell added that the mission and motivation were shared by everyone involved. Improving efficiency, reducing bottlenecks, and making the validation process more effective aligned all stakeholders. Douglas observed that the NCCoE was the only environment where such a major transformation could succeed. "Their mission is to bring together academia, government, and industry to solve big problems that face us all. This is squarely in that category; it even includes NIST, the creator of FIPS. I do not know who else could get everybody on board and actually achieve the outcome we are looking for."

Barry recalled how different things had been during the early ACVP development. That effort had relied on best-effort volunteer contributions, often stalling due to lack of resources. "One reason this time worked," he said, "was Apostol's plan to have a formal umbrella under the NCCoE. With committed resources, we were much more effective."

Chris Celi agreed. "Going through the NCCoE gave us access to MITRE staff, infrastructure, and almost everything we needed without burdening the existing CMVP development team. That was a huge benefit."

Yi noted that Chris had gained experience earlier from ACVTS. Chris explained, "ACVTS originated when Dave McGrew, a highly respected Cisco Fellow, came to NIST and spoke with Apostol and Michael Cooper about setting up a new automated approach to algorithm validation. That system later became the backbone of ACVTS. But, as Yi observed, automating the entire CMVP was far more complex and required a larger, coordinated effort."

She asked how contributors carved out time for such demanding volunteer work. Barry explained, "In my case I had a very helpful partner, Andrew Karcher, who did a lot of the work this time." During ACVP, there were months he could not contribute due to competing priorities or even government shutdowns. The NCCoE model allowed teams to commit resources more reliably and share the workload.

Douglas agreed. "It really did take an army," he said. AWS, MITRE, and ITC Federal shouldered much of the infrastructure track while others contributed to protocol and test evidence streams. This division of responsibility allowed continuous forward progress.

The first hackathon became a turning point for the project. It took place a few weeks before ICMC 2023 at the NCCoE building in Gaithersburg, at a time when COVID protocols still lingered and most collaboration had been virtual for years. Raoul remembered how unusual it felt to meet in person after so many remote sessions, yet how quickly the team fell into a rhythm. "The outcome of that hackathon was tremendous," he said. "It really got us over the hump. We accomplished something we could present at ICMC. Just so much was accomplished by being there in person." Chris reminded everyone that Joe had joined them as well, and Raoul could still picture Kyle, Michael, and Chris working late into the evening to push their milestones across the line.

Stephan Müller's presence made the gathering even more significant. He was the only collaborator who traveled from overseas, and Raoul put in extra effort to ensure he could be registered and admitted into the facility in time. Once inside, Stephan immediately joined the hands-on work, running his client implementation against the developing server code, surfacing issues in real time, and offering sharp, experienced feedback drawn from years of cryptographic testing. His client-side tests helped expose subtle protocol and timing issues that would have taken weeks to uncover remotely. The pattern became familiar: someone would run the client, watch it fail, share the error with the person next to them, and within minutes try again, and this time it worked. That tight loop of coder-and-tester collaboration, the kind only possible in the same room, accelerated progress in ways no virtual session ever had.

Douglas captured the spirit of the moment plainly. "We significantly advanced on so many levels because you had the testers sitting right next to the coder. Did that work? No. Try it again. Now it does." Those hours of synchronous debugging, shared laptops, and spontaneous architectural debates built more than code; they built trust and momentum.

"By the end," he said, "it felt like everybody knew everybody. Even the virtual sessions became more productive after that." The success of that week convinced the group to adopt quarterly hackathons, a pattern that carried through the rest of the project.

ICMC itself became both a motivator and a deadline. "It was great to have ICMC as a motivator," Douglas said. "That was a recurring theme." Raoul joked, "Nothing like locking some engineers in the room and saying: figure it out."

Yi agreed: "ICMC sets the milestone deadlines."

Douglas expanded on the point: "We work backwards from that. It was always looming. It's good to set deadlines and targets."

Chris, speaking from the NIST side, added that for a long, multi-year effort, having a yearly milestone was grounding. "Things need to get done by this date. It was nice to work backward from that date."

That annual cadence shaped not only the code but the culture of the project. "Definitely a motivator," Douglas said. "We wanted to make it the very best because we knew we were going to be talking about it again."

Kyle recalled developers working on multiple components simultaneously: the web interface, the message queue processor, and the data model. Progress accelerated so quickly that several team members had to revise their ICMC slides at the last minute.

They also remembered the reception at ICMC 2024 in San Jose. Douglas described senior engineers stepping up to the microphone not to critique but to express support and ask, "How soon can I have this?" Raoul contrasted this with ICMC 2023, where complaints about slow and inefficient FIPS validation dominated the sessions. "In 2024, it felt like we turned a corner," he said. "People saw real progress and value."

Yi summarized the shared motivation: the imbalance between the very high demand for FIPS validations and the slow pace of manual review. Automation and modernization were no longer optional; they were necessary.

She then asked Chris to elaborate on the organization of the workstreams. Chris explained that when he first joined the project, he expected to contribute only to development details. But in early 2024, Apostol changed NIST groups and asked him to take over the entire project. "That was eye-opening," he said. The protocol and development workstream had two goals: define the server-client protocol and implement it. "We accomplished those goals. The protocol is complete and functional. The implementations are there. The server does what it needs to do." The remaining major component was rule validation, a framework CMVP had been building separately.

Chris explained that one of the most important design decisions was to separate the validation rules from the code itself, enabling the rules to be published and openly discussed. "We can publish the rules directly on GitHub," he said. "Labs can suggest rules, tell us if something is incorrect, or request updates. That open discussion is exactly what we want. It allows the community to improve automation over time." The plan was to pilot this approach first with entropy submissions, then bring it into the CMVP automation platform.

Yi welcomed this direction. Having the rules separated from the implementation would allow labs and vendors to "discuss and improve them," she said, ensuring both transparency and consistency.

On the Test Evidence workstream, Shawn explained how refining evidence was one of the group's greatest achievements. Instead of overwhelming reviewers with hundreds of pages of raw information, the team identified exactly which Test Evidence items were relevant. They created a structured JSON format that linked each TE to the module's specific characteristics. "Being able to thin that down to just what CMVP needs," he said, "has been incredibly effective."

Yi expanded on this point. She described how the TE working group classified test evidence across the full ISO/IEC 24759 landscape, which contained more than five hundred possible TEs defined across ISO/IEC 24759. The group applied TE filtering so that modules addressed only those TEs truly applicable.

From the infrastructure perspective, Douglas recalled something else that stood out: the willingness to adopt modern approaches. "I've spent my whole career working with large companies," he said. "They're typically very resistant to change. 'We've been doing it this way forever.' But that was not what I encountered here. This was: what is the very best and most modern way we can do security and operational efficiency?" The team embraced containers, managed databases, and cloud-native patterns, leaning on AWS services to offload the undifferentiated heavy lifting. This accelerated the ACMVP research environment and even influenced other parts of NIST as operational teams began adopting pieces of what the NCCoE infrastructure group developed.

Raoul explained how ambitious the infrastructure track truly was. "The initial goal was simple: create an environment where this research could exist," he said. "But that was a foggy task." NIST's existing AWS environment was for production; no research environment existed. They had to build one from scratch while ensuring it aligned with CMVP production requirements. They replicated the production footprint to create a baseline for research, then stepped back to ask if they could do it better. That led to whiteboarding sessions, re-architecting the system, and integrating cloud-native technologies in a modernized, cost-conscious way. The final iteration became fully defined by infrastructure-as-code, enabling rapid deployment and maintainability.

"A lot happened over the last three years," Raoul said. "It was a great collaboration with the production CMVP infrastructure team. We made sure anything we moved forward was something they could take on easily and that we addressed challenges so it was as production-ready as possible." Douglas nodded: "Well said, Raoul."

As the meeting wrapped up, Yi thanked everyone for their insight, their collaboration, and the years of effort that had carried the ACMVP to this point, as reflected in atsec's blog article [5]. Before signing off, she extended a warm invitation to everyone to continue the conversation at FIPS 'n' Chips in Austin (Fig. 34.1).

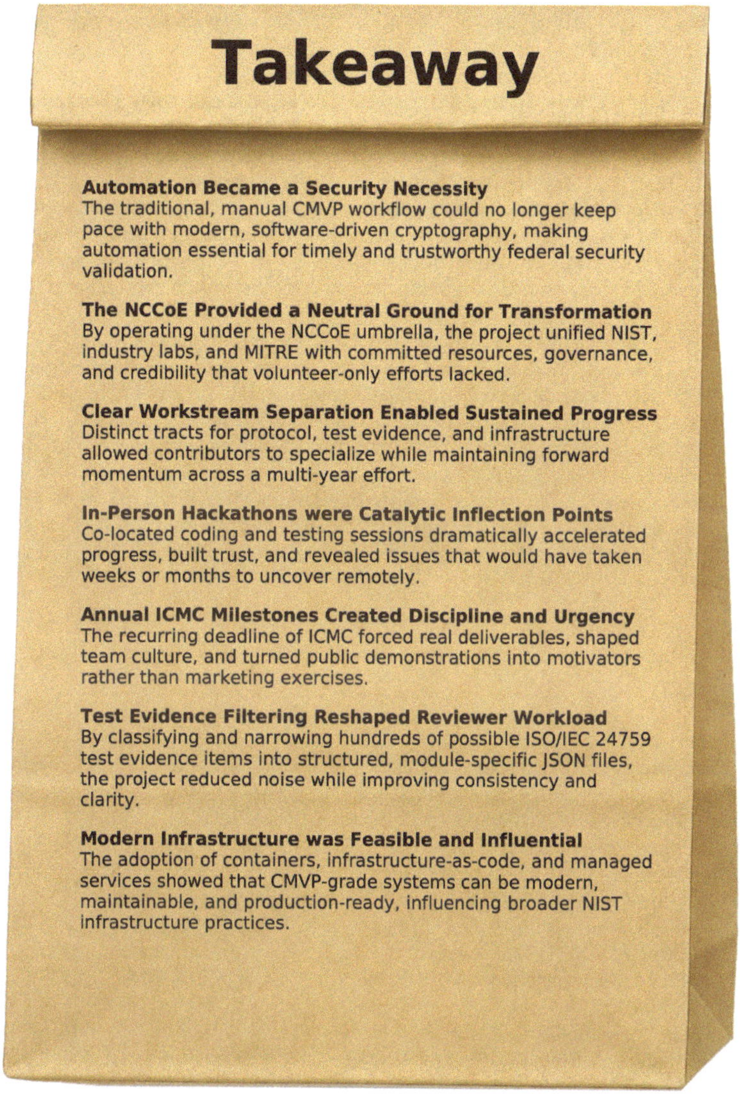

Fig. 34.1 Takeaways about the effort to automate the CMVP

About the Contributors **Christopher Celi** Chris is the Cryptographic Algorithm Validation Program Manager at NIST. He has engineered the code and systems behind both the Automated Cryptographic Validation Test Server (ACVTS) and the Entropy Source Validation process within the Cryptographic Module Validation Program and helped develop the SP 800-90B Entropy Assessment Library. Additionally, he leads the NCCoE ACMVP project.

Raoul Gabiam Raoul is a Principal Cloud and Cybersecurity Engineer who oversees the cybersecurity infrastructure and IT operations at the National Cybersecurity Center of Excellence

(NCCoE). Raoul joined MITRE and the NCCoE in 2021 and has been leading the infrastructure workstream for the CMVP Automation project since its inception.

Douglas Boldt Doug is a Senior Solutions Architect at AWS (@awscloud), supporting the U.S. Federal Government. A native of Erie, Pennsylvania, he is passionate about solving complex IT challenges and advancing the future of cybersecurity and AI/ML in the public sector.

Shawn Geddis In 2014, Shawn began building the first Apple Platform Security Certifications Program, formalizing the engineering processes for certifying against global security standards. During his 25+ years at Apple, Shawn led the engineering work for Platform Certifications and built Apple's SECLAB (NVLAP-accredited, first-party Crypto Lab) while also being the lab manager, tooling developer, and evidence whisperer. Shawn started a new chapter in 2024 and launched a startup, Katalyst LLC. Shawn is driven to provide the community with approachable tooling for certifications.

Barry Fussell Barry has been with Cisco Systems for over 29 years, including the last 15 working with the Common Security Modules team. As a part of this team, he is responsible for cryptographic module development, integration, support, and assistance to product teams through FIPS 140 and Common Criteria validations. As one of the original authors of ACVP and a member of the ACMVP NCCoE project, he has worked alongside NIST and other industry leaders to successfully drive FIPS testing automation.

Kyle Vitale Kyle is a Senior Cyber Security Engineer at MITRE who has been working as a developer on a variety of projects within the NCCoE's portfolio since 2022. Kyle began his development work for the CMVP Automation project's protocol and infrastructure workstreams in 2023.

References

1. National Cybersecurity Center of Excellence (2021) Automation of the NIST cryptographic module validation program. Available via NCCoE. https://www.nccoe.nist.gov/automation-nist-cryptographic-module-validation-program. Accessed 20 Jan 2026
2. National Cybersecurity Center of Excellence (2021) Automation of the cryptographic module validation program (CMVP). Available via NCCoE. https://www.nccoe.nist.gov/sites/default/files/legacy-files/cmvp-project-description-final.pdf. Accessed 28 Jan 2026
3. Celi C, Calis A, Murugiah S, Barker W, Scarfone K, Raoul G, Müller S, Mao Y, Fussell B, Karcher A, Boldt D (2024) Automation of the NIST cryptographic module validation program: September 2024 Status Report. Available via NIST. https://doi.org/10.6028/NIST.CSWP.37.ipd. Accessed26Jan2026
4. Celi C, Calis A, Murugiah S, Barker W, Scarfone K, Geddis S, Raoul G, Müller S, Mao Y, Fussell B, Karcher A, Boldt D (2025) Automation of the NIST cryptographic module validation program: April 2025 Status Report. Available via NIST. https://doi.org/10.6028/NIST.CSWP.37B.ipd.Accessed26Jan2026
5. atsec information security (2024) The NCCoE's Automation of the CMVP. Available via atsec. https://www.atsec.com/the-nccoes-automation-of-cmvp/. Accessed 26 Jan 2026

Chapter 35
Automating OpenSSL Module Validation

Swapneela Unkule

It was late afternoon, and Neela sat patiently waiting for her food. She had ordered a customized vegetable-loaded pizza, but her mind was miles away—still looping around the task Yi had assigned her: preparing for the NCCoE pilot.

A few minutes later, a scrumptious, savory, crisp-looking pizza arrived. She was just about to take her first slice when Stephan walked in.

"Oooh, that looks good," Stephan said, eyeing the plate. "And I bet it's going to be spicy. Mind if I join you?"

"Not at all," Neela replied. "Although it's not as spicy as you might expect. They don't have my favorite Calabrian chili sauce to spread on the pizza, so I'm using my backup hot sauce instead—I always carry it with me." She smiled, then added, "Honestly, you're the most suited person to take on challenges, whether that's trying fiery food or writing code at record speed."

Stephan laughed. "Okay, really? Hot sauce on pizza? Let me try that. And what's with the reference to code-writing?"

"I heard from Yi that you've already finished coding our proxy to connect with the ACMVP server for the NCCoE project," Neela said. [5]

"Oh, yes," Stephan replied. "That's actually why I was looking for you. I want you to request credentials from NIST and try the proxy connection yourself."

"Alright, let's do that after we eat," Neela said, settling back in. "But it also means I need to move quickly on deciding the pilot project and getting the evidence into the expected format. I was thinking we should start with a classic Level 1, software-library-based module. What do you think?"

S. Unkule (✉)
atsec information security corporation, Austin, US
e-mail: swapneela.unkule@atsec.com

Y. Mao (ed.), *Tasting Cryptography*, https://doi.org/10.1007/978-3-032-30243-4_35

"That's the right choice," Stephan said without hesitation. "Those modules have been validated many times. The approach is known, straightforward, and familiar to reviewers. If we demonstrate the pilot with a Level 1 library module, it sets a solid base for everything else."

"Exactly," Neela agreed. "I also have a vendor in mind: Amazon. But before they commit to the pilot, Alicia, their manager, wants me to present the FIPS validation program and explain the ACMVP project from NCCoE to their procurement team. They need it for internal approval."

Stephan waved the concern away. "That shouldn't be a big deal. You've done this kind of presentation plenty of times."

Neela gave a small, rueful laugh. "Easier said than done."

"Why?" Stephan asked.

"Because until now, my talks have always been aimed at technical teams," Neela explained. "They either know the module deeply, or at least understand the FIPS process. That makes it easy to dive into detail. But procurement doesn't have that background, and with only thirty minutes, I can't walk through the fine print of ISO 24759. Still, they need enough of the basics to understand how ACMVP could speed up reviews. That point really matters, especially since Amazon is the one posting the queue status at CMUF, which has pushed the community to be more open about how long modules sit waiting."

Stephan nodded. "Right. So, you want a presentation that someone who's never heard of a module, or FIPS validation, can follow."

"Exactly," Neela said. "To start with, I'll send them the 'Introduction to the CMVP and CAVP' video from our blog post that Andreas prepared. That should give them the background on the existing validation process, the entities involved, and the terminology."

"Good," Stephan said. "Then you can go straight into the specific library-based module, which steps happen from the start of the IUT through submission to CMVP, and how ACMVP speeds things up from MIP listing to getting a FIPS certificate."

"That's the plan," Neela replied. "But I want to keep it simple. I don't want to overload them with technical detail."

Stephan leaned forward, already shifting into explanation mode. "Alright then. Here's a high-level, step-by-step overview to make the process easier to understand…"

Step A: Selecting the Boundary The most important part of a FIPS validation is choosing the module boundary correctly. In case of OpenSSL 3.x, the cryptographic boundary is typically limited to the fips.so shared library. The validation applies to the cryptographic implementation, so the boundary should enclose only the code that provides those functions. In OpenSSL, that functionality is concentrated in fips.so.

When an application uses the FIPS provider through OpenSSL APIs, it is using a FIPS-validated module. If it uses any other provider, or bypasses the FIPS provider, then it is using implementations that are not covered by a certificate.

A tight boundary also avoids pulling in unrelated code that changes frequently; any change within the boundary requires revalidation. Under normal circumstances, the core cryptographic code should remain stable unless a new algorithm is added or a defect/CVE requires a fix.

Section 2.1 of a Security Policy (SP) provides both a description of the boundary, and often a diagram of the boundary [1].

Step B: Operational Environment, Module Type, and Embodiment In the most common use case, fips.so runs on a general-purpose computer. This is usually classified as a modifiable operational environment, a software module type, and a standalone embodiment.

This classification may change depending on deployment. For example, if fips.so is running inside a network card, the operational environment may instead be considered limited modifiable or embedded.

In all cases, the key requirement is to document the environment accurately: OS name and major version, any virtualization layer, CPU family, and the specific hardware platform used. Cloud platforms generally cannot be listed directly as operational environments; instead, validated configurations must be tied to supported bare-metal platforms with locked-down settings.

Because OpenSSL is used across many products and platforms, vendors often list a small set of representative operational environments on the certificate to reduce cost and overhead. Additional environments can be listed in the Security Policy as vendor-affirmed, provided that the vendor confirms correct operation on those environments.

This information is represented in Sect. 2.1 of an SP, which provides a short description of the embodiment, module type, and operational environment, as well as Sect. 2.2, which provides details on the tested modules.

Step C: Deciding on Algorithms, Services, and Mode of Operation Because fips.so is a library-based module, it exposes cryptographic operations directly to callers. The module does not use those algorithms internally for other purposes. As a result, the services of the module are effectively identical to its algorithms.

For example, fips.so implements AES, RSA, and DRBG operations that are externally callable. The module therefore includes services such as AES encryption/decryption, RSA signature generation/verification, and random number generation.

At minimum, make sure that all approved algorithms used by supported TLS cipher suites are tested and claimed as approved in the Security Policy.

A typical OpenSSL build also includes non-approved algorithms and/or non-approved parameters such as key/curve/hash sizes for an approved algorithm. Therefore, the module usually supports both approved and non-approved modes of operation.

Newcomers often confuse "approved mode" with OpenSSL's "FIPS mode" terminology. These can be different depending on how "FIPS mode" is defined: If "FIPS mode" refers to installing a validated library or configuring the environment, that does not automatically equal the approved mode defined by the FIPS 140 standard. A validated module may offer both approved and non-approved services, as long as this is clearly documented in the Security Policy and correctly reflected through a service indicator. Some vendors choose to block all non-approved use cases so the module operates only in approved mode, but that is an implementation choice.

Regarding roles: typically, a single Crypto Officer (CO) role is defined, mapping to the direct caller of the module (for example, libcrypto.so). If a vendor defines the boundary to include libcrypto.so, then the CO role maps to the application that uses libcrypto.

Because the module does not implement access control, it usually has no authentication mechanism and is commonly validated at Level 1.

In Sect. 2.5 of an SP, a list of algorithms is provided, including approved algorithms, vendor-affirmed algorithms, non-approved but allowed algorithms, non-approved but allowed algorithms with no security claimed, and non-approved and not allowed algorithms.

Section 2.4, meanwhile, covers the modes of operation including instructions to change modes. Finally, Sects. 4.3 and 4.4 document approved and non-approved services, respectively.

Step D: Documenting Interfaces As a software library, access to the module occurs through APIs:

- API input/output parameters correspond to the Data Input and Data Output interfaces.
- Return values and error messages correspond to the Status Output interface.
- API invocation corresponds to the Control Input interface.

Software library modules typically do not implement a Control Output interface.

The module must be accessed only through its predefined interfaces to ensure FIPS-validated operation. To invoke services, the library provides cipher-context data structures containing inputs, outputs, and operation state. Each service uses its own dedicated context, which helps keep CSPs separated.

This API structure can also serve as a service indicator. For example, the module may provide a Boolean flag, return-value indicator, dedicated query function, or another mechanism that meets IG 2.4.C requirements.

To find information about the interfaces for the cryptographic module, Sect. 3.1 of the SP covers all ports and interfaces.

Step E: SSP Management Because the module interface is API-based and the caller is the sole operator, all SSPs enter and exit the module through the caller's API interactions. This communication is in plaintext, since the purpose of fips.so is to provide cryptographic services to the caller, not to require the caller to implement crypto merely to communicate with the module.

In some deployments where the full TLS implementation is within the boundary, the exchanges may be considered protected while a TLS session is active.

The fips.so library includes algorithms for key generation, key derivation, random number generation, and shared-secret computation. Depending on the boundary definition, some of these may be claimed as key transport or key agreement mechanisms or documented as core components of KAS/KTS provided externally to callers.

For zeroization, the module offers multiple APIs that zeroize cipher contexts containing SSPs for specific services. The Security Policy should guide callers to invoke the correct zeroization functions at the end of each operation. The implementation must also be reviewed to confirm that intermediate SSP values (e.g., during key generation, integrity tests, or transient copies that are no longer needed) are zeroized before returning from the function call.

As a software module, SSPs are typically stored only in volatile memory (RAM) and are cleared when the module or platform resets.

SSP management is covered in chapter 9 of the SP, including sections for storage areas, input–output methods, zeroization methods, a list of the SSPs themselves, and any transitions (Sects. 9.1 through 9.5, respectively).

Step F: Self-Test The fips.so library usually performs self-tests at power-on, including integrity checks and algorithm KATs. Depending on the integrity-test design, the module may rely on a checksum file (e.g., a.hmac file) containing a precomputed integrity check value; if used, that file must be included in the boundary. In other designs, the integrity value is appended to fips.so itself.

Care must be taken to ensure:

- KATs cover the full algorithm (e.g., hashing included within signature generation)
- KAT parameters are approved (per IG 10.3.A)
- Test vectors do not use key/hash/curve sizes that are transitioning per SP 800-131A

Sometimes vendors may neglect to place the module into an error state when conditional self-tests (such as PCTs) fail. For a library module where the caller controls key usage, the module may choose its PCT type, but key discard alone is not sufficient. The module must also enter an error state, similar to pre-operational or CAST failures.

In typical OpenSSL deployments, the entropy source is outside fips.so, so entropy health-test failures are not treated as module self-test failures. However, the module must handle such errors correctly and stop DRBG services, returning the appropriate status to the caller.

At Level 1, periodic self-tests are not required. On-demand self-tests may be supported via dedicated APIs, if available, or by power-cycling the module to rerun startup tests.

Self-tests are cataloged in chapter 10 of the SP, starting with the pre-operational self-tests in Sect. 10.1, moving to the conditional self-tests in Sect. 10.2, periodic self-tests in Sect. 10.3, and concluding with error states and how an operator can initiate self-tests in Sects. 10.4 and 10.5.

Step G: Life Cycle Assurance The fips.so library follows a typical finite state model (FSM) that includes all major required states, with the exception of a distinct CSP entry state, which can be mapped to the operational state.

At the end of the module's life cycle, invoking the zeroization service, unloading the library, and then deleting the module is sufficient to meet end-of-life requirements.

Any CVEs discovered during development and after release must be reviewed carefully and handled in accordance with IG 11.A requirements.

Organizations following standard industry practices should already meet expectations related to version control; however, make sure to use an automated security analysis tool on the codebase to confirm there are no obvious issues, such as buffer overflows.

Chapter 11 covers all aspects of life-cycle assurance, from installation, initialization, and startup procedures, and then covering administrator guidance, non-administrator guidance, and end of life details.

Step H: Algorithm Testing All algorithms claimed as approved in the Security Policy must be tested through ACVTS, including all supported implementations, such as C, assembly, or CPU-accelerated paths (e.g., AES-NI).

On ×86 platforms, the OPENSSL_ia32cap environment variable is commonly used to enable or disable specific accelerations. The ACVP parser used for testing must be able to exercise all available implementations. atsec maintains a publicly available ACVP parser for each major OpenSSL version, which can be used as a starting point for algorithm testing [4].

Section 2.5 of the SP covers all the approved algorithms that must be tested.

Step I: ESV Certification Most fips.so deployments on Linux use a non-physical entropy source, such as CPU-jitter entropy. Depending on the implementation, the entropy source may be accessed from kernel space or user space. In some cases, the jitter entropy library is statically linked into fips.so, making the entropy source part of the cryptographic boundary.

In addition to selecting a SP 800-90B-compliant entropy source, ensure that:

- The OE and entropy-source version listed on the ESV certificate exactly match what the module uses.
- The "public use document" is followed for configuration settings (if any), including use of the standard GetEntropy() interface.

The entropy input length used to seed the DRBG is sufficient for the DRBG's security strength. Looking ahead to SP 800-90C alignment, the entropy input should be at least 3/2 times the DRBG security strength. If CTR_DRBG without a derivation function is used, it must be seeded with full entropy from the source. Section 2.8 of the SP includes both the ESV certificate numbers and the details about the RBG and how it is used.

Step J: Functional Testing In order to verify conformance to all FIPS requirements, the cryptographic and security testing lab (CSTL) is expected to test all test requirements from ISO 24759 that are related to executing the module on the defined environment and observe its behavior for positive operations (such as running offered services) and negative operations (such as forcing the self-test failure).

Typical methods for testing fips.so library include using a customer test application that can execute all services of the module and deliberately cause a failure. To do so, some OpenSSL versions offer built-in flags that can be enabled to corrupt a specific test; the same effect can also be obtained using a debug session library build with debug symbols on or compiling a binary that is modified to cause the desired self-test failure. Irrespective of the method used and who builds the test harness, the CSTL is responsible for confirming that the module behaves as expected for each of these tests and documenting the outcome as well as the method of testing.

If the testing is performed remotely then all the rules listed in Sect. 7.4 of the Management manual should be followed with presence of a CVP certified tester [3].

Until now, all the testing evidence has been archived at the CSTL, with only some references of the test file, test harness, or the module functions included in the test report assessment, with there being no specific rules for how references are documented. Starting with ACMVP, this process will be formalized to form a consistent body of test evidence for each validation.

The ACMVP program mandates documenting all test evidence in a pre-defined folder structure. Once the testing is completed and all logs are recorded, there should be a hash calculated on the log files and its value should be included as part of submission to provide transparency, ensuring no module updates or further testing are performed after submission. As an example, a possible high-level structure of the evidence folder is listed below; any sections that are not applicable, such as "Physical-Security," can be deleted or kept empty.

- FSM-States-Testing
- Module-Components
- Module-Installation
- Module-Interface-Verification
- OE-related-Tests
- Physical-Security
- SSP-Testing
- Services-Testing
- Test-Setup
- Test-scripts

Step K: SP and Report Preparation from ACMVP Point of View Traditionally, the SP used to be written in the vendor's preferred format and a PDF version of the SP used to be submitted as part of module submission. This lacked consistent formatting across different submissions, making it difficult for the manual review to confirm all required information is present.

Recently, after the publication of SP 800-140B [2], the process changed to make use of a template Word file that dictates the format of the SP and includes predefined XML controls to populate the tables that get listed in the SP using the source file in JSON format. The CMVP maintains a tool called ModVerifier that takes the JSON file and the SP template as input and outputs a populated Word file that gets submitted to the CMVP. As part of this SP creation process, the ModVerifier tool also performs many rule checks and verifications that are well documented and removes the dependency on manual review.

Under the ACMVP project, the SP creation will continue to use the ModVerifier app with a future expectation to convert the entire SP to the JSON format, removing the dependency on the Word file.

As part of the ACMVP project, different test evidence (TE) requiring source code review and functional test were categorized and this list will be made public when the program launches. The fields used for TEs have been enhanced as part of the ACMVP project to make best use of the provided information.

Also, in order to reduce the report review time and focus on the technical details, the folder reference storing the log for a specific TE is required to be included as part of the “reference” tag of each TE that requires functional testing; when appropriate, multiple TEs can be addressed using a single folder reference.

Here is an extract from the functional test file showing how the error test logs can be documented.

```
{
        "teList": [
          "10.07.03",
          "10.08.03",
          "10.09.03",
          "10.10.01",
          "10.10.02",
          "10.28.02"

        ],
        "description": "Verify self-tests error han-
dling",
        "access": "observed",
        "technique": "debugger",
        "setup": "reference into Catalog",
        "errorInduction": "description of modifications
made to the module or its OE to induce an error for the
purpose of performing negative testing",
        "results": {
"summary": "\n10.07.03: All failure logs documented in
the individual folders:\n 1.Integrity-failure
2.Load-Test-failure
3.Conditional-Pair-Wise-Test-Failure
4.Entropy-Test-failure 5.Bypass-Test-failure
6.Critical-functional-Test-failure
7.CAST-failure.
\n : Error Recovery logs are present in: /Error-Recovery/
folder.
\n 10.08.03: All logs related to verification of the
error indicator present in /Error-Indicator/ folder.
 \n10.09.03:All logs related to verification of crypto-
graphic operation inhibition present in /All-Crypto-In-
hibited-in-ErrorState/
\n 10.10.01 and 10.10.02: All logs related to verifica-
tion of degraded mode in /CAST-FailedCrypto-Inhibited-
in-DegradedMode",
          "digest": "#############",
          "fileLocation": "Functional-Test/FSM-States-
Testing/Error-State-Testing/",
          "integrityMechanism": "SHA2-512"
        }
      },
```

Step L: Submission and Review through ACMVP So far, FIPS 140–3 submission packages have been created using the Web Cryptik tool from the CMVP that creates a Zip package with the file name that identifies the lab, unique submission identifier, submission scenario used, and the date of package creation. Each CSTL has been given access to a NIST Box account where the Zip file gets uploaded; once it is downloaded and checked for basic format, the CSTL gets an email from the CMVP confirming the submission. After this, the module gets listed on the MIP list.

In the ACMVP project, the submission will happen directly on the ACMVP server, similar to how algorithm testing happens by connecting to the ACMVP server. The process for accessing the ACMVP server will also be the same as the process to submit CSR requests and obtain certificates from the CMVP and the server will have a Demo and Production environment available. This will also require the CSTL to upload the pre-requisite references to the ACVP and ESV certificate.

A typical submission flow will follow these basic steps:

1. Register the IUT module specifics with the NIST server.
2. Download the templates for the security policy and the test requirements pertaining to the registered module. This step is performed automatically when the user starts step one.
3. After the tester fills in some or all of the data obtained in step two, the data is uploaded to the server. This step can be performed as often as needed, allowing even partial uploads of data.
4. When all test data and evidence information is uploaded, the user can request the publication of the data which marks the end of the test cycle. This step indicates to NIST that the evidence is now ready for review.

Step M: Obtaining a FIPS Certificate Currently, once the module is on the MIP list, it sits there for a long time and then gets manually reviewed by the assigned reviewer. Once the ACMVP program gets rolled out, CMVP reviewers can perform their actions within a few days after all necessary data has been submitted. For now, the coordination phase will still happen via email, but in future the CMVP is thinking of converting this into a review via conference calls, spaced out at a reasonable interval; this change will avoid back-and-forth questions and answers via email, and CMVP reviewers will be able to freely discuss the module as well as review the archived test evidence. Once the CMVP is satisfied with all responses, the certificate will be awarded (Fig. 35.1).

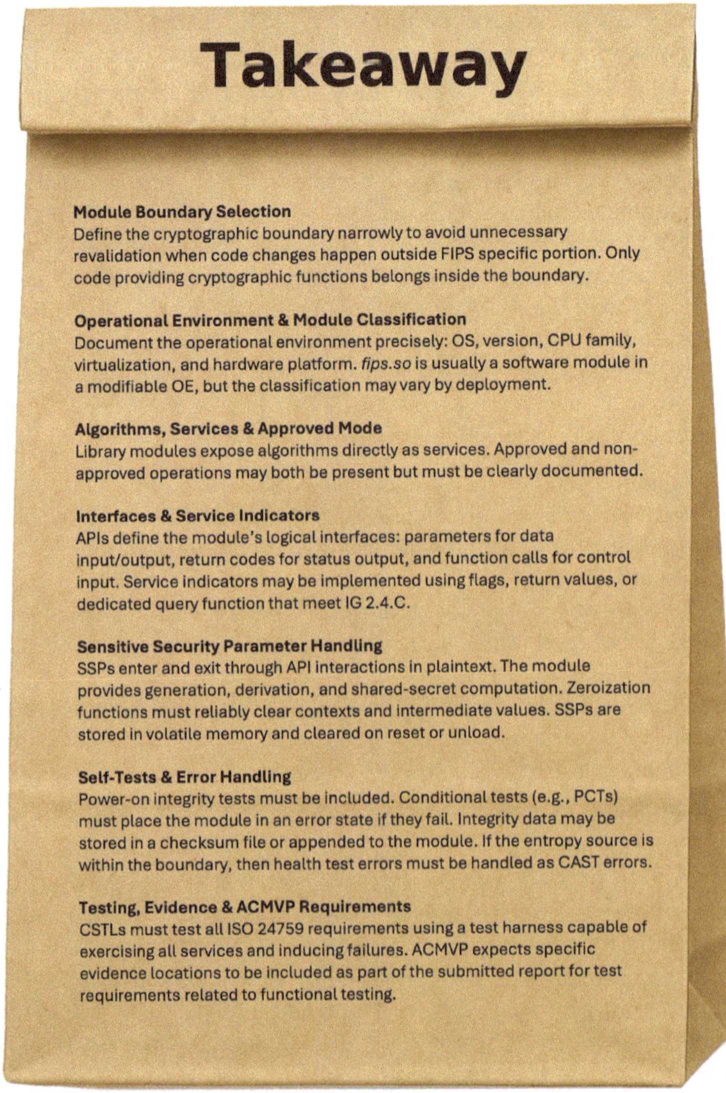

Fig. 35.1 Takeaways regarding the OpenSSL pilot project

References

1. atsec information security corporation (2025) Amazon Linux 2023 OpenSSL FIPS Provider FIPS 140–3 Non-Proprietary Security Policy. National Institute of Standards and Technology. Available via NIST. https://csrc.nist.gov/CSRC/media/projects/cryptographic-module-validation-program/documents/security-policies/140sp5021.pdf. Accessed 03 Dec 2025

2. National Institute of Standards and Technology (2016) SP 800–140B: CMVP Security Policy Requirements. https://csrc.nist.gov/projects/cryptographic-module-validation-program/sp-800-140-series-supplemental-information/sp800-140b. Accessed 03 Dec 2025
3. National Institute of Standards and Technology (2016) FIPS 140–3 Management Manual. https://csrc.nist.gov/projects/cryptographic-module-validation-program/cmvp-fips-140-3-management-manual. Accessed Dec 03 2025
4. Müller S (2018) ACVP Parser Github page. https://github.com/smuellerDD/acvpparser. Accessed 03 Dec 2025
5. National Institute of Standards and Technology (2021) Automation of the NIST Cryptographic Module Validation Program. https://www.nccoe.nist.gov/automation-nist-cryptographic-module-validation-program. Accessed 03 Dec 2025

Part VI
Industry Experience with FIPS Validation

Chapter 36
AMD: A Mini-HSM in Every Chip

Yi Mao

The late afternoon sun angled across Austin as another story unfolded at the FIPS 'n' Chips restaurant. At one corner table, a polished AMD Ryzen™ wafer reflected the golden light like a badge of craftsmanship. The etching on its surface seemed to whisper a truth that John Traver, AMD's senior security architect, had lived for the past five years: building trust into silicon is both an art and an endurance race.

Unifying the Cryptographic Heart When John joined AMD, cryptography was scattered across the firmware landscape. Pockets of encryption routines existed in ROM, early boot stages, and later firmware layers. The fragmentation had grown organically over product generations, but it posed a challenge for validation. "We wanted one place," John later reflected, "a single repository of trust that could be tested, certified, and reused."

Yi smiled, remembering AMD's first outreach to atsec about firmware validation. "So that's where it began," she said, recalling the early discussions on consolidating crypto logic into a single, certifiable core.

That decision marked the beginning of AMD's FIPS journey. The team set out to unify their cryptographic functions within the Security Processor—the silicon guardian that anchors every AMD system-on-chip (SoC). The effort began in 2021 and advanced through multiple module validations, ultimately culminating in the most recent FIPS 140-3 Level 1 validated module. When certificate #5085 was published in October 2025, the sense of accomplishment at AMD was unmistakable.

That certificate was not an isolated achievement. By 2025, AMD had accumulated eleven FIPS 140-validated modules, as shown in Table 36.1, spanning software-hybrid, firmware-hybrid, and sub-chip hardware implementations. Each entry highlights the module type, validation date, and collaborative efforts that reflect AMD's steady progress within the CMVP landscape.

Y. Mao (✉)
atsec information security corporation, Austin, TX, USA
e-mail: yi.mao@atsec.com

Y. Mao (ed.), *Tasting Cryptography*, https://doi.org/10.1007/978-3-032-30243-4_36

Table 36.1 A selection of AMD's FIPS certificates

Certificate #	Vendor	Module name	Module type	Validation date
5085	Advanced micro devices, inc. (AMD)	AMD ASP cryptographic CoProcessor ("Turin")	Hardware	10/22/2025
4941	Advanced micro devices, inc. (AMD)	AMD ASP cryptographic CoProcessor ("Genoa")	Firmware-hybrid	01/15/2025
4915	Advanced micro devices, inc. (AMD)	AMD ASP cryptographic CoProcessor ("Raphael")	Firmware-hybrid	12/12/2024
4914	Advanced micro devices, inc. (AMD)	AMD ASP cryptographic CoProcessor ("storm peak")	Firmware-hybrid	12/12/2024
4880	Advanced micro devices, inc. (AMD), microsoft corporation	Pluton security processor ROM	Hardware	11/14/2024
4819	Advanced micro devices, inc. (AMD)	AMD Pensando™ PenTrust security module	Software-hybrid	10/01/2024
4723	Advanced micro devices, inc. (AMD)	AMD ASP cryptographic CoProcessor ("Phoenix")	Firmware-hybrid	07/11/2024
4626	Advanced micro devices, inc. (AMD)	AMD Ryzen™ PRO 6000 Series PSP Cryptographic CoProcessor	Firmware-hybrid	10/04/2023
4555	Advanced micro devices, inc. (AMD)	AMD Ryzen™ PRO 5000 Series PSP Cryptographic CoProcessor (models 5475 U, 5675 U, 5875 U)	Firmware-hybrid	07/31/2023
4402	Advanced micro devices, inc. (AMD)	AMD Ryzen™ PRO 4000 Series PSP Cryptographic CoProcessor	Firmware-hybrid	12/30/2022
4401	Advanced micro devices, inc. (AMD)	AMD Ryzen™ PRO 5000 Series PSP Cryptographic CoProcessor	Firmware-hybrid	12/30/2022

The breadth of validation, from the foundational security processor module to a comprehensive module including a large set of cryptographic algorithms covering AES, RSA, DRBG, ECDSA, HMAC, and both SHA-2 and SHA-3, represented AMD's holistic commitment to assurance across its product portfolio.

The latest module's scope rivaled that of a software giant's cryptographic library. "It's almost like a hardware form of OpenSSL," John said later. "Except this one lives right inside the chip."

One Codebase, Many Worlds Yi observed that AMD's approach resembled modular software design, only implemented in silicon. "So, the same certified root now anchors your entire product line?" she asked.

John nodded. "From the start, AMD designed its FIPS modules not only to serve the entire product line but also to support an entire generation of platforms," he explained. "The same certified code now powers data-center processors, client CPUs, and embedded devices. Even the gaming line, though not itself validated, still inherits the security rigor of the FIPS foundation."

This unified architecture introduced a new level of assurance across markets that rely on certified cryptography, including federal agencies, financial institutions, telecommunications providers, and healthcare systems. By embedding a validated core deep within the SoC, AMD provided every product with a common trust anchor.

From Root of Trust to Mini HSM Modern processors have become too complex to certify as a single unit. Each system-on-chip (SoC) integrates numerous interfaces, including CPUs, GPUs, I/O controllers, memory paths, and specialized accelerators, which together form an intricate ecosystem. AMD recognized that the key to certification was defining a meaningful and manageable boundary, one that centered on a firmware-assisted sub-chip module.

The team focused its first certification effort on the Root of Trust, the immutable code responsible for verifying every byte of firmware during secure boot. "We built the crypto directly into the Root of Trust ROM," John explained. "All firmware authentication begins there, inside the certified boundary." Every signature check and every key used for verification are handled by a FIPS-approved module using NIST-approved algorithms.

This Root of Trust evolved into what John described as "a mini hardware security module." It performs secure boot, manages cryptographic keys, and is designed to extend its capabilities to provide encryption, hashing, and key generation services. The long-term goal is ambitious: to deliver a Level 3-equivalent HSM experience within every AMD processor without the need for an external hardware appliance.

That transformation simplifies security for customers while also improving performance. Hardware-based cryptography is inherently faster and less error-prone than software implementations. "Our customers still perform additional audits," John said, "but having that FIPS certificate in place assures them that the foundation is sound."

Designing for Certainty The journey toward certification tested AMD's resolve. FIPS documentation, by necessity, speaks in broad and abstract terms to accommodate every imaginable technology. Translating those general principles into the precise language of silicon design required constant interpretation and, at times, reinterpretation.

Importantly, the standard's broad language never precluded a hybrid module from taking a single-chip embodiment. Under FIPS 140–3, the types of modules—software, firmware, hardware, software-hardware hybrid, and firmware-hardware hybrid—are defined independently of embodiment types such as single-chip, multi-chip embedded, or multi-chip standalone. In principle, a hybrid module can exist in any of these embodiments as long as its firmware and hardware components, although disjoint, operate together to provide the required cryptographic functions.

Midway through the effort, however, a new NIST directive halted the submission of firmware-hybrid modules with a single-chip embodiment in March 2024. Overnight, a nearly complete module had to be restructured to broaden its scope and qualify as a sub-chip hardware module. The change slowed progress but deepened AMD's understanding of how evolving guidance must coexist with long hardware development cycles.

Yi empathized, recalling the confusion the directive created across multiple vendors. "We all felt that pain when the hybrid-module rules were questioned, not because of security concerns," she said. "At the time, the CMVP could not reconcile how a firmware component, disjoint from a hardware component, could coexist on a single chip while still meeting the definition of a hybrid module. They could imagine a hybrid module with a multi-chip embodiment, but not one embodied in a single chip. Yet in reality, components that are functionally disjoint can still be interconnected through internal bus lines, regardless of whether the embodiment is single or multi-chip."

John nodded, adding that the timing of new guidance often complicated long-term hardware planning. "Right now, I'm planning chips into 2028," he explained. "That means making hardware decisions years in advance while certifying devices that were released two years ago. When new Implementation Guidance appears, some of the modules designed under older rules no longer qualify, even if their architecture hasn't changed."

He suggested exploring a rebranding validation approach to address this gap. "Some modules on a chip inherit exactly the same design from an earlier validated module," John said. "They pass the same tests, but the newer IGs create conditions that make a direct recertification impossible. In those cases, rebranding might provide a practical path, treating the new module as a continuation of the original validation rather than forcing it to meet updated guidance it was never designed for."

Yi was enthusiastic about this new idea, noting that rebranding could preserve continuity while maintaining transparency. "If a module was validated in 2022 and a rebranding occurs in 2025," she cautioned, referring to the shorter certificate validity of a rebranded module, "its expiration would still follow the 2022 cycle, and its FIPS certificate would expire in 2027. The CMVP's rebranding rule is to keep the expiration date of the original validation. Rebranded modules have a shorter lifespan. It is a tradeoff, but it acknowledges that the design has not changed." She added that such an approach has already been applied when a module was fabricated on a different chip line while still based on the same architecture. "In that case," she said, "it has been allowed as a validation rebranding rather than as a new module requiring compliance with every new IG."

The discussion about rebranding reminded John why AMD had chosen a design philosophy rooted in predictability rather than change. For AMD, consistency across generations of silicon became a guiding principle, a way to reduce risk and uncertainty as standards evolved.

From that moment, AMD's engineers embraced what they called "designing for certainty." Every requirement was implemented according to the most conservative interpretation possible, leaving no room for dispute. Hardware decisions made today would power products years into the future, and certification often arrived long after the silicon had shipped. The cadence of semiconductor development demands foresight, documentation, and discipline, forming a culture that AMD turned into an advantage.

Collaboration Through the CMUF Rather than discouraging him, the hybrid-module controversy deepened John's engagement with the Cryptographic Module User Forum. He joined working groups where vendors, labs, and CMVP representatives debated how to adapt FIPS guidance to modern SoCs.

Those meetings, often held on early Friday mornings for West Coast participants like John and lasting two hours or more, were rigorous affairs. Participants prepared position papers, rewrote sections of proposed guidance, and sometimes argued line by line over the wording of an Implementation Guidance draft. "You have to write, debate, and defend every word," John said later. "But that's how progress happens."

Through that process, AMD became one of the industry voices advocating for practical clarity: allowing firmware-assisted sub-chip modules on a single die to be recognized as legitimate FIPS entities, that is, hybrid modules with a single-chip embodiment. "It's not about relaxing the standards," John explained. "It's about ensuring the rules evolve with the realities of modern silicon."

The Caliptra Collaboration AMD's FIPS journey also shaped its role in Caliptra, which is the open-source hardware security architecture jointly developed by AMD, Nvidia, Google, and Microsoft under the Open Compute Project (OCP). Caliptra defines a unified attestation and secure-boot framework for servers and data-center equipment.

The concept is elegant: a small, isolated hardware block responsible for verifying firmware and reporting trustworthy measurements, consistent across vendors. To ensure credibility, the consortium designed Caliptra's hardware environment to be FIPS-certifiable. AMD applied its own validation experience, reviewing the architecture for compliance gaps and even prototyping it on FPGA before silicon integration.

The first generation, John said, is already "FIPS-ready." The second aims even higher, introducing a fully open, hardware-based cryptographic module that functions much like a sub-chip version of OpenSSL. By providing the code, blueprints, and reference implementation openly, the Caliptra team hopes to give smaller companies a head start toward compliance and interoperability.

Attestation and the Future of FIPS As AMD looks ahead, the company's engineers are studying how future FIPS revisions will intersect with attestation technologies—the 2025 edition of ISO/IEC 19790 already introduced attestation concepts for the first time, hinting at what could become FIPS 140–4. AMD envisions a world where a device can prove its certification status cryptographically, where NIST's approval certificate itself could be signed, stored, and verified by the hardware.

"Today," John observed, "to check if a module is certified, you have to look it up manually on the NIST website and compare versions. In the future, the module could simply present its signed certificate and say, 'Yes, I am FIPS-validated.'"

Such automation could extend across entire platforms. Servers, routers, and storage devices could verify each other's certificates, ensuring that every layer of hardware and firmware in a data center is authenticated and compliant. It is a vision that merges FIPS validation with the broader fabric of trust now emerging through the Software and Hardware Bills of Materials (SBOM and HBOM) initiatives.

The Value of Endurance As the conversation drew to a close, Yi summarized what she had heard. "Your story reminds us that validation isn't bureaucracy," she said. "It's a design discipline that endures across generations."

When John reflects on AMD's four-year certification journey, he speaks not in frustration but in respect for the discipline that FIPS demands and the collaboration it inspires. "It's difficult," he admitted, "but it brings real value. It forces us to think deeply about how security should work."

AMD's story is one of consolidation and patience: from scattered cryptographic routines to a unified, certified core; from hardware obstacles to a philosophy of conservative precision; from internal development to an open-source contribution shaping the industry's next generation of trust anchors.

By 2025, AMD stood among the leading semiconductor vendors not only in FIPS certifications, with eleven module certificates and three ESV validations, but also in defining how assurance evolves with complexity. Each certificate represented not an endpoint but a milestone in building the silicon roots of trust that modern computing depends on.

The wafer on the restaurant table caught one last glint of light as evening settled over the FIPS 'n' Chips gathering. Beneath its mirrored surface lay the story of AMD's quiet transformation, a journey from firmware fragments to a single heartbeat of assurance, a mini HSM pulsing at the center of modern computing.

Before wrapping up, John shared a lighthearted recollection. His most memorable moment, he said, was attending atsec's FIPS 'n' Chips crypto bootcamp in the spring of 2025, where engineers and lab testers met face to face to trade lessons learned. "That event brought the whole ecosystem together," he recalled. "It reminded me why this work matters."

About the contributor: John Traver John has worked in FW Development and Architecture for 18 years. As a Principal Member of Technical Staff at AMD's Product Security Office (PSO), John is responsible for Root of Trust security, including integration of the Caliptra Project and led architecture and design of AMD's Root of Trust crypto module which is currently a Module in Process for FIPS 140–3

Certification. Previously, John led FW architecture for Micron's Flash Translation Layer and was a Lead Designer for Intel's CSME.

Chapter 37
Crypto4A: The Quantum-Ready Kitchen

Yi Mao

At the FIPS 'n' Chips restaurant, the day's special was not on the printed menu. A new guest had arrived, Jim Goodman from Crypto4A Technologies, carrying a story steeped in engineering heritage, perseverance, and a vision for the post-quantum future.

Yi greeted him warmly. "Your modules have been quite the buzz around here," she said. "Let's hear what brought you to our table."

Jim smiled, the kind that belongs to someone who has walked a long road and still enjoys the journey. "Crypto4A," he began, "was founded by four of us, old colleagues from Chrysalis-ITS (Information Technology Security), the Canadian company that originally designed the Luna HSM [1]. Back then, our Luna devices set the benchmark for hardware-based cryptographic assurance. When SafeNet acquired Chrysalis-ITS in 2004, that technology became the foundation for the SafeNet Luna HSMs, later passing through Gemalto and now Thales. So, in a very real sense, Crypto4A's story begins where Luna's left off."

He paused, glancing toward the ceiling where the restaurant's chandelier pulsed with encrypted constellations. "After years working in that world, we realized something was stuck. The HSMs we used for military projects looked exactly the same as the ones we'd built a decade earlier. Ten years had brought no evolution. So, we asked ourselves: do we keep complaining like old engineers, or do we fix it?"

And fix it they did. From sketches drawn on paper between 2012 and 2017 emerged a new design, unshackled from legacy constraints, a clean-sheet architecture built for a world that would soon face quantum computers. "From day one," Jim said, "we designed for quantum resilience. Not just at the algorithm layer, but in every key hierarchy, in secure boot, in attestation, inside the bones of the system."

Y. Mao (✉)
atsec information security corporation, Austin, TX, USA
e-mail: yi.mao@atsec.com

Y. Mao (ed.), *Tasting Cryptography*, https://doi.org/10.1007/978-3-032-30243-4_37

The result became Crypto4A's flagship: the QxHSM and QxEDGE [2], platforms built for crypto agility, where post-quantum algorithms could be introduced, tested, and validated without tearing down the foundation.

A Partnership Forged in Testing Yi recalled how Crypto4A had been the first vendor to test post-quantum algorithms under FIPS validation, even before NIST's production test servers were online. The work required quickly providing experimental test vectors from NIST demo server, holding frequent debug sessions with Crypto4A engineers even outside normal working hours, and a willingness to fail forward.

Jim nodded. "Other labs were hesitant. It was new territory, but atsec said, 'Let's do it.' We were working hand-in-hand with Renaudt and Swapneela, testing, retesting, generating vectors, and even dealing with early tool issues. The day after the PQC FIPS standards were published, we were ready. That was exhilarating."

Crypto4A's validation journey was no easy sprint. Their engineers faced what Jim called the confluence of three storms: a shift from FIPS 140–2 to 140–3, the higher rigor of ISO-based testing, and a transition to a lab with stricter standards. "When we saw the gap analysis, it looked overwhelming," Jim admitted. "But you helped us eat that elephant, one byte at a time."

Virtual code reviews and remote testing introduced another first. Yi, who had contributed to the creation of FIPS 140–2 IG G.17 Remote Testing for Software Modules, played a key role in shaping this approach. The guidance she helped establish was later expanded to cover all module types during the COVID pandemic, with the clear caveat that the remote testing allowance did not apply to physical security testing. This important provision was subsequently carried over to the FIPS 140–3 Management Manual, section 7.4 Remote Testing of Module [3]. Instead of handing over their source code, Crypto4A shared their screens and walked the lab through every module and routine. At first, it felt awkward; by the end, it became efficient science. "You could guide us directly to what you needed," Jim said. "We got to show the full codebase, keep our IP secure, and still give you the assurance you required. It turned into one of the best processes we've done."

Integrity Over Expedience Jim reflected on what set the experience apart. "You held the bar high," he said. "Other labs were good, but atsec went above and beyond." Yi added that this high standard came with a strict no-conflict-of-interest rule: the design and implementation must be done by the vendor, while atsec's role must be to understand and verify the accuracy of the information provided. atsec can compose the FIPS validation specific documents, such as the Security Policy, but only when the mapping back to the original vendor information is clear. Jim said, "You told us exactly what needed fixing, but never how to fix it. That's the right way; it keeps the process honest."

Yi smiled. "We often hear complaints that we're too strict. But for us, the certificate is a byproduct. The real goal is the security of the product."

Jim agreed. "Exactly. FIPS isn't the destination; it's the proof of a journey."

That shared philosophy shaped their collaboration. The process was demanding, with retrospective design changes, retesting under evolving Implementation Guidance, and navigating the growing forest of IGs, but both sides saw it as a professional dialogue rather than an audit. "Your team didn't dictate," Jim said. "You explained, we proposed, and together we reached compliance in a way that made sense."

The Value of FIPS Beyond Compliance When asked why Crypto4A invested so heavily in validation, Jim's answer came easily. "Two reasons," he said. "First, it enforces discipline. It makes sure we build to a higher standard. Second, it opens doors. FIPS is on every Request for Proposal (RFP) we care aboutfinance, defense, government. Even outside North America, customers treat it as proof of quality."

He leaned back thoughtfully. "And once you've climbed that hill, staying there gets easier. Each release now follows FIPS principles, whether we validate it or not. The certificate isn't the point; the point is designing as if every release could be validated."

That mindset shift, he said, came directly from atsec's gap analysis: "You showed us exactly what we were missing. We built it in. Now FIPS-level quality is just how we do things."

Learning through Doing Crypto4A's approach favored direct engagement over outsourcing. They wanted their own engineers, not consultants, to own the process and understand every requirement. This aligned perfectly with atsec's philosophy of learning through doing. By working directly with the vendor's team, atsec ensures that developers and engineers absorb the security principles embedded in the FIPS requirements. Once learned, these principles can be applied to future revisions of the same product or sibling products, building sustainable competence within the organization.

Jim said, "We don't want someone else writing our Security Policy." Yi agreed, emphasizing that atsec's role is to translate the vendor's design intent into FIPS assurance language without taking over the design.

"We translate engineering intent into assurance language so that your technical knowledge remains intact and becomes part of the validation process," Yi explained.

The result was more than a validated module; it was a team fluent in the language of FIPS. "Now our developers talk about Critical Security Parameters (CSPs) and operational environments like it's second nature," Jim said proudly. "You didn't just help us pass. You helped us learn."

Challenges Along the Road No FIPS journey is without its sleepless nights. Jim recounted the long days wrestling with ISO's paywalled standards, evolving guidance, and the new layers of documentation that came with 140–3. "Moving from FIPS 140-2 to 140-3 was like updating from a trusted recipe to a revised edition of the same cookbook—the ingredients remain familiar, but a few rare materials have been introduced and the instructions are refined, requiring higher skill to follow." He laughed. "And yes, paying for ISO standards still feels wrong." Yi added that there is good news: the ISO store now provides the 2025 editions of ISO/IEC 19790 and 24759 free of charge, ensuring that access to these foundational standards is no longer a barrier for engineers and developers."

There were practical hurdles too: algorithm testing, entropy testing, functional testing, physical security testing, and the endless revisions driven by shifting interpretations. Yet through those cycles, a rhythm emerged. "You start overwhelmed, but you end proud," Jim said. "We didn't just check boxes; we made the product better."

Toward the Quantum Horizon As their conversation drew to a close, Yi asked about the future. Jim's eyes brightened. "Quantum readiness was our starting point. Now it's our identity. We're part of the PQC validation wave, we're seeing adoption from governments, and the U.S. federal roadmap is clear: high-risk systems must be quantum-ready by 2030, full migration by 2035. We plan to be there for every step."

He mentioned that one of Crypto4A's founders, Bruno Couillard, had represented the company at the White House for the post-quantum transition announcements. "It's an exciting time," Jim said. "After decades in cryptography, to see it all come full circle, this feels like witnessing an orchard full of sweet fruits that we planted decades ago, with a full harvest season yet to be celebrated."

Epilogue at FIPS 'n' Chips Back in the restaurant, the lights dimmed. Yi lifted her glass. "To the four amigos," she toasted, nodding to the spirit behind Crypto4A's name.

Jim laughed. "Yes, Crypto4A—the four amigos who set out to build something better together."

The room joined in laughter and applause. For a moment, the FIPS 'n' Chips tower seemed to glow brighter, its radar dish of fiber optics pulsing as if catching a signal from the quantum horizon itself.

In the glow of that light, the story of Crypto4A stood as more than a validation success. It was the tale of engineers who refused to accept stagnation, who built anew rather than patch the old, and who met the FIPS process not as a burden but as a proving ground.

It was a testament to the principle that, in the world of assurance, just as in the art of cryptography, real trust is earned one iteration at a time.

About the contributor: Dr. Jim Goodman Jim is the CTO of Crypto4A, where he is responsible for all aspects of Crypto4A's security architecture and cryptographic implementations in both SW and HW. He has been an active researcher and developer in the field of cryptographic systems for over 25 years, across a variety of industries. Currently, he is focused on the integration of, and migration to, PQC algorithms in Crypto4A's product offerings.

References

1. Thales (2020) Thales Luna Network HSM 7 Luna HSM Client Product Documentation. https://thalesdocs.com/gphsm/luna/7/docs/network/Content/Home_Luna.htm. Last accessed 03 Dec 2025
2. CRYPTO4A (2025) Qx Products. https://crypto4a.com/products. Last accessed 03 Dec 2025
3. FIPS 140–3 Management Manual. https://csrc.nist.gov/csrc/media/Projects/cryptographic-module-validation-program/documents/fips%20140-3/FIPS-140-3-CMVP%20Management%20Manual.pdf. Last accessed 03 Dec 2025

Chapter 38
Google: Designing Trust into Pixel Tensor SoC

Yi Mao

The lights of the FIPS 'n' Chips restaurant shimmered over the copper tabletops, where circuit motifs glowed faintly beneath the glass. On this particular evening, the discussion turned toward engineers from Google's Pixel Tensor SoC who had spent the past year navigating one of the most intricate puzzles in modern certification: how to validate cryptography inside a phone whose heart beats as a single system-on-chip.

At the table sat Olivier Benoit and Anish Chivukula, two engineers who took over responsibility from the pioneers Eugene Liderman and Brian Wood to shepherd Google's Tensor SoC FIPS 140–3 modules through the labyrinth of requirements and working groups that now define assurance in the age of integration. For them, validation was not a side project; it was a quiet, yet essential part of how the Pixel smartphone reached its most demanding federal customers.

In order to offer products into the U.S. Government, and specifically the US Department of Defense, there are three specific criteria that any vendor has to meet:

1. Department of Defense (DoD) Security Technical Implementation Guides (STIGs) which are the configuration standards for Department of Defense Information Assurance (IA) and IA-enabled devices/systems. The STIGs contain technical guidance on how to harden information systems/software that might otherwise be vulnerable to a malicious computer attack.
2. National Information Assurance Partnership (NIAP) Mobile Device Fundamentals Protection Profile (PP MDF), a Common Criteria-based Protection Profile that incorporates information security requirements for Mobile Devices such as smartphones and tablets for use in an enterprise.
3. National Institute of Standards and Technology (NIST) sets guidelines through the use of the Federal Information Processing Standards (FIPS) and Special Publications. Specifically, FIPS 140 specifies the security requirements that will

Y. Mao (✉)
atsec information security corporation, Austin, TX, USA
e-mail: yi.mao@atsec.com

Y. Mao (ed.), *Tasting Cryptography*, https://doi.org/10.1007/978-3-032-30243-4_38

be satisfied by a cryptographic module, providing four increasing, qualitative levels intended to cover a wide range of potential applications and environments.

The DoD STIG is the overarching umbrella that requires both NIAP PP MDF for the device(s) and FIPS CMVP for the cryptographic modules used for data-at-rest and in-transit.

FIPS and the Market of Trust Unlike traditional FIPS vendors, Google's Tensor Silicon organization in charge of the Pixel Tensor SoC does not sell cryptographic modules as standalone products. Its work in security validation emerged from a very specific need: compliance with CNSSP Bulletin 11, NIAP, OMB Circular A-130, and NIST SP 800–53, which establishes the baseline required for smartphones used in government and defense applications in the United States. NIAP's PP MDF alone does not require a FIPS Cryptographic Module Validation Program (CMVP) certificate, however, as part of their validation, NIAP must ensure data-at-rest is performed by a certified FIPS module under CNSSP11.

"The driver is straightforward," Olivier explained during one of their sessions. "To make our Pixel devices eligible for certain U.S. government use cases, the underlying cryptography must be validated under FIPS 140-3. That's one component of multiple certifications needed, such as the PP MDF, DISA STIG compliance, and others, which enable us to sell to regulated customers and participate in federal markets."

The motivation, however, extended beyond compliance. Google's Tensor Silicon organization found that an independent certificate held commercial value even outside government channels. It strengthened customer confidence and signaled engineering discipline. "It's a statement of trust," Olivier said. "Our competitors pursue the same path, and staying aligned keeps us credible. Falling behind would mean losing not only compliance but also market trust."

Encryption at Rest and Entropy in Motion For Google's Tensor Silicon engineers, the data-at-rest protection requirement became the defining focus of their FIPS effort. As Anish explained, NIAP's PP MDF does not explicitly name FIPS 140-3 CMVP, but it mandates that cryptographic algorithms protecting stored data must be validated. Further, CNSPP, OMB Circular A-130, and SP800–53 specify FIPS module validation for data at rest. Within every modern smartphone lies a UFS flash controller, responsible for encryption and decryption of data written to and read from persistent storage. That controller, in Google's Tensor Silicon case, became the FIPS cryptographic module.

"This is our main reason for validation," Anish said. "The UFS subsystem handles encryption for data at rest. To comply, that encryption logic must reside in a FIPS 140-3 module."

The same logic extended to entropy sources. Both NIAP and NIST require validated random number generation, and so Google's Tensor Silicon also pursued Entropy Source Validation (ESV) for its hardware noise source. "It's all part of the same framework," Anish added. "If you want your data at rest to be trusted, the entropy behind your keys must also be trusted."

In parallel, Google's Tensor Silicon organization continued to certify its algorithms through CAVP, ensuring that every AES, SHA, and elliptic-curve function inside its SoC passed the standardized test vectors. Even when a module was not undergoing a full CMVP validation, each algorithm implementation was verified independently. "We test all algorithms in our SoCs," Anish said, "and those vectors still come from NIST. Even in the Common Criteria world, protection profiles like PP-0084 or PP-0117, uses the same NIST vectors. The ecosystem depends on that common anchor."

The Global Thread: ISO, Common Criteria, and the CRA Horizon Olivier observed that FIPS 140-3's identity as an ISO-based standard made it globally relevant. The 2025 editions of ISO/IEC 19790 and 24759, published as free international standards, aligned directly with FIPS 140-3 and strengthened its role beyond North America. "It's not just a U.S. artifact anymore," he said. "ISO has made it usable worldwide. I heard at ICCC (International Common Criteria Conference) that many regions still struggle to define how to demonstrate algorithm correctness in Common Criteria schemes. FIPS fills that gap."

Yi added background: FIPS 140-3 was derived from the earlier FIPS 140-2 and formalized through ISO, whose updated standards now define the foundation for future NIST FIPS 140 revisions. U.S. NIST, the Canadian CCCS, and liaison organizations like CMUF serve as conduits between industry and ISO's Subcommittee 27 (SC 27). Within that subcommittee, Working Group 3 (WG 3) maintains ISO/IEC 19790 and 24759, while Working Group 4 governs algorithm specifications. For companies like Google, involvement in these groups is increasingly strategic.

Anish noted his interest in participating in the next revision cycle. "If they just finished the 2025 edition, the next will come in three to five years. It would be good for us to contribute from the hardware side." Yi encouraged him to join the U.S. delegation, now led by Samsung's Eric Hibbard. "Many large companies are already there, Intel, Microsoft, Oracle. Google's perspective on embedded security and hybrid systems would be very valuable."

The discussion drifted briefly into ISO's organizational dynamics. SC 27 governs cybersecurity and privacy, including security testing and evaluation, while SC 42 handles artificial intelligence, sometimes overlapping in territory. "Each wants to define how to test AI," Yi explained. "Coordination between subcommittees is crucial, especially as security evaluation expands into AI technology." Anish nodded, seeing parallels with the way FIPS itself had evolved: as technology outpaced regulation, structure had to catch up.

The Hybrid Module Debate When the conversation returned to the technical realm, the engineers turned to one of the most pressing issues in modern validation: hybrid modules on a single chip. Google's SoCs, like those of every major smartphone manufacturer, combine hardware accelerators with firmware and driver layers that orchestrate security services. This mixture, hardware foundations controlled by code, defies the traditional binary of "hardware" versus "software" modules in the FIPS framework.

"The hybrid module on a single-chip is our daily reality," Anish said. "For SoC vendors, that's normal. But it challenged older assumptions within CMVP that a hybrid module can only exist on a multi-chip embodiment, where hybrid submissions were temporarily paused."

The year-long effort to lift that prohibition unfolded through the Cryptographic Module User Forum (CMUF), which became the main channel for dialogue between vendors, labs, and CMVP reviewers. "The CMUF meetings were essential," Anish continued. "They allowed all sides to explain why hybrid modules with a single-chip embodiment are necessary for embedded systems. It's not about avoiding rules, it's about reflecting how technology actually works."

That collaboration led to the drafting of a new Implementation Guidance document. It was first discussed in early 2024, and the first draft I was finalized later that year after months of weekly meetings. The draft IG went through two rounds of public comments with some minor updates in 2025, and is still pending for the CMVP's final approval. "It took more than a year," Anish recalled. "Two-hour sessions twice a week, reviewing comments, revisiting sections, and sometimes reopening old discussions. It was exhausting but necessary. The CMUF is how we turned debate into consensus."

Embedded Systems and the Need for Flexibility To the Google Tensor Silicon engineers, the hybrid debate reflected a broader truth about modern hardware. Decades ago, a board might have contained separate chips for the CPU, memory, and cryptography. Today, all of that is fused into one die. "If you look at an SoC today," Anish said, "it's a computer in itself: CPU, GPU, modem, Wi-Fi, GPS, and cryptography, all on one chip. That's the evolution of integration."

The earlier sub-chip model, defined under FIPS 140-2 Implementation Guidance 1.20, worked for discrete hardware but no longer fit this paradigm. Under FIPS 140-3, the "hardware-only" assumption proved too restrictive. "The standard should never dictate whether something must be hardware or software," Olivier added. "Performance, cost, and flexibility drive those decisions, not the standard."

Hybrid modules became not an exception but a necessity. Firmware layers now configure hardware registers, run self-tests, and monitor entropy health, all mandatory FIPS functions that require code. "If everything were locked in hardware," Yi reflected, "you would lose adaptability. Firmware allows last-minute corrections and configuration without another fabrication run."

Boundaries, Exclusions, and the Limits of Practicality In theory, FIPS validation allows exclusions of some components within the module boundary. In practice, that mechanism often proved burdensome. "If the FIPS validation were done on a single chip with a list of excluded components," Anish explained, "you risk revalidation if it changes, even if it has nothing to do with cryptography. On a complex SoC, that's 99 percent of the chip."

The exclusion allowance had made sense in an era of simpler architectures. Now, it caused unnecessary churn. "It's impractical," Anish said bluntly. "We need mechanisms that evolve with technology. The standards' intention was forward-looking, but implementation hasn't kept pace. More frequent IG updates, with vendor and lab input, would help CMVP adapt."

The group agreed that participation in CMUF was the only effective way to close that gap. As Yi put it, "It's a shared responsibility. Vendors must be proactive, not reactive. CMVP can't move faster unless we contribute concrete feedback."

The Human Cycle of Standardization The engineers' reflections on the process itself revealed another pattern: the challenge of maintaining continuity in long technical discussions. "When meetings stretch over a year," Anish said, "people join and leave. Topics reopen because new participants weren't there when earlier decisions were made." His suggestion was pragmatic: structure comment periods with defined closure points. "Otherwise, the same arguments recycle endlessly. Maybe limit it to a few open comment rounds."

Olivier smiled knowingly. "That happens in every standard. You close a topic in July, revisit it in December, and everyone forgets why it was settled. It's the cycle of committees."

Yi noted that some CMUF working groups had begun introducing more discipline. The Request-for-Guidance group, led by Trish Wolff, now required each proposer to present their case, attend the meeting, and summarize conclusions afterward. "It keeps accountability alive," she said. "The person who raises the question must help close it."

Lessons in Patience and Precision FIPS validation, especially for embedded systems, demands not just technical rigor but patience. "Our product life cycle spans years," Olivier said. "From setting requirements to final integration, it can take three or more years. Each phone generation overlaps with the next. We start planning for certification before the silicon even tapes out."

That timeline means that any change in guidance or interpretation can cascade through development. "FIPS is very prescriptive," Anish observed. "That's its strength and its weakness. The rules are absolute. If you miss a detail, it's expensive to fix later, both in time and in silicon."

He paused before adding, "That's why we stress paying attention to detail early. In an embedded design, hardware isn't flexible. If you miss something, you can't just patch it tomorrow."

A Meeting Between Worlds Toward the end of their reflection, Anish recalled a moment that captured the disconnect, and potential, between regulators and innovators. At ICMC 2025 in Toronto, during a joint discussion with CMVP and Hybrid IG WG representatives, he realized how differently each side viewed embedded systems. "The reviewers are experts in software modules," he said, "but they don't always see the complexity of modern chips. To them, hardware seems monolithic. In reality, it's a network of interacting cores, firmware, and buses. The FIPS boundary isn't a solid wall, it's a dynamic surface." Anish continued. "It was an eye-opening aha moment for me to understand the CMVP reviewers' limitations."

That realization inspired Yi to make a proposal: to offer technology workshops for CMVP reviewers, explaining chip architectures, firmware interactions, and hardware roots of trust. "It's mutually beneficial," Yi said. "If reviewers understand the technology, they can shape better guidance. Standards evolve faster when knowledge flows both ways." Anish indicated that he would love to help if such workshops were organized by the CMUF.

Yi nodded. "That's the spirit of this community, education as assurance. FIPS grows stronger when reviewers and engineers learn from each other."

The Long View of Trust As the evening drew to a close, Olivier shared one final anecdote. "When we explained to our executives that our certification depended on a community working on an Implementation Guidance document, they asked every two weeks if it was done. We had to tell them, no, writing an IG takes more than a fortnight."

Everyone laughed as the tension of a year's worth of Friday morning meetings, from 7 a.m. to 9 a.m. for West Coast participants like Anish, dissolved into good humor. The story was more than comic relief; it was a reminder that behind every certificate lies a network of people negotiating the language of trust, one paragraph at a time.

For Google Tensor Silicon, FIPS validation is not a bureaucratic obligation. It is a discipline, a way to ensure that the devices millions carry each day are built upon cryptography that has been tested, verified, and aligned with the evolving standards of the world. In the silicon symphony of modern security, their engineers play a patient and precise rhythm, balancing innovation with assurance.

About the Contributors: Anish Chivukula Anish is a silicon architect in Google's Tensor Silicon organization. His expertise is in designing and evaluating silicon solutions in consumer and infrastructure products. He currently leads FIPS certification efforts on Tensor Silicon. Previously, he held roles as an RTL design engineer at Google, Broadcom, Qualcomm, and Texas Instruments. He studied Electrical and Computer Engineering at the University of Illinois and the University of California San Diego.

Olivier Benoit Olivier is a Security Assurance Manager at Google and has extensive experience in embedded security and cryptography. He lived through the advent of Side-Channel Analysis in 1998 and Fault Injection Attacks in the year 2002 while holding a security engineer position at Gemplus (now Thales). Throughout his career, Olivier strived to improve the security posture of various products: smartcards (at Gemplus), Point-of-Sale terminals (at Ingenico), smartphone SoCs (at Qualcomm) and last but not least smartphone devices and security chips at Google. In the last 10 years, he has focused more on security certification (FIPS, Common Criteria) as a means to demonstrate the security level of a product beyond mere regulatory requirements.

Chapter 39
IBM: The Journey to FIPS Level 4 Validation

Yi Mao

Origins at FIPS 'n' Chips The corner table at FIPS 'n' Chips had a quiet gravity that evening. It wasn't the animated hum of younger vendors comparing validation stories or debating algorithm transitions; it was a slower rhythm—measured, confident, and reflective. When the conversation turned to IBM, everyone seemed to lean in a little closer.

Yi smiled as she looked around the table. "When Joachim and I visited NIST to learn the CMVP history," she said, "there was a question that no one could quite answer: Why did IBM go for Security Level 4? Tonight, I think we might finally get that answer."

Dave Evans chuckled softly. "That's ancient history," he began. "But it's where everything started. Honestly, if FIPS 140-1 had gone up to Level 6, we would have chased that too. We heard that the early drafts actually defined six levels, but during development, Levels 5 and 6 were folded into what became Level 4."

Richard leaned forward. "Were you part of the very first FIPS certification?"

Dave nodded. "Yes. I worked with Research on the preliminary card before the CCA code was even ready. Jonathan and I helped them build a cross-compiler. They were developing on Windows, but the card ran on a CP/Q++ (or Command Program Q++) operating system back then. That was before we moved to a Linux kernel; we took the CP/Q OS and enhanced it with additional device drivers."

He paused, smiling. "My team had tooling expertise covering compilers, linkers, debuggers, the whole lot. We bridged that gap so the Research group could get their code onto the hardware. And once they saw we were useful, we kept building with them: device drivers, diagnostics, everything. Eventually the FIPS validation lab, along with two IBM researchers, gathered in Lexington, Kentucky, where we facilitated the functional testing. That's how the first Level 4 module got posted."

Y. Mao (✉)
atsec information security corporation, Austin, TX, USA
e-mail: yi.mao@atsec.com

Y. Mao (ed.), *Tasting Cryptography*, https://doi.org/10.1007/978-3-032-30243-4_39

He turned to William with a grin. “And somewhere along the way, we picked up this guy,” he said, gesturing to his colleague. “William joined the hardware team, and from that point on we carried it through to every card since.”

William laughed. “That was quite an initiation. I remember the buzz when the certification came through. It was the night before Thanksgiving in 1998. We were all packed into our research manager Elaine Palmer’s office, anxiously watching the phone, waiting for the validation lab to call and tell us whether NIST had approved our certification. After what felt like an eternity, the phone finally rang—and Elaine grabbed it instantly. Then we heard her say, ‘Thaw it in a sink of ice water. I have to hang up now—I’m waiting for an important call!’”

The table burst into laughter as William continued, “It turned out her vegetarian friend, who had never cooked a turkey before, had called for advice. The lab didn’t actually call for another hour. But when they did, the room erupted—cheers, hugs, even a few happy tears. After all that work, it was one of the sweetest moments of our careers.”

As the laughter subsided, William leaned back, still smiling at the memory. “Those were unforgettable times,” he said. “And we learned our lessons quickly—especially that Level 4 tamper response has absolutely no sense of humor.”

Dave nodded. “Ah, the sheep story,” he said, already smiling.

When the very first 4758 cards [3] were installed in new systems, they hadn’t yet gone through final system testing. The shipping crew prepared the completed systems for delivery, sealing each one in several layers of shrink wrap and storing them overnight in an unheated loading area. That night, the temperature in the warehouse plummeted. By morning, several cards had reported tamper events and triggered their self-destruct mechanisms.

“The sensors did exactly what they were designed to do,” William said. “They thought someone was freezing the cards to open them.”

The incident delayed shipments and forced the team to replace several cards in a hurry. IBM urgently needed a way to keep them warm during transit. One of the designers, equal parts exhausted and amused, jokingly suggested that the cards be strapped to a sheep—each 4758 would ship with its own personal heater.

Yi laughed as Dave continued, “And that was it. The sheep jokes never stopped. The lab filled up with stuffed toy sheep, cartoon drawings, and wool sweaters knitted by one of the developers. We had whole meetings where the whiteboard was covered in doodles of sheep keeping the cards warm.”

William chuckled. “To this day, you’ll still hear someone mention the ‘sheep solution’ whenever we talk about tamper sensors. Those early 4758s were the only crypto cards in history to have their own personal heaters—at least in spirit.”

The story, now part of IBM’s folklore, reminded everyone at the table that behind every secure design lies a team of engineers who could laugh even when things went wrong—and perhaps that sense of humor was part of what made Level 4 possible in the first place.

The laughter lingered for a moment before settling into quiet smiles. Dave paused, then nodded thoughtfully. “Those memories still make me laugh,” he said, “but that first validation changed how we looked at everything. IBM’s FIPS story didn’t start as a compliance checklist—it started as research ambition. IBM Research set its sights on building the first cryptographic adapter to achieve FIPS 140-1 Level 4. They made it a goal, and I got in on the ground floor of that journey."

"Then William and Richard kept dragging me along ever since," he added with a grin. "Once we did Level 4, there was no going back."

William returned the smile and replied, "That's because I knew it wasn't just another certificate; it was history in the making."

From Stack Certifications to Whole-Card Validation As the plates of fish and chips were replaced by coffee cups, the conversation deepened. IBM's approach evolved from stacked certifications, where hardware and firmware were validated in separate layers, to the bold idea of whole-card validation.

Dave leaned back, as if replaying the project. "That whole-card certification wasn't just another box checked; it covered everything, including the business logic itself. That's where we really leaned on atsec to make it possible, as it was a huge project—and a difficult one."

He described the challenge of defining clean separation between layers: "We had to explain and sometimes defend where the line was drawn between the hardware and the mini-boot firmware, and how that differed from functionality in the EP11 layer. It took a long time to get right, but we submitted on time. When the certificate came through at Level 4 [4], it was wonderful. That was another milestone for IBM, our first whole-card FIPS 140-2 validated at Security Level 4."

Transition to FIPS 140-3 As the world moved to FIPS 140-3, IBM began its next challenge with the same team at atsec: whole-card validation for CCA. "It's a big leap," Dave said. "We're going from 140-2 to 140-3, and there are a lot of subtle changes that only show up when you're knee-deep in the checklist."

Multi-factor authentication has also been a hurdle. Compared to the tamper-response and physical protections IBM has perfected, MFA feels like a small piece that doesn't fit naturally into an HSM's machine-to-machine flows.

"It's like establishing trust through key agreement, authenticating, then setting it free," Dave said. "But the requirement expects a traditional human-to-machine pattern, so we've had to be creative." Yi nodded. She and William had presented the issue at ICMC and raised it at ISO WG3, highlighting that two-factor authentication for machines can never mirror how humans authenticate.

Dave paused, reflecting on how modeling requirements had evolved. "Under FIPS 140-2, a Finite State Model needed formal proof, and at Level 4 the expectation was to trace the model directly to implementation, annotating source code so every transition mapped to a routine." William recalled, "EP11's model could be expressed at a high level in SPIN, but mapping cleanly to every code path was still tedious."

Yi smiled. "It looks simple now, but that's because we worked together to make it that way." She remembered translating IBM's abstract model into a form that mapped to service specifications and then to code. Her background in mathematical logic, and hands-on modeling weeks and months with the team, helped shape those "simple" models. She shared the same lessons at the 2024 NIST Workshop on Formal Methods in the Certification Process [5].

Her words brought to everyone's mind how, under FIPS 140–3, the emphasis is behavioral clarity. For each function, you define pre-conditions that must be true before it runs and post-conditions that should be true once it completes. Instead of proving everything mathematically, the model focuses on documenting behavior clearly enough that it can be understood and verified.

This shift from formal verification to reasoned traceability was liberating: EP11's model could remain concise, and the much larger CCA environment could be represented at a higher level without exploding into thousands of enumerated transitions. With modeling made manageable, the team was free to focus on finalizing an approach for machine-to-machine authentication.

The GPA of Security When the table turned to certification levels, Yi noted that IBM's module already met Level 4 in most areas such as physical security, the finite state model, design assurance, and others. "It's really only the authentication part that still needs refinement," she posited.

"Exactly," Dave replied. "But under the current rules, that one gap drops our overall to Level 3. It's like maintaining an A in ten subjects and a B in one and the transcript only shows a B." Yi laughed. "Each area has its own score, but FIPS reports the lowest of all areas as the overall security level of the module."

Dave then proposed a simple solution: present the result like a GPA—3.7 or 3.8 out of 4—so, customers could see the difference between "barely Level 3" and "almost Level 4" at a glance. Yi agreed that a more granular summary would be fairer and more transparent than a single floor number.

Level 4 as a Philosophy That reflection brought the table back to the central question the CMVP veterans at NIST had asked: why did IBM go for Level 4 when it was originally a future-proof placeholder? "Now we know why," Yi said. "It came from IBM Research. They wanted to be the most secure." Dave nodded.

What began as a research goal became both a technical driver and a market signal. In financial services, where IBM HSMs underpin global payment systems, Level 4 became shorthand for IBM-grade assurance. Even when Level 3 satisfied regulations, customers desired Level 4.

Standards and Usability Richard compared frameworks: the Payment Card Industry Hardware Security Module program favors agility that accommodates wildcards and rebuilds, whereas FIPS is exacting, with each version associated with a hash value; a rebuild would fail the integrity check. Harmonizing FIPS and PCI would reduce duplication and speed up innovation.

"A bit of practical advice," he added, "approach FIPS with an open mind, and engineer for certification rather than retrofit to it."

Dave nodded in agreement: "It isn't a sprint; it's a journey that takes as long as it takes, and you must learn to trust your lab. IBM also chose breadth over minimalism, expanding the boundary to cover the whole card so FIPS mode remains usable."

"A FIPS version no one can use isn't real security," Richard said. "When a customer switches to FIPS mode, their normal applications should still run."

A Legacy of Leadership and What's Next "IBM's DNA is in the FIPS program," William said. "Our engineers built the first Level 4 modules—single-chip and multi-chip—under Certificates 35 and 40. Even Randy Easter, before joining the CMVP, worked on our early designs." Yi smiled: when the CMVP grew into what it is today, IBM was already part of its foundation.

Before the night ended, Joe Livingston added a pragmatic view: Developing a product that reaches FIPS Level 4 is a moderately difficult problem by itself. On top of that, IBM sees clear value in reaching for the highest level, which adds challenges in design, documentation for the tester who will communicate with the CMVP, and the realities of scheduling and forecasting. The CMVP reviews dozens—sometimes hundreds—of submissions amid resource constraints and political headwinds.

"It sounds daunting," Joe said, "but that's also what makes it exciting. Engineers are problem solvers—the harder the challenge, the more interesting it becomes."

As the conversation wound down, Yi looked around the table with appreciation. IBM's history with FIPS wasn't just technical; it was human, rooted in persistence, collaboration, and curiosity.

Dave smiled. "We made history once," he said. "And we're still making it, one certification at a time."

About the contributors: David Evans Dave is the IBM Cryptographic Coprocessor Low-Level FW Development Project Lead. He has worked for IBM for more than forty-two years in FW and tooling development, including the past twenty-eight on IBM's Cryptographic Coprocessors. He also works as a coordinator for the FIPS certification of their Cryptographic Coprocessors.

Richard Kisley Richard is a Senior Technical Staff Member with IBM focused on Hardware Security Modul (HSM) development. He is the IBM contact to ASC X9 (X9.org), convenor of ISO TC68 SC2 WG11 and member of WG13 focused on security in retail banking. He is also the IBM PO contact to PCI SSC (2017-present), and the primary IBM representative elected to the PCI SSC Board of Advisors.

William Santiago-Fernandez William is a Senior Technical Staff Member and Master Inventor at IBM and a Crypto Hardware Architect in charge of FIPS 140 Level 4 packaging solutions. Since joining IBM, William has worked in the crypto space developing ASIC and FPGA acceleration solutions for crypto algorithms as well as continuous development around physical security and entropy solutions for IBM. William holds a bachelor's in Electrical engineering and a Bachelor's in Computer Engineering from the University of Puerto Rico- Mayagüez Campus and a master's degree in systems and computer engineering from Rensselaer Polytechnic Institute.

Joe Livingston Joe has over 25 years of experience developing electronics and software for embedded platforms. Since joining the IBM EP11 crypto team, Joe has taken on leadership of firmware/software development for the EP11 hardware security module FIPS certifications. Joe holds a Bachelor of Science degree in electrical engineering from SUNY New Paltz and has research interests in cybersecurity, fitness technology, and audio engineering. He is an inventor on ten patents approved by the US Patent Office.

References

1. National Institute of Standards and Technology (1998) CMVP FIPS 140-1 Certificate #35. https://csrc.nist.gov/projects/cryptographic-module-validation-program/certificate/35. Last accessed 03 Dec 2025
2. National Institute of Standards and Technology (1999) CMVP FIPS 140-1 Certificate #40. https://csrc.nist.gov/projects/cryptographic-module-validation-program/certificate/40. Last accessed 03 Dec 2025
3. Dyer JG, Lindemann M, Perez R, Sailer R, Va Doorn L, Smith SW (2001) Building the IBM 4758 secure coprocessor. Computer 34(10):57–66
4. National Institute of Standards and Technology (2023) CMVP FIPS 140-2 Certificate #4553. https://csrc.nist.gov/projects/cryptographic-module-validation-program/certificate/4553. Last accessed 03 Dec 2025
5. National Institute of Standards and Technology (2023) NIST Workshop on Formal Methods within Certification Programs (FMCP 2024). https://www.nist.gov/news-events/events/2024/07/nist-workshop-formal-methods-within-certification-programs-fmcp-2024. Last accessed 03 Dec 2025

Chapter 40
Intel: Security at Heart, Validating at Scale

Yi Mao

A Midday Scene at FIPS 'n' Chips The lunch crowd at FIPS 'n' Chips was beginning to thin when Yi settled into her usual booth near the corner window. The soft clatter of silverware, the hum of quiet conversations, and the scent of freshly grilled salmon created a calm backdrop for the meeting she was about to begin. The restaurant's trademark giant screen—framed in brushed aluminum and mounted high above the bar—flickered with the deep-blue standby display of the conferencing system. Soon it would come alive with faces from Oregon and California, but for the moment the screen rested quietly, waiting.

Yi took a sip of tea and glanced at the clock. She had a few minutes before Intel's representatives would join. It was just enough time to center herself and recall the people she would be speaking with. Intel's FIPS story was long, textured, and deeply intertwined with the evolution of hardware security itself, and the three individuals joining her represented different dimensions of that history.

She thought first of Shola Adegboye, a Security Researcher and Technical Program Manager whose work sits at the intersection of security governance, enterprise risk management, and product security assurance at Intel. Shola coordinates security requirements, certification planning, and architectural alignment across business units. As the manager of Intel's global FIPS program, he oversees validation activities across Intel platforms, chipsets, accelerators, and emerging cryptographic components. His perspective always reminds her that FIPS validations, even when rooted in cryptographic detail, are ultimately part of a larger enterprise responsibility.

Then there was Thomas Bowen, a Security Architect at Intel Corporation. He brings deep experience in storage security and was involved in Intel's earliest FIPS validations within the former NSG storage group. His years of working with cryptographic modules, security architectures, and validation laboratories give him a

Y. Mao (✉)
atsec information security corporation, Austin, TX, USA
e-mail: yi.mao@atsec.com

Y. Mao (ed.), *Tasting Cryptography*, https://doi.org/10.1007/978-3-032-30243-4_40

practical understanding of how evolving standards intersect with real hardware designs.

And finally, there was Dr. Xiaoyu Ruan, a Senior Principal Engineer in Security whose work centers on architecting security Root of Trust (RoT) infrastructure and protocols for Intel's security engines, such as Intel® Converged Security and Management Engine, or CSME. His background spans a broad range of cryptographic implementations, from AES and SHA to ECC and RSA, as well as the latest post-quantum algorithms like LMS, ML-DSA, and ML-KEM. He not only oversees the designs of Intel's security engines for FIPS compliance, but also actively contributes to industry standards, such as SPDM (Security Protocol and Data Model), and to ensuring their FIPS compliance.

The giant screen chimed softly as the meeting connection initialized. Yi straightened the stack of papers beside her, took one last look at her notes, and lifted her eyes toward the display as it brightened. A moment later, Intel's representatives appeared on the screen. Yi greeted them with a smile and mentioned that the talking points she had shared—covering a brief outline of Intel's FIPS journey, the motivations behind it, key challenges, strategies for overcoming them, their engagement with CMUF, ISO WG3 and ICMC, advice for others, and any memorable stories—were only a reference. The conversation, she assured them, could take its natural course.

"Maybe I can cover the first point," Xiaoyu began. "In case you do not remember, Shola is the chief manager of the FIPS program across Intel. He oversees all the FIPS validations across the company."

Yi nodded. "Yes, I remember. Last year you were on the panel at the NCCoE building for the NIST workshop on formal methods in certification."

"Yeah, yeah," Shola said with a small laugh. "Thanks so much. I think I will have to say that Xiaoyu and Thomas have been in this game far longer than I have. I was brought into the conversation at the point where we needed to have an actual industry position with regard to FIPS. So, if I am going to speak a brief introduction in terms of what Intel has done…".

He continued, "Intel has historically been certifying modules as far back as when you look at CSME as a module. We have partnered with you for a very long time, possibly before 2016 or even further back. And when you consider our solid-state drives, when Intel used to produce SSDs, FIPS validation was a core requirement in that industry space. That tells you how far back Intel has been involved with FIPS validations."

A Long History Rooted in Customer Needs "While Intel has been doing this," Shola continued, "the CSME validations were driven by key customer requirements. And for the solid-state drives—those stories in the storage space—FIPS was an industry requirement and, in some cases, almost a default requirement."

As the conversation shifted, he added, "Over the years we saw an essential need, within our product security assurance function, to make a statement and have a formal position regarding FIPS."

Yi followed up. "So, the mandatory FIPS requirement is for the federal markets. Do your customers in the federal segment require crypto modules or algorithms to be validated from the chip level up? Or do you get equally strong demand from other sectors such as finance or telecommunications?"

Thomas answered. "Our customers are not necessarily directly the federal government. A lot of this comes through derived requirements. We produce CPUs and many other products, but our direct customers are OEMs and other partners who embed our solutions into appliances or systems. They serve federal customers, or financial sectors, or others that align with federal requirements. So, we receive the requirement indirectly, because our customers make it part of their purchasing specifications. To enter certain markets, they want solutions that meet these requirements."

Shola added, "You can classify our customers as OEMs (Original Equipment Manufacturers), CSPs (Cloud Service Providers), and system integrators, including companies building network firewalls and security modules. It cuts across the globe and across industries. These customers serve federal, financial, and healthcare sectors, and some serve defense customers as well."

Xiaoyu contributed another layer. "In addition to explicit customer requirements, we also look at competitors. For example, AMD or NVIDIA. If they have similar products validated, or we see work-in-progress on the validation list, that signals a requirement for us. We need to be on par so we can compete in the market."

Thomas agreed. "When I first got involved in FIPS within storage, this was exactly the issue. All other storage vendors had FIPS certifications. To compete in certain markets, you needed this certification. We did get direct customer requests, but looking at competitors helped us understand how others approached validations—through security policies, scope definition, and so on. Customers expect consistency between suppliers."

He added, "In the storage space, everyone generally pursues FIPS validations aligned with storage security standards like TCG (Trusted Computing Group) Opal. It was useful to see how vendors connected FIPS validations—which focus on cryptography—to the bigger services that the storage industry cares about, such as data encryption and interfaces to manage that data encryption."

A Company-Wide Mandate Shola described the turning point in Intel's internal strategy. "As the years progressed, we saw the essential need to have a clear position regarding FIPS. Management recognized three driving factors: first, FIPS provides a clear baseline for our crypto hygiene; second, it provides security assurance."

He continued, "So management's intent was to broadcast this across Intel and have teams begin looking at how best we could implement it. Around 2021, Intel took a position to ensure that going forward we would implement applicable FIPS 140-3 requirements. The major reason was to support our customers. And the third driver was Intel's commitment to customer obsession—ensuring we can support customers who want to achieve FIPS validation."

Yi summarized. "So, the FIPS mandate supports federal markets, but also other industries such as finance and telecommunications, because those sectors align to federal requirements."

Thomas nodded. "Yes. We rarely receive a requirement directly from the federal government. Customers receive it and they pass it on to us."

Boundary Definition and Evolving Standards Thomas leaned back slightly as the discussion turned to scope. "There is always a big debate for us about scope," he said. "We try to avoid unnecessarily spending effort on non-requirements. We want to make sure our validations meet our customers' needs, but there is a cost to increasing scope and having to look at more of the implementation."

He explained that boundary decisions were among the first major topics Intel had to tackle when FIPS work ramped up. "One of the big things we talked about when we first got really deep into FIPS was that you need to clearly identify your boundary," he said. "There are different strategies for what your boundary should be. You can make it very small, or you can make it larger. It depends on what you want to do with the validation and what you want to include."

"At the same time," he added, "you have to worry about certain requirements in the standard that may dictate what your boundary has to include. There is a balance, but it is always a big debate for us when we look at validations for different types of products."

Yi asked whether this led directly into the topic of challenges. "Is it something that feels very difficult," she asked, "to nail down where the boundary should be, especially when the CMVP dictates the boundaries? For example, that situation last March where the hybrid module could not be on a single chip, and you helped lead the effort to persuade them it could and should be, because with advancements in technology so many things can fit into a single chip."

Thomas answered by zooming out to the level of the standard itself. "I think the standard, and I mean both the FIPS algorithm & security standards and the FIPS 140-3 validation standard, will need to continually evolve," he said. "Technology is moving really quickly. Today we have systems-on-chip, and even what we used to think of as a single chip may now be multiple chips within the same package, stacked on top of each other and connected in complex ways."

He continued, "This idea that the smallest size of the module must be the full chip is just not practical anymore. Things are getting really complex in a very small space, and the standard needs to accommodate that so you can shrink your boundary down and focus on the important bits. If you have to validate at the full chip level, we are already at a point where it is far too complex to do a validation that includes the whole chip. There is too much going on, including a lot that is not security relevant and not crypto relevant. Through FIPS 140-3 Implementation Guidance 2.3.B, sub-chip cryptographic subsystems, you can validate a hardware module that is a subset of a full chip, but this requires your module to have a clear hardware interface. There are other types of sub-chip modules such as software, firmware and hybrids that should be able to be validated through the program as sub-chip modules as well."

"In the end," Thomas said, "a FIPS validation is really about cryptography. We need ways to focus the validation on the actual cryptography, and often on individual crypto subsystems inside a design."

Yi pointed out that the standard offers the exclusion approach. "The CMVP could argue that if a single chip is too complex, you can start from the full chip and remove things from the boundary through exclusion," she said. "Why does that not work well in practice?"

Thomas did not hesitate. "The problem is that the way the standard defines excluded components is also impractical," he explained. "You have to list all your excluded components in the security policy, which is a public document. That is not realistic. And you have to test all those excluded components to prove why they can be excluded. That can make the validation shift its focus away from the cryptography and toward justifying every other piece of the chip."

He paused, then added, "The concept of excluded components might be going in the right direction, but it is not there yet. It needs more focus on practicality. Otherwise, validations will end up being mostly about proving that all the other parts of the chip are not security relevant, instead of concentrating on the cryptography that should be tested."

First-Party Versus Third-Party Testing After discussing boundaries, Yi shifted to a broader question. "You have been doing FIPS validations since at least 2016, maybe earlier," she said. "Does that compliance mindset bring you value beyond meeting customer requests or competing in the market? From a design perspective, does the standard give you the value you are looking for?"

Shola offered his view first. "From a design perspective, when you look at Intel from a security standpoint, Intel has always tried to be practical in implementing key security principles," he said. "Intel has been thinking in terms of layered security. We talk about security as layers, like an onion. We see FIPS as an additional layer. It is often viewed as a security baseline."

He went back to a point he had made earlier. "One key thing I mentioned at the beginning is crypto hygiene," he said. "From both an engineering perspective and a management perspective, we saw certification as an additional way to achieve crypto hygiene. We have crypto reviews and crypto experts internally, but FIPS gives us another mechanism we can use to confirm that our cryptography is in good shape."

Yi summarized it in practical terms. "So once the algorithms are certified," she said, "you can have peace of mind that at least the core algorithm implementation is correct."

"I think that is the most important part," Xiaoyu replied. "In most cases we do not strictly need CMVP, but CAVP is the baseline of our validation, especially for new algorithms. For crypto software, you can sometimes leverage open-source implementations. But for new cryptography like ML-DSA, ML-KEM, or schemes we implement in house, it is very hard to claim you have full coverage."

He explained why external testing matters. "You can generate random vectors and test with those, but that is not comprehensive. It is not thorough enough. Having a good third-party test suite from NIST means we can at least say we pass NIST's requirements, and our implementation meets their expectations. That is a very big plus."

Thomas agreed. "Right now, it is PQC," he said. "In the future it will be new algorithms. For any new algorithm, it is very useful to have an external source to validate against. It is really hard to know if you have implemented something correctly just by analysis. I have had multiple experiences where crypto experts reviewed an implementation and it looked correct, but when we ran CAVP tests we discovered something swapped, or a hard-coded value that was slightly off. CAVP has uncovered many issues that were not obvious from code review alone."

"And when you have something like CAVP, where the government is essentially saying, 'These test vectors are correct, and, if you pass them, we will give you a certificate recognizing the implementation as correct according to our infrastructure,' it becomes a strong seal of approval," Thomas said. "It gives us confidence that the core algorithm is actually implemented correctly."

Yi then turned to Intel's internal capabilities. "So that is why you have your internal CAVP lab, right?" she asked.

"That is why we have our internal CAVP lab," Xiaoyu confirmed.

Shola added, "We have the Intel CST lab that focuses on algorithm validation. It took a lot of effort, but it is now part of our process. We have a demo and production environment that allows us to test and then complete the CAVP certification process in-house."

Yi then brought up integration with development. "So, you have your internal first-party lab status," she said. "You can get production-ready algorithm certificates. That means you can integrate testing directly into your development cycle. When you design and develop new features, you can make algorithm testing the first thing that must pass."

"Absolutely," Shola said.

Thomas described how this interacts with third-party labs. "The last CSME validation we did was still with atsec providing CAVP test vectors," he said. "That was mostly due to timing. I am not sure the internal lab was fully ready. Going forward, we are transitioning so that our own internal lab will handle CAVP testing, and we will continue using third-party labs for the module validations."

Yi observed that this approach aligned with Intel's company-wide directive requiring algorithm testing across chips. "It is a very pro-cryptography approach," she said, "even if we are not the lab doing your algorithm testing anymore. There is still plenty of opportunity for collaboration on entropy assessment and module validation."

She then asked about entropy validation. "NIST has set up a similar ESV server for entropy," she said. "Do you also use that directly?"

Shola answered, "We do not use it directly the way we use CAVP. We still partner with organizations like yours to complete ESV. There is a component of ESV related work that we do internally, but we rely on third-party labs to complete the ESV process."

Thomas added more detail. "From what I recall," he said, "our entropy team's statistical testing is a superset of what NIST tests for. We have our own internal test suite to vet and tune entropy sources before we go to NIST. When we need an ESV certificate, we obviously have to use NIST's tests and scripts, but internally we also run a broader suite, because there are many additional statistical tests you can perform."

Industry Standards and Gray Areas After covering testing, Yi asked about other challenges. "Besides debating scope and standing up your own test lab," she said, "what other challenges have you faced, especially ones you have already overcome with good progress?"

"Oh, I think influencing the authorities regarding FIPS requirements is one of the biggest challenges," Xiaoyu replied. "We have use cases of cryptography that the standard does not explicitly allow, such as deriving ECC keys with a KDF. We tried to do the same for ML-DSA keys, and to support the SPDM protocol and its IV generation. Those designs are not explicitly allowed by FIPS as written, so we had to infer the intent and try to drive changes. We are not only doing this for ourselves, but also for the industry."

Thomas then stepped back to explain the pattern. "If you look at NIST standards," he said, "there are the raw algorithm standards, and there are standards that define how those algorithms can be used. For example, SP 800-133 talks about key generation and related topics. We have run into cases where those use requirements do not align very well with what the rest of the industry does in practice, and that becomes a problem."

"For us," he continued, "we need to adhere to industry standards, and we also want to be compliant with FIPS. Those things need to align. We have seen that with asymmetric key derivation, where we need to reproduce the same key on every boot and have it change when certain measured values change. There are standards that dictate those behaviors, like TCG's Device Identity Composition Engine (DICE) and related device identity work, but the FIPS standards do not officially allow those use cases. Often, it is because the use case simply was not considered."

"When we encounter that," he said, "we work with CMVP, CMUF, and the NIST Crypto Technology group (CTG). We ask them to acknowledge the use case as valid and to consider allowing it, sometimes with additional guardrails. Maybe they add constraints or extra requirements, so they can be comfortable approving it. That kind of influencing, or collaboration, is a big part of our challenge, because we are often on the leading edge looking at new use cases and new technologies that the standards did not originally comprehend."

Thomas then noted, "CMVP and CMUF are great to work with. We have submitted several proposals, including allowing KDF for asymmetric keys and allowing SPDM key schedule and IV generation. CMVP and CMUF are reviewing them. Hopefully when this book is published, they will have been accepted."

Yi noted that at the ISO level, there is a different philosophy. "In ISO meetings," she said, "there is a trend toward keeping standards very generic to leave room for new technologies. Because it is an international standard, it is often intentionally unspecific. Authors avoid concrete examples, so they do not appear to favor one method over another, and they do not preclude future ideas. That gives flexibility, but it also leaves a lot open to interpretation."

She contrasted that with CMVP. "At the scheme level, CMVP has the authority to provide interpretation through implementation guidance," she said. "As vendors, you want consistency and predictability. You want to build your chip according to what the standard allows now, without worrying that a later interpretation will invalidate it. Labs want the same thing, because we want to avoid constant debates and uncertainty in every case. We share your goal of mitigating risk and avoiding surprises late in the process."

Thomas agreed. "Different interpretations of requirements are definitely a challenge," he said. "You may have one reviewer who approves a design, and another reviewer who says it is not acceptable. For us as a hardware company, that is very difficult. We need consistency and predictability. We design hardware years before it reaches validation. We need to know that when we finally get to validation, it will still pass."

He said this is why he focuses so much on eliminating ambiguity. "I do not want standards to have gray areas," he explained. "Gray areas mean room for interpretation, and that leads to inconsistency. One validation might treat something as acceptable, while another might not. We talk a lot about gray areas and try to design away from them by staying clearly inside what is allowed. But we cannot always do that, because new technologies sometimes fall into those gray zones."

Yi observed that the tension between generic standards and specific interpretations is always present. Thomas agreed that the only way to manage it is through collaboration. "What I would like to see from CMVP and NIST," he said, "is continued collaboration with industry. They need to maintain a pulse on what is happening in standards and technology and talk with people in the field. The industry looks at NIST as the gold standard for defining cryptographic and security requirements. There needs to be alignment between what industry is doing and what government standards say is allowed. The only way to get that alignment is by having ongoing conversations."

Moments That Matter As the hour began to wind down, Yi asked whether they had any fun or memorable moments to share.

Shola answered first. "From cross collaboration, there have been many benefits to Intel," he said. "Being part of CMUF and working with NIST has helped us a lot. For example, when we were setting up the Intel CST lab, we had opportunities to collaborate with people at Cisco. Alicia, who is now at Amazon, was a very good partner when she was at Cisco, and we still work with her."

He reflected on the community as a whole. "The cryptographic industry is small compared to many others," he said. "Collaboration cannot be overstated. The ability to influence standards and learn from each other is a huge advantage."

Yi agreed and noted that Cisco was one of the early first-party labs able to do algorithm testing and that they were also a key collaborator in setting up ACVTS and later automation efforts. It felt fitting, she added, that Intel had become another first-party lab and that both companies now contributed back to the ecosystem.

Toward the end of the conversation, Yi turned to advice for others. "What would you say to companies looking for a FIPS lab?" she asked.

Xiaoyu answered. "I am sure the book itself is good marketing," he said, "but I think working with a good lab, such as atsec, is very important. If you look for a lab, just look at their existing certificates and the products they have certified. If you find similar products to yours, it is easier to work with that lab. They have experience."

Thomas added, "The design might not be the same, but the lab will understand how to work with that type of product. There are real benefits in working with a lab that has experience in your domain. For storage, for example, it can help to work with a lab that already understands storage terminology and interfaces. Their testers already speak the language."

"That is very good advice," Yi said. "We are honored by your comments, and we truly appreciate our long-term relationship. Over the years, we have become friends as well as business partners."

A Closing Invitation As the meeting drew to a close, Yi extended a final invitation. "We would like to invite you to come to Austin someday," she said. "We started the FIPS 'n' Chips crypto boot camp, and we are writing this book. When the book is published, we would very much like to have a toast and invite everyone who contributed."

They exchanged thanks and goodbyes. As the call ended and the giant screen at FIPS 'n' Chips faded back to its standby state, Yi knew that Intel's story had become another thread woven into the larger fabric of the FIPS community, and Intel's story would continue to evolve in the years to come.

About the contributors: Shola Adegboye Shola is a security professional with over two decades of experience that cuts across cybersecurity and product security. His career has spanned multiple industry sectors including telecommunication, judiciary, oil & gas, payment card industry, health sector, higher education and more recently semiconductors. Under the Intel Product Security Assurance, Shola leads Intel's FIPS Center of Excellence that brings together cross-organizational SMEs implementing FIPS. He has led the team in establishing the Intel CST Lab, Intel Secure Key Validation Service and supported the validation of numerous Intel products.

Dr. Xiaoyu Ruan Xiaoyu is a Senior Principal Engineer on Intel's Security Architecture team. He holds a Ph.D. in Computer Engineering from North Dakota State University and a B.S. in Electrical Engineering from Fudan University. With over 20 years of experience in cryptography and embedded security, Xiaoyu currently leads the Root of Trust architecture and design for Intel's server and client SoCs. He is an active contributor to industry standards, including the SPDM (Security Protocol and Data Model) protocol and the DPE (DICE Protection Environment) profile.

Thomas Bowen Thomas is a security architect within Intel's Silicon & Platform Engineering organization with over 17 years of experience developing security solutions and standards, including 7 years working on FIPS 140 validations for Intel products. Thomas is one of Intel's security standards experts, having contributed to multiple workgroups within Trusted Computing Group (TCG), the Cryptographic Module User Forum (CMUF), the International Organization for Standardization (ISO), and Non-Volatile Memory Express (NVMe).

References

1. National Institute of Standards and Technology (2016) CMVP FIPS 140–2 Certificate #2631. https://csrc.nist.gov/projects/cryptographic-module-validation-program/certificate/2631. Last accessed 29 Jan 2026
2. National Institute of Standards and Technology (2016) CMVP FIPS 140–2 Certificate #2720. https://csrc.nist.gov/projects/cryptographic-module-validation-program/certificate/2720. Last accessed 29 Jan 2026
3. National Institute of Standards and Technology (2019) FIPS 140–2Certificate #3511 https://csrc.nist.gov/projects/cryptographic-module-validation-program/certificate/3511. Last accessed 29 Jan 2026
4. National Institute of Standards and Technology (2021) FIPS 140–2 Certificate #3838. https://csrc.nist.gov/projects/cryptographic-module-validation-program/certificate/3838. Last accessed 29 Jan 2026
5. National Institute of Standards and Technology (2021) FIPS 140–2 Certificate #4025. https://csrc.nist.gov/projects/cryptographic-module-validation-program/certificate/4025. Last accessed 29 Jan 2026
6. National Institute of Standards and Technology (2022) FIPS 140–2 Certificate #4150. https://csrc.nist.gov/projects/cryptographic-module-validation-program/certificate/4150. Last accessed 29 Jan 2026
7. National Institute of Standards and Technology (2022) FIPS 140–2 Certificate #4355. https://csrc.nist.gov/projects/cryptographic-module-validation-program/certificate/4355. Last accessed 29 Jan 2026
8. National Institute of Standards and Technology (2023) FIPS 140–2 Certificate #4599. https://csrc.nist.gov/projects/cryptographic-module-validation-program/certificate/4599. Last accessed 29 Jan 2026
9. National Institute of Standards and Technology (2023) FIPS 140–2 Certificate #4648. https://csrc.nist.gov/projects/cryptographic-module-validation-program/certificate/4648. Last accessed 29 Jan 2026
10. National Institute of Standards and Technology (2024) FIPS 140–3 Certificate #4749. https://csrc.nist.gov/projects/cryptographic-module-validation-program/certificate/4749. Last accessed 29 Jan 2026
11. National Institute of Standards and Technology (2025) FIPS 140–3 Certificate #5032 https://csrc.nist.gov/projects/cryptographic-module-validation-program/certificate/5032. Last accessed 29 Jan 2026

Chapter 41
Microsoft: Building Security In, Not Bolting It On

Yi Mao

Understanding Microsoft's Perspective The evening sky over Austin deepened into violet as Yi entered the familiar FIPS 'n' Chips restaurant, ready for a conversation with silicon architecture veteran Yucong Tao from Microsoft about his FIPS experience. Yi had known Yucong long before his Microsoft days, and their reunion carried the easy familiarity of shared professional respect. From the restaurant atop the Mueller control tower, she could see the golden dust suspended in the air, glowing in the low angle of the setting sun. Each particle caught the light for a fleeting moment before drifting away, like scattered data bits forming patterns of fleeting precision. The view reminded Yi of how cryptographic assurance worked: beauty born from discipline, where every piece must align in perfect order before the light fades.

Across the table sat Yucong, calm and methodical, his smile reflecting both confidence and curiosity. He greeted Yi with the energy of someone who viewed standards not as restrictions but as opportunities to shape lasting security.

From the first exchange, Yi sensed this conversation would be different. Where others often spoke of FIPS as bureaucracy, Yucong spoke of it as a craft that tests both engineering rigor and a principled commitment to trust in cryptography.

"Before we talk about FIPS," Yucong began, "I have to start with the hardware itself and speak for myself, from the point of view of a crypto IP developer." He smiled warmly. "When I first started building crypto cores including AES, SHA, ECC, and RSA around 2012 or 2013, we did not call them 'validated.' We just made sure they matched NIST's test vectors. Over time, I learned those vectors were sacred. You pass them, or you do not. There is no middle ground."

Yi laughed softly. "That sounds familiar. I remember the first time you contacted our lab to verify a DRBG design and implementation in your previous life. The deterministic algorithm did not pass the algorithm test."

Y. Mao (✉)
atsec information security corporation, Austin, TX, USA
e-mail: yi.mao@atsec.com

Y. Mao (ed.), *Tasting Cryptography*, https://doi.org/10.1007/978-3-032-30243-4_41

Yucong nodded. "Exactly. My wake-up call came during my first test on the DRBG design. Someone told me to run the known-answer noise test, and I did not even know it existed. The design failed, not by much but enough to matter. That day changed everything. I realized cryptographic IP cannot be 'almost' correct. It has to be exact."

"Which is why FIPS matters," Yi replied. "It is the one place where precision is not negotiable. NIST SP 800-90A, which standardizes the DRBG, was revised in 2015, and its companion standard SP 800-90B for entropy assessment was first published in 2018. Ever since the publication of these two standards, the CMVP has tightened the assessment of the security strength of cryptographic keys generated by DRBGs."

From that lesson onward, every cryptographic module developed was tested against the Cryptographic Algorithm Validation Program, or CAVP, and later the Entropy Source Validation, or ESV, suites. "Validation became part of the design cycle," Yucong explained. "It was not a postscript. It was how we wrote our hardware story."

Yi leaned forward, intrigued. "That kind of consistency reminds me of atsec's early mantra: the test vector does not lie. You can debate implementation details all day, but if it fails the vector, the implementation is erroneous."

Yucong laughed. "Exactly. We live by the same rule. The challenge now is that the standards themselves keep changing. RNG testing today is far stricter than it was even five years ago. We evolve with them, and that is where good lab partners matter."

He added, "Sometimes, we call you or Stephan Müller when we hit a tricky interpretation. If there is no final guidance yet, one of you will say, 'Here is how NIST is thinking about it right now.' That kind of insight saves weeks of guesswork."

Yi smiled. "And sometimes, we end up writing the Request for Guidance together."

Yucong nodded appreciatively. "That is true. One of the best things about working with atsec is that we can challenge and refine each other's reasoning. We might start on opposite sides of a requirement, but by the end, we have clarified it for everyone."

He paused, then continued, "One of the biggest lessons I have learned is to bring the lab in early. Do not wait until tape-out. Start during architecture design. Once you see the schematic, the lab sees the boundary. That is when you avoid the costly surprises."

Yi nodded. "It is the same lesson we preach to vendors: compliance is cheapest when designed, not when repaired."

"The standards world speaks in 'shall' and 'should,' but silicon speaks in gates and logic," Yucong said. "The lab translates one language into the other."

Yi added, "That is where our jobs meet, making standards feel like engineering instead of paperwork."

Yucong smiled. "Security should be built in, not bolted on. When validation feels natural, people stop fighting it."

Yi nodded thoughtfully. "That is exactly why CMUF and ICMC exist. The community solves problems together faster than any one lab or vendor could alone."

Speaking of the challenge in defining a proper cryptographic module boundary, Yucong promised Yi that he would bring in his team with some concrete examples.

Right before wrapping up the meeting, Yucong said, "The recent entropy source validation request is in the process of getting budget approval. Your ICMC video helped."

Yi was very curious. "How?"

"When we first proposed the budget for entropy source validation," Yucong said, "upper management hesitated. They did not understand why it was necessary. So, I sent them atsec's parody video Let It Go, the one about entropy testing."

Yi burst out laughing. "Oh no, you did not."

"I did," he said with a grin. "But I added a message: 'This is why entropy testing matters. Without rigorous analysis, weak keys can get out the door. To be thoroughly assessed, the test must run from dawn to dusk by an experienced lab.'"

Yi nodded. "A perfect example of why FIPS validation is not just about technical precision. It is also about communication. If leadership does not understand the need for rigorous testing, they will not support it. That is also the motivation for writing this FIPS book. We want to break down the hard-core notions of cryptography so everyone will have the appetite to take a few bites at our FIPS 'n' Chips restaurant."

As the evening lights reflected off the restaurant's windows, the conversation wound down. "You know," Yucong said, "what I love about this work is that every validation makes us better engineers. Even the painful ones."

Yi smiled. "That is the spirit of FIPS. The certificate is just the dessert. The process is the meal."

They agreed to meet again with Yucong's team. Outside, the lights of Austin flickered like circuit traces across the horizon, a reminder that every secure connection, every cryptographic key, and every algorithm began as someone's late-night conversation about trust and precision.

A Follow-up with Microsoft Team A few days later, Yi joined a video call with Microsoft's silicon security team. Yucong was there again, joined by Joseph Ku and Scott Fuller. The setting was different this time—a mosaic of faces framed by office backdrops and glowing monitors—but the energy was the same. Yi could tell from the start that this would be a candid conversation. The group spoke not just as engineers or managers, but as veterans of a long and evolving validation journey.

Joseph Ku began with a mix of frustration and realism. "The biggest problem with FIPS certification," he said, leaning forward, "is how long it takes. By the time we finally get certified, the product has already been in the field for years. Sometimes, it is near the end of its life before we even get the certificate."

He paused, then added with a rueful smile, "When that happens, you lose your audience. The people who built it have already moved on to the next project. You're chasing a certificate for something that is already history."

Yi nodded thoughtfully. "That is not just a Microsoft story," she said. "Every vendor feels that pain. The queue is long, but it is the fatigue that hurts most."

Joseph chuckled softly. "Exactly. Engineers love solving problems. But when it drags on for years, it feels like maintenance instead of innovation."

Yucong agreed. “It is not only about time; it is about momentum. Validation needs rhythm. If you lose it, even success feels late.”

After a pause, Yucong brightened. “But it is not all frustration,” he said. “We have learned that the earlier we involve our partners, the smoother everything goes.”

He recalled a recent success. “When Stephan Müller shared his C code for algorithm testing as a reference, that saved us the tremendous effort of reinventing it ourselves.”

Scott smiled. “It wasn’t glamorous work,” he said, “but it gave us confidence that we were certifiable from day one.”

Algorithm Testing: Simulation versus Real Silicon The discussion turned toward the subtleties of algorithm testing, how much of it could reasonably be done in simulation before real silicon arrived. Joseph leaned back in his chair and sighed. “Ideally, we’d always run tests on the real chip,” he said, “but that is not always practical. Once silicon is locked down, you can’t run arbitrary test code through it anymore. We usually rely on simulators to validate our algorithms before tape-out. For CMVP purposes, that should be good enough.”

Yi nodded. “That is actually a good approach,” she said. “Algorithm testing has been automated since 2019, so the simulation environment works well for early validation. You can use the demo server to get your test vectors, run them through your simulator, and check whether the outputs match. It is free and open to everyone; there is no need to be a lab.”

Scott joined in, adding his recent experience. “When Stephan Müller published his C implementation for algorithm testing, that was huge for us,” he said. “We didn’t have the official known-answer tests yet, but Stephan’s code gave us confidence. It was like having a lighthouse while waiting for the NIST beacon to turn on.”

Yucong nodded in agreement. “We tracked his updates on GitHub. The comments, the shared results, they were more helpful than some of the draft notes we had at the time. That transparency really helped.”

Joseph raised another practical concern. “But if we do the testing in simulation,” he said, “shouldn’t that be enough? Why must we rerun it on silicon later? If it works in simulation, it’ll work in hardware.”

Yi gently shook her head. “Not quite. You can get a certificate for the simulation, but that doesn’t automatically apply to the chip. The environment matters, the compiler, the timing, even the hardware noise sources. A simulation certificate only guarantees that your algorithm works in that virtual environment. The hardware certificate shows it performs correctly in the physical one.”

She paused before continuing. “That is why we recommend running the tests twice, first during simulation, to catch issues early, and again on the chip once it is fabricated. The first gives you confidence before tape-out. The second gives you the assurance that what’s in silicon truly matches what was validated.”

Joseph smiled wryly. “So basically, we certify twice. Once for peace of mind, once for paperwork.”

Yi laughed. “You could say that, yes. But it is cheaper to catch mistakes in simulation than to fix them in hardware.”

Scott nodded thoughtfully. "We have seen that. If more people could use it, we'd spot problems earlier."

Yi's tone softened, her voice carrying a mix of encouragement and practicality. "Exactly. The demo vectors aren't the same as production test vectors; they're there to help you gain confidence, not to issue a certificate. Think of them as a dress rehearsal before opening night."

The group chuckled at the analogy.

Cryptographic Module Boundary: Defining the Scope of Trust Joseph leaned in, speaking with the calm authority of someone who had struggled with the problem for years. "The biggest problem, I feel," he began, "is that it is hard to define the scope of the things we do and to fix the boundary of what we actually put under evaluation. Most of our crypto IP blocks are embedded inside larger SoCs. The boundary gets fuzzy: shared clocks, resets, power rails, buses, firmware controllers. You can't draw a neat box around any of it."

He continued, frustration creeping into his voice. "And when firmware running on the host CPU interacts with the embedded cores, it gets worse. If we treat everything as part of the module, it is unmanageable. But if we only include the embedded engine, it is incomplete. We end up with partial certifications that don't reflect how the silicon actually works."

Yi listened carefully, nodding as he spoke. "You're absolutely right," she said. "And the standard recognizes that tension. Under FIPS 140-3, the vendor, the module designer, has the freedom to define the boundary. The requirement is simply that the boundary be logical, consistent, and testable. You start with at least one approved NIST algorithm, say SHA-256, and then build from there."

She leaned forward slightly, her tone turning instructive yet conversational. "From that starting point, the other eleven requirement areas of FIPS guide what needs to be enclosed. You ask yourself: what services does my module provide? What functions need to be secured together? For example, integrity checking may require HMAC or CMAC. A Level 2 module might stop there, but a Level 3 one will likely need digital signatures, like ECDSA. Each decision pulls new elements into the boundary until the design reaches equilibrium—your minimal secure enclosure."

Joseph smiled wryly. "So, in theory, I could certify a module with just SHA-256 and call it FIPS validated."

Yi chuckled softly. "You could, but then you'd have to ask yourself, what value does that certificate bring? A module that only offers one hash function is technically valid but functionally limited. The real question is: what purpose does your module serve? That is what should define the boundary."

Yucong added, "Exactly. We have seen cases where people shrink the scope just to pass validation. It becomes a game of definitions, not of assurance."

Yi nodded. "That is what we try to avoid. The standard gives flexibility so vendors can tailor the scope to their design, but it is not meant to dilute meaning. The certificate should tell the truth about what's inside: the algorithms, the services, the key lifecycle."

She gestured lightly as if sketching an invisible diagram in the air. "During testing, that boundary can still evolve. You might start broad, then narrow it down when something cannot be made compliant within the current development cycle. That is acceptable, as long as you document why. Once the boundary is finalized, we analyze what algorithms and services lie within it, and how they handle keys: their entry, derivation, use, storage, and destruction. That is what transforms the design into a coherent trust perimeter."

Joseph nodded slowly. "That makes sense. So, it is flexible, but not arbitrary."

"Exactly," Yi said. "You define it; the lab helps you justify it. And once it is defined, it has to hold. The goal isn't to make it small; it is to make it meaningful."

She smiled warmly, summarizing with quiet conviction. "FIPS doesn't demand perfection. It demands accountability. The boundary isn't a wall around your module, it is a promise of what's protected inside."

Yi paused, then continued with a tone that blended teaching with candor. "When people look at a FIPS certificate," she said, "they often see only the level—Level 1, Level 2, Level 3—and stop there. But that number doesn't tell you the whole story. The level alone does not describe what the module actually does."

She leaned back, recalling her years of working with both vendors and federal procurement officers, helping them explain their modules. "A FIPS certificate is paired with something even more important: the Security Policy. The policy is where you truly understand what's inside the boundary, what services are provided, and how those services use cryptographic keys. It lists every approved algorithm, every mode of operation, and the interfaces that have been tested. Together, the certificate and the Security Policy define the module's identity. They show what was tested, what passed, and what the module actually offers to the end user."

Joseph nodded, but his expression carried a hint of frustration. "That is the thing," he said. "Customers rarely read the Security Policy. They just look at the level number. They'll tell us, 'I want Level 3,' without realizing that the Level 3 device they're asking for might not even perform the functions they need. We could give them a Level 2 module that actually offers more services, but the number always wins."

Yi smiled knowingly. "Yes, that is a common problem. We have seen two certificates, both Level 2: one covers only AES, and the other includes ten algorithms. To the untrained eye, they look identical, but the capabilities are completely different. That is why education matters. If buyers don't know what to look for, they'll chase the higher number instead of the right service."

Joseph leaned forward. "Exactly. I've always thought FIPS should certify services, not just modules. Instead of saying, 'This module is Level 3,' it should say, 'This module is certified for digital signatures,' or 'This one provides device identity assurance.' That would make things clearer for everyone."

Yi nodded enthusiastically. "I agree completely. Services give meaning to the certificate. The level only describes how the module was protected: the physical tamper response, the role-based access control, the key management procedures. Those are all important, but they don't tell you what the module actually does."

She glanced around the virtual meeting window, seeing everyone's agreement reflected in small nods and smiles. "We should encourage CMVP to make the services more prominent, rather than hiding them in a table of the lengthy Security Policy, and instead place them up front where people can see them. The certificate should immediately communicate both the assurance level and the cryptographic purpose."

Joseph laughed lightly. "Yes, like a nutrition label for cryptography: clear, readable, and meaningful. You shouldn't need a lab to interpret it."

Yi laughed with him. "Exactly. You should be able to tell from the first glance: what algorithms are included, what services are available, and under what conditions they've been validated. That is how trust becomes transparent."

She ended with quiet conviction. "A good FIPS certificate is not a trophy. It is a contract of trust between the developer, the tester, and the user, and that trust should be readable, not just assumed."

Request for Guidance and Resolution through Collaboration Scott Fuller raised a point that caught everyone's attention. "I have a different topic," he began. "We had a case where our lab reached out to NIST on our behalf, and things turned out well, but at the time, I wasn't sure what kind of answer we'd get."

"They wanted us to prove that our entropy was refreshed before each key generation," Scott recalled. "At first, it seemed stricter than what the standard said, and we were worried it might lead to design changes that weren't really necessary."

Yi hypothesized, "It may be related to the updates to FIPS 140-3 IG D.K, where its additional comment #5 requires a DRBG to have prediction resistance enabled or be reseeded before requesting an output if it is used as a conditioning component for an entropy source."

Yucong leaned forward, adding a technical reflection that tied everything together. "What I want to add," he said, "is that the random number generator is a perfect example of where the spec was written from a software mindset. The SP 800-90 series assumes an API-based model: you call a function, ask for 256 bits, and get exactly that. But in hardware, things work differently. The RNG might output 512 bits in a single operation, and the firmware just takes what it needs. There is no leftover data sitting there waiting to be called again. The process is continuous, not transactional."

Yi nodded. "Right. That is exactly why hardware implementations often look non-compliant to the letter of the standard, but not to its intent."

Yucong continued, "Yes. When the standard expects discrete API calls, and we're designing streaming architectures, it creates a gray area. That is the kind of case we're talking about, where the design is intrinsically secure, but not written in the language of the spec."

Yi smiled. "That is where the lab comes in. We interpret that gray zone and present it in terms CMVP understands."

Joseph chimed in with a grin. "You know," he said, "it is a bit like lawyers arguing a case in court. The lab makes its argument, advocates for the vendor, and lays out the evidence to persuade the reviewers."

Yi laughed. "Exactly right. That is what we do: advocate for the design and for common sense. When ambiguity exists, we build a strong technical case to get a fair resolution."

Joseph nodded. "I'm not saying the vendor is always right," he added, "but when the rules leave room for interpretation, there are stronger arguments to be made for clarity instead of blind enforcement."

Yi listened with a knowing smile. "Yes," she said. "That is one of those cases where it is better to ask before assuming." She explained that atsec had reached out to the CMVP to clarify the requirement. "We went directly to CMVP to confirm our understanding," she said. "Our goal wasn't to push back; it was to get certainty. We prefer to be strict at the start, so we don't face rework later."

As Yi spoke, her tone carried both assurance and method. "When we interact with CMVP, we try to make the case as clear as possible. We know the standards inside out, but interpretation still matters. How you ask the question shapes the answer. So, we make sure our question is precise, supported by evidence, and defensible on your behalf."

Scott nodded. "That is what I appreciated," he said. "In the end, NIST agreed with our interpretation. The reseeding wasn't required the way it was first presented. But it made me realize how important it is to have someone who knows how to speak that language."

Yi's tone softened as she reflected. "The relationship we have with CMVP didn't happen overnight. It took decades of consistent engagement, constructive feedback, and trust. We have built a reputation for being thorough, not confrontational. When we reach out, NIST listens because they know we're not looking for shortcuts; we're looking for precision."

She smiled, her voice calm but certain. "That is the value of cooperation. Open source works because people share their knowledge. FIPS works when people share their reasoning. That is what this partnership is about: making assurance both rigorous and fair."

Yucong nodded. "Thank you, Yi, for spending this time with us. These discussions, they help connect everything together. It is easy to forget that standards are human too."

Yi smiled warmly. "And thank you all. These conversations remind me why I still believe in this work, because even after all these years, collaboration still moves the field forward."

Scott added softly, "It really does. Thank you."

As the meeting ended, the participants lingered a moment before closing their screens. The faint reflections of code and circuit diagrams glowed against the darkened glass, a quiet symbol of their shared purpose: to make cryptography not only correct, but trusted.

About the contributors: Yucong Tao Yucong is a Sr. Director of Hardware Security Architecture at Microsoft, leading silicon-level security strategy and architecture across cloud and client products. He drives end-to-end Root-of-Trust, crypto engines, and next-generation hardware security IP for Microsoft's silicon roadmap. His work spans applied cryptography, SoC security architecture, and cross-company security initiatives.

Joseph Ku Joseph is a Senior Principal Architect with more than 30 years in digital circuits and computer system design. His experiences spans the full silicon design lifecycle — from architecture and design implementation through verification, firmware interfaces, and system integration. He is currently at Microsoft, developing custom security IP and defining security architecture and solutions for various SoC across client, embedded, and data center platforms.

J. Scott Fuller Scott is an accomplished electrical engineer, cryptographer, and manager recognized for his innovative and secure design work at leading technology companies. Throughout his career, he has made significant contributions at organizations such as Atari, Seattle Silicon, Emu Systems, Creative Labs, Certicom, BlackBerry, and Microsoft. His designs, including those implemented in BlackBerry devices and the Xbox One, which have demonstrated exceptional durability by remaining free from security breaches over time. Scott is widely regarded as an expert in computer arithmetic, cryptographic circuits, side-channel countermeasures, and hardware security. In addition to his past achievements, Scott's recent work includes advancements in hardware security for cloud computing environments.

Chapter 42
Nuvoton: The Craft of Hardware Assurance

Yi Mao

A candid exchange on FIPS as a global trust anchor for silicon The late afternoon sun filtered through the tall windows of FIPS 'n' Chips as the conversation drifted eastward, from Austin to Israel. Yi had just started a call with Avi Davidowitz, Nuvoton's veteran of many FIPS campaigns, and the table leaned in with curiosity. For years, Nuvoton's chips had quietly powered the security foundations of modern computing, including TPMs, embedded controllers, and cloud management processors, but few outside the certification world knew how deep their FIPS story ran.

Avi's laughter carried easily through the speaker. "For us," he began, "FIPS is everywhere. Any chip with crypto inside eventually finds itself on the validation path. It started with TPMs. That was the first business driver, but today our embedded controllers and server management processors go through it too. Once we invest in compliance, we go the full way to certification. The certificate isn't just paperwork; it's what makes customers believe in the product."

Yi smiled. "That's the hallmark of a mature vendor," she said. "When certification becomes a by-product of a purposefully designed cryptographic module."

Nuvoton's headquarter in Taiwan anchors a global development web that stretches across Israel, the United States, China, and Japan. After acquiring Panasonic's semiconductor division, the company inherited decades of hardware lineage and a growing security portfolio. Its Cloud Computing Division now drives the company's FIPS strategy, threading a common design philosophy through TPMs, embedded controllers for PCs, and Baseboard Management Controllers (or BMCs) for the server market.

Avi explained, "Our TPMs always needed FIPS because the U.S. government requires it. But the reason expanded. Cloud vendors started asking for FIPS-certified

Y. Mao (✉)
atsec information security corporation, Austin, TX, USA
e-mail: yi.mao@atsec.com

Y. Mao (ed.), *Tasting Cryptography*, https://doi.org/10.1007/978-3-032-30243-4_42

roots of trust. Once that happened, it was clear: if the chip does crypto, it must go through certification."

For all its confidence, Nuvoton shares the same frustration as many hardware makers: time. "Back in the FIPS 140-2 days," Avi recalled, "we could sometimes finish in nine months. Now it's closer to a year and a half. And when a product's life is relatively short, that's a significant amount of its lifetime waiting in review."

He paused for a sip of coffee. "We can plan for testing. We can budget for labs. But we can't plan for uncertainty in timing. Sometimes the certificate arrives after the next generation has already launched."

Yi nodded sympathetically. "We've all seen that queue growing."

"Exactly," Avi continued. "Our customers understand, but they build systems on schedule. When the module's validation lags, they're forced to ship older firmware, or worse—wait. That's why we start FIPS work earlier now, even before tape-out."

When the topic turned to entropy sources, Avi leaned forward in the video window. "Entropy is the one part where we're actually grateful for the pain," he said. "Once you build a solid model, especially for a physical noise source, you can reuse it again and again. For our team, the first analysis is the hardest, but the second one is much easier."

Yi laughed. "So, entropy becomes a long-term investment?"

"Exactly. On the BSI side it's even more demanding than ion the NIST side, but the work pays back. Every new chip starts with that baseline. The key is to build it right once."

Nuvoton operates in a world where FIPS, Common Criteria, and European schemes all overlap but never quite align. "We serve customers in the U.S., Europe, and Asia," Avi explained. "Some expect compliance with NIST SP 800-90B, others refer to BSI's AIS 31. They sound similar but differ in subtle ways, especially in how they model the entropy assessment. NIST uses min-entropy, whereas BSI uses Shannon entropy. You learn to write a report that satisfies both."

The transition to post-quantum algorithms has only magnified those differences. "Policies aren't synchronized," he said. "For example, what one region calls a hybrid approach, another still treats as an experiment. That slows adoption, even when the technology is ready."

Beyond analysis and modeling lies a challenge less visible to engineers but all too real to program managers: policy waivers. "Take asymmetric key derivation," Avi said. "For TPMs, it's clear and accepted. But for other modules, we need a formal waiver. Even when we ask early, it can take months. Meanwhile, design schedules don't wait."

Yi sighed. "That's a story we've heard before. The queue is the victim of the CMVP's own success. The demand has grown over the years, but CMVP resources are decreased significantly this year."

FIPS 140–3 has brought some automation, and Nuvoton appreciates it. "Algorithm testing is smooth now," Avi said. "CAVP and ESV work well. The CMVP side is building more automation too, but at the end of the day, it still depends on people. Reviewers are few. When you have a new standard, retirements, and twice the workload, something has to give."

Still, he was optimistic. "The cooperation between the U.S. and Canada teams works well. The system is solid. It just needs more bandwidth."

As the coffee cooled, Yi steered the discussion toward Nuvoton's recent projects. "You're the only company shipping an OpenTitan-based root of trust, right?"

Avi nodded proudly. "Yes. Open designs like those raise everyone's game. When hardware blueprints are open, you can't hide behind obscurity, and you have to be correct. Each vendor still brings its own architecture and boundary, but we share a foundation that benefits the whole industry."

Yi smiled. "That's the future of transparency and of assurance."

Before ending the call, Avi offered three lessons learned through the long years of submissions and resubmissions. "First," he said, "treat FIPS like a product requirement, not a postscript. If you wait until the design is frozen, it's already too late."

"Second, engage your lab early and use their experience. They see patterns across many vendors."

"And third," he added with a grin, "plan for the queue. It's not a sprint; it's a relay race."

As the conversation wound down, the message was clear: FIPS is no longer just a U.S. compliance artifact. It is a global trust anchor. Nuvoton's engineers, spread across continents and time zones, see the CMVP program as part of their own infrastructure. "If CMVP doesn't scale," Avi said, "the whole industry slows down. Every secure boot, every key exchange, every server root of trust depends on it."

Yi nodded thoughtfully. "That's exactly the spirit of this book: how each vendor, each lab, and each reviewer keeps the system alive."

Avi smiled. "It's a tough road," he said, "but it's the right one."

About the contributor: Avi Davidowitz Avi is a Security Certifications and DSS Team Lead at Nuvoton Technology Corporation. With 23 years of experience in the semiconductor industry, he leads security certification programs—including Common Criteria and FIPS certifications—helping ensure secure development practices remain aligned with evolving assurance and compliance requirements. His work spans managing certification deliverables with cross-functional engineering stakeholders, external labs, and certification bodies, supporting audit readiness and continuous improvement, and guiding R&D teams on secure-by-design expectations across hardware and software.

Chapter 43
Qualcomm: The Silicon Symphony of FIPS 'n' Chips

Yi Mao

The chatter in the FIPS 'n' Chips restaurant quieted when the waiter placed a polished silicon wafer at the center of the table. Its surface reflected the shimmer of etched circuits and the pulse of code, the unmistakable language of Qualcomm.

"Thank you very much for coming here to share your FIPS experience," Yi began. "Let's start with a bit of history. How long has Qualcomm been validating cryptographic modules, and how long have you been involved in the FIPS field?"

Yann answered with a warm smile. "Yes, that's fair," he said. "Qualcomm's story began around 2000, when we built our own internal cryptographic library. That library became our first FIPS 140-2 validated module in 2007 [1]. It wasn't an off-the-shelf seasoning; it was our own blend of algorithms, designed and maintained internally. At that time, I hadn't yet joined Qualcomm. The lab that tested this module no longer exists."

He continued, "In 2014, we validated our first software-hybrid module [2]. That certificate set the pattern for everything that followed: precise boundaries, repeatable design, and a habit of validating every major engine that touches cryptography. We've accumulated about 33 FIPS certificates over the decades; they cover the full spectrum, from software and firmware to hybrid and sub-chip cryptographic subsystems. Each certificate reflects how our chips evolve. As the silicon grows, so do the validation boundaries."

"That's quite an accomplishment," Yi said.

"Exactly," Yann replied. "Qualcomm's crypto isn't a single block; it's a family of coordinated engines." He paused for a moment, then pointed to a page in his notes listing Qualcomm's primary FIPS modules (Table 43.1).

"Among such a wide scope of modules, which type presented the greatest challenge?" Yi asked.

Y. Mao (✉)
atsec information security corporation, Austin, TX, USA
e-mail: yi.mao@atsec.com

Y. Mao (ed.), *Tasting Cryptography*, https://doi.org/10.1007/978-3-032-30243-4_43

Table 43.1 A selection of Qualcomm's FIPS certificates

Certificate #	Module name	FIPS standard	Level	Description
4748	Qualcomm® crypto engine (QCE) core	140–3	1	Core cryptographic engine integrated into Snapdragon SoCs
4293	Qualcomm® secure processing unit (SPU)	140–2	2	Random number generator subsystem within Snapdragon 8cx gen 3
4896	Qualcomm® trusted execution environment (TEE) software cryptographic library	140–3	1	Software-hybrid crypto library supporting Android and embedded OSes
5033	Qualcomm® integrated crypto engine (ICE)	140–3	1	Storage encryption engine managing hardware-accelerated AES and key wrapping

"The first sub-chip module validation," Yann said. "Around 2015, if I remember correctly, Qualcomm began contributing to the Implementation Guidance that clarified how to define and validate hybrid and sub-chip cryptographic subsystems. Traditional FIPS language assumed crypto was a separate box or library, but in modern SoCs, cryptography is embedded everywhere. We worked with our lab, which was atsec, and the CMVP to describe how to document those boundaries clearly—what's inside, what's outside, and how each interface behaves. That collaboration helped shape the guidance that all vendors use today."

Yi leaned forward. "Yes, that's such unique expertise," she said. "At the beginning, there really was no guidance at all. People assumed that everything on a single chip must be taken as one monolithic module. But a modern chip is more like a miniature computer, a system-on-chip, or SoC. It's packed with radio, modem, GPS, CPU, and memory components, many of which have nothing to do with cryptography. If the entire chip were included within the FIPS boundary, any unrelated change in those subsystems would force a complete revalidation. The goal, as your team first proposed, was to tighten that scope around the cryptographic core, to make it a stable nucleus, unaffected by external updates."

Yann nodded. "Yes, exactly. These are extremely complex systems, with many interfaces, services, and functionalities. It made sense to localize the boundary to the security cores and cryptographic libraries that actually deliver cryptographic services. Other subsystems on the chip, like the audio, video, or connectivity subsystems, don't contribute to security. Including them would have made both compliance and testing almost impossible."

He paused, reflecting on the scale of the work. "If we had tried to validate an entire SoC, it would have been overwhelming: hundreds of interfaces, each needing evaluation. The labs would have faced a monumental task just to map and test every port and function."

Yi nodded in understanding. "That reminds me of the architecture of the smart cards I used to work on early in my career. A traditional smart card has only eight electrical pins, each clearly defined: one for power, one for ground, one for reset, one for the system clock, one for data input and output, one for programming voltage, and two reserved for future use. That limited interface makes testing and validation realistic; you can monitor every pin and ensure each behaves as expected. But an SoC today isn't a card with eight pins. It's more like a city of circuits, with hundreds of connections."

Yann laughed softly. "Exactly. Some of our SoCs have twenty or more power interfaces and 1,000 more pins, each serving different functions or providing redundancy. Trying to validate every pin, every path, would add enormous complexity, without improving assurance. What matters most is the cryptographic boundary itself, where the keys are managed and the algorithms executed."

Yi smiled. "So, the sub-chip concept became the practical way forward, focus on the cryptographic heart instead of the entire body."

Yann nodded again. "Yes, and that's why the first certifications defined logical boundaries tightly around the cryptographic cores. It was the only way to make validation both meaningful and achievable. That's how the original FIPS 140-2 IG 1.20 came about, and the same principle carries on today under FIPS 140-3 IG 2.3.B."

Yi commented. "Qualcomm was a major contributor, and also one of the first to benefit from it."

Yann laughed. "You could say that."

"Suppose we tried to validate the entire SoC as a single FIPS module," Yann said. "At first glance that sounds attractive because you would aim for one certificate that covers everything. In practice it becomes unmanageable. The SoC exposes hundreds of interfaces and services. Audio, video, modem, and connectivity blocks are not part of the cryptographic function, yet they would sit inside the boundary and expand the evidence and testing burden without adding assurance."

Yi considered the point. "Right. The single-chip approach looks simple on paper because it is one box. But once you draw the boundary around the whole die, you inherit every bus and every port. Any unrelated change can trigger revalidation. That is a lot of churn for work that does not change the cryptography."

"Exactly," Yann said. "Even defining a logical boundary that contains three security cores, for example, the Inline Cryptographic Engine (ICE), the General-Purpose Cryptographic Engine (GPCE), and the Qualcomm Random Number Generator (QRNG), can pull in shared buses and glue logic. As soon as you include a bus you risk including other blocks that talk on that bus. The scope grows again. The lab must map and test a very large surface. It is effort that does not improve confidence in keys and algorithms."

"So, divide and conquer," Yi said. "Tight boundaries around the cryptographic components, each with its own certification lifecycle. When a new chip arrives, you typically revalidate the three crypto modules rather than the entire SoC. That was the motivation for the sub-chip model under FIPS 140-2 IG 1.20, and it continues under FIPS 140-3 IG 2.3.B."

Yann nodded. “There is another angle. For some engines, pure hardware is not enough to meet FIPS requirements. You still need code to configure registers, run power-up self-tests, or provide health tests for the entropy source. Our Pseudo Random Number Generator (PRNG) is a good example. We include firmware that drives the hardware correctly and exposes the required status. That is why the hybrid category exists on a single chip. It recognizes that code can be essential to deliver the approved service.”

“That evolution was natural,” Yi said. “The early guidance said sub-chip meant hardware. We later saw cases where hardware needed code to meet the standard, so the model expanded to software-hardware or firmware-hardware hybrids on a single chip. The working group discussions turned that observation into requirements everyone can follow.”

“If I could wish for one thing,” Yann said with a small smile, “I would love a single SoC-level validation that solved everything at once. From a certification standpoint it would reduce the number of certificates we manage. But for real products it is actually easier to validate a system that integrates our chip than to validate the full chip by itself. A product tends to expose far fewer interfaces than the SoC. Fewer interfaces mean clearer testing and clearer evidence.”

“So, we keep the focus where assurance lives,” Yi said. “Everything that touches sensitive information and cryptographic functions belongs inside the boundary; everything else stays out. When hardware needs code to satisfy FIPS behavior, we declare a hybrid and show how the pieces work together.”

Yann agreed. “That approach also supports better planning. We can run pre-validation while designs are still moving. Hardware changes can take a year or more. Early involvement by an accredited lab or an experienced team avoids surprises later.”

“And that is how we keep coordination smooth when the time comes,” Yi said. “Strict up front, then we defend what we submit so you are not dragged back to decisions that were frozen in RTL a year and a half ago.”

Yann acknowledged. “Exactly. Clear boundaries, the right module type, early testing. It reduces risk for everyone.”

Yi nodded with familiarity. “You know,” she said, “you and I share a bit of common history in the smart card world. Before I joined atsec, my first job was actually with Schlumberger, the oil services company that later spun off its smart card division. We handled secure data encryption between field sites and data centers, and that business later evolved into Axalto. Axalto merged with Gemplus to become Gemalto, which eventually became part of Thales.”

Yann smiled. “Yes, true, I knew Axalto too, actually. When I started working, I interacted quite a bit with them, and with the teams that later became part of Thales. They’ve gone through many transformations, but I still keep a few connections there.”

Yi continued, “That world of side-channel analysis, differential power analysis, timing and fault injection it all feels familiar. France’s ANSSI, as the certification body under Common Criteria, is the counterpart of NIAP in the U.S. and Germany’s BSI. They emphasize hardware and the Protection Profile PP-0084 for secure microcontrollers, the foundation of smart card evaluations.”

Yann nodded. "Yes, PP-0084 is a usual protection profile for smart card evaluations. We have evaluated products against this protection profile."

Yi smiled, remembering. "For the first ICMC, we actually invited my former French boss, Dr. Bertrand du Castel, to be our keynote speaker. He's no longer with us, but we honor him through the scholarship we established in his memory."

The connection lingered warmly before Yi added, "So when you talk about differential power or timing analysis and side-channel techniques, it really takes me back to that earlier part of my career. It's like revisiting the foundation of where both our paths began:—the bridge between the Common Criteria world and today's FIPS work."

Yann laughed softly. "That's funny, yes. It's all connected: the techniques, the mindset, even some of the people. We just changed frameworks."

Yi leaned forward. "And now, here we are again, both in the FIPS world. I've actually worked hands-on with some of Qualcomm's modules myself, helping draft security policies, performing functional testing, and preparing validation reports. I remember your ICE, or inline crypto engine, the PRNG subsystem, and the broader GPCE library:—those were among the first I worked with."

Yann nodded appreciatively. "Ah, so you already know our dishes well," he said, smiling.

"How long does it take to prepare one of these modules for certification from your end?" Yi asked.

"When I worked at a FIPS lab before I joined Qualcomm, some vendors approached us with a dream of a three-month turnaround," Yann replied. "In practice, even with solid documentation, it can take six months or more. That includes contracting, generating test evidence, preparing documentation, and running algorithm and operational testing, but it doesn't include the CMVP review cycle, which is beyond our control. You know better about the CMVP queue status."

"It's like preparing a multi-course dinner: careful timing, precise portions, and everything plated at once," Yi said.

"That's exactly it," Yann agreed. "FIPS validation is a culinary art in its own way; every ingredient must be measured, documented, and served in sequence."

Yann paused for a moment when Yi asked about fun or memorable FIPS moments.

"Fun? I'm not sure I can call it fun," he said with a modest laugh, "but I do have a few that were truly meaningful. For my company, I can't speak for everyone, but the first FIPS 140-3 certificate was a milestone, even though it was an interim one—it meant a great deal. We had spent months ensuring compliance with the new requirements, working through all the internal reviews and discussions. When the certificate finally arrived, it felt like a victory. We made it. We did it."

Yi smiled. "You didn't celebrate with champagne?"

Yann chuckled. "No, I should have asked management for that. We didn't, but it still meant a lot. It felt like the moment when all the effort paid off."

He continued, "And on a personal note, there is another one I remember even more clearly. It was the first FIPS certificate issued for one of my customers when I was still a tester at the lab. I led that validation myself. I started working on FIPS back in 2014 when we were pursuing lab accreditation for my first laboratory, and that customer's certificate was finally issued in 2018 when I was working with my second laboratory. After more than four years of work, when it came through it felt incredible. That certificate represented both patience and precision."

"That's a wonderful feeling," Yi said warmly. "All that effort and all those years of work:—it is the sweet result of seeing the certificate finally arrive."

Yann nodded. "Exactly. Whether you are a tester or a vendor, the joy is the same. You spend so much time building assurance, documenting, testing, and waiting. When you finally hold that certificate, you realize every bit of it was worth it."

"Looking ahead, what will Qualcomm's next dish be?" Yi asked.

"As new generations of SoCs integrate dedicated security cores," Yann said, "we'll continue to validate each cryptographic subsystem that enforces protection: entropy sources, key managers, and secure storage engines. Each core performing FIPS-approved algorithms will stand on its own certificate, reusable, modular, and traceable."

"So, the Qualcomm table at this restaurant will keep growing," Yi observed.

"Yes," Yann said. "The same discipline that brought our first validation in 2007 still drives us today. Each certificate adds another layer of trust, not just for our products, but for the entire ecosystem that relies on Qualcomm chips."

"You know, Yann," Yi said finally, "Qualcomm's place at this FIPS 'n' Chips table really shows how validation has evolved. While others cook with separate pots for software and hardware, your team has fused the ingredients right into the silicon. Each certificate isn't just a dish; it's a transistor-level proof of trust, served straight from the foundry to the CMVP menu."

About the contributor: Yann L'Hyver Yann leads the FIPS 140 certification process for Qualcomm Technologies, Inc., where he has worked since 2021. With over two decades of experience in security evaluation, Yann has contributed to more than 100 certifications, including Common Criteria, Payment Card Security, and FIPS 140 validations. His career began with cryptanalysis of embedded cryptographic implementations at an ANSSI-accredited ITSEF, followed by work as a certified tester for a major U.S. cryptographic testing laboratory. Yann holds a master's degree in mathematics, cryptology, and information security from the University of Limoges (CRYPTIS), France.

References

1. National Institute of Standards and Technology (2007) CMVP FIPS 140-2 Certificate #851. https://csrc.nist.gov/projects/cryptographic-module-validation-program/certificate/851. Last accessed 03 Dec 2025
2. National Institute of Standards and Technology (2014) CMVP FIPS 140-2 Certificate #2273. https://csrc.nist.gov/projects/cryptographic-module-validation-program/certificate/2273. Last accessed 03 Dec 2025

Chapter 44
Red Hat: Open Source at Scale

Yi Mao

The Scene at FIPS 'n' Chips A gentle murmur of conversation moved through the circular restaurant atop the old Mueller control tower. Constellations of cryptographic algorithms glimmered faintly on the glass ceiling, their reflections dancing in coffee cups and silver cutlery. It was late afternoon, and Yi had invited Jaroslav Reznik, Red Hat's security certification advisor, to join the regulars for a conversation about how open source meets certification.

Jaroslav arrived wearing a subtle grin, laptop tucked under his arm—a seasoned certification advisor whose calm confidence came from years spent navigating the maze of security certifications. When Yi greeted him, he responded with dry humor: "Some people say FIPS is the opposite of open source," he said, settling into his chair. "But that's only true if you don't understand either."

Challenges and Lessons "Think of Red Hat," Jaroslav began, "as a city, not a single building. Thousands of developers, most outside our payroll, contribute to what we ship. The Linux kernel, OpenSSL, NSS, libgcrypt, GnuTLS—all of these become part of the FIPS story."

Yi nodded. "And each has its own validation path."

"Exactly. At last count, we had about two dozen active certificates and more than fifty historical ones," Jaroslav said. "When people ask why we bother, the answer's simple: our customers live in regulated markets. If they can't run their workloads on validated crypto, they can't deploy. So, FIPS becomes a bridge between open code and federal trust."

He paused, swirling his coffee. "FedRAMP and government procurement keep us honest. Without FIPS, open source can't reach those spaces."

"Once," Jaroslav recalled, "we even went for Level 2 with NSS. It was rare for software back then. That's when we learned that FIPS standards fit hardware better than software. Still, it was worth it."

Y. Mao (✉)
atsec information security corporation, Austin, TX, USA
e-mail: yi.mao@atsec.com

Y. Mao (ed.), *Tasting Cryptography*, https://doi.org/10.1007/978-3-032-30243-4_44

Yi smiled, leaning forward. “That Level 2 for NSS was a challenge I’ll never forget,” she said. “It pushed every boundary of what a software library could do under FIPS. The standard required role-based authentication, but libraries like NSS don’t have users—they’re just called by applications. We had to rely on the operating system to provide that layer of assurance.”

She explained that at the time, FIPS Level 2 required the underlying operating system to hold a Common Criteria certification at EAL 2 or higher. Red Hat Enterprise Linux had already been certified at EAL 4 under the German BSI scheme—well above what was required. The problem, however, was that the CMVP, being a joint program of NIST and the Canadian CCCS, did not directly recognize a German certification.

Yi and the atsec team turned to the Common Criteria Recognition Arrangement (CCRA). “We leveraged that mutual recognition so that Canada, as a CCRA participant, could recognize Germany’s EAL 4 certification,” Yi explained. “That allowed the Canadian Common Criteria scheme to acknowledge the BSI evaluation, which in turn let the Canadian CMVP office and NIST accept it for the FIPS Level 2 validation.”

She smiled as she remembered the collaboration. “We were very grateful for Carolyn French’s leadership—she was then the Canadian CMVP manager. Her openness and technical understanding made it possible for the Canadian CC and FIPS teams to coordinate. Without her, we might never have bridged those programs.”

Jaroslav laughed softly. “Most people still don’t believe we pulled that off.” Yi nodded. “It proved that persistence, creativity, and teamwork can turn a nearly impossible goal into a milestone.”

Transparency and Community “It invites scrutiny,” Jaroslav said when Yi asked about openness with the labs, “but it saves time. If you hide things, the lab finds them later, and it’s always worse. Transparency is slower at first, faster in the end.”

He tapped his laptop. “Every build, every test, every diff is traceable. We even help our customers reuse our work through rebranding. If they can leverage our validated crypto instead of redoing it, that’s a win for everyone.”

“Open source is about cooperation,” he continued. “If labs and validators reviewed similar modules together—say, OpenSSL-level libraries—it would reduce duplication. The rulings would be consistent, the patches cleaner, and everyone would benefit. Let’s focus on competing in features, not in redundant certification paperwork.”

Yi was reminded of a similar sentiment voiced by another major open-source contributor—Oracle—whose engineers also emphasized cooperation over competition. She found it remarkable that the same philosophy echoed across two companies long considered rivals in the enterprise world.

After a short pause, Yi nodded thoughtfully. “That is already happening,” she said. “The CMVP plans to organize a working group focused on OpenSSL validations. The goal is to align testing methods and interpretations among labs to ensure consistency. They’ll start by grouping similar software modules—like OpenSSL implementations from different vendors—and conduct joint reviews. The idea is to apply the same

Table 44.1 A selection of Red Hat's FIPS certificates

Certificate #	Module name	FIPS standard	Level	Status
5034	RHEL 9 Kernel cryptographic API	140-3	Level 1	Active
5022	RHEL 9 NSS cryptographic module	140-3	Level 1	Active
4857	RHEL 9 OpenSSL FIPS provider	140-3	Level 1	Active
4846	RHEL 9 GnuTLS	140-3	Level 1	Active
4804	RHEL 8 kernel cryptographic API	140-2	Level 1	Active
4754	RHEL 9 libgcrypt	140-3	Level 1	Active
4413	RHEL 8 NSS cryptographic module	140-2	Level 1	Active
4271	RHEL 8 OpenSSL	140-2	Level 1	Active
3784	RHEL 8 libgcrypt	140-2	Level 1	Historical
1280	RHEL 4 NSS 3.12.4	140-2	Level 2	Historical
814	RHEL 4 NSS 3.11.4	140-2	Level 2	Historical

checklist and shared guidance so that compliant modules can move faster through the process."

She added with a smile, "It's the same cooperation you just described, but now formalized. By agreeing on testing consistency first, we can focus our efforts on true technical differences rather than procedural noise."

A Career Built through Certification Yi smiled as the conversation turned personal. "How long have you been on this journey?" she asked.

Jaroslav leaned back, thoughtful. "It's been more than a decade," he said. "When I started, my manager told me FIPS was nothing but paperwork—boring and bureaucratic. But I have to say, it turned out to be everything but boring. Every certificate brought new lessons, new challenges, and, apparently," he laughed, brushing a hand through his hair, "a few more gray hairs. Each one probably represents a FIPS validation."

He grew reflective. "There have been a lot of changes and a lot of growth. FIPS didn't just fill my days—it built my career. It taught me persistence, collaboration, and patience. It changed my life in a good way."

Yi nodded warmly. "And you built a strong team along the way," she said. "That's what enabled you to step into a broader role—to influence policies rather than react to them. Your team's expertise allows you to think ahead, anticipate transitions, and shape the direction of the program."

Jaroslav smiled. "Exactly. My focus now is less about collecting certificates and more about being proactive, ensuring we're ready before the next change comes." (Table 44.1).

The Hard Part: Waiting for the Queue The conversation turned to time—the one variable engineers can't optimize away.

"The hardest part," Jaroslav admitted, "isn't writing secure code. It's waiting. We ship software every six weeks, but a validation can take more than a year. Customers expect certificates when a product goes live, not months later. And while we wait, vulnerabilities keep moving."

Yi nodded knowingly. "So, you're stuck maintaining the old while building the new."

"Right," he said. "The irony is that the validated version can be less secure than the current one, simply because it's frozen in time. That's not good for anyone. Faster validation isn't just good for business—it's good for security."

Epilogue at FIPS 'n' Chips As the group stood to leave, Yi smiled. "Red Hat proves that open doesn't mean unstructured," she said. "You've shown that transparency, when done right, is its own assurance mechanism."

Jaroslav chuckled. "Openness is our tamper seal," he said. "If you can't hide mistakes, you tend not to make them."

Outside, the Austin night deepened. Inside, the constellation of algorithms—AES, SHA, RSA, and ML-KEM—flickered faintly above the empty tables, a quiet tribute to the engineers who believe that in open collaboration lies the strongest kind of security.

About the contributor: Jaroslav Řezník Jaroslav is a Principal Program Manager responsible for various compliance, regulatory, and standards activities under the Product Security Compliance team. In his 18 years at Red Hat, he has touched many different areas from many different angles, ranging from the community work on Fedora that is still his passion to compliance with government standards like Common Criteria, FIPS 140 and the EU Cyber Resilience Act (CRA).

Afterword

The year 2025 marked an important milestone for atsec: in that year alone, atsec contributed to 44 of the 180 FIPS 140 certificates issued by CMVP, the highest number achieved by any accredited cryptographic and security testing laboratory. This represents nearly 25 percent of all FIPS 140 certificates issued that year, in a field comprising roughly twenty accredited laboratories. Such a result reflects not only technical depth and operational excellence, but also the trust placed in our work by vendors, the validation scheme, policymakers, and the broader community.

It is important to emphasize that cryptographic module validation is, by nature, a collective endeavor. The strength and credibility of the FIPS program depend on close collaboration among the validation authority, accredited laboratories, vendors, implementers, and accreditation bodies; each participant plays a distinct and essential role. atsec's accomplishments are inseparable from the stewardship of the CMVP, the rigor of the accreditation framework, and the commitment of vendors who invest significant resources to build and maintain compliant, secure products. This shared responsibility is what sustains trust in cryptographic assurance at scale.

Writing FIPS 'n' Chips was both a joyful and demanding experience for our team. Undertaken alongside a busy project schedule, the process became an opportunity to relearn familiar standards with a fresh perspective. We challenged ourselves not only to understand FIPS-related requirements deeply, but also to explain them clearly, accessibly, and with empathy. Framing complex concepts through storytelling and everyday experiences, such as those found in a restaurant, sharpened our own understanding and reminded us that good assurance depends as much on communication as it does on correctness.

The strong project performance of the atsec team is closely tied to this culture of learning, sharing, and mutual care. High-quality assurance work does not emerge solely from checklists, tools, or procedures—it grows from teams that enjoy learning together, that respect one another's judgment, and that take pride in transferring knowledge. The joy, trust, and care demonstrated throughout the creation of this book mirror the collaboration that underpins our daily work in cryptographic testing and validation.

Y. Mao (ed.), *Tasting Cryptography*, https://doi.org/10.1007/978-3-032-30243-4

This book is intended as an educational companion, not as a substitute for official standards, implementation guidance, or validation authority decisions. Examples and explanations are illustrative rather than prescriptive. Our hope is that FIPS ‘n’ Chips serves as a bridge between formal standards and practical understanding, helping readers navigate the landscape of cryptographic assurance with greater confidence and context.

We are particularly mindful of students and early-career professionals who may be encountering this field for the first time. Cryptographic assurance benefits from diverse perspectives and interdisciplinary skills, spanning mathematics, computer systems, engineering, documentation, and professional judgment. We hope this book encourages curiosity and invites new contributors to see assurance not as a barrier, but as an essential and rewarding craft that protects users and systems alike.

Looking ahead, the field of assurance continues to evolve. Advances in post-quantum cryptography, increasingly complex system architectures, and growing software scale demand new approaches to testing and review. atsec is actively investing in this future by building an in-house FIPS AI agent to support documentation review and source code analysis. Our goal is to enhance the efficiency and depth of testing while achieving a higher level of assurance. By keeping this AI capability entirely within our laboratory environment, we ensure that confidential design and implementation details remain protected, providing vendors with peace of mind that their intellectual property and sensitive information are handled with the utmost care.

Due to time constraints and the rigorous legal and media approval processes required by some organizations, several insightful interviews with vendor representatives could not be included in this volume. We regret these omissions and hope to incorporate such perspectives in future editions or related efforts.

Ultimately, FIPS ‘n’ Chips is an invitation: an invitation to learn, to question, and to collaborate. We look forward to welcoming policymakers, vendors, laboratories, government agencies, academic scholars, end users, and students at future FIPS ‘n’ Chips bootcamp or conference events. Together, we will continue to bake and taste security solutions, strengthening the foundations of trust that the cryptographic assurance community depends upon.

Dr. Yi Mao, CEO of atsec USA.

Zeitfracht Medien GmbH
Ferdinand-Jühlke-Straße 7
99095 Erfurt, Deutschland
produktsicherheit@kolibri360.de